MASCULINITIES AND PLACE

Gender, Space and Society

Series Editors: Peter Hopkins, Newcastle University, UK and
Dr Rachel Pain, Durham University, UK

The series on Gender, Space and Society aims to publish innovative feminist work that analyses men's and women's lives from a perspective that exposes and is committed to challenging social inequalities and injustices. The series reflects the ongoing significance and changing forms of gender, and of feminist ideas, in diverse social, geographical and political settings.

The themes it covers include, but are not restricted to:

- The constitution and transformation of gender in different political and economic regimes around the world.
- Men's and women's lived experiences of femininities and masculinities in diverse spaces and environments.
- The ways in which gender is co-constituted and intersects with a range of other social identities, such as race, ethnicity, nationality, class, age, generation, religion, (dis)ability, sexual orientation, body size and health status in different places and times.
- Challenging distinctions and offering new understandings of the relationships between public/private, economic/social (re)production, geopolitical/intimate and so on.
- Destabilising the binary man/woman, and developing more complex ways of understanding gendered social and spatial relations.
- Developing theoretical perspectives that shed light on the changing nature of gender relations, such as indigenous, postcolonial, queer, Marxist, poststructuralist and non-representational feminist theories.
- Exploring innovation in methodology, praxis, knowledge co-production and activism as means of challenging social injustices.

Masculinities and Place

Edited by
ANDREW GORMAN-MURRAY
University of Western Sydney, Australia
PETER HOPKINS
Newcastle University, UK

Routledge
Taylor & Francis Group
LONDON AND NEW YORK

First published 2014 by Ashgate Publishing

2 Park Square, Milton Park, Abingdon, Oxfordshire OX14 4RN
711 Third Avenue, New York, NY 10017

Routledge is an imprint of the Taylor & Francis Group, an informa business

First issued in paperback 2018

British Library Cataloguing in Publication Data
A catalogue record for this book is available from the British Library

The Library of Congress has cataloged the printed edition as follows:
Masculinities and place / [edited] by Andrew Gorman-Murray and Peter Hopkins.
pages cm. -- (Gender, space and society)
Includes bibliographical references and index.
ISBN 978-1-4724-0979-9 (hardback)
1. Masculinity--Research. 2. Men's studies. 3. Space in economics-Research.
I. Gorman-Murray, Andrew. II. Hopkins, Peter (Peter E.)
HQ1088.M372 2014
155.3'32--dc23

2014020762

ISBN 978-1-4724-0979-9 (hbk)
ISBN 978-1-138-54723-0 (pbk)

Contents

List of Figures and Tables

Figures

Tables

Notes on Contributors

Stuart Aitken is a Professor of Geography and Chair, Department of Geography, San Diego State University, USA.

Stephen Atherton is a Lecturer in Education in the School of Education and Lifelong Learning, Aberystwyth University, Wales.

Lawrence D. Berg is a Professor of Critical Human Geography in the Community, Culture and Global Studies Unit, University of British Columbia, Canada.

Stefano Bettani is a doctoral candidate in the Department of Geography at the University of Washington, Seattle, USA.

Alp Biricik is a doctoral candidate in the Department of Gender Studies, Linkoping University, Sweden.

Michael Brown is a Professor in the Department of Geography, University of Washington, Seattle, USA.

Andrew Childs is a doctoral candidate in the Department of Geography, University of Washington, Seattle, USA.

Rosie Cox is Reader in Geography and Gender Studies in the Department of Geography, Environment and Development Studies, Birkbeck, University of London, UK.

Kavita Datta is Reader in Geography in the School of Geography, Queen Mary University of London, UK.

Isabel Dyck is Professor Emeritus in the School of Geography, Queen Mary University of London, UK.

Kim England is Professor in the Department of Geography, University of Washington, Seattle, USA.

Joshua Evans is an Assistant Professor in the Centre for Social Sciences, Athabasca, Canada.

Levi Gahman is a doctoral candidate in the Community, Culture and Global Studies Unit, University of British Columbia, Canada.

Chris Gibson is a Professor of Geography, in the Department of Geography and Sustainable Communities, University of Wollongong, Australia.

Andrew Gorman-Murray is a Senior Lecturer in Social Sciences in the School of Social Sciences and Psychology, University of Western Sydney, Australia.

Abby Hardgrove is a researcher in human geography in the School of Geography and Environment, University of Oxford, UK.

Jeff Hearn is a Research Professor Research Professor, University of Huddersfield, UK and Professor, Swedish School of Economics, Helsinki, Finland.

Anna Hickey-Moody is a Senior Lecturer in the Centre for The Arts and Learning in the Department of Educational Studies at Goldsmiths, University of London, UK.

Peter Hopkins is a Professor of Social Geography in the School of Geography, Politics and Sociology, Newcastle University, UK.

Tanja Joelsson is a doctoral candidate in the Department of Gender Studies, Linkoping University, Sweden.

Jessica Keppel is a Research Assistant in the School of Social Sciences and Psychology, University of Western Sydney, Australia.

Jane Kenway is a Professor in the School of Education, Monash University, Melbourne, Australia.

Larry Knopp is a Professor and Director of Interdisciplinary Arts and Sciences, University of Washington, Tacoma, USA.

Nathaniel Lewis is a Lecturer in Human Geography in the School of Geography and Environment, University of Southampton, UK.

Jeff May is a doctoral candidate in the Department of Geography and Program in Planning, University of Toronto, Canada.

Robyn Mayes is a Research Fellow in the John Curtin Institute of Public Policy at Curtin University, Australia.

Linda McDowell is a Professor of Human Geography in the School of Geography and Environment, University of Oxford, UK.

Cathy McIlwaine is a Professor of Geography in the School of Geography, Queen Mary University of London, UK.

Angela Meah is a Postdoctoral Research Fellow in the Department of Geography, Sheffield University, UK.

Paula Meth is a Senior Lecturer in Town and Regional Planning, Sheffield University, UK.

Greg Noble is a Professor in the Institute for Culture and Society, University of Western Sydney, Australia.

Neil J. Nunn is a doctoral candidate in the Community, Culture and Global Studies Unit, University of British Columbia, Canada.

Barbara Pini is a Professor in the School of Humanities at Griffith University, Australia.

Geir-Henning Presterudstuen is a Research Fellow in the School of Social Sciences and Psychology, University of Western Sydney, Australia.

Michael Richardson is a Teaching Fellow in the School of Geography, Politics and Sociology, Newcastle University, UK.

Esther Rootham is a Post-Doctoral Fellow in the Department of Geography, National University of Singapore, Singapore.

Paul Tabar is an Associate Professor and Director of Lebanese American University's Institute for Migration Studies, Lebanon.

Anna Tarrant is a Postdoctoral Research Fellow in the Faculty of Health and Social Care, Open University, UK.

Elen-Maarja Trell is a Leverhulme Early Career Fellow in the Department of Sociology and Social Policy, University of Leeds, UK.

Bettina van Hoven is an Associate Professor in the Department of Cultural Geography, University of Groningen, Netherlands.

Andrew Warren is a Lecturer in Human Geography in the Department of Geography and Sustainable Communities, University of Wollongong, Australia.

Robert Wilton is a Professor in the School of Earth Sciences and Geography, McMaster University Canada.

Acknowledgements

The editors are very grateful to all of the chapter authors for their excellent contributions to this collection and for their patience as we have compiled the book. We are very grateful to Valerie Rose and Katy Crossan at Ashgate for their support, and to Jessica Keppel who provided invaluable editorial assistance.

Andrew Gorman-Murray extends special thanks to Peter Hopkins for embarking on this project and enabling an excellent collaborative experience. Thanks also to colleagues at the University of Western Sydney for their support. Andrew acknowledges the support of the Australian Research Council, who funded the Discovery Project *Men on the home front: spatialities of domesticity and masculinity* (DP0986666), which helped provide a catalyst and resources for this book project.

Peter Hopkins is very appreciative of the award of a University of Western Sydney International Visiting Fellowship in 2011. During this fellowship, both editors met for the first time and had the initial discussions that led to this edited collection. Peter is particularly thankful to Andrew for collaborating so professionally on this edited collection. Many thanks also to those who presented at the 'Relational masculinities: embodiment, homespaces and the family' sessions at the Association of American Geographers Annual Conference in New York in February 2012, some of whom have contributed to this collection; in particular, Peter thanks Michael Richardson for co-organising this session with him.

Chapter 1
Introduction: Masculinities and Place

Andrew Gorman-Murray and Peter Hopkins

Tracing masculinities and place

The emergence of research about masculinities and place can be traced through two sets of interconnected literatures that we explore briefly in this introduction. The first of these is research that can be loosely defined as being about the geographies of masculinities (e.g. Berg and Longhurst 2003, Hopkins and Noble 2009, McDowell 2003, van Hoven and Hörschelmann 2005). This has emerged largely from feminist social and cultural geographical work that draws attention to structures, processes and places of inequality and injustice that sustain unequal gender relations. The second area of scholarship, which is 'increasingly interdisciplinary' (Kimmel 1987: 11) in nature, is variously referred to as 'men's studies' (Kimmel 1987), the sociology of masculinities (Whitehead 2002), 'studies of men and masculinities', or 'critical studies on men' (Connell, Hearn and Kimmel 2005: 3). This work started to develop before research about the geographies of masculinities although both areas of scholarship have close connections not only in their focus upon advancing understandings of masculinities and men's lives but also in their close relationship to, and interconnections with, feminism. In setting up this collection then – and before we say more about social and geographical research about men and masculinities – we first discuss some of the significant contributions of feminist geographies in order to contextualise the focus of this book upon masculinities and place.

Particularly from the 1980s onwards, feminist geographers have developed an increasingly sophisticated set of critiques about the discipline of geography, the nature of geographical knowledge and the gendering of social relations (including in university departments, in publishing, at conferences, and in other activities related to academic geography) (e.g. Bondi et al. 2002, Jones, Nast and Roberts 1997, Laurie et al. 1999, Moss 2002, Moss and Falconer Al-Hindi 2008, WGSG 1997). Rose (1993:1) observes that 'the academic discipline of geography has historically been dominated by men' and van Hoven and Hörschelmann (2005:1) note that 'geography has long been a discipline dominated by men and one about men'. A crucial point made by feminist geographers is that geographers exclude women from their work because of the ways in which they produce knowledge:

> Masculinist work claims to be exhaustive and it therefore assumes that no-one else can add to its knowledge; it is therefore reluctant to listen to anyone else.

> Masculinist work, then, excludes women because it alienates us in its choice of research themes, because it feels that women should not really be interested in producing geography, and also because it assumes that it is itself comprehensive. (Rose 1993: 4)

As Bonnett (1999) notes, this definition sees masculinism working within and across geography – including in learning and teaching settings and in terms of opportunities for career progression – as well as with regards to the production of geographical knowledge. Although there has arguably been much progress with regards to challenging sexism and patriarchy in geography, concerns about masculinism and male-domination persist within the discipline (e.g. Crang 2003, Maddrell et al. 2011, Seager 2000).

Second, and in addition to demonstrating the masculinism of geography, feminist geographers have made major contributions to exploring the complex ways in which everyday socio-spatial relations are gendered in ways that marginalise and stigmatise women while empowering and emboldening men. Moss and Falconer Al-Hindi (2008: 1), for example, note that 'feminist geographers have focused their research on, for, and about women, their work, their homes, and the organization of their everyday lives'. Too numerous to mention here, there now exists a vibrant, exciting and sophisticated body of scholarship about the complexities, and ambiguities of the relationships between gender, space and power (e.g. McDowell 1999). Arguably, research about geographies of gender – although most evident in social and cultural geographies – is now an important theme in many sub-fields of geography, including economic, development and rural geographies and migration studies (e.g. Cornwall, Edstrom and Greig 2011, Laurie 2011, Little 2002, Walsh 2011, Yeoh and Willis 2004). A significant emergence from this work has also been research about the intersections between gender, sexuality and place (e.g. see Brown 2012 for an overview of work in this area) and indeed, work about geographies of masculinity, which we say more about below.

Third, feminist geographers have contributed a range of methodological approaches and insights to geography that have significantly enriched the discipline through the critical use of important methodological tools and by encouraging researchers to reflect critically about their research practices, politics and ethics when undertaking research (e.g. Bondi et al. 2002, England 1994, Katz 1994, Kobayashi 1994, Moss 2002). One of the important methodological considerations emphasised by many feminist geographers is about engaging reflexively with the research process and considering the role of positionality in research (Kobayashi 2003, Mohammad 2001). As Kobayashi (2003: 346) notes, 'self reflexive scholars are above all concerned about the potential for recreating or reinforcing the forms of social exclusion that are at the very heart of both our research and our social acts'. In addition to this, feminist geographers have also played a significant role in advancing understandings about the centrality and importance of emotions in social life (Davidson, Bondi and Smith 2005) and this has arguably contributed to the destabilising of masculinism in the discipline (as discussed above). Overall, this body of scholarship has provided the foundation for researchers to be able to conduct emotionally sensitive and politically engaged research about gender issues while also being reflexive about their engagements with others, their role in the research process and the complex ways in which the multiple positionalities of researcher and researched interconnect in the field.

Geographies of masculinities and critical men's studies

The reason we have explored some of the key contributions of feminist geography here is because without this, geographers would probably not be researching masculinities and we would not have produced this edited collection. Feminist geographies have provided the space, context, approaches and tools for geographers to critically research and explore the relationships between masculinities and place. Moreover, feminist geographers have also re-shaped the discipline of geography and challenged how geographical knowledge is produced; this in turn has opened up spaces for geographies of masculinities to develop. van Hoven and Hörschelmann (2005: 7) note: 'feminist work has been crucial for the development of critical "men's studies" in as far as the latter seek to deconstruct homogenous understandings of gender and sexuality and aim to challenge gendered power relations.' Feminist geographies and geographies of masculinities are relational; the growth and establishment of the former has enabled the latter to develop. Indeed, many (if not most) geographers who write about masculinities – and many of the contributors to this collection – associate with feminist geographies or have, at least, strong feminist leanings.

In an overview of the field that sought to 'place' masculinities and geographies, Berg and Longhurst (2003: 353) note:

> While Anglo-American geography has a long history of androcentrism and masculinism (Rose 1993) and therefore geographers have long been preoccupied with the activities of men, it took somewhat longer for a critique of hegemonic masculinities to develop in the discipline. It was not until 1989, then, that we began to see the beginnings of an outline for the study of masculinities.

It was Peter Jackson (1989, 1991, 1994) who was one of the first geographers to offer an explicit focus on masculinity through his work about cultural politics, plural masculinities (Jackson 1991), and black masculinity and advertising (Jackson 1994, see also Jackson, Stevenson and Brooks 1999, Stevenson, Jackson and Brooks 2000). Jackson (1991: 199) sees the interest in masculinity 'as a response to the challenge of feminism and, to a lesser extent, the rise of increasingly politicized gay consciousness' although this is somewhat contested as Longhurst (2000) regards the study of masculinities as being about the shifting focus of feminism rather than a response to it. In the late 1990s, following on from Jackson's earlier work, social and cultural geographers started to focus more attention on masculinities, particularly in feminist cultural and social geographies and in work about sexuality (Longhurst 2000). Berg and Longhurst (2003) observed that by the early 2000s, other geographers were also exploring issues of relevance to masculinities, including those working in urban geographies, employment, disability and post-colonialism.

Building upon this earlier work, there was a steady increase in research about geographies of masculinities during the late 1990s and early 2000s with two important monographs about economic change and working-class young men in the UK (McDowell 2003, Nayak 2003), reviews of the field (Berg and Longhurst 2003, Little 2002, Longhurst 2000), and the publication of the edited collection *Spaces of Masculinities* in 2005 (van Hoven and Hörschelmann 2005). Although the field has arguably developed since the early 1990s to the mid-2000s, van Hoven and Hörschelmann (2005: 5) felt that 'there been a notable lack of attention to the formation of masculine identities and spaces'. They continued that 'a focus on the relational formation of male identities and masculine spaces seems long overdue in both feminist and gender-oriented geographical work' (van Hoven and Hörschelmann 2005: 5). A key focus for geographers interested in masculinity has been about exploring the contested constructions of gender identities and how these are constructed, negotiated and contested in different localities or places (van Hoven and Hörschelmann 2005) and how this changes over time; indeed, a key challenge for geographers interested in masculinities has been to respond to the ways in which gender relations change over time and how younger men may no longer be able to fit quite so comfortably into categories of understanding that are now somewhat dated given their contemporary experiences of gender relations. Understandably then, a key focus of work here has been on how young men construct and contest their masculine identities and how these are informed by their own identities, such as their class, sexuality, race and ethnicity. Examples of work in this area include Nayak's (2006) and McDowell's research about working-class masculinities and Hopkins' (2006) study of youthful Muslim masculinities.

Around ten years before geographers started to develop an interest in masculinities, social scientists researching gender relations began to develop a strong interest in studying men and masculinities. Whitehead (2002: 1–2) refers to the 'rapidly growing international study of men and masculinities, now recognised as the *sociology of masculinities*' and notes that 'the depth and breadth of this sociology is staggering'. Similarly, Hopkins and Noble (2009: 811) discuss the 'rapid growth within the social sciences and humanities of the new field of "masculinity studies"'. It is clear that many geographers interested in masculinity have drawn upon work in this field: 'present-day critical analyses of masculinities owe much to the early work of Bob Connell' (Berg and Longhurst 2003: 352).

Michael Kimmel (1987: 10–11), a leading contributor to this field, noted the following about 'men's studies':

> Men's studies responds to the shifting social and intellectual contexts in the study of gender and attempts to treat masculinity not as the normative referent against

> which standards are assessed but as a problematic gender construct. Inspired by the academic breakthroughs of women's studies, men's studies addresses similar questions to the study of men and masculinity. As women's studies has radically revised the traditional academic canon, men's studies seeks to use that revision as the basis for this exploration of men and masculinity. Men's studies seeks neither to replace nor to supplant women's studies; quite the contrary. Men's studies seeks to buttress, to augment women's studies, to complete the radically redrawn portrait of gender that women's studies began.

Aligning itself closely with women's studies, men's studies – or what we refer to here as 'critical men's studies' – is therefore about studying masculinities in a critically engaging way such that the power, authority and control often associated with masculinities is questioned and challenged. Regarding men's studies, Whitehead (2002: 2) clarifies that it 'does not concern itself with, other than critically, "men's studies". By that I mean those more populist writings that either portray men as needing to reject feminism … or ignore feminist theories altogether in their research about men'. As with geographies of masculinities, the emergence of critical men's studies has close connections with the emergence of feminist research: 'The new feminism of the 1970s not only gave voice to women's concerns, it challenged all assumptions about the gender system and raised a series of problems about men' (Connell 2000: 3).

Having now traced the development of research about masculinities and place, we ask an important question for this collection: what is masculinity? This is a notoriously difficult question to answer. Berg and Longhurst (2003: 352) note that 'we should not speak of a singular masculinity, but rather, of multiple masculinities' while also clarifying that masculinities are 'temporally and geographically contingent'. One of the most frequently used definitions of masculinity is offered by Connell (1995: 71); masculinity is 'simultaneously a place in gender relations, the practices through which men and women engage that place in gender, and the effects of these practices in bodily experience, personality and culture'. Connell (2000: 29) also clarifies how masculinities 'are configurations of practice within gender relations, a structure that includes large-scale institutions and economic relations as well as face-to-face relationships and sexuality. Masculinity is institutionalised in this structure, as well as being an aspect of individual character or personality'.

Adding to this complexity, van Hoven and Hörschelmann (2005: 10–11) note that rather than only being attached to men's bodies, 'masculinity can attach to bodies, objects, places and spaces well beyond the confines of biology and sex. Masculinity evokes images of maleness, yet they are by no means necessarily shared by men and can, on the other hand, be adopted by or attributed to women'. Masculinity can therefore be associated with a variety of types of bodies, places and contexts. Nayak and Kehily (2013: 197) discuss female masculinity noting that 'an interesting approach to gender relations considers what happens when women engage with masculinity as part of themselves rather than a male Other'. Partly as a result of these challenges around defining masculinities, researchers have often focused on how masculinities are conceptualised (e.g. Connell 1995, Connell and Messerschmidt 2005) and there now exists a range of language, terminology and typologies of different types of masculinities and the particular qualities or attributes associated with these. We now turn to consider how masculinities have been conceptualised.

Conceptualising masculinities

Growing cross-disciplinary interest in men and masculinities has impelled breadth and depth in the way masculinities are conceptualised. In the early post-WWII era, sex-role theory prevailed as a key schema for understanding and explaining (and policing) gender (Carrigan, Connell and Lee 1987, Berg and Longhurst 2003). This reinforced a binary model of masculine/feminine gender identification and behaviour based on a taken-for-granted biological distinction between male and female bodies. Gender identity and social role was calibrated to biological sex characteristics. With the spread of feminist philosophies in the 1960s and 1970s, sex-role theory gave way to social constructionist understandings of gender, in which masculinity and femininity were no longer seen as innate characteristics of sex differences but as behaviours that were taught and learnt (Mac an Ghaill and Hayward 2007). To paraphrase Simone de Beauvoir (2009 [1949]), one is not born but becomes a man or a woman, and normative gender roles and performances are acquired through socialisation within the context of institutions such as the family, school, media and workplace.

The understanding of gender and gender differences as social constructions led to different ways to conceptualise masculinities as *relational* achievements – that is, masculinity/masculinities is/are constructed *in relation to* other entities, including bodies, identities, institutions, ideas, social norms and categories, and historical and geographical contexts (Berg and Longhurst 2003, Hopkins and Noble 2009). This relationality, moreover, is an ongoing and ever-changing process, as masculinities are continuously reconstructed in and through these social and material relations. There are, accordingly, different relational frames to consider in regard to conceptualising typologies of masculinities and their identity work.

Masculinity is conceptualised as both an identity and as an ideology (van Hoven and Hopkins 2009). Masculinity provides a personal sense of self, and this identity is always constructed in the context of a broader social order. In this articulation of the personal and the social, masculinity is constituted in the first instance as part of a gender order suffused with notions of difference, power and hierarchy (Carrigan, Connell and Lee 1987). In frameworks of gender power, masculinity is conceptualised not just in relation to femininity, but masculinities are also understood as plural and hierarchical identities. The work of R.W. Connell (1998, 2000, 2005a, 2005b) has been especially influential. Connell elaborated the concept of *hegemonic masculinity* to describe how power relations suffuse the gender order in a way that not only differentiates masculinity and femininity, but structures relations of dominance between men. Hegemonic masculinity is the normative archetype that occupies the apex of the gender order, channelling power and creating an ideal of masculinity that men might try to (but rarely) achieve. As Connell and Messerschmidt (2005: 832) state in their assessment of the concept:

> Hegemonic masculinity was not assumed to be normal in the statistical sense; only a minority of men might enact it. But it was certainly normative. It embodied the currently most honoured way of being a man, it required all other men to position themselves in relation to it, and it ideologically legitimated the global subordination of women to men.

This 'conceptual system' has been critiqued for its tendency 'to reduce the complexity and nuance of what men actually do', but it nevertheless remains an informative and useful tool for explaining gender dynamics and power (Hopkins and Noble 2009: 813). Crucially, maintaining the gender order and its power through the hegemonic masculine ideal relies not only on the subordination of all women and feminine subjectivities, but also the subordination of most masculine subjectivities to this ideal.

Plural masculinities were thus recognised through this conceptual framework, which some have used to proffer a typology of masculinities (Beasley 2005). A range of non-hegemonic masculinities are identified in relation to the hegemonic idea, including *complicit*, *subordinate*, *protest* and *marginal* masculinities (Connell 2005a). Regardless of whether a typological understanding is salient, what is significant here is that these masculinities are constructed and defined not only in terms of gender identity and power, but in relation to other social categories as well (Hopkins and Noble 2009). To construe an aspirational archetype, hegemonic masculinity relies not only on the social construction of gender norms, but also on ideals of race, class, sexuality, age and bodily ability, *inter alia*. In contemporary Western societies, for instance, the archetype does not just rely on masculinity as a gender identity, but on hegemonic masculinity as an embodiment of race (whiteness), class (middle-class aspirations, professional skills and technical competence), sexuality (heterosexuality, evidenced through marriage and fatherhood), age (working-age, not older-aged or retired) and physical attributes (height, strength, muscularity). Non-hegemonic masculinities are usually rendered subordinate or marginal due to the *intersection* of 'aberrant' social attributes with masculinity, such as working-class status, homosexuality, non-whiteness, retirement or physical disability. Masculinities, then, are constructed in relation to, and at the intersection of, a range of social categories aside from (but certainly including) gender.

As a gender identity, masculinity is also conceptualised and constituted through ideas about the relations between mind, body and emotions (Barker 2007, Johnston and Longhurst 2010). Masculinity and femininity are embodiments of gender identity and behaviour, which despite insights from social constructionism, are still seen as differently articulated to male and female sexed bodies. This gender embodiment is not only physical. Normative ideas of masculine and feminine embodiment, from at least the eighteenth century, have imputed hierarchical binary distinctions of mind/body and rationality/emotion upon male/female bodies (McDowell 1999). Enlightenment thinking – particularly Descartes' (Longhurst 1997) – produced a 'scaling' of sexed bodies, in which women were imagined as tied to bodily cycles of menstruation and pregnancy, which were seen to affect their mind and emotions, while men were seen to transcend the exigencies of embodiment, and posited as rational and 'in control' of body and mind (Young 1990, Johnston and Longhurst 2010). Women are considered 'in touch' with their bodies and emotions (in a more positive spin) while men are 'hard-bodied' and 'impermeable' (Longhurst 2001). Masculinities studies have thus urged more attention to men's bodies and emotions (Evers 2009). Seidler (2007: 15–16) argues that men's disengagement from emotional and sensuous embodiment is problematic for gender relations, and in turn contends that pursuing gender equality requires men to connect with their emotions and gain an appreciation of emotional embodiment: 'our bodies carry our emotional histories', and 'by developing an engagement with their bodies … men could give voice to emotions that would otherwise remain dis/connected.'

Another emerging and increasingly important way in which masculinities (and gender) are conceptualised – and one which is, indeed, central to this book – is in relation to space, place and geographical context. Until recently, there has been little work addressing 'the *spatial* dimensions of masculinity' (Hopkins and Noble 2009: 812), let alone work that incorporated spatial thinking into conceptualisations of masculinities (Berg and Longhurst 2003). This is, as Hopkins and Noble (2009: 812) suggest, 'the specific nature of geography's contribution to the field', and they go on to argue that: 'Indeed, it is the peculiar domain of geography to explore not simply how masculinities are played out in different spaces, but how those spaces shape the very nature of the experience of masculinity, and how it articulates with other key dimensions of social relations' (Hopkins and Noble 2009: 814). The plurality of masculinities, and modulations in the gender order, are arguably intertwined with spatial variations (and also temporal/historical ones). This has several important and inter-related implications for conceptualising masculinities (and gender).

Differences across geographical context vitally shape gender dynamics and masculinities, as van Hoven and Hopkins contend (2009: 492): 'Since the performance of masculinity interrelates with space, place, and time, that is, the same person can reveal a different kind of masculinity and/or femininity at different times and in different contexts, it is more appropriate to speak of masculinities.' This speaks to differences at a variety of scales, from the local (between spaces of work, home and leisure, for example) to the global (between different national, cultural, social and legal contexts) (see also Jackson 1991, Connell and Messerschmidt 2005). This helps to understand and clarify a new ('third') phase in masculinities studies, where masculinities can be understood as *strategic* accomplishments, as 'performances which are undertaken in particular contexts, drawing on specific resources and capacities' (McDowell 2003 cited in Hopkins and Noble 2009: 814, see also Batnitzky, McDowell and Dyer 2009). Or, as Connell and Messerschmidt (2005: 836) put it: '[m]asculinities are configurations of practice that are accomplished in social action and, therefore, can differ according to the gender relations in particular social settings.'

As Berg and Longhurst (2003: 352) first argued a decade ago: 'Masculinities, then, are highly contingent, unstable, contested spaces within gender relations. It is this very contingent and unstable character that makes the process and spaces of identity production so important in both the construction of masculinities, and … in the construction of ways of understanding masculinities.' In this context, geographers, cultural theorists and social scientists have begun to examine, analyse and theorise masculinities in relation to a diverse range of spaces. This diversity is epitomised in van Hoven and Hörschelmann's 2005 collection, *Spaces of Masculinities*, which alongside other work in the growing field of geographies of masculinities, has examined the construction and contestation of different performances and discourses of masculinities in workplaces (Massey 1996, McDowell 2003, 2005), the military (Atherton 2009, Woodward 2003, 2006), homes (Atherton 2009, Gorman-Murray 2008, 2011a, 2013), commercial leisure venues (Law 1997, Caluya 2008), sports fields (Hall 2005, Waitt 2006), discursive media spaces (Jackson 1994, Gorman-Murray 2011b), cities and urban neighbourhoods (Erhkamp 2008, Warren and Gibson 2011), rural areas (Pini 2008, Pini and Mayes 2013) and practices of internal and international migration (Walsh 2011, Annes and Redlin 2012, Yi'En 2012). As Nayak (2006) and Hopkins and Noble (2009) suggest, 'it is only in the situated, empirically grounded analysis of actual men in actual places that we can grasp the shifting dynamics of power' (Hopkins and Noble 2009: 813), and this range of work has gone some considerable way towards evidencing the spatial imperatives and nuances in masculinities and in gender dynamics. The present collection builds on and extends these spatial dimensions and insights for conceptualising masculinities.

Researching masculinities

A significant topic that continues to remain under-explored in research about men and masculinities are the methodological, ethical, practical and political issues involved in conducting research about masculinities (although see Haywood and Mac an Ghaill, 2003 for a useful discussion of some of these issues). Aside from a few exceptions, Meth and McClymont (2009: 909–10) observe a 'lack of explicit engagement with questions of methodology' in work about men and masculinities in geography and that: 'Masculinities researchers within geography have shied away from examining different methods in terms of the quality and depth of empirical findings, particularly in terms of their propensity to enliven understandings of men.' Some of the exceptions that Meth and McClymont

(2009) refer to include Vanderbeck's in-depth discussion of negotiations of his masculinity during ethnographic fieldwork with young people in a British voluntary organisation and McDowell's (2001b, 2001c) discussion about how she negotiated complex ethical issues in her research with white working-class young men in the UK. More recently too, Tarrant (2014: this volume) has written about her negotiations as a young woman researcher studying older men's masculinities and Richardson (2014: this volume) has critically reflected on his position as a young man researching men from different generations. Although critical reflections on the ethical and methodological issues involved in researching men and masculinities is therefore being given more attention from geographers, an explicit focus upon the politics, ethics and methods of such research is still relatively limited within the discipline. This raises questions about how 'do we begin to conceptualise the methodological, conceptual and political challenges thrown up in researching men's lives?' (Hopkins and Noble 2009: 817).

Perhaps one possible explanation for the tendency to shy away from considering different methodological and ethics issues relates to the ways in which the majority of those researching masculinities associate themselves with feminist geography and therefore have a rich, sophisticated and engaging tapestry of reflexive methods and ethically sound principles for conducting research? That being said, there are mixed views with regards to whether or not men are able to conduct feminist research:

> we believe that that feminist research can explore both masculinities and femininities and that ways in which they are produced simultaneously with other attributes of social identity, such as age, physical ability and location. Additionally, it has been argued by some that men may also conduct feminist research as long as they have feminist goals, but this is a contested arena as others believe that feminist research can only be conducted by those whose feminist consciousness comes from their personal experience, the experience of being a woman. (Madge et al. 1997: 99)

However, we agree with Butz and Berg (2002: 90) who contend that 'a feminism that refuses to accept the possibility that men might be active participants in the transformation of masculinity is both practically and theoretically problematic'. That being said, we also feel that it is important for masculinities researchers in geography to start (or continue) to reflect critically on various ethical and methodological issues involved in researching masculinities, including the methods they use in their research and the ethical issues they negotiate in the field. Although none of the chapters in this collection focus solely on methods, they do offer a series of insights into the employment of different methods in masculinities research (e.g. interviews, focus groups, diaries, ethnography) and the politics and ethics connected with conducting such research.

Introducing the parts of the book

We now briefly explore the seven main parts that the chapters of this collection are organised around in order to provide background context for the themes and issues that are explored in more depth in each of the chapters. We prefer to do this rather than only providing a descriptive summary of each chapter. As with many edited collections, the chapters speak across multiple themes and reach into debates that are discussed in other chapters and parts and so we consider these seven parts to be strongly interconnected and overlapping. These thematic parts are preceded by a set of chapters that focus explicitly on further theorising masculinities and place. In doing so, they extend the discussion of how to conceptualise masculinities that was started earlier in this Introduction, and also provide (again, along with this Introduction) the groundwork for the interconnections that reach across the subsequent parts and chapters. Hearn, Biricik and Joelsson (2014: Chapter 2) examine the relationship between theorising, men/masculinities and space/place, observing the distinctions and interrelations between local, national and transnational contexts. Hickey-Moody and Kenway (2014: Chapter 3) further draw out these complex interconnections between different scales, from the local to the global, in their analysis of the spatial assemblages of bodies, actions, senses and youthful masculinities in a regional Australian town. Berg, Gahman and Nunn (2014: Chapter 4) discuss the interlocking spatial processes of neoliberalism, masculinities and other forms of oppression, in order to elucidate the relational nature of social power, knowledge production and academic masculinities in the neoliberal academy. The discussions in the subsequent seven parts take these ideas forward. The themes of the parts are: intersectionality and relationality, home, domestic labour, the family, place and care, health and well-being, and work. We now discuss each of these in turn.

Part 2: Intersectionality and relationality

As noted earlier, researchers studying masculinity have often been drawn to explore how masculinities change (or not) as they are simultaneously negotiated alongside other markers of identity such as class, age, disability, sexuality and ethnicity. Ten years ago, Berg and Longhurst (2003: 357) observed a trend that involved 'a focus not on masculinities per se but on the mutually constitutive relationships between masculinities and other axes of identity such as class, disability, sexuality and "race"' (Berg and Longhurst 2003: 357). More recently, Hopkins and Noble (2009: 812) note: 'We might add that, as with feminism, the study of masculinities had been shaped by a greater engagement with the ways in which gender intersects with other social categories – in particular, those associated with racial and cultural diversity – as well as broader theoretical questions around subjectivity, intersectionality and power.' Taking debates about masculinities, intersectionality and relationality forward, the contributors to this part tease out the complexities of thinking through the intersections of masculinity, ethnicity and migration, masculinity and community, and masculinity and rurality.

The first chapter in this part focuses specifically upon the experiences of a Lebanese–Australian young man and his negotiations of masculinity and 'home' and offers rich insights into some of the challenges of using intersectionality to understand subjectivities (Noble and Tabar 2014: Chapter 5). Continuing with the focus on migration, the second chapter in this part draws attention to the experiences of Brazilian migrants in London, paying specific attention to issues of rights and everyday citizenship. It explores how Brazilian migrants work with ideas of hegemonic masculinity and how they negotiate experiences of exclusion in relation to their female counterparts and to other Latin Americans in general (Datta and McIllwaine 2014: Chapter 6). Taking a rather different focus, on 'community', the third chapter offers an ethnographic insight into the performance of masculinities in the leather community in the US, exploring the particular masculinities that are valorised at International Mr Leather events (Childs 2014: Chapter 7). Also exploring travelling typologies of masculinities, the final chapter in this part troubles the association between hegemonic masculinity and the figure of the 'cowboy' in rural places and does so by discussing some of the contradictions, intersections and specificities surrounding the performance of cowboy masculinities (Gibson 2014: Chapter 8). This chapter clearly demonstrates the complex ways that cowboy masculinities are relational and intersectional, shaped as they are by discourses of race, colonialism, rurality and work.

Part 3: Home

Similar to 'the body', home has been considered the geography 'closest in' (Rich 1986, Smith 1993). Home, as Blunt and Dowling (2006) contend, is a spatial imaginary that is both material and discursive, a site that encompasses personal feelings and cultural meanings. Home can reach across scales from the domestic to the global, but here we are thinking of home as a residential space, or house-as-home, including experiences of marginal housing and homelessness. Gender is deeply implicated in both ideas about and experiences of the house-as-home (Chapman 2004). Notions of femininity and of women's identities and practices are bound to the home in cultural imaginaries (McDowell 1999, Blunt and Dowling 2006). But homes are also sites in which masculinities are constituted and performed, with certain normative expectations about the relations between men and the home as a site of leisure and/or responsibility (Tosh 1999). Work in masculinities studies has recently begun to examine, more thoroughly, the relationship between masculinity and the home, the domestic practices and desires of men, and the shifting gender imaginaries and patterns of domesticity more broadly. The three chapters in this part attend to different elements of masculinities and home, and importantly, show how masculine domesticity interconnects with sites, institutions, practices and cultural meanings beyond the home.

The first chapter examines the inculcation of domestic skills during British men's military training, as well as their experiences of home and domesticity following demobilisation (Atherton 2014: Chapter 9). The second chapter explores how the home symbolises and facilitates black South African men's wider relationships with men and women, the state and the market, and is thus consequential for their experiences (and practices) of violence (Meth 2014: Chapter 10). The final chapter investigates the complex experiences of 'home' and being 'not-at-home' for young men of colour who have been homeless in Toronto, Canada, including domestic imaginaries, house-hopping and attachments to neighbourhood as 'home ground' (May 2014: Chapter 11).

Part 4: Domestic labour

Following neatly from these discussions of masculinities and the home, the next set of chapters examine masculinities and domestic labour, or 'house' work. Domestic labour is inherent in practices of homemaking, yet within the households of heterosexual couples and nuclear families, the burden of domestic labour still tends to fall to women, being seen as the 'natural' work of wives and mothers. While time-use surveys from a number of countries show that men's contributions to domestic labour in such households has been increasing since the 1970s, they still tend to do far less, proportionally, than women (Chapman 2004). To bring about a more equal distribution of housework, it is therefore important to attend to those men who do such work, and to understand the motivations and outcomes of such activities, as well as how masculine labour in the home can either reinforce or reconfigure the traditional gender order. The three chapters in this part advance this important work.

The first chapter investigates how gender, hegemonic masculinity and the attribution of masculine and/or feminine responsibilities is undone in the *way* men *perform* particular elements of domestic labour – in this case, men's practices of domestic foodwork, which has traditionally been associated with femininity but is an increasing domain of masculine activity with households and homemaking (Meah 2014: Chapter 12). Picking up on another dimension of domestic work that is conventionally seen as a feminine activity, the second chapter examines shifting relations between Australian masculinities, domestic materiality and interior design, and the consequences this has for understanding contemporary masculinities, domestic practices and gendered meanings of home (Gorman-Murray 2014: Chapter 13). The final chapter turns attention to a form of domestic labour that is, conversely, considered more 'traditionally' masculine: DIY activities (Cox 2014: Chapter 14). However, Cox's work with New Zealand homeowners shows the gendering of DIY – and its meaning for masculine identity – is complex, involving notions of responsibility and a duty of care that can both sustain or challenge conventional gender relations, identities and domestic practices.

Part 5: The family

These next three chapters focus specifically upon the construction and contestation of masculinities in the context of the family. Arguably, the family offers an important forum where gender relations are formed, renegotiated and reconstructed through interpersonal contact with direct and/or extended family members. Research in this area has been supported by the development of work in children's geographies (to which feminist geographers have made a significant contribution), which has focused attention on the micro-geographies of children's and young people's everyday lives and the relations and tensions experiences within the family (e.g. Evans and Holt 2011). In particular, attention to relational geographies of age (Hopkins and Pain 2007), which explore the relations within and between different age groups, has encouraged stronger relations to be built between children's geographies and those studying other age groups.

Attention to the significance of intergenerational relations has emerged as an important way of advancing relational geographies of age (Vanderbeck 2007) and there are now many studies adopting an intergenerational focus with some considering masculinities in the process (Hopkins 2006, Richardson 2013, Tarrant 2010a, 2010b, 2013a, 2013b). Two of the chapters contribute to this ongoing focus on intergenerational relations and masculinities, focusing specifically on grandfathers' intergenerational contact with their grandchildren in homespaces (Tarrant 2014: Chapter 15) and masculinities and intergenerational relations amongst men of Irish descent in the North East of England (Richardson 2014: Chapter 16). The final contribution to this theme is slightly different in focus and draws attention to the spatialities of practices of fathering and fatherhood (Aitken 2000, 2009) to use ethnopoetics as a methodology to demonstrate the emotional intensities evident within accounts of fathering and space (Aitken 2014: Chapter 17).

Part 6: Place and care

Building on chapters about home, domestic labour and the family, the next two parts advance work about geographies of masculinities through focus on place and care, and health and wellbeing. Reviewing work about geographies of care, Conradson (2003: 451) notes that 'we see how relations and practices of care – things such as listening, feeding, changing clothes and administering medication – are implicated in the production of particular social spaces'. Furthermore, Atkinson, Lawson and Wiles (2011: 563) observe that care offers geographers 'a richness of possibilities through which to engage critically with a range of politically charged discourses', and we would contend that this includes discourses around men, masculinity and social relations. However, men (and debates about masculinity) tend not to be central to discussions about geographies of care. As Barker (2011: 418) observes from data collected as part of research about geographies of care and the school run: 'fathers as a social group can still be thought of as existing outside of everyday gendered carescapes'. The chapters in this part make an important contribution to understanding how performances of masculinities mediate experiences of, and expressions about, place and care.

In the first chapter, England and Dyck (2014: Chapter 18) examine how men embody care work in the home – as care recipients, caregivers and care workers – and the implications for 'doing gender' and challenging particular conventional hues of hegemonic masculinity and gender relations. Drawing attention to the links between care, caring and communities, the second chapter focuses upon the site of the 'gay bar' and its role as a caring place for men (Brown et al. 2014: Chapter 19). In particular, the chapter explores the themes of caring about, taking care of, caregiving and care receiving in relation to men, masculinities and the spaces of the gay bar. Following from this, the final chapter in this part explores the friendship experiences of young men from rural Estonia and in particular, how their participation in boat trips and dance classes enabled them to perform different aspects of masculinity in relation to available physical resources and social groups in both locations (Trell and van Hoven 2014: Chapter 20).

Part 7: Health and wellbeing

Although geographers have explored gender and health issues, research about masculinity and health is relatively rare aside from some research about men with HIV and AIDS (e.g. Wilton 1996): 'Health geographers have yet to interrogate men's overall (un)healthiness, their health behaviors, experiences, and outcomes, including how sociospatial practices or hegemonic masculinities affect men's health, men's spatial and affective relationships with and in support for health, and the contexts within which men's health takes place' (Thien and Del Casino 2012: 1147). Thien and Del Casino (2012) continue by setting out an agenda for health and masculinities research, identifying three areas requiring further work. First, they suggest that research should focus on the gendering of men's health and the places in which it occurs; second, studies could usefully explore men's affective relationships with health and health support systems; and third, researchers might explore how variations of hegemonic masculinities interrelate with men's health. This final point is particularly significant given that: 'Being men and being healthy seem to be contradictory sociospatial states. For example, rejecting health care, minimizing or dismissing health needs, and engaging in (socially sanctioned) risky behaviors are ways in which some men have historically demonstrated manliness while compromising their health' (Thien and Del Casino 2012: 1147).

This part of the edited collection offers an important set of insights into the relations between men, masculinities and health. Although some elements of the chapters focus specifically upon traditional ideas of health in terms of the absence of disease, much of the contributors' discussions are about the promotion of wellbeing, including aspects of mental health as well as the physical conditions of their participants. Building upon a larger project (Wilton, DeVerteuil and Evans 2013), the first chapter explores how men respond to the process of negotiating drug/alcohol addiction treatment (Wilton and Evans 2014: Chapter 21). Following on from this, Lewis (2014: Chapter 22) draws attention to issues of HIV risk and prevention in Nova Scotia, Canada, and investigates the anxieties around masculinity, sexuality and HIV–AIDS that reinforce each other and operate across multiple scales. Drawing attention to issues of mental health, the final chapter in this part examines the social spaces that create and reinforce discourses of hegemonic masculinities in Aotearoa New Zealand, with a particular focus on issues of emotion, hope and healthiness (Keppel 2014: Chapter 23).

Part 8: Work

In contrast to the spaces of home and domesticity, the arena of paid work – encompassing workplaces, labour practices and career investment and attainment – has been associated with men throughout the twentieth century (and earlier) and has been given attention within masculinities studies. Indeed, with regard to thinking about the geographies of masculinities – in both popular as well as scholarly thought – the persistent ideology of separate spheres (public/private = work/home) has proffered a social and cultural viewpoint through which men are taught to derive satisfaction, fulfilment and affirmation from paid employment: 'in twentieth century industrial society men's identity has been predominantly grounded in the workplace' (Smith and Winchester 1998: 328, Pease 2002). Thus, paid work in the public sphere has provided a crucial basis for understanding masculine power and identity. Moreover, given diversity and change in the workplace – including the shifting gender composition of employment, increased female participation, decreased manual labour and increased service-sector employment (both low-paid and high-end) – the arena of paid work has also been a key site for understanding changes in masculinities, and masculine identities, attitudes and behaviours. Here, McDowell's extensive scholarship on gender dynamics, masculinities and paid work has been influential in grasping how hegemonic masculinity continues to hold power and persuasion in high-end professions, such as finance and banking (McDowell 1997, 2010), and how masculinities are challenged in low-paid and often casualised service jobs, such as retail and restaurant service (McDowell 2003, 2009). Meanwhile, in rural industries, Pini's (2008) research has been critical in understanding how hegemonic masculine ideals – and men who epitomise those ideals – continue to dominate the management and employment structures of primary sectors such as agriculture and mining.

These complexities, continuities and changes are picked up and examined in the four chapters in this part. In the first chapter, McDowell, Rootham and Hardgrove (2014: Chapter 24) continue their important work, examining the marginality of working-class young men in a service-dominated economy with high rates of youth unemployment, highlighting how masculinity is marked as disadvantaged, dangerous and a failure. The second chapter discusses the complex changes in masculinities in the market economy of post-colonial Fiji, demonstrating the conflict between traditional and capitalist modes of gender work and engagement in economic processes (Presterudstuen 2014: Chapter 25). The third chapter, likewise, examines competing masculinities in the context of the surfboard industry, where both 'blokey' and alternative 'soulful' modes of masculine identity are evident (Warren 2014: Chapter 26). In the final chapter, Pini and Mayes (2014: Chapter 27) explore the contemporary construction of hegemonic masculinity in the Australian mining industry, constituted through the intersecting discourses and practices of corporatism, rurality and frontier imaginaries.

A final statement

This book provides, we believe, an insightful collection of critical work on the intersection of masculinities and place, delving into and explicating the ways in which masculinities are constituted and contested in diverse geographical contexts at a range of scales. The seven thematic parts highlight some of the key developments in research on masculinities and place over the last decade. But of course, spaces and spatial practices are not discrete but interconnected; the public and private spheres of work and home, for instance, interpenetrate, and the social power, relations and politics of each cannot be fully appreciated without acknowledging their mutual influence. Likewise, the chapters in this collection, as noted earlier, should not be taken as constrained to and by each part: rather, they speak across the themes – and spaces and places discussed therein – and draw them together. Taken collectively, the different contributions to this collection evidence how the field of masculinities studies has advanced in recent years, particularly in its focus on masculinities as situated and strategic, constructed within and mutually with space and place. The contributors are, as ever, careful to discuss how gender inequity and social power is embedded and actualised in place. Therefore, as with all scholarship that trains a critical eye on gender relations and social power, we hope that these chapters and their observations reach beyond the academy and make some contribution to political and practical work towards gender equity in contemporary society.

References

Aitken, S.C. 2000. Fathering and faltering: 'sorry but you don't have the necessary accoutrements'. *Environment and Planning A*, 32(4), 581–598.

Aitken, S.C. 2009. *The Awkward Spaces of Fathering*. Farnham: Ashgate.

Annes, A. and Redlin, M. 2012. Coming out and coming back: rural gay migration and the city. *Journal of Rural Studies*, 28(1), 56–68.

Atherton, S. 2009. Domesticating military masculinities: situated identities, relations and intersectionality. *Social and Cultural Geography*, 10(8), 811–820.

Atkinson, S., Lawson, V. and Wiles, J. 2011. Care of the body: spaces of practice. *Social and Cultural Geography*, 12(6), 563–572.

Barker, C. 2007. *The Hearts of Men: Tales of Happiness and Despair*. Sydney: UNSW Press.

Barker, J. 2011. 'Manic mums' and 'distant dads'?: Gendered geographies of care and the journey to school. *Health and Place*, 17(2), 413–421.

Batnitzky, A., McDowell, L. and Dyer, S. 2009. Flexible and strategic masculinities: the working lives and gendered identities of male migrants in London. *Journal of Ethnic and Migration Studies*, 35(8), 1275–1293.

Beasley, C. 2005. *Gender and Sexuality: Critical Theories, Critical Thinkers*. Thousand Oaks: Sage Publications.

Berg, L. 1994. Masculinity, place and a binary discourse of 'theory' and 'empirical investigation' in the human geography of Aotearoa/New Zealand. *Gender, Place and Culture: A Journal of Feminist Geography*, 1(2), 245–260.

Berg, L. and Longhurst, R. 2003. Placing masculinities and geography. *Gender, Place and Culture: A Journal of Feminist Geography*, 10(4), 351–360.

Blunt, A. and Dowling, R. 2006. *Home*. London: Routledge.

Bondi, L., Avis, H., Bankey, R., Bingley, A., Davidson, J., Duffy, R., Einagel, V., Green, A-M, Johnston, L., Lilley, S., Listerborn, C., Marshy, M., McEwan, S., O'Connor, N., Rose, G., Vivat, B. and Wood, N. 2002. *Subjectivities, Knowledges, and Feminist Geographies: The Subjects and Ethics of Social Research*. Oxford: Rowman and Littlefield.

Bonnett, A. 1999. Masculinity/masculinities/masculinism, in *A Feminist Glossary of Human Geography*, edited by L. McDowell and J. Sharp. London: Arnold, 159–162.

Brod, H. 1987. A case for men's studies, in *Changing Men: New Directions in Research on Men and Masculinity*, edited by M. Kimmel. London: Sage Publications, 263–277.

Brown, M. 2012. Gender and sexuality I: intersectional anxieties. *Progress in Human Geography*, 36(4), 541–550.

Butz, D. and Berg, L. 2002. Paradoxical space: geography, men and duppy feminism, in *Feminist Geography in Practice: Research and Methods*, edited by P. Moss. Oxford: Wiley-Blackwell, 87–102.

Caluya, G. 2008. 'The rice steamer': race, desire and affect in Sydney's gay scene. *Australian Geographer*, 39(3), 283–292.

Carrigan, T., Connell, R.W. and Lee, J. 1987. Toward a new sociology of masculinity, in *The Making of Masculinities: The New Men's Studies*, edited by H. Brod. Boston: Allen and Unwin, 63–102.

Chapman, T. 2004. *Gender and Domestic Life: Changing Practices in Families and Households*. Basingstoke: Palgrave Macmillan.

Connell, R.W. 1998. Masculinities and globalization. *Men and Masculinities*, 1(1), 3–23.

Connell, R.W. 2000. *The Men and the Boys*. Cambridge: Polity Press.

Connell, R.W. 2005a. *Masculinities*. Cambridge: Polity Press.

Connell, R.W. 2005b. Growing up masculine: rethinking the significance of adolescence in the making of masculinities. *Irish Journal of Sociology*, 14(2), 11–28.
Connell, R.W. 2011. *Confronting Equality: Gender, Knowledge and Global Change*. Cambridge: Polity Press.
Connell, R.W. and Messeschmidt, J.W. 2005. Hegemonic masculinity: rethinking the concept. *Gender and Society*, 19(6), 829–859.
Connell, R.W., Hearn, J. and Kimmel, M. 2005. Introduction, in *Handbook on Studies on Men and Masculinities*, edited by M. Kimmel, J. Hearn and R.W. Connell. London: Sage Publications, 1–12.
Conradson, D. 2003. Geographies of care: spaces, practices, experiences. *Social and Cultural Geography*, 4(4), 451–454.
Cornwall, A., Edstrom, J. and Greig, A. 2011. *Men and Development: Politicizing Masculinities*. London: Zed Books.
Crang, M. 2003. Malestream geography: gender patterns among UK geography faculty. *Environment and Planning A*, 35(10), 1711–1716.
Datta, K., McIllwaine, C., Herbert, J., Evans, Y., May, J. and Wills, J. 2009. Men on the move: narratives of migration and work among low-paid migrant men in London. *Social and Cultural Geography*, 10(8), 853–874.
Davidson, J., Bondi, L. and Smith, M. (eds) 2005. *Emotional Geographies*. Aldershot: Ashgate.
Day, K. 2006. Being feared: masculinity and race in public space. *Environment and Planning A*, 38(3), 569–586.
de Beauvoir, S. 1949. *The Second Sex*, translated by C. Borde and S. Malovany-Chevallier (2009). New York: Vintage Books.
Edley, N. and Wetherell, M. 1997. Jockeying for position: the construction of masculine identities. *Discourse and Society*, 8(2), 203–217.
Ehrkamp, P. 2008. Risking publicity: masculinities and the racialization of public neighborhood space. *Social and Cultural Geography*, 9(2), 117–133.
England, K. 1994. Getting personal: reflexivity, positionality, and feminist research. *Professional Geographer*, 46(1), 80–89.
Evans, R. and Holt, L. 2011. Diverse spaces of childhood and youth: gender and other socio–cultural differences. *Children's Geographies*, 9(3–4), 277–284.
Evers, C. 2009. 'The Point': surfing, geography and a sensual life of men and masculinity. *Social and Cultural Geography*, 10(8), 893–908.
Frosh, S., Phoenix, A. and Pattman, R. 2002. *Young Masculinities*. New York: Palgrave Macmillan.
Gorman-Murray, A. 2006. Homeboys: uses of home by gay Australian men. *Social and Cultural Geography*, 7(1), 53–69.
Gorman-Murray, A. 2008. Masculinity and the home: a critical review and conceptual framework. *Australian Geographer*, 39(2), 367–379.
Gorman-Murray, A. 2011a. Economic crises and emotional fallout: work, home and men's senses of belonging in post-GFC Sydney. *Emotion, Space and Society*, 4(4), 211–220.

Gorman-Murray, A. 2011b. 'This is disco-wonderland!': gender, sexuality and the limits of gay domesticity on *The Block*. *Social and Cultural Geography*, 12(5), 435–453.

Gorman-Murray, A. 2013. Urban homebodies: embodiment, masculinity and domesticity in inner Sydney. *Geographical Research*, 51(2), 137–144.

Hall, C.M. 2005. Shifting spaces of masculinity: from Carisbrooke to the MCG, in *Spaces of Masculinities*, edited by B. van Hoven and K. Hörschelmann. London: Routledge, 155–164.

Haywood, C. and Mac an Ghaill, M. 2003. *Men and Masculinities*. Buckingham: Open University Press.

Hopkins, P. 2006. Youthful Muslim masculinities: gender and generational relations. *Transactions of the Institute of British Geographers*, 31(3), 337–352.

Hopkins, P. and Noble, G. 2009. Masculinities in place: situated identities, relations and intersectionality. *Social and Cultural Geography*, 10(8), 811–819.

van Hoven, B. and Hörschelmann, K. 2005. Introduction: from geographies of men to geographies of women and back again?, in *Spaces of Masculinities*, edited by B. van Hoven and K. Hörschelmann. London: Routledge, 1–16.

van Hoven, B. and Hopkins, P. 2009. Masculinities, in *International Encyclopedia of Human Geography*, edited by R. Kitchin and N. Thrift. Oxford: Elsevier, 492–495.

Jackson, P. 1989. *Maps of Meaning*. London: Unwin Hyman.

Jackson, P. 1991. The cultural politics of masculinity: towards a social geography. *Transactions of the Institute of British Geographers*, 16(2), 199–213.

Jackson, P. 1994. Black male: advertising and the cultural politics of masculinity. *Gender, Place and Culture: A Journal of Feminist Geography*, 1(1), 49–59.

Jackson, P., Stevenson, N. and Brooks, K. 1999. Making sense of men's lifestyle magazines. *Environment and Planning D: Society and Space*, 17(3), 353–368.

Johnston, L. and Longhurst, R. 2010. *Space, Place and Sex: Geographies of Sexualities*. Lanham: Rowman and Littlefield.

Jones, J.P., Nast, H. and Roberts, S. (eds) 1997. *Thresholds in Feminist Geography: Difference, Methodology, Representation*. Maryland: Rowman and Littlefield.

Katz, C. 1994. Playing the field: questions of fieldwork in geography. *Professional Geographer*, 46(1), 67–72.

Kenway, J. and Hickey-Moody, A. 2009. Spatialized leisure-pleasures, global flows and masculine distinctions. *Social and Cultural Geography*, 10(8), 821–836.

Kimmel, M. 1987. Rethinking 'masculinity': new directions in research, in *Changing Men: New Directions in Research on Men and Masculinity*, edited by M. Kimmel. London: Sage Publications, 9–24.

Kimmel, M. 2008. *Guyland: The Perilous World Where Boys Become Men*. New York: Harper Collins.

Kobayashi, A. 1994. Coloring the field: gender, 'race', and the politics of fieldwork. *Professional Geographer*, 46(1), 73–80.

Kobayashi, A. 2003. GPC ten years on: is self-reflexivity enough? *Gender, Place and Culture: A Journal of Feminist Geography*, 10(4), 345–349.

Laurie, N. 2011. Gender water networks: femininity and masculinity in water politics in Bolivia. *International Journal of Urban and Regional Research*, 35(1), 172–188.

Laurie, N., Dwyer, C., Holloway, S., and Smith, F. 1999. *Geographies of New Femininities*. Harlow: Pearson Education.

Law, R. 1997. Masculinity, place, and beer advertising in New Zealand: the Southern man campaign. *New Zealand Geographer*, 53(2), 22–28.

Little, J. 2002. Rural geography: rural gender identity and the performance of masculinity and femininity in the countryside. *Progress in Human Geography*, 26(5), 665–670.

Longhurst, R. 1997. (Dis)embodied geographies. *Progress in Human Geography*, 21(4), 486–501.

Longhurst, R. 2000. Geography and gender: masculinities, male identity and men. *Progress in Human Geography*, 24(3), 439–444.

Longhurst, R. 2001. *Bodies: Exploring Fluid Boundaries*. London: Routledge.

Mac an Ghaill, M. 1996. Introduction, in *Understanding Masculinities*, edited by M. Mac an Ghaill. Buckingham: Open University Press, 1–16.

Mac an Ghaill, M. and Haywood, C. 2007. *Gender, Culture and Society Contemporary Femininities and Masculinities*. New York: Palgrave Macmillan.

MacInnes, J. 1998. *The End of Masculinity*. Buckingham: Open University Press.

Maddrell, A., Strauss, K., Thomas, N., and Wyse, S., 2011. *Careers in UK HE Geography Survey*. Paper presented at the RGS-IBG Conference, London.

Madge, C., Raghuram, P., Skelton, T., Willis, K. and Williams, J. 1997. Methods and methodologies in feminist geographies: politics, practice and power, in *Feminist Geographies: Explorations in Diversity and Difference*, edited by C. Madge, et al. Harlow: Addison Wesley, 86–111.

Massey, D. 1996. Masculinity, dualisms and high technology, in *BodySpace: Destabilizing Geographies of Gender and Sexuality*, edited by N. Duncan. London: Routledge, 109–126.

McDowell, L. 1995. Body work: heterosexual gender performances in city workplaces, in *Mapping Desire*, edited by D. Bell and G. Valentine. London: Routledge, 75–95.

McDowell, L. 1997. *Capital Culture: Gender at Work in the City*. Malden: Wiley-Blackwell.

McDowell, L. 1999. *Gender, Place and Identity: Understanding Feminist Geographies*. Cambridge: Polity Press.

McDowell, L. 2000. Learning to serve? Employment aspirations and attitudes of young working-class men in an era of labour market restructuring. *Gender, Place and Culture: A Journal of Feminist Geography*, 7(4), 389–416.

McDowell, L. 2001a. Men, management and multiple masculinities in organisations. *Geoforum*, 32(2), 181–198.

McDowell, L. 2001b. Working with young men. *Geographical Review*, 91(1–2), 201–214.

McDowell, L. 2001c. 'It's that Linda again': ethical, practical and political issues involved in longitudinal research with young men. *Ethics, Place and Environment*, 4(2), 87–100.

McDowell, L, 2002a. Masculine discourses and dissonances: strutting 'lads', protest masculinity, and domestic respectability. *Environment and Planning D: Society and Space*, 20(1), 97–119.

McDowell, L. 2003. *Redundant Masculinities? Employment Change and White Working Class Youth*. Oxford: Wiley-Blackwell.

McDowell, L. 2005. The men and the boys: bankers, burger makers and barmen, in *Spaces of Masculinities*, edited by B. van Hoven and K. Hörschelmann. London: Routledge, 19–30.

McDowell, L. 2009. *Working Bodies: Interactive Service Employment and Workplace Identities*. Oxford: Wiley-Blackwell.

McDowell, L. 2010. Capital culture revisited: sex, testosterone and the city. *International Journal of Urban and Regional Research*, 34(3), 652–658.

Meth, P. and McClymont, K. 2009. Researching men: the politics and possibilities of a qualitative mixed-methods approach. *Social and Cultural Geography*, 10(8), 909–926.

Mohammad, R. 2001. 'Insiders' and/or 'outsiders': positionality, theory and praxis, in *Qualitative Methodologies for Geographers: Issues and Debates*, edited by M. Limb and C. Dwyer. London: Arnold, 101–120.

Mort, F. 1998. Cityscapes: consumption, masculinities and the mapping of London since 1950. *Urban Studies*, 35(5–6), 889–907.

Moss, P. 2002. *Feminist Geography in Practice: Research and Methods*. London: Blackwell.

Moss, P. and Falconer Al-Hindi, K. 2008. An introduction: feminisms, geographies, knowledges, in *Feminisms in Geography: Rethinking Space, Place and Knowledges*, edited by P. Moss and K. Falconer Al-Hindi. Maryland: Rowman and Littlefield, 1–29.

Nayak, A. 2003a. Last of the 'real Geordies'?: White masculinities and the subcultural response to deindustrialisation. *Environment and Planning D: Society and Space*, 21(1), 7–25.

Nayak, A. 2003b. *Race, Place and Globalisation*. Oxford: Berg.

Nayak, A. 2006. Displaced masculinities: chavs, youth and class in the post-industrial city. *Sociology*, 40(5), 813–831.

Nayak, A. and Kehily, M.J. 2013. *Gender, Youth and Culture: Global Masculinities and Femininities*. New York: Palgrave Macmillan.

Noble, G. 2009. 'Countless acts of recognition': young men, ethnicity and the messiness of identities in everyday life. *Social and Cultural Geography*, 10(8), 875–892.

O'Donnell, M. and Sharpe, S. 2000. *Uncertain Masculinities: Youth, Ethnicity and Class in Contemporary Britain*. London: Routledge.

Pease, B. 2002. *Men and Gender Relations*. Croydon: Tertiary Press.

Pini, B. 2008. *Masculinities and Management in Agricultural Organisations Worldwide*. Aldershot: Ashgate.

Pini, B. and Mayes, R. 2013. Gender, sexuality, and rurality in the mining industry, in *Rurality, Sexuality and Geography*, edited by A. Gorman-Murray, B. Pini and L. Bryant. Lexington: Lanham, 187–198.

Rich, A. 1986. Notes towards a politics of location, in *Blood, Bread and Poetry: Selected Prose 1979–1985*, edited by A. Rich. New York: Norton, 210–231.

Richardson, M. (in press). Embodied intergenerationality: family position, place and masculinity. *Gender, Place and Culture: A Journal of Feminist Geography*.

Rose, G. 1993. *Feminism and Geography: The Limits of Geographical Knowledge*. Cambridge: Polity Press.

Seager, J. 2000. 'And a charming wife': gender, marriage, and manhood in the job search process. *Professional Geographer*, 52(4), 709–721.

Seidler, V. 2007. Masculinities, bodies, and emotional life. *Men and Masculinities*, 10(1), 9–21.

Smith, G.D. and Winchester, H.P.M. 1998. Negotiating space: alternative masculinities at the work/home boundary. *Australian Geographer*, 29(3), 327–339.

Smith, N. 1993. Homeless/global: scaling places, in *Mapping the Futures*, edited by J. Bird. Routledge: London, 87–119.

Stevenson, N., Jackson, P. and Brooks, K. 2000. The politics of 'new' men's lifestyle magazines. *European Journal of Cultural Studies*, 3(3), 366–385.

Tarrant, A. 2010. 'Maturing' a sub-discipline: the intersectional geographies of masculinities and old age. *Geography Compass*, 4(10), 1580–1591.

Tarrant, A. 2010. Constructing a social geography of grandparenthood: a new focus for intergenerationality. *Area*, 42(2), 190–197.

Tarrant, A. 2013a. Grandfathering as spatio-temporal practice: conceptualizing performances of ageing masculinities in contemporary familial carescapes. *Social and Cultural Geography*, 14(2), 192–210.

Tarrant, A. 2013b. Negotiating multiple positionalities in the interview setting: researching across gender and generational boundaries. *Professional Geographer* [online: 12 July] Available at: http://www.tandfonline.com/doi/pdf/10.1080/00330124.2013.805621 [accessed: 26 November 2013].

Thien, D. and Del Casino, V. 2012. (Un)healthy men, masculinities and the geographies of health. *Annals of the Association of American Geographers*, 102(5), 1146–1156.

Tosh, J. 1999. *A Man's Place: Masculinity and the Middle-Class Home in Victorian England*. New Haven: Yale University Press.

Valentine, G. 1999. What it means to be a man: the body, masculinities, disability, in *Mind and Body Spaces: Geographies of Illness, Impairment and Disability*, edited by R. Butler and H. Parr. London: Routledge, 167–180.

Vanderbeck, R.M. 2005. Masculinities and fieldwork: widening the discussion. *Gender, Place and Culture: A Journal of Feminist Geography*, 12(4), 387–402.

Vanderbeck, R.M. 2007. Intergenerational geographies: age relations, segregation, and re-engagements. *Geography Compass*, 1(2), 200–221.

Waitt, G. 2006. Boundaries of desire: becoming sexual through the spaces of Sydney's 2002 Gay Games. *Annals of the Association of American Geographers*, 96(4), 773–787.

Waitt, G., Jessop, L. and Gorman-Murray, A. 2011. 'The guys in there just expect to be laid': embodied and gendered socio-spatial practices of a 'night-out' in Wollongong, Australia. *Gender, Place and Culture: A Journal of Feminist Geography*, 18(2), 255–275.

Waitt, G. and Warren, A. 2008. 'Talking shit over a brew after a good session with your mates': surfing, space and masculinity. *Australian Geographer*, 29(3), 353–365.

Walsh, K. 2011. Migrant masculinities and domestic space: British home-making practices in Dubai. *Transactions of the Institute of British Geographers*, 36(4). 516–529.

Warren, A. and Gibson, C. 2011. Blue-collar creativity: re-framing custom car culture in the imperilled industrial city. *Environment and Planning A*, 43(11), 2705–2722.

Whitehead, S.M. 2002. *Men and Masculinities.* Cambridge: Polity Press.

Wilton, R. 1996. Diminishing returns? The geography of everyday life with HIV/AIDS. *Health and Place*, 2(2), 69–83.

Wilton, R., DeVerteuil, G. and Evans, J. 2013. 'No more of this macho bullshit': drug treatment, place and the reworking of masculinity. *Transactions of the Institute of British Geographers* [online: 17 August] Available at http://onlinelibrary.wiley.com/doi/10.1111/tran.12023/abstract [accessed 26 November 2013].

Woodward, R. 2003. Locating military masculinities: space, place and the formation of gender identity and the British Army, in *Military Masculinities: Identity and the State,* edited by P.R. Higate. Westport: Praeger, 43–56.

Woodward R. 2006. Warrior heroes and little green men: soldiers, military training and the construction of rural masculinities, in *Country Boys: Masculinity and Rural Life*, edited by M.M. Bell, H. Campbell and M. Finney. Philadelphia: Pennsylvania State University Press.

Yeoh, B. and Willis, K. 2004. Constructing masculinities in transnational space: Singapore men on the 'regional beat', in *Transnational Spaces*, edited by P. Jackson, P. Crang and C. Dwyer. London: Routledge, 147–163.

Yi'En, C. 2012. Transnational masculinities *in situ*: Singaporean husbands and their international marriage experiences. *Area*, 41(1), 76–82.

Young, I.M. 1990. *Justice and the Politics of Difference.* Princeton: Princeton University Press.

PART 1
Introducing and Theorising Masculinities and Place

Chapter 2

Theorising, Men, Masculinities, Place and Space: Local, National and Transnational Contexts and Interrelations

Jeff Hearn, Alp Biricik and Tanja Joelsson

Introduction

This chapter examines the interrelations of theorising, men, masculinities, space and place, with emphasis on the local, the national and the transnational, and their interrelations. While studies on men have always been on feminist agendas (Hanmer 1990), over the past 35 years or more there has been a relatively rapid, if geographically uneven, growth of focused studies on men and masculinities (Kimmel, Hearn and Connell 2005, Flood et al. 2007). Yet although there has been an increase of less or more critical studies on men and masculinities, a social un-placed or de-placed model has often been dominant in theorising on men and masculinity, with sex role theory perhaps the biggest culprit.

Lefebvre's (1974: 26) famous argument that 'social (space) is a (social) product' has, in recent years, prompted further analyses of the construction of space parallel to the unequal class relations under late capitalism and neoliberalism. Agnew (2005: 82) builds on this, suggesting 'space refers to location somewhere and place to the occupation of that location. … Place is specific and space is general'. Arguably, space is a more abstract concept than place, while space has tended to become associated with movement to a greater extent (see Cresswell 2004: 8–10). Recent debates on how place and space are socially constructed (Cresswell 2004: 30, 39), and how social relations are part of the production of space and place (Massey 1994), are central to critical analysis of men and masculinities. Yet while masculinities theory initially recognised the analysis of the social spatiality of the male body as part of its initial formulation (Connell 1983), many subsequent applications of masculinities have neglected spatiality.

This neglect has many consequences, at all levels from the immediate to the local, the national, the transnational and global, and even gendered geopolitics above and beyond the Earth, as in climate change or militarisation of space above the planet. Many places are produced, occupied, populated, dominated and controlled by men. To name some obvious sites, military institutions, men-only clubs, gay men's clubs, pornography theatres and sports stadia are places where male homosociality is produced, often celebrated harmoniously, by some at least.

Patriarchy, or patriarchies, as non-deterministic social systems in which males or men tend to be dominant over females or women, remains a highly relevant approach to explore symbiotic co-constructions of hegemonic versions of being men, masculinities, place and space (see also Berg, Gahman and Nunn 2014: this volume).

In reviewing studies on men and masculinities, Raewyn Connell (2000: 2–3) has remarked:

> We now have a growing library of studies from around the world, across a number of the social sciences, in which researchers have traced the construction of masculinity in a particular milieu or moment. They include studies of marital sexuality, homophobic murders, a body-building gym, street gangs, a clergyman's family, an insurance office, a high school, a film, a political movement, professional sports, a police station, a literary genre, a media debate … I call this the 'ethnographic moment' in masculinity research, in which the local and specific is emphasised.

The 'ethnographic moment' in studies on men and masculinities has highlighted the multiplicity of masculinities, relations among masculinities, the importance of collectivity, social learning of and about masculinities and femininities, complexities, contradictions and change. This attention to the ethnographic moment has both strengths, in the recognition of the local and of place, location and locationality, but it can also feed into ideographic decontextualisation or limitation to a single national, societal context, as a form of 'methodological nationalism' (Beck 2000) or even 'methodological essentialism'. But 'the ethnographic moment' does not necessitate limiting attention to the local. Ethnographic research can also challenge analysis of wider, global, and indeed transnational, processes and power dynamics (see also Datta and McIlwaine 2014: this volume). Recent critical research on men and masculinities has moved towards more international, transnational, global, and postcolonial perspectives and processes (Cornwall, Edström and Greig 2011, Ruspini et al. 2011, Hearn, Blagojević and Harrison 2013).

In the remainder of this chapter, the relations of men, masculinities, space and place are considered in more concrete terms and contexts, through an ethnographic study of younger greaser men at the *local* level in Sweden, followed by focused analyses of gay men's relations with mandatory military service in the Turkish *national* context, and older men seen within the *transnational* domain. While these are discrete cases in different locations, they also point to connections and interrelations across the 'levels' of context and analysis (see also Hickey-Moody and Kenway 2014: this volume).

Where is the local? Greasers in a Swedish peri-urban community

We begin with the local level, as both a concrete focus and as requiring contextualisation beyond itself. Young men's risk-taking with motor vehicles regularly generates public debate as a traffic safety issue, often resulting in various policy suggestions, such as curfews or raising the minimum age for attaining a driving licence. Seldom are these suggested solutions based on critical ethnographic research where intersections on age, gender, class and place are highlighted. In Joelsson's (2013) ethnographic study of the greasers[1], or more precisely 'Volvo greasers', in Lillby, a peri-urban[2] community in Sweden, risk-taking practices with motor vehicles, such as speeding and drifting, are reported as central practices. Through contextualisation as an analytical tool, intersecting norms and conceptions around age, gender, class and place are practiced at the local level, highlighting the situated character of risk-taking practices.

Situated risk-taking and masculinity

In the greasers' narratives and practices an inconsistent topography of risk emerges: certain practices are created as high risk, while others are practiced on a regular everyday basis. This risk landscape is in many senses fluid in the greaser's narratives, and the negotiation of which practices remain in their everyday repertoire depends on their social, temporal and geographical surroundings. Creating the risky and dangerous practices within the realm of 'fun' in general is part of the accepted way of doing a greaser.

The greasers are most often portrayed in media and popular representations as physically superior to the other young men in the community: daring, confrontational, aggressive. The connection between working-class men/masculinity, toughness and living a risk-taking life appear to have some explanatory value with reference to the greasers. Canaan (1991) argues that young 'working class' men's bodies are their main source of power and self-esteem, due to manual labour and blue-collar jobs (see also Vaaranen 1999, Hatton 2007). Recognising

1 The emic term 'greasers' refers to a member of a group interested in motor vehicles, usually specific kinds of cars such as Volvos, but also mopeds, EPA tractors (older cars, sometimes trucks, converted into agricultural machines) and quad bikes. It has loose cultural ties to 1950s and 1960s greaser culture (Joelsson 2013, cf. O'Dell 2001, Rosengren 2000). Joelsson's study is based on ethnographic fieldwork with greaser men and women between 15 and 19, as well as formal interviews with pupils at the local high school and youth centre staff in the local community.

2 The term peri-urban refers to a different kind of urban, at the urban fringe, where lifestyles and values do not differ substantially from the lifestyles and values in conventional urban settings. The designation of (the anonymised) Lillby as peri-urban rather than rural concerns the problematic urban-rural dichotomy, hence destabilising that relationship and its inherent hierarchy.

close links between working-class men, masculinity and car-related practices, Hatton (2007: 172) argues that:

> Taking risks or willing to take risks, affected the status of the young men within the group and to appear 'hard' or a 'real' man gaining the reputation through hard living, risk taking, fighting, and so on was thought to be preferable than being regarded as 'gay', 'girly', a 'wimp', or 'wanker' being the terms usually levelled at someone who did not demonstrate desirable qualities of masculinity.

In line with Hatton (2007), the greaser men can be linked with a certain kind of masculine position that values and amplifies physical strength, toughness and offensiveness. These practices are, however, not necessarily to be interpreted in terms of a working-class position. The practices the greasers carry out with their motor vehicles are naturalised, and even framed as desired acts constituting a (masculine) self within greaser culture, where some elements correspond to what other researchers have interpreted as class-related. Such an analysis falls short if spatiality is not taken into account.

Thus far, the situatedness of risk has been emphasised (Bunton, Green and Mitchell 2004), by illuminating how the greasers relate to risk-taking as practice. It is important to recognise the difference between young people's own perceptions of risk and 'objective' definitions circulating in official policy. As Bunton, Green and Mitchell (2004), *inter alia*, have stressed, young people tend to construct their risk hierarchies within their social and cultural context where education, family and the peer group are heavy influences. What is further needed is the contextualising of practices so that socio-cultural incentives for risk-taking with motor vehicles are made visible, including acknowledging and accounting for how place co-constitutes greaser culture, and thus spatially frames greasers' risk-taking.

Spatial boredom

Violations with motor vehicles in public space occur in all age groups eligible for driving, but the conception of the reckless teenage driver (cf. Best 2008) has had pervasive consequences for how a dangerous driver is imagined, as well as how problems associated with this age category are remedied. The perception of the most dangerous driver is most notably *young* and *male*, but also, increasingly, placed and positioned in rural or peri-urban backwaters. But how does space and place relate to risk-taking with motor vehicles? A very common way in which the greasers talk about the attraction of hanging out at the parking lot in Lillby relates to the experience of boredom: having 'nothing to do' or 'nowhere (else) to go'. It is further framed as a strategy to cope with and avoid what they call 'restlessness'. Conceptions of rural or peri-urban areas are particularly poignant when youth cultures are discussed: the *råners*, a Norwegian group similar to the Swedish greasers, 'are associated with rural areas that are understood as backward and boring, and as a dull rather than idyllic space for young people' (Laegren

2007: 29). Indeed ideas associated with urban and rural place often evolve around dichotomies between modernity and backwardness or tradition, and progress and stagnation respectively (see Kenway and Hickey-Moody 2009, Stenbacka 2011, Waara 1996).

The experience of boredom is part of the greasers' narratives and practices, and is used as a resource by the young greasers to constitute themselves as 'fun' and social, through engaging in fun practices, such as partying and risk-taking with motor vehicles. They also recreate social distinctions with other young people by labeling non-greasers as boring. Spatial boredom is a resource for the young greasers to draw upon, rather than a mental state or an effect of geographical conditions, in the way that many approaches conceptualise the phenomenon of boredom. Spatial boredom refers to the co-constitution of place and culture: of how cultural conceptions on age, class, place and gender are related to and actively engaged with at the level of practice. The greasers actively engage with conceptions of themselves as rural and backward, and manage to create a position of spatial and social dominance with regard to other local youth, while meanwhile recreating pervasive notions around gender and place. Their orientation towards their neighbourhood and peers entails distancing from the home, which can be interpreted as distancing from both the adult world and a feminised sphere. The neighbourhood comes to portray values connoting danger, risk – and masculinity (see Rose 1993, Domosh and Seager 2001). The social norms associated with masculinity in greaser culture encourage appropriation of public space, and distancing from feminised private space, by exercising and encouraging risk-taking with vehicles.

It is not only the gendering of place that is reinforced, however, but also place in relation to time. Whereas place is conceived of as stasis and immanence, and therefore feminine in line with the home, time is perceived as flux, fluidity and transcendence (cf. Massey 1994). Yet again, the passive character of the home can be seen as the place from which the greasers need to 'flee' in order to be able to build their fun personas. It is impossible to be anything other than boring if confined to the stasis of the home. Furthermore, the (potential) activities associated with the neighbourhood are conceived of in terms of movement and activity – of time moving fast, of 'something happening'. The co-constitution of place and person is here vital in the greasers' creation of themselves as fun through fun practices.

Place matters to and affects the greasers of Lillby: the place they live in is marginalised and stigmatised within regional and national politics; they are positioned in society in relation to conceptions of youth as an idealised and problematic life phase; as young people, they are placed within society with regard to these notions of youth, and the politics of youth have effects with spatial implications, such as the institutionalisation of leisure time and space; and all the above-mentioned together affect their possibilities to act. A thorough analysis of the spatial, and its socio-cultural context, represents a crucial engagement for understanding the persistence of social formations and power orders related to, *inter alia*, age, class and gender. Thus, what may appear as a simply local place and context exists in relations with wider societal, national place and space, with consequent implications for theorising men and masculinities there in the local.

Where is the national? The case of non-normative male sexualities in Turkey

Our next case both focuses on and problematises the national context. Since the Gay Liberation Movement in the 1970s and its associated academic developments, themselves both strongly national and international in character, various theorisations on the interconnections of sex/gender, sexuality, space and time have been elaborated. An important spatial metaphor, 'the closet', has been theorised to analyse the dimensions of sexual oppression and hegemonic versions of heterosexuality (Brown 2000, Kosofsky Sedgwick 1990). Many researchers have addressed the subordination of non-normative male sexualities in heteronormative environments and in specific male homosocial environments, places and sites in urban contexts, such as gay men's cruising areas/parks, bars, clubs and saunas. Under the influence of Michel Foucault's arguments on power, sexuality and subjectivity, place-based cases have shown how sexual subjectivity and spatiality are symbiotically constructed in relation to power differentials, such as age, gender and race (Bell and Valentine 1995, Browne and Lim 2007). Such theorisations, through the experiences of non-normative sexual subjects, have problematised the construction of (mainly urban) space within sexually central and peripheral spatial relations.

New theoretical insights on intersections of sexual identity politics, globalisation and transnationalisation have also been developed (Grewal and Kaplan 2001, Plummer 2008). Referring to the followers of Lefebvre, Halberstam (2005: 5) has argued that most neo-Marxist macro analyses and theorisations on spatiality have privileged 'class/global/political' over 'body/local/personal', and ignored sexuality as a category of analysis, thus missing various dimensions of transnational capitalism. Halberstam has suggested concepts of 'queer time' and 'queer space' to examine subjects' spatial experiences outside heteronormative time and space constructions.

Militarism, masculinity, and sexuality

In Turkey, a country founded as a modernisation project on the relics of the Ottoman Empire in 1923, the rite of passage of 'becoming a real man' means to develop a symbiotic relation with the hegemonic masculinity system. In Turkish, *erkek* [man] and *erkeklik* [masculinity] both derive from the word *erk* [*iktidar*/power] (Türker 2004), and have strong semiotic ties for the construction of *ataerkil* [patriarchy] as well as *er* [man or soldier]. *Erkek adam* is a common expression to signify what 'the real man' is. However, to become an *erkek adam* is not an easy process (Biricik 2008). Broadly speaking, the social and cultural construction of the 'ideal [Turkish] man' starts early in childhood with the performance of circumcision.

In teenage years, the first sexual intercourse with a woman, known as 'becoming national' (*milli olmak*), is counted as a 'man's must' before starting the mandatory military service. Marriage and setting up a job to become a breadwinner father are two major steps in becoming a man after the fulfilment of military service. Although men experience each rite of passage at different times of their life, they find social and cultural support from their families, friends and state institutions (Sinclair-Webb 2000, Helvacıoğlu 2006, Biricik 2009, 2012).

Discussing gendered dynamics of mandatory military service in Turkey, in particular, demonstrates how militarism, as a modern, patriarchal form of violence, operates through male bodies and builds its own militarised space. Every man who is over 19 years old must fulfil his mandatory military service. There are few exceptions, such as men with physical and/or bodily disabilities who are not counted as 'fit' for the army, and therefore labelled as 'rotten' and exempted. Although homosexuality is not criminalised in the Turkish military system, the system nevertheless considers homosexual men as 'rotten'/'unfit' for the military service, and therefore they are exempted from the military service too.

Recent research on homosexual men's lived experiences during mandatory military service in Turkey demonstrated that military institutions, as places dominated by men, have become spaces where hegemonic masculinity intersects with a militarised medical gaze through violent medical examinations (Biricik 2009). In de Certeau's (1984) sense, against the militarised Turkish state's strategy of building a citizens' army, some men resist mandatory military service by developing gendered tactics.

With few exceptional cases, homosexual men's oral statements of their sexual orientation are not counted valid or sufficient, and they are also asked to prove their sexual orientation by the medical authorities. The so-called medical examinations may vary due to time and cities in Turkey, but the medical authorities ask applicants to complete a series of psychological tests, go through a rectal examination – applied by military doctors to examine the loss of (masculine) control on the rectal area as the result of being passive during sexual intercourse – and submit photographs taken during sexual intercourse where the applicant must clearly perform being 'passive'. In some cases, applicants are obliged to stay in military hospitals for 'medical' observation at sections called 'pink rooms'. In addition to medical examination, recently authorities oblige applicants to bring their families to meet military hospital authorities and 'confess' that they are aware of the applicant's sexual orientation (read: 'perversion') (Biricik 2012). This all clearly exemplifies how militarism and masculinity fit together well in militarised places, such as military hospitals, and how such a convergence reconstitutes and empowers values of hegemonic masculinity and expands its operating space.

On 30 October 2010, the *Der Spiegel* magazine published an article on debates around Turkish militarist medical examinations of gay men, bringing the issue to wider international attention with the headline 'Porn for the Generals'. Based on the narratives of two gay men, a lawyer and a military doctor, *Der Spiegel* claimed that the Turkish military hospitals had the biggest 'porn' archive in Turkey.

On 9 November 2010 the European Commission progress report on Turkey stated that Turkish military medical treatments on gay men were against human rights. In the face of international and supranational institutions' critiques and observations, on 12 November 2010 the Turkish Armed Forces (TAF) published a press statement on a private internet newspaper (OdaTv.com), claiming none of their military institutions had any 'porn archives' and no such medical examinations were ever carried out in military hospitals. A few days after TAF's defence, Lambda–Istanbul, a gay, lesbian, transgender advocacy group based in Istanbul, released a press statement. The group underlined that so-called medical examinations of gay men were still practised at military institutions and TAF must update its medical examinations and related health criteria according to international standards (Biricik 2013).

Although laws do not restrict homosexuality in Turkey, social and cultural values aim primarily to protect the heterosexual family structure through discourses of honour and morality. Such a system surely dignifies the values of hegemonic masculinity and protects patriarchal social and economic structures. Since the 1990s, LGBT movements, often in coordination with feminist/women rights and anti-militarist organisations, have contested heteronormative and patriarchal constructions of society and state by making sexual identity politics visible in public space.

Today, even though the number of active LGBT organisations is less than double figures in Turkey, a country with more than 70 million citizens, ICT-based LGBT activism, networking and communication have enormously created its own (virtual) communities, (virtual) solidarity sites/places (for example, Facebook, Twitter), and increased visibility of non-normative sexual subjectivities in national and transnational public space. This mirrors the high level of online activity in Turkey (CamScore 2009, Turkish Statistical Institute 2012), with over 31 million Facebook subscribers (Socialbakers 2012); at the same time, governmental Telecommunications Communication Presidency controls restrict access to 20,792 websites from Turkey, as of 16 October 2012 (Erişime Engelenen Siteler 2012), and some transnational gay-dating websites, such as gayromeo.com and planetout.com, are restricted by Turkish law. The interrelations of the national and the transnational are clear here, and arguably becoming more pronounced and more recognisable.

Where is the transnational? Older men in globalising contexts

The final example brings us to transnational contexts. Men's structural power within transnational processes may increasingly be enacted *by and upon* men, who are themselves contradictory, fractured, mediated through globalising information, media and cyberspace. Most conceptualisations of the transnational invoke two elements: the *nation* or *national boundaries*; and *'trans'* (across) relations, as opposed to inter- or intra-relations (Hearn 2004). In speaking of transnational relations, *the nation is simultaneously affirmed and deconstructed.* One way of conceptualising this is as transnational patriarchies, or simply transpatriarchies, in international business and financial corporations; sex trade; information and communication technologies (ICTs); militarism; oil, energy and environment; circulations of representations; transgovernmental machineries (Hearn 2009). Transpatriarchies comprise acutely contradictory processes, with multiple forms of difference, presence and absence for different men, and interplays of transnational privilege and threat to aspects of being men.

Older men, transnationalisation, place, space

Considered within such a broad context, the category of older men is contradictory (Hearn 1995). In many societies age has been a source of patriarchal power, in relation to women, older women, and younger men. With contemporary contradictions of ageing, older men benefit through sexism while disadvantaged by ageism. Older men can be seen as an 'absent presence' (Hearn 1998), both visible and invisible, even a contradictory another Other. However, this relation of men's aged and men's gender power is becoming yet more complex. Men's generational power in communities has been widely overtaken by inter/national institutions, with growing power of corporate, transgovernmental, military and media organisations, and their patterns of domination by groupings of men. It is increasingly problematic to see nation-states as the given starting point of analysis.

Transnational constructions of older men are not distant phenomena, but happen and are experienced locally, in several ways (Hearn and Sandberg 2009). First, transnational processes have *political economic* effects, such as work restructuring through transnational corporate policies, exerting powers over individuals and nation-states in relation to older men. The individual autonomous older man has widely been superseded not only by the (patriarchal) nation, but by transpatriarchal forces beyond the nation. Second, there are *geographical* effects. While national boundaries can be extremely rigid for some people, transnationalisations involve movements of people, and greater cross-cultural social relations for older men. Older men meanwhile live in *particular* local places, sometimes more than one, made local through concentrations of *effects* of global forces. Places have significance as localities of 'origin', family, work, friendship, leisure, sexuality, affection, and much more. While greater cultural contacts have positive implications for some, transnational ageing brings legal complications, as in different legal traditions on pensions. Third, transnationalisation processes provide social contexts for *personal* experience. Re-formations of older men's identities occur through personal relations within globalising contexts. Increased availability of visual and textual images of older men from advertising, film, ICTs, and international travel produce contradictory global influences and artifacts, for use in becoming a particular 'type of (older) man'.

Rich older men

Ageing may not necessarily reduce men's power; age is a source of financial, and indeed corporate, power for some men, so that ageing also brings greater economic divergence from dispossessed men through, for example, forced migration. At the extreme end of riches, men are overwhelmingly dominant. According to the *Forbes* (2013a) list, the eight richest persons globally are men; and only one of the richest ten is a woman, and her estate is now managed by others. The average age is also close to 75 years. George Soros is an interesting case in point, in terms of transnational processes. His *Forbes* (2013b) biography reads:

> Hedge fund legend George Soros is chairman of Soros Fund Management, the $24 billion firm that manages his personal fortune as well as the money belonging to his foundations, which support causes ranging from human rights to education and public health. He is not involved in day-to-day operations, … but Soros remains involved. … The firm's performance trailed the U.S. stock market in 2012, but was firmly in positive territory, thanks partly to a big bet against the yen. Born in Budapest, Soros survived the Nazi occupation of Hungary and went on to study at the London School of Economics before launching storied hedge fund firm Quantum Fund Management in 1969. Outspoken on world economic policies and an unapologetic proponent of European integration, Soros has recently declared that the euro is 'here to stay'. Since 1979 Soros has given away $8.5 billion to human rights, education and public health groups; $6 billion has gone to international causes and estimated $400 million to fight poverty. His efforts have resulted in the creation of organisations such as Revenue Watch, which works to ensure that citizens benefit from their country's natural resources. In August 2012, at his 82nd birthday party at his summer home in Southampton, Soros announced that he and his girlfriend, Tamiko Bolton, are engaged. Bolton is 42 years Soros' junior and will become the financier's third wife. The couple plans to marry in the summer of 2013.

This kind of rich older man might be seen to exemplify Connell's (1998) concept of transnational business masculinity. Such an approach can be extended by reference to intersections of diverse forms of local and national place, and transnational space and spatialisation, as well as age, generation, gender, sexuality, money, charity, natural resources, and indeed post-socialism, postcolonialism and neoliberalism. This complexity points to the inadequacy, in terms of space and place, of even most 'critical' gendered analyses of transnational business, management and leadership (see Hearn 2013). The shifting and interrelated local, national and transnational locations of transnational men and masculinities matter (Reis 2004).

Concluding remarks: where are theorisations on men and masculinities going?

In this chapter we have examined the questions of place and space in the analysis of men and masculinities in different – local, national, transnational – contexts. In contemporary local, national and transnational social processes, centres of dominance and inequality, spatial and place-bound, may be reinforced, relocated, fragmented, deconstructed. Moreover, social space operates not only at geographical, local, national and transnational levels, but also on bodily experience. These are analytical and theoretical issues, and also emotional, lived, fictive ones of central importance to the further critical analysis of men and masculinities.

In the light of these turns to place and space, where are theorisations on men and masculinities moving today? There seem to be at least five major moves here, some inter-linked, some seemingly in different directions. First, we note the centrality of the immediate spatiality of the body. This could in some ways be seen as a return to the body, not least because the first formulation of the concept of hegemonic masculinity was made in relation to embodiment (Connell 1983), a form of spatiality still often neglected in studies of men and masculinities (Hearn 2012). Second, there is the continuing significance of the local, locality, place and indeed nation, understood as specificities not abstractions. As illustrated in the first two cases studies, the immediacy and potency of local and national space and place for gendered lives persists, not only and most obviously for young men, but also in the construction of the adult male national citizen. Third, and what may appear apparently contradictory, we note the growing impacts of the transnational and transnational space. This occurs in myriad ways – within, between and beyond nations (Hearn, Blagojević and Harrison 2013) – creating both greater powers and potentials for some men, and marginalising and undermining others. Fourth, there is the complexity of intersections of locality, nation, and transnationalisations, whereby particular ways of being men and doing masculinities may be formed by and through combinations of elements across these different domains. Finally, we draw attention to the prospect of new possible conjunctions of the local/national/transnational places and spaces, for example, through ICTs, themselves subject to apparently rapid change and uncertainty in real time. These moves make for much to be done in re-theorising of men and masculinities in place(s) and space(s).

References

Agnew, J. 2005. Space: place, in *Spaces of Geographical Thought: Deconstructing Human Geography's Binaries*, edited by P. Cloke and R. Johnston. London: Sage Publications, 81–96.

Beck, U. 2000. *What is Globalization?* Cambridge: Polity Press.

Bell, D. and Valentine, G. (eds) 1995. *Mapping Desire: Geographies of Sexualities*. London and New York: Routledge.

Best, A. 2008. Teen driving as public drama: statistics, risk and the social construction of youth as a public problem. *Journal of Youth Studies*, 11(6), 651–671.

Biricik, A. 2008. Erkek adam ezberini bozmak üzerine: Türkiye'de toplumsal cinsiyet sisteminin resmi söylem üzerinden kurgulanması [Contesting the memorization of 'manly man': The construction of gender system through official discourse in Turkey], in *Cinsiyet Halleri: Türkiye'de Toplumsal Cinsiyetin Kesişim Sınırları [States of Sex: The Crosscutting Borders of Gender Relations in Turkey]*, edited by N. Mutluer. Istanbul: Varlık, 232–246.

Biricik, A. 2009. Rotten report and reconstructing hegemonic masculinity in Turkey, in *Conscientious Objection: Resisting Militarized Society*, edited by Ö.H. Çınar and Ç. Üster. London: Zed, 112–117.

Biricik, A. 2012. 'Rotten report' and the reproduction of masculinity, nation and security in Turkey, in *Making Gender, Making War: Violence, Military and Peacekeeping Practices*, edited by A. Kronsell and E. Svedberg. New York: Routledge, 76–89.

Biricik, A. 2013. 7. Ok – militarism: Vatandaþlýk, borçluluk ve çürükle°tirmek üzerine [7. Arrow – The militarism: Citizenship, indebtedness and rotting], in *Erkek Millet Asker Millet: Türkiye'de Militarizm, Milliyetçilik, Erkek(lik) ler [Manly Nation, Soldier Nation: Militarizm, Nationalism, Men and Masculinities]*, edited by N.Y Sünbüloðlu. Istanbul: Ýletiþim, 369–392.

Brown, M.P. 2000. *Closet Space: Geographies of Metaphor from the Body to the Globe*. London: Routledge.

Browne, K. and Lim, J. 2007. *Geographies of Sexualities: Theory, Practices and Politics*. Aldershot: Ashgate.

Bunton, R., Green, E. and Mitchell, W. 2004. Introduction: young people, risk and leisure, an overview, in *Young People, Risk and Leisure. Constructing Identities in Everyday Life*, edited by W. Mitchell, R. Bunton and E. Green. Basingstoke: Palgrave Macmillan, 1–24.

Caanan, J. 1991. Is 'doing nothing' just boys' play? Integrating feminist and cultural studies perspectives on working-class young men's masculinity, in *Off-centre: Feminism and Cultural Studies*, edited by S. Franklin, C. Lury and J. Stacey. London: Harper Collins, 109–125.

CamScore.com. 2009. *Turkey has seventh largest and most engaged online audience in Europe* [Online: CamScore]. Available at: http://www.comscore.com/Insights/Press_Releases/2009/5/Turkey_has_Seventh_Largest_Online_Audience_in_Europe [accessed: 12 March 2013].

Connell, R.W. 1983. Men's bodies, in *Which Way Is Up?* Edited by R.W. Connell. Sydney: Allen and Unwin, 17–32.

Connell, R.W. 1998. Masculinities and globalization. *Men and Masculinities*, 1(1), 3–23.

Connell, R.W. 2000. Understanding men: gender sociology and the new international research on masculinities. Clark Lecture, University of Kansas, 19 September. Available at: http://www.engagingmen.net/files/resources/2010/Caroline/

Understanding_Men__Gender_Sociology_and_the_New_International_Research_on_Masculinities.pdf [accessed: 19 September 2000].

Cornwall, A., Edström, J. and Greig, A. (eds) 2011. *Men and Development: Politicising Masculinities*. London: Zed.

Cresswell, T. 2004. *Place: A Short Introduction.* Oxford: Wiley-Blackwell.

de Certeau, M. 1984. *The Practice of Everyday Life*. Berkeley: University of California Press.

Domosh, M. and Seager, J. 2001. *Putting Women in Place: Feminist Geographers make Sense of the World*. New York: Guilford.

Erişime Engellenen Siteler. 2013. [Online: Access Restricted Websites]. Available at: http://engelliweb.com/ [accessed: 12 March 2013].

Forbes. 2013a. *Billionaires list* [Online: Forbes]. Available at: http://www.forbes.com/billionaires/list/ [accessed: 12 March 2013].

Forbes. 2013b. *George Soros* [Online: Forbes]. Available at: http://www.forbes.com/profile/george-soros/ [accessed: 12 March 2013].

Flood, M., Gardiner, J.K., Pease, B. and Pringle, K. (eds) 2007. *International Encyclopedia of Men and Masculinities*. London: Routledge.

Grewal, I. and Kaplan, C. 2001. Global identities: theorizing transnational studies of sexuality. *GLQ: A Journal of Lesbian and Gay Studies*, 7(4), 663–679.

Halberstam, J. 2005. *In a Queer Time and Place: Transgender Bodies, Subcultural Lives*. New York: New York University Press.

Hanmer, J. 1990. Men, power and the exploitation of women, in *Men, Masculinities and Social Theory*, edited by J. Hearn and D. Morgan. London: Unwin Hyman/Routledge, 21–42.

Hatton, Z. 2007. *The Tarmac Cowboys: An Ethnographic Study of the Cultural World of Boy Racers*. Plymouth: University of Plymouth, School of Law and Social Science.

Hearn, J. 1995. Imaging the aging of men, in *Images of Aging: Cultural Representations of Later Life*, edited by M. Featherstone and A. Wernick. London: Routledge, 97–115.

Hearn, J. 1998. Theorizing men and men's theorizing: men's discursive practices in theorizing men. *Theory and Society*, 27(6), 781–816.

Hearn, J. 2004. Tracking 'the transnational': studying transnational organizations and managements, and the management of cohesion. *Culture and Organization*, 10(4), 273–290.

Hearn, J. 2009. Patriarchies, transpatriarchies and intersectionalities, in *Intimate Citizenships: Gender, Sexualities, Politics*, edited by E. Oleksy. London: Routledge, 177–192.

Hearn, J. 2012. Male bodies, masculine bodies, men's bodies: the need for a concept of gex, in *Routledge Handbook of Body Studies*, edited by B.S. Turner. London: Routledge, 307–320.

Hearn, J. 2013. Contextualizing men, masculinities, leadership and management: gender/intersectionalities, local/transnational, embodied/virtual, theory/

practice, in *The Oxford Handbook of Gender in Organizations*, edited by R. Simpson, R. Burke and S. Kumra. Oxford: Oxford University Press.

Hearn, J., Blagojević, M. and Harrison, K. (eds) 2013. *Rethinking Transnational Men*. New York: Routledge.

Hearn, J. and Sandberg, L. 2009. Older men, ageing and power: masculinities theory and alternative spatialised theoretical perspectives. *Sextant: Revue du Groupe Interdisciplinaire D'Etudes sur les Femmes et le Genre*, 27, 147–163.

Helvacıoğlu, B. 2006. The smile of death and the solemncholy of masculinity, in *Islamic Masculinities*, edited by L. Ouzgane. London: Zed, 35–56.

Joelsson, T. 2013. *Space and Sensibility: Young Men's Risk-taking with Motor Vehicles*. Linköping: Linköping University Electronic Press.

Kenway, J. and Hickey-Moody, A. 2009. Spatialized leisure pleasures and masculine distinctions. *Social and Cultural Geography*, 10(8), 837–852.

Kimmel, M., Hearn, J. and Connell, R.W. (eds) 2005. *The Handbook of Studies of Men and Masculinities*, Thousand Oaks: Sage Publications.

Laegren, A.S. 2007. Exploring masculinity, technology and identity in rural Norway, in *Global Perspectives on Rural Childhood and Youth: Young Rural Lives*, edited by R. Panelli, S. Punsch and E. Robson. New York: Routledge, 29–40.

Lefebvre, H. 1974. *The Production of Space*. Oxford: Wiley-Blackwell.

Lupton, D. 2004. Pleasure, aggression and fear: the driving experience of young Sydneysiders, in *Young People, Risk and Leisure. Constructing Identities in Everyday Life*, edited by W. Mitchell, R. Bunton and E. Green. Basingstoke: Palgrave Macmillan, 25–42.

O'Dell, T. 2001. Raggare and the panic of mobility: modernity and hybridity in Sweden, in *Car Cultures*, edited by D. Miller. Oxford: Berg, 105–132.

Plummer, K. 2008. Studying sexualities for a better world? Ten years of sexualities. *Sexualities*, 11(1/2), 7–22.

Reis, C. 2004. *Men Managers in a European Multinational Company*. Mering and München: Rainer Humpp Verlag.

Rose, G. 1993. *Feminism and Geography: The Limits of Geographical Knowledge*. Cambridge: Polity Press.

Rosengren, A. 2000. *Hot Rod-Byggare och Andra Bilentusiaster*. Stockholm: Carlsson.

Ruspini, E., Hearn, J., Pease, B. and Pringle, K. (eds) 2011. *Men and Masculinities around the World: Transforming Men's Practices*. New York: Palgrave Macmillan.

Sedgwick, E.K. 1990. *Epistemology of the Closet*. Berkeley: University of California Press.

Sinclair-Webb, E. 2000. Our Bulent is a commando: military service and manhood in Turkey, in *Imagined Masculinities: Male-Identity and Culture in the Modern Middle East*, edited by E. Sinclair-Webb and M. Ghoussoub. London: Saqi, 65–91.

Socialbakers.com. 2012. *Facebook Statistics by Country* [Online: Social Bakers]. Available at: http://www.socialbakers.com/facebook-statistics/ [accessed: 12 March 2013].

Stenbacka, S. 2011. Othering the rural: about the construction of rural masculinities and the unspoken urban hegemonic ideal in Swedish media. *Journal of Rural Studies*, 27(3), 235–244.

Türker, Y. 2004. Erk ile erkeklik [Power and masculinity]. *Toplum ve Bilim*, 101(Eylül), 8–10.

Turkish Statistical Institute. 2012. *Information and Communication Technology (ICT) Usage Survey on Households and Individuals* [Online: Turkish Statistical Institute]. Available at: http://www.turkstat.gov.tr/PreHaberBultenleri.do?id=10880 [accessed: 12 March 2013].

Vaaranen, H. 1999. The emotional experience of class: interpreting working-class kids' street racing in Helsinki. *The Annals of the American Academy of Political and Social Science*, 595(1), 91–107.

Waara, P. 1996. *Ungdom i gränsland*. Umeå: Borea Bokförlag.

Chapter 3

Spatio-temporal and Spatio-sensual Assemblages of Youthful Masculinities

Anna Hickey-Moody and Jane Kenway

> You go down the rock pool and we are all there. You bring your bathers and go swimming down the rocks and you can go around the other side where there is a beach and everything, and you jump off the rocks and swim into the beach and do it again and again.
>
> (Nick, Eden)

> It has got lots of beaches, it has got a beautiful river mouth that is good for fishing, good waves, good caravan park, good little shop there. It has also got a swamp out the back of my friend's place that has got lots of different birds – some bird watchers go over there ... There is heaps of walking tracks and a motorbike track, a footy field. There used to be a bowling club there but now they are turning the tracks into a school.
>
> (Daniel, Eden)

These anecdotes of being in place and experiencing place change demonstrate a love of landscape and locality, as well as an experiential attention to detail that arises from this affection. The passages quoted above are taken from stories of place told by young men living in a coastal town in New South Wales, Australia. While the boy's stories demonstrate their fondness for the places in which they live, they only begin to gesture towards the ways their subjectivities are embedded, or mixed into, the local landscapes and the impact that being this embedded has on their biographies. Through conceiving subjectivity as a mixture, or an assemblage of folds that aggregate spaces, times and materialities, we can begin to understand the material connectedness of these young men to the landscapes they inhabit. Such an intensive relationship, either in the form of connectedness or other responses to landscape, is a profound theme that runs through the narratives of most of the young men in our research, not only those from Eden. Reconciling the impact on biography that such intense connectedness to place can have, we think through the lived and historical connections to locality that make up these young men's subjectivities. In doing so, this chapter develops two related theories of subjectivity we call *spatio-temporal* and *spatio-sensual assemblages*. These theories hold in relief the ways that young men's selves are assembled in place through histories of writing themselves into landscapes and feeling intimate connections to place (see also Hearn, Biricik and Joelsson: this volume).

The material presented in this chapter draws on ethnographic studies conducted in four diverse, dynamic 'out of the way', yet globalising, places in Australia. While the spatial stories of these places are unique, in other ways they resonate profoundly with those of other non-metropolitan places around the globe. Certainly their industrial and agricultural biographies correspond to other places with similar economic bases in comparable Western countries, namely forestry, fishing, mining (coal, opal), viti and horticulture. Under the imperatives of late modern global trade economies, environmental pressures and cultural globalisation, each place is having to rethink and reconfigure its economic base, its view of sustainable living, its sense of place identity and what this means for local inhabitants. Indeed, in contemporary times, many out of the way places around the Western world are similarly rethinking themselves in response to shifting centres of economic and industrial power and the uneven uptake of environmental impact agendas. As such, the tools for theorising subjectivity that we develop here may be of use in considering the experiences and life worlds of many young men across the globe.

Assemblages of subjectivation

Assemblage is an English translation for the French word *agencement,* which also means layout or arrangement. We use the term to explain how any body and embodied subjectivity exists in relation to specific connections with other people and places: bodies are assembled in place through relationships to others and landscapes. In the material we present, we show how connections between place, time, communities and practices fold in to constitute young men's experiences of being in their body in place. Thinking through this connectedness, and by locating particular youth in place and time, we bring into view the different components that fold in to constitute young men's subjectivities. We also hold the located and embedded nature of their subjectivities in relief. The concept of the assemblage as a method for theorising subjectivity brings with it a model of the dividual, the individual as one part, segment or shard, of a greater whole. The territory from which the dividual is abstracted constitutes half the mixture of their subjectivity. Guattari's (1995: 98) writing explains this foregrounding of context quite clearly, as he states:

> [S]ocial relations, economic and matrimonial exchanges, were, in the group life, hardly discernible from what I proposed calling territorialized assemblages of enunciation. Through diverse modes of semiotization, systems of representation and multireferenced practices, these assemblages managed to crystallize complementary segments of subjectivity. … individuals found themselves enveloped by a number of transversal collective identities or, if one prefers, found themselves situated at the intersection of numerous vectors of partial subjectivation.

The 'territorialized assemblages of enunciation' or 'transversal collective identities' to which this quote refers are subjective mixtures: composites of space, time, feeling, relationality that fold in to make up subjects. Through such a frame of reference, all social subjects are, by constitution, part of a number of transversal collective identities – boys are or become 'themselves' in relation to place, leisure communities, families, biographies, employment, each of which constitutes a vector of *partial subjectivation*, a wedge in the composite formation of their subjectivity. If we take subjectivity as composite, as a compilation of connections to place, possibilities for relationality, the materiality of young men's experience (the way they feel in their body when they work the land, the smell of the earth, the sensation of swimming in the surf), then histories of writing themselves into landscape can be seen as literally constituting parts of the mixture that make up who they are. The spaces, times and senses of themselves as a mixture are thus quite specific to their 'local' community. Such assemblages have specific temporal and sensual natures.

Various spatio-temporal and sensual assemblages are created by virtue of being in place. These affect young men's identifications and dis-identifications with particular rural and urban spaces. With a conceptual lens that looks beyond the individual foci of the young men in question and theorises the material connections between boys and the ways they use their possessions and travel to communicate and engage in meaningful activity, we theorise spatio-sensual assemblages. These are the connections boys embody in place and the ways young men's identities are embedded in the sensorium of relations that characterise their lives. We argue that intense connections to place are material products of particular spatio-temporal and spatio-sensual assemblages.

Embodied, place-based gendered identities

The body is central to the method of theorisation we advance. Others with concerns about boys and place also emphasise the role of the body. For example, in 'Topologies of masculinity: gendered spatialities of preadolescent boys', Nespor (2000: 33) offers a model of the body in place as 'a location, a set of densities' the production of which 'is always tenuous, the result of ongoing struggle'. Here, the body as configured in relation to context is also seen as crucial in the assemblage of subjectivity. The terms on which such a struggle to become a located set of densities takes place, and the contexts in which points are assembled into bodies, are the places, spaces and speeds in which and through which young men live. Lived spatial rivalries and specific cultural conflicts embodied by these rivalries, along with the sensuous nature of places, formed core components of the coordinates that folded in to produce the composite mixtures of subjectivity experienced and performed by the young men in our study.

Indeed, as much as experiences of being in place, cultural constructions of place, impacted on the boys keenly. Massey (1994) argues, many – if not most –

people are still located in a routine or 'home base', a locality to which they return regularly and spend a significant proportion of their time. The local remains important and should not be lost in some globalisation theory's obsession with the fast, the new and the large scale. However, neither should current understandings of locality or place be constrained by conventional notions of borders and boundaries (Massey 1994). They must recognise a complex and mobile range of links to other places and to other types of space, including virtual spaces associated with mediascapes (Appadurai 1996) and the ideoscapes (Appadurai 1996) attached to corporate globalisation. Massey (1994) develops the notion of a 'progressive sense of place': a concept that is both spatial and temporal. She argues that places can be understood as 'particular moments' in the 'articulation of social relations which necessarily have a spatial form' (1994: 120). Here, place is conceived as an inter-textual, or compiled, spatial form constructed through social relations with other places and objects. This 'progressive sense of place' is in line with McDowell's (1999) conceptualisation of place as a set of 'fluid, socio-spatial relations'. Both McDowell and Massey argue that places are constructed through time and the ongoing intersection of the past and the present, the 'in here and the out there' (Bingley 2003). Building upon McDowell (1999) and Massey's (1994) conceptualisations of place as multifaceted, lived connections of time, biography and sensory surroundings, the notions of spatio-temporal and spatio-sensual assemblages allow us to consider the embodied nature of place-based gendered identities.

The first of these concepts, spatio-temporal assemblages, articulates the ways diverse spaces: cyberspace; outback space; shopping malls; scrub-land and so on, operate within distinct temporal zones. Life online can be much faster than life in a paddock. Our research suggests that young men are connected to the different temporal frameworks of the various places they inhabit.

Spatio-temporal assemblages

The qualitative natures of places evoke specific temporalities: time zones that engender different ways of being and feeling in place – temporality and temperament are symbiotic. This enmeshment of place and pace is brought together in evocative ways in May and Thrift's (2001) edited collection. But we want to focus on Knopp's (2004: 131) discussion of the 'ontology of place' and specifically the 'ontological weight' of being and becoming in place. Knopp contends that a cartographic imagination should have the capacity to focus upon: 'the messy and most ephemeral aspects of the experiences and practices we call 'place' (including those involving non-human forces). Rather than objects that need to be specified theoretically or even fully understood, places … are 'disclosive', in the sense that they evoke, enable and denude simultaneously. They are conjunctions of time and space-specific material practices and events at the same time that they are generative (and reflective) of meaning (see Knopp 2004).

There are parallels here between Knopp's (2004: 126, 128–131) imagining of place, in which he draws on a 'topological imagination [which] focuses on connections, flows, simultaneity, situatedness, contingency, and "becoming"' and Nespor's (2000: 32) theory of multiple '"gender topologies" ... masculine and feminine spaces'. Both angles of vision account for the complexity and speed or slowness of place: it is multi-dimensional and has capacity for motion, yet it is also situated and powerful in its material fixity. We take up Knopp's (2004: 129) suggestion that place is an assemblage of 'conjunctions of ... time and space-specific material practices' and consider specific temporal zones alongside the spatial coordinates that are required to imagine and understand place. It is our contention that various spatio-temporal assemblages happen by virtue of being in space and they affect young men's identifications and dis-identifications with particular places. In terms of dis-identification, 'dead zones' is a name we use to explain some young men's experiences of being in place and to refer to a specific kind of spatio-temporal folding. Dead zones are slow, binding, heavy and bounded. Charlie's story offers an example of what dead zones look and feel like. Aged 14, Charlie has only recently moved to Coober Pedy from rural Victoria. He has been having difficulty adjusting to life in the desert. For him, Coober Pedy is a dead zone, largely due to his reading of the landscape: 'There is nothing here; it is just dirt'. Other young people in the town echo Charlie's reading of the barren locale, saying: 'Coober Pedy is a hole' ... it is 'a crusty town, a dust bowl', 'a waste-land in the middle of nowhere'. The burnt red desert landscape of Coober Pedy and its surrounds, framed by flat broad blue horizons, offers a forceful testimony to their claims. But there is more to the construction of a dead zone than just a desolate landscape. Charlie elucidates:

> Coober Pedy is probably the worst place I have ever been in. Coober Pedy has nothing. The other places I have been to, you walk up the street and there are trees around, and pavements, seats. You can go and see your friends and have fun up-town, buy roller blades or something ... Here, all you see is people sitting around, doing nothing.

This narrative highlights the key aspects of dead zones, most of which apply to some young people's views of our other research locations. Also characterising spaces like dead zones in non-metropolitan places, Bone, Cheers and Hil (1990) illustrate the perspective of one 17-year-old girl in the Whitsundays, who feels that life in regional coastal towns can also be pretty dead when you're not a tourist: '[There's] not much to do ... no jobs ... everything requires money ... it's a boring place ... no privacy'. As this quote suggests, the first element of a dead zone is boredom, the belief that there is 'nothing to do'; there are no desirable activities available for young people. But there is also a sense of not being able to escape, of being trapped in a slow place that weighs a young person down and makes them feel like they are being held back. In such places, boredom narratives abound. They are a frequent knee-jerk, anguished first response to inquiries about local life. 'Nothing to do' is associated with 'nowhere to go': no resources and available spaces to hang out with friends, form relationships, meet new people, build a biography amongst one's peers. 'Nowhere to go' also means there are no desirable spaces in which young people can gather and undertake activities of their choice away from the adult gaze of the community panopticon that oppresses the young in small places. This sentiment is evident in the words of Seaneen MacInearny (age 15 from Renmark), who complains that: 'Country life is so boring and you know, you don't have any freedom … you're basically under surveillance all the time, it doesn't matter who you are … you can't even walk down the street without someone seeing you, that knows you.'

Narratives about 'nothing to do' and 'nowhere to go' are associated with those of 'no-one here': no available like-minded people with whom to share activities. The lack of varying spatial areas, harshness of the landscape and climate and the sluggish pace of local life mean that few boys see Coober Pedy's spatio-temporal dead zone as a preferred space of identity. Nonetheless, boys' embodied masculine identities are, in many ways, assembled in relation to these sluggish territorialities. The ways time affects identity formation in out of the way 'dead zones' such as Coober Pedy is evident in the kinds of men that live there. The adult masculinities that are fashioned in the unhurried but harsh frontier landscapes of Coober Pedy are usually 'no rush, no problems' – relaxed, convivial, robust and resilient within specific limits. Males who are not fashioned in this manner are seen as out of place in Coober Pedy and may attract suspicion, derision and hostility.

As young people grow older, their readings of place shift and so too do notions of live and dead zones. For older boys, relationships 'stretch out', as Giddens (1990: 19) suggests, to include other townships and cities. Such widening spatial assemblages may be accompanied by a sense of local inadequacy, re-enforcing the notion of home as a dead zone. Jonathan Nichols, age 15 from Morwell, describes this 'age trap': 'If you are under ten, there is heaps you can do; places that you can go. For anyone over ten or 15, there is just nothing to do. At least up at Melbourne, you can go to *Timezone* or something'. In this case, the stretching out of adolescence retains the dead zone of homeland and is accompanied by a sense of place being emptied out. Dead zones do not always involve an increasing sense of world-wide and imaginary 'proximity' as Tomlinson argues (1999: 9); rather proximities are likely to be very real and nearby (*Timezone* in the local capital Melbourne, for example). A spatial paradox is that they may be geographically near yet figuratively far away, or at least very hard to access. While '[m]obility practices are common for many people in contemporary individualistic societies and cultures, especially those with the means to be physically mobile, such as those with class, race, and/or gender privilege' (Knopp 2004: 123–124), such practices are often unobtainable for young men without jobs, cars and money for bus fares. They can only escape from place in their imaginations.

Such imaginative escape and virtual forms of escape facilitated by the internet are powerful agents. This is partially evidenced by the fact that what is considered a dead zone for some is not necessarily so for others. The Coober Pedy example above shows that landscape can play a major role in the construction of temporal dead zones but, as we now demonstrate, it can also be a feature of live zones. Some young people have a very deep attachment not so much to the scapes of the global cultural economy, but to the scapes of the local in which they live, be they land, street, or waterscapes. Nick Bradley, aged 13 from Eden, is quoted at the start of the chapter and his words ring with delight as he describes his attachment to the 'live zone' of his local landscape and going down to the rock pool with his bathers. Jumping off the rocks and swimming into the beach again and again can be seen as a practice of writing oneself into place, of inscribing one's subjectivity and imprinting one's body on the land and seascape. Nick certainly doesn't feel bound by a dead zone of place, rather he is very much brought to life and invigorated by what he experiences as the live zone of the place in which he lives.

Boys like Nick focus on their homes, street or neighbourhood. While they tend to know very little beyond, they often know their own place intimately and love its sights, smells, textures. Their sense of place involves 'topographical intimacy' (Lippard 1997: 33) which is experienced kinaesthetically as well as temporally. For them, places are alive and in their place they feel alive. Daniel Fitzsimmons, age 13, also quoted at the beginning of the chapter, has a detailed knowledge of his neighbourhood and its beaches, river mouth, caravan park and shop. Daniel's description of his neighbourhood is also a description of how he spends much of his life and it demonstrates a sensory engagement with his surroundings. He, and others like him, are embedded in their immediate landscape and have little wish or thought for activities or relationships that are more 'stretched out' (Giddens 1990: 19). The ways they assemble space and time are connected, astute and their place feels light, populated and alive.

Even downtrodden and desolate places can be construed as live zones. What 'enlivens' is either connection to landscape or the easiness and busy familiarity associated with place-based relationships. For example, Morwell is a deindustrialising township that has suffered greatly. But some young people still construct Morwell as a 'live zone'. In so doing they draw on local family traditions, deep roots within the community and strong sense of home. Take the case of Mark Thinley, age 15, who has lived in Morwell all of his life. He has a very strong attachment to it and would not consider living anywhere else. His family has lived in the town for three generations and he has a large extended family. He belongs here and feels sorry for anyone who does 'not have the satisfaction of living in a nice place like Morwell' or has not had the opportunity to get 'attached to any one place like I have'. Mark experiences Morwell as a live zone, a rich base for who he is and for what he wants to do. Others feel the same. Such feelings arise from local socioscapes; the connections between time, blood and belonging. Cherie Mathers, age 16, says she loves: 'the closeness with everyone. Practically everyone's parents have grown up here, and their parents have grown up here, and we have all just grown up with each other. That is probably the most special thing about it'.

Friendship is an important factor in perceptions of live zones and can attach both males and females fondly to a place even if there is 'nothing to do'. Constructions of masculinity articulate strongly with local mateship and male connections and, for many, this is the traditional anchor of male identity.

Andrew Morrissey, age 14, invests a great deal of his masculine identity in who his friends are and what they do together. Robert Godard, age 16, similarly expresses the importance of friendship for males in Renmark: 'You've got to have fun with other kids up here. You've got to have friends, especially as a boy. If not, it's going to make life difficult for you because you're classed as a loser'. As this quote suggests, gendered assumptions often underlie constructions of live and dead zones and boys associate certain scapes more with males than females, often seeing non-city locations as dead zones for girls because there 'is not enough shopping' and because they associate outdoor lifestyles with masculinity. Girls are generally constructed as antithetical to the masculine landscape and are represented as inactive and passive in relation to it. For instance, with regard to the beaches at Eden, the boys say that the girls have 'got nothing better to do than sunbake'. However, boys' readings of gender, landscapes and of live and dead zones for the girls, are usually based on traditional constructions of femininity that some young women are challenging, especially around Eden. The case of 'surf chicks', 'snow chicks' and 'country chicks' illustrates this point. Eileen DeCarli, age 13, explains the differences she perceives between these groups of girls and the ways her subjectivity as a 'country chick' is assembled in relation to the sensory nature of her surroundings. Eileen says:

> I'm not really into the beaches and surfing and getting a tan. It is just not my thing. My best friend Rhianna is into all that. I'm more country, I get wood, I collect rocks for the garden, and soil and manure, and I'm just a country person. I'm no pretty girl that is afraid of breaking a nail. And I like skiing, I'm a country person, I've grown up there all my life in the snow … I'm not the kind of girl that is into bikinis and getting a tan and surfing and being 'cool'.

This suggests that some young women do construct themselves in relation to the outdoors and its sensorium. Eileen's statement that 'I get wood, I collect rocks for the garden, and soil and manure, and I'm just a country person' is perhaps an example of what Knopp (2004: 125) calls a 'humble ontology'. Such a way of being calls attention to the subtle, embedded and sensory connections people make with place, gender identities and identifications.

There are many ways people, institutions and localities produce and secure the meaning and identity of their place, themselves and others. These include the establishment of sensory and temporal boundaries and the invocation of binary spatial comparisons and rivalries in relation to other locales. Massey (1994: 5) argues that 'the need for the security of boundaries, the requirements for such a defensive and counter positional definition of identity, is culturally masculine' (Massey 1994: 7). In constructing such culturally masculine boundaries, mediascapes of the global first world cultural economy regularly craft images of place that mobilise a country/city binary, normalise and prioritise the city and its moiré's and morals. Metropolitan and non-metropolitan places and people are often presented as the antitheses of each other and are arranged in moral hierarchies.

The young men in our study had in common a view of the city that involves a profusion of speeds, mobilities and rhythms. In contrast to the thick, slow, substantial assemblages of life in out-of-the way places, city life is seen as fast-paced, thin or superficial, random in flow and teeming with bodies and signs. Pro or anti-metropolitan sentiments often hinged, in part, on such matters: speed and abundance can delight or deter. The speed of life for many boys in out of the way places is very different from that of the metropolis. The pace you live at and the time you live through are fundamental factors in determining that of which you are and are not capable. People cannot escape their own time, as Bergson (1992: 93) reminds us: 'the living being essentially has duration; it has duration precisely because it is continuously elaborating what is new and because there is no elaboration without searching, without groping. Time is this very hesitation'. If time is the pauses in between becoming a person, the second before acting or thinking – the machining of the acts that are one's subjectivity, then the time of place, the slowness or speed of one's surroundings are a constitutive part of the tenor of the pause. They are the time through which one becomes. For young men who have identity investments in the large, unbounded spaces they associate with non-metropolitan zones, the 'hesitation' of their being, the time on and through which they live, is assembled in ways often fundamentally incompatible with the speeds of city life. They do not, and possibly cannot, connect with the ways time, space and the senses are configured in the city. Located and locally embedded configurations of time, space and the senses form the bedrock of these young men's senses of self. But there are additional views overlaying these beliefs. These quite frequently include two extremes – the city as a utopia of boundless opportunities or, alternatively, the city as a fearful hellhole. Interestingly, quite a few boys in places beyond the metropolis hold the latter view.

A powerful set of constructions of the city by the young men who live outside it revolves around notions of danger and depravity and can largely be understood as masculine. These interpretations are particularly associated with violence, crime and drugs. The city is seen as a menacing space to be feared, a place of perpetual hazard and the temptations of drugs, peopled mainly by criminals, bums and 'druggies'. Toby, age 13 from Eden, typifies this view, explaining that metropolitan spaces are to be avoided because of: 'Murders, there is more murders and all that sort of thing, kidnapping, getting punched'. Jordan, 13, of Coober Pedy states: 'there are a few kids I know who have gone to Adelaide and they are just druggies. It is the Adelaide people who make them become druggies'. Such views of the city may well be informed by the action and crime movies that many young males consume voraciously (Browne and Hamilton-Giachritsis 2005, Chensvold 1995). Such films often produce a view of the city male as either degenerate, menacing, vicious or violent (Beltran 2005, Giroux 2001). But such hostile perceptions could also be a response to the radically different speeds, sounds and senses that accompany metropolitan life. City spaces constitute machinic assemblages of very different natures to those of the out of the way places in which we conducted our research.

A very select few boys in out of the way places were quite invested in alternative ideas presented in mediascapes of the city male as a forceful and fearless defender of good order. Such films offer young men entrée into a fast paced reality and the pleasure of vicarious danger and heroic control. They also promote hegemonic masculinities that either evoke in their audience impossible identifications and/or fear and anxiety. For these young men, the city comes to embody these affective intensities and speeds that are then mingled with the place myths of danger produced by peers and parents. As a consequence, many such boys feel that their masculinity would be put under severe pressure in the city, that while they might be 'the big man' in a country town, the city would expose their weakness and vulnerability and also potentially corrupt them. They could never live up to the ideal of the morally strong city man and would be corrupted by the metropolitan underclass. Some of these young men who see the city as populated by hegemons or as filled with dangerous and depraved others, who would need to be warded off, proclaim they are simply not interested in ever moving to the city to study or work.

The contrasting view is of the city as a fast, fabulous, feminine, utopia associated with the possibility of lots of new relationships and particularly with consumer desires. Here, metropolitan space is experienced as a spectacle of stores, products and images of endless opportunities for desirable consumption and entertainment. Yet even when the city is seen as a place that can satisfy young men's shared desires for globalised youthful consumer culture, the senses of the city are not as amenable to the sensory assemblages through which many young men from non-metropolitan places produce themselves. For example, John Horton of Eden is profoundly connected to water and space through physical activity. For John, the act of surfing [surf+board+boy+wind+movement] constitutes 'a *machinic assemblage* of bodies, of actions and passions, an intermingling of bodies reacting to one another' (Deleuze and Guattari 1987: 88) that is fundamentally masculine. John explains that: 'Boys are more into physical stuff, surfing and stuff, while girls are more into not physical stuff. Like just shopping. I reckon girls would fit in better in the city than the country'. For some young men in out of the way places, the spatio-temporal and spatio-sensual assemblages of family and home soil, or the landscapes of the bush or the beach, are what holds them in place and what they articulate their masculinity in relation to. They could not be who they are in the city or, to put it another way, they could not be sufficiently male in the 'feminine' city.

As we have intimated, it is not just the physical busyness and fast pace of the city that young men in out of the way places characterise as feminine. The feminisation of city space is a response to cultural difference and fear of the unknown. Metropolitan spaces are full of girls 'talking and chatting with friends', they are also shaped by flows of corporate signs which bring specific cultural significances and economies of relation into young people's lives. For some young men, these flows are welcome augmentations to the existing connections they have with popular culture. To others, they are sense-less: disruptive, anxiety provoking cultural mores. Such young men are those who characterise city spaces, or places heavily populated with corporate presences, as 'girl zones'.

Thus, a 'progressive sense of place' beyond the metropolis cannot be solely constructed in terms of reworking city/ country boundaries. It also needs to involve the gendered dimensions of places, the temporalities and senses of places, their *sensuousness* and the relationships between different places beyond the metropolis. Such relationships link back to wider cultural and economic codings of space. Particular sorts of economic change have implications for specific understandings of place. Global economic flows and territorial spaces coexist and interrelate in a complex fashion and can be experienced very differently, even in places of close proximity.

For example, Eden ascribes to itself an identity as a 'workingman's town'. This spatial identification has a long history in the fishing and logging industries. Place-based masculinities in Eden are produced through comparisons with the neighboring town of Merimbula. The adult males in Eden consider themselves decent, 'down to earth blokes' who work hard to 'make a quid' and who don't live a fancy life. They subscribe to a 'no frills' form of masculinity that involves more than a little contempt for any consideration of the aesthetic. In comparison, Merimbula is booming as a tourist location, its economy is firmly rooted in the service industries, which are considered feminine by Eden's working men. There is much rivalry and ridicule between these towns. Eden boys call those in Merimbula 'fairy bread eaters', while Merimbula boys call those in Eden 'concrete munchers' (senior boys focus group). Clearly these place-based cultural constructions extend beyond oral characterisations.

It seems that these spatial rivalries are integral to the formation of youthful masculine identities. The story of Paul Jones, age 15 from Eden, illustrates how this place-based masculinity is produced. Paul has lived in Eden all his life, as did his father. He is very proud of his town and gets quite defensive if anything critical is said about the place. He also constructs his masculinity in direct contrast to his readings of Merimbula and especially Merimbula boys:

> I consider the Merimbula people to be wimpy and dickheads. The Merimbula people probably think it about us, but they are surfy people, and Eden is more like stronger people and we are into footy and stuff … Everyone from Eden thinks that Merimbula is sort of poofter people, we don't do the same things.

Paul's sense of his own masculinity is established through contrast and, at times, conflict with Merimbula boys, whom he derides as individualistic, feminine and gay in contrast with the more acceptable team masculinity of Eden males. He also observes that Eden and Merimbula boys do not mix at school. For him, and many others, Eden and Merimbula boys are working from a completely different identity base and have nothing in common. This spatial friction is often played out on the sports field, especially through football in the case of Eden, but also in the school grounds. Paul delights in talking about the fights between Merimbula and Eden boys, and is quite proud of the fact that the Merimbula boys are scared of his group of friends because they have beaten up several Merimbula boys in the past. Paul has big investments in the Eden-Merimbula enmity and clearly uses it as a resource for identity. Some older boys think that 'as you get older, you just get over it' (Simon Jackson). It is possible, however, that this is easier for the more privileged boys of Merimbula than for those in struggling Eden.

Young men in Merimbula are more likely to grow up connecting to the global flows of commodities, people and corporate signs and thus to more diverse articulations of masculine gender identities. As such, Merimbula boys are also more accustomed to the ways spaces, cultural beliefs and people's occupations come to be reconfigured in relation to flows of capital, commodities and bodies. These boys are already part of spatio-sensual assemblages that are fast paced and accommodate multiple media flows, objects and images. The ontology of people occupying such positions is markedly different from those located in the thick space of the country life where, as Shaw (2001) explains, the slow life is understood as the good life.

Spatio-sensual assemblages

Machinic assemblages of bodies, of actions and passions, are physical acts composed of human and non-human bodies. They are acts that shift materialities and are accompanied by assemblages of enunciation: new stories and new knowledges about the bodies being machined. We have noted that young men in Eden and Merimbula construct themselves in direct opposition, and are often constructed by others as such. Indeed, spatial rivalries are integral to the formation of their masculine identities. That the Merimbula boys are also somewhat more accustomed to the ways spaces, cultural beliefs and people's occupations come to be reconfigured in relation to globalised media, flows of capital, commodities and bodies. We now want to elucidate the ontological or machinic aspects of these boy's connections to their place. Merimbula boys are already part of spatio-sensual assemblages that are fast-paced, loud, brightly coloured. The ontology of occupying such positions is markedly different from those deeply located in the thick space of the local indigenous landscape, flora and fauna. The former, faster, thin assemblages typify or produce the 'escape velocity' Virilio (1997: 119) characterises as aiming to: 'Gradually break down all resistance, all dependence on the local, to wear down the opposition of duration and extension … To eradicate the gap, to put an end to the scandal of the interval between space and time that used to separate man so unacceptably from his objective.' Extensive assemblages of media flows, cosmopolitan lives and city spaces are experienced by some as exciting. For these boys, metropolitan styles and spatial affects bring excitement to place. Metropolitan flows of corporate commodities extend and enrich the range of ways they connect to various nearby spaces, people and the ways boys imagine themselves. Yet, for others, city-style spaces and global cultural flows rupture their consciousness and ways of being in the world in an intrusive manner. For these boys, the gap between urban and regional, costal or rural remains too big to bridge. This is not because of a conceptual divide between peripheral and metropolitan places, but because of the qualitative natures of the assemblages these men belong to. The speeds they live at, the senses they exist in relation to, are erased by metropolitan velocity in ways that some are not able to overcome.

References

Appadurai, A. 1996. *Modernity at Large: The Cultural Dimensions of Globalization* Minneapolis: University of Minnesota Press.

Beltran, M.C. 2005. The new Hollywood racelessness: only the fast, furious (& multiracial) will survive. *Cinema Journal*, 44(2), 50–67.

Bergson, H. 1992. *The Creative Mind: An Introduction to Metaphysics*. New York: Citadel Press.

Bingley, A. 2003. In here and out there: sensations between self and landscape. *Social and Cultural Geography*, 4(3), 329–345.

Bone, R., Cheers, B., and Hil, R. 1990. Paradise lost: young people's experience of rural life in the Whitsunday Shire. *Rural Society Journal*, 3(4), 9–12.

Browne, K. and Hamilton-Giachritis, C. 2005. The influence of violent media on children and adolescents: a public health approach. *The Lancet*, 365(9460), 702–710.

Chensvold, C.M. 1995. Speed, Nietzsche & the American Cultural Palate. *Films in Review*, 46(1–2), 8–12.

Deleuze, G. and Guattari, F. 1987. *A Thousand Plateaus: Capitalism and Schizophrenia*. Minneapolis: University of Minnesota Press.

Giddens, A. 1990. *The Consequences of Modernity*. Cambridge: Polity Press.

Giroux, H. 2001. Private satisfactions and public disorders: fight club, patriarchy, and the politics of masculine violence. *JAC: Journal of Composition Theory*, 21(1), 1–31.

Guattari, F. 1995. *Chaosmosis: An Ethico-Aesthetic Paradigm*. Bloomington: Indiana University Press.

Knopp, L. 2004. Ontologies of place, placelessness, and movement: queer quests for identity and their impacts on contemporary geographic thought. *Gender, Place and Culture: A Journal of Feminist Geography*, 11(1), 121–134.

Lippard, L. 1997. *The Lure of the Local: Senses of Place in a Multicentered Society*. New York: The New Press.

Massey, D. 1994. *Space, Place and Gender*. Cambridge: Polity Press.

May, J. and Thrift, N. 2001. *Timespace: Geographies of Temporiality*. London: Routledge.

McDowell, L. 1999. *Gender, Identity and Place: Understanding Feminist Geographies*. Cambridge: Polity Press.

Nespor, J. 2000. Topologies of masculinity: gendered spatialities of preadolescent boys, in *Masculinities at School*, edited by N. Lesko. Thousand Oaks: Sage Publications, 27–49.

Shaw, J. 2001. Winning territory: changing place to change pace, in *Timespace: Geographies of Temporality*, edited by J. May and N. Thrift. London: Routledge, 120–132.

Tomlinson, J. 1999. *Globalization and Culture.* Cambridge: Polity Press.

Virilio, P. 1997. *Open Sky.* London: Verso Publishers.

Chapter 4

Neoliberalism, Masculinities and Academic Knowledge Production: Towards a Theory of 'Academic Masculinities'

Lawrence D. Berg, Levi Gahman, and Neil Nunn[1]

Introduction

Feminist and social geographers have long concerned themselves with critically interrogating the spatial politics of neoliberalism (Berg and Roche 1997, Castree et al. 2006, Berg 2011, 2013) and masculinity (Zelinsky 1972, Zelinsky, Monk and Hanson 1982, Rose 1993, Pratt 2000, Berg 2001, Berg and Longhurst 2003, Dyck 2005, Johnson 2008) as they pertain to processes of knowledge production. Less often, however, are these systems of control brought together in an attempt to gain a broader understanding of emplaced knowledges and the spatial politics of difference. In this analysis we take these topics – the masculine and the neoliberal – into consideration while attending to their role in the co-production of and emergence with other forms of oppression. We hope to do this by elucidating the complex and contradictory relationships amongst processes of neoliberalisation of the academy, gendered subject formation, and the production of emplaced knowledges. If, as Raewynn Connell argues, masculinity is 'a set of practices by which men locate themselves in gender relations, articulate with that place in gender, and produce gendered effects on others and themselves', then masculinity surely impacts the production of knowledge (e.g. Rose 1993, Berg 2001, Butz and Berg 2002). At the same time, the academy is being dramatically transformed by processes of neoliberalisation, in which new forms of academic subjectivity are being produced via more hierarchical power relations that interlock with already-existing forms of exclusion including patriarchy, classism, ableism, heterosexism, and racism.

Theories of interlocking oppression suggest that in order to understand a particular system of social control, it is essential to consider its constitution and relation with other forms of oppression. According to Sherene Razack (1997: 12), any given system of control always relies on other forms of control and oppression to give it meaning. This interlocking approach allows us to pay attention to how

1 Names are listed alphabetically. Each author contributed equally to the chapter. Correspondence to: Lawrence.berg@ubc.ca.

particular forms of difference evolve in relation to other forms of oppression (see Holmes 2012, Razack 1997, 2002, Min-ha 1997, Ruddick 1996, Jiwani 2006, Valentine 2007). Our objective in this chapter is thus to bring together discussions of academic practice, social difference and control, and attempt to elucidate the complex and contradictory relationships between processes of neoliberalisation of the academy, the production of emplaced knowledges, and gendered academic subject formation.

Motivated by similar concerns, Rosalind Gill (2009: 230) questions how we might 'make links between macro-organisation and institutional practices on the one hand, and experiences and affective states on the other, and open up an exploration of the ways in which these may be gendered, racialised and classed'. Such concerns characterise our efforts to explore deeper the way that a key form of systemic oppression and control – namely gendered academic social relations – can be linked to other systemic forms of hierarchical social relations in the academy.

We begin this analysis by first discussing the ways that masculinity can be understood in academic knowledge production, then consider the ways that other forms of social relations (particularly those that are neoliberal and neoliberalising) can be understood in a complex, mutually constitutive manner that is fraught with contradictions and paradox.

Masculinity and knowledge

How best, then, approach masculinity in the context of knowledge production? Since the 1970s feminist geographers and their supporters have made important contributions to rethinking the way that masculinity operates in academic knowledge creation (e.g. Zelinksy, Monk and Hanson 1982, Rose 1993, Berg 2001, Moss 2002) by exploring the fluid, performative, discursive and material aspects of the quotidian, and connecting these details to broader questions of intersecting difference and hegemonic masculine control (Dyck 2005).

In the opening statement of her foundational work, *Feminism and Geography,* Gillian Rose (1993: 1) argues: 'The academic discipline of geography has historically been dominated by men, perhaps more so than any other human science'. For over four decades, feminist scholars and their supporters have been attuned to the ways in which knowledge production is gendered, particularly through processes of male privilege (e.g. Browne 2008, Hanson 2004, Kobayashi 2002, McDowell 1979, 1990, Monk and Hanson 1982, Rose 1993, Zelinsky 1973). For example, the 'Women in Geography' special focus section of *The Canadian Geographer* (46(3), 2002) makes a convincing case that, among Canadian universities, the discipline of geography has had one of the worst gender equity records (Berg 2002, Kobayashi 2002,Yasmeen 2002). Historically, geography departments in Canadian universities have lagged far behind the national ratios of female to male full professors in other disciplines (Berg 2002, for similar arguments about UK geography, see McDowell 1979, 1990).

Feminist geographers have noted that the gendered character of geography has had significant consequences for the nature of knowledge that is produced (Monk and Hanson 1982, Rose 1993). Kobayashi (2002) explains that it is normatively defined masculine values and deeply embedded cultural practices that limit significant change in the culture of the discipline. Hall et al. (2002) argue that often women are not perceived as 'serious' academics due to choices in research topics, gaps in career trajectories, social and 'caring' service, or involvement in community politics. Berg suggests (2002: 253) that the so-called meritocracy that defines academic promotion and status in Geography is actually the result of a system constituted by 'masculine norms of academic behaviour'. Studies such as these have been important as they confirm claims of male dominance (and unearned privilege that goes with that dominance) in the discipline made by geographers decades prior (e.g. McDowell 1979, Zelinsky 1973, Zelinsky, Monk and Hanson 1982), and thus they contribute to the feminist project of contesting normative gendered ideals that reproduce male privilege in the discipline.

Others have written about the relationship between masculinity and science in human geography, arguing that the 'trope of discovery' is deeply infused in geographical ways of coming to know the world (Rose 1993, Berg 1994). This work has illustrated the way that geography, much like many of the social sciences, has been constructed on a mind/body distinction that is deeply implicated in the way that many geographers come to see themselves as knowing subjects that seek to obtain 'objective' knowledge of the world that they study (Rose 1993, Berg 1994, Mansvelt and Berg 2005). This is both a spatialised and a gendered ontology that constitutes 'the Geographer' as a knowing masculine subject that is able to transcend lived space in order to maintain an objective view of the world (Berg 1994, 2001). Donna Haraway (1988: 581) has famously referred to this way of constituting objectivity (and the gendered subject that knows) as 'the god trick of seeing everything from nowhere'.

Given that this type of objectivity is not possible, its maintenance as a dominant mode of knowing in Geography (until very recently) must surely have something to do with power relations. Accordingly, the relationship between power, knowledge and the production of truth has been a central point of interest for geographers who have sought to explore the character of masculine privilege in academic knowledge production (McDowell 1990, Rose 1993, Moss 2002). For these and other critics, normative knowledge has been established by those who dominate the research process, with their power validated through processes like citations (Browne 2008), peer review (Berg 2001) and other key aspects of knowledge production in the academy. While not always poststructuralist itself, work that points out the imbrication of power and knowledge certainly runs parallel with that of poststructuralist theorists (e.g. Derrida 1976, Foucault 1984, Irigaray 1985a, 1985b, Gregory 1994, Rose 1995a), and we align ourselves with that tradition as well. In this regard, and drawing on work by feminist geographers (e.g. Rose 1993, McDowell and Sharp 1999), we argue that the hegemonic idea of knowledge in Geography is implicated in the (re)production of forms of normativity that privilege the masculine and devalue the feminine. Of course, these academic norms are also implicated in the reproduction of racism, colonialism, ableism, ageism and various other forms of marginalisation (see Nocella, Best and McLaren 2010, Smith 1999). As Gillian Rose (1993, 1997) argues, masculinist knowledge in the academy is relational – discursively formed through intersections between power and academic knowledge – existing in our relationships with each other, and manifest through the subject positions we adopt as scholars. This intersection between power and knowledge, then, is a useful point of departure to examine the ways in which institutions produce masculinity, and therefore manufacture other forms of privilege and authority that evolve through processes of knowledge production.

Hegemonic masculinities

As researchers who engage with questions of masculinity in many contexts, we are keenly aware of the way that exploring masculinity in institutions of knowledge production can be generative of a whole host of insights about neoliberal (and other) hierarchies of social control. In an attempt to gain a hold on the way that masculinity as a gendered system operates, we continue this discussion by theorising the concept of hegemonic masculinity, considering its relationship and emergence with other systems of oppression and marginalisation.

Raewyn Connell's well-cited definition of hegemonic masculinity is a useful starting point. For Connell (2005: 77), hegemonic masculinity can be defined as: 'The configuration of gender practice, which embodies the currently accepted answer to the legitimacy of patriarchy, which guarantees (or is taken to guarantee) the dominant position of men and the subordination of women.' Hegemonic masculinity is a dominant feature in most societies, most men are privileged by hegemonic masculinity, and mostly men have historically been, and continue to be, the leading figures in control of the most highly valued or most powerful institutions in society: the military, the police, business, trades, education, and sport. With that in mind, it is not surprising that such framings of masculinity come to be seen in a simple dualism of 'men versus women'. However, the key point underpinning the concept of hegemonic masculinities is that gendered identities work in more complex and often contradictory ways (e.g. Butz and Berg 2002, Connell and Messerschmidt 2005, Pacholok 2009, Nunn 2013). More specifically, masculinities take different forms and are inscribed with different kinds of social power that are then placed in hierarchical relation to each other (and to various forms of femininity). As we argue in this study, much can be gained from a broader framing of masculinity. Gendered social relations, and relations of power more generally, operate in complex manners: social control is fluid and emergent and can operate in and through a wide spectrum of temporalities, subjectivities and materialities. With that in mind, Connell (2005: 44) describes hegemonic masculinities as 'configurations of practice structured by gendered relations', recognising that such practices are situated in places significantly influenced by 'bodily experience, personality, and culture' (2005: 71), suggesting that masculinities are mutually and relationally constituted by subjects seeking to embody their various forms. Most importantly for us as geographers, masculinities are also constituted by (and constitutive of) the spaces and spatialities within which they operate (Berg 2006, Berg and Longhurst 2003).

In order to best understand the dynamics at play in these social relationships it is key to recognise that a plurality of masculinities exists. In addition, these relationships, replete with contrasting power dynamics, inherently give rise to processes of domination and subordination through an array of interactions that occur between and amongst non-normative identities (Ashe 2007, Connell and Messerschmidt 2005, Hearn 2004). The normative hegemonic figure – male, heterosexual, able-bodied, white, citizen – is framed in comparison to what it is not, its 'Other'. This Other is often constructed as inferior, lacking and deficient (Anderson 2009, Ashe 2007, Hopkins 2007). The practical elements of such social relations are readily apparent in neoliberal capitalist societies in the arenas of production, labour, domesticity and interpersonal relationships, where men are typically framed as rational, decisive, assertive, knowledgeable, ruggedly individualistic and better fit to occupy positions of leadership (Kimmel, Hearn and Connell 2005, Demetriou 2001).

Notwithstanding these dominant framings of what it means to be a man, it is important to keep in mind Gillian Rose's (1993) important arguments about the complexities of multiple masculine and feminine subject positions. In this regard, Rose (1993) argues that different men become masculine in different ways, thus only certain men will be attracted to the academy generally (and to Geography more specifically). Academic men will also react in different ways to the masculinism of the academy and to that of their specific academic discipline. As a discursive practice, disciplines like Geography encode certain disciplinary actions that enact specific masculinities. Rose (1993: 10, see also Berg 1994) cogently summarises this aspect of the relationship between Geography and the politics of identity:

> I am not suggesting that no man can escape the masculinities that I identify as central to geography; nor that women cannot occupy a masculine position; nor that women are incapable of producing geographical knowledge. Rather, I argue that both men and women are caught in a complex series of (historically and geographically specific) discursive positions, relations and practices. The relationship of individual men to the masculinism of geography may be highly problematic and unstable.

Building on this, we wish to explore further the concept of hegemonic masculinities, considering how it might be a useful conceptual tool to understand masculinities in knowledge production and their interlocking relationships with other forms of domination and subordination in the academy. Developed through the work of Antonio Gramsci and emerging through concerns regarding the cultural influence that capitalism has on society, the concept of hegemony suggests that members of the dominant faction in society come to dominate not by physical coercion, but rather by gaining the consent of those who are dominated (Gramsci 1971, see also Joll 1977, Connell 1995, 2005, Hearn 2004). Writers like Connell (1995, 2005) and Hearn (2004) have used the concept of hegemony to better understand the relationship between dominant forms of masculinity and femininity and subordinate forms of masculinity. In a similar way, we think that the concept of hegemony can also be used to aid in understanding other forms of oppression in academia by offering insights about the ways that individuals within the academy unwittingly grant privilege to oppressive structures, even while it may not be in their long-term interest to do so (Francese 2009, Connell 1995, Gramsci 1992).

In many instances, it is not through extraordinary means that such structures are created and maintained, but rather it is through banal and prosaic everyday *practices* that normative gender identities are (re)produced and maintained. Hegemonic systems (ableism, racism, classism, heterosexism, speciesism) that operate through landscapes of knowledge production work by gaining the willing acquiescence – and in many cases full support – of those subjects often most oppressed by these systems. We argue that hegemonic systems of domination define the academic landscape, and in turn, analyses of these systems offer an important lens through which to consider the interlocking nature of academic oppression (after Nocella, Best and McLaren 2010, see also Berg 2002, Kobayashi 2002, McDowell 1979, 1990, Moss and McMahon 2000, Rose 1993). Moreover, we suggest that such practices are instantiated in the academy through banal practices that would, on first analysis, seem relatively harmless.

Returning to the idea that there is no single, uniform or standardised masculinity, we are reminded of masculinity's amorphous character; it occurs in multiple forms, is constantly shifting, and is temporally and spatially fluid (see Ashe 2007, Connell 2009). Connell (2005) suggests that this continual flux is what allows masculinity to maintain a hegemonic position in gender. Masculinities, along with other hegemonic projects like neoliberalism, ableism and classism, are continually in the process of adapting to new cultural norms, technologies and forms of counter-hegemonic resistance. Jamie Peck's description of the adaptive power of neoliberalism provides a useful model for understanding hegemonic masculinity. In this regard, Peck (2010: 109) has coined the term 'zombie neoliberalism' as a way of reminding us that there is really no longer any specific intention and design behind neoliberalism 'but the limbs are still moving, and many of the "defensive reflexes" carry on'. The same could be said about dominant systems of control like hegemonic masculinity. Ontologically, many hegemonic processes that operate in the discipline of Geography are constructed through adaptive, ephemeral and persistent systems of (re)production. This is the strength and character of hegemonic systems, but it is also their weakness. For example, the very fluid and ephemeral character of hegemonic masculinity means it is also always in danger of coming undone. Much work goes into preventing this undoing.

The interlocking character of neoliberalism in the academy

> To study the implementation of neoliberalism does not involve that we only study the 'application' of policies. It also requires us to consider the process of their production, the historicity of places and institutions where neoliberalism is deployed and the historicity of dispositions that embody it. (Hilgers 2013: 78)

While neoliberalism as a system characterises much of the social world, its nebulous character is shaped and continues to be reshaped by 'compromise, calculation, and contradiction' (Peck 2010: 106). Or as Wendy Larner (2003) argues, neoliberal spaces are hybrid, multiple and emergent through performance and contestation. All of this suggests that we need to attend to the everyday banal practices through which spaces, institutions and subjects emerge in order to gain a deeper understanding of neoliberalism as 'policy, ideology and governmentality' (Larner 2000) in the academy.

Geographers have done an exemplary job of mapping the large-scale historical geographies of neoliberalism in the academy (e.g. Berg and Roche 1997, Castree and Sparke 2000, Castree et al. 2006), and the world more generally (e.g. Brenner, Peck and Theodore 2010, Larner 2000, 2003, Peck 2010, Peck and Tickell 2002, Springer 2010). Given its global pervasiveness, it is not surprising that discussions have turned to the social relations that are produced through neoliberal systems and how these social relations (re)shape and (re)produce geographies (Dowling 2008, Dyck 2005). Similarly, our discussion turns to the ways in which neoliberalisms are felt through academic experiences and the paradoxical and violent ways that they are sustained in relation to other systems of control. Attempting to explore the emergent relationship between neoliberalism and masculinity, we highlight some key aspects of neoliberalism in the academy and further hint at some of its interlocking relationships with other forms of domination and subordination. Interlocking analyses go beyond simply analysing the way that systems of oppression operate together. As Razack argues, 'interlocking systems need one another' and, in fact, in such systems, one form of oppression always exists 'symbiotically' with other forms of oppression (Razack 1998: 13). She goes on to argue (Razack 2008) that interlocking forms of oppression *are* each other and *give content to* one another. With this approach in mind, we can begin to see not only the pervasiveness and normalised influence of masculine traditions of knowledge production and neoliberal academic systems, but the inseparability of masculinism and neoliberalism.

What, then, are some of the ways we observe and experience neoliberalism interlocking with other forms of oppression in the academy? Generally speaking, in academia, as with other spaces and scales more broadly, there has been a shift from Keynesian welfare-based government to policies that support private enterprises and initiatives (Hubbard 2004). We live in a time of increasing corporatisation and privatisation of the university, that are manifested in structural transformations of higher education, including the instrumentalisation, commodification and marketisation of education, the 'entrepreneurialisation' of faculty, and the transformation of students into consumers. A number of scholars have argued that this has significantly compromised the academy's capacity to serve as a 'space of critical intellectual citizenship' (Castree and Sparke 2000: 223, see also Berg and Roche 1997, Strathern 2000). Philip Morowski (2012) has gone so far as to refer to these processes as academic ponzi schemes.

Neoliberalism produces disciplined academic subjects who come to accept forms of surveillance and assessment as the norm. This can be seen through the increasingly normative nature of audit systems like the 'Research Assessment Exercise' (now 'Research Excellence Framework') in the UK, the 'Research Assessment Exercise' in the Netherlands, 'Excellence in Research' in Australia, the 'Performance-Based Research Funding' scheme in New Zealand, and a wide variety of similar schemes being developed in places like Denmark, Iceland, Finland and Germany. This is all part of turning the academy into a space of calculation that can then be made into an educational 'marketplace' with attendant winners and losers. Part of this includes the process of rendering individual and institutional (department, faculty, university) performance knowable and quantifiable through a series of measures of so-called 'outputs'. These kinds of processes have become increasingly common in academia today, and they are a central part of disciplining the neoliberal academic subject. Gill (2010: 231) describes this as 'technologies of selfhood that bring into being endless self-monitoring, planning, prioritising "responsibilised" subjects required by the contemporary university'. This is a model of hyper-competition that produces academics as particular kinds of 'individuals', and then rewards those who are willing to produce the outputs required to make the cut (and punishes those who are unwilling to do so). Those academics who occupy feminine, raced, working-class and/or disabled subject positions are all disadvantaged in this system, often because under the so-called 'merit' system that guides much of neoliberalised academic assessments and audits, their work is rarely accorded the same value as that of academics positioned as white, middle-class, able-bodied, masculine subjects (Kierstead, D'Agostino and Dill 1988, McDowell 1990, Bagilhole 1993, Nast and Pulido 2000, Winkler 2000, Bagilhole and Goode 2001, Berg 2002, Kobayashi 2002, Ben-Moshe and Colligan 2010, Cotera 2010).

The current division of labour also ensures that feminine and racialised subjects bear a majority of the responsibility for work related to both social reproduction (pregnancy, childcare, paid and unpaid domestic work) and university reproduction (student guidance, student counselling, collegial counselling, etc.), and both of these interfere with what is deemed to be the far more important work of academics: obtaining external grant funding, publishing in peer-reviewed journals and books, and travelling to present conference papers and invited lectures at other universities and international conferences. Neoliberal audit systems rarely even count the intangibles of social and university reproduction, while they usually over-value funding and publishing activities in the university. Troublingly, women who are able to negotiate these problematic distinctions in the academy often find that they have to adopt a masculine subject position in order to be taken seriously (as an academic), but in so doing, they then fail to fit the masculinist ideal of academic femininity. The penalty for such transgressions, as Moss and McMahon (2000) so aptly put it, is that they are often viewed as occupying a position 'somewhere between a flake and a strident bitch'.

Neoliberalisation of the academy produces a space of competition that creates the conditions of possibility for the rise of a particular form of atomistic individualism that leads to secrecy and silence among colleagues. Academics are systematically pit against each other through funding audits, competitions and peer-reviews, and often required to serve as auditors themselves. Serving on funding and promotional review committees provides banal and prosaic processes through which normative forms of neoliberal control are exercised in academic lives. Cronin (2000: 274) labels this as 'compulsory individuality' and speaks to its relationship with broader systems of oppression. She argues that the ideal of individuality is: 'an exclusive and politically privileged category, access to which is restricted for the overlapping groups of women, lesbians and gay men, black people, [members of] working classes, children, and the disabled' because the 'very exclusion of these intra-categorical "differences" forms the boundaries for the interiority of "the individual"'.

Precarity too is a defining feature of contemporary academic life, and perhaps is most felt by younger, early career academics. Statistical data about the employment patterns of academics point to a systematic casualisation of the workforce, an increasing casualisation of employment, and the degradation of pay and working conditions for academics with only recently a rise in organised resistance from trade unions or other bodies (Bauder 2006, Brown, Goodman and Yaukawa 2010, Bryson 2004, Dobbie and Robinson 2008, Dominelli and Hoogvelt 1996, Rossi 2005). All of this leads us to question what the costs of a transition away from secure work to poorly paid and casualised contract employment might be? It is perhaps the same 'sacrificial' ethos, in which academics and graduate students are expected to sacrifice their time to the institution that silences accounts of the personal costs of insecure and precarious work within universities (see Meyerhoff, Johnson and Braun 2011 for a deeper discussion of time and the university). A system in which, truly, only the 'strong' – or those with flexible personal situations and hidden systems of support – survive. This is a particularly powerful example of how oppression interlocks. Clearly those less 'flexible and adaptive' (i.e., those with children, those with particular health needs, those who have to deal with racism in their workplace and communities) find themselves at a clear disadvantage. Despite their profound impact upon academic lives, these things are rarely spoken of within the academy, and if they are, they tend to be treated as individual, personal experiences rather than systemic, structural failures of the contemporary university.

Towards a theory of neoliberal academic masculinities?

For geographers, space is implicated in, and intimately tied to, the contradictions that arise in the practices of scholars who are complicit in the neoliberalisation of the academy (Cronin 2000). More specifically, we suggest that theories of neoliberal academic masculinity might take into consideration the necessarily paradoxical and interlocking character of social domination, as well as both the material and discursive spaces where academic masculinities are produced. Discursively, the academy is granted prominence as one of the most respected social and cultural institutions in Western societies, due in part to the pressure that is placed on members of those same societies to obtain a university degree (Giroux 2002). Of course, there are widespread differences in the social and cultural capital wielded by universities in different national contexts. University professors in Canada and the USA, for example, have much higher status than university lecturers in Australia and New Zealand – spaces where practical knowledge is given much more prominence than the merely 'theoretical' ideas produced by academics (see Berg 1994). Nonetheless, at the wider abstract level of the 'Western academy', such regimes of truth afford cultural capital to academics who 'produce knowledge', and participate in the reproduction of dominant (liberal and neoliberal) social norms. The naïve yet widespread belief that entering academia is a path towards 'expanding intellectual horizons' as well as more instrumental outcomes like obtaining a 'good job', are precisely what grants power to academic masculinities.

The authoritative academic masculine ideal is typically formed through the achievement of positions of prestige (full professorships, endowed professorships, headships, etc.), external grant funds, and publications in highly ranked (usually by 'impact factor') journals. Such legitimisation is significant because it provides academics with the benefits, dividends and prestige that becoming an academic affords. A significant question arises in such contexts: what gendered, raced, classed and (en)abled subject positions have full access to this privilege? In the case of the gendered academy, the elite positions in the university are disproportionately reserved for white, heterosexual, middle-class, (en)abled masculine subjects. This means that both men and women can occupy these positions in the university, but women must do so as (academically) masculine subjects. Of course, it also means that men are much more likely than women to occupy the key positions of authority in the university (see Berg 2002, McDowell 1979, 1990).

While these hierarchical relationships (and physical structures) certainly do not go unnoticed, largely, they are often unchallenged at the level of practice, and when they are challenged the challenges come from within neoliberalism. Such neoliberal contestations are evident in the ways in which academics regularly point to individual acts of 'excellence' in their research, their publications, and their teaching – all in order to situate themselves as scholars who are willing to confront and challenge the neoliberal academy. But given the virulent forms of individualism produced by and encouraged in the neoliberal academy, such assertions are typically made at the individual level. Acting individually allows scholars to disaffiliate themselves from the neoliberalism of the institution, all the while posing little (if any) threat to the academy, the masculinism it supports, or the neoliberal repression and violence reproduced within it. In fact, *individuals* are precisely what the neoliberal academy wants.

Paradoxically, while neoliberalism is theorised, critiqued and problematised by a host of differing perspectives that attest to the harmful individualising capacities of such a system, it nonetheless remains a powerful status quo. The permeation of masculinist traditions in the academy is largely due in part to the atomising demands that result from the pursuit of personal merit and individual accomplishment. The splintering effects that result from obedience to neoliberal ideology produces subject positions that are disconnected and atomised. In this way, academics are encouraged to think and act as 'individuals' by way of engagement in hyper-competitive academic rituals. In order to be successful in the academy it is vital to consent to the hierarchies of rank, status and reputation, despite any critical opposition one may have to such constructs. The demand is to perform, and exist, as a highly successful individual. In light of this, academic masculinity remains intimately tied to neoliberal ideology and we cannot understand one without understanding the other. Neoliberalised academic practices employ the rhetoric of rugged individualism and personal work ethic while also diluting conversations of systemic oppression through the suggestion that equitable meritocracies exist within universities. As a result, radical collective praxis that could potentially bring about widespread transformation of the academy becomes less likely, and in many cases even vigorously disciplined. What results is a systematic reproduction of hierarchical academic masculinities that produce subjects who (re)produce the punitive demands of the neoliberal academy.

Academic masculinities

So far we have outlined the context within which we might think relationally about the production of academic masculinities, but with the exceptions of some very broad brush strokes, we have yet to paint a specific picture of what these academic masculinities might look like. A useful place to start specifying how academic masculinities might be defined is with Raewynn Connell's (1995: 71) working definition of masculinity more generally: 'Masculinity … is simultaneously a place in gender relations, the practices through which men and women engage that place in gender, and the effects of these practices in bodily experience, personality and culture'. In a later iteration, as quoted earlier, Connell (2005: 77) argued that hegemonic masculinity should be understood as 'the currently accepted answer to the legitimacy of patriarchy', the 'configuration of gender practice' that is taken to guarantee 'the dominant position of men and the subordination of women'.

Drawing on both of these definitions, we argue that *academic masculinity should be understood as simultaneously a place in gendered academic relations that embodies the currently accepted answer to the legitimacy of patriarchy in the academy, the practices through which academics engage with that place in gendered academia, and the gendered effects of these practices that operate to maintain the dominant position of men and the subordination of women in the academy.*

The above definition allows us to think academic masculinities relationally, and to connect them to the wider systems of gender relations within which they arise (after Berg and Longhurst 2003, also see Hopkins 2007). In so doing, we can come to understand that there is no single hegemonic academic masculinity, but rather, there are geographically, culturally and temporally contingent academic masculinities. Although processes of academic capitalism, globalising neoliberalism and the so-called 'internationalisation' of the academy are leading to more ubiquitous forms of academic masculinity, it is important to remember that time and space still matter to the constitution of academic masculinities. Academic masculinities are highly contingent, unstable, contested spaces within gender relations, and it is this contingency and instability that makes both the process and spaces of academic subject formation so important in the construction of academic masculinities (Berg and Longhurst 2003).

Attempting to make sense of these complex and contradictory social spaces, perhaps it might be useful to understand the neoliberal academy as a space characterised by 'slow violence', a form of violence that is neither 'spectacular nor instantaneous, but rather incremental and accretitive' (Nixon 2011: 2). The concept of slow violence disrupts common ideas of violence being both acute and highly visible and offers a way to account for the seeming complacency and contradictions that exist within the neoliberal academy (see also Holmes 2012).

Universities in the space now known as Canada are situated on land stolen from indigenous peoples, they are populated by over-employed tenured professors and under-employed sessional lecturers, service workers and labourers, as well as students from middle- and upper-middle-class backgrounds. These people all work in buildings named after powerful white men, many of whom gained their social power through various forms of capitalist structural violence and accumulation by dispossession. These universities are the embodiment in both practices and in actual bricks and mortar of the materialities of gendered social relations as they interlock with, for example, colonialism, racism, ableism and neoliberal capitalism.

Academic masculinities are, in part at least, both the product of these repressive university systems and implicated in their reproduction. These facts are important for academic men to keep in mind, and particularly for critical and progressive male scholars who wish to support women and other marginalised colleagues as they contest academic and other forms of repression (Nocella, Best and McLaren 2010). One of neoliberalism's many dangers for academics is that it can fool us into confusing our unearned privileges with advantages that we might have somehow earned through our hard work. Neoliberalised forms of academic audit and assessment especially operate to fool those of us male academics who are privileged by our unearned privilege into thinking that our position in the academy is actually the result of our own individual meritorious actions as 'excellent' scholars. As we have illustrated here, however, that kind of thinking needs to be problematised, especially the virulent (and violent) form of gendered, raced, classed, and (en)abled individualism that underpins such neoliberal thinking.

We end this discussion with no cut-and-dry descriptions of specific academic masculinities. Rather, our goal has been to argue for the need to understand academic masculinities as relational and processual, as complex and contradictory, and to provide a better understanding of the need for an interlocking analysis of their conditions of possibility under neoliberalised academic relations. We wish to open up wider discussions about the mutual constitution of academic masculinities in particular places, and how they interlock with the neoliberalising academy and the different forms of domination and subordination found in particular places. In short, we are calling for the analysis of the geographies of actually-existing academic masculinities as they are (re)produced through the quotidian and the banal, and how these processes are always already geographical.

Acknowledgements

We are grateful to Andrew Gorman-Murray and Peter Hopkins for their helpful comments on the penultimate draft of this chapter We are also indebted to them for their patience and understanding when it comes to missed deadlines!

References

Anderson, E. 2009. *Inclusive Masculinities: The Changing Nature of Masculinities*. New York: Routledge.

Ashe, F. 2007. *The New Politics of Masculinity: Men Power and Resistance*. New York: Routledge.

Bagilhole, B. 1993. How to keep a good woman down: an investigation of the role of institutional factors in the process of discrimination against women academics. *British Journal of Sociology of Education*, 14(3), 261–274.

Bagilhole, B. and Goode, J. 2001. The contradiction of the myth of individual merit, and the reality of a patriarchal support system in academic careers. *The European Journal of Women's Studies*, 8(2), 161–180.

Bauder, H. 2006. The segmentation of academic labour: A Canadian example. *ACME: An International E–Journal for Critical Geographies*, 4(2), 228–239.

Ben-Moshe, L. and Colligan, S.E. 2010. Regimes of normalcy in the academy: the experiences of disabled faculty, in *Academic Repression: Reflections from the Academic Industrial Complex*, edited by A. Nocella, S. Best and P. McLaren. Edinburgh: AK Press, 374–385.

Berg, L.D. 1994. Masculinity, place, and a binary discourse of theory and empirical investigation in the human geography of Aotearoa/New Zealand. *Gender, Place and Culture: A Journal of Feminist Geography*, 1(2), 245–260.

Berg, L.D. 2001. Masculinism, emplacement, and positionalities in peer review. *Professional Geographer*, 53(4), 511–521.

Berg L.D. 2002. Gender equity as boundary object: or the same old sex and power in geography all over again? *Canadian Geographer*, 46(3), 248–254.

Berg, L.D. 2006. Masculinities, in *Encyclopedia of Human Geography*, edited by B. Warf. Thousand Oaks: Sage Publications, 296–298.

Berg, L.D. 2013. Hegemonic geographies and their 'others': towards an interlocking approach to emplacing geographical knowledges. *Dialogues in Human Geography*, 3(2), 200–204.

Berg, L.D. and Longhurst, R. 2003. Placing masculinities and geography. *Gender, Place and Culture: A Journal of Feminist Geography*, 10(4), 351–560.

Berg, L.D. and Roche, M.M. 1997. Market metaphors, neo-liberalism and the construction of academic landscapes in Aotearoa/New Zealand. *Journal of Geography in Higher Education*, 21(2), 147–161.

Boggs, C. 1984. *The Two Revolutions: Gramsci and the Dilemmas of Western Marxism*. London: South End Press.

Brenner, N., Peck, J. and Theodore, N. 2010. Variegated neoliberalization: geographies, modalities, pathways. *Global Networks*, 10(2), 182–222.

Brown, T., Goodman, J. and Yasukawa, K. 2010. Academic casualization in Australia: class divisions in the university. *Journal of Industrial Relations*, 52(2), 169–182.

Browne, K. 2008. Power and privilege: (re)making feminist geographies, in *Feminisms in Geography: Rethinking Space, Place, and Knowledges*, edited by P. Moss and K. Falconer Al-Hindi. Lanham: Rowman and Littlefield, 140–148.

Bryson, C. 2004. What about the workers? The expansion of higher education and the transformation of academic work. *Industrial Relations Journal*, 35(1), 38–57.

Buttigieg, J.A. (ed.) 1992. *Antonio Gramsci: Prison Notebooks*. New York: Columbia University Press, 233–238.

Butz, D. and Berg, L.D. 2002. Paradoxical space: geography, men, and duppy feminism, in *Feminist Geography in Practice*, edited by P. Moss. Oxford: Wiley-Blackwell, 87–102.

Castree, N. and Sparke, M. (eds) 2000. *Professional Geography and the Corporatization of the University: Experiences, Evaluations and Engagements*, *Antipode* (Special Issue), 32(3), 222–339.

Castree, N., Aspinall, R., Berg, L.D., Bohle, H-G., Hoggart, K., Kitchin, R., et al. 2006. Research assessment and the production of geographical knowledge. *Progress in Human Geography*, 30(6), 747–782.

Connell, R.W. 1995. *Masculinities: Knowledge, Power and Social Change.* Berkeley: University of California Press.

Connell, R.W. 2005. *Masculinities*. 2nd Edition. Berkeley: University of California Press.

Connell, R.W. 2009. *Gender: In World Perspectives.* Cambridge: Polity Press.

Connell, R.W. and Messerschmidt, J.W. 2005. Hegemonic masculinity: rethinking the concept. *Gender and Society*, 19(6), 829–859.

Cotera, M.E. 2010. Women of color, tenure, and the neoliberal university, in *Academic Repression: Reflections from the Academic Industrial Complex*, edited by A. Nocella, S. Best and P. McLaren. Edinburgh: AK Press, 328–336.

Cronin, A. 2000. Consumerism and compulsory individuality: women, will and potential, in *Thinking Through Feminism. Transformations: Thinking Through Feminism*, edited by S. Ahmed, et al. London: Routledge, 273–287.

Demetriou, D. 2001. Connell's concept of hegemonic masculinity: a critique. *Theory and Society*, 30(3), 337–361.

Derrida, J. 1976. *Of Grammatology.* Baltimore: Johns Hopkins University Press.

Dobbie, D. and Robinson, I. 2008. Reorganizing higher education in the United States and Canada: the erosion of tenure and the unionization of contingent faculty. *Labor Studies Journal*, 33(2), 117–140.

Dominelli, L. and Hoogvelt, A. 1996. Globalization, contract government and the Taylorization of intellectual labour in academia. *Studies in Political Economy*, 49, 71–100.

Dyck, I. 2005. Feminist geography, the 'everyday', and local-global relations: hidden spaces of place-making. *The Canadian Geographer*, 49(3), 233–243.

Foucault, M. 1984. *The Foucault Reader*. New York: Pantheon Books.

Francese, J. (ed.) 2009. *The Politics, Culture and Social Theory of Gramsci: A Multidisciplinary Perspective*. New York: Routledge.

Gill, R. 2009. Breaking the silence: the hidden injuries of neo-liberal academia, in *Secrecy and Silence in the Research Process: Feminist Reflections*, edited by R. Flood and R. Gill. London: Routledge.

Giroux, H.A. 2002. Neoliberalism, corporate culture, and the promise of higher education: the university as a democratic public sphere. *Harvard Educational Review*, 72(4), 425–464.

Gramsci, A. 1971. *Selections from the Prison Notebooks of Antonio Gramsci*, translated and edited by Q. Hoare, and G.N. Smith. New York: International Publishers.

Gregory, D. 1994. *Geographical Imaginations.* Cambridge: Wiley-Blackwell.

Hall, J., Murphy, B., Moss, P., Yasmeen, G., et al. 2002. Focus: equity for women in geography. *Canadian Geographer*, 46(3), 235–240.

Haraway, D.J. 1988. Situated knowledges: the science question in feminism and the privilege of partial perspective. *Feminist Studies*, 14(3), 575–599.

Hearn, J. 2004. From hegemonic masculinity to the hegemony of men. *Feminist Theory*, 5(1), 49–72.

Hilgers, M. 2013. Embodying neoliberalism: thoughts and responses to critics. *Social Anthropology*, 21(1), 75–89.

Holmes, C. 2012. *Violence denied, bodies erased: towards an interlocking spatial framework for queer anti-violence organizing*. Unpublished PhD dissertation, Kelowna, University of British Columbia, Canada.

Hopkins, P. 2007. Young people, masculinities, religion and race: new social geographies. *Progress in Human Geography*, 31(2), 163–177.

Horne, W.R. 2002. Integrating gender into mainstream teaching. *Canadian Geographer*, 46(3), 254–257.

Hubbard, P. 2004. Revenge and injustice in the neoliberal city: uncovering masculinist agendas. *Antipode*, 36(4), 665–686.

Irigaray, L. 1985a. *Speculum of the Other Women*. Ithaca: Cornell University Press.

Irigaray, L. 1985b. *This Sex Which is Not One*. Ithaca: Cornell University Press.

Jessop, B. 2005. Gramsci as a spatial theorist. *Critical Review of International Social and Political Philosophy*, 8(4), 421–438.

Jiwani, Y. 2006. *Discourses of Denial: Mediations of Race, Gender, and Violence*. Vancouver: UBC Press.

Joll, J. 1977. *Antonio Gramsci*. New York: Viking Press.

Kierstead, D., D'Agostino, P. and Dill, H. 1988. Sex role stereotyping of college professors: bias in student's rating of instructors. *Journal of Educational Psychology*, 80(3), 342–344.

Kimmel, M., Hearn, J. and Connell, R.W. (eds) 2005. *The Handbook of Studies on Men and Masculinities*. Thousand Oaks: Sage Publications.

Kobayashi, A. 2002. A generation later and still two per cent: changing the culture of Canadian geography. *Canadian Geographer*, 46(3), 245–248.

Larner, W. 2000. Neo-liberalism: policy, ideology, governmentality. *Studies in Political Economy*, 63, 5–25.

Larner, W. 2003. Neoliberalism? *Environment and Planning D: Society and Space*, 21(5), 509–512.

Malszecki, G. and Cavar, T. 2004. Men, masculinities war and sport, in *Feminist Issues: Race, Class, and Sexuality*, edited by N. Mandel. Scarborough: Pearson Education Canada.

Mansvelt, J., and Berg, L.D. 2005. Writing qualitative geographies, constructing geographical knowledges, in *Qualitative Research Methods in Human Geography*, 2nd edition, edited by I. Hay. Toronto: Oxford University Press, 248–265.

McDowell, L. 1979. Women in British geography. *Area*, 11(2), 151–154.

McDowell, L. 1990. Sex and power in academia. *Area*, 22(4), 323–332.

McDowell, L. and Sharp, J.P. 1999. *A Feminist Glossary of Human Geography*. New York: Arnold.

McGann, P. 2002. Eating muscle – material semiotics and a manly appetite, in *Revealing Male Bodies*, edited by N. Tuana and W. Cowling. Bloomington: Indiana University Press.

Meyerhoff, E., Johnson, E. and Braun, B. 2011. Time and the university. *ACME: An International E-Journal for Critical Geographies*, 10(3), 483–507.

Min-ha, Trin T. 1997. Not you/like you: postcolonial women and the interlocking questions of identity and difference, in *Dangerous Liaisons: Gender, Nation, and Postcolonial Perspectives*, edited by A. McClintock, A. Muftir and E. Shohat. Minneapolis: University of Minnesota Press.

Mirowski, P. 2012. The modern commercialization of science is a passel of Ponzi schemes. *Social Epistemology: A Journal of Knowledge, Culture and Policy*, 26(3–4), 285–310.

Moss, P. 2002. *Feminist Geography in Practice*. Oxford: Wiley-Blackwell.

Moss, P. and McMahon, M. 2000. Between a flake and a strident bitch: making 'IT' count in the academy. *Resources for Feminist Research*, 28(1–2), 15.

Nast, H.J. and Pulido, L. 2000. Resisting corporate multiculturalism: mapping faculty initiatives and institutional-student harassment in the classroom. *The Professional Geographer*, 52(4), 722–737.

Nixon, R. 2011. Slow violence, gender, and the environmentalism of the poor, in *Environment at the Margins: Literary and Environmental Studies in Africa*, edited by B. Caminero-Santangelo and G. Myers. Athens: Ohio University Press, 257–285.

Nocella, A.J., Best, S. and McLaren, P. (eds) 2010. *Academic Repression: Reflections from the Academic Industrial Complex*. Edinburgh: AK Press.

Nunn, N. 2013. 'It can be dangerous for the uterus': hegemonic masculinity and cooperative recycling in São Paulo, Brazil. *Gender, Place and Culture: A Journal of Feminist Geography*, 20(6), 794–810.

Pacholok, S. 2009. Gendered strategies of self: navigating hierarchy and contesting masculinities. *Gender, Work and Organization*, 16(4), 471–500.

Peck, J. 2010. Zombie neoliberalism and the ambidextrous state. *Theoretical Criminology*, 14(1), 104–110.

Peck, J. and Tickell, A. 2002. Neoliberalizing space. *Antipode*, 34(3), 380–404.

Peralta, R. 2007. College alcohol use and the embodiment of hegemonic masculinity among European American men. *Sex Roles*, 56(11–12), 380–388.

Pratt, G. 2000. Science, geography and, in: *The Dictionary of Human Geography*. 4th Edition. R.J. Johnston, et al. Malden: Wiley-Blackwell, 332–334.

Razack, S. 1998. *Looking White People in the Eye: Gender, Race and Culture in Courtrooms and Classrooms*. Toronto: University of Toronto Press.

Razack, S. (ed.) 2002. *Race, Space, and the Law: Unmapping a White Settler Society*. Toronto: Between the Lines.

Razack, S. 2008. *Casting Out: The Eviction of Muslims from Western Law and Politics*. Toronto: University of Toronto Press.

Rose, G. 1993. *Feminism and Geography: The Limits of Geographical Knowledge*. Minneapolis: University of Minnesota Press.

Rose, G. 1995. Distance, surface, elsewhere: a feminist critique of the space of phallocentric self/knowledge. *Environment and Planning D: Society and Space*, 13(6), 761–768.

Rossi, U. 2005. The struggles of precarious researchers and demands for social change in (post-) Berlusconian Italy. *ACME: An International E–Journal for Critical Geographies*, 4(2), 277–286.

Ruddick, S. 1996. Constructing difference in public spaces: race, class, and gender as interlocking systems. *Urban Geography*, 17(2), 132–151.

Springer, S. 2010. Neoliberalism and geography: expansions, variegations, formations. *Geography Compass*, 4(8), 1025–1038.

Strathern, M. (ed.), 2000. *Audit Cultures: Anthropological Studies in Accountability, Ethics, and the Academy.* New York: Routledge.

Tuhiwai-Smith, L. 1999. *Decolonizing Methodologies: Research and Indigenous Peoples*. London: Zed Books.

Valentine, G. 2007. Theorizing and researching intersectionality: a challenge for feminist geography. *The Professional Geographer*, 59(10), 10–21.

Winkler, J. 2000. Faculty reappointment, tenure, and promotion: barriers for women. *The Professional Geographer*, 52(4), 737–750.

Yasmeen, G. 2002. Attracting and keeping women and visible minorities in Canadian geography departments. *Canadian Geographer*, 46(3), 240–244.

Zelinsky, W. 1973. The strange case of the missing female geographer. *The Professional Geographer*, 25(2), 151–165.

Zelinsky, W., Monk, J. and Hanson, S. 1982. Women and geography: a review and prospectus. *Progress in Human Geography*, 6(3), 317–365.

PART 2
Masculinities, Intersectionality and Relationality

Chapter 5

'I am lord, … I am local': Migrant Masculinity, Sex and Making Yourself at Home

Greg Noble and Paul Tabar

Do migrants have sex?

In reading much of the scholarship over many decades on migration and diasporic communities, you might be mistaken for thinking that the success of migrants in fulfilling the economic and social functions of reproduction – the aims of immigration policies in many countries – was accomplished without recourse to (hetero)sexual activity. This blindness was partly addressed by the increasing scholarship on gender and migration, and an interest in families and the sexual divisions of migrant labour, but this literature not only focused overwhelmingly on women's experience, it also tended to talk about sex primarily in terms of domestic violence and the sex industry or, more generally, as a means of gender subordination (Willis and Yeoh 2000, Palmary et al. 2010). The many calls to bring gender into migration studies have been successful in critiquing the presumption of the masculine migrant subject and in drawing attention to the specificity of women's experiences, but, as several commentators have pointed out, there has been a resulting tendency to neglect and over-simplify men's experiences and, through a politicised contrasting of men's and women's experiences, cast migrant men as 'tyrannical patriarchs' (Ryan and Webster 2008: 4–5, Herbert 2008: 189). Ironically, this can only foster the wider social view of migrant men – particularly those of Muslim and Middle Eastern backgrounds – as sexually perverse (Dagistanli and Grewal 2012). There are two issues here for us: a diminishing of the social role of sexual practices and a neglect of the specificity of men's experiences.

An impressive body of recent work, including that of Ahmad, Mai and others, brings very forcefully onto centre stage questions of sexuality previously underexplored. It reminds us that migrants aren't just economic categories or rational beings, or social problems, but humans with desires, emotions, love lives and sexual energies (Ahmad 2011: 3, 5, Mai 2011, Kitiarsa 2008). As Mai and King argue in calling for a 'sexual turn' in migration studies, these supposedly subjective dimensions can have profound effects on people's mobility, the decision to migrate and their capacity to settle (2009: 296–297). But while there has been an important recognition of the experiences of gay migrants, for example, the focus in this work – as in some of the earlier work foregrounding women's experience – continues to be on issues such as sex trafficking, illegal migration and sex work, within a broader framework drawn largely from feminist and queer theory that foregrounds the deconstruction of heteronormative discourses and gendered relations of power. This, of course, is not a criticism – this is much needed work – but it leaves unaddressed a range of other questions around sexual subjectivities and mobility, especially for heterosexual men.

Over twenty years ago, Chambers (1991) argued that we knew very little about the effects of migration on men's sexual identities. Adkins (2002), a decade later, suggested we don't understand more broadly what happens to sexuality under conditions of mobility. Walsh, Shen and Wills (2008) made a similar point in a special journal issue in relation to heterosexuality and migration in Asia. Hibbins and Pease (2009: 7–8), in their introduction to a collection on migrant men, suggest that despite two decades of escalating 'men's studies', there is still a shortage of empirical work on the connections between migration, ethnicity, masculinity and sexuality (see also Datta and McIlwaine 2014: this volume, Gibson 2014: this volume). Herbert (2008), in an all-too-rare exploration of the life histories of East African Asian men, demonstrates the complex entanglements of gendered identities, domestic relations, work, class, sexuality and settlement. We think these are pressing questions because sexual subjectivities play a key role within what is often referred to as the 'intersection' of gender, class and ethnicity. Moreover, sexual life, like any aspect of social life, contributes to the negotiation and renegotiation of identities, especially important for people uprooted from their place of origin (Ricatti 2011, Malam 2008), and thus central to the mediation of a sense of belonging and the process of emplacement in the country of settlement, for men as for women, entailing complex relations between mobility and place (Hubbard 2002, Cheng 2012).

The sensuousness of settlement

These issues are particularly pressing for us because sex reared its head in an interview we conducted with a man we shall call Abbas. Abbas was one of a small number of older Lebanese–Australians we asked to reflect on their experiences migrating to Australia in the 1970s and 1980s. We were interested in their accounts of settlement primarily in terms of the sensuous dimensions of living in a strange land – a key theme of non-academic accounts but rarely foregrounded in scholarly analysis. We have elsewhere argued that this process entails the 'ethnicisation' of the migrant's habitus, learning to belong as an embodied difference, as a subordinated member of the field of national belonging (Noble and Tabar 2013). Focusing on these phenomenological dimensions was important, we felt, because the ability of a migrant to fashion a viable life in the new place of settlement rests on their capacity to learn how to adjust to quite different physical and sensory worlds. We asked interviewees to describe what struck them as different in the landscapes they found themselves in – the sights, sounds, tastes and smells they encountered – and how they navigated local spaces, new rules for social interaction and bodily conduct, and so on. They recounted sensations of disorientation and reorientation as they learnt to live differently, and to be the difference.

One of the questions we asked the participants was if there was a moment when they felt 'at home' in Australia. Many talked of conventional markers of accomplishment – getting a job, learning English, buying a house, having kids, etc. – but Abbas startled us with his response: 'My first bloody sexual contact, the first time I had sex with a woman made me feel I'm the master of the whole eternity. I am lord, know what I mean? I am local.' It wasn't just the emphasis on sexual experience as the source of a sense of homeliness, nor the language which seemed to evoke a patriarchal sense of 'mastery', but the specification of feeling 'local'. Abbas's admission urged us, we felt, to think about the relationships between masculinity, ethnicity, sexuality and making one's self at home in a particular time and place.

Abbas was 25 when he arrived in Australia in 1977. He had migrated from a village in southern Lebanon, where he had worked on his family's tobacco farm. He had begun attending technical college in Lebanon, but it was interrupted by the civil war. He migrated in the wake of the war and the occupation by the Israeli army of his village. When he arrived in Sydney, he did not know a single word of English, and only had $10 in his pocket. Moreover, it was his first encounter with a modern Western, urban society. He described his early years with a strong sense of displacement, but he gradually found his feet, getting a job as a shunter on the railways and attending English language classes. While he never became wealthy – he became and remained a train guard for most of his working life – he nevertheless succeeded in making himself a comfortable life in Australia. He eventually married – returning to his village to get a wife – and has four children. We interviewed him, several times, as a 60-year-old man reflecting on his early life in Australia.

Two things stand out very clearly from the beginning of his interviews: first, a sense of disorientation in those early years, but a largely pragmatic acceptance of this disorientation; and second, an equally strong emphasis on his sexual life, especially in these early years. Abbas, a heterosexual male, recounts story after story involving his sexual adventures with women, and particularly significant is the way he responds to questions about how he experienced Australia and learning to live here in sensuous and sensual terms. Abbas talked at length about how Australia was a very different place to that in which he grew up: 'it felt like someone was in a sunk ship and you find yourself suddenly on island … trees, air, rocks, everything was different'. Or, as he says in a second interview[1]: 'Generally I felt like Gulliver in the land of talking horses – the novelty of things was

1 We spoke with Abbas several times, so material for an event comes from different interviews. In the first interview we did not ask about sex, but in the second we asked him to elaborate on the experiences referred to in the first.

overwhelming.' He doesn't seem to despair about this (not at this point, anyway); in fact, he says he felt like he had been 'born again'. But when we asked him what specifically he noticed as different, he responded: 'the way people dress; shorts, barefoot, topless, it was very interesting to watch people the way they dress; the way they go around … especially girls, whoosh!' The novelty of the new landscape extended to women themselves. Abbas noted the:

> physical difference to womans we used to know, … they are more revealing, the way they look, colour of eyes, their blondeness, well maintained physical shapes, all these things reflect on you, as a new arrival. As someone who wasn't new to women, to sexual relationships, but it felt like, it's different, … It looks like a world you'd like to discover, but you scared to discover, … you are not armed, you do not how to go in, you keep on asking yourself.

Abbas recounts a key incident early in our first interview:

> … once we [he and his cousin] were coming from the beach, on the train, there was a girl about 17, and she was half naked, … beautiful girl, she started gazing at us. She felt threatened … Then she was bloody insulting us. But we did not know a word … I knew from the expression on her face. So we stopped … We didn't know what she was saying, we didn't know how to answer, we didn't know what to do … We were fucking scared at the same time. Got out at the train station and we ran away!

As he elaborates later, 'we were both frustrated sexually, we kept unintentionally gazing at her … I knew she was very unhappy, very uncomfortable'.

The sensuous nature of difference quickly becomes sexualised for Abbas; where others talked about the physical differences of Sydney, he gravitates quickly to the socio-sexual codes and practices of Western modernity of Australian urban life. Of course, he is not alone: several others talked, for example, about being confronted by bodily display on streets, nudity on beaches, and learning not to engage in physical intimacy between men (Noble and Tabar 2013); but it is the sustained focus on sex which marks out Abbas's comments. New social codes as well as new urban spaces have to be 'learnt' and internalised by the migrant and this process is potentially anxiety-producing, and is experienced as a threat or a challenge that has to be met in one way or another. Significantly, and a point we will return to below, is that Abbas registered that fact that while this moment aroused fear as well as desire in him, he also recognised that it was also a fearful moment for the young woman.

Abbas's anxiety is caused, of course, not simply by the dissonance between competing 'traditional' and 'modern' sexual codes (Khalaf 2006), or an abstract disconnect between the social values of village society and those of Western modernity, or the wider sense of social and economic dislocation. He is struggling to get used to the visceral processes of navigating the physical and social spaces of a city and its infrastructure, learn English, get a job, and so on. But significantly for Abbas, not only does he continue to see his sensuous engagement with modernity in highly sexualised terms, he responds to the challenge partly *through* his sexual life.

The dephallicised male migrant

As Hage (2006) notes, migration is often experienced or represented as an emasculating experience for men. This parallels an existing literature on the intertwining of masculine sexuality, racial marginalisation and the psychology of colonialism, explored by Fanon (1952/1986), Nandy (1983) and Sinha (1995), but it also parallels an emerging literature examining racial and sexual hierarchies as emasculating experiences amongst gay migrants (Ayres 1999, Caluya 2007). Hage challenges the simplistic formulae of emasculation through his recounting of the story of Adel, a Lebanese migrant in Boston who complains that his conditions of miserable existence have resulted in impotence. Hage recounts Adel's assertion that 'migration smoothly fucks a person's heart ... without them even noticing'. He hates his job as a mechanic, he doesn't have enough money to go out, he envies his wife's more prestigious job, his kids don't respect him because he is uneducated, and so on. Hage questions Adel's simple view that his failure to succeed as a migrant lies behind his erectile dysfunction, but suggests that what is interesting is the relationship between Adel's mode of sexual identification and his social identification, what Hage glosses as his conception and projection of his social viability. He outlines what he calls Adel's 'migratory process of de-phallicisation', premised on Adel's internalisation of modernistic aspirations, a Western gaze premised on acquisition and social, economic and educational success.

We are not convinced by Hage's argument that Adel's predicament rests on a peculiarly Mediterranean masculinity, but we do see some merit in his claim that there is a particular form of 'actual phallocentrism' typical of male sexual culture found in village society and its valorisation of the penis. He recounts a village rite in which a boy's pants are removed by the male elders and 'they put you behind a girl your age and they keep pressing you and rubbing you on her until you get a little erection'. This exemplifies not a primal moment, but an example of the preoccupation with the physical penis which creates a fusion between social and sexual male viability.

There are many challenging ideas in Hage's argument, but the main issue we wish to draw from Hage's analysis is that it allows us to think of two points that are relevant here. Hage notes that the literature on migration for men often relies on a sense of the process as emasculating, but he is suggesting we need a much more situated and subtle understanding of the connection between masculine heterosexuality and migration, and fewer generalisations: as he says, 'penis-centred masculinity is not a one way traffic of empowerment'. Adel's 'phallic trajectory', he continues, cannot be presented simplistically as the possession of phallic power in Lebanon and the loss of phallic power through migration; there are always phallicising and de-phallicising tendencies operating. In suggesting that not all males will experience such a process, then, we need to think in much more nuanced, and empirically grounded, ways about the role of sexual experience in practices of settlement. This is especially important at this moment given the moral panics around Lebanese/Arab/Muslim boys and the pathologisation of their sexuality as violent, animalistic, misogynistic and racist (Poynting et al. 2004, Dagistanli and Grewal 2012) and the larger history of racialised sexuality through which sexual fears and desires articulate with regimes of racial and class inequality (Fanon 1952/1986, Stoler 1992).

Rephallicisation? Or, learning to be a new kind of man

Abbas's account suggests he has a different kind of experience to Adel, despite also coming from a patriarchal village culture and also articulating a sense of the 'suffering' of the immigrant, the anguish arising from displacement and the struggle to achieve emplacement (Sayad 2004). As he says at the end of his first interview:

> Migration, especially at this age, … you have to work, learn language, whatever … it's a misery, generally speaking, migration is a misery … everyday there is a new question you have to answer, everyday day there is an issue you have to deal with … and you don't feel fucking, you don't feel comfortable.

But misery does not define his overall perspective on making himself at home in Australia nor produce the kind of social and sexual dysfunction of which Adel complains. Sex seems to offer Abbas different kinds of opportunities for responding to the 'questions' migration asks. There are moments in Abbas's narrative where he voices what might be seen as a patriarchal, peasant masculinity, but there are also moments when he seems to embrace the values and opportunities a modern, Western society offers. So, for example, in the context of talking about the shock of being confronted by Western codes of dress, sexual display and physical open-ness, he adds, with a laugh, 'but it didn't take much time to start to imitate them'. His admission of *imitation* is significant here: as we've suggested, new sexual codes, like new social codes and spaces, have to be 'learnt'. So rather than simply stress the dissonance between codes and the consequent inability to negotiate coherent identities (Khalaf 2006: 7–8), we want to think about how these competing logics may be addressed through practices and pedagogies of emplacement, including sexual practices as a form of making one's self at home.

Most importantly, there are moments when Abbas's sexual learning becomes quite explicit, and it is often at the hands of women. He recounts a key moment in his brief attendance at a night school learning English with a female English teacher:

> Less than a year, and I remember very well, I was very very attracted to that woman, she was petite, dark chocolatey skin, she looked beautiful to me, naturally I prefer the dark-skinned girls. And I was sitting there in the classroom, looking at her, I wasn't listening to what she was saying. My mind was somewhere else, fantasising about that, and she caught me. I wanted her. I was looking under the table, the only thing I could see was her legs, and I was looking at her legs, during the course of teaching, she called my name, she said 'can you see my feet?' [out loudly] about 20 people in class – Chinese, Vietnamese, Lebanese – I pretended I was stupid, I said 'yes, of course' [laughs], she said 'can you please come over?', she put me on the podium, and started explaining to them about me, Abbas is this, that, talking about the way I look, my body, my waist, my length, then asked me to go back and sit down, by this time I realised I was doing something I shouldn't have done, I knew it, but she was very understanding.

Abbas got the point: as she used his body to teach English words to the class, she was also teaching him what it means to be sexually objectified. We may speculate that she was also teaching him that a woman could be his intellectual superior, and that sexual desire requires restraint and care for others' sensibilities. Abbas learnt even more about himself through his sexual experiences with other women. He recounts another key moment within his first year here:

> … we were at a party … a social gathering [in fact it is a club], I happened to be there with [a friend]. I was sitting at a table, … and there was this girl there. Like every girl, she looks good, she was beautiful, and during the course of that party, she start talking to me, and I didn't understand a word she was saying … [his friend] acted as an interpreter … he said to me, look, this girl wants to drive you home, at the end of this she was very enthusiastic, he knew what she wants but I didn't, she drove me back to my street, then at the car, this was my first sexual experience with a woman on her initiative, she started it, and she tried to come inside with me, and I said can't do that […] and we practiced sex in the car. She kept on coming after a couple of months, and finally it seems like she lost interest, she found I was not up to a relationship.

As Abbas admits, this was his first experience of a woman initiating sex, learnt in the context where his own lack of English competence means he had to be led. Significantly, she was an 'anglo'.[2] While it lasted for some time, he also eventually learnt that 'he was not up to a relationship'. Rather than this producing a maudlin sense of failure, he seems to accept this and moves on; he sees it as a lesson and goes on to talk about the importance of learning English. In contrast to Adel's experience, Abbas is undergoing some kind of 're-phallicisation' or remasculinisation (Caluya 2007), not so much in terms of an increase of phallic

---

2 'Anglo' is commonly used to refer to Australians of English-speaking or 'Anglo-Saxon' background.

power per se, but in learning how to be a different kind of man in response to changing and challenging circumstances.

These experiences are significant when we contrast them to Abbas's comment about sex helping him feel at home in Australia. The language of 'mastery' and 'lordship' points towards what seems to be a patriarchal discourse of masculine power and possession of the feminine, and that is how we read it at first. Indeed, there is much to see in Abbas that suggests he hasn't strayed far from a peasant masculinity: as an old man he can be quite dismissive towards women while fetishising their appearance, and he is somewhat homophobic. We don't want to romanticise Abbas as some kind of sensitive new age man. There *is* a sense of a masculine pride in his sexual history, which ostensibly echoes the fantasy of sexual potency we have come across amongst some young Lebanese men (Tabar, Noble and Poynting 2010: 108) and the macho code Mercer (1994: 137) theorised as the recuperation of power by marginalised Afro-American men. But we don't think Abbas's comments amount to a hypermasculine bravado or a 'predatory' approach to sexuality; his comments about his first few years reflect as much an orientation to a 'permissive' discourse, where sexual encounters are valued for their own sake, not simply to confirm the masculine ego, and in which women have agency (Wight 1996: 157, Hollway 1984). He admits that he 'was very preoccupied with women', talks of 'going fishing' for women at clubs and the good feeling when other men asked for advice on how to approach girls – but this is later in his history. In any case, he doesn't boast of conquests or his prowess explicitly, although he is clearly enjoying recounting his history as a kind of accomplishment.

Despite his embracing of permissive sexual values, Abbas retains elements of a sexual conservatism. This is seen most clearly in his decision to eventually return to his village to choose a wife with the blessing of his uncle, the patriarch of the family, and to return to the village on a fairly regular basis, every three-four years. There is, however, a degree of ambivalence in his retelling of this, and he puts the decision down to family pressure:

> I never felt the specific need to get married. There were always women around me. Until they started whingeing at home … I was 35 … [getting a woman here] never crossed my mind, people were always talking about the corrupt women in Australia, the way they dress, … their relationships and this puts you off, the idea was to marry a girl from my background, … but it took a long time to materialise.

Abbas himself never voices this view of 'Australian' women as corrupt, and his decision seems more about fitting with his family's expectations, and delaying the decision as long as possible. When he eventually went back to Lebanon to get married:

> It wasn't a good experience, there was no one there … when I am here I felt like I was going home, but when I got there I lost it … It had changed for the worse

> [social life] doesn't exist … people pass you in the street and don't say hello, an entirely different world … they didn't treat me as one of them, I didn't feel it, they look at you as an alien, … whose luggage is full of money.

The space that opens up between the sexual conservatism of his peasant roots, and his enthusiastic embracing of sexual openness, suggests more than immobilising dissonance between sexual codes. The acknowledgement of the fear and anger of the woman on the train, the 'lesson' he learns from his teacher and his naiveté in contrast to the worldliness of the woman in the car, all indicate there is something approaching a self-reflexivity in his accounts of his dealings with women in his early years in Sydney. Reflecting on his affair with the Anglo woman, Abbas comments that:

> I thought then, it seems to me like a break through, you are in a situation where you are in need of something but it doesn't occur you can achieve this thing so fast, and the other thing, the initiative of women towards you which was something new. I've been through things like this before, in Lebanon, I have been proposed to, plus sex wasn't something new to me – sexually active since early age, 17, a married woman. The context was the person. For me, having sex, someone coming from a third world background, having sex with a woman from the first world, you're from the third world, gives you the feeling that you are doing something that contribute to your personality, … and makes you feel more, after that you don't feel you are totally the underdog, in terms of your relationship with that person, that person represents the whole society at that time for you, you are narrowing the gap between you and that person and the whole society …

Abbas frames the affair not just as an encounter between a marginalised and dominant ethnicity – indeed, he rarely talks in terms of the ethnic backgrounds of the women unless asked – he sees it as an engagement with modernity, a closing of the gap between his third worldness and her first worldness. She represents 'the whole society'. In emphasising the sexual agency of the woman it is clear he is coming to terms with a different kind of sexual morality and politics. And he sees it as an accomplishment, a feeling that it contributes to his subjectivity, his 'personality', in such a way as to refuse the status as 'underdog'. Yet this is not the same kind of recuperation of power by marginalised masculinities described by Mercer (1994). His relations with women do entail a sense of 'success' denied to him in other contexts, but the language of mastery, we speculate, indicates more the affective consequences of his achievements, of feeling like a 'lord', than a simple discourse of sexual possession or resistance to racial oppression.

This closing of a social gap also returns us to the other element of Abbas's comment: this experience made him feel 'local', a process of emplacement and belonging (rather than possession) which is both physical and symbolic. Crucial to this feeling was a local club (not Lebanese or Arabic-specific) where he socialised with his mates and met women:

> The experience down the club was something out of this world … fucking beautiful, beautiful people, feel like you are in a celebration, everyone is happy, everyone is dressed, everyone is doing what they wanna do, you wanna eat you eat, wanna gamble you gamble, you wanna swim you swim; you feel like you've got everything, you feel like you're the master of everything.

The club allows him to participate in a space in which he is not marginal; and yet it is a microcosm of modern, Western affluence where everything is available. It is a place of pleasure and potential. It is where what once seemed distant as a migrant – spatially and socially – is now within reach. When he was asked how this made him feel about being in Australia, he replied that:

> you don't think beyond the immediate circumstance, you think you are more happy with yourself, you start comparing yourself with others, people going there night after night leaving empty handed, … . it gives you a sense of confidence, on a personal level, and you become sort of an advisor to others.

When we asked him if these experiences helped him settle into Australia, he saw 'both sides': 'Made me waste a large bit of my income, dining and all this bullshit business, but there's the positive side, explain yourself, practice your role as a human, as a man'. Despite this, and despite his frequent indication that he would never return to Lebanon, Abbas comments frequently that he never quite feels at home in Australia. He explained that:

> It didn't feel like it was my decision, just … settlement; you go to work and you come home and do what you got to do, … then, I used to think I was not going to be in Australia for a long time, … anything that makes you feel like this is a root, I didn't want to think about it.

The space of subjectivity

And yet Abbas *has* set down roots in Australia, even if he is uncomfortable with calling it 'home'. Perhaps it is truer to say that he has made a place for himself through the ensemble of social practices which amount to home-making. His subjectivity is defined by the learned capacity to *be* in Australia, and it is marked by an ambivalence common to experiences of migrancy (Abdelhardy 2011: 44). Abbas's sexual practices are central to his achievement of a certain degree of ontological security, the sense of familiarity with and confidence in the world about him, and his place in it, an ongoing *accomplishment* which produces the sense of order and continuity which makes social action possible (Giddens 1991:

36). But this chapter has also suggested that in learning to make himself 'at home' in Australia, Abbas has learnt to be masculine differently, not through assimilating Western values but through sexual practices which are marked by ambivalence and reflexivity (Adkins 2002). We don't want to present Abbas's sexual trajectory as typical of all migrants, nor as representative of 'Lebanese masculinity'. However, we do want to speculate upon three issues to emerge from our reading of Abbas's history that might move towards a wider discussion of the entanglement of sexual energy, migration, libidinal investment and male subjectivity (Ahmad 2011: 5).

First, sexuality is a resource. It is not simply a way of reproducing heteronormative categories and relations of the world, it is also, phenomenologically, an ensemble of intersubjective social practices which mediate relationships and experiences and make us capable social participants in particular social spaces of encounter (Moore 2010: 10, Hubbard 2002). We know from the therapeutic literature that sex can function as a 'coping strategy', such as for victims of abuse or emotional isolation, and may fulfil desires for control amongst some men (Cortoni and Marshall 2001), but we think the issue is more complex than focusing on psychologically damaged men. We also know that sex functions importantly as a masculine rite of passage to adulthood (Kimmel 2008) and as a way of renegotiating hierarchies of race and masculine sexuality (Malam 2008), but we want to extend our understanding of the resourceful and productive aspects of sexual practices: they are a way of knowing the world and others, and being in the world (see also Childs 2014: this volume). Centrally, sexual activity can provide a sense of what Ahmed (2006: 1) calls *orientation*, or how we 'reside in space' and, indeed, move through space and time.[3] Sexual orientation, she argues, is also a 'matter of residence'. Abbas's sexual history, we argue, is a key way he fashions a life, marshalling the resources necessary for making himself at home in Australia, and making his way through the world. The sexualisation of his experiences of settlement, and the details of his sexual life, are ways he develops the capacities to control the sensuous difference of a new world: it is key to his social viability. The imperatives of developing these capacities are heightened when the context is migration into the 'first world' of Western modernity, and where settlement can be experienced as an emasculating dislocation. But sexual orientation also has temporal dimensions: it is also prone to the variable 'times of migration', patterns of strangeness and displacement, routine and asynchronicity (Cwerner 2001) which can only be grasped through methodologies which grapple with complexities of life over time, and a sense of the complex relations between mobility and dwelling (Cheng 2012). Consequently, we need to think of sexual activity, like any social practice, as a *pedagogic* process through which we transform old ways of doing things and acquire new capacities, values, understandings, and a process through which we can imagine a future (Gaetano 2008). This is especially so for the migrant who embarks on practices of home-making and whose ways of being 'masculine' are not as viable as they were in the country of origin.

3 Ahmed, of course, is using this argument to make a case for *queer* orientation.

Second, subjectivity has to be recognised not as a single position but in terms of the multiple and shifting configurations of identification, relations and practice, which are both structural and subjective. 'Intersectionality' has become the key way we have come to grapple with this complexity (Brah and Pheonix 2004). It has also, however, come under criticism because of its inability to ultimately grapple well with that complexity, nor to analyse this complexity in lived experience (McCall 2005). There is a tendency to construe 'intersectionality' as the adding up of different categories of identity, which represent positions within different relations of power, as if at some magical crossroads of life, things like class, gender and ethnicity are vectors which 'intersect' (Taylor, Hines and Casey 2010: 2–5). So whereas in the past we reductively read off people's views general truths about class or gender or ethnicity, we now tend to read off slightly more complicated versions based on configurations of class AND gender AND ethnicity, and so on. People continue to be mere bearers of master identities (Staunaes 2003). As Moore (2012: 11) argues, in specifying multiple axes of difference, intersectionality still disassembles lived experience into a series of entities that it reassembles in more nuanced ways. Yet people have personal trajectories which are often idiosyncratic of larger histories of social relations. How would we explain Abbas's trajectory, particularly given its similarity to and yet difference from Adel's? And how does Abbas himself explain his life? Class, gender, age and ethnicity, as well as his sense of the relation between 'third' and 'first' worlds, interweave in the ways he makes himself 'at home' in Australia, but not in any grand narrative nor in any simple or consistent way. This is not to deny the structural dimensions of relations of power, but to recognise that lived experience is marked by a messy heterogeneity of elements which produce subjectivity, but not in any simple or formulaic way (Guattari 1995: 4). This suggests we think of categories of gender, class and ethnicity not just as discrete vectors which 'intersect' or relations that oppress, nor as structural determinants of experience, but as different types of resources which existing humans deploy to inhabit their complex social worlds.

Third, this subjectivity is not only not a single position nor an intersection of vectors, but is a temporalised 'space' through which the coordinates of shifting understandings and capacities are mapped out, navigated and acquired, over time. By this, we mean not simply that Abbas oscillates between the conservative values of a patriarchal peasant society and a Western permissiveness, nor that class, gender, ethnicity and age constitute the parameters of his experience, but that he lives out of his existence in the space that these heterogeneous elements constitute. The partial reflexivity he demonstrates in thinking through the significance of his sexual history demonstrates at one level the spatial nature of subjective being. On the one hand, we live in diverse orders of time and space – what Plummer (2003) depicts as living simultaneously in traditional, modern and postmodern worlds – in which control of the body is a key mechanism for managing the plurality of existence. This has particular resonance for thinking about masculine subjectivity, which has often been defined in terms of armoury, fortresses and models of attack and defence, in contrast to feminine subjectivity defined through relationality or an ethic of care (Easthope 1986). Abbas's use of his body is not, we suggest, an evocation of masculine subjectivity as a quest for wholeness or a defence against the threat of dissolving social boundaries (Theweleit 1987), but a recognition that the multiple and indeed fragmentary nature of modern male subjectivities is an aspect of active self-making and social exploration, premised on pleasure which embraces, not anxiously resists, the multiplicity of being (Srivastava 2010: 836).

We don't wish to burden Abbas's story with too much responsibility for resolving these big, conceptual questions, but its retelling reminds us that we need to study migrants' trajectories to understanding the relation between their embodied experience and the social mechanisms to which they are subject in order to make sense of the ways they make themselves at home in particular places and times (Sayad 2004: 29).

References

Abdelhardy, D. 2011. *The Lebanese Diaspora: The Arab Immigrant Experience in Montreal, New York, and Paris*. New York: New York University Press.

Adkins, L. 2002. *Revisions: Gender and Sexuality in Late Modernity*. Buckingham: Open University Press.

Ahmed, S. 2006. *Queer Phenomenology: Orientations, Objects, Others*. Durham: Duke University Press.

Ahmed, S. 2011. *Masculinity, Sexuality and Illegal Migration: Human Smuggling from Pakistan to Europe*. Farnham: Ashgate.

Ayres, T. 1999. China doll: the experience of being a gay Chinese Australian, in *Multicultural Queer: Australian Narratives*, edited by P.A. Jackson and G. Sullivan. New York: The Haworth Press, 87–97.

Brah, A. and Phoenix, A. 2004. 'Ain't I a woman?': revisiting intersectionality. *Journal of International Women's Studies*, 5(3), 75–86.

Caluya, G. 2007. The (gay) scene of racism: face, shame and gay Asian males. *Australian Critical Race and Whiteness Studies* e-journal, 2(2).

Chambers, D. 1991. *Contemporary Problems in the Study of Masculinities: A Comparison Between Australia and Britain*. Kingswood: Women's Research Centre University of Western Sydney: Nepean.

Cheng, Y.E. 2012. Transnational masculinities *in situ*: Singaporean husbands and their international marriage experiences. *Area*, 44(1), 76–82.

Cortoni, F. and Marshall, W. 2001. Sex as a coping strategy and its relationship to juvenile sexual history and intimacy in sexual offenders. *Sexual Abuse: A Journal of Research and Treatment*, 13(1), 27–43.

Cwerner, S. 2001. The times of migration. *Journal of Ethnic and Migration Studies*, 27(1), 7–36.

Dagistanli, S. and Grewal, K. 2012. Perverse Muslim masculinities in contemporary orientalist discourse: the vagaries of Muslim immigration in the

West, in *Global Islamophobia: Muslims and Moral Panic in the West*, edited by G. Morgan and S. Poynting. Farnham: Ashgate, 119–142.

Easthope, A. 1986. *What a Man's Gotta Do: The Masculine Myth in Popular Culture*. London: Paladin, Grafton Books.

Fanon, F. 1952/1986. *Black Skin White Masks*, translated by Charles Markmann. London: Pluto Press.

Gaetano, A. 2008. Sexuality in diasporic space: rural-to-urban migrant women negotiating gender and marriage in contemporary China. *Gender, Place and Culture: A Journal of Feminist Geography*, 15(6), 629–645.

Giddens, A. 1991. *Modernity and Self-Identity*. Cambridge: Polity Press.

Guattari, F. 1995. *Chaosmosis: An Ethico-Aesthetic Paradigm*, translated by P. Bains and J. Pefanis. Bloomington: Indiana University Press.

Hage, G. 2006. Migration, marginalized masculinity and dephallicization: a Lebanese villager's experience, in *Sexuality in the Arab World*, edited by S. Khalaf and J. Gagnon. London: Saqi, 107–129.

Herbert, J. 2908. Masculinity and migration: life stories of East African Asian men, in *Gendering Migration: Masculinity, Femininity and Ethnicity in Post-War Britain*, edited by L. Ryan and W. Webster. Aldershot: Ashgate, 189–203.

Hibbins, R. and Pease, B. 2009. Men and masculinities on the move, in *Migrant Men: Critical Studies of Masculinities and the Migration Experience*, edited by M. Donaldson, R. Hibbins and B. Pease. New York: Routledge, 1–20.

Hollway, W. 1984. Gender difference and the production of subjectivity, in *Changing the Subject: Psychology, Social Regulation and Subjectivity*, edited by J. Henriques, et al. London: Methuen, 227–263.

Hubbard, P. 2002. Sexing the self: geographies of engagement and encounter. *Social and Cultural Geography,* 3(4), 365–381.

Khalaf, S. 2006. Living with dissonant sexual codes, in *Sexuality in the Arab World*, edited by S. Khalaf and J. Gagnon. London: Saqi, 7–34.

Kimmel, M. 2008. *Guyland: The Perilous World Where Boys Become Men*. New York: HarperCollins.

Kitiarsa, P. 2008. Thai migrants in Singapore: state, intimacy and desire. *Gender, Place and Culture: A Journal of Feminist Geography*, 15(6), 595–610.

Mai, N. 2011. Tampering with the sex of "angels": migrant male minors and young adults selling sex in the EU. *Journal of Ethnic and Migration Studies*, 37(8), 1237–1252.

Mai, N. and King, R. 2009. Love, sexuality and migration: mapping the issue(s). *Mobilities*, 4(3), 295–307.

Malam, L. 2008. Bodies, beaches and bars: negotiating heterosexual masculinity in southern Thailand's tourism industry. *Gender, Place and Culture: A Journal of Feminist Geography*, 15(6), 581–594.

McCall, L. 2005. The complexity of intersectionality. *Signs: Journal of Women in Culture and Society*, 30(3), 1771–1800.

Mercer, K. 1994. *Welcome to the Jungle: New Positions in Black Cultural Studies*. New York: Routledge.

Moore, H. 2012. Sexuality encore, in *Understanding Global Sexualities: New Frontiers*, edited by P. Aggleton, et al. Abingdon: Routledge, 1–17.

Nandy, A. 1983. *The Intimate Enemy: Loss and Recovery of Self under Colonialism*. Delhi: Oxford University Press.

Noble, G. and Tabar, P. 2013. Learning to be Lebanese, in *Palestinian, Lebanese and Syrian Communities in the World*, edited by A. Escher, P. Tabar and T. Batrouney. Stuttgart: Franz Steiner Verlag, forthcoming.

Palmary, I., Burman, E., Chantler, K. and Kiguwa, P. (eds) 2010. *Gender and Migration: Feminist Intervention*. London: Zed Books.

Plummer, K. 2003. *Intimate Citizenship: Personal Decisions and Public Dialogues*. Seattle: University of Washington Press.

Poynting, S., Noble, G., Tabar, P. and Collins, J. 2004. *Bin Laden in the Suburbs: Criminalising the Arab Other*. Sydney: Sydney Institute of Criminology Series.

Ricatti, F. 2011. *Embodying Migrants: Italians in Postwar Australia*. Bern: Peter Lang.

Ryan, L. and Webster, W. 2008. Introduction, in *Gendering Migration: Masculinity, Femininity and Ethnicity in Post-War Britain,* edited by L. Ryan and W. Webster. Aldershot: Ashgate, 1–17.

Sayad, A. 2004. *The Suffering of the Immigrant,* translated by D. Macey. Cambridge: Polity Press.

Sinha, M. 1995. *Colonial Masculinity.* Manchester: Manchester University Press.

Srivastava, S. 2010. Fragmentary pleasures: masculinity, urban spaces, and commodity politics in Delhi. *Journal of the Royal Anthropological Institute*, 16(4), 835–952.

Staunaes, D. 2003. 'Where have all the subjects gone?': bringing together the concepts of subjectification and intersectionality. *NORA: Nordic Journal of Women Studies*, 11(2), 101–110.

Stoler, A. 1992. Sexual affronts and racial frontiers: European identities and the cultural politics of exclusions in colonial Southeast Asia. *Comparative Studies in Society and History*, 34(3), 514–551.

Tabar, P., Noble, G. and Poynting, S. 2010. *On Being Lebanese in Australia.* Beirut: Lebanese American University.

Taylor, Y., Hines, S. and Casey, M. 2010. Introduction, in *Theorizing Intersectionality and Sexuality*, edited by Y. Taylor, S. Hines and M. Casey. Basingstoke: Palgrave Macmillan, 1–12.

Theweleit, K. 1987. *Male Fantasies.* vol. 2. Minneapolis: University of Minnesota Press.

Walsh, K., Shen, H. and Willis, K. 2008. Heterosexuality and migration in Asia. *Gender, Place and Culture: A Journal of Feminist Geography*, 15(6), 575–579.

Wight D. 1996. Beyond the predatory male: the diversity of young Glaswegian men's discourses to describe heterosexual relationships, in *Sexualizing the Social: Power and the Organisation of Sexuality*, edited by L. Adkins and V. Merchant. London: Palgrave Macmillan, 145–171.

Willis, K. and Yeoh, B. (eds) 2000. *Gender and Migration.* Cheltenham: Edward Elgar.

Chapter 6
Negotiating Masculinised Migrant Rights and Everyday Citizenship in a Global City: Brazilian Men in London

Kavita Datta and Cathy McIlwaine

Introduction

This chapter explores the relationship between transnational migration and masculinised migrant rights among Brazilian migrant men in a global city. While the current interest in migrant rights to the city focuses on the importance of making claims and recognising migrant identities, it is curiously gender-blind, particularly in relation to migrant men's rights. In addressing this neglect, this chapter focuses not only on the constructions of hegemonic masculinities in relation to Brazilian and Latin American identities, but also on the negotiation of migrant rights manifested through everyday citizenship practices in terms of overall gendered patterns of inclusion and exclusion in the city in relation to civic participation and access to financial services. In so doing, the chapter explores how masculinities intersect with processes of exclusion in relational ways *vis-à-vis* their female Brazilian counterparts and, to a lesser extent, other Latin Americans, and how this affects migrant men's lived experiences of citizenship through their ability to exercise their rights. We argue that while recognising migrants' rights is central to understanding their citizenship practices, much more attention needs to be paid to the gendered nature of this. Indeed, while women's rights have been acknowledged in partial and incomplete ways, we argue that men's have been even more neglected. Thus, it is essential not only to recognise that women and men migrants are not always able to exercise their rights to the same extent but that their experiences of exclusion and inclusion in the polity, economy and society also vary. Conceptually, it is therefore critically important to recognise how gendered identities underpin migrants' rights and citizenship practices and especially the paradoxical and fluid nature of men's positioning materially and ideologically in relation to women (see also Noble and Tabar 2014: this volume).

Masculinising transnational migration, migrant rights and everyday citizenship

A large and growing body of research has established that gender identities, ideologies and practices are formulated and negotiated in manifold ways as people move across borders yet maintain ties with their home countries through 'transnational social spaces' (Mahler 1999, McIlwaine 2012). While women (as migrants or non-migrants) have been the focus of much of this work, research on male migrations is also evident. Shaped by broader understandings of masculinities, research has paid particular attention to male migrants' labour market position in host countries (Datta et al. 2009, Sarti and Scrinzi 2010), the reconstruction of male gendered identities particularly in relation to marriage, fatherhood and spaces of reproduction (Kilkey, Plomien and Perrons 2013, Montes 2013, Pribilsky 2012), as well as the intersections between migrant masculinities, race and sexuality (Hondagneu-Sotelo and Messner 1997). Collectively, this research has been critical in highlighting that masculinities are dynamic social constructs which are sensitive to space, place and time, and derived from complex relational and intersectional identities (Connell and Messerschmidt 2005). In particular, researchers have underscored how hegemonic masculinities may be marginalised and subverted upon migration, and the multiple ways in which migrant men re-negotiate their identities in relation to both native and migrant men and women who occupy a range of race, class and sexuality positions (Sarti and Scrinzi 2010).

Academic and policy attention to migrant rights is more recent with scholars highlighting the myriad ways in which rights shape migration decisions, opportunities and outcomes. There is increased recognition of the multiple exclusions that migrants face and the ways in which they attempt to resist and/or accommodate these. The imperative to develop a rights-based approach to migration was recognised internationally at the 2008 Global Forum on Migration and Development which emphasised the shared responsibility of both home and host states to protect migrant rights (Ruhs 2009). More agency-inscribed understandings have articulated migrant rights in relation to operationalising *access* to, for example, labour markets, legal residence, state welfare, as well as *opposition* or *resistance* to socio-economic, political and cultural exclusion.

In turn, migrants' rights are often understood as either human rights or citizenship rights. Yet, a growing critique of the significant gap between migrant rights in principle and practice, and the role of the state in shaping differential realisations of rights, has led to greater consideration of migrant rights within the context of citizenship, which is understood as both a legal status and the exercise of rights (Basok 2004). An important aspect of this research is the extent to which there has been a shift towards post-national citizenship (Soysal 2000) whereby traditional models of national citizenship are being superseded by more contemporary modes of membership rooted in universal notions of human rights. Although this is now thought to be a rather celebratory interpretation in light of the increasingly powerful role that nation-states play in restricting movements and regulating citizenship rights (Kofman 2005), it has led to some useful conceptualisations such as that of 'denizenship'. This is where migrants claim membership in multiple polities in which they may be residents, part-time residents, or absentee, and where residence can afford such migrants access to a range of important resources (Brubaker 1989). Yet, while these debates highlight the blurred distinction between citizens and non-citizens, they often fail to consider those who may be especially vulnerable to rights abuses, including irregular migrants (Varsanyi 2006). More importantly in this context, the gendering of migrants' rights has also received little attention, particularly with reference to *male* migrants. In a rare study in Canada, Basok (2004) illustrates that it is not only women migrants' rights which are under threat such that female Filipino domestic workers may be better placed to demand and exercise their rights as they have the prerequisite language skills, live in urban areas and can draw upon the support of feminist organisations in contrast to predominantly male Mexican seasonal agricultural workers who are more isolated geographically, socially and economically. Moreover, understanding of these processes requires a consideration of the construction of masculinities and femininities among migrants in relation to rights, again, something that is rarely explicitly done.

It also entails a consideration of the nature of everyday citizenship practices that are not necessarily predicated on formal state membership and which closely intersect with wider processes of exclusion. Citizenship is also an identity where people conceive of themselves as belonging to a wider polity (Joppke 2007). Thus, citizenship practices are formed through the act of living in a community on a daily or 'ordinary' basis (Staeheli et al. 2012). Everyday citizenship identities and practices are essential for the creation of well-being and belonging among migrants who are unable to make formal claims on their host state, especially through their engagement with civil society organisations (Ehrkamp and Leitner 2003). In terms of the gendering of such practices, it is often suggested that women migrants are often more likely to have limited citizenship despite their central role in much economic migration, especially in relation to emotional labour and global care chains. Yet, and significantly in this context, this research tends not only to neglect the experiences of male migrants, but also fails to consider the relationality of migrant men's and women's citizenship practices. While we strongly reinforce that women migrants experience exclusion from exercising their citizenship rights, the lack of attention paid to migrant men's citizenship practices within such research is especially marked (although see Kilkey, Plomien and Perrons 2013).

The importance of place in shaping everyday citizenship practices – and in particular the city as a container and creator of migrant rights – is important (Ehrkamp and Leitner 2003). Varsanyi (2006) illustrates the strong historical and etymological connections between the city and citizenship with urban scholars debating the politics of the 'right to the city' in terms of right of access and right to transform (Harvey 2003). Arguably, debates on 'urban citizenship' have been revived in the context of global city research whereby membership and residence in cities is seen as providing a space in which transnational and cosmopolitan political identities develop (Keith 2005). A significant body of research has documented the impacts of migration on these urban forms as well as the crucial influence of migrant men and women in the production of cosmopolitan, culturally hybrid urban spaces (Bonnerjee et al. 2012, Wills et al. 2010). Such shaping of urban landscapes often revolves around appropriating public space in temporary and/or permanent ways that allows migrants to claim rights and citizenship and facilitate full civic participation (Blunt and Bonnerjee 2013, Veronis 2006) while also potentially contributing to the racialisation and gendering of public spaces in the city (Ehrkamp 2008, Keith 2005). Migrant urban spaces are further intermediated by a new politics of migration that is organised around highly diverse migrant civil society and faith-based organisations which seek to navigate the multiple dislocations brought on by migration (Wills et al. 2009). Again, these activities are deeply gendered and classed (McIlwaine and Bermudez 2011) even if this is not always acknowledged.

Methodological framework and background: Brazilian migration to London

This chapter draws on two projects which included Brazilian migrant men and women (Datta 2012, McIlwaine, Cock and Linneker 2011). Both projects included a wider number of migrant communities, and investigated different aspects of migrants' lives: *Migrants and their Money* explored migrants' diverse everyday financial practices in London and how these were shaped by both an exclusion from the financial fabric of the city as well as a preference for alternative ways of 'doing finance', while *No Longer Invisible* outlined the nature of migrant living and livelihoods among Latin Americans in the city. The projects deployed mixed methods frameworks ranging from questionnaire surveys, in-depth interviews and focus group discussions. In total, this generated a questionnaire survey on financial exclusion with 119 Brazilians (54 men and 59 women), 21 in-depth interviews (nine men and 11 women migrants) and one focus group discussion, as well as a questionnaire survey on livelihoods among the Latin American communities with 233 respondents (128 women, 105 men), ten in-depth interviews (five women, five men) and one focus group.

Migration from Latin America to Europe, and specifically from Brazil, has been a relatively recent phenomenon with most movement occurring since 2000 (McIlwaine 2011). Although there are significant Brazilian communities in Spain, Italy and Portugal, the UK has become an increasingly attractive destination for Brazilians (Evans et al. 2011). Indeed, it has been estimated that it now receives the highest proportions of Brazilians in Europe, comprising around 180,000 with unofficial estimates ranging from 200,000 to 300,000 (Sheringham 2013). With the vast majority concentrated in London, Brazilians are increasingly making their mark on the urban landscape (see below). Although some Brazilians migrated to the UK in the 1970s, flows burgeoned for economic reasons after 2000. The spread of neoliberal macro-economic policies throughout Latin America in the 1980s and

1990s led to increasing inequalities and sustained this migration. Although Brazil has since experienced an economic boom, the effects of the growth have not been evenly spread, with life for the poor and lower middle classes changing very little (Sheringham 2013). As a result, Brazilians, especially those from the southeast, continue to be attracted to economic and educational opportunities in London despite the global economic downturn (Evans et al. 2011).

A brief 'profile' of the Brazilian community in London reflects a youthful and economically active population with the *No Longer Invisible* research identifying the mean age of Brazilians as 34 years (also Evans et al. 2011). The population is also feminised with around three-quarters of the population comprising women (Kubal, Bakewell and de Haas 2011). Brazilians are also well-educated, especially women, with 80 per cent having post-secondary education (20 per cent with postgraduate studies) compared with 69 per cent of men. In terms of immigration status, Evans et al. (2011) found that around a third were irregular (29 per cent), with 44 per cent holding an EU passport, and a further 17 per cent residing on a spouse visa. The *No Longer Invisible* research showed that men were more likely to be irregular than women (42 per cent compared to 34 per cent) and women were more likely to be British citizens than men (11 per cent compared with 2 per cent). Employment rates were also very high with Brazilians' work concentrated in hotel/catering (22 per cent), business/administration (21 per cent) and cleaning (17 per cent) (Evans et al. 2011: 19). Women were more likely to work in professional and managerial jobs than men (19 per cent compared to 12 per cent) while men were more likely to work in elementary jobs than women (60 per cent compared to 43 per cent) (McIlwaine et al. 2011).

Aspects of the urban landscape of London have been transformed by Brazilian migration, albeit in distinct neighbourhoods. Following initial settlement in Bayswater, which came to be called 'Brazilwater', Brazilians have since moved further north to Brent and south to Stockwell. A wide range of shops, restaurants, cafes and money transfer agencies have been established in these places as part of what Brightwell (2010) calls the 'economy of longing' ('*a economia de saudade*'). There is little gender differentiation in using these facilities, with men and women visiting them equally, although women are more likely as men to visit cafes and restaurants (60 per cent of all those who visit). Similarly, Brazilian music and dance have also become popular with several samba schools and Brazilian evenings held at nightclubs throughout the city (Margolis 2013).

Negotiating migrant rights in London among Brazilian male migrants

Bearing these processes of in/exclusion in mind, the remainder of this chapter explores the ways in which migrants assert their rights and create everyday citizenship practices in London with a specific focus on their civic participation and access to financial services. This is prefaced by a consideration of the construction of hegemonic and Latin American masculinities from a relational perspective, given that these identities underpin the ways in which men and women exercise their rights in the city.

Brazilian and Latin American migrant hegemonic masculinities

The ways in which Brazilian men negotiate their rights and citizenship practices closely interrelates with constructions of gender identities in relation to the notion of 'Brazilianness' as well as what Beserra (2005) calls '*latinidad*' (referring to the latino character and condition). This broadly corresponds to a complex racialisation and sexualisation of identities that are at once stereotypical but also fluid and situational (Margolis 2013). In the context of migration, this depends on whether migrants are in Brazil or living elsewhere, as well as the historical context, migrants' social background and their skin colour (Piscatelli 2008). While hegemonic Brazilian femininities tend to revolve around an exoticised submissiveness, domesticity and predilection for sexual activity and sensuality, for men, hegemonic masculinities are similarly sexualised and hyper-eroticised, while also focusing on aggression, possessiveness and other characteristics linked with machismo (ibid.). This is compounded for both women and men by associations with various national symbols such as carnival, soccer, coffee and dance. It is also clear, and perhaps not surprising, that Brazilians feel much more Brazilian after migration (McDonnell and de Lourenço 2009, Rezende 2011).

Our own work in London from the *No Longer Invisible* research corroborates these nationalised and gendered identities and shows how men assert their Brazilian and Latin American subjectivities in different ways from women. For example, Rogerio noted that in London, Brazil is viewed as: 'A tropical country, colourful country, different from theirs, we are smart, we are open, women are sensual.' The main issue to arise in relation to Brazilianess was in terms of whether migrants were identified as Brazilian or Latin American. Research in the US has illustrated that Brazilians often reject the terms 'Hispanic' and 'Latino' because these are historically inappropriate and inherently racialised, with Hispanics perceived to be close to Blacks and therefore lower down an ethno-racial hierarchy (Beserra 2005). As such, Brazilians often resist this association as a form of distancing from discrimination and as a way of asserting superiority. Yet interestingly, it has been shown that men are less likely than women to disclaim Hispanic, Latin American and Latino/a identifications and stress their Brazilianess, again as a way of resisting perceived marginalisation (McDonnell and de Lourenço 2009).

This emerged in London on a number of counts. When asked about their ethnicity, men were more likely than women to state they were 'Latin American' (25 per cent compared with 19 per cent of women). For example, Carlo commented: 'Yes, I think I considered myself to be Latin American after coming to London, because while I lived in Brazil, this vision of regionalism changes depending where you are. When you leave South America, Brazil is not very different from other Latin American countries.' In contrast, Mariana noted: 'I don't identify with that [being Latin American] either, I have friends who are Colombian, one talks to me as if I know what the country is like … but I identify with Brazil, I'm Brazilian.' Language was not surprisingly very important within this as a Brazilian lawyer, Angelina noted: 'Brazilians don't consider themselves Latin because they don't speak Spanish. If you ask if they are from Latin America they say no. Because of the language we are not comfortable with being Latin American.'

Wider reasons for why women, in particular, asserted a Brazilian identity related to the sense that 'Latin American' was a derogatory term, as noted by Sandra: 'It is because of the status of the region, when you talk about Latin American the first thing that always comes to my mind is Colombia, yes I think of their dress, the ponchos, the hats.' Yet men were less concerned with distancing themselves from Latin American identities, arguably predicated on links with marginalised work. Indeed, men working in elementary jobs were more likely than their female counterparts to identify with other Latin Americans (50 per cent compared with 41 per cent). This contrasts with other research where a Latino identity negatively affects Brazilians working in low paid jobs and in a lower class positions (Beserra 2005); we found that men embraced a Latin American identity more readily than women as part of an acceptance of their more marginalised status whereas women were more active in resisting this and asserting their Brazilian identity. These processes also played out in terms of their civic engagement in relation to inclusion and exclusion from various institutions of the city and access to financial services.

Placing rights to the city through civic participation

Research on the exercise of migrants' rights in relation to their civic participation has burgeoned in recent years, highlighting how migrants simultaneously engage in homeland and immigrant or diaspora politics through both formal and informal means (Bermudez 2010, Østergaard-Nielsen 2003). Intersecting work has also explored how migrant organisations form an important part of diasporic civil society that operates across different scales and with variegated outcomes for democratisation processes and migrants rights (McIlwaine 2007). Although this work acknowledges the importance of differentiation among diasporic civil society according to social identities, there has been little empirical research exploring its gendered or racialised nature. Similarly, gendered research on political and civic engagement is under-developed, especially the case in the European context and in relation to the specific experiences of men. This said, there has been some important work on the concentration of women migrants in informal organisations while men are more involved with formal politics back home in the context of Latin Americans in the US (Montoya, Hardy-Fanta and Garcia 2000). More specifically, and bearing in mind the importance of relationality and intersectionality, McIlwaine and Bermudez (2011) showed that while Colombian migrant men in London have much stronger involvement in formal and transnational activities, with women participating more in informal politics (see also Jones-Correa 1998), working-class women appeared to gain most from changing gender regimes, partly linked with their active engagement with migrant community organisations, with working-class men losing out the most.

These issues also emerged in our research with Brazilian men and women in that engagement in formal and informal political and civic engagement emerged as gender differentiated, again linked with the marginalised masculinities of Brazilian men. In contrast to much research to date, men were less likely to exercise their formal political rights locally or transnationally in that they were less likely to vote in home country elections than women (21 per cent compared with 26 per cent) and in British elections (21 per cent compared with 24 per cent). Lucia, who participated in a focus group and was university educated, working as a waitress and as a freelance journalist, reflects on this:

> I've already told my partner that as soon as I get hold of my British passport, I want to go into politics and I want to be the first foreigner MP and fight for the rights of foreigners or immigrants, whatever, and I will be able to tell them that I know it is like for them, because I've been through the same, I've been here without a visa, there is no foreigner MP here.

Although both men and women participated equally as members in migrant organisations, men were more likely to use their services than women (24 per cent compared with 18 per cent). This could be related to men's greater need for assistance rooted in their greater likelihood of being irregular and working in precarious jobs. However, it also reflects generally low levels of use (McIlwaine et al. 2011). This is partly because Brazilians tend not to use organisations serving the Latin American community as a whole, but only those for them such as the Casa do Brasil em Londres, ABRAS and ABRIR, linked with issues of trust, as Orlandina notes: 'Yes, because like in Brazil, we don't trust institutions, and there are not that many [organisations] anyway.'

More informally, men engaged in more leisure-based and culture-oriented forms of civic engagement associated with carnivals and festivals. For example, men were more likely to attend summer carnivals than women (38 per cent compared with 32 per cent). This could be viewed as men asserting their identities as Brazilians and Latin Americans in a positive manner that is missing from their everyday working lives. Their inability to exercise anything approaching formal citizenship rights in London means that they turn to more informal and leisure-oriented pursuits, albeit ones that tend to reinforce hegemonic masculinities through dance, in particular, with many Brazilian men in London working as dance and capoeira teachers. The problems that migrant men face in exercising their rights in relation to civic participation are further reinforced from a material point of view through the obstacles they face in exercising their rights to financial resources, to which we now turn.

A right to financial access?

Migrant men's and women's rights to financial access in host cities has been insufficiently addressed (although see Datta 2012) even while this is increasingly crucial in global cities like London, which are characterised as finance-led or 'financialised' (French, Leyshon and Wainwright 2010). The permeation of finance at the macro-level of global, national and city economies, as well as the micro-level of the everyday, has meant that the consequences of being excluded from formal financial circuits has significant socio-economic and political consequences (Datta 2012). As such, commentators note that financial access is increasingly salient to the exercise of many citizenship rights (Dymski 2006).

While there is little research on migrants' financial practices in host countries beyond the money that they send back as remittances, nascent research suggests that financial access among migrant communities is restricted. This is attributed to a number of factors which migrant communities share with other financially excluded groups but which are also distinct (immigration status, transnational financial needs, lack of documents, compromised credit histories, language proficiency and lack of familiarity with financial systems). For example, it is estimated that 75 per cent of Mexican immigrants in the US do not have bank accounts.

Alongside migrant status, gender also shapes financial access and usage, with women more prone to partial or full financial exclusion. Feminist researchers have been at the forefront of documenting the heavily gendered nature of finance, ranging from accounts of 'hyper-masculine capitalism', the masculinisation of the global financial services industry, to gendered accounts of the contemporary global financial crisis (Griffen 2013, McDowell 2010, Pollard 2012). Research primarily conducted in the global South documents the exclusion of (poor) women from formal financial services and the concomitant focus of microfinance schemes on female clients for motives which range from female empowerment to an understanding of women as more reliable clients. Notwithstanding this, specific research on the gendered nature of financial exclusion among migrant groups in advanced economies is scarce.

Drawing on the *Migrants and their Money* project, we explore how Brazilian migrant men and women negotiate their financial rights to the city by documenting their relational and differential access to core financial resources as well as the strategies they deployed to engineer access to these services. The research uncovered that 83 per cent of Brazilians were banked, with marginally more women migrants owning bank accounts (84 per cent) than their male counterparts (82 per cent). While both men and women acknowledged the importance of bank account ownership, male migrants viewed banking access in a more instrumental manner, in that it facilitated access to the labour market[1], the welfare system, and wider

1 This is largely attributable to the fact that the majority of salaries and benefits are now paid directly into bank accounts.

financial resources such as affordable credit. Thus, Decio noted the importance of bank account ownership as soon as he started to search for employment, recalling that 'to get those first cleaning jobs I needed an account, the employer asked for one because he was going to pay my wages into it'. Somewhat in contrast, female migrants recognised the wider *strategic* importance of banking access, with women like Rosana arguing that '[bank accounts are] very important because it makes you feel like a citizen', on which her compatriot Marcia elaborated:

> If you don't have a bank account, they will presume that you are here illegally or that your name is on a credit blacklist ... It is a little discriminatory, but it has got more weight than having your name in the police books, so it is really the bank that determines whether you are a person of good character or not.

Migrants' access to saving opportunities and affordable credit revealed a more differentiated gendered experience. While only 66 per cent of Brazilian men were able to save, this rose to 81 per cent among Brazilian women. This is all the more marked given that both men *and* women worked in a range of low paid jobs but echoes broader research which emphasises that women are more likely to prioritise saving over immediate consumption. Indeed, just over half of all participants (51 per cent) had accessed formal credit in the preceding year, primarily through over drafts, credit cards and personal loans, with loan sizes varying from £1,500 to £20,000. Again, there were important gendered distinctions, particularly in *attitudes* towards credit and debt. While women like Josana argued that 'I personally have never asked for loans, here or in Brazil, I do not know how it works ... I think it is also a risk, it is a rope with which to hang yourself in the future', many of her male counterparts highlighted that access to banking credit was an important and necessary resource, both to survive in an expensive city but also in terms of accumulating assets, both in London and transnationally in Brazil (see Datta 2012).

Turning to the strategies which migrant men, and to a lesser extent women, deployed to access banking and wider economic and financial resources, the main obstacles identified related to banks' requirements for documents verifying the identity of prospective clients (primarily via passports), proof of residential address (through utility bills), as well as perceptions that high street banks considered Brazilians to be 'high risk' customers. Migrant men like Valerio commented that only the self-proclaimed global bank, HSBC, explicitly targeted Brazilian clients as evidenced by advertisements 'showing a person with the Brazilian flag painted on their faces'. In his opinion, other high street banks were much more circumspect with Brazilians as they did not want to take the risk of inviting 'illegal immigrants, come here and open an account with us'. Within this context, Brazilians were depicted as suffering from a matrix of vulnerabilities, which arose, inter alia, through their transient residential status, current or past periods of irregularity, as well as the high risk behaviour of a few 'bad' Brazilians who had secured formal credit and then absconded.

Given these obstacles, a variety of strategies were deployed to engineer access to banking services. While these ranged from sheer persistence to using migrant networks to locate banks and bank tellers who would be sympathetic to migrant customers, which were particularly prevalent among female migrants (see Datta 2012), we focus particularly upon three strategies that all involved an element of invisibilising migrant/national identities: the attainment of dual nationality; the purchase of false documents, including National Insurance Numbers or bank accounts; and sharing bank accounts with migrant compatriots. It is important to emphasise that while some Brazilian women also utilised these strategies, they were more evidenced in male migrants' narratives.

Successive UK governments have sought to restrict non-EU entry into the country through the intensification of both external and internal controls on migration (Vasta 2008). In turn, these controls are reliant upon the 'paper regimes', which are critical in the construction of shared national identity, while also actively marginalising those who are deemed as 'aliens', particularly in terms of access to work and welfare (ibid.). In the face of such exclusions, migrants may develop 'innovative identities and cultures of resistance around papers and documentation' as they seek to escape the power of the 'state's gaze by becoming invisible' (ibid.: 3). A strategic acquisition of 'papers' was evident among a number of Brazilian men and women who had claimed European citizenship prior to arriving in the UK. Part of a growing intra-European onward migration flow, over half of Brazilian men and women had arrived in London via Portugal, Spain, Italy and Germany (Datta 2012, McIlwaine 2012). Further, while some had initially moved to these European countries assuming that they would remain here, several had done so to facilitate their subsequent entry into the UK, in order to access employment and educational opportunities through what McIlwaine (2012) refers to as 'mobilising civic capital' and 'institutional cultural capital' across transnational spaces.

Importantly, European passports also enabled an invisibilisation, or what Broeders and Engbersen (2007: 1598) refer to as an 'obliteration of legal identity', with Brazilian migrant men in particular reporting that a European passport facilitated their movement across Europe in contrast to a Brazilian one. This was expressed graphically by Jacinto, who noted that his 'Brazilian passport docs not exist for me here [in London], only when I go back to Brazil, there is not a single rubber stamp on it, if I use the Brazilian passport here they think I am an illegal so I only use the German passport'. European passports also played a pivotal role in securing access to bank accounts in the UK as well as labour markets more widely (McIlwaine 2012).

For those Brazilian migrants unable to claim dual nationality, accessing relevant identification documents entailed illegal practices of purchasing false documents and/or bank accounts. Achieved through the inter-mediation of 'middlemen' who advertised their services in Brazilian media, services ranged from the sale of National Insurance numbers, bank accounts and loans. Rafael admitted that he had: 'Got the phone number of a Brazilian guy that sells bank accounts from a [Brazilian] magazine. He charges £150. Even without visa he managed to open an account for me. He paid someone who works at [high street retail bank]. He opened my account for me in one day.' Other Brazilian men and women reported the practice of sharing bank accounts whereby migrants were depositing their wages in someone else's account as well as account holders who were sharing their own accounts. While the majority of migrants presented this as a temporary arrangement until they had secured the documents necessary to open their own accounts, men like Amaldo had used his friends' account for two years before he opened his own account. Sharing was premised upon the availability of banked friends who were willing to participate in this activity, and therefore largely dependent upon the social networks or capital at migrants' disposal.

This section has documented the importance of financial access for transnational migrants arriving in a financialised city like London, access which is increasingly critical in shaping migrant rights to wider social and economic resources. It has highlighted the relational and differential access that Brazilian migrant men and women have to core financial services, reflecting gendered financial behaviour, particularly in relation to savings and credit. Importantly, while there is some distinction in the strategies deployed by Brazilian men and women in engineering financial access, it is equally important to acknowledge shared experiences of exclusion.

Conclusion

This chapter has addressed the ways in which the exercise of the rights of Brazilian migrant men are underpinned partly by the nature of their gendered identities and partly by the processes of exclusion they experience in relation to their female counterparts and to other Latin Americans more widely. In exploring how their rights are manifested through the creation of various everyday citizenship practices in relation to civic participation and access to financial resources, the chapter highlights how, although Brazilian men and women both experience marginalisation, in many cases men's exclusion is more marked. This has ramifications not only for their well-being in terms of accessing services, advice and resources, and thus influences their ability to claim rights, but also for how they relate with other Latin Americans, with men being more likely to relate than women. Arguably, because women are often more able to exercise their rights to better paid work, migrant association services and financial resources, they are more able to integrate into the wider urban polity and society than men. Yet, it also illustrates the importance of challenging essentialist notions of hegemonic masculinities and femininities in the context of migration to cities whereby identities shift as migrants' material circumstances change and as they exercise their rights in differential ways.

London, as a cosmopolitan multicultural place, affords migrants the space to assert their gendered and migrant identities in flexible and complex ways. This plays out positively in relation to multicultural expressions of Latin American and Brazilian identities through music, food as well as the built environment in specific places in the city, albeit in gender-bifurcated ways. Yet, while London as a city might accept and benefit from Brazilian migrants' assertion of their cultural citizenship practices, it is much more reticent in acknowledging their wider economic, financial and civic rights because of wider processes of gendered exclusion. For migrant Brazilian men in particular, these obstacles result in an invisibilisation of their national identity in favour of a broader Latin American or European association.

Acknowledgements

We would like to thank the Trust for London, the Latin American Women's Rights Service and Friends Provident Foundation for funding the projects included here.

References

Basok, T. 2004. Post-national citizenship, social exclusion and migrants rights: Mexican seasonal workers in Canada. *Citizenship Studies*, 8(1), 47–64.

Bermúdez, A. 2010. The transnational political practices of Colombians in Spain and the United Kingdom: politics 'here' and 'there'. *Ethnic and Racial Studies*, 33(1) 75–91.

Beserra, B. 2005. From Brazilians to Latinos? Racialization and Latinidad in the making of Brazilian carnival in Los Angeles. *Latino Studies*, 3(1), 53–75.

Blunt, A. and Bonnerjee, J. 2013. Home, city and diaspora: Anglo-Indian and Chinese attachments to Calcutta. *Global Networks*, 13(2), 220–240.

Bonnerjee, J., Blunt, A., McIlwaine, C. and Pereira, C. 2012. *Connected Communities: Diaspora and Transnationality*. London: Queen Mary University of London. Available at www.geog.qmul.ac.uk/docs/research/61819.pdf.

Brightwell, M.G. 2010. Saboreando o Brasil em Londres: comida, imigração e identidade. *Travessia: Revista do Migrante*, 66, 221–231.

Broeders, D. and Engbersen, G. 2007. The fight against illegal migration. identification policies and immigrants' counter strategies. *American Behavioral Scientist*, 50(12), 1592–1609.

Brubaker, R. (ed.) 1989. *Immigration and the Politics of Citizenship in Europe and North America*. Lanham, Md.: The German Marshall Fund of the United States and University Press of America.

Connell, R.W. and Messerschmidt, J.W. 2005. Hegemonic masculinity: rethinking the concept. *Gender and Society*, 19(6), 829–859.

Datta, K. 2009. Risky migrants? Low paid migrants coping with financial exclusion in London. *European Urban and Regional Studies*, 16(4), 331–344.

Datta, K. 2012. *Migrants and Their Money: Surviving Financial Exclusion in London*. Bristol: Policy Press.

Datta, K., McIlwaine, C., Herbert, J., Evans, Y., May, J. and Wills, J. 2009. Men on the move: narratives of migration and work among low paid migrant workers in London. *Social and Cultural Geography*, 10(8), 853–873.

Dymski, G.A. 2006. Targets of opportunity in two landscapes of financial globalization. *Geoforum*, 37(3), 307–311.

Ehrkamp, P. and Leitner, H. 2003. Beyond national citizenship: Turkish immigrants and the (re)construction of citizenship in Germany. *Urban Geography*, 24(2), 127–146.

Evans, Y., Tonhati, T., Dias, G., Brightwell, M.D.G., Sheringham, O., Souza, A. and Souza, C. 2011. *For a better life: Brazilians in London, 2010*. London: GEB, Brazilian Migration to the UK Research Group. Available at: http://www.red-redial.net/doc_adj/4342–for-a-better-life-geb-may-2011.pdf [accessed 15 May 2013].

French, S., Leyshon, A. and Wainwright, T. 2011. Financializing space, spacing financialization. *Progress in Human Geography*, 35(6), 798–819.

Griffen, P. 2013. Gendering global finance: crisis, masculinity and responsibility. *Men and Masculinities*, 16(1), 9–34.

Harvey, D. 2003. The right to the city. *International Journal of Urban and Regional Research*, 27(4), 939–941.

Hondagneu-Sotelo, P. and Messner, M.A. 1999. Gender displays and men's power: the 'new man' and the 'Mexican immigrant man', in *American Families: A Multicultural Reader*, edited by S. Coontz, M. Parson and G. Raley. London and New York: Routledge, 342–358.

Jones-Correa, M. 1998. Different paths: gender, immigration and political participation. *International Migration Review*, 32(2), 326–349.

Joppke, C. 2007. Transformation of citizenship: status, rights, identity. *Citizenship Studies*, 11(1), 37–48.

Keith, M. 2005. *After the Cosmopolitan? Multicultural Cities and the Future of Racism*. London and New York: Routledge.

Kilkey, M., Plomien, A. and Perrons, D. 2013. Migrant men's fathering narratives, practices and projects in national and transnational spaces: recent Polish male migrants to London. *International Migration*, [Online] doi: 10.1111/imig.12046.

Kofman, E. 2005. Citizenship, migration and reassertion of national identity. *Citizenship Studies*, 9(5), 453–467.

Kubal, A., Bakewell, O. and de Haas, H. 2011. *The Evolution of Brazilian Migration to the UK*. Oxford: Oxford University Press.

Mahler, S. 1999. Engendering transnational migration: a case study of Salvadorans. *American Behavioral Scientist*, 42(4), 690–719.

Margolis, M. 2013. *Goodbye, Brazil: Émigrés from the Land of Soccer and Samba*. Wisconsin: University of Wisconsin Press.

McDonnell, J. and de Lourenço, C. 2009. You're Brazilian, right? What kind of Brazilian are you? The racialization of Brazilian immigrant women. *Ethnic and Racial Studies*, 32(2), 239–256.

McDowell, L. 2010. Capital culture revisited: sex, testosterone and the city. *International Journal of Urban and Regional Research*, 34(3), 652–658.
McIlwaine, C. 2007. From local to global to transnational civil society: re-framing development perspectives on the non-state sector. *Geography Compass*, 1(6), 1252–1281.
McIlwaine, C. 2010. Migrant machismos: exploring gender ideologies and practices among Latin American migrants in London from a multi-scalar perspective. *Gender, Place and Culture: A Journal of Feminist Geography*, 17(3), 281–300.
McIlwaine, C. 2011. Super-diversity, multiculturalism and integration: an overview of the Latin American population in London, UK, in *Cross-Border Migration among Latin Americans*, edited by C. McIlwaine. New York: Palgrave Macmillan, 93–117.
McIlwaine, C. 2012. Constructing transnational social spaces among Latin American migrants in Europe: perspectives from the UK. *Cambridge Journal of Regions, Economy and Society*, 5(2), 271–288.
McIlwaine, C. and Bermudez, A. 2011. The gendering of political and civic participation among Colombian migrants in London. *Environment and Planning A*, 43(7), 1499–1513.
McIlwaine, C., Cock, J.C. and Linneker, B. 2011. *No Longer Invisible: The Latin American Community in London*. London: Trust for London.
Montes, V. 2013. The role of emotions in the construction of masculinity: Guatemalan migrant men, transnational migration and family relations. *Gender and Society*, 27(4), 469–490.
Montoya L.J., Hardy-Fanta, C. and Garcia S. 2000. Latina politics: gender, participation, and leadership. *Political Science and Politics*, 33(3), 555–561.
Òstergaard-Nielsen, E. 2003. The politics of migrants' transnational political practices. *International Migration Review*, 37(3), 760–786.
Piscitelli, A. 2008. Looking for new worlds: Brazilian women as international migrants. *Signs: Journal of Women in Culture and Society*, 33(4), 784–793.
Pollard, J. 2012. Gendering capital: financial crisis, financialization and (an agenda for) economic geography. *Progress in Human Geography*, 37(3), 403–423.
Pribilsky, J. 2012. Consumption dilemmas: tracking masculinity, money and transnational fatherhood between the Ecuadorian Andes and New York City. *Journal of Ethnic and Migration Studies*, 38(2), 323–343.
Rezende, C.B. 2011. Seeing oneself through the eyes of the other: gender, race and Brazilian identity abroad, in *Brazilian Subjectivity Today*, edited by S. Simai and D. Hook. Buenos Aires: EDUVIM, 108–129.
Ruhs, M. 2009. *Migrant rights, immigration policy and human development*, New York: United Nations Development Programme Human Development Reports, Research Paper 2009/23.
Sarti, R. 2010. Fighting for masculinity: male domestic workers, gender, and migration in Italy from the late nineteenth century to the present. *Men and Masculinities*, 13(1), 16–43.

Sarti, R. and Scrinzi, F. 2010. Introduction to the special issue: men in a woman's job, male domestic workers, international migration and the globalization of care. *Men and Masculinities*, 13(1), 4–15.

Sheringham, O. 2013. *Transnational Religious Spaces: Faith and the Brazilian Migration Experience*. Basingstoke: Palgrave Macmillan.

Soysal, Y.N. 2000. Citizenship and identity: living in diasporas in post-war Europe? *Ethnic and Racial Studies*, 23(1), 1–15.

Staeheli, L., Ehrkamp, P., Leitner, H. and Nagel C. 2012. Dreaming the ordinary: daily life and the complex geographies of citizenship. *Progress in Human Geography*, 36(5), 628–644.

Veronis, L. 2006. The Canadian Hispanic Day Parade, or how Latin American immigrants practice (sub)urban citizenship in Toronto. *Environment and Planning A*, 38(9), 1653–1671.

Varsanyi, M. 2006. Interrogating 'urban citizenship' *vis-à-vis* undocumented migration. *Citizenship Studies*, 10(2), 229–249.

Vasta, E. 2008. *The paper market: 'borrowing' and 'renting' of identity documents*, Oxford: COMPAS Working Paper Series, WS-08-03.

Wills, J., et al. 2009. Religion at work: the role of faith-based organisations in the London living wage campaign. *Cambridge Journal of Regions, Economy and Society*, 2(3), 443–461.

Wills, J., et al. 2010. *Global Cities at Work: New Migrant Divisions of Labour*. London: Pluto Press.

Chapter 7

'Where you are is what you wear': The Leather Community, International Mr Leather and Hyper-masculinity

Andrew Childs

Introduction

Few scholars have discussed personal experiences of strapping on leather (with the exception of those who have written about the history of the leather community in general, see Bean 2004, Stem 2012) and fewer still have written about the intersection of leather, place, sexuality and masculinity. In this chapter I draw on current trends within geographies of the body (Dyck 1999, Valentine 1999, Bordo 2003, Longhurst, Ho and Johnston 2008, England and Dyck 2011) and especially from geographies of masculinity (Berg and Longhurst 2003, Connell 2005, Vanderbeck 2005, Henry and Berg 2006, Valentine 2007, Hopkins and Noble 2009) to portray how the gay leather community propagates a certain type of hyper-masculinity. I link this main theme with work on how different communities territorialise space (Hansen 2005, Atherton 2009, Valdivia 2009) to portray how the leather community territorialises their bodies and creates a place and culture that is simultaneously welcoming and exclusionary. Combining this scholarly work with my ethnographic interviews and participant observations, I hope to extend the understanding of masculinity within the leather community and how this community territorialises the body, thus rendering the body as a place. The key instrument, of this 'placing' of the body within the leather community, is wearing leather and having frequent events to re-claim their image and highly essentialised understanding of masculinity. As a performance (Butler 1993) wearing leather for many of these men is about limiting or granting access to parts of their body, sexual identity, community and idolising and idealising a hyper-masculine gender type. Ultimately, I conclude that men in this community use leather to inscribe discourse(s) upon their body, turning their bodies into largely sexualised places.

I focus on one event – IML (International Mr Leather) – as the case study for this chapter because it encompasses many dimensions of the leather community and enables me to explore the relationships between leather, masculinity, sexuality and place. IML is an annual event held over Memorial Day weekend (the weekend preceding the final Monday in May) in Chicago. It is primarily a gay event, though it welcomes all genders and sexual identities.[1] IML started in 1979 when a local Chicagoan saw the need for a leather contest and celebration of the leather lifestyle. It has numerous sponsors – including many corporate sponsors – and the organisers hold the events at a large conference-like hotel. There were about 20,000 visitors for the 2013 IML. The attendees were mostly white men in their 30s and 40s. There were representatives from other ethnicities, but the predominant race was white. One would encounter women peppered throughout the hotel though not in great numbers. Almost all of the men are 'geared up'[2] in leather, donning everything from leather boots to leather hats. 'Bud Lite' banners festoon the lobby and Expo area and bartenders peer out onto long lines of patrons eagerly paying for overpriced drinks. In conducting research on IML from a feminist perspective, I am sensitive to debates about positionality in the field and in the research process, and cognisant of the way my positionality in this project informs the dialectic between researcher and researched (Vanderbeck 2005, Hart 2006, Longhurst, Ho and Johnston 2008). As Haraway (1996) keenly reminds us that all knowledge is situated, I write this chapter as a gay, white male who likes to wear leather, who is in his mid-30s, and is a geographer interested in masculinity and place.

Methods

The bulk of this ongoing research project is based on ethnographic interviews (n=12 to date) and my own participant observation at IML 2013. I observed people at the leather expo for three days. In the beginning of my observations I focused on people's attire, the proportions of men versus women, and what people were selling. By the end of the third day, I was writing down more seemingly irrelevant details as I had discovered that minor things in one moment seemed relevant to me later. For the expo, I walked around asking people questions and making conversation. I carried a small notepad with me where I jotted down notes (though I usually would not take notes conspicuously in front of people to whom I had just spoken). After I finished observing for three to four hours each day, I would return to the room and expand my notes in another notebook with greater detail. While those were the formal occasions upon which I took notes, the entire time I participated in IML I was an observer. Often, I would find out something I thought interesting and would make a mental note or digitally write it onto my phone's notepad and then expand upon it later in my room. I realised that having too rigid of a time when I wanted to interview meant that I might miss valuable information. Thus, by the end of IML I was carrying my small notepad and phone with me everywhere.

1 For a more detailed understanding of IML, see http://www.imrl.com.

2 'Gear' is a common reference to one's leather apparel.

For interviews, I used snowball sampling by establishing a rapport with a key informant and branching out from there. I conducted, recorded, and transcribed all of the interviews in Seattle, Washington. Usually I conducted the interviews in public places like a coffee shop with half of the interviews conducted before IML and the other half after. Attending IML influenced some of my questions. Specifically, I wanted to find out more about what it was like to participate in the pageant so I tried to focus on this part of my questioning in the interviews I conducted after IML. Eleven of my respondents are male and one is female. Because I am trying to understand processes and how IML has changed, I focused on men, usually in their forties. I did have some basic questions such as: How did you become involved in the leather community? How has the leather community changed since your involvement? Describe your experience in competing at IML? But I also learned that letting the respondents speak freely and asking open-ended questions that linked to what they were already discussing was the best tactic. Ultimately, I let my respondents tell a story while probing (usually by asking, 'could you say more about that?') when they discussed something especially relevant.

Whips, harnesses and slings, oh my!

Meandering through the leather market at IML in Chicago, the first thing I saw was a man on all fours wearing a dog mask and a dog tail inside of a dog pen. The booth to his left displays slings, leather harnesses and candles that say they are scented like sex (whatever that is supposed to smell like?). Down one aisle, I strolled passed a porn booth with a live demonstration involving a man using leather whips on another man in a leather sling. I turned right down another aisle and one of the largest leather clothing companies in the United States was selling its goods: leather jockstraps, leather armbands, leather shirts and leather harnesses. These are the common sights I witnessed at the IML expo. Generally, the leather expo is an enormous convention type place where vendors and consumers come together usually in a conference area of a hotel – to accommodate the multitude.

There is a clear socio-spatial dialectic (Soja 1988) between the participants and the leather expo. As an observer at the expo, one becomes accustomed to the performances around them and their spatial dynamics. In turn one might find themselves participating in certain performances that encourages others to take part and increases the intensity of the expo as a sexually charged place. While scholars have documented the spatial dynamics of gay bars (Castells 1983, Valentine 1994, Brown 2009), the expo is arguably a more public place than a bar. It is well-lit, not primarily a place for alcohol or drug consumption and it is full of vendors selling leather products. The expo also functions as a catchall for kink and fetish. Puppy play (where people behave like dogs), furries (dressing up like animals), electrocution with nodes, and any other fetish or kink are all performed in the leather expo. IML generally and the expo specifically, normalises many types of behaviors, and as Bean (2004) and Stein (2012) note, this normalisation leads to a very strong sense of inclusion between different types of people. One respondent put it this way: 'While everyone might value different types of kink or fetishes, the fact that most are welcome is certainly a hallmark of IML and the expo.'

Many critics of gay culture in general and gay bars and leather places in particular, however, claim that gay bars and places of leather performance (like IML) are homonormative, classist, racist, sexist places that are primarily concerned with sexual gratification and drugs (Rushbrook 2002, Bell and Binnie 2004, Duggan 2003, Johnson and Samdahal 2005, Caluya 2008, Brown 2009, Browne and Bakshi 2011). In contrast, some scholars (Brown et al. 2014: this volume) have argued that gay bars are also places of care. The expo at IML is no exception. The expo is a welcoming and an inclusive side to IML which translates into an overall more diverse picture of the leather community. Conversely, you might walk through the expo wearing your favourite leather strategically placed and notice someone that is not compatible to you because of the placement and style of their clothing. There might even be people into certain fetishes you find repulsive! In this visualised manner, the expo can be an ostracising, highly territorialised place, especially if you cannot find like-minded individuals easily. Nevertheless, there is very little disciplining of self-expression, and while participants are mostly white there is a sprinkling of different ethnicities. The culture of the Expo urges you to express yourself freely-especially in a sexual manner-where you can relatively easily transcend personal boundaries. Thus, the expo is both a welcoming and simultaneously exclusive place. When I asked one respondent about the types of people (specifically gender) one might find at the expo and whether the community was welcoming in general, he responded with:

> I would say the community as a whole is, yes. I think there are individuals in the community that get a little uppity. So kind of … If you're a new person coming in, wherever your entry point is you may have a different reaction from people … Not just women but I mean every form of gender you can think of. So socially when there's not necessarily play going on, I mean you'll have every … There's a spectrum again. You go from male to female and everything in between. Wherever or whoever you identify as on that line is represented and welcome at most social functions.

Perhaps ironically, a community that is deeply concerned with masculinity seems to care very little about gender, transgender, and performances of gender that might defy traditional conceptualisations of masculinity. This is a community nevertheless, and communities by definition have borders so there remains a feel of exclusivity-especially if you are simply not into leather. Perhaps one of my respondents put it best when they said:

> … so say you have a group of 30 leather men. Maybe three of them again have this sort of like really strict requirements of how they're going to accept you. The rest of them are going to be open arms and be fine. But if you happen

> to encounter one of those people first you may get a reaction that's like, 'oh my God the leather community is awful you know?' Because they tend to be very vocal.

This quote highlights the contradictory nature of the leather community with its simultaneously welcoming and potentially ostracising tendencies. This ambivalence between welcoming and exclusion are not usually based on gender, race, class or sex. Instead, the exclusive tendencies of the leather community rest upon a division between the old guard and the new guard (traditional versus non-traditional) and how one person versus another has territorialised their body as an object of desire or an object off-limits.

Out with the old, in with the new?

IML celebrates leather, hyper-masculinity, pageantry and sexual gratification in one place. The participants at IML value these things and convene publicly to demonstrate this shared sense of community. Moreover, many of the attendees have formed national and international networks of friendships and use IML as a place to reconnect with those friends. One respondent noted: 'Often I only see people at IML that I don't see anywhere else throughout the year. It's a gathering place, a meeting place and that is what I mostly use it for now.' While many of my respondents spoke fondly of their experiences at IML, others lamented the changes they see in IML. Some of the respondents claimed that the true history of IML has been exaggerated and that the original purpose for the event has been lost in the swirl of partying, drinking, sex and drugs. One respondent claimed:

> IML is an interesting situation. For example it started off as a contest with this little party thrown in afterwards on the weekend so these guys could get together and have a good time. It was a bar contest. And as it progressed it became, in the 35 years that it's been in existence it's become less about the contest and more about the party. So even though this year there's probably going to be over 20,000 men in Chicago strictly for this event, I would say 200 or 300 of them will actually go to the contest.

A mythologising of IML's history was a commonplace occurrence among my respondents. When I asked people if they knew how long the contest had been in existence or how it started, very few gave me an answer, or they gave me answers that contradicted each other. This historical ignorance allows IML to function epiphenomenally as throngs of people lusting for immediate gratification piggyback on the cultural and historical work that the harbingers of the tradition strive so diligently to maintain. Buried, hidden or forgotten histories, however, are nothing new to cultural geography (Mitchell 1996, DeLyser 2008). Cultural geographers have noted how place and nostalgia combine to make a landscape or an experience into a myth. In this way, IML functions as a key cultural guardian of the leather community's tenets for those who value the history, but also as a place where thousands of participants bask in the ephemera of sexual encounters that might be spiked with alcohol or drugs. Ironically, IML, an event that was specifically designed to commemorate and celebrate the history and legacy of the leather community, is also where that history is actively ignored, if not erased. Some in the community see no need to revere history. One respondent noted:

> Hey history is great but I'm not going to, I refuse to be stuck in this kind of historical, you know, archetype that I don't care about ... I appreciate whoever it was that started it or wherever it came from, or when it began – that's great, I'm glad it happened – but that was then.

For this respondent, acceptance into the leather community or participation at IML rested upon different criteria than knowledge of history. His new guard attitude is at odds with the old guard mentality.[3] The old guard (which comprises members who adhere to strict rules and require a comprehensive knowledge of the community in order to participate in the community) tend to be older folks who guard and transmit the history of the community and IML – the border patrol of the leather nation. Knowledge of history for the community and IML is analogous to the manner in which states require new citizens to accumulate and demonstrate the history and traditions of their new state (Adams 1995, Hansen 2005). In other words, the old guard functions as cultural police-granting access to the community based on a shared and embraced history of IML and the leather community. Policing the traditional and historical borders of IML is one method that the old guard institutes to territorialise IML as a place.

The old guard implicitly values embodied knowledge. Bordo (2003) and Irigaray (2003) aver that place underwrites embodiment and embodied knowledge is as much about location within networks, lived experience, sensualness and sexual difference. Likewise, men place themselves in the community based upon how active or inactive they are when it comes to wearing leather or what we might call a location within the leather network. For example, when I asked my respondents how often they 'do' leather, many responded 'every day'. This response is typical for the old guard. For these respondents, wearing leather is not something one dons for special events-taken out of the closet and then hung back up. Even if they are not wearing something made out of leather necessarily, many of the respondents speak of leather as a mindset-what Filault and Drummond (2007) call an attitude. For example when I asked one of my respondents if he wore something leather every day he said:

3 The 'old guard' and the 'new guard' are terms people in the leather community use to refer to people who are concerned or not so concerned with the traditions, customs and history of the leather community.

> Not necessarily something every day. My leather is more of an internal leather. Like my thinking, my thought process, my way of looking at things goes that way … So when I say I do it every day, I do … It's part of my life every day. It's not necessarily a piece of leather but there is an aspect of it every day.

As this response suggests, leather is as much a mindset as it is a material reality. And while the old guard might have established the rules for membership ardency, the new guard pays little attention to these regulations. This tension between the old and new obviously exists but as one respondent noted, most of the members 'can do their own thing you know. And if the old guard suits you, you do it and if it doesn't, you don't do it. And most of the community is in the middle somewhere'.

Whoso would be a man would be a hyper-masculine man

IML also privileges a certain flavour of hegemonic masculinity (Connell 2005, Filault and Drummond 2007). Moreover, many of my respondents use the term hyper-masculine in much the same way that Bell et al. (1994) and Vanderbeck (2005) use it to denote that not only do they privilege masculinity but a macho form of it. Filault and Drummond (2007) describe the macho man look as broad and hairy chested, bulging muscles, bulging pelvic regions, wearing working-class clothes and bodies indicative of the use of supplements or even steroids. They also describe the macho attitude as stoic, strong and even misogynistic. Interestingly, Filault and Drummond (2007), as well as other scholars of masculinity (notably Bell et al. 1994, Vanderbeck 2005), do not define the term 'hyper-masculine' – a point I will return to later. Filault and Drummond's (2007) description of the macho male corresponds with my respondent's descriptions. When I asked one respondent to describe hyper-masculine, they responded with:

> The uniform of the United States Marines is hyper-masculine. It makes a guy look extremely male. The cut of the outfit, the adornments, the hat, the rigidness is a very masculine look. At the same time and not to sound like I am being racist or bigoted but the Nazi uniform was extremely sexual in appearance. A lot of people would not necessarily agree with that because of whatever, whatever but their outfits that they were dressed in were extremely, extremely masculine … So it also has a sense of like hyper-masculinity plus it also feeds off of a lot of visual stimulus that gay men have seen in the past: Tom of Finland, AMG, Athletic Models Guild, anything that is, anything that represents something like Rough Trade, anything that accentuates body shape. (See Figure 7.1 for examples of Tom of Finland and Rough Trade)

This description underpins how numerous attendees define hyper-masculine in essentialised terms. Geographers and other social scientists are careful not to essentialise but instead define gender and masculinity in relational terms (Longhurst

2000, Berg and Longhurst 2003, Connell 2005, Connell and Messerschmidt 2005, Aitken 2006, Atherton 2009, Hopkins 2009, Simpson 2009). A possible, unintended consequence of using terms like hyper-masculine is that it smuggles in latent essentialisms. While men and women active in the leather community certainly essentialise masculinity, scholars illustrate my point concerning the difficulty of defining hyper-masculinity (notably Bell et al. 1994, Vanderbeck 2005, Filault and Drummond 2007). None of these scholars explicitly define hyper-masculine like my respondents and these scholars are trying to discover how men construct, maintain, and challenge masculinities and how masculine ideals change over time, not how to define some essential element of masculinity. Yet using the term hyper-masculine runs the risk of essentialising so it might be helpful to define it. Defining hyper-masculine, however, proves to be a challenge. For my own research, I could not find any definition of hyper-masculine so I used Connell's (2005) definition of masculine and machismo and added characteristics based on my research to arrive at the following definition: a masculine ideal stressing the domination of women by men, competition between men, aggressive display especially with the body and sexuality, predatory sexuality, lack of emotional language, behaviour, or appearance and non-feminine mannerisms.

Figure 7.1 Hyper-masculine achetypes

The attendees of IML appear to have less of a problem defining hyper-masculinity; even still I noticed a level of uneasiness in nearly all of my respondents about the term. Perhaps they too realise that once we start to define masculinity in absolute terms instead of the post-modern tendency towards relational terms (see Sayer 1997) that the definition fails. As Sayer (1997) contends, however, if we are to explain anything then some measure of 'non-deterministic essentialism' is necessary-otherwise gender is an evanescent concept. Therefore, when we use the term hyper-masculine or any term that smuggles in what I have referred to as latent essentialisms, we need to discuss how some of the elements that term implies are potentially deterministic. Conversely, while we may find terms like hyper-masculine useful we should define them and maintain that our use of them does not foreclose other epistemologies of masculinity. The reticence of my respondents to define hyper-masculinity, and the refusal of scholars to define it, demonstrate at least a nascent understanding that the use of such a term imperils alternative epistemologies of masculinity.

My body is a nation

IML is about celebration and commemoration. It is not primarily a place for political rallying and while the concept of 'pride' is present at IML, based on my observations most attendees are concerned with enjoying the experience and sexual gratification. The lack of an overt political agenda renders IML rife for easy corporatisation. Like many gay pride parades one acquires a sense that corporate sponsors have appropriated IML. Oswin (2005) notes that the process of appropriation by capitalism is a normalisation of homosexuality, and at IML one can certainly see a normalisation of a certain type of hyper-masculinity that underpins a hegemonic, male aesthetic (Filault and Drummond 2007). Moreover, Oswin points out that queerness is not always radical or even progressive and that in certain manifestations it may serve to entrench race, gender and class divides (see also Nast 2002). Thus while the celebration of a particular type of kink or fetish is something I value, IML simultaneously privileges white, male, somewhat affluent bodies.

Duggan (2003) describes this normalisation process as 'homonormative'. If there is a certain type of hegemonic, hyper-masculinity at play at IML, there is also a standard of conduct. Clothing especially, subtly yet strongly regulates and normalises comportment and behaviour. When everyone starts to look relatively similar, it is easy to have similar expectations. Aside from clothing, language and bodily appearance are also similar. There is a strong use of familial language (dad/son, mom/daughter) and there is a colour-schemed signification of fetish and kink (there is an entire colour 'hanky code' that signals to others what kind of sexual fetish you enjoy, see Figure 7.2). In much the same way that states territorialise their sovereignty with discreet borders, rules and regulations (Adams 1995, Hansen 2005), these men regulate their bodies in a similar fashion. If you wear your leather armband on your right arm, you are signalling that you are a bottom and are looking or interested in a top (armband on the left). If you and another person have the same color armband or suspenders, etc. then it is a clear, tacit signal that you are into the same fetish. A shared attraction and sexual compatibility underwrites the sense of community that participants feel and the body as a territorialised space legitimises sexual compatibility.

Hanky Code

HANKY	WORN ON LEFT	WORN ON RIGHT
WHITE	jerk me off	I'll do us both
WHITE VELVET	voyeur	will put on a show
WHITE w/MULTICOLOR Dots	hosting an orgy	looking for an orgy
CREAM	cum fetish (mine)	cum fetish (yours)
BLACK/WHITE check	safe sex top	safe sex bottom
BLACK/WHITE stripes	kissing	kissing
BLACK	SM top	SM bottom
BLACK VELVET	has/takes videos	will perform for the camera
CHARCOAL	latex fetish	latex fetish
GREY, Dark	bondage – ties	fit to be tied
GREY, Light	stone – I'll fuck you	stone – just fuck me
SILVER LAME	celebrity/titleholder	starfucker
GREEN (Hunter) W/ Green (Kelly) Stripe	sugardaddy	looking for sugardaddy
GREEN, Kelly	hooker (for rent)	trick (looking to buy)
GREEN, Mint	looking for orphan	looking for mummy
GREEN, Light	dirty talk	dirty talk
GREEN, Lime	dines off tricks (wants food)	dinner plate (will buy dinner)
AQUA	watersex	watersex
BLUE, Teal	genital torturer	genital torturee
BLUE, Robin's Egg	69	69
BLUE, Light	gives oral	wants oral
BLUE, Light w/ light PINK stripe	sucks dildo	suck my dildo
BLUE, Navy	fucking / TOP	fucking / BOTTOM
VELVET, NAVY	watches masturbation	will masturbate for audience
PURPLE	piercer	piercee
LAVENDER	X dresser / dragster	likes X dressers / drag
MAUVE	worship my navel	has a navel fetish
FUCHSIA	spanker	spank me
MAGENTA	suck my pits	armpit lover
MAROON	cuts	bleeds
w/ MAROON stripe	into blood	into blood
RED, Dark	2-handed fister	2-handed fistee
RED	fist fucker	fist fuckee
RED/WHITE Stripes	shaver	shavee
RED CROSS	HIV positive	HIV positive
PINK, Dark	tit torturer	tit torturee
PUCE	bruiser	bruise me
PINK, Light	dildo wielder	dildo fuckee
YELLOW, Pale	spits	spit on me
YELLOW, Bright	watersports – pisses	watersports – drinks/wears
MUSTARD	hung (carries)	size queen
GOLD	2 looking for one	1 looking for two
GOLD LAME	likes muscles	likes muscles
ORANGE	looking to lead	open to suggestion
CORAL	suck my toes	shrimper (sucks toes)
RUST	cowboy	cowboy's horse
BEIGE	rimmer	rim me
TAN	cigarplay – Clinton	cigarplay – Lewinsky
BROWN	scat – gives	scat – receives

Figure 7.2 The hanky code

This priority of the body and its sexual prowess turns much of the feminist critique about the mind/body dualism (Rose 1993, Bordo 2003) on its head, at least at IML. While Western philosophy has castigated the body as the realm of women and celebrated the mind as the domain of men, rationalism and logic have little currency at IML. Meeting one's 'animalistic desire' and 'primal needs' are but two descriptions my respondents used to explain their intentions at IML. In fact, most attendees freely admit to hedonism being a prevailing virtue. While Rose (1993) and Bordo (2003) succeed in tracing the historical linking of rationalism to men and animalistic desire to women, the culture of IML stands as an oasis, a temporary suspension of this mind/body fallacy where the body, sexual gratification and sexuality reign supreme.

Bordo (2003) reminds us that the defining and shaping of the body is the focal point for the shaping of power. The body as the focal point of power is certainly true at IML as it is the key instrument folks use to attract one another in an environment where attraction is fundamental. These men's bodies are power or at least how they understand, define and materially shape it. We should not view their bodies as merely receivers of the discourse of hyper-masculinity, a tabula rasa passively awaiting discursive inscription: their bodies have generative powers *as well as* receptive ones. Tom of Finland, Rough Trade and other popular cultural icons of the leather community homogenise and normalise the body. Their images, for all their supposed sexuality and virility, homogenise by demonstrating sameness of race, class and especially gender. These men's bodies are not only normalised, however, but also depoliticised. Rather than trying to disrupt the dominant, heterosexual, hegemonic male aesthetic, these bodies reinforce that aesthetic and celebrate it (Filault and Drummond 2007) as they constantly endeavour to achieve the unachievable body type ideal (Butler 1993) and perform the virtues of stoicism, strength and, at times, misogyny.

There he is, Mr IML!

Masculinity and its perceived essence are central to much of the pageantry of IML. The pageant is run very similarly to a beauty pageant such as Ms America. There are contestants from all over the world but primarily from North America, and each contestant participates in competitions to determine the winner. Each contestant at IML has to first win a local competition. Around the globe, bars, social clubs and local leather organisations sponsor myriad competitions. The competitions are feeder competitions and winning a competition that is a feeder competition for IML ensures your entry into the IML pageant. At the local and IML level, some of the pageant's categories are: closed and open interviews, a prepared speech, jockstrap competition (wearing a jockstrap on stage), bar wear (what you might wear to a bar) and formal leather wear (this might include chaps, leather shirt, vest, boots, sash, belt and hat). Many of the contestants bring a friend or partner along just to prep the clothing they must wear for each round. In the interviews and speech section, the contestant should highlight any philanthropic work they have done but also what type of kink and fetish they prefer along with their history of involvement in the leather community. One respondent characterised the pageant as:

> I did always look at the contest as, I was like, it's like a beauty pageant but with jocks instead of you know a bathing suit section. And I never quite really understood that there was such a big political aspect to it. I thought it was just sort of like a beauty pageant where, 'who's the hottest guy in this outfit and what is he into, and what is his kink, and what's his specialty?' You know just general statistics. I didn't realise at the time that it was a lot of politics, a lot of history, a lot of background knowledge that an individual would need to know to be able to compete in these things.

Again, a strong sense of history is important and obligatory for success in the pageant. A sense of history, however, is not the only ingredient for success. Much of the pageant is predicated upon the masculine look of the contestant, their ability to represent the leather community and their pedigree. One prior contestant proclaimed: 'IML is representative of a very large community. Being able to be someone the straight or non-leather community can look to and not be afraid of I think is a very large part of it.' Moreover, the winner of the pageant reigns for a year and embarks on a speaking circuit. They are usually invited to smaller local contests as judges or keynote speakers. All of my respondents that had participated in the IML pageant stressed the need for the contestants to be able to travel most weekends out of the year and that keeping a full-time job was next to impossible. Often other bars or organisations will pay for your travel expenses but having spending money beyond that is difficult if you have not saved nor have a portable job.

Conclusion: onward to the past

As I have argued, IML is simultaneously a welcoming and ostracising place and privileges a hyper-masculine, hegemonic male aesthetic. If we are to believe Butler's (1993) claim that there is no original gender type – as I believe – then we can cast IML in the light of a moment of gender articulation. Of course this gender articulation rests upon the fallacy that there is an original, hyper-masculine type and attempts to conjure such an image (see also Gibson 2014: this volume). Thus, these men, through their hyper-masculinised performances are like swimmers against the current of history and its flow of changing norms. In their pageantry and pursuit of *the* archetypal body and attitude, they ceaselessly reach back into the past to summon the true, hyper-masculine male. Perhaps this is the greatest irony of IML: while it celebrates the myriad forms of gender it relentlessly promotes and reifies the myth of the quintessential, hyper-masculine male.

References

Adams, P. 1995. A reconsideration of personal boundaries in space-time. *Annals of the Association of American Geographers*, 85(2), 267–285.

Aitken, S.C. 2006. Leading men to violence and creating spaces for their emotions. *Gender, Place and Culture: A Journal of Feminist Geography*, 13(5), 491–507.

Atherton, S. 2009. Domesticating military masculinities: home, performance and the negotiation of identity. *Social and Cultural Geography*, 10(8), 821–836.

Bean, J. 2004. *International Mr. Leather, 25 Years of Champions*. Las Vegas: Nazca Plains Corporation.

Bell, D., Binnie, J., Cream, J. and Valentine, G. 1994. All hyped up and no place to go. *Gender, Place and Culture: A Journal of Feminist Geography*, 1(1), 31–47.

Bell, D. and Binnie, J. 2004. Authenticating queer space: citizenship, urbanism and governance. *Urban Studies*, 41(9), 1807–1820.

Berg, L.D. and Longhurst, R. 2003. Placing masculinities and geography. *Gender, Place and Culture: A Journal of Feminist Geography*, 10(4), 351–360.

Bordo, S. 2003. *Unbearable Weight: Feminism, Western Culture, and the Body*. Berkeley: University of California Press.

Brown, G. 2009. Thinking beyond homonormativity: performative explorations of diverse gay economies. *Environment and Planning A*, 41(6), 1496–1510.

Browne, K. and Bakshi, L. 2011. We are here to party? Lesbian, gay, bisexual and trans leisurescapes beyond commercial gay scenes. *Leisure Studies*, 30(2), 179–196.

Butler, J. 1993. Imitation and gender insubordination, in *The Lesbian and Gay Studies Reader*, edited by H. Abelove, M.A. Barale and D.M. Halperin. New York: Routledge, 307–320.

Caluya, G. 2008. 'The rice steamer': race, desire and affect in Sydney's gay scene. *Australian Geographer*, 39(3), 283–292.

Castells, M. 1983. *The City and the Grassroots*. Berkeley: University of California Press.

Connell, R.W. 2005. *Masculinities*. Berkeley: University of California Press.

Connell, R.W. and Messerschmidt, J.W. 2005. Hegemonic masculinity: rethinking the concept. *Gender and Society*, 19(6), 829–859.

Delyser, D. 2008. 'Thus I salute the Kentucky Daisey's claim': gender, social memory, and the mythic West at a proposed Oklahoma monument. *Cultural Geographies*, 15(1), 63–94.

Duggan, L. 2003. *The Twilight of Equality? Neoliberalism, Cultural Politics, and the Attack on Democracy*. Boston: Beacon Press.

Dyck, I. 1999. Body troubles: women, the workplace and the negotiations of a disabled body, in *Mind and Body Spaces*, edited by R. Butler and H. Parr. New York: Routledge, 119–137.

England, K. and Dyck, I. 2011. Managing the body work of home care. *Sociology of Health and Illness*, 33(2), 206–219.

Filault, S.M. and Drummond, M.J. 2007. The hegemonic aesthetic. *Gay and Lesbian Issues and Psychology Review*, 3(3), 177–183.

Hansen, T. 2005. *Sovereign Bodies: Citizens, Migrants, and States in the Postcolonial World*. Princeton: Princeton University Press.

Haraway, D. 1996. Situated knowledges: the science question in feminism and the privilege of partial perspective, in *Human Geography: An Essential Anthology*, edited by J.A. Agnew, D.N. Livingston and A. Rogers. Oxford: Blackwell Publishers, 108–128.

Hart, G. 2006. Denaturalizing dispossession: critical ethnography in the age of resurgent imperialism. *Antipiode*, 38(5), 977–1004.

Henry, M.G. and Berg, L.D. 2006. Geographers performing nationalism and hetero-masculinity. *Gender, Place and Culture: A Journal of Feminist Geography*, 13(6), 629–645.

Hopkins, P.E. 2009. Responding to the 'crisis of masculinity': the perspectives of young Muslim men from Glasgow and Edinburgh, Scotland. *Gender, Place and Culture: A Journal of Feminist Geography*, 16(3), 299–312.

Hopkins, P.E. and Noble, G. 2009. Masculinities in place: situated identities, relations and intersectionality. *Social and Cultural Geography*, 10(8), 811–819.

Irigaray, L. 2003. What other are we talking about? *Yale French Studies*, (2004)104, 67–81.

Johnson, C. and Samdahal, D. 2005, 'The night they took over': misogyny in a country-western gay bar. *Leisure Sciences*, 27(4), 331–348.

Longhurst, R. 2000. Geography and gender: masculinities, male identity and men. *Progress in Human Geography*, 24(3), 439–444.

Longhurst, R., Ho, E. and Johnston, L. 2008. Using the body as an instrument of research: kimch'i and pavlova. *Area*, 40(2), 208–217.

Mitchell, D. 1996. *The Lie of the Land: Migrant Workers and the California Landscape*. Minneapolis: University of Minnesota Press.

Nast, H. Queer patriarchies, queer racisms, international. *Antipode*, 34(5), 874–909.

Oswin, N. 2005. Towards radical geographies of complicit queer futures. *Acmee: An International E-Journal for Critical Geographies*, 2(2), 79–86.

Rose, G. 1993. *Feminism and Geography: The Limits of Geographical Knowledge*. Cambridge: Polity Press.

Rushbrook, D. 2002. Cities, queer space, and the cosmopolitan tourist. *GLQ: A Journal of Lesbian and Gay Studies*, 8(1–2), 183–206.

Sayer, A. 1997. Essentialism, social constructionism, and beyond. *The Sociological Review*, 45(3), 453–487.

Simpson, R. 2004. Masculinity at work: the experiences of men in female dominated occupations. *Work, Employment and Society*, 18(2), 349–368.

Soja, E. 1980. The socio-spatial dialectic. *Annals of the Association of American Geographers*, 70(2), 207–225.

Stein, S. 2012. *Twenty-Five Years of Living in Leather: The National Leather Association, 1986–2011*. Palm Coast: Adynaton Publishing, 1–178.

Valdivia, G. 2009. Indigenous bodies, indigenous minds? Towards an understanding of indigeneity in the Ecuadorian Amazon. *Gender, Place and Culture: A Journal of Feminist Geography*, 16(5), 535–551.

Valentine, G. 1999. What it means to be a man: the body, masculinities, disability, in *Mind and Body Spaces*, edited by R. Butler and H. Parr. New York: Routledge, 167–181.

Valentine, G. 2007. Theorizing and researching intersectionality: a challenge for feminist geography. *Professional* Geographer, 59(1), 10–21.

Vanderbeck, R.M. 2005. Masculinities and fieldwork: widening the discussion. *Gender, Place and Culture: A Journal of Feminist Geography*, 12(4), 387–402.

Chapter 8
Cowboy Masculinities: Relationality and Rural Identity

Chris Gibson

Introduction

One of the more dominant, formulaic and enduring compositions of masculinity is the cowboy. In this chapter I discuss cowboy masculinities through a historical geographical lens. I contrast a hegemonic masculinity associated with the cowboy, with a more complex, relational perspective. The former requires critique of the commercializing and socially conservative forces at work in producing normative masculinity, while the latter is dependent on interpreting the cowboy figure not as a singular stereotype, but as a palette of discourses, representations, commodifications and material cultural interactions – from which diverse, unfolding and often contradictory subject positions emerge. Necessary for this kind of interpolation of masculinity is sensitivity to an 'array of vectors of relationality' (Hopkins and Noble 2009: 815) that operate at any given time, and in any given place. As I hope to illustrate below, even a cursory unpicking of the historical and geographical variability of cowboy masculinities demonstrates their contingent assembly: coming together in diverse times and places as outcomes of relations between men and women but also the relations between men and other men, between popular cultural depictions and the lived experiences of cattle workers, between bodies, boots and clothes, and between men and the rural landscape (see also Childs 2014; this volume). Against a dominant and simplistic stereotype of what constitutes a cowboy, I discuss the historical emergence and proliferation of cowboy masculinities as dependent on complex intersections and assemblages.

Cowboy masculinities vividly combine the visual and the material: the travelling cowboy body on the colonial frontier or on the international rodeo circuit, the star of western films, the clothes, hats and boots. But material embodiments of cowboy masculinities are also embodied, performed and interpreted in specific geographic contexts (Gorman-Murray, Waitt and Gibson 2008) where they variously reinforce or trouble contingent norms. In the case of the cowboy this includes embodied performances of masculinity in rural work, in film, on stage or in the rodeo ring, at nightclubs and at festivals, in America and beyond – where an assortment of clothes, boots, holsters, horses, saddles and spurs visualise and hyperbolise identities. The story of cowboy masculinities is also one of the specificities of the cowboy body in mythical and material space: the western film set, the ranch, but also deep in the city, in bars and busy city streets. Cowboy masculinities depend on material fabrications such as clothes and boots for an element of hyperreality, self-referential visual cues that reproduce cowboy myth. But these reproductions necessarily resonate in and through specific times, places and translations – where their meanings and affordances vary considerably.

In what follows, I hope to bring some of this variability to light, albeit in truncated form, in the process demonstrating that the processes that bolster hegemonic masculinities are always countered by more complex intersectionalities, subversions and counter-narratives. Diversity and contradiction are leitmotifs. And as cultural geographers have shown, such intersections are complex, spatial and material as well as discursive: located 'within and between embodiment, desires, practices and feelings' (Waitt and Warren 2008: 356, see also van Hoven and Hörschelmann 2005, Berg and Longhurst 2003). Masculinity is thus co-constituted through intersections of identification, practice, style and discourse, in material spaces (Gorman-Murray 2008, Hopkins and Noble 2009). Throughout this chapter I thus seek to 'place' analysis of cowboy masculinities – on the American frontier, in contemporary subcultures, in remote Aboriginal communities in the Australian outback. Cowboy masculinities are co-constituted through practices, styles and discourses in a distinct set of material spaces. Through such groundings a more pluralist sense of cowboy masculinities emerges. What makes this analysis most pertinent is that, in the case of the cowboy, a form of masculine identity has persisted throughout over a century and half's worth of popular culture, and travelled enormously widely as a motif of rural manhood. The cowboy is a pervasive figure that needs to be cast in critical geographical light.

The cowboy: a hegemonic masculinity?

The perspective developed here is influenced by feminist and cultural geographic analyses of masculinity. Following Raewyn Connell (2005), masculinity as a sense of maleness is culturally constructed and malleable, but also bound up in patriarchal and relational processes that define masculinity 'in relation to femininities and other social identities (class, race, sexualities)' (Gorman-Murray 2008: 369). *Hegemonic masculinities* (Connell and Messerschmidt 2005) become embedded in social life, norms, laws and politics, while simultaneously oppressing subordinated masculinities, femininities, minority identifications and non-heterosexualities. For some men, hegemonic masculinities represent (impossible) ideals; others contest them in a multitude of ways, dramatically or prosaically.

The cowboy can be read in this frame. There is a dominant stereotype of the cowboy reproduced in all kinds of commodified cultural products, from films, books and cartoons, to children's toys, clothing and costumes. The stereotype – a gallant, rugged outdoor man working alone on the range, wearing jeans, underslung-heeled boots, chaps, press-stud shirts, Stetson-style hat and holsters – has been remarkably durable for more than a century. Along with sailors, pirates and superheroes, the cowboy stereotype has provided a script for the performance of a normative, and heroic, masculinity that has been subsequently appropriated, mutated and differentially interpreted across diverse global places (cf. Bell 2000, Basso, McCall and Garceau 2001, Stanley 2012).

This stereotype of the cowboy is unambiguously open to critique, as an outcome of the exercise of patriarchal power. The origins of the heroic cowboy figure are bound up within the colonial mastery over indigenous peoples, animals and landscapes. One precedent was the Spanish *vaquero* (a term that later morphed into English as 'buckaroo'), an important figure of conquest, nature management and permanent occupancy in the colonial expansion of North America. Cattle were introduced to ensure the survival of Spanish colonies in the 1500s and 1600s, and then later, after stray herds grew and spread northwards, ranching activities expanded and vaqueros dispersed with them (Dary 1989). Vaqueros also closely followed the expanding colonial mining industry, indirectly securing Spanish control over mineral resources through feeding miners and providing tallow to make candles for mines. The stereotype of cowboy masculinity thus has its origins in a form of agricultural work premised on controlling animals, securing territory and naturalising conquest.

The later evolution of the cowboy as a distinctly Anglo-American variant on the vaquero was similarly entwined with the masculine domination of nature. In a much-repeated, cherished and nationalistic history told about American cowboys, masculinity is intricately interwoven with late-nineteenth-century frontier expansion. 'In the legendary West, Europeans became Americans who tamed a wilderness' (McCall 2001: 5). The westward expansion of the frontier was a narrative of white male mastery of nature – hence Frederick Jackson Turner's idealised frontier space was what *made American men*. In Australia, too, the figure of the cowboy was appropriated and fused with emergent local masculinities forged on that continent's own pastoral frontier. American Wild West shows (that themselves featured active working cowboys) travelled across the Pacific in the late nineteenth century, coincidentally when Australian nationalism intensified, as pastoralism expanded and a sense of permanence fuelled confidence in the fledgling national populace. Cowboy mythology thus mutated and was absorbed on another continent where colonial domination of nature, indigenous peoples and territory fused with emergent masculinities.

Later depictions in pop culture further entrenched hegemonic cowboy masculinity, which became increasingly formulaic, heroic, and conservative. Film producers went to great lengths to market their cowboy stars as clean-cut and 'authentically' Western. Hollywood studios 'marketed these men as indigenous heroes whom they had not created but had merely discovered' (Smith 2003: 203). In the hands of movie producers cowboys became national heroes, patriarchal father-figures. Gene Autry publicised his 'Cowboy Ten Commandments' ('he must never shoot first … '; 'he must be gentle with children, the elderly, and animals … '; 'he must be a good worker'; 'he must keep himself clean … ') and Roy Rogers had ten 'rules' for membership of his Riders Club ('be neat and clean', 'always obey your parents', 'protect the weak and help them … ') (Tucker 2000). Such heroes became saleable at the very time that gender roles in American society (and on farms in particular) were shifting, with increasing mechanisation and sedentarism in farming, and further integration of women into working life and public affairs (Garceau 2001). Intersections of evolving gender, class and working identities contributed to the atmosphere out of which the heroic, hegemonic cowboy figure emerged.

The extent of popular culture commodification of the heroic cowboy figure was remarkable: Remington and Russell paintings, dime novels, postcards, children's toys and stories, cigar boxes, cigarette advertisements, western wear manufacturing, accompanied by silent and then talkie films, hillbilly and country music, and television. Metropolitan cultural industries generated a stock of images, ideas about bodily deportment, and fables of heroic acts that were hyperbolised, standardised and commodified. This did not so much reconstruct the frontier as nostalgic past, but commodify and formularise the cowboy persona at the very time that ranch work was being transformed. According to Laura McCall (2001: 1–2), this was 'a time when standards of ideal manhood were undergoing profound change', a transition from 'Victorian norms of manliness that emphasised self-restraint, chastity, sobriety, self-denial, sentiment, and delayed gratification' to newer ideals of 'physical prowess, the masculine primitive, and a deliberate linkage between white supremacy and male dominance'. Theodore Roosevelt 'became a vigorous proponent of this new ideal, leading "Rough Riders" in the Spanish-American War and exhorting American men to take up "the strenuous life"'. Roosevelt even undertook a complete personal makeover from 'weakling' to his running for the mayor of New York as the 'Cowboy of the Dakotas' (McCall 2001: 1), 'refashioning himself as the embodiment of iconic western masculinity' as a result of a self-imposed exile in the Dakotas pursuing ranching, branding cattle and working the range. The setting was a tumultuous period in American masculinity, that:

> stemmed from a presumed breakdown in masculine authority … Some cite the crucible of the Civil War, others the closing of the frontier and its attendant loss of opportunity for the self-made man. Unstable economic conditions, the emergence of giant industrial combinations, and … the sheer dullness of urban-industrial culture … Dendangered the nonconformist entrepreneurial spirit. Working-class and immigrant men competed with middle-class men for control of the political arena. Women publicly challenged men to quit alcohol and give them the vote. In reaction to the growing sentimentalization and feminization of American culture, beleaguered men responded with muscular Christianity, the strenuous life, and pseudoscientific theories that stressed the mental and physical superiority of white males. The rugged, individualistic maverick of the West became a fashionable antidote to urban malaise. (McCall 2001: 5)

Importantly, this mythology was always mediated by commercial interests, especially metropolitan cultural and entertainment industries. As Smith (2003: 170) describes, depictions of cowboys in films, dime novels and paintings:

> popularized the notion that the western wilderness, free of the effeminizing forces of the city, challenged and therefore stimulated white men's masculinity. Their ideas appealed to middle-class men who found their work increasingly deskilled under corporate capitalism and who were threatened by the movement of women into the public sphere. Such Americans abandoned Victorian ideals of self-denial and restraint and celebrated strength and virility as the basic qualities of manhood.

Such critiques can also be applied to the twentieth-century practice of rodeo – organised competitions of bull-riding, rope-work and rounding-up stock that became especially popular in America, Canada and Australia (Hicks 2002). Elizabeth Lawrence (1982: 7), for instance, views rodeo as embodying 'the frontier spirit as manifested through the aggressive conquest of the West, and deals with nature and the reordering of nature according to this ethos. It supports the value of subjugating nature, and re-enacts the taming process where the wild is brought under control'. Contemporary forms of hegemonic cowboy masculinity maintain the hubristic assumption of a supreme domination over wild, feminine nature.

Cowboy masculinities in time and place

While there remains an important role for such critiques in challenging patriarchal power, my argument is that a focus on only the hegemonic cowboy masculinity (in the singular) nevertheless overlooks ambivalences and counter-possibilities. Historical geographical interpretation of cowboy masculinit*ies* provides room for alternative renderings of the past, and enables cowboys (in the plural) to be situated in more nuanced fashion within the jumble of people, objects, processes and relationships that constitute geographical places. Although hegemonic, heroic cowboy masculinity deserves critique, there is also the need for interrogation and critique of the inconsistencies that surrounded the cowboy figure in both Spanish and American colonial experiences, as well as later multivalent qualities of cowboy iconography and performed masculinities. Bringing these to light is itself an important political and performative act – decentring the cohesion of the stereotype of the cowboy and instead providing space to consider other kinds of masculinities enabled by the cowboy figure: for instance, those present among different national traditions, among indigenous peoples, within gay subcultures, and ethnically diverse communities.

The hegemonic cowboy figure also needs unpicking historically. Against a dominant and mythologised cowboy narrative, feminist historians have since sought to show a more dynamic, multicultural picture of colonial oppression, conflict and change: 'The romanticization and continuing currency of iconic Western manhood … veil many struggles against colonialism, conquest, and notions of white male supremacy' (McCall 2001: 6). Vaqueros were far from a romanticised figure: rounding up, moving and branding cattle were considered some of the lowest forms of work, and vaqueros were effectively indentured labour: employed by cattle ranchers to undertake menial work and rewarded often in rations rather than cash. Although a genealogical point of origin for the later American cowboy, the vaquero was unrecognisable in terms of the cowboy's later romantic mythology of the lonesome but free wanderer. Their lives were tightly constrained and surveilled under the authoritarian rule of ranchers and regional stockmen's associations.

In the American West, too, the cowboy was not so much a homogenous frontier figure embodying an emergent national individualism (as Turner's frontier thesis suggested), but rather a type of marginal agricultural worker, more likely drawn from diverse ethnic and national backgrounds, fulfilling a duty for the growing meat processing industry in a very specific time and place: the cattle drives of the 1860s and 1870s. Cowboys normally worked in camps as teams, and along established routes, rather than as wandering individuals; their job was to round up otherwise freely wandering cattle and transport them to railheads in Kansas. Their presence in newly emergent frontier towns was notable (more on that below), but exceptional. Much of the cowboy's working life was spent in a repetitive, unglamorous and uncomfortable form of itinerant work – the job of conquest already done by others.

In the American West cowboys were certainly not all ethnically white, either. Because Spanish ranchers looked down on cattle work, they contravened an earlier colonial decree to deny Native Americans access to horses – so as not to submit themselves to such menial work. Seizing on the proselytising activities of padres, ranchers 'chose to teach their new converts – Indians, Negroes, and other non-Spaniards – to ride horses and look after cattle' on their behalf (Dary 1989: 13). Significant numbers of African-Americans, Native Americans and Mexicans were attracted to the lifestyle and comparative freedom working as cowboys on the Texas cattle trails – up to a third of all post-Civil War cowboys, according to Iber (2000) – but nevertheless suffered the consequences of both hierarchical views on race and appalling working conditions.

The metropolitan cultural industry's heroic, hegemonic cowboy was also a highly malleable figure – later inviting appropriations and subversions. The cowboy would come to be a highly multivalent identity through which macho, camp and conservative masculine bodily identities could be performed. And there were limits to the hyper-masculinity of commercialised, popular culture cowboys. As Smith (2003: 170) describes, the hyper-masculine cowboy figure – isolated, morally relativist, tough to the point of being sadistic, stoic to the point of causticity – would have alienated female-dominated movie-palace audiences. Therefore:

> the cowboy actor and his screenwriters modified the message: if the natural environment made men strong and virile, it also caused them to become dangerous and unpredictable. Only through the influence of white women and Christianity would the frontiersman renounce his life of instinct, take up Victorian ideals of manliness, and become a responsible and contributing member of a western community. (Smith 2003: 170)

Hence the Broncho Billy films of the 1910s had a repeated script of the outlaw figure 'tamed' by Christian women, making the cowboy figure more palatable for urban middle-class nickelodeon audiences, but also reflecting emerging codes of masculine domesticity. Later incarnations in film, music and television negotiated this tension between conservatism and rebellion, through 'competing images of the cowboy as social outcast and the cowboy as socially respectable' (Garceau 2001: 153). In the 1950s the Nashville music industry fused hillbilly music, cowboy iconography and southern Baptist Christianity to create the 'country' music genre (Peterson 1997), but it too gave rise to outlaw figures such as Willie Nelson and Johnny Cash. For every prototype of the hegemonic, nationalistic, heroic cowboy there were darker doppelgangers.

Intersections, intimacies and interrelationships

Further revealing the contingency of cowboy masculinities are insights that emerge from historical work on sociological dimensions of frontier life – notably the interpersonal relations cowboys pursued and maintained with each other, with women, and with other men, in everyday life (Gibson 2013). Laura McCall (2001: 6) suggests that the frontier experience was 'a laboratory of gender where competing systems of social organization came into contact, often generating conflict as well as consensus'. No more was this apparent than in the embodied experiences of working cowboys themselves, on the plains and in cow-towns, as workers, and as social and sexual beings. Vernacular experiences of men in the 1860s, 1870s and 1880s – working alone or in men-only travelling camps on the great cattle trails – provide a much more heterogeneous record of interrelationships and ambivalences than suggested by the formulaic, heroic script of cowboy masculinity. According to historians, long months of isolation and the forming of peculiar bonds of friendship in the company of other men were followed by the intense hedonism of 'cutting loose' in the saloons, dance halls and red-light districts of cow-towns. Isolation and repression fuelled a dysfunctional view of women and an astringent, humourless and violent masculinity.

Homosexuality was present on the nineteenth-century cattle drives and on the frontier, with same-sex relations often referred to euphemistically as 'mutual solace' (Wilke 1995). Nevertheless sodomy laws and heteronormative mores prevailed, repressing expressions of homoeroticism. As with pirates and sailors, same-sex sexuality was a lived response to isolation (Rupp 1999). Boundaries were decidedly blurred between sexual orientations and between intimate acts and asexual companionship practices (Packard 2006). Contrary to the myth of stoic individualism, 'cowboys created distinctive relationship patterns suited to nomadic life ... the record is poignant with their need for human companionship' (Garceau 2001: 154). So-called 'bunkies' were cowboys who paired up as sleeping partners, a survival strategy to share body warmth on freezing nights but also an intimate expression of same-sex bonding (Rupp 1999: 55). Cowboys in the nineteenth century were also drawn from a diversity of cultures (including Mexican, African-American and Chinese) within which same-sex relations were viewed differently. The picture is of a much more heterogeneous interplay of emergent masculinities, experiments and emotional bonds.

Yet another historical dismantling of the heroic cowboy figure is warranted around the presumed relationships that also existed between men and animals – at roundups, on ranches, at rodeos. Although superficially reinforcing the masculine domination of nature through the taming of the wild beast, the rodeo can be re-read – especially in circumstances as diverse as outback Australia, where participation of Aboriginal stockmen is widespread – as a specific form of human-animal encounter, replete with nuances. Within rodeo the animal's agency is of course essential: bulls in nearly every case discharge their human rider violently, causing frequent injuries in the process, and they are named and followed by fans, much as sports enthusiasts might follow the careers of individual human competitors in tennis or golf. As Richard Davis writes in the context of Aboriginal Australia – where cowboy activities such as rodeo provide a means to articulate engaged relationships with the nonhuman world – 'a more substantial response ... is possible if rodeo competition is regarded as more than human dominance over animals, as many riders experience a relationship to the animal they ride where the boundaries between animal and human are fluid' (Davis 2005: 151). Even in this most rugged form, where hegemonic masculinity seems most strongly buttressed, there are instances of men extending relations of care and respect, and maintaining deep emotional links to the land, to their country.

In Australia's remote north, where Aboriginal communities have fused cowboy culture into their own ceremonial life, a hybrid modernity has thus been negotiated as a consequence of colonialism and the imposition of pastoral stations over their traditional lands; hence 'Aboriginal men used cattle work to regain or retain their pride as men, in a colonial context' (McGrath 1987: 46). Landscape was an active agent in the construction of personal identities, including those of working cowboys and rodeo riders (McWilliam 2005). In this context too, the skill and athleticism of Aboriginal cowboys has provided a means to negotiate race, gaining respect from non-Aboriginal pastoralists. Nevertheless, 'there was the inevitable reinforcement of the connection between Indigenous masculinity, Nature and physicality' (Hunter 2008: 83). Cowboy masculinities have thus become a vehicle to further racialise the 'savage' Aborigine 'though a focus on Aboriginal bodies and "traditional" skills' (Hunter 2008: 83). Masculinity, race and Indigeneity intersect in complex and context-specific ways.

Bodies, boots and clothes

Finally, cowboy masculinities – both heroic and vernacular variants – are relationally entwined with the development of a particular 'look', most obviously realised in clothing and accessories. The evolution of cowboy material culture reflected Spanish-Mexican antecedents, though cowboy clothing as we have now come to know it – western snap shirts, chaps, blue jeans, boots, hats – settled into a formula in the 1930s and 1940s as elements of working cowboy clothing were transformed into an emblematic on-stage genre. During this time of intense commercialisation a specialist cultural/fashion industry grew, supplying the various essential costume elements. Wild West performers, rodeo riders and western silent film stars such as Tom Mix and Buck Jones sewed their costumes themselves, or had them made by expert tailors such as Nathan Turk, Rodeo Ben, and Nudie Cohn, conveniently concentrated in Hollywood. Film heartthrob William S. Hart chose costumes that appeared 'authentic' to the frontier experience, epitomizing the 'austere realist', but he was an exception. Working cowboys bought stock clothes from dry goods stores, whereas rodeo, film and recording stars had tailors produce evermore stylised and exaggerated designs.

Cowboy clothing enabled manhood to be refashioned. Lines and embellishments were steadily dramatised in order to amplify masculinity and sex appeal. Western shirts from the start were 'form-fit and flattering to the slim physique' (Weil and DeWeese 2004: 35). Although true that tight-fitting shirts and snaps were practical for working cowboys (they were less likely to snag, and snaps enabled shirts to pop open when caught, without damage), 'when Western Wear came into being it was mainly popular with young, slim men' (Weil and DeWeese 2004: 35) for whom it enhanced muscular body shapes (Figure 8.1). Other elements in the twentieth-century evolution in the design of western clothing aided a masculine sexual ideal: leather cuffs once worn to protect the wrists from rope burns lent distinctive lines to the sewn cuffs and plackets on later cowboy shirts (distinctive 6-snap cuffs known as 'shotgun cuffs' that amplified the impression of strong wrists and forearms); flap pockets, piping and bib fronts reflected a military influence; and distinctive, stylised front yokes emphasised broad shoulders and pectoral muscles. Lines of hats, shirts and boots from companies such as Rockmount, Miller, Justin, Tony Lama, ACME and Nocona carried suitably macho, adventurous frontier names: 'The Idaho', 'The Ranger', 'The Laredo', 'The Thunderbird', 'The Stallion', 'The Sharpshooter', 'The Rodeo King' (Figure 8.2). The cowboy boot, in particular, would become an especially multivalent object, the wearing of which enabled macho, camp and conservative masculine bodily identities to be performed (Gibson forthcoming). Clothing and boot design in the process pushed boundaries between rugged individualism and camp effeminacy, between a conservative rancher 'look' and other more subcultural and subversive variants (fusing with punk, rockabilly, biker and gay identities).

Figure 8.1 Lee Western Wear advertisement, 1962 – 'Gives You That Slim, Trim Fit'

Source: Miller Stockman mail order catalogue No. 133, p. 46 [private collection of the author].

Figure 8.2 Cowboy hat advertisement, 1946. Western wear manufacturers marketed lines of hats, shirts and boots that were individually named, evoking frontier individualism and enabling personal customization of masculine identities

Source: Miller Stockman mail order catalogue No. 71, p. 17 [private collection of the author].

Following John Travolta's film *Urban Cowboy* (1978) was a global fad for western wear and boots, which fused with the growth in urban country music bars and disco clubs (George-Warren and Freedman 2006). Again, the themes of transmogrified masculinity and escape from repressive conditions of urban life resonated. Blue jeans became astonishingly tight, and slim fit western shirts for both sexes became even slimmer (produced using fabrics such as satin, polyester and denim that enhanced the appearance of svelte figures). A far cry from the clean-cut, clean-shaven appearances of early silent western film stars, the 'plainsman hunter' look boomed, with long-hair, horseshoe moustache and/or goatee beard (also popular with bikie gangs). This was an open invitation to camp, and unsurprisingly it became a *de rigueur* model of deportment in the urban gay subcultures of the 1970s and 1980s. Conservative elements of the cattle industry and western wear industries reacted negatively: their western shirts became plainer, lost their decorative yokes and replaced snaps with regular buttons; working cowboys shifted their preferences to plain 'roper' boots without Cuban underslung heels, while custom-made boots became more elaborate, an art-form now the province of collectors, film stars and Houston oil-barons.

Meanwhile in Aboriginal Australia wearing cowboy clothes and boots took on a rather different inflection. As Richard Davis (2005: 154) vividly described:

> Scratch an Aboriginal man long enough in the Fitzroy Valley region of the Kimberley and you will undoubtedly find he was or is a cowboy. Even those men who no longer are fit enough to handle the rigours of long hours of station work, will express their cowboy experience and pride in their dress: a large hat with upturned brim, press-stud shirt, blue jeans and riding boots. This gear says he is able to handle himself in the saddle and with cattle, is conversant with a stoic work ethic, and likely he also has a cosmological knowledge and experience of land that cattle are moved across.

In such circumstances becoming a cowboy, participating in rodeo and wearing cowboy clothes had, for some young Aboriginal men, replaced ceremonial means to initiation in tribal life: 'some young Aboriginal cowboys actively seek to identify their relationships to land as cowboys, rather than through the mythico-ritual aspects associated with initiation' (155). Across the Pacific, cowboy masculinities became even more composite, context-dependent, and contested.

Conclusion

There is more to the cowboy than holsters, guns and hegemonic expressions of masculinity. I have sought to briefly discuss here some of the contradictions, intersections and specificities surrounding the performance of cowboy masculinities. At times the promotion of cowboy masculinities has been motivated by profit, as in the commodification of heroic cowboys by film, television and music industries; in other examples it has been cultural, and strategic, pursued by men constrained by experiences of colonialism and race, who nevertheless reconstruct manliness with whatever materials and resources are at hand (cf. Hopkins and Noble 2009: 814). Cowboy masculinities are revealed as relational and intersectional – entwined with identifications and discourses of race, colonialism, gender, class, rurality and work.

Pursuing the more complex, relational processes through which cowboy masculinities are produced does not mean abandoning a critique of the operation of power, or acting as an apologist for cowboy aggression or conservatism. There is always the potential for the cowboy figure to be appropriated by conservative and oppressive forces (take, for example, the appropriation of elements of cowboy rhetoric by ex-Texan Governor, George W. Bush, within an overtly aggressive and imperialist US Presidential style). Such appropriations demand censure. Likewise the point is not to simply place men back into the 'limelight' of feminist analysis, but rather to appreciate how masculinities intersect with structures of power and oppression (Longhurst 2000), including where dominant or formulaic (singular) masculinities are appropriated or subverted.

Although I have sought here to open up the cowboy figure to historical geographical interpretation, thus developing a more heterogeneous picture, I do nevertheless freely admit that interpretation of cowboy masculinities brought together here remains necessarily partial – reflecting my own interests as a geographer with personal passions for Americana and for Australian cowboy variants. I focused on cowboys and masculinity, leaving untold equally important stories of cowgirls and femininities (but see Jordan 1984). There are even more diverse examples such as the Mexican *charro*, Hawaiian *paniolo*, Argentinean and Uruguayan *gaucho*, Chilean *huaso*, Peruvian *chalan* or French *gardian* (but see for example Rainger 2000). Opportunities abound for scholars of masculinity to further probe intersections and identifications within these different national and cultural contexts. The agenda is not just to enchant our understanding of the cowboy figure, but through it to trace the interrelationships between normative (and often commercially propagated) hegemonic masculinities and vernacular juxtapositions and counter-expressions.

References

Basso, M., McCall, L. and Garceau, D. 2001. *Across the Great Divide: Cultures of Manhood in the American West*. New York: Routledge.

Bell, D. 2000. Farm boys and wild men: rurality, masculinity, and homosexuality. *Rural Sociology*, 65(4), 547–561.

Berg, L.D. and Longhurst, R. 2003. Placing masculinities and geography. *Gender, Place and Culture: A Journal of Feminist Geography*, 10(4), 351–360.

Connell, R.W. 2005. *Masculinities*. 2nd edition. Cambridge: Polity Press.

Connell, R.W. and Messerschmidt, J.W. 2005. Hegemonic masculinity: rethinking the concept. *Gender and Society*, 19(6), 829–859.

Dary, D. 1989. *Cowboy Culture: A Saga of Five Centuries*. Lawrence: Kansas University Press.

Davis, R. 2005. Eight seconds: style, performance and crisis in Aboriginal rodeo, in *Dislocating the Frontier: Essaying the Mystique of the Outback*, edited by D.B. Rose and R. Davis. Canberra: Australian National University Press, 145–164.

Garceau, D. 2001. Nomads, bunkies, cross-dressers, and family men: cowboy identity and the gendering of ranch work, in *Across the Great Divide: Cultures of Manhood in the American West*, edited by M. Basso, L. McCall and D. Garceau. New York: Routledge, 149–168.

George-Warren, H. and Freedman, M. 2006. *How the West Was Worn: A History of Western Wear*. New York: Harry N. Abrams.

Gibson, C. 2013. The global cowboy: rural masculinities and sexualities, in *Sexuality, Rurality, and Geography*, edited by A. Gorman-Murray, B. Pini and L. Bryant. Lanham: Lexington, 199–218.

Gibson, C. (in press) Texan boots, *Tourist Studies*.

Gorman-Murray, A. 2008. Masculinity and the home: a critical review and conceptual framework. *Australian Geographer*, 39(3), 367–380.

Gorman-Murray, A., Waitt, G. and Gibson, C. 2008. A queer country? A case study of the politics of gay/lesbian belonging in an Australian country town. *Australian Geographer*, 39(2), 171–191.

Hicks, J. 2002. *Australian Cowboys, Roughriders & Rodeos*. Rockhampton: Central Queensland University Press.

Hopkins, P. and Noble, G. 2009. Masculinities in place: situated identities, relations and intersectionality. *Social and Cultural Geography*, 10(8), 811–819.

van Hoven, B. and Hörschelmann, K. (eds) 2005. *Spaces of Masculinities*. London: Routledge.

Hunter, K. 2008. Rough riding: Aboriginal participation in rodeos and travelling shows to the 1950s. *Aboriginal History*, 32(1), 82–96.

Iber, J. 2000. Vaqueros in the Western cattle industry, in *The Cowboy Way: An Exploration of History and Culture*, edited by P.H. Carlson. Lubbock: Texas Tech University Press, 21–32.

Jordan, T. 1984. *Cowgirls: Women of the American West: An Oral History*. New York: Doubleday.

Lawrence, E.A. 1982. *Rodeo: An Anthropologist Looks at the Wild and the Tame*. Knoxville: University of Tennessee Press.

Longhurst, R. 2000. Geography and gender: masculinities, male identity and men. *Progress in Human Geography*, 24(3), 439–444.

McCall, L. 2001. Introduction, in *Across the Great Divide: Cultures of Manhood in the American West*, edited by M. Basso, L. McCall and D. Garceau. New York: Routledge, 1–24.

McGrath, A. 1987. *Born in the Cattle: Aborigines in Cattle Country*. North Sydney: Allen and Unwin.

McWilliam, A. 2005. Absence and plenitude: appropriating the Fitzmaurice River frontier, in *Dislocating the Frontier: Essaying the Mystique of the Outback*, edited by D.B. Rose and R. Davis. Canberra: Australian National University Press, 177–196.

Packard, C. 2006. *Queer Cowboys: And Other Erotic Male Friendships in Nineteenth-Century American Literature*. New York: Palgrave Macmillan.

Peterson, R. 1997. *Creating Country Music: Fabricating Authenticity*. Chicago: University of Chicago Press.

Rainger, J.G. 2000. French cowboys: the gardians of the Camargue and Buffalo Bill, in *The Cowboy Way: An Exploration of History and Culture*, edited by P.H. Carlson. Lubbock: Texas Tech University Press, 167–178.

Rupp, L.J. 1999. *A Desired Past: A Short History of Same-Sex Love in America*. Chicago: University of Chicago Press.

Smith, A.B. 2003. *Shooting Cowboys and Indians: Silent Western Films, American Culture, and the Birth of Hollywood*. Boulder: University Press of Colorado.

Stanley, P. 2012. Superheroes in Shanghai: constructing transnational Western men's identities. *Gender, Place and Culture: A Journal of Feminist Geography*, 19(2), 213–231.

Tucker, A.B. 2000. Reel cowboys: cowhands and western movies, in *The Cowboy Way: An Exploration of History and Culture*, edited by P.H. Carlson. Lubbock: Texas Tech University Press, 179–200.

Waitt, G. and Warren, A. 2008. 'Talking shit over a brew after a good session with your mates': surfing, space and masculinity. *Australian Geographer*, 39(3), 353–366.

Weil, S. and DeWeese, D. 2004. *Western Shirts: A Classic American Fashion*. Salt Lake City: Gibbs Smith.

Wilke, J. 1995. Frontier comrades: homosexuality in the America West, in *Out in All Directions: The Almanac of Gay and Lesbian America*, edited by L. Witt, S. Thomas and E. Marcus. New York: Warner Books, 164–172.

PART 3
Masculinities and Home

Chapter 9
The Geographies of Military Inculcation and Domesticity: Reconceptualising Masculinities in the Home

Stephen Atherton

In this chapter I challenge the traditional theorisations of military identities through both an examination of domesticity as a conceptual term and an analysis of the inculcation of domestic skills during military service. This examination counterpoints the hegemonic masculinities that one would expect to encounter in the highly masculinised institution of the military and seeks to identify how domesticity is used as a means of 'breaking in' new soldiers to the military hierarchy. One key objective following on from the military's inculcation of domestic skills is to explore how the skills are subsequently utilised outside of military domestic spaces. Once demobilised, many of the soldiers in this study returned to a 'family home', yet they had to readjust to civilian life and acclimatise to new domestic routines and spaces. This chapter begins with an outline of current scholarship focusing on the nature of military masculinities, before an analysis of masculinities in the home. Specifically I note how scholarship on 'the home' in relation masculinity has shifted from feminist approaches to analysing domestic divisions of labour, into more recent work that has focused on the changing nature of masculinities and domesticity through the proliferation of masculine subjectivities and the home. I then draw upon my own research to examine issues of domesticity and the changing sense of 'home' for army men during their military service and subsequently following demobilisation.

Military masculinities

The Armed Forces are considered as 'masculine institutions' insofar as the majority of their population is male, but also because they are a significant reservoir for the articulation of masculinity within society at large (see Addelston and Stirrat 1996, Barrett 2001, Connell 1995, Sasson-Levy 2003). There have been numerous studies of the nature of masculinities produced within the military that have focused on traditional 'hard bodied' approaches to understanding the performances and identities of these men (see Agostino 1998, Atherton 2009, Barrett 2001, Connell 1995, 2000, Gill 1997, Enloe 2000, 2004, Higate 2000, 2003, Hockey 1986, 2003,

Kronsell 2005, Lahelma 2005, Morgan 1994, Sasson-Levy 2003, Woodward 1998, 2003, 2004, Woodward and Winter 2007). As Jackson notes, such men are expected to 'take a few knocks and still come through smiling' (1991: 204). According to Francis (2002), the military has long been a source of escapist fantasy for men, fuelled by song and spectacle. In the eighteenth century, English gentlemen looked to the military as the antithesis of an increasingly 'effeminate' urbanity, spoiled by trivia and luxury (Carter 1997). In Belgium, in the 1830s, Hoegarts (2010: 252) comments on how military manoeuvres against a picturesque backdrop provided a grand spectacle of militarism and patriotism, royally recounted in newspapers of the period: 'No longer solely related to the space of the Barracks and a clearly delineated exercise field, a self-declared national masculinity became tied to the nation's soil and allowed itself to be formed and deformed by the "nation".'

Higate and Hopton (2004) suggest that over the course of the twentieth century this relationship between masculinity and militarism has been strengthened, as popular fiction and non-fiction have sought to encompass particular ideas around what it is to be manly. They note, for example, that:

> In the earlier span of the 1914–1918 war recruitment of volunteer soldiers owed much to Victorian ideologies that defined masculinity in terms of strength, courage, determination and patriotism. In turn, this image of masculinity was reinforced by wartime propaganda that glamorized military culture and military success and that tacitly encouraged brutality toward war resisters. (2004: 433)

The perceived glamorisation of these particular identities highlighted the requirements of the military but also sought to marginalise those who were deemed to be subordinate. A common theme amongst academics writing on the military is that a unique set of militarised, masculine identities are produced and performed through the day to day activities of the soldier (see Barratt 1996, 2001, Collinson and Hearn 1994, Woodward and Winter 2007). Here, it is the institutionalised, routinised behaviours expected within the military that are seen as productive of particular subjectivities. Hence, Barratt (1996: 141) writes: 'The military is a gendered institution. Its structure, practices, values, rites and rituals reflect accepted notions of masculinity and femininity. But it is also a gendering institution. It helps to create gendered identities.'

Barrett (2001) makes a specific connection to Irving Goffman's theory of the institution, in that it destabilises existing identities and reconstitutes them according to its requirements. In a similar vein, Hale (2008) suggests that military culture has its own distinctive identity and, moreover, that this is a heavily circumscribed one. Key to this process is the heavily regimented routine of military life, but also the constant association of particular meanings with these performances, which confer a strong sense of surety. Importantly, Hale argues that this subjectification – or militarisation – is not a one size fits all process, nor is it a wholesale conversion. Rather, she identifies that there are key events that are significant within the transition from civilian to soldier, each requiring a process of individual learning and the development of skills that are useful for soldiering. She suggests that recruits are set a number of challenges that are intended to 'break' them and those that do not perform sufficiently well are thus deemed unsuitable for the process of militarisation insofar as they do not conform to the required standards for a military role.

Masculinities and the home

As much work within feminist geography has made clear, the home is much more than a physical dwelling space; it is linked through ideologies and practices to local networks and community and, on a larger scale, to national identities (McDowell 1997b). For many feminist geographers the modern-day home is part of a broader spatial geography of public and private (Rose 1993, Duncan 1994), with the latter being more closely circumscribed in terms of mobility (England 1993). In many feminist critiques the home has been described as place of leisure for men, but an oppressive site of labour for women (Ahrentzen 1997, McDowell 1997a, 1997b, 1999, Rose 1993).

In more recent scholarship the proliferation of new masculine subjectivities within the home has led to a re-examination of the relationship between masculinities and domesticity. For example, Meah and Jackson (2013) identify the complex negotiations of masculinities in the kitchen, but note that there has been a shift in men's relationships with these spaces. They suggest that men enter such spaces on their own terms as a 'lifestyle choice' rather than to prepare food in the traditional familial sense. Meah and Jackson (2013: 15) note, 'Indeed, new kitchens are no longer simply concessions made by husbands to wives but, rather, spaces in which masculine identities are also inscribed.' Walsh (2011) notes that while little work has been conducted on home-making practices of heterosexual men, there has been a body of work that focuses on the nature of the masculinities of gay men in relation to the home (see Gorman-Murray 2007, 2008). As I have previously identified (Atherton 2009), there is very little research into the experience of homosexual men within domestic spaces in the military.

There has also been a recent and significant body of work that has analysed men's emotional links to the home. This work identifies issues such as an emotional sense of belonging (Gorman-Murray 2011), fatherhood (Aitken 2009) and grandfathering (Tarrant 2010, 2013). Tarrant (2013) notes that grandparents are often present within familial domestic spaces yet are an under-researched group within geography. She notes that, traditionally, ageing was deemed to 'de-gender' males, but when grandparents are required to look after grandchildren, new masculinities of care emerge that challenge these traditional conceptualisations. Cox (2013) suggests that caring has been conventionally associated with femininity. However, in her research with 'handymen', Cox (2013) notes that masculine identities emerge as these men had a duty of care to their family to maintain the home. Gorman-Murray (2011) similarly notes that performing domestic maintenance tasks can reaffirm men's identities and masculinities in situations where the global financial collapse has caused unemployment and therefore a challenge to the traditional role of 'breadwinner'. In her work on migration, masculinities and domesticity, Walsh (2011) notes that some of the men in her study developed an idealised sense of home and domesticity in a response to short-term residence abroad and would therefore not manifest the emotional link identified in the previous studies cited. Home-making emerged as a key issue in Walsh's (2011) research and was also important in Gorman-Murray's (2013) research into masculine homebodies, which sought to identify insights into gendered dimensions of domesticity and work/life balance. What all of these recent studies have in common is a challenge to the traditional concepts of hegemonic masculinity (Connell 1995) and instead invite a more fluid, contextual and place-based approach to the study of masculinities.

Domestication and the military

As noted earlier in this chapter the military is more often than not seen as a distinct and separate entity from the rest of society. And, the military has often been discussed as distinct from the 'domestic realm' (see Gagen 2009). As I have previously noted, 'within the military, much has been made of the need to protect "hearth and home" and yet its very reproduction depends upon the successful subsuming of home-making skills' (Atherton 2009: 827). Furthermore, military accommodation and associated activities have tended to be viewed as unique and somewhat isolated. Within training Barracks, for example, recruits can initially expect to be housed in dormitories and divided from their families. Later in a soldier's career they may choose to live in Army accommodation with or without their families. For Soeters, Winslow and Weibull (2006), these Army houses are as much about maintaining separation and distinction as the repertoires of masculinities discussed earlier in this chapter. They suggest that:

> Military organizations represent a specific occupational culture which is relatively isolated from society. Military people not only work in separated Barracks and bases, but they also live (here frequently and sometimes their wives and children as well). Cadets and recruits get their training in specific schools and academies, where a sense of uniqueness is emphasized … (2006: 237)

In his detailed analysis of Naval accommodation and domesticity, Colville (2009: 512) suggests that living areas aboard naval vessels were aimed at distancing junior officers from feminised stereotypes:

> This process of prising apart male and female identity was considered most urgent among junior officers, who might still bear the imprint of maternal cosseting. With its extrovert communality and suppression of compassionate love, the male

> domesticity of the gunroom (as with its public school equivalent) was intended to distance midshipmen from feminised contexts that would weaken resolve and impede progress to manhood. Within this space, feminised stereotypes of domestic perfection were overturned through a rhetoric of scruffy dilapidation.

Here Colville suggests that the 'scruffy dilapidation' identified with particular rhetorics of masculinity, which new recruits were expected to adhere to. This apparent de-feminisation of living space in the Navy is in sharp contrast, however, with the scrupulous neatness expected of Army Barracks. And, according to Hockey (1986), it is because of the association of cleanliness and femininity that many soldiers feel they have been rendered effeminate by Army routine and discipline. He notes that:

> … while some of the activities they encounter match the expectations they hold, there is a variety of other activities used by superiors primarily to inculcate discipline … there is for example, a sudden immersion in activities of a domestic nature … involving and the path a logical concern cleanliness, neatness and uniformity. These are activities which, set against an 'action-image', are seen as female character. (1986: 51)

The inculcation of discipline is intended to motivate troops and to exemplify the dominance of officers over the ordinary 'squaddie'. Hockey (1986: 51) suggests that: 'While the shaming ineptness they show in the first month motivates nearly all recruits to smarten themselves up, this aspiration is rarely in strict conformity to the standards of neatness, cleanliness and uniformity demanded by their training team superiors'. The nature of these domestic activities included 'washing dishes, moving stores, cleaning equipment and accommodation, or some other tasks designated by superiors' (Hockey 1986: 51) and were perceived as taking the soldier away from their real duties. Hockey (1986: 53) notes how:

> Unofficial evening fatigues may be given to him on the occasions when the various support and administrative echelons of the depot require manpower, to fulfil various tasks. NCOs may also order the recruit to complete fatigue tasks within their own living accommodation, such as cleaning toilets, or giving the floor polish. Again such activities clash with the action image of real soldiering, as well as taking up precious time and energy.

Therefore it is clear that there is a level of complexity that underpins the apparent hegemonic masculinities that are created within the Army. With the seemingly 'effeminate' nature of the work that is involved within domestic spaces there is in fact an overriding element of power and hierarchy within these activities. These activities are seen as a measure of discipline, but are also used to punish and to break the spirit of new recruits so that they can be inculcated into the military mindset.

This hierarchical, power-laden relationship is firmly inscribed into domestic, military space, as access is strictly circumscribed according to rank. Therefore, a further level of complexity is added to the already difficult situation of the soldier in military training. Not only are they forced to produce what they perceive of as 'effeminate' work, but equally they are confined to particular spaces that their rank and position within the hierarchy dictates.

Researching military men

To explore these issues of masculinity and domesticity I engaged in extensive interviews with 32 members of the armed forces (and partners where possible) who had all been regular squaddies and had left the Army in the past 25 years. The 25-year period was decided upon firstly because, as noted by Connell (2005) and Jackson (1991), for example, there have been significant theoretical developments in how masculinities are analysed. Developments in understanding the multiple and fluid performances of masculinities and indeed the development of alternative theoretical personas such as the 'new man', have substantially reworked this object of analysis. Secondly, the past 25 years have seen a change in how the military is viewed socially. Kronsell (2005) notes that following the Cold War the military was essentially 'feminised' and the key operations were 'peace keeping'. Yet, following 9/11 and the war on terror, Kronsell suggests that we have seen the re-masculinisation of the military and a changed perception of soldiers in society and media. To place these experiences within modern and historical contexts I also analysed several tranches of archival reports dating back to the 1940s, which identified Ministry of Defence and government policies in relation to army training, accommodation and, most surprisingly, the distinct emphasis on family that was present in post-World War II literature. Indeed, it is this institutional emphasis on the family, in addition to the various routines of domestication experienced in barracks spaces that were the most unexpected findings from this research.

The inculcation of domestic routines to 'break in' new recruits

During basic training, recruits are placed in dormitories that house between eight and 20 men. Once basic training is completed individual rooms are assigned but amenities such as bathrooms, kitchens, common rooms and laundry rooms are shared between recruits in the same building. And, as Hockey (1986) notes, during their service in the Army many men are deeply immersed into domestic routines that are constructed as feminine. Regular inspections are made of domestic spaces and everything within the domestic space has its place. Andy (aged 23, demobilised for four years, lives with his parents) identified that these punishments are very much seen as a means of breaking in new recruits (see also Atherton 2009):

> … they check for dirt and you know it has to be spotless they find anything and you're for it. Sometimes they were real bastards and would move out the lockers and see if you had cleaned behind them, if you hadn't then they would mess up the whole room untidy everything and give you an hour to put it right and do the cleaning that they wanted as well. If you didn't do it right then they would make you do push ups or runs to punish you more.

And:

> They check everything, your lockers, your beds and you know it all has to be tidy, ironed and folded.

According to Tom (aged 40, divorced, demobilised for five years):

> You got all your meals cooked for you but sometimes you had to use your own eating kit and wash it but they … err … well they had to know that under combat conditions you could survive so you could cook for yourself and look after yourself … I mean most of it was your appearance, you had to look a certain way, dress a certain way everything worn in the correct place. It was quite terrifying at first, you know, having your boots inspected for dirt of scuffs but you get used to it eventually, you know how to please them.

A different sense of 'home'

For some of the men in this study *home* was not the concrete space in which they inhabited during military service, but was an imagined space that held emotional connection. Peter (aged 37, lives with partner, demobilised for ten years), suggested that the domestic routines during training were very much a part of the Army's attempts at home-making. Yet, as I have previously noted (see Atherton 2009), Peter challenged the very concept of barrack spaces being *home*:

> **Peter**: You get moved around so much. It's like for a few months you'll be in one set of digs then you'll be moved somewhere else, even like abroad, as far away from home as you can imagine.
>
> **Interviewer**: So really you never thought of the barracks as home?
>
> **Peter**: No I didn't really have a home. The Army likes you to think that they're your home if that makes sense, but for me I'm at home when I'm out with my mates on leave, going back to my roots and my old drinking places.

Here, Peter distances himself from the idea of home as the place wherein he eats and sleeps. This is in part because of his identification of his military role as a career, to be performed outside of the home. There are also clear parallels with Walsh's (2011) work where migrant males developed an idealised sense of home, when they knew that the domestic space they currently inhabited was short term. For Peter, the Barracks remained a site wherein he was trained and disciplined; and not a space where he would expect to perform home-making practises. Peter says: 'I was so much more relaxed, I was on leave and so the whole town was going to know about it. We tore it up, me and my mates, different pubs, women, clubs you know we had a right good time'. Equally Tom felt that the army base where he was stationed was not *home*:

> I met my wife who was stationed at the Barracks up the road … When we met it was difficult, you know, we had to try to meet when we had time off. I mean I was lucky that I had a relatively normal job, normal hours you know after all the training you become useful to them and they give you more leeway. When [my wife] got pregnant we moved into a place together, that was our first real home. I enjoyed my time on base but actually getting our own place was great. I could still travel to work and do my bit for queen and country [laughs] but as I said I was lucky. I know other careers where you couldn't do that.

Here, Tom relates home to the place where he and his wife were able to settle down and look after their child. The military home was in many ways an 'artificial' home where Tom felt no emotional attachment (see also Atherton 2009).

For Kevin (aged 31, divorced, demobilised for two years), home was also 'outside' of the Army, when he could be with his girlfriend and his family. In the following, he describes the problems in being away from his family, which then leads into a discussion about his own sense of home:

> **Kevin**: All in all the military doesn't want you to leave them so they try to make you feel as at home as they can.
>
> **Interviewer**: So what did they do? Did they try to make it less formal or was it more about the atmosphere?
>
> **Kevin**: They try to keep us occupied I suppose it was very difficult because they didn't really appreciate that we all had a home you know I had a girlfriend out there and I wanted to be at home with her not stuck here but at the same time I was really enjoying being in the Army so I was really caught between a rock and a hard place so to speak.
>
> **Interviewer**: So did you in effect feel that your home was outside of the Army and therefore what was the Army, was it a work place?

> **Kevin**: More than a work place in that we didn't go to work we lived at work but it isn't home is it really? Because that's like not at work and that's where you go to chill out so really it's away from the Army.

This disassociation is exacerbated by the fact that, as mentioned earlier, throughout their period of military training, military men may be forced to move up to three times in order to achieve various states of training. Specific military bases deal with certain aspects of training and so soldiers may be on base in the initial basic training period, yet then be moved to a more specialist base in the area of which they wish to pursue their Army career. Once qualified as an Army member it is then likely that the soldier will be stationed in a variety of bases throughout the United Kingdom and then possibly even abroad.

For Alan (aged 52, married with three children, demobilised for 11 years), for example, it was far better that his family stayed put in one place, 'at home', while he travelled between various bases working as a soldier. As he describes it:

> My missus and the kids stayed put, better for them and better for me because I didn't have to worry about them moving all over the place with me. I kept a clear head I could focus on being a soldier, bloody hell staying alive looking after yourself is bad enough without adding the family nearby. They were two different worlds, we knew it wouldn't be for ever and so I saw her and the little ones on leave, to be fair I ended up having most Christmases with them but I could not have dealt with having to move them with me.

Alan's approach to dealing with the enforced mobility of troops within the military is particularly interesting as he is clearly a compassionate, family man who wanted his family to have geographic stability while he worked for a living. He is evidently constructing his role as a father and husband within the context of a stereotypical provider/protector masculinity. However, his suggestion that it was self-preservation that dictated these actions is equally interesting as it identifies the simultaneous production of a warrior persona, who puts his body on the line in the course of duty.

Domesticity following demobilisation

Earlier I noted the constructions of masculinities within the Army and how these were reiteratively performed, to a certain degree, within military domestic spaces. Much of the training in Army Barracks is based upon routine and the times that one must eat, sleep, shower, train and rest, for example, were dictated and enforced to such an extent that they became ingrained into the daily lives of the soldiers. Upon discharge from the military these routines still played a prominent part of many of the men's daily lives. For example, Brian (aged 27, married, demobilised for one year after eight years of service) described the lingering effects of his military training:

> I was still waking up at five in the morning. You get used to having no sleep so much that you well just can't get out of it. I didn't start work until nine so I go for a run in the morning until the missus wakes up to make breakfast.

Here Brian highlights the division of household labour within his home as he bides his time until his wife is able to prepare breakfast. In the Army all of Brian's meals were cooked for him; when it came to performing this domestic skill, Brian simply did not expect it to be his responsibility. This allowed him to retain his hyper-masculine identity by continuing to train his body through exercise.

For Liam (aged 27, lives alone but in a relationship, demobilised for five years), dis-engaging from the military routine was particularly difficult, a situation exacerbated by a mild obsessive-compulsive disorder (amongst other medical health issues) that had led to him being medically discharged:

> They really committed to you that you have to keep everything clean. Do I mean committed? I think so yeah committed. It had to be committed anyway because if you didn't big problems. So I left yeah and God I couldn't stop it just kept on going. You know getting up at the same time clean myself make sure the clothes clean smart it's not necessarily a bad thing but I may be went a bit far in those first few months. And partly I suppose as I was on my own it made it harder to break out of that routine had someone else been there they could have had a word and made me stop.

And:

> It started with very little things like every morning I'd pull out the settee and Hoover underneath it. Sounds ridiculous doesn't it all it's true sorry all of its true a bit hard to explain but you know I clean for about an hour every day and that presented its own problems really because it began to really affect me you know mentally. So gone a bit obsessed with it all and I'd be hoovering maybe the same room to three times a day and that's not good.

What is particularly interesting here is that Liam perceived the routines in the home as an extension of the Barracks themselves. So by hoovering the same room three times a day, or pulling out the settee every day to clean, he was not consciously performing domestic labour for the sake of domestic labour; rather he was reproducing the skills that had been taught and perpetually reinforced, during his time with the Army.

For Steven (aged 36, married, demobilised for six–seven years), particular elements of domesticity were a problem. In the following excerpt he discusses some of the issues he had cooking and cleaning following demobilisation:

> I was a horrible horrible cook really horrible. Cause it's all done for you isn't it? You know in the Army they cook for you give your meals on time every day. Learn a bit about cleaning and you have to do certain things within your own place especially in that first period they really crack down on any kind of dirt you name it. When I got out I didn't have a clue what to do and know anything, just about managed to boil a kettle. Typical man as those that say. Man I tell you if you can see my flat in those days well Sarah (his wife) will tell you she's come round and cleaned and tided the thing. The thing was I thought I'd already clean and tidied up.

His partner, Sarah, explained further:

> He was absolutely hopeless nothing was tidied away, things just lying around waiting for someone to put them back. I think he was quite embarrassed the first time I saw his flat but then I started to clean it for him and I think I was almost a replacement mother tidying up after the naughty little boy [laughs]. Still useless now bless him but he does try. He can't cook at all, he'll tell you he can, but there's no way you'd want to eat anything he cooks. It does have its uses, all the heavy lifting and putting up shelves doing all the bloke's jobs.

This interview highlights the gender perceptions of household work within this particular family home. In particular, Sarah sees Steven fitting very much into the male stereotype of household work, by stating that she has to cook and clean, but also that he has the 'masculine' jobs. These jobs seemed to be based on embodied skill and strength such as lifting putting up shelves. Steven, it seems, was not inculcated with the set of domestic skills that are generally enforced during military training.

Conclusion

As noted at the beginning of this chapter, a hegemonic masculinity has been predominant in the military (Barret 2001, Enloe 2000, 2004, Higate 2000, 2003, Hockey 2003, Kronsell 2005, Morgan 1994, Woodward 1998, 2003, 2004, Woodward and Winter 2007). In many studies, such as Woodward (2004), particular spaces such as the Barracks have been identified simply as militarised, such that there is a failure to see how these same spaces are often articulated as home. Moreover, as Gagen (2009) notes, these military domestic spaces are eschewed as 'real' homes by servicemen. Within my research, however, I have used domesticity as an analytic entry point in order to underscore that these subjectivities and the spaces they animate and inhabit, are not 'closed off' or distinct from civilian ones, but interweave time and again.

I note how military domestic spaces contain strict routines and demand the highest levels of cleanliness and tidiness. The inculcation of these domestic routines demonstrates the power and control that the higher echelons of the military hierarchy have over individual troops. Through analysing domesticity within military spaces one can better understand the means used to control soldiers within this environment. By enforcing domestic skills upon new recruits particularly the army inculcates domestic routine, embodied practices, while using these practices to 'feminise' troops as punishments for various misdemeanours. The process of empowerment and subsequent disempowerment is a tool that the military has developed to create obedient soldiers who are fit for purpose. What is particularly interesting here is how these domestic routines create a repertoire of behaviours that are unexpected and seemingly out of place. What is more, using soldier's narratives I demonstrate the varied and fluid subjectivities that prevail within these spaces, subjectivities that do not correspond with the circumscribed norms that exist. Within barracks, officers messes, single quarters, married quarters and Army housing, domesticity permeates; the military and domestic worlds are clearly interwoven and certainly not separate entities.

Undoubtedly, the Army does materially provide for certain forms of domestic life to emerge, whether in married quarters, the single Officers Mess, or Barracks. And, it has certain expectations as to how all manner of domestic practices will be carried out. Regardless of the fact that such activities are necessary for the functioning of the military itself, as some of my interviewees observed there is a distinct 'feminisation' at work here, as domestic chores become a matter of punishment and routine. What has become apparent from my fieldwork, however, is that domesticity is not thus simply wrapped up into a hegemonic masculinity; rather, the performance of domesticity becomes part of what Valentine (2007) has called 'geometries of oppression' (see also Meth 2014: this volume). That is, domesticity permeates the notion of a 'brotherhood' that works to exclude others. It becomes the preserve of apprentices and lower ranks, rather than officers. Domesticity becomes a 'welfare' issue when applied to families and dependents. And, its successful negotiation marks the good recruit from the bad. In all of these areas and more, domesticity becomes a means of applauding some person, or action, or words and denigrating others. Domesticity thus undercuts any notion of a monolithic, or closed off, military masculinity.

References

Addleston, J. and Stirrat, M. 1996. The last bastion of masculinity: gender politics at the citadel, in *Masculinities in Organizations*, edited by C. Cheng. Beverley Hills: Sage Publications, 54–76.

Agostino, K. 1998. The making of warriors: men, identity and military culture. *Journal of International Gender Studies*, 3(2), 58–75.

Ahrentzen, S. 1997. The meaning of home workplaces for women, in *Thresholds in Feminist Geography: Difference, Methodology, Representation*, edited by J. Jones, H. Nast and S. Roberts. Lanham and Oxford: Rowman and Littlefield, 77–92.

Aitken, S.C. 2000. Fathering and faltering: 'sorry, but you don't have the necessary accoutrements'. *Environment and Planning A*, 32(4), 581–598.

Aitken, S.C. 2009. *The Awkward Spaces of Fathering*. Aldershot: Ashgate.

Atherton, S. 2009. Domesticating military masculinities: home, performance and the negotiation of identity. *Social and Cultural Geography*, 10(8), 821–836.

Barrett, F. 1996. The organizational construction of hegemonic masculinity: the case of the US Navy. *Gender, Work and Organization*, 3(3), 129–142.

Barrett, F. 2001. The organizational construction of hegemonic masculinity: the case of the US Navy, in *The Masculinities Reader*, edited by S. Whitehead and F. Barrett. Cambridge: Polity Press, 77–100.

Carter, P. 1997. An 'effeminate' or 'efficient' nation? masculinity and eighteenth-century social documentary. *Textual Practice*, 11(3), 429–443.

Collinson, D. and Hearn, J. 1994. Naming men as men: implications for work, organization and management. *Gender, Work and Organization*, 1(1), 2–22.

Colville, Q. 2009. Corporate domesticity and idealised masculinity: Royal Naval Officers and their shipboard homes, 1918–39. *Gender and History*, 21(3), 499–519.

Connell, R.W. 1995. *Masculinities*. Cambridge: Polity Press.

Connell, R.W. 2000. *The Men and the Boys*. Cambridge: Polity Press.

Connell, R.W. 2005. *Masculinities*. 2nd edition. Cambridge: Polity Press.

Cox, R. 2013. The complications of 'hiring a hubby': gender relations and the commoditisation of home maintenance in New Zealand. *Social and Cultural Geography*, 14(5), 575–590.

Duncan, S. 1994. Theorising differences in patriarchy. *Environment and Planning A*, 26(8), 1177–1195.

England, K.V.L. 1993. Suburban pink collar ghettos: the spatial entrapment of women? *Annals of the Association of American Geographers*, 83(2), 225–242.

Enloe, C. 2000. *Maneuvers: The International Politics of Militarizing Women's Lives*. Berkeley: University of California Press.

Enloe, C. 2004. *The Curious Feminist – Searching for Women in a New Age of Empire*. Berkeley: University of California Press.

Francis, M. 2002. The domestication of the male? Recent research on nineteenth-and twentieth-century British masculinity. *The Historical Journal*, 45(3), 637–652.

Gagen, E. 2009. Homespun manhood and the war against masculinity: community leisure on the US home front, 1917–1919. *Gender, Place and Culture: A Journal of Feminist Geography*, 16(1), 23–42.

Gill, L. 1997. Creating citizens, making men: the military and masculinity in Bolivia. *Cultural Anthropology*, 12(4), 527–550.

Gorman-Murray, A. 2007. Contesting domestic ideals: queering the Australian home. *Australian Geographer*, 38(2), 195–213.

Gorman-Murray, A. 2008. Queering the family home: narratives from gay, lesbian and bisexual youth coming out in supportive family homes in Australia. *Gender, Place and Culture: A Journal of Feminist Geography*, 15(1), 31–44.

Gorman-Murray, A. 2011. Economic crises and emotional fallout: work, home and men's senses of belonging in post-GFC Sydney. *Emotion, Space and Society*, 4(4), 211–220.

Gorman-Murray, A. 2013. Urban homebodies: embodiment, masculinity and domesticity in inner Sydney. *Geographical Research*, 51(2), 137–144.

Hale, H.C. 2008. The development of British military masculinities through symbolic resources. *Culture and Psychology*, 14(3), 305–332.

Higate, P. 2000. Tough bodies and rough sleeping: embodying homelessness amongst ex-servicemen. *Housing, Theory and Society*, 17(3), 97–108.

Higate, P. 2003. 'Soft clerks' and 'hard civvies': pluralizing military masculinities, in *Military Masculinities: Identity and the State*, edited by P. Higate. London: Praeger, 22–42.

Higate, P. and Hopton, J. 2004. War, militarism and masculinities, in *Handbook of Studies on Men and Masculinities*, edited by M. Kimmel, J. Hearn and R.W. Connell. London: Sage, 432–447.

Hockey, J. 1986. *Squaddies: Portrait of a Subculture.* Exeter: University of Exeter Press.

Hockey, J. 2003. No more heroes: masculinity in the infantry, in *Military Masculinities: Identities and the State*, edited by P. Higate. London: Praeger, 15–27.

Hoegaerts, J. 2010. Manoeuvring men: masculinity as spatially defined readability at the Grandes Manoeuvres of the Belgian Army, 1882–1883. *Gender, Place and Culture: A Journal of Feminist Geography*, 17(2), 249–268.

Jackson, P. 1991. The cultural politics of masculinity: towards a social geography. *Transactions of the Institute of British Geographers*, 16(2), 199–213.

Kronsell, A. 2005. Gendered practices in institutions of hegemonic masculinity. *International Feminist Journal of Politics*, 7(2), 280–298.

Lahelma, E. 2005. Finding communalities, making differences, performing masculinities: reflections of young men on military service. *Gender and Education*, 17(3), 305–317.

McDowell, L. 1997a. *Capital Culture: Gender at Work and in the City.* Oxford: Wiley-Blackwell.

McDowell, L. 1997b. Introduction: homeplace, in *Undoing Place: A Geographical Reader,* edited by L. McDowell. London: Arnold, 13–21.

McDowell, L. 1999. *Gender, Identity and Place: Understanding Feminist Geographies.* Oxford: Wiley-Blackwell.

Meah, A. and Jackson, P. 2013: Crowded kitchens: the 'democratisation' of domesticity? *Gender, Place and Culture: A Journal of Feminist Geography*, 20(5), 1–19.

Morgan, D. 1994. Theatre of war: combat, the military and masculinities, in *Theorizing Masculinities*, edited by H. Brod and M. Kaufman. London: Sage Publications, 165–183.

Rose, G. 1993. *Feminism and Geography: The Limits of Geographical Knowledge*. Minneapolis: University of Minnesota Press.

Sasson-Levy, O. 2003. Military, masculinity and citizenship: tensions and contradictions in the experience of blue-collar soldiers. *Identities*, 10(3), 319–345.

Soeters, J., Winslow, D. and Weibull, A. 2006. Military culture, in *Handbook of the Sociology of the Military*, edited by G. Caforio. New York: Kluwer Academic/Plenum Publishers, 237–254.

Tarrant, A. 2010. Constructing a social geography of grandparenthood: a new focus for intergenerationality. *Area*, 42(2), 190–197.

Tarrant, A. 2013. Grandfathering as spatio-temporal practice: conceptualizing performances of ageing masculinities in contemporary familial carescapes. *Social and Cultural Geography*, 14(2), 192–210.

Valentine, G. 2007. Theorizing and researching intersectionality: a challenge for feminist geography. *The Professional Geographer*, 59(1), 10–21.

Walsh, K. 2011. Migrant masculinities and domestic space: British home-making practices in Dubai. *Transactions of the Institute of British Geographers*, 36(4), 516–529.

Woodward, R. 1998. 'It's a man's life!': soldiers, masculinity and the countryside. *Gender, Place and Culture: A Journal of Feminist Geography*, 5(3), 277–300.

Woodward, R. 2003. Locating military masculinities: space, place and the formation of gender identity in the British Army, in *Military Masculinities: Identity and the State*, edited by P. Higate. London: Praeger, 43–56.

Woodward, R. 2004. *Military Geographies*: Oxford: Wiley-Blackwell.

Woodward, R. and Winter, T. 2007. *Sexing the Soldier: The Politics of Gender and the Contemporary British Army*. London: Routledge.

Chapter 10
Violence and Men in Urban South Africa: The Significance of 'Home'

Paula Meth

Introduction

Violence is rife in South Africa and men are most commonly the perpetrators. But men's experiences of violence are far more complex than this, as they too are particularly vulnerable to violence, even if and when they might enact violence themselves. I have argued elsewhere that violence is omnipresent (Meth 2009) and cannot thus be tied to particular spaces, such as the street. In addition men's experiences of violence in and of the home are not simply that of domestic violence, although this is significant. Rather, through a focus on the home as a fluid category, the intersections between violence and masculinities are explored. This reveals the significance of differing notions and experiences of home – in relation to legislative changes, unemployment, informal housing, and rural homes (see also Atherton 2014: this volume, May 2014: this volume) – for experiences and views of violence by African men. The ways in which the home both symbolises and also facilitates men's wider relationships with men and women, the state and market begins to provide partial explanations for violence experiences.

This chapter focuses on the homes of black South African men living in poverty. It concentrates on the city of Durban, where informal living dominates much of the urban housing offered, and where levels of violence and HIV are both devastatingly high. South Africa is well known for its exceptional levels of interpersonal and generic crime, and its high occurrence of violence, particularly rape, murder and grievous bodily harm. Violence is acutely gendered with much of the sexual and interpersonal violence carried out by men against women, but where men are victims of much violent crime, usually perpetrated on the street, but not exclusively. The post-apartheid state has invested heavily in both policing and housing, as both are key election concerns. The former has led to a rise in more aggressive policing, which has been assisted to some degree by the formalisation of many housing settlements, whereby police and their vehicles can access the spaces of a settlement more readily. Housing change – usually the formalisation of informal settlements – but also the construction of greenfield developments is relatively recent, and although is extensive in scale, has not kept pace with the national and growing demand for housing.

The themes of masculinities, violence and home are explored through the life of one man, Bhekithemba Khathi, a resident of Cato Crest in Durban and a participant in a research project conducted in 2006–2007 (insights in the chapter draw on projects conducted in this settlement between 2003 and 2011).[1] Bhekithemba's stories crosscut and illustrate the role of home in relation to men and violence in urban South Africa. At the time of the project, he had already lived in Cato Crest for seven years. He was born in the rural area of Nongoma in 1976 into a very poor household and was given the task of keeping watch over the family cows, thus preventing him from attending school until the age of 12. Nongoma is about 290 kilometres from Durban and during apartheid would have fallen within the homeland of KwaZulu. Bhekithemba was eventually educated up to the equivalent of UK school year five. Bhekithemba was not working at the time of the research project but he had worked previously in Johannesburg in the mines and at other jobs in Durban, working as a cashier, delivery man and a cleaner. He also conducts occasional work in his rural home for which he is paid in cows. His connections with his rural home are typically intensely strong, and he has very traditional views which are also shaped by his strong Christian religious beliefs. He has an estranged wife and children, who all live in his rural home in Nongoma.

A fluid understanding of home

This chapter contributes to work which questions the binaries implicit in understandings of men and violence, and the role of home. The focus here is on the home and how the home is constructed in relation to masculinities, but it is important to also re-state a conceptual affiliation to work which understands men's experiences of violence beyond a victim/perpetrator binary. Although men are primarily responsible for violence perpetration, simultaneously they are also remarkably vulnerable to violence, and can experience violence as both perpetrator and victim. This recognition is central to a nuanced understanding of home. Home must be thought about in (at least) three ways: (1) As a gendered space tied to wider socio-political processes; (2) As a site where gendered vulnerability (for women and men) but also empowerment is enacted; and (3) As site which is spatially significant, both in terms of its spatial relationship to the 'outside' but also its own spatial qualities.

Home is a contested and changeable concept and it has long been recognised within Geography as a significant space for analysis and political intervention. Tyner's analysis of the home explores the ways in which interpersonal violence is tied to broader social and political processes, in particular, capitalism, racism

1 Bhekithemba is a pseudonym. Meth and McClymont 2009 outlines the mixed qualitative methods approach used in this project, including the use of diaries, interviews, photography and drawing. The paper explores how different methods allowed men to participate in varying ways, particularly when sharing very private and/or painful issues.

and patriarchy (2012: 26). He argues that these structures 'work to discipline the spaces of the home' (2012: 26). This argument certainly applies to interpretations of home in the South African context, however cultural processes are also central to the meaning of home. In this, as in other contexts, the home is heavy with symbolism for men, as it reveals the politics of men's relationships with women as well as children and other men, and it focuses attention on men's relationships with the state (Meth 2009) and other figures of power and authority. The realities of the wider socio-economic context of racialised poverty in South Africa are also typified through men's relationship with the home. High levels of unemployment and the challenges of living informally are two key exemplars, and both contribute to an understanding of why and how violence occurs, and whether this is violence against men or women.

Hence although 'Home as Haven' persists as a notion, there is much recognition of the home is a site where power can be exercised unequally and violently and is thus a site of vulnerability. Tyner (2012: 29) argues that '[t]he home becomes a site where appropriate roles, behaviours, and expectations are both taught and learned. These … furthermore, are gendered, sexed, aged, and even raced'. The gendering of these spaces as well as the entrenchment of patriarchal societies results in homes often being spaces of patriarchal violence (although Tyner (2012: 27) acknowledges same sex violence too). His arguments on home focus, however, only on interpersonal violence and overlook the ways in which more generic violence can spill over into the home space (as well as how this generic violence can also become interpersonal). There is thus a need to incorporate an analysis of violence and the home which moves beyond a focus on male perpetrated domestic violence. Despite this being key, it is one of a range of processes and experiences and must be explored in relation to other violence practices. Men are obviously vulnerable to violence and crime on the street and in public spaces, but as argued in Meth (2009) in the context of particular spaces of poverty in South Africa, violence is omnipresent, for both men and women, and men's experiences of violence within the home extend beyond domestic violence against women.

Finally, our understandings of homes have not only been broadened to recognise their socio-political complexity, homes are also spatially and physically diverse and relational, in important ways that interconnect with their socio-political complexity. In Meth (2003) I explored the ways in which ideas of home draw on norms and notions which are insufficient to understand informal living and importantly the domestic violence experiences of women, but also the violence experiences of men. These informal and insecure homes – which may include squatter settlements, but also street sleeping, living in abandoned or hijacked buildings – typify the homes of millions across the world living largely in cities in the global South. The qualities of informal living are significant for residents, shaping parenting, sexuality, safety, privacy and emotion (Meth 2009, 2013). Furthermore, the meanings of home are culturally and spatially constructed in relation to migration and employment practices. In South Africa, many African urban residents have a claim or right to land in a rural area, often described as their 'real home'. Relating to complex historical patterns of migration for employment in urban areas (see Bank 2011), some men and women live 'temporarily' (often their whole adult lives) in urban centres, remitting wages back to family in rural homesteads. This pattern constructs home in an urban context *in relation to* the rural home, and so too are patriarchal (and other) norms constructed, transported, unsettled and practiced between radically different sites. Men's notions of what is and what is not socially acceptable are often pinned to these differing homes, with violence both an outcome of challenges to their ideas, as well as a pervasive reality that men must confront. Bank's ethnography (2011) supports this complex interpretation of tradition, space and identity, arguing 'the presence of "the rural in the urban" is never simply a matter of the transposition of rural cultural materials into the city, but involves reworking, reconstituting and renegotiating *ideas about the rural in the urban*' (2011: 12).

Power in the home – changing politics

Changing political and legislative practices directly shape gender relations within the home (Meth 2009). South Africa has experienced a number of changes in gendered (and other) legislation since the fall of Apartheid (Bonthuys and Albertyn 2007), relating to the adoption of a progressive constitution. These changes have included legislation governing the definition and significance of domestic violence (Schneider and Vetten 2006). These shifts in legislation shape relations within the home, and have worked to unsettle masculine and feminine identities and power practices. This state-directed intervention is key to an understanding of men, violence and the home as it identifies the historical significance of politics (tied to cultural norms) in shaping violence in the home, as well as the ways in which changing state practices are interpreted and experienced by citizens, often leading to anger and resentment. Described by others as a perception of the 'burden of rights' (see Posel 2004: 233) this anger is not isolated to gender legislation, but includes frustrations (by women and men) over the rising rights of criminals, nonetheless, the changes to domestic violence legislation was a key concern for men living in this settlement (Meth 2009). Bhekithemba argues for example:

> This government was making a mistake to giving women all rights because if you try to control your wife by putting the law, she said you abuse her. The time I'm growing up my father was a head of everything at home. My mother was obeyed the law of my father all the time and even children were obeyed the laws of his father. The government want to rule everything even at your home, he tell you what to do which is wrong. (Diary)

When questioned about whether and why he beats his wife, Bhekithemba resorts to his role as the head of the household to justify his decisions. He explained that his wife had become pregnant with another man's child and he beat her because of this. When asked why she did not report him to the police he explained: 'No, because she was knows the truth and reason to beat her … I understand domestic violence is illegal but I was trying to build my family and she was apologising to me because I told her about that rule of the house' (Life history interview). His views on women informing his understanding of family and tradition are clearly formulated:

> I'm quite old fashion because I'm still believed in traditional things. In tradition the women supposed to respect men … The women and men will never be equal because even the bible stresses that the man is the head of the household and everyone must respect the rules for him. I think the domestic violence is cause by those rights of government. Before that rights come, women were respect their husband and in my family will never be equal. (Life history interview)

For men in this settlement, the home persists as the spatial embodiment of patriarchal power. Men employ the home to delineate their power practices, as the space where they can exert their rules and their culturally-derived ideas of respect and hegemony. As is evident here, home, however, is not isolated from men's wider political subjectivities, as citizens in a changing society. As stated earlier, one key understanding of the home relates to its significance as a gendered space tied to socio-political realities. In all contexts these changing realities, particularly in relation to changing legislation, works to construct men and women's relationships with their homes in different ways. Changing legislation can underpin a real, or perceived, change in rights, at times curtailing or enabling violence, but is more significant than this. Policies about welfare and employment are absolutely central and thus the following section explores how the meanings and experiences of home for men are shaped by socio-economic realities, particularly rising unemployment and reformed welfare regimes, which are in part, a function of wider political processes.

Unemployment and home

Unemployment is recognised to be a key factor in men's explanations of violence, particularly domestic violence (Mosoeta 2011: 61), as well as a justification for involvement in crime. Unemployment is a spatially embodied reality and it shapes the daily rhythms of both men and women's lives. For unemployed men living in informal or poor housing, daily routines, movement, and engagement are often reduced to within and near the home, alongside efforts to find employment or livelihoods, which might take men out of their home or neighbourhood, or could occur within the home. Poverty and unemployment in relation to the home is significant for explorations of violence for two reasons. First, poverty and unemployment directly cause violence, as they fuel tensions, desperation and need. Second, unemployment structures the movement patterns of adults differently, with the home often re-centred in daily life. Here the impacts of wider political and economic decisions directly impinge on men's relationships with, and within, the home.

With regard to the first, the significance of employment for the construction of masculine identities has been highlighted by multiple authors (Mosoetsa 2011: 60, Morrell and Swart 2005: 102), and relates not simply to a desperation for household hegemony, but also the challenges of fatherhood, particularly where men are unable to provide (Richter and Morrell 2006). Employment trends are gendered in South Africa, as they are elsewhere. Domestic service employment is strictly populated by women, and industries employing men (such as mining, manufacturing etc.) have suffered substantial losses in employment over the past few decades (see Mosoetsa 2011: 9–10 for details). Household decisions, culturally the preserve of African men, are shaped and informed by income-power which may mean that adult females are potentially in positions of greater authority. Furthermore, changing welfare regimes in South Africa in the post-apartheid period means that differential income streams are available to mothers of young children, and pensioners, with women accessing a pension five years before men (Mosoetsa 2011: 7). All these wider economic changes shape men's access to resources and experiences of employment, having a knock on effect on their identities as breadwinners: 'It is not any easy thing to be a father and it is difficult to me because sometime I couldn't find job to support them. Sometimes I'm always thinking about them, if food is finish in my house I always worried about them because they finished before me … ' (Life history interview).

In Zulu culture, similar to many other patriarchally-enscribed societies, the senior male is viewed as the household head, the ideals of urban living rest on this masculine authority being shored up through an income, often externally secured. In reality, much urban livelihood (if any at all) is secured through informal means, which may use the home as a partial resource to secure an income (home may be a site for storage of goods for sale, a site for the creation of items etc.). In Cato Crest, despite parts of the settlement undergoing formalisation, there is little in the way of leisure or social space for residents, although *shebeens*[2] are certainly present, and are a popular space for men in particular. When they are not busy with other activities, many men simply make do with hanging about their homes, increasing their time spent with wives or girlfriends as well as children. Mosoetsa describes the home as a 'sanctuary for the poor and unemployed' (2011: 58) and thus unemployment directly shapes men's engagement and patterns of use of their houses and homes. It is evident then that wider political and economic decisions and processes map onto the ways in which men relate to their homes, as well as their everyday use of their homes. Violence is part of these processes, arguably an outcome of poverty and the gendered stresses of unemployment and subsequent challenges to men's power. But violence also arises in relation to the frustrations of everyday life, and cramped conditions with few affordable alternatives for

2 Informal drinking venues.

socialising. Low levels of employment for men results in more men spending time in their home environment during the day. A key feature of these constrained living conditions is that of informality, explored here in its physical sense. This chapter argued earlier that the spatial particularities of home are significant for men's experiences of violence, both in terms of domestic violence but also the violence experiences of men. This is explored now as the ways in which masculinities are constructed in relation to informal homes, is revealed to both entrench men's violence as well as their vulnerability.

Informal housing

Men's ambivalence towards informal housing was very similar to the views of women (see Meth 2003, 2013). Both pointed to the vagaries of a poor living environment, the vulnerability to criminals, the shame of living like animals, their perceptions of state neglect (see Meth 2009) and anger relating to this, and their mutual anxieties and fears about their children (Meth 2013). Elsewhere I have pointed to the ways in which the spatial realities of living informally really do shape vulnerability to generic violence (Meth 2012) simply because of physical limitations such as impermanent roofing materials, a lack of window guards and an absence (and presence) of locks on doors. But informal living also shapes the formation of the wider community, in both positive and negative ways. The ease of construction within informal settlements was often cited as a drawback, meaning that 'anyone' could set up home in the settlement, thereby undermining communal ties, raising densities and reducing neighbourly knowledge. Younger residents could also set up their own homes more easily in such contexts, fuelling concerns about their early sexualisation as well as their vulnerability. More positively, some pointed to this latter possibility as a benefit, as children could escape violent homes more easily because alternative living was relatively simple to construct.

Earlier, the impacts of the material realities of living informally on leisure and privacy were discussed. This is not necessarily an exclusive feature of informal living (see Meth 2013), but it is a pervasive concern. Residents suffer from a lack of housing space, as well as an inflexible layout. The specifics of housing size really does matter as it serves to shape the mental and physical well-being of residents and actively contributes to tension and stress in the home. The spatiality of the home is significant in shaping men's notions of masculinity and in turn their justifications for violence. In explaining different occasions when he beat his wife, privacy and anxieties about privacy are drawn on by Bhekithemba. He describes his discovery of his wife at home with visitors:

> I beat her because I told her I don't want many people in my house.
>
> **Interviewer**: You mean you do not like visitors in your house?

> Yes I got a reason for that; [in the] informal settlement [there] is no privacy and we doing all things in that one room. The under wear-clothes are hanging there and people watch everything. If I got the house may be two rooms it should be better for visitors. I told her to stop visiting people because one day they will like to visit her in my house. (Life history interview)

The significance of spatiality and privacy reinforces the cultural significance of the home, as well as the ways in which this is gendered and leads to violence. Privacy is obviously a relative concept, but ties to notions of decency (Ross 2010) and ideas of appropriate behaviours for residents. In this chapter, its absence is tied to informal housing, yet exact measurements of informal homes are very tricky, as many are fluid in form. Some residents pointed out that their informal homes were actually larger than those provided by the state, raising concerns about the quality of formal housing for which they may be eligible. But privacy and ideas of decency also relates to aesthetic and practical concerns, which are also significant for experiences of gendered violence. Aside from size, informal housing is also often constructed of very temporary and flimsy materials, usually wood or plastic or metal. If we widen an understanding of violence to incorporate structural violence (that of structural inequalities and processes), then the violence of 'risks in and of the home' facing men and women living informally (or in severe poverty) are clearly evident. Of particular significance is the daily vulnerability to elements such as flooding, heat and fire. These concerns shaped men's views of living informally, and informed their emotional registers, particularly that of fear, as evidenced by Bhekithemba:

> It is hard to live with the family in this area because these informal houses are dangerous in term of the fire. One day I saw the house burn with man, his wife and children. All were died inside that *mjondolo*.[3] I couldn't sleep at night after that incident because I was fear may be my house will burn while I sleep. We live here because we don't have work to rent the proper house. We always fear because other people are careless to watch candles and paraffin stove while they [are] drunk. (Diary)

Finally, the properties of informal settlements that lead to the concentration of crime and violence caused concern for men. Most pointed to the densities of such settlements as well as the ease of construction, as causing rising crime rates. Bhekithemba's account illustrates his views on crime, informal living and the true meaning of home:

> The informal settlements also cause crime in this area. Criminals … [are] hiding here because informal settlement is a place to hide because it's not a proper house [for people to live in] … If you going out in this area always we met with

3 Local term for shack.

> the new faces because many people are still coming in this area to hide. The police [do] not [have] access to walk between the *mjondolos.* (Diary)

Bhekithemba's concerns about crime rates within informal settlements are fundamental to understanding the significance of home in relation to violence and masculinities. This is because in these informal contexts the absolute vulnerability of all residents in all places really shapes and in turn challenges how we might theorise masculinities and violence in relation to place. Informality, as a descriptor of particular home spaces, illustrates that men (as well as women's) experiences of violence are spatially significant. Home is a key space, in the context of South Africa, for the enactment of violence by and of men.

Vulnerability in the home (as well as the street)

This chapter opened with acknowledgement of Tyner's (2012) work on interpersonal violence and the home. It made the point that in particular contexts men were also very vulnerable in the home, but their vulnerability outside the home is also significant for their home-life experiences (violence on the street spills over into the home) particularly where home can and does provide a safe haven (or at least an opportunity for spatial closure) for vulnerable men (and women). Below, Bhekithemba recalls his fear in relation to a violent incident on the street as he travelled towards home. These were not his only accounts of street violence; among other stories he describes his friend who arrived as his home 'trembling' with fear from a similar gun attack:

> One day I was coming from work and the criminals were asking me the money. They were carrying guns and point me with that gun. I was fear and trembling. I was trying to give them the money I was had … [the] other man was calling me a dog and asking where is [the] other money? I was told them that only that money I had. Other man said you are useless, you have to die; others said leave that dog and go. (Diary)

Men's vulnerability on the street is a globally recognised reality, and is shaped by their race, age, sexuality, and class. In societies where extreme social breakdowns have occurred (perhaps through war, civil instability, or extreme inequality and poverty) the home can also be a site of vulnerability for men. This is the case in South Africa, and in particular in this settlement of Cato Crest. Research over the past ten years has revealed high levels of rape, murder and child rape and murder, with both men and women describing the settlement as suffering from a loss of humanity:

> [T]here was a family who was abused by the criminals in this area. The criminals were point the man with the guns and one-man criminal raped the wife in front

> of the husband, he was wish to help his wife but he can't because the criminals were point him with the guns. All the men raped her. When they finished raping they ask her husband to do what they done to her. The time the man is raping his wife, the criminals were packing all things they like in that house. (Diary)

Such violence is directly tied to men's experiences of the home, in this case, the informal house. The vulnerability of a home to exceptional violence relates to its material qualities (doors that can be kicked down, roofs the can be lifted etc.), but also its positioning within a wider political context, where police protection is limited and often problematic. Such inhumane events work to undermine men's constructions of themselves as capable protectors, but also serve to classify and label the spaces where this violence occurs in negative terms. These negative spaces are the informal settlement and home in particular, but the 'urban' more generally. Constructions then, of masculinities as well as of places, unfold through violence. In this case, as was common across the research the extreme violence enacted within this urban setting contributes towards the construction of the rural home as safe, proper, and traditional. This notion persists despite there being much evidence of high levels of violence in rural areas and homes too, fuelled historically by regional political violence and economic instability.

Rural homes: tradition, religion and culture

Many men involved in the project pointed to their traditional rural homes as their preferred location, as the bastion of traditional values and practices, as possessing more entrenched (and appropriate) gendered divisions of labour and proper ways of living, perhaps as timeless outposts of patriarchy. In the rural home, these cultural norms of gendered inequality, construct hegemonic masculine behaviours, which are entrenched through forces of tradition. For men, their identities are not being challenged or undermined in such home spaces, rather their rural homes are sites for the celebration of masculinity, which may draw on violence to 'build [one's] family'. Bhekithemba, like many men in his settlement, has chosen to keep his estranged wife and children living in their rural home with his extended family. His references to his rural home draw on tropes of Zulu culture, his religious affiliation (the Shembe Church, a significant African Christian Church in South Africa), and ideas of tradition. He maintains a regular connection to his rural home:

> I miss it my place but I always visit there because my parents are there and my children. I went there every month if I'm working. If I'm not working I go there may be once after two month. … Actually I don't like to have a house here in Durban because I love my rural area [more] than urban area … It is my plan to not call my wife to live here with me. (Life History interview)

He goes on to contextualise his desires for his rural home, explaining why people compromise by living in difficult urban conditions:

> You know my sister; many people live in informal settlements because they want to save the money … not all people who live informal settlements are poor. Many people are affording to buy a house but they like to live in the cheaper place and most people are coming from rural areas and they got homes there. (Life history interviews)

While living in the city, he drew on cultural and religious practices to fulfil his longings for his traditional cultural heritage. He describes entertainment in Cato Crest: 'We saw the different party of Zulu singers and Zulu dance. I really enjoy to see that because the songs they sing are reminding me about my root where I was growing up at Nongoma' (Life History interview). And: 'this church (Shembe Church) is reminding me about the culture of where I come from. They are wearing traditional [clothing]' (Life History interview).

Bhekithemba follows the rules of his church closely by 'not making the fire if it is Saturday … not cooking and eating hot food if it is Saturday. All the Christian of Shembe is not drinking a tea if it is Saturday. They cooked food after 6 o'clock pm. Every one eats cold food' (Life history interview). This devotion is significant because his belief in Shembe is central to his management of violence in his urban home, where the name of Shembe is frequently evoked in an effort to ward off criminals. In a story of an encounter with multiple young men in his urban settlement, Bhekithemba tells how he challenged their repeated requests of him for cigarettes and a lighter:

> I tell him I'm not smoking. On that time I was not fear because these boys were young and my hope was in Shembe to protect me. I carry on with my journey and I was near my house. I found other boys and one was asking me a cigarette, I also ask him who was teaching you a cigarette. He said do you understand what you saying or not, I repeated what I've said. One boy said I know this man a Christian of Shembe is better to leave him. On that time I was not walking I was facing them because I was feeling someone with me that was Shembe. (Diary)

Here Bhekithemba's masculine identity as a devout Shembe follower constructs his ability to cope with violence, an account repeated by several other Christian men in this settlement. In Cato Crest he keeps a photograph of Shembe on his wall, 'for protection [of] my house' (Life History interview).

Bhekithemba's attraction to tradition and his rural home also shaped his political affiliations, which in turn definitively shapes his vulnerability to urban violence, where political party patronage is central to much masculine vulnerability. He described how he joined the Inkatha Freedom Party (IFP) when he was younger, explaining his reasoning as follows:

> The things that were made me to join IFP [was that they] were wearing traditional clothes, singing traditional songs and were carrying traditional stick. I was really attracted because all those things were reminding me about my culture and where I come from. I was joining that politics without any explanation to what is all about.

This admission of political naivety is significant. Cato Crest is an ANC (African National Congress) stronghold and has a long history of violent clashes between political rivalries. Bhekithemba's IFP credentials (based on his desire for tradition) place him in a marginalised and vulnerable position.

Finally, Bhekithemba employs his ideas of rural tradition to explain his views on appropriate gendered behaviours, referring here to how women dress. He describes a romantic relationship he had with a female urban doctor, and how this floundered because of her decision to wear trousers (pants) in his rural area.

> **Interviewer**: Why did you break it up?
>
> She was not listening to me, as I believe in traditional things. [She came home with me to] Nongoma and she noticed that [the] place is too rural [and that] she cannot fit. She did not like to stop wearing pants. I told her she must wear pants at work (i.e. in an urban area) not if she walk with me. I think the thing was made to break it up was the pants …
>
> **Interviewer**: What is wrong with the pants?
>
> In my culture the woman must not wear the pants such as a man. (Life history interview)

Despite the apparent flippancy of this quotation, it illustrates the gendered spatial divisions which shape Bhekithemba's masculine identity and points to his views on women as a product of his ties to his tradition and culture. These views link back to his ideas of gendered power relations introduced at the start of this chapter, and in relation to domestic violence. This final section on tradition and religion and their link with 'the rural' points to the significance of culture in shaping men's experiences of home, as well as the ways in which home is shaped by wider socio-political forces, including geographical. This chapter examines violence in relation to the urban informal settlement and men and women's homes within such spaces, but it does not suggest that rural homes are non-violent spaces for women or men. More work is needed on that matter, (although see Mosoetsa's 2011 work in two peri-urban townships) but of importance here is how men make sense of the idea of home in relation to their constructions of masculinity in rural settings compared with urban, and how in turn these work to shape violence.

Conclusions

This chapter has explored the experiences of violence and its relationship to the home through the life of one man, Bhekithemba. The chapter has offered a more nuanced insight into the role that home plays in men's experiences of violence. Bhekithemba's masculine identity is key here, as it shapes the insights into home and the ways in which home is invoked and experienced in order to build and entrench patriarchal masculinity, but also how it serves to illustrate his marginalised masculinity as a poor, informally-housed, black South African.

Through analysing his experiences of violence, the chapter has shown that home is not simply the locus of domestic violence, although this was a reality. Home is the site of unstable and changing patriarchal power practices, where shifting national norms and legislation directly impinge on men's emotional and material access to violence as a tool to enforce gendered power inequalities. But home is also both a haven and a site of vulnerability for men themselves in the context of wider masculine aggression where violence against men is the norm. Men's journeys home were stressful and they suffered potentially lethal encounters. Home at times provided refuge from such aggression, but could not always work in this way, as generic violence spilled over into the home devastating women and men. The chapter also stressed the significance of the spatial and material, of the role of informality in shaping men's experiences of violence in relation to the home; and turned to the idea of the traditional rural home to establish the counter point in men's constructions of an optimal patriarchal landscape. Bhekithemba's yearnings for tradition, culture and religion all focused on his stated desires to return to his rural home, but he employs these in different ways to manage his urban home. They are central to his experiences of violence, both structuring his rationale for domestic violence, and controlling his encounters with urban aggression. The rural home, despite being spatially dislocated, is fundamental to masculine encounters with violence in urban contexts.

References

Bank, L. 2011. *Home Spaces, Street Styles: Contesting Power and Identity in a South African City*. London: Pluto Press.

Bonthuys, E. and Albertyn, C. (eds) 2007. *Gender, Law and Justice*. Cape Town: Juta & Co Ltd.

Meth, P. 2003. Rethinking the domus in domestic violence: homelessness, space and domestic violence. *Geoforum*, 34(3), 317–327.

Meth, P. 2009. Marginalised emotions: men, emotions, politics and place. *Geoforum*, 40(5), 853–863.

Meth, P. 2012. *Poor Homes, Gender and Violence: The Role of Design*. Royal Geographical Society – Institute of British Geographers Annual International Conference (Edinburgh: University of Edinburgh, 3 July 2012).

Meth, P. 2013. Parenting in informal settlements: an analysis of place, social relations and emotions. *International Journal of Urban and Regional Research*, 37(2), 537–555.

Meth, P. and McClymont, K. 2009. Researching men: the politics and possibilities of a qualitative mixed methods approach. *Social and Cultural Geography*, 10(8), 909–925.

Morrell, R. and Swart, S. 2005. Men in the third world: postcolonial perspectives on masculinity, in *Handbook of Studies on Men and Masculinities*, edited by M. Kimmel, J. Hearn and R.W. Connell. London: Sage Publications, 90–113.

Mosoetsa, S. 2011. *Eating From One Pot: The Dynamics of Survival in Poor South African Households*. Johannesburg: Wits University Press.

Posel, D. 2004. Afterword: vigilantism and the burden of rights: reflections on the paradoxes of freedom in Post-Apartheid South Africa. *African Studies*, 63(2), 231–236.

Richter, L. and Morrell, R. (eds) 2006. *Baba: Men and Fatherhood in South Africa*. Cape Town: HSRC Press.

Ross, F. 2010. *Raw Life, New Hope: Decency, Housing and Everyday Life in a Post-Apartheid Community*. Cape Town: University of Cape Town Press.

Schneider, V. and Vetten, L. 2006. *Equal or Different? Comparing Women and Men's use of the Domestic Violence Act (No. 116 of 1998): Report for the Centre for the Study of Violence and Reconciliation* [Online: International Relations and Security Network]. Available at: http://www.isn.ethz.ch/Digital-Library/Publications/Detail/?ots591=0c54e3b3-1e9c-be1e-2c24-a6a8c7060233&lng=en&id=103417 [accessed: 25 June 2013].

Tyner, J. 2012. *Space, Place and Violence*. New York: Routledge.

Chapter 11
'My place of residence': Home and Homelessness in the Greater Toronto Area

Jeff May

Introduction

This chapter explores the experiences of 'home' and being 'not-at-home' for Canadian-born, young men of colour who have experienced homelessness in the Greater Toronto Area (GTA). I enter into scholarly debates about normative meanings and experiences of home. Previous research has shown that despite their lack of conventional 'homes', many homeless people articulate broader place-making practices that emphasise the inherent spatiality of home-making – that is, home as a creation and experience of place (Johnsen, May and Cloke 2008, May 2000, Moore 2007, Robinson 2005, Whitzman 2006).

'Homeless' is rearticulated in this chapter as being 'not-at-home' to emphasise the affective character of homelessness, that is, the loss of homed meaning that many young men of colour suggest they experience (see also Meth 2014: this volume). Despite experiences of being not-at-home, young men of colour articulate clear ideas of what an ideal home could or should look like. That picture looks very much like the ones painted by scholars who have done work on idealised conceptions of home (Blunt and Dowling 2006, Brueckner, Green and Saggers 2011, Despres 1991, Domosh 1998, Gorman-Murray 2006, 2008, Mallett 2004, McDowell 1997, Meth 2003, Somerville 1992). I also utilise bell hooks' 'homeplace', which she argues has often been denied many people of colour: 'An effective means of white subjugation of black people globally has been the perpetual construction of economic and social structures that deprive many folks of the means to make homeplace' (1990: 46). 'Home', and the ability of people to create it, is inherently political.

Young men of colour experiencing homelessness are excluded from making home in the idealised, normative sense, but articulate clear ideas of what that ideal looks and feels like. In this chapter, I explore that normative sense through a discussion of their experiences of home and homelessness, and the ways they create and experience alternative forms of belonging and home. Through this discussion I illustrate how 'home' is a racially, gendered, and spatially-constructed privilege. Despite the fact that they articulate disaffected experiences and senses of normative home-spaces, these young men also articulate place-making practices that indicate the creation of alternative home- and belonging-spaces. These place-making practices are tied to youthful masculine identities, and through these broader home- and belonging-spaces, young men of colour achieve a sense of themselves *as* young men in the city.

This chapter is arranged into four parts. First, I discuss the literature and scholarly context, and second, I outline the parameters for the study. Third, in 'My place of residence', I briefly discuss interviewees' conceptions of 'ideal' homes, followed by a deeper, comparative discussion of their lived experiences of home, homelessness and being not-at-home. Finally, in the fourth part, 'Common ground', I illustrate some of the broader ways young men of colour create home and a sense of belonging through relationships with people and neighbourhood and community spaces.

Geographies of home

Home and meaning

It is widely acknowledged that home involves a relationship between place/site and meaning, and scholars point out the critical importance of the establishment of personal meaning for experiencing home (Blunt and Varley 2004, Blunt and Dowling 2006, Brueckner Green and Saggers 2011, Gorman-Murray 2007, Manzo 2003, Somerville 1992, Valentine 2001). Personal meaning must be continually remade and home is often understood as a process that involves continual engagement with home-making practices (Blunt 2005a, Blunt and Dowling 2006, Gorman-Murray 2007, 2008, Waitt and Gorman-Murray 2011, Walsh 2011).

Much recent work on home and meaning is focused on women's experiences of home (Anderson 2011, Meth 2003, Quinn 2010, Robertson 2007, Yantzi and Rosenberg 2008). However, there is some recent literature on men's experiences of home that accounts for the different ways that men create and connect with home (Atherton 2009, Blunt and Dowling 2006, Gorman-Murray 2007, 2008, Mifflin and Wilton 2005, Walsh 2011). Gorman-Murray (2008) argues for the mutuality of home (or domestic) space and masculinities, and he follows Blunt and Dowling (2006) in noting there is yet little work in this area. He suggests this is problematic, as men's experiences of home spaces contribute to their sense of selfhood, personally and politically.

Idealised Western notions of 'home' have often been shown to be normatively based on white, middle-class, single-dwelling, nuclear family, suburban, owner-occupancy homes (Brueckner, Green and Saggers 2011, Gorman-Murray and Dowling 2007, Gorman-Murray 2007, Veness 1993). Such norms are political in character and are produced in local Western contexts through the dissemination of white, middle-class, heterosexual values. hooks indicates that 'in the contemporary situation … the paradigms for domesticity in black life mirrored white bourgeois norms (where home is conceptualised as politically neutral space)' (1990: 47). The idealisation of home as politically neutral space has been challenged quite broadly within feminist, anti-racist, critical race, and queer analyses of the meaning of home.

Somerville (1992) provides a still-cited evocation of some central 'meanings' of home, including shelter, hearth, heart, privacy, roots, abode, and paradise. Notably, these meanings combine material and affective senses. Many scholars have argued lived experiences of home do not often map onto idealised imaginations of home (Blunt and Dowling 2006, Brueckner, Green and Saggers 2011, Domosh 1998, Gorman-Murray 2006, 2008, Mallett 2004, McDowell 1997, Meth 2003, Watson and Austerberry 1986). The latter are often rooted in normative ideologies as suggested above.

Home/homelessness/belonging

There is important work on home and belonging on which I draw for wider understandings of 'home', including that concerned with the multi-scalarity of home. Home as multi-scalar means that while home is often connected to residence, it is also enacted at broader scales, such as neighbourhood, city, nation, and diaspora (Atherton 2009, Blunt and Dowling 2006, Gorman-Murray 2007, 2008, hooks 2009, Walsh 2011). hooks offers her classic evocation of 'homeplace', suggesting these were 'places where all that truly mattered in life took place – the warmth and comfort of shelter, the feeding of our bodies, the nurturing of our souls' (1990: 41). The development of homeplace is explicitly political, with hooks suggesting it is both a place of 'radical politics' and 'a site of resistance and liberation struggle' (1990), in contrast to the apolitical idealisation assumed in normative meanings of home.

hooks returned to the idea of homeplace in her 2009 book *Belonging*, in which she broadens the discussion of home to include a more localised connection between people and place. In *Belonging*, she articulates the need to develop a 'culture of belonging' (2009: 182) in the context of widespread alienation from 'home' for many people of colour. hooks directly relates this alienation to widespread social and economic whiteness in North America and thus helps articulate the tensions between idealised and normalised white, middle-class, heterosexual nuclear family values of 'home' and the lived experiences of many people of colour, which may or may not match up with these ideals.

Researchers working on homelessness also open up 'home' to include a wider sense of belonging. May (2000) attempts to open up homeless people's understandings of home from 'home as residence' to 'home as place', which articulates a wider sense of 'home' and relationship between home and space. Robinson (2005), in her analysis of the spatiality of grief in the lives of homeless youth, illustrates how bereavement is spatial, in the sense that youth experiencing homelessness have lost a 'place in the world' (2005: 49). Robinson's argument uses the experience of homelessness to examine connections to place and space. She argues that their homelessness colludes with their grief to make youth less able 'to "put down roots", to feel at-home in terms of a sense of experiencing connectedness to physical place and community' (Robinson 2005: 52). Other recent studies on people experiencing homelessness also account for the multiple ways and spaces in which people achieve a sense of belonging (such as the library – Hodgetts et al. 2008, historical public spaces – Sheehan 2010, squats – Johnsen, May and Cloke 2008, and hostels – Cloke, May and Johnsen 2008).

Research on lived experiences of homelessness can illustrate the relationships between senses of belonging, feelings of 'home', and different spaces and places. Such research can explore the 'micro-tactics of belonging' (Robinson 2002: 37) created and exercised by people experiencing homelessness. It is in this context that my present research enters these debates.

The study

This chapter is based on 40 interviews with Canadian-born young men of colour (aged 17–26) recruited in four GTA locations between June 2010 and March 2011. To recruit participants, I volunteered at Evergreen Yonge Street Mission in downtown Toronto (18 participants) and Our Place Peel Emergency Youth Shelter (OPP) in Mississauga (11 participants), and observed Identification Clinic drop-in at East Scarborough Storefront (ESS) (four participants) and Red Cross Church of the Epiphany Homeless Drop-In (six participants) in Scarborough. Interviews varied from half an hour to one and a half hours and were conducted in locations chosen by both me and the participant based on walking access and where we might have a candid conversation. Locations included restaurants, coffee shops, parking lots, park benches and empty shelter office rooms. Participants were recruited by posters, word-of-mouth, staff solicitations and personal contact, and self-identified as having experienced homelessness. They were paid $15 for participation. Names used in this chapter are participant-chosen pseudonyms.

Interviewees were asked to reflect both on ideal homes and actual homes. Both these were approached with a series of questions about what makes 'home' and about homes they have had or places they have lived. I attempted to elicit from interviewees ideas about physical homes and emotional/affective understandings of home. I asked questions about current and past housing experiences, while trying to encourage interviewees to discuss the many forms of housed and homeless experiences they have had. The themes in the following section emerged from these discussions.

'My place of residence'

'A home should be ... '

When the young men of colour in this study talk about idealised homes they suggest uniformly positively-valenced meanings. These include fun, eating food, 'head space', peace, sharing feelings with people, routine, 'a place to put your stuff', security, 'belongingness', certainty, permanence, comfort, love, freedom, personal space, privacy, a partner, family, relaxation, safety, being alone, or a 'loving mom'. Thus, in describing what an ideal home is, these young men consistently articulate feelings and senses that emphasise permanence, comfort and safety. These match up with previous scholarly work that has evinced normative and conventional definitions of ideal homes (Blunt and Dowling 2006, Domosh 1998, Gorman-Murray 2006, 2008, Mallett 2004, McDowell 1997, Meth 2003). Notably, however, depictions of ideal homes do not always include family or even other people. Sometimes these young men will indicate that an ideal home does not include family, other times it does, and still other times it includes family but also personal and private space (cf. Gorman-Murray 2006, 2007).

Lived experiences of home

Young men of colour experiencing homelessness have a wide variety of housing experiences. They stay in shelters, apartments, foster homes, they 'househop', are in gaol or prison, sleep outside ('rough sleeping'), and all of these with family, friends, parents, or alone. In discussions about lived homes they have had, they articulate a variety of things, many of which are negatively-valenced. These things include: childhood/past, negativity, dark/no light, trapped, bad future, 'institution', anger, disgust, stress, being 'spaced out from people' (family and friends), being alone, a 'place of residence', harassment, annoyance, confusion, threats, conflict, and captivity. This list emphasises the danger, anger, and frustration of (bad) homes. Some of this comes from living in abusive family situations, but some comes from living situations in which they might have lived alone or unaffordably. These articulations are overwhelmingly negative, suggesting that it is not only the experience of homelessness that weighs heavily on the mind. Rather, the experience of being housed can produce a strong feeling of being not-at-home. These include strong emotions (annoyance, stress, disgust, anger), as well as more specific articulations of a troubled materiality (captivity, conflict, threats, harassment, 'spaced out from people'), and more metaphorical projections (trapped, dark/no light).

Often, these young men experience 'home-as-residence' as a passing sensation they try to hold on to. Bonton (23 years old) and I are discussing what home feels like when he narrates a long story about visiting his brother, where conflict arises as he gets close to feeling 'at home'. He describes going to live with his brother and a fight they got into around Christmas:

> I went to his house, stayed there a night and he told me 'where do you stand between family and friends?' 'I go you guys are my family no matter what. I'll do whatever it takes, right?' And they look at me and they go 'well, you don't really come around, so how are you family? We see more friends than you!' We

> were about to burn a couple joints and we got into an argument. It was about, over this, our friends, like, who was who. My brother wanted me to stay, but inside it broke me down so much that I couldn't stay in the premises of them so I ended up leaving. You know, at the same time I left and as soon as I walked out the door he's like 'if you leave right now, never come back'. But I do come back, you know what I mean? It works both ways. But … it doesn't work, it doesn't work at all.

Bonton appreciates family ties and brotherhood. Family ties keep him coming back, despite not feeling appreciated by them. That 'it doesn't work' cripples Bonton's ability to achieve a feeling of home with his brother, despite his efforts. The sense of being not-at-home is demonstrated through overt masculine conflict. Despite desire and effort, Bonton is unable to achieve a feeling of home.

The emptiness and lack of family love and company comes through in discussions of lived home experiences for these young men. Dwayne (21 years old) and I transition from talking about his ideal home to some of the places he has lived recently. He suggests they lack a feeling of being-at-home, but instead impel a sense of emotional emptiness: 'I have three brothers and one sister down in Toronto living with my dad, single parent, you know? So, I been growing up with them basically my whole life so when I left that I tried to find a comfortable spot. The emptiness always remained there.' The emptiness results from the lack of material family contact in Dwayne's recent residences. He has tried to achieve a youthful masculine independence, but in the process has lost the 'family' feeling of home. Seth (20 years old), too, describes a situation of affective emptiness when he suggests that he feels like a 'nowhere man': 'I was homeless and I was walking around, wandering around the streets and looking for places. I kind of felt like pretty much a nowhere man. Someone who doesn't really have a straight future, but um, he's just doing what he can right now.' The placelessness implicated in being a 'nowhere man' suggests that, for Seth, homelessness destabilises him, ungrounds him, and affects his sense of youthful manhood. The experience of homelessness contributes to this, producing a distinct feeling of being not-at-home.

This placelessness, the lack of connection with an idealised home environment, reduces some young men to what they perceive as elementary existence. Thus, not only is Seth 'nowhere', but he becomes a 'nowhere *man*', with the placelessness folding into his sense of masculine self. Others, such as Blackjack (23 years old) and John (19 years old), identify the lack of 'belongingness' and the emotional alienation of homelessness when they distinguish between having a home and not having a home:

> **Blackjack**: Yeah, you have family, you kind of have a sense of belongingness, you know. But when you're homeless, you don't really have belongingness, you're just kind of doing your own thing, but nothing really going on so you're just there. Like, really, you're just there.

> **John**: A place where you know you can feel comfortable, you know, secureness. You're not, it's not you have to share it with someone. It's where you have belongingness.

For Blackjack and John, a home provides a sense of 'belongingness'. Blackjack explicitly mixes family and home. He identifies homelessness with the lack of 'belongingness' and the elementary spatial existence of just being in a space: 'you're just there'. John also identifies some of the idealised meanings of home, including security, privacy, and comfort, suggesting they contribute to feelings of belonging.

Perhaps because of the traumatic experiences of previous family (and other) homes, these young men articulate a variety of feelings about living with other people. TJ (19 years old) is unsuccessful at living with others, suggesting that when he househops it never lasts very long. However, he can articulate what someone needs to do in order to successfully live with other people, including when househopping:

> You can't really be in someone's house and be disrespecting them. You can't really be in someone's house and not washing dishes. You think you can come in my house and not wash dishes? The dishes will outside the house and so will your things, you know what I mean, like? Go wash the dishes and go wash your clothes, like, at the end of the day you have to be at someone's house cleaning, working. When they come home they shouldn't have a whole bunch of shit to do. You're there, right? If you can't do the dishes, clean up the bathroom. If you bathe in the fucking bathtub and you can't clean out the bathtub when you're done, you're nasty. You don't live where you fucking sleep. You're just there at the present time.

TJ's statement 'you don't live where you fucking sleep' is revealing, suggesting the impossibility of creating a homespace, of making home when househopping. TJ knows how to live with other people but he also acknowledges he cannot do the things necessary ('if you can't do the dishes … '). He uses 'live' in the sense of making home, a person 'lives' in a space in which they have an emotionally-invested sense of belonging. His inability/unwillingness to wash the tub/dishes at his friend's house mirrors his inability to cook, clean and otherwise provide for family at his parents' house:

> When you're with your mom and your dad, don't take advantage. Clean, cook. If you're a fucking hustler, bro, show your mom you can bring fucking money in the house, know what I mean, like, don't just be hustling and buy your stupid shit and don't give your mom fucking money so you can get kicked out the house.

His rationalisation about how to live with others very likely has to do with his disaffection with conventional or normative meanings of home as much as it does with his unwillingness to abide by homemaking practices derived from that meaning. As such, he can understand it intellectually, but his inability to feel at home in such environments alienates him from those same environments.

Young men feel they are imposing when they ask friends or family if they can stay for a few nights. Curious about this, I ask Sean if it is difficult to ask:

> Well, it is, kind of, when you're at the moment asking them, can I stay with you? But they usually say yes, you know? Because they know what I'm going through. And, but what happens is I stay too long, you know? And then they start to get fed up. Especially if you're not working, you know? Yeah. Kind of get fed up.

'Too long' is a big part of the problem. Often unstated, the length of stay and feeling of imposition plays on their sense of propriety. Although people often agree, as Sean suggests, when the length of stay drags on, patience wears thin. The constant search for a place to sleep becomes all-consuming, inhibiting the househopper from looking for or finding work.

For some youth, the disengagement from previous routines provides a sense of liberation. Indeed, several young men articulated freedom at having separated from the overbearing control of parents or family. Seth was one of these young men:

> It kind of feels nice househopping cuz when I was living with my mom she would always call me all the time to see, to pinpoint where I was and she'd always get me to baby-sit for the kids. When I was househopping I didn't have to do that anymore, I didn't have any responsibilities. I was free to go wherever, whenever.

Seth suggests he enjoys this freedom ('it kind of feels nice'), but it is relative. The lack of responsibilities and the freedom to 'go wherever, whenever' supposedly is liberating, but as the other stories I have presented suggest, househopping brought new responsibilities and restrictions:

> When I stayed with my friend I would hear his parents giving him a hard time about it. It's their house, not his house, so … that would make me feel guilty like I'm intruding on their family. Always the feeling of intruding and not being … it makes me feel that, deep down, I'm not really wanted here.

This feeling of intrusion contributes to a continued feeling of being not-at-home, despite his earlier suggestions of freedom (which many young men articulated as part of ideal homes). This is perhaps not contradictory. Seth might identify the freedom of househopping as ideal in an effort to capture a sense of being at home he did not feel when living with his mom. That it seems illusory is less important than his yearning to escape the not-at-home feeling.

The gap between these young men's articulations of ideal and lived homes indicates their alienation from structures that empower home-making. Their transience and unstable housing situations flow from their oft-identified feeling of being not-at-home even when they are housed. Sometimes they ultimately adopt notions of home that lack the affective grounding of the ideal homes they desire, such as Zgune Cluned (22 years old), who suggests 'Can I sleep there? Can I go there the next day? Can I eat? Home. Pretty much.'

'Common ground'

There is clearly a great disjuncture between idealised notions and lived experiences of 'home' for the young men of colour in this study. The stories they tell about their lived experiences of 'home' often make the house-as-home the primary referent. Despite their experiences of alienation and being not-at-home in the many home-spaces of their lives, they often tell stories about spatialised home-making and place-making practices that occur outside the conventional house-as-home. This broadened sense of 'home' moves beyond the space of the house or apartment to take shape in 'friendly spaces' and neighbourhoods/communities. This finding indicates that despite the importance of house-as-home in idealisation and lived experience, home is often experienced at multiple scales, including residence and neighbourhood (Blunt and Dowling 2006). The alternate belongings suggested here allow for alternative developments of feeling at-home in the context of homelessness.

Friendly spaces

The first of these alternative 'home-spaces' are what I loosely call 'friendly spaces', meaning social spaces formed through relationships with friends and peers. In the following quote, Bonton and I are discussing friends with whom he 'grew up' and the emotional and physical support network they provide. Doing the interview in College Park, a parkette in downtown Toronto, he looks around and takes in ten people he knows and suggests that network functions as a 'family' removed from blood ties:

> Mostly all my friends, he's over there, my next friend's over there, he's just over there, like right now I'm looking at like ten people I know in this park alone. I grew up with these guys, so every time I see them I feel that they're a little bit more family to me cuz like, we always see each other and you know, they're there. When I'm down they'll try to cheer me up, when they're down I'll cheer them up, you know, we'll smoke weed together, we chill, we party, we relax, like, you know. If you don't have nowhere to go at least one of us will try to pick up and try to put us somewhere.

The latter point is in regards to housing, but the broader conception involves home-making in the space of College Park and downtown generally. Bonton suggests his friends provide some of the idealised meanings of 'home' discussed previously. This sentiment is representative of several discussions I had with young men about groups of friends, particularly in downtown spaces. The seemingly simple function – 'they're there' – creates a social network that contrasts with what Blackjack suggested in saying 'you're just there'. The collegiality of male street youth provides a sense of home even outside home-as-residence spaces (cf. Robinson 2005).

Other young men found belonging in territorial friendships based on local proximity. DH (26 years old) discusses his childhood and teenage years and reflects on how relationships with other young men in the area allowed him to achieve a 'common ground' and 'family feeling':

> Okay, my childhood I was pretty much neglected. When I was introduced to my area and I saw the sense of stability, the sense of common ground and the family feeling of it, you know? You tend to nurture it, you know? You wanna be involved, so if one of the older guys, we call them the older heads, one of them if they tell you, oh, this guy did something to me, we have to do something about it, you wanna be the first one be like I'ma do it! Because you wanna make sure. It's like having a father figure in place or having a mother figure in place to nurture you to health.

DH's analysis of his life is a psycho-social interpretation of the spatiality of friendship and social place-making. His explicitly spatial metaphor 'common ground' is only a metaphor insofar as it abstracts *from* the local space of the suburban neighbourhood he is talking about to incorporate social relationships into a home-making spatiality. Notably, DH, like Bonton, invokes notions of 'home' such as nurturance and family, which mirror what scholars articulate about idealised notions of home.

The connections between people and places in localised relations are what allow for the manifestation of these 'nurturing' relationships. As such, DH articulates a spatial politics tied to the small-scale space of the 'area' – here, home-making and a sense of belonging are produced outside of the space of the 'house-as-home'.

Neighbourhood and community

Many young men of colour have very close emotional ties to particular neighbourhoods in the GTA. These ties come up in discussions of 'home', but also in discussions of family, work, school, and practices of navigating street-space. After 'house-as-home', the larger scale 'neighbourhood' was the second most common reference for a home-space, eliciting the multi-scalarity of home. Moreover, neighbourhood affiliations and emotional and affective ties were commonly cited as integral to making a space called home.

For example, Roger and I are discussing if and where he feels at home. He cites the neighbourhood of Jane and Weston in the Weston area of Toronto as a 'home':

> I consider a neighbourhood like my home. Yeah. Jane and Weston, that's where I was born and raised. That's my house, that's my home. I'm most comfortable in that area ... Memories from kids growing up. Just reminds me of all my good, happy days when I didn't have to give a shit about nothing. Just had to chill with my friends. Hang out, go to school, get suspended, come home. Nothing.

Roger no longer lives in the same neighbourhood, but because it is the area in which he grew up, the feeling of home remains. Some of the aspects of the neighbourhood that help create the feeling of home are comfort, happiness, lack of responsibility, friends, and food. There is thus a temporal-spatial relationship Roger has with Jane and Weston, since many of the feelings and aspects of the neighbourhood that generate 'home' are unlikely to remain if and when he returns. Home is a past neighbourhood space for Roger in this case.

While Roger does not return with any regularity to his old neighbourhood, the feeling of home lingers. Others who suggested a 'home' feeling tied to a particular neighbourhood talked explicitly about going back and what that return might mean. Omega (19 years old) has a similar temporal-spatial relationship with the neighbourhood in which he grew up, but feels that he could return because he maintains a 'cool' (and perhaps patriarchal) relationship with the place and the people in it:

> The neighbourhood. Yeah, everyone knew me. I walked past the neighbourhood, walk through the plaza, I see two people I already know, say from school, say hi to them, we'll meet up from there, all three of us go to the plaza. We'll go to the plaza, get something to eat, come back, I'll see my best friends, now it's five of us instead of three of us, you know, like I'm cool with the neighbourhood since I was a kid. Now I moved out. I could still go there sometimes, say hi, what's up. See some of the people ... all the people I knew, like right now they'd probably be like your [Jeff's] age or like, twenty-five or twenty-four. Like, I knew a lot of them. I'm the type of guy who was friendly.

The emotional comfort expressed here is similar to that suggested by Roger. Omega navigates the neighbourhood with friends, suggesting the integral character of interpersonal relationships for crafting a neighbourhood space as 'home'. The socio-spatial trajectory he describes suggests that movement through the neighbourhood might result in the comfort and familiarity that often come with feelings of home. I did not clarify whether 'I could still go there sometimes' meant he does return, but as in Roger's story, the neighbourhood-as-home again appears to be a home in the past, but providing an affective anchor (a spatial referent) in the city. This resonates with what Blunt (2005b) has argued about 'productive nostalgia', in which longing for past homes is oriented towards the creation of present and future homes.

Solo (19 years old) reflects on the role gang culture plays in being comfortable with a neighbourhood. Notably, he suggests that while gang territoriality helps forge strong neighbourhood affiliations, he implies that it also has an effect even outside the gang. Having heard from many young men the important role 'neighbourhood' plays in the feeling of comfort in the city, I ask Solo about it:

> Yeah, you can definitely get used to your neighbourhood. I've been part of a gang and the neighbourhood is everything. You don't come over here if you're not from here. When you grow up with nothing, it becomes everything you've got. The name becomes very, means a lot to you, you know? Cuz you have nothing else, you know? Other kids have cars, scholarships to go to college. You have nothing, you have your moms giving you business and a little weed to get your mind straight, that's it. Other than that you have your name and your word and those two things mean a lot, you know? And so, you just find a couple other kids that are like you around the neighbourhood and next thing you know, we're like family. And I won't let anyone disrespect your name and you won't let anyone disrespect my name and we'll keep it like that.

Here, neighbourhood works its way into personal subjectivity through fraternal relationships. Solo suggests that a person 'has' her or his 'name and word' and they work to protect that association. He also indicates the creation of alternative families, as neighbourhood friends quickly become 'like family'. The sense of belonging and feeling of home is thus palpably spatialised, associated and felt in the space of the neighbourhood.

The association of people in social space might actually help tie people to particular areas where they have built (or made) a feeling of home. DH suggests it has to do with being raised within a community and developing a kind of familial love for the community:

> We were raised in a community. You either fight with the communities or you have love for the communities, you know? For me to go to another block and mingle with them and be friends with the … I can't do that, cuz I've known my people for so long, and my people, we already fight with each other. Why am I gonna be doing that in another place, to go find new friends to do the same stupid shit I'm doing with new people? I might as well do with my own people and ride with my people.

Again, the socio-spatial relationship between particular people ('my people') and place creates the affective and emotional (as well as practical and pragmatic) ties between young men and their neighbourhoods. Many young men articulated these neighbourhood connections even when they have long moved away from the area (as had Roger and Omega).

Conclusion

The young men of colour I talked with articulate a range of experiences of home. They feel alienated by the disjuncture between their idealised notions of home and their lived experiences of being not-at-home. Having grown up in the Canadian context of Toronto, they have been exposed to the normative discourse of the idealised white, middle-class, nuclear-family household that privileges the site of the house or apartment. Their lived experiences of homes point to a set of affective responses suggesting the feeling of being not-at-home (including captivity, confusion, and stress). However, despite this distinct feeling of being not-at-home regarding the site of the house or apartment, the young men in this research articulate feeling 'home' as a localised connection with other spaces, such as 'friendly spaces' and neighbourhood/community.

These latter connections support research that argues for a broader conception of 'home' than normative conceptions allow (hooks 1991, Blunt and Dowling 2006). Moreover, the stories these young men tell about being alienated from home-spaces suggest that such normative ideals can actually be damaging to young people. The connections between place and people suggest the intensely spatial character of these alternate home feelings. Robinson, in her research with homeless youth, zeroed in on the words of one interviewee, who suggested that home should be 'spaceful' (2005). Robinson indicates that such spaces encourage 'different ways of inhabiting the world' (2005: 57). My research provides further evidence of this notion, by illustrating the various 'spaceful' ways young men of colour create 'home' despite being alienated from what even they cite as 'normal' forms of home. Further, this research illustrates that young men achieve a sense of themselves as young men through their relationships with home-spaces. Building upon Gorman-Murray's argument in 'Masculinity and the home' – that 'as one 'makes home', one accumulates a sense of self' (2008: 369) – this research demonstrates that this identity work happens even in broadened home- and belonging-spaces.

Finally, the idealised versions of 'home' these young men articulate are different from what hooks argues for 'homeplace'. This is because the idealised versions of home suggested here are based on normative white, middle-class, nuclear family values that specify narrow emotional criteria for the creation and maintenance of home. It is thus particular aspects of their idealised notions of home that serve to produce the feeling of being not-at-home, despite the fact that many of them can simultaneously articulate a sense of belonging and feeling of home in a variety of spaces. Despite suggesting a variety of home-space associations, young men of colour *feel* this norm and feel the failure of not living up to it. What results is a complicated alienation from the city in which they exist, leaving them to dream of what many of the city's denizens have, a place in which they can 'live where [they] fucking sleep'.

References

Anderson, V.R. 2011. Homes and being 'at home' in New Zealand: women's place-making in internationalised higher education. *Gender, Place and Culture: A Journal of Feminist Geography*, 19(3), 1–17.

Atherton, S. 2009. Domesticating military masculinities: home, performance and the negotiation of identity. *Social and Cultural Geography*, 10(8), 821–836.

Blunt, A. 2005a. Cultural geography: cultural geographies of home. *Progress in Human Geography*, 29(4), 505–515.

Blunt, A. 2005b. *Domicile and Diaspora: Anglo-Indian Women and the Spatial Politics of Home*. Oxford: Wiley-Blackwell.

Blunt, A. and Dowling, R. 2006. *Home*. New York: Routledge.

Blunt, A. and Varley, A. 2004. Geographies of home. *Cultural Geographies*, 11(1), 3–6.

Brueckner, M., Green, M. and Saggers, S. 2011. The trappings of home: young homeless people's transitions towards independent living. *Housing Studies*, 26(1), 1–16.

Cloke, P., May, J. and Johnsen, S. 2008. Performativity and affect in the homeless city. *Environment and Planning D: Society and Space*, 26(2), 241–263.

Despres, C. 1991. The meaning of home: literature review and directions for future research and theoretical development. *Journal of Architectural Research*, 8(2), 96–155.

Domosh, M. 1998. Geography and gender: home, again? *Progress in Human Geography*, 22(2), 276–282.

Gorman-Murray, A. 2006. Gay and lesbian couples at home: identity work in domestic space. *Home Cultures*, 3(2), 145–168.

Gorman-Murray, A. 2007. Reconfiguring domestic values: meanings of home for gay men and lesbians. *Housing, Theory and Society*, 24(3), 229–246.

Gorman-Murray, A. 2008. Masculinity and the home: a critical review and conceptual framework. *Australian Geographer*, 39(3), 367–379.

Gorman-Murray, A. and Dowling, R. 2007. Home. *M/C Journal*, 10(4), http:journal.media-culture.org.au/0708/01-editorial.php.

Hodgetts, D., Stolte, O., Chamberlain, K., Radley, A., Nikora, L., Nabalarua, E. and Groot, S. 2008. A trip to the library: homelessness and social inclusion. *Social and Cultural Geography*, 9(8), 933–953.

hooks, b. 1990. *Yearning: Race, Gender and Cultural Politics*. Boston: South End Press.

hooks, b. 2009. *Belonging: A Culture of Place*. New York: Routledge.

Mallett, S. 2004. Understanding home: a critical review of the literature. *The Sociological Review*, 52(1), 62–89.

Manzo, L. 2003. Beyond house and haven: toward a revisioning of emotional relationships with places. *Journal of Environmental Psychology*, 23(1), 47–61.

May, J. 2000. Of nomads and vagrants: single homelessness and narratives of home as place. *Environment and Planning D: Society and Space*, 18(6), 737–759.

McDowell, L. 1997. *Undoing Place? A Geographical Reader*. London: Arnold.

Meth, P. 2003. Rethinking the domus in domestic violence: homelessness, space and domestic violence in South Africa. *Geoforum*, 34(3), 317–328.

Mifflin, E. and Wilton, R. 2005. No place like home: rooming houses in contemporary urban context. *Environment and Planning A*, 37(3), 403–421.

Moore, J. 2007. Polarity or integration? Towards a fuller understanding of home and homelessness. *Journal of Architectural and Planning Research*, 24(2), 143–159.

Johnsen, S., May, J. and Cloke, P. 2008. Imag(in)ing 'homeless places': using auto-photography to (re)examine the geographies of homelessness. *Area*, 40(2), 194–207.

Quinn, B. 2010. Care-givers, leisure and meanings of home: a case study of low income women in Dublin. *Gender, Place and Culture: A Journal of Feminist Geography*, 17(6), 759–774.

Robertson, L. 2007. Taming space: drug use, HIV, and homemaking in downtown Eastside Vancouver. *Gender, Place and Culture: A Journal of Feminist Geography*, 14(5), 527–549.

Robinson, C. 2002. 'I think home is more than a building': young home(less) people on the cusp of home, self and something else. *Urban Policy and Research*, 20(1), 27–38.

Robinson, C. 2005. Grieving home. *Social and Cultural Geography*, 6(1), 47–60.

Sheehan, R. 2010. 'I'm protective of this yard': long term homeless persons' construction of home place and workplace in a historical public space. *Social and Cultural Geography*, 11(6), 539–558.

Somerville, P. 1992. Homelessness and the meaning of home: rooflessness or rootlessness? *International Journal of Urban and Regional Research*, 16(4), 529–539.

Valentine, G. 2001. *Social Geography: Space and Society*. Essex: Pearson Education.

Veness, A. 1993. Neither homed nor homeless: contested definitions and personal worlds of the poor. *Political Geography*, 12(4), 319–340.

Waitt, G. and Gorman-Murray, A. 2011. 'It's about time you came out': sexualities, mobility and home. *Antipode*, 43(4), 1380–1403.

Walsh, K. 2011. Migrant masculinities and domestic space: British home-making practices in Dubai. *Transactions of the Institute of British Geographers*, 36(4), 516–529.

Watson, S. and Austerberry, H. 1986. *Housing and Homelessness: A Feminist Perspective*. London: Routledge.

Whitzman, C. 2006. At the intersection of invisibilities: Canadian women, homelessness, and health outside the 'big city'. *Gender, Place and Culture: A Journal of Feminist Geography*, 13(4), 383–399.

Yantzi, N. and Rosenberg, M. 2008. The contested meanings of home for women caring for children with long-term needs in Ontario, Canada. *Gender, Place and Culture: A Journal of Feminist Geography*, 15(3), 301–315.

PART 4
Masculinities and Domestic Labour

Chapter 12
Reconceptualising 'Masculinity' Through Men's Contributions to Domestic Foodwork

Angela Meah

'Masculinity' has conventionally been conceptualised in terms of traits or qualities perceived to be associated with men and, therefore, in binary opposition to those associated with women and 'femininity'. This is supported by this dictionary definition:

> Definition of **masculinity**: *[mass noun]* possession of the qualities traditionally associated with men (Oxford Dictionaries 2013).

Typically 'masculine' qualities might include virility, strength, robustness; men were formerly hunters, protectors, providers, while women were gatherers, carers and servers; men are 'rational', women are 'emotional'. Men occupy the public world of work, while the domestic is women's domain. While masculinity and femininity are clearly relational, implicating relations of privilege and power, scholarship on gender has highlighted that power is not something that is either experienced or practiced by all women or all men in the same way, but rather that male domination is a 'dynamic system constantly reproduced and reconstituted through gender relations under changing conditions, including resistance by subordinate groups' (Carrigan, Connell and Lee 1985: 598). Indeed, in their rethink of hegemonic masculinity, Connell and Messerschmidt (2005) suggest that dominant masculinities take on different forms in different cultures, spaces and time and are not necessarily oppressive.

A generation ago it was possible to clearly distinguish particular roles, responsibilities or spaces within the home as either 'feminine' or 'masculine', but the boundaries between these distinctions have become increasingly blurred in recent years as the 'standardised biographies' that once traced our progression through life have been dismantled (Giddens 1992). As an outcome of changing social mores, economic factors and an ageing population, there has been an emergence of more diverse family forms, resulting in an increase in the number of reconstituted families, solo living, and extended periods of house-sharing (Smart and Neale 1999, Sellaeg and Chapman 2008, Allan, Crow and Hawker 2011). Consequently, in the United Kingdom, the 'nuclear' household with two parents and their dependent children living under the same roof is no longer the statistical norm and domestic roles have consequently required reconceptualisation (Jackson

2009). At the same time, however, individuals' engagement with physical and emotional spaces outside the home has also facilitated a reconstitution of people's relationship to activities which take place within it (Meah and Jackson 2013). Indeed, where once the strongly demarcated spatial structures of work and home were regarded as perpetuating power and gender imbalances (Smith and Winchester 1998: 328), the changing nature of paid work – marked both in terms of a decline in manufacturing in the global North, and women's increased labour market participation – have provided fertile conditions for the reconceptualisation of gender-based subjectivities, witnessed most markedly through a blurring of the male 'breadwinner'/female 'housewife' model (Meah in press).

Time-use data from the UK would appear to indicate a shift in the gendered distribution of household tasks, Kan, Sullivan and Gershuny (2011) reporting that men's total domestic work time has increased from 90 minutes per day in the 1960s to 148 minutes per day in the early 2000s, with time spent on cooking, cleaning and laundry increasing from around 20 minutes per day to more than 50 minutes per day over the same period (see also Bianchi et al. 2000 reporting on the US). Some scholars have interpreted these findings as a cause for optimism, while others argue that, regardless of shifts in the ideologies surrounding women and men's domestic roles and responsibilities, men's failure to fill the shortfall in household labour wrought by women's participation in waged work outside the home suggests that there is little evidence of *actual* change (McMahon 1999, Singleton and Maher 2004, Segal 2007). Indeed, within my own study of gender and foodwork in the UK[1], there was little evidence of any significant transformation in gender roles and relations amounting to a 'democratisation' of domesticity (Meah and Jackson 2013). Debates about the 'oppressive' character of the home and the gendered power dynamics within it are well-worn, and elsewhere (Meah in press) I have made an attempt to 'unsettle' the resounding Anglo-American feminist refrain of female domestic oppression. In this chapter, my aim is to move away from the gendered myopia that has tended to characterise much Anglo-American scholarship on food by focussing specifically on men. Indeed, although perceptions about what is and is not strictly 'women's work' might be shifting (Swenson 2009), Julier and Lindenfeld (2005) highlight that there have been very few academic analyses of how ideologies surrounding women, men and food are changing, and – until recently – there has been a 'lack of research based on men's own accounts of involvement in "foodwork"' (Metcalfe et al. 2009: 95). Rather than reporting who is doing what, why and with what frequency, my concern is with examining how participation in the kitchen is experienced by some of the men who took part in my study of domestic foodwork practices, exploring the meanings that these practices might have in the wider context of their everyday lives and the

1 This research was part of an international programme of research on 'Consumer Culture in an Age of Anxiety' (CONANX) funded by an Advanced Investigator Grant awarded to Peter Jackson by the European Research Council (ERC-2008-AdG-230287-CONANX).

implications regarding masculine subjectivities (see also Gorman-Murray 2014: this volume, Cox 2014: this volume). By exploring what men and women are seen to do via *observed practice,* my aim is to contest the either-or-ness suggested by the terms 'masculinity' and 'femininity', highlighting that gendered practice is more fractured and nuanced than currently allowed by these categorisations.

Performing gendered subjectivities within 'slippery' spatial boundaries

The idea that 'masculinity' and 'femininity' are not fixed or monolithic categories is not a new one. Indeed, academic scholarship has increasingly emphasised the multiple, fluid, dynamic and contested nature of *masculinities* and *femininities* (Connell 1985, 1987), constituting a process of 'endless becoming' (Nilan 1995). Feminist geographers have been among those contributing to developing a more nuanced understanding of the operationalisation of power in the different spaces occupied by women and men – for example, work, home, leisure – highlighting the role of place in processes of identification (see Valentine 1993, McDowell 1999, Browne 2004, van Hoven and Hörschelmann 2005, Johnston and Longhurst 2010), as well as the slippage which may occur between masculine and feminine subjectivities as individuals move between these spaces.[2] Indeed, as Gillian Rose (1995: 546) reminds us, 'not even sexed difference should be taken for granted' since subjectivities are spatially embodied. Linda McDowell's (1997) work on bankers, for example, pertinently challenges the codification of certain types of jobs as exclusively 'masculine' preserves with little or no slippage between the different spaces occupied by men and women and related identities required therein. McDowell highlights the metaphor of performance, and of masquerade, in her interviews with male and female bankers (1997: 161), her analysis drawing upon Judith Butler's (1990, 1993) theorisation of the social construction of gender as embodied performance, making possible transgressive and spatially specific performances. Developing Butler's arguments further, Gregson and Rose (2000) suggest that the instability and slippage evident between performances and the spaces in which these take place point toward potential for both subversion and disruption, as well as highlighting a much more complex and messy relationship between power, different spaces and the (gendered) performance(s) which take place therein. For these authors, the emphasis is with exploring the 'relationality' of performance and how the blurring of clear distinctions between positions and spaces is a source of performative instability (Gregson and Rose 2000: 442–443).

This way of rethinking the practices which take place within the kitchen, and a blurring of its boundaries with other seemingly unrelated spaces, is a useful conceptual tool for re-examining the negotiation and performance of masculine subjectivities as men move within the domestic environment and beyond. Indeed,

2 See also Robinson and Hockey (2011) for a sociological account of performances of masculine identities as men move across public and private spaces.

as Alison Blunt (2005: 510) has pointed out, 'the home itself is intensely political, both in its internal intimacies and through its interfaces with the wider world'.

Over the last decade or so I have spoken with dozens of people (admittedly largely women) about 'family' practices, including gendered emotional and domestic distributions of labour (see Robinson and Hockey 2004, Hockey, Meah and Robinson 2007, Meah and Watson 2011, Meah and Jackson 2013, Meah in press). Data from generations aged 60+ point toward the persistence of a traditional division of the domestic into 'masculine' (outside) and 'feminine' (inside) domains (see Cameron 1998). Indeed, in the UK there exists a stereotype of the man who takes pride in his shed, his garage, his workshop, where everything has its place, who will service the household's cars, check the tyre pressures, and religiously wash, wax and polish, activities which his female counterpart may be ill-equipped, or disinclined, to do. Consciously or otherwise, gendered subjectivities are invoked as clothes are ironed and alloys are polished. Reporting shifts in the domestic participation of a group of Norwegian men over a 15-year period, Helene Aarseth (2009: 430) indicates the persistence – at least until the 1990s – of gendered discourses in the articulation of certain tasks as more 'naturally' undertaken by women than men. One participant, for example, is reported as suggesting that cleaning and dusting are not activities that he felt he had a 'gut-feeling for', whereas his wife did. However, 15 years after his initial interview, it appeared that responsibility for cleaning the house was distributed among all members of the household, with tasks regarded as gender-neutral. For commentators such as Andrew Gorman-Murray (2008: 369), such reports are evidence of a shifting relationship between masculinity and domesticity, at least ideologically pointing toward both the way in which ideals of home and changing homemaking practices have (re)figured masculine identities, and also how men's changing enactments of domesticity can refashion dominant discourses of home.

Within this chapter, I want to explore the ways in which changing homemaking practices are contributing toward refiguring masculine identities. I do so by specifically focussing on foodwork, understood here as referring to all aspects of planning, provisioning and clearing up, as well as the activity of cooking. My discussions draw upon data collected via a multigenerational household study undertaken largely in the South Yorkshire and Derbyshire areas of the UK between February 2010 and August 2011. Combining both qualitative and ethnographic methods in the form of provisioning go-alongs (Kusenbach 2003), videoed meal preparation and generally 'hanging out' (Evans 2012) in participants' kitchens, I spoke with 23 members of eight extended families (17 households), aged between 17 and 92. Seven of the participants were men. Three were responsible for everyday cooking in their relationships, while a fourth had increasingly taken on responsibility for cooking as he approached retirement, while his wife continued to work. One lived alone, while another in an all-male house-share. Only one man did not routinely involve himself in any of the routine foodwork in his household. All but one of the men are White British, the other was a British-born Pakistani; and households represented a largely middle-class constituency, although social mobility was evident in the older generations in particular. Additionally, I also undertook a series of focus groups[3] which were more socially and ethnically diverse. While the 'sample' is small, and findings cannot, therefore, be extrapolated across a general population, participants were observed in detail as they interacted with food, family members and various retailers. By accessing the wider social context in which men's foodwork practices took place, this enables us to begin move beyond masculinity as ideology (relying exclusively on reported behaviour), to understanding masculinity in relational practice.

Unsettling the gendered geography of domestic kitchens

Foodwork occupies a peculiar position within domestic activities. Although the kitchen is generally regarded as 'women's domain', there is ample evidence to suggest that men have, historically, been involved in various aspects of foodwork. In many pastoral societies in the global South, for example, men are responsible for activities which take place *outside* of the kitchen, including killing animals and butchering domestic meat, as well as roasting meat in fields, forests and other open spaces (see Goody 1982, Holtzman 2002). Of course, one doesn't have to look so far to find evidence of men's involvement in particularly 'masculine' forms of foodwork. Adler (1981: 46), for example, reports that although occasional domestic cooking by men can be dated back to the mid-nineteenth century, the repertoire of male cooking is believed to have expanded in response to the popularity of outdoor barbeques following the Second World War. Men, he suggests, demonstrate a predilection toward outdoors and open-fire cooking which invoke memories of campfire cooking in boyhood, an observation also echoed by Aarseth (2007) in relation to Norwegian men who enjoy cooking as an extension of their interest in outdoor activities such as hiking, hunting and fishing. Inness' (2001: 17) observations regarding US men's cookbooks dating to the 1950s indicates that 'Men and Cooking' is not the oxymoron that it might initially appear. Indeed, she suggests that although American boys were 'instructed at an early age that their masculinity was imperilled in the most feminine of home environments: the kitchen' (2001: 39), as an antidote to this, a 'male cooking mystique' was created within men's cooking literature which would reinforce their sense of masculinity and reassure them that 'a trip to the kitchen wouldn't feminise them' (2001: 18).[4] Conversely, however, Jay Mechling (2005) has pointed out the paradox that the American Boy Scouts movement apparently endorsed the philosophy that teaching

3 37 participants aged 23–89 contributed to the seven focus groups. These included 13 men.

4 The Male Cooking Mystique encouraged men to resist women's attempts to force their preference for 'fluffy frippery' on them, by insisting on cooking and eating foods associated with 'masculinity and manliness' (Inness 2001: 18–19) (see also Roos, Prättälä and Koski 2001, Sobal 2005), namely meat, preferably grilled or barbecued.

boys cooking skills and an ethic of *caring* for others – usually a 'feminine' preserve – could actually *enhance* their masculinity. He writes:

> From a feminist perspective, boys' everyday experiences with cooking and eating are formative in the boys' understanding of caring and being cared for, of serving and being served, and therefore, of naturalized patterns of gender dominance and submission. Yet, under certain circumstances, boys can be urged by men and other boys to cook and serve, to nurture others, without surrendering male privilege. (2005: 69)

Clearly, foodwork cannot be distinguished from gendered stereotypes and subjectivities. As Deutsch (2005) and Swenson (2009) have noted, the proliferation of food-related cooking programmes in the US, in particular, has inspired some men to become more than just recreational 'burgermeisters' (Deutsch 2005: 92), while the conventions employed by broadcasters simultaneously uphold existing gender binaries: men's cooking is competitive or leisurely, while women's cooking remains domestic work (Swenson 2009: 42).[5] Coterminous with the advent of consumer-based living and the explosion in popularity of cookery programmes and the cookbook genre, cooking is increasingly emerging as a recreational, leisure activity (Roos, Prättälä and Koski 2001, Holden 2005, Short 2006, Brownlie and Hewer 2007, Aarseth 2009, Swenson 2009, Cairns, Johnston and Baumann 2010). Indeed it has been demystified – by the likes of Jamie Oliver – and reconstituted as a 'cool', masculine lifestyle activity (see Hollows 2003, Brownlie and Hewer 2007), a claim which is unlikely to be made of doing the laundry or cleaning the toilet.[6]

These ideas had currency within some of my focus group discussions. Here, women in their 40s discuss the role of television in transforming the character of cooking, highlighting, as Swenson (2009: 47) observes, that it has been instrumental in invoking a sense of 'masculine domesticity' which has given men a culturally approved place at the stove:

---

5 See also Holden (2005), writing about representations of masculinity in Japanese food programming.

6 Exceptionally, William Beer (1983) has compared housework with 'adventure', invoking a traditionally masculine form of identification in approaching housework as 'unexplored territory', not unlike Everest. Likewise, Sarah Pink (2004) reports that some of her Spanish informants suggested that their engagement in housework was no less performative of their masculinity as other activities, and reflective of a specifically 'meticulous' masculine identity. Stephen Atherton (2009) reports that such meticulous attention to detail is also characteristic of the domestic discipline demanded of the barrack environment in the British Army, where 'men are deeply immersed into domestic routines that are constructed as feminine' (Hockey 1986). However, these male-dominated and rigidly disciplined artificial constructs of 'home' are unlikely to bear any resemblance to traditional domestic life and are often rejected outside in civilian spaces.

Marie:[7] But [TV chefs] have made cooking cool as well. It used to be seen as,

Louise: A drudge.

Marie: A drudge, women's work, something like that. Now that it's the blokes doing it, and it seems quite cool, but when,

AM: Do any of your husbands cook?

Louise: Yeah, mine does, very, very good cook. Well I cook 'cause I have to and I don't particularly enjoy it, but I do, I cook it, I don't buy pre-packed things but Tim cooks at weekends, and he loves it and he's really good.

Louise: For me it's a drudge, I've got the kids, you've got work, you've got this, you've got that, I just, I just don't enjoy it, full stop.

Helen: I enjoy it if I've got time.

These women draw upon a vocabulary of duty, responsibility and obligation in speaking about their relationship with cooking which is contrasted with the image of Jamie Oliver, who has made cooking 'cool', and Louise's husband – a weekend cook – reinforcing long-standing arguments that men's cooking is festal (Adler 1981), or undertaken mostly out of choice, rather than through a sense of duty and obligation (Swinbank 2002, Meah and Jackson 2013). That said, however, the only male participant in this group, 79-year-old Jim, reports that 'I don't get the chance' to cook because it's his wife who is always cooking; 'if I was left on my own, I should be able to cook'.[8]

Enacting masculine subjectivities across blurred spatial boundaries

One woman who contributed to this focus group reported that her husband is 'sort of in charge of the food'. This couple, along with his parents, went on to take part in the household study. Sally (39) and Stuart (42) were interviewed separately before I went on to hang out with him shopping and preparing food. Sally had reported her husband's enthusiasm for and interest in cooking had rubbed off on and inspired her. I expected to meet someone who would recreate vivid memories of the food of his childhood and the evolution of his passion for cooking. I was surprised to discover that Stuart's interest in cooking was relatively recent; indeed

7 All names are pseudonyms.

8 Elsewhere (Meah and Jackson 2013, Meah in press) I have discussed the territorial tensions emerging from men's presence in 'women's domain', sometimes leading to a sense of 'crowding', or estrangement and loss of power for women.

he had been inspired to change his cooking and provisioning practices 'because he saw it on a Jamie Oliver programme'. My interest here is not with why Stuart came to be 'in charge' of foodwork in his household. Rather I want to focus on the processes by which his activities are undertaken and how these challenge ideas about gendered subjectivities being fixed to/in the spaces with which they are associated.

Smith and Winchester (1998) have highlighted how men's engagement with physical and emotional spaces outside the home has also facilitated a reconstitution of their relationship to activities which take place within it. Rather than emasculating men in the way that was perhaps feared among older generations of men and women (Cameron 1998, Segal 2007), they suggest that men's engagement with the domestic can, conversely, provide opportunities to engage with alternate expressions of masculinity to those available in competitive, public spaces, such as the workplace; for example, in doing care through parenting, or exercising creativity through cooking. But workplace and domestic subjectivities, for example, do not have to exist in isolation from each other. For example, in his study of an urban firehouse in the US, Deutsch (2005) reports how domestic values and family ideologies are invoked and reproduced in the workplace as fire-fighters demonstrate caring subjectivities in preparing food for each other. In my study, the 'flow' operated in the other direction where we see an extension of the skills associated with the workplace within the home environment. Stuart works in IT; during his interview he opened up his laptop to demonstrate the databases he had created to store his favourite *Good Food* recipes, and to plan the family's meals, a response to he and Sally getting 'sick of eating the same things', and their over-consumption of red meat. Clearly, Stuart's workplace skills are invoked and this facilitates both his enjoyment of food provisioning and consumption, but also the effectiveness with which he can undertake his responsibilities. The recipe database enables him to avoid having to spend time leafing through recipe books and magazines, while the meal planner – dating back three years – not only allows him to see when they last ate a particular ingredient or dish, but also facilitates the creation of a shopping list – relative to the required ingredients – which is linked to and stored on his mobile phone, which he refers to while shopping. Utilising work-based skills and competencies enables Stuart to accomplish several things which may or may not be regarded as gendered, but nonetheless attract attention since they are tasks or responsibilities which are culturally associated with women: he is the caring husband/father concerned that his family eats a varied repertoire of dishes; he is able to complete meal planning, provisioning and cooking efficiently, enabling him to spend time with his family; he is able to plan food consumption thriftily to avoid waste and to ensure that the household resources are not strained. While Stuart's workplace identity clearly plays a role in reconstituting the way in which his masculinity is expressed within the home, likewise, his culinary endeavours are a source of unexpected capital in the workplace since he reports making flapjacks to share at meetings and exchanging preserves with colleagues, surely unsettling perceptions of domestic masculinities as viewed from the perspective of the workplace.

Foodwork as a haven from hegemonic masculinities

While Stuart clearly demonstrates the flow between different workplace and domestic subjectivities, Smith and Winchester (1998) also observe that for some men, the domestic sphere can represent an opportunity to retreat from the everyday pressures and expectations of work-based identities. Indeed, Beer (1983: 107) suggests that participation in domestic activities offers tangible results: 'concrete pleasures and immediate gratification' distinct from the alienating routines and lack of creativity associated with paid work. There was more evidence in support of these observations within my data and cooking emerged, among men of all ages, as providing an opportunity to relax, be creative, to lose oneself in mundane activities which are neither mentally or physically taxing. For example Laura (63) reported how her husband, Ted (65) had previously suffered with myalgic encephalopathy (ME), prompting her to speculate:

> **Laura**: … I think cooking kind of helped him get over the M.E., although I don't know whether he would say that. He always seemed to really kind of be in a good state when he was cooking, you know. He could come in from work and you know, quite tired and yet …
>
> **AM**: He was energised by it?
>
> **Laura**: Yeah, yeah, he always seemed very focussed and calm and that kind of calm, focussed energy when cooking.

This was explored during my work with Ted – the principal cook in the household – whom I interviewed and spent several hours observing on two separate occasions; during both, he was 'under-the-weather', but as soon as he started cooking, the calm, quiet focus Laura spoke of could be observed. Here, he reflects on his enjoyment of what, ordinarily, might be regarded as mundane and repetitive activities, but which are transformed into something perhaps more meditative and satisfying:

> I love [baking bread] 'cause of the kneading, I love kneading. I get this (…) [9] this mess of stuff into this beautiful silky ball (.) dough and then … chopping vegetables (.) to make er (…) a base for a dish, and I just I'd, I'd chop, I'd just start chopping and immediately my mood would change.

9 (.) Indicates a short pause/hesitation; (…) indicates a longer pause/hesitation.

When performed as part of everyday foodwork, for many women these kinds of activities are perhaps associated with repetitive, routine drudgery, with resentment often resulting from having to take responsibility for decisions about what to eat rather than the cooking itself (see Short 2006).[10] However, for Ted, appreciating that 'one of the very pleasures of life is sitting down at the table with food that you've just cooked', transforms foodwork into something to be enjoyed, rather than endured, and represents a distraction from the pressures experienced during their working lives.

Ted and Laura's son, Jonathan (38) is another example here. He reports how discovering cooking, via the British cookery programme *Ready Steady Cook,* gave him a sense of purpose and productivity which were absent to him as an unemployed graduate living at his parents' home. He says:

> I wasn't depressed, but I was back in (.) finished at [university] … So finished without a job … and not really accomplishing much else … And *Ready Steady Cook* had just started … I kind of joined in with that a little bit I suppose … Getting quite a bit of confidence from being able to churn it out really … I was obviously (.) I was doing bits of work, but effectively a sort of a layabout, but cooking these things for Dad, who was like 'Oh that's good! That's fabulous! How did you, where did you learn to do that?' And there was a bit of a shift, you know (.) from him doing all the cooking to me being prepared to say, 'Well I want to cook because I've got something I want to try'.

While these activities arguably help promote Jonathan's sense of confidence, enabling him to feel that he's making a contribution and also facilitates a form of male sociality (Hollows 2003, Brownlie and Hewer 2007) between himself and his father and – he also reports – his subsequent housemates, motivations for cooking were quite different for another of my participants. Azam (35) was divorced, had lost access to his children, was unemployed and being treated with medication for depression when I met him. He lived alone, but was in regular contact – by telephone – with his mother and sisters. He reported that he had learned to cook curries since becoming single in order to facilitate his self-imposed isolation: he did not want to have to see other people, but also wanted to make sure that he ate reasonably well, as opposed to relying on 'junk'. While it had perhaps not been an intended outcome, Azam speculates that had he not got into cooking: 'I would be in a lot worse state than I am … it's very therapeutic because I've really stared to enjoy it. When I, when the taste started getting better, I enjoyed it even

10 Baking (cakes) occupies a slightly different category since it is no longer part of everyday cooking. Women focus group participants identified it as 'fun', and something that grandmothers often do with grandchildren, while Liz (55), a household study participant, reported: 'I find it relaxing to bake, I mean I can come in from work and start baking 'cause … that's my way of coming down', an observation not dissimilar to that made by Ted.

more; I've been able to cook sometimes as good as my mum.' When probed about this and whether cooking gave him a sense of achievement when confronted with personal 'failure', he agrees that this was the case: 'Cooking gives me good karma. It makes me feel better, especially when I'm eating it or sharing it with people.' This observation was echoed among other male participants, but was not absent in women's accounts either. In a very particular example, when observing Azam's mother preparing food during Ramadan, she explained that Muslims are taught that they will receive 'blessings from Allah' from sharing their food with others.

Azam's case is more interesting when we consider what both he and his mother observe about how men's cooking is regarded within South Asian cultures. Azam explained that his brother-in-law was also learning to cook and that when she had heard about this, this man's mother sees cooking as a 'woman's job'. As reported by Cameron had 'taken the piss taken out of him' as she (1998: 299) it is women, in this case, who find challenges to the organisation of domestic life most unsettling.

Queering 'masculinity' and 'femininity' in practice

In 'Crowded kitchens' (2013), Peter Jackson and I briefly reported how specialist equipment play a role in actively configuring their users (Shove et al. 2007: 23), reminding us both that things are 'consumed not for their own sake, but for what they make possible' (Shove et al. 2007: 22) and, more simply, that 'special cooking gadgets proclaim the special cook' (Adler 1981: 48). In deliberating the question of what, exactly, is it that constitutes masculinity and femininity in the context of the kitchen, I decided that it might be useful to revisit some of the observations I made about how different users engaged with knives and chopping boards, for example. I had a sense that my observations of men were characterised by display, particularly as several were seen to display pseudo-professional knife skills, while women tended to be more understated in their performances and concerned with getting the job done quickly, as opposed to meticulousness or precision.

However, on re-examining a selection of the photos I took of my male participants preparing food, I was struck by a number of things which effectively 'queer' what we understand of 'masculine' (and 'feminine') behaviour and practice. Take Figure 12.1, which features Ted, equipped with his expensive Japanese knife (a birthday gift from son Jonathan, he informed me), chopping the ingredients that will form the base of a Tuscan peasant dish, one of his speciality dishes. He is using a large wooden chopping board; *his* chopping board. Speaking of this piece of equipment, his wife, Laura, complains that it is something that she feels she has to 'lug about; I feel it's … macho'. As with other items of equipment in the couple's kitchen, its size and weight excludes her from its use.

Figure 12.1 Ted's 'macho' chopping board and knife

Contrast the image of Ted with his *'macho'* equipment with Figure 12.2. Here he is pictured wearing his apron, carefully making delicate puff-pastry panadillas. Do the apron and delicate nature of his culinary endeavours render him 'unmanly' in this instance?

Figure 12.2 Ted sporting an apron – a challenge to his masculinity?

Likewise, in Figure 12.3, we see Azam slowly, patiently and painstakingly peeling a head of garlic with an ordinary kitchen knife (not a 'flash', or specialist one).

What is perhaps more extraordinary about this image is that since Azam had already peeled and chopped his garlic and onions prior to my arrival – something which I had specifically wanted to observe – I exploited the fact that I knew him and 'insisted' that he peel and chop a few cloves of garlic again. Without objection or resistance, he proceeded to peel the entire head of garlic with precision and care. This contrasted with both other men, who were observed 'bashing' garlic with the blades of their big knives, and – interestingly – with Azam's mother, Nazra (55). Indeed, in Figure 12.4, Nazra is pictured in perhaps the most 'macho' of demonstrations. Lacking her son's patience and meticulousness, time-pressed Nazra can be seen literally bashing away, first at chillies, then at a whole head of garlic, complete with skin, because she 'can't be bothered' to spend time peeling and chopping individual cloves with a knife in the way that her son does.

Figure 12.3 Azam – patient, precise, 'feminine' … ?

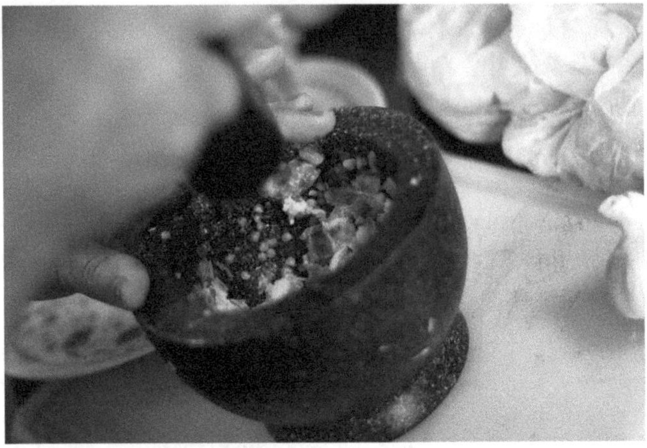

Figure 12.4 Nazra's 'macho' display

In each of these images, my participants – male and female – subvert, or 'queer', our expectations of 'proper' masculine and feminine behaviours via mundane acts of food preparation. In doing so, they expose the subtlety with which gender is enacted or performed in domestic kitchens.

Conclusion

The observations made within this chapter must be considered provisional since they are based both on the experiences of a very small group of men and may not reflect the meanings and significance that cooking had for the participants themselves. Nonetheless, my aim has been to illustrate how individuals' shifting relationships, both with other family members, and with those spaces outside of the home, particularly work, have impacted upon the domestic. Indeed, masculine and feminine subjectivities are not immutable. Not only are they are increasingly required to respond to the vagaries of daily domestic routines which place demands on all household members, but changing social and structural conditions have required a fundamental reconceptualisation of questions regarding what constitutes 'masculinity' and 'femininity' and the assumed 'naturalness' of sex-based domestic roles and practices. These shifts have consequently prompted such questions as: is it 'demeaning' for a man to cook, as it may have been regarded by earlier generations (Hockey, Meah and Robinson 2007); and is it still 'unmanly' for men to iron (Cameron 1998)? Likewise, gendered subjectivities are not neatly or discretely contained in the workplace, leisure spaces or the home, but slippage in our occupational and domestic subjectivities occurs as we move within and between these spaces. In adopting a more spatially curious (Allen 2004: 19) approach which emphasises the slippage which occurs as men and women move between the range of spaces they inhabit, drawing upon skills, competencies and modes of sociality associated with one domain when engaging with another, it is perhaps more appropriate to conceptualise gendered subjectivities not just as multiple and fluid, but as more amorphous than previously imagined. Indeed, my observations of men and women 'doing gender' in their kitchens expands the possibilities of the either-or-ness which currently constrains how we conceptualise 'masculinity' and 'femininity'.

References

Aarseth, H. 2009. From modernized masculinity to degendered lifestyle projects: changes in men's narratives on domestic participation 1990–2005. *Men and Masculinities*, 11(4), 424–440.

Adler, T.A. 1981. Making pancakes on Sunday: the male cook in family tradition. *Western Folklore*, 40(1), 45–54.

Allan, G., Crow, G. and Hawker, S. 2011. *Stepfamilies*. Basingstoke: Palgrave Macmillan.

Allen, J. 2004. The whereabouts of power: politics, government and space. *Geografiska Annaler: Series B, Human Geography*, 86(1), 19–32.

Atherton, S. 2009. Domesticating military masculinities: home, performance and the negotiation of identity. *Social and Cultural Geographies*, 10(8), 821–836.

Beer, W. 1983. *Househusbands: Men and Housework in American Families*. New York: Praeger Publishers.

Bianchi, S., Milkie, S., Sayer, L. and Robinson, J. 2000. Is anyone doing the housework? Trends in the gender division of household labor. *Social Forces*, 79(1), 191–228.

Blunt, A. 2005. Cultural geography: cultural geographies of home. *Progress in Human Geography*, 29(4), 505–515.

Browne, K. 2004. Genderism and the bathroom problem: (re)materialising sexed sites. (re)creating sexed bodies. *Gender, Place and Culture: A Journal of Feminist Geography*, 11(3), 331–346.

Brownlie, D. and Hewer, P.A. 2007. Prime beef cuts: culinary images for thinking 'men'. *Consumption, Markets and Culture*, 10(3), 229–250.

Butler, J. 1990. *Gender Trouble: Feminism and the Subversion of Identity*. London: Routledge.

Butler, J. 1993. *Bodies that Matter*. London: Routledge.

Cairns, K., Johnston, J. and Baumann, S. 2010. Caring about food: doing gender in the foodie kitchen. *Gender and Society*, 24(5), 591–615.

Cameron, J. 1998. The practice of politics: transforming subjectivities in the domestic domain and the public sphere. *Australian Geographer*, 29(3), 293–307.

Carrigan, T., Connell, R.W. and Lee, J. 1985. Toward a new sociology of masculinity. *Theory and Society*, 14(5), 551–604.

Connell, R.W. 1987. *Gender and Power*. Cambridge: Polity Press.

Connell, R.W. and Messerschmidt, J.W. 2005. Hegemonic masculinity: rethinking the concept. *Gender and Society*, 19(6), 829–859.

Deutsch, J. 2005. 'Please pass the chicken tits': rethinking men and cooking at an urban firehouse. *Food and Foodways*, 13(1), 91–114.

Evans, D. 2012. Beyond the throwaway society to ordinary domestic practice: what can sociology say about food waste? *Sociology*, 46(1), 41–56.

Giddens, A. 1992. *The Transformation of Intimacy*. Cambridge: Polity Press.

Goody, J. 1982. *Cooking, Cuisine and Class: A Study in Comparative Sociology*. Cambridge: Cambridge University Press.

Gorman-Murray, A. 2008. Masculinity and the home: a critical review of a conceptual framework. *Australian Geographer*, 39(3), 367–379.

Gregson, N. and Rose, G. 2000. Taking Butler elsewhere: performativities, spatialities and subjectivities. *Environment and Planning D: Society and Space*, 18(4), 433–452.

Hockey, J. 1986. *Squaddies: Portrait of a Subculture*. Exeter: Exeter University Press.

Hockey, J., Meah, A. and Robinson, V. 2007. *Mundane Heterosexualities: From Theory to Practices*. Basingstoke: Palgrave Macmillan.

Holden, T.J.M. 2005. The overcooked and the underdone: masculinities in Japanese food programming. *Food and Foodways*, 13(1–2), 39–65.

Hollows, J. 2003. Oliver's Twist: leisure, labour and domestic masculinity in The Naked Chef. *International Journal of Cultural Studies*, 6(2) 229–248.

Holtzman, J. 2002. Politics and gastropolitics: gender and the power of food in two African pastoralist societies. *The Journal of the Anthropological Institute*, 8(2), 259–278.

van Hoven, B. and Hörschelmann, K. (eds) 2005. *Spaces of Masculinities*. London: Routledge.

Inness, S.A. 2001. *Dinner Roles: American Women and Culinary Culture*. Iowa City: University of Iowa Press.

Jackson, P. (ed.) 2009. *Changing Families, Changing Food*. Basingstoke: Palgrave Macmillan.

Johnston, L. and Longhurst, R. 2010. *Space, Place, and Sex: Geographies of Sexualities*. Maryland: Rowman & Littlefield Publishers.

Julier, A. and Lindenfeld, L. 2005. Mapping men onto the menu: masculinities and food. *Food and Foodways*, 13(1–2), 1–16.

Kan, M.Y., Sullivan, O. and Gershuny, J. 2011. Gender convergence in domestic work: discerning the effects of interactional and institutional barriers from large-scale data. *Sociology*, 45(2), 234–251.

Kusenbach, M. 2003. Street phenomenology: the go-along as ethnographic research tool. *Ethnography*, 4(3), 445–485.

McDowell, L. 1997. *Capital Culture: Gender at Work in the City*. Oxford: Blackwell.

McDowell, L. 1999. *Gender, Identity and Place: Understanding Feminist Geographies*. London: Polity Press.

McMahon, A. 1999. *Taking Care of Men: Sexual Politics in the Public Mind*. Cambridge: Cambridge University Press.

Meah, A. (in press) Reconceptualising power and gendered subjectivities in domestic cooking spaces. *Progress in Human Geography*.

Meah, A. and Watson, M. 2011. Saints and slackers: challenging discourses about the decline of domestic cooking. *Sociological Research Online*, 16(2), 45–51.

Meah, A. and Jackson, P. 2013. Crowded kitchens: the 'democratisation' of domesticity? *Gender, Place and Culture: A Journal of Feminist Geography*, 20(5), 578–596.

Mechling, J. 2005. Boy scouts and the manly art of cooking. *Food and Foodways*, 13(1–2), 67–89.

Metcalfe, A., Dryden, C., Johnson, M., Owen, J. and Shipton, G. 2009. Fathers, food and family life, in *Changing Families, Changing Food*, edited by P. Jackson. Basingstoke: Palgrave Macmillan, 93–117.

Oxford Dictionaries. 2013. *Masculinity* [Online: Oxford Dictionaries]. Available at: http://oxforddictionaries.com/definition/english/masculinity [accessed 3 January 2013].

Nilan, P. 1995. Masculinity as a social practice and cultural 'becoming'. *Journal of Interdisciplinary Gender Studies*, 1(1), 57–69.

Pink, S. 2004. *Home Truths: Gender, Domestic Objects and Everyday Life*. Oxford: Berg.

Robinson, V. and Hockey, J. 2011. *Masculinities in Transition*. Basingstoke: Palgrave Macmillan.

Roos, G., Prättälä, R. and Koski, K. 2001. Men, masculinity and food: interviews with Finnish carpenters and engineers. *Appetite*, 37(1), 47–56.

Rose, G. 1995. Geography and gender, cartographies and corporealities. *Progress in Human Geography*, 19(4), 544–548.

Segal, L. 2007. *Slow Motion: Changing Masculinities, Changing Men*. Basingstoke: Palgrave Macmillan.

Sellaeg, K. and Chapman, G.E. 2008. Masculinity and food ideals of men who live alone. *Appetite*, 5(1), 120–128.

Short, F. 2006. *Kitchen Secrets: The Meaning of Cooking in Everyday Life*. Oxford: Berg.

Shove, E., Watson, M., Hand, M. and Ingram, J. 2007. *The Design of Everyday Life*. Oxford: Berg.

Singleton, A. and Maher, J. 2004. The 'new man' is in the house: young men, social change, and housework. *The Journal of Men's Studies*, 12(3), 227–240.

Smart, C. and Neale, B. 1999. *Family Fragments?* Cambridge: Polity Press.

Smith, G. and Winchester, H. 1998. Negotiating space: alternative masculinities at the work/home boundary. *Australian Geographer*, 29(3), 327–339.

Sobal, J. 2005. Men, meat and marriage: models of masculinity. *Food and Foodways*, 13(1–2), 135–158.

Swenson, R. 2009. Domestic divo: televised treatments of masculinity, femininity and food. *Critical Studies in Media Communication*, 26(1), 36–53.

Swinbank, V. 2002. The sexual politics of cooking: a feminist analysis of culinary hierarchy in Western culture. *Journal of Historical Sociology*, 15(4), 464–494.
Valentine, G. 1993. (Hetero)sexing space: lesbian perceptions and experiences of everyday spaces. *Environment and Planning D: Society and Space*, 11(4), 395–413.

Chapter 13
Materiality, Masculinity and the Home: Men and Interior Design

Andrew Gorman-Murray

Men on the home front

This chapter begins an investigation of men's engagements with day-to-day interior design and decoration – with the arrangement, appearance, colour and texture of domestic interiors, including fixtures, furnishings and ornamentation. The focus is not professional design and decoration. Rather, I draw on data from a study of 'ordinary' men's meanings and everyday practices of homemaking in twenty-first century inner-city Sydney. This context is one of changing gender, work, lifestyle and household patterns, thus enabling empirical observations that help refine knowledge of, and reconceptualise, the relationships between masculinity, domestic life and the modern home. The material includes in-depth interviews, reflective diaries and home tours conducted with 52 men. From analysing this data I suggest that there has been, arguably, a shift in men's material and ontological connections to the domestic sphere in twenty-first century Sydney. Against traditional stereotypes of feminine domesticity, the men in this study are active in practices of interior design and decoration, deciding the style and appearance of their homes alone and alongside their partners. Consequently, these men are ever more engaged with the aesthetics of domestic materiality, emphasising its importance for expressing identities, cementing relationships and fostering feelings of comfort and wellbeing. With these shifting gendered practices of homemaking, new (domestic) masculine subjectivities are possible. As I have argued elsewhere, as men make homes they create and reconstitute masculinities (Gorman-Murray 2008a).

Through developing this argument I seek to make a number of contributions to scholarship on masculinities and place, focusing on domestic material culture. Men's everyday homemaking practices have been marginal in research endeavours not only in geography but across design, humanities and social science disciplines (Blunt and Dowling 2006, Lees-Maffei 2008, Walsh 2011), and so most fundamentally I help to redress this under-representation and under-theorisation. As such, I contribute to trans-disciplinary interest in shifting relationships between gender and domesticity in the contemporary Western home. I use approaches from social and cultural geography – specifically, critical geographies of home (Blunt and Dowling 2006, Brickell 2012) – to better understand the factors underpinning interior design practices in twenty-first century society. The first two sections outline a conceptual scaffold and methodology. I then analyse the empirical material, interrogating the meaning of men's changing concerns with interior design. In doing so, I elaborate the wider contextual associations of this change, contemplating how shifting patterns of gendered domesticity are embedded in trends unfolding across the West, including transformations in employment and relational meanings of home and/to self. This analysis of masculinity and interior design complements chapters in this volume on masculinity and domestic foodwork (Angela Meah) and masculinity and DIY home maintenance (Rosie Cox).

Domestic materiality, gender and interior design

I draw together and extend two themes informed by recent geographical conceptualisations of home and identity. The first is the materiality of home and its connections to identity, comfort and wellbeing. One of the key points of Blunt and Dowling's (2006) critical geography of home is that the space of the home is both material and imaginative. Home is a physical location, constituted in Western society at the site of the house. But home is not reducible to location and shelter: home is a matrix of cultural associations and personal meanings and relationships intersecting in and with the space of the house. These material and imaginative dimensions of home are inseparable: for a house to become a home it must be imbued with meanings, feelings and experiences by occupants. And since the home *is* a material space, a critical dimension of homemaking is modifying and maintaining its materiality, including interiors, furnishing and objects – domestic materiality is entwined with and shaped by personal and familial activities (Tolia-Kelly 2004, Dowling 2008, Dowling and Power 2011). Indeed, the home provides a material locus of comfort and wellbeing for the constitution and reconstitution of individual and collective identities (Gorman-Murray 2008b, Miller 2008). As Young (2005: 149) argues, home is 'the material anchor for a sense of agency and a shifting and fluid identity'. In this chapter, I focus on how men's material homemaking practices enable comfort and wellbeing, which in turn articulates identities and affirms relationships.

This leads into the second theme I wish to advance in this analysis: the gendered dimensions of meanings of home(making). Blunt and Dowling (2006) contend that home is a key location, and homemaking is a critical set of practices, for constructing, reinforcing and contesting wider subjectivities and social relations, including gender, sexuality, family, class, race and ethnicity. As feminist scholars have stressed, home is one of the most significant sites for constituting gendered subjectivities, and homemaking is a critical expression of gendered practices (McDowell 2002). In particular, home is imagined as a site for enacting normative heterosexual gender roles. Public policy and popular culture reinforces the heterosexual nuclear family home as the ideal version of home, bound tightly with the ideology of separate gendered spheres of home and work (Johnson 2000). In this discourse, paid work is positioned as the basis of men's self-worth, while domestic spaces and activities are seen as women's domain (Domosh and Seager 2001). This in turn gives rise to the binary subject positioning of male breadwinners and female homemakers (Chapman 2004). In this gendered framing of the domestic, homemaking is seen as a feminine undertaking, and men are rendered 'out-of-place' at home while paradoxically providing economic resources for family upkeep. From this perspective, men have limited engagement with homemaking.

But gendered subjectivities and spaces, and associated masculine and feminine practices, are malleable and multiple (Robinson and Hockey 2011). While the ideology of breadwinners and homemakers influences masculine and feminine associations with the home, its coverage is incomplete (Cameron 1998). In working-class families, for instance, wives have often participated in the labour market to ensure sufficient financial provision for their families (McDowell 1999). Moreover, the gendering of home has been complicated since the late-twentieth century by men's uptake of particular domestic practices, such as cooking (Meah and Jackson 2013). Indeed, drawing together the two themes of materiality and gender, domestic materiality has provided a practical and ideological seam for refashioning gendered connections with the home. While wives, at least 'ideally', attend to housework – that is, cooking, cleaning and childcare – husbands have been charged with home maintenance, particularly carpentry, cabinetry and plumbing – for example, fixing broken window frames, unblocking drains and building furniture (Cameron 1998).[1] The 'handyman' husband is not out-of-place at home; for him, home is a place on which to work. Gelber (2000: 85) has chronicled the development of this domestic masculinity in the Anglophone West, focusing on the US: beginning in the early-twentieth century, DIY grew in significance so that '[b]y the 1950s being handy had … become an expected quality in good husbands', and 'household repair, maintenance, and construction projects … became a requirement of masculinity' (see also Carter 2011 on Australia). In this light, material homemaking constitutes masculine, as much as feminine, subjectivities (Gorman-Murray 2011a, Walsh 2011, Cox 2013).

Interior design is a fundamental aspect of domestic materiality linked to the pliable gendering of domestic practices. Stretching from the present day back to Victorian times, attention to interior design has been understood as a feminine concern (Domosh and Seager 2001, Fellows 2004, Lees-Maffei 2008). In the Victorian era, the middle-class home was understood as both a moral bulwark against worldly temptations and an aesthetic statement of family status, and bourgeois wives were expected to sustain these ideals through interior decoration (Sparke 1995, Friedman 1998). Style, colour, ornamentation and arrangement were utilised as instruments for shaping moral character and expressing social standing.

1 All domestic practices are material to the extent that people have physical need for shelter, food and clothing. Thus, cooking, cleaning and laundry are also arguably material practices. What I am interested in here, however, is the materiality of the dwelling and contents.

Sparke (1995) contends that this legacy was then taken up by housewives in 1950s post-war America and Britain (and across the West), who were ideologically charged with decorating, furnishing and making homely their newly-built suburban houses (see also Johnson and Lloyd 2004 on Australia). Yet, there have also been masculine associations with interior design, particularly beyond the ideal of the hetero-nuclear home. In post-war America, the bachelor pad became a 'cultural icon' in which interior design was configured as a distinctly masculine practice underpinned by stylistic expression and (hetero)sexual seduction (Cohen 1996, Osgerby 2005, Fraterrigo 2008). Recently there has been discussion of gay men's interior design (Gorman-Murray 2006, 2011a, Lambert 2006), including whether their presumed aptitude for domestic styling is empowering or 'feminising' (Hart 2004, Ramsey and Santiago 2004), but also empirical studies investigating their domestic design practices in the context of wider processes of marginalisation (Fellows 2004, Gorman-Murray 2007).

Further configurations of masculine interior design are emerging. These changes are captured in various media forms, and thus the media is a key site for encapsulating and articulating new connections between masculinity, domesticity and the modern home (Carter 2011). Key here is the rise of a 'mixed gender address' in interior decorating and homemaker magazines and lifestyle television programmes across the Anglophone West since the 1980s, with both women *and men* equally targeted as image-conscious, style-attentive individuals (Attwood 2005, Lewis 2008). As Attwood (2005: 97) contends: 'increasingly, in contemporary consumer culture, the home is presented as an important site of self-expression for both women and men. The "feminine" worlds of fashion, beauty and the home are being opened up to men, acquiring new centrality and changing status within the culture.' This is buttressed by the presence of men engaged in conventionally feminine homemaking practices in popular lifestyle programmes and magazines in the UK, the US and Australia, from cooking to interior decoration, as both experts and everyday practitioners (Hollows 2003, Rosenberg 2008, Gorman-Murray 2006, 2011a). Attwood (2005) and Lewis (2008) argue that this gathering masculine address re-genders the domestic: in the contemporary West, men are increasingly positioned as homemakers, and the home has become a central arena for masculine self-expression. As I have similarly discussed elsewhere, masculine subjectivities and homes are co-constitutive (Gorman-Murray 2008a). The relationality of masculinity and domestic materiality provides a conceptual underpinning for the present analysis.

New design-oriented domestic masculinities are further reinforced in other media forms. Recent commentaries and advice books in Australia, the US and the UK suggest that more types of men – straight, gay, husbands, fathers and bachelors – are increasingly concerned with interior design and decoration (Minor 2004, Jellie 2005, Kalyn 2008, Martin 2008). These assertions link men's identities, happiness, comfort, and relationship satisfaction to active decision-making about the design of interior spaces. Minor (2004), for instance, contends that a man's personal investment in décor provides material support for his sense of self, with flow-on affects for both his wellbeing and intimate domestic relationships. He further suggests that greater numbers of 'ordinary' men in Sydney are designing and decorating their own domestic spaces. But while there has been scholarly interest in men's increasing contribution to domestic labour and parenting (Chapman 2004, Singleton and Maher 2004, Johansson and Klinth 2008), there has been little attention to their involvement in interior design and what this means for the constitution of masculinities (Gorman-Murray 2008a; aside from studies of bachelor pads and gay men's homes, noted above).[2] These unfolding changes in men's homemaking need empirical and scholarly assessment to understand how meanings of home, gendered subjectivities and domestic practices – and the connections between these – are shifting in contemporary society. This is the aim of this study; next, I outline data collection methods.

Methodology

The data utilised in this analysis are drawn from a project on men's changing practices of homelife in contemporary inner-city Sydney. The project is prompted by growing concern amongst commentators and policy-makers about men's wellbeing and sense of self-worth – a so-called 'crisis of masculinity' induced by shifting employment conditions, gender roles and household and family structures since the 1980s (McDowell 2005, Barker 2007). While the 'crisis' rhetoric is debatable and rightly disputed (McDowell 2000, Singleton 2007), the social and economic changes, and their effects, are not. Yet simultaneously, these transformations lie alongside persistent cultural valuations of homelife, a basic manifestation of the 'Great Australian Dream', reinforced through popular discourse like lifestyle television, homemaker magazines and interminable reports on the health of the real estate industry (Dolgopolov 2003, Allon 2008, Lewis 2008). In this national ideal, home is epitomised as a site and source of self-fulfilment, happiness, emotional health and ontological security. In these twin contexts, this project seeks to understand how men value and use their homes for personal and lifestyle goals in the pursuit of work/life balance, and how domestic spaces and activities contribute to a sense of self-worth, wellbeing and 'healthy' masculinity.

This is not a simple equation by any means. In light of gender transformations and the 'crisis' of masculinity, there is no universal and homogenous masculinity (Connell 2005, Segal 2006). Rather, there are masculinit*ies* – a fluid set of subjectivities differentiated by intersections of gender with sexuality, class, age, *inter alia*. They are also distinguished by household and family formation, including

2 Gosling et al.'s (2005) US study of material attributes in young college students' accommodation shows some gender differences in décor, with women's personal living spaces often more colourful and stylish, containing flowers, and men's less organised, containing mechanical equipment. They suggest this reflects *conventional* gender roles. My concern, however, is with *changing* masculinities.

bachelorhood, cohabitation and fatherhood (Pitt and Borland 2008, Aitken 2009). These social and spatial intersections produce multifaceted relationships between masculinity and domesticity. Fifty-two men participated in this project, varying across household type (including single, couple and family homes), age and occupation.[3] Table 13.1 summarises these characteristics. While there are a range of household, dwelling and tenure types represented, there are some demographic tendencies: 88 per cent are of European heritage (82 per cent Anglophone), 85 per cent are (or were) employed in managerial or professional jobs (with associated middle-class performativities), and only two respondents are over 70 years of age. This is partly because of the spatial concentration of the sample. Fieldwork was focused on inner-city Sydney, from the coast in the east to Strathfield in the west, from Sydney Harbour in the north to Botany Bay in the south, to provide socio-spatial coherence. Indeed, some similarities did emerge across the sample, such as men's interest in interior design, the focus of this chapter.

Men were recruited in June–September 2009 through advertisements in local newspapers. Participation involved three stages, offering a depth of narrative and visual information. First, participants completed a semi-structured interview about their homelife. A range of themes was explored: work/home relations, work at home, leisure at home, interior design, domestic labour, parenting, home maintenance, gardening, entertaining, neighbourhood involvement, and the ideal home. Next, participants recorded a time-use diary of their homelife for one week. For each day they were asked to chronologically document their activities – what, where, how long, with whom – and to write a reflection for each activity considered significant to their wellbeing, feelings, and sense of self (Meth 2003). Finally, a follow-up visit was conducted one week after I had read the diary. This involved asking specific questions about the diary, discussing life satisfaction, including work/life balance, and importantly, a guided home tour. Home tours allowed me to 'see' the spaces and activities discussed in the first two stages, probing for further details about homelife (Tolia-Kelly 2004). This provided a valuable visual component to the research, and photos were taken with permission. Men's partners, if applicable, were invited to participate in the follow-up. Together, the interviews, diaries and tours afforded rich layers of insight into men's homelife. In this chapter, I focus on what these data reveal about men's changing engagements with interior design – a practice, I argue, that offers a powerful lens for interpreting emerging domestic masculinities, and subsequently for the shifting gendered meanings of home in contemporary society.

Materialising masculinity: men and interior design in Sydney homes

Men's role in interior design was explicit in this project. In each interview I discussed interior design, asking men if it was important for their wellbeing

3 Sexual orientation also varied, with 13 gay men and 39 heterosexual men.

Table 13.1 Respondent characteristics

Household	*Number (Proportion)*
Couple-only family	15 (29%)
Couple family with children	16 (31%)
Single-parent family	1 (2%)
Single-person	15 (29%)
Group (unrelated cohabitating adults)	5 (9%)
Dwelling	
Semi/detached house	26 (50%)
Apartment	26 (50%)
Tenure	
Owned	25 (48%)
Rented (private)	17 (33%)
Rented (public)	3 (5%)
Personal agreement[1]	7 (14%)
Age	
18–30	7 (13%)
31–50	24 (46%)
51–70	19 (37%)
71+	2 (4%)
Birthplace	
Australia/New Zealand	35 (67%)
Asia	6 (12%)
North/South America	4 (8%)
UK/Europe	7 (13%)
Occupation (Australian Standard Classification)	
Managers/Professionals	36 (69%)
Tradesperson	3 (6%)
Service Workers	3 (6%)
Retired[2]	10 (19%)

[1] Informal agreements between family members: e.g. adult sons living with parents; leasing property owned by a family member, or only one partner in a couple as property owner.
[2] Former occupation: eight managerial/professional, one trades, one service.

and sense of self, and how they participated in interior design practices. I found that, across the sample, interior design was important: 45 men, 87 per cent of respondents, said that they were concerned with and participate in interior design, and that it was important for their wellbeing. Men across all household types were engaged with interior design decisions and actions – bachelors, partners and fathers – thus arguably supporting Minor's (2004) anecdotal assertion that the feminine stereotype of interior design and decoration is being reworked in contemporary Sydney. In this analysis I want to focus on men's interest in interior design in relation to several themes raised in the earlier conceptual discussion: gender norms and roles, self-expression, comfort, wellbeing and relationship-building. These elements are interwoven. For example, wellbeing is enabled by a combination of self-expression and physical comfort; gendered practices are re-sculpted in the context of relationships with spouse and/or house. I consider both bachelors and partnered men to show the increasing significance of masculine interior design across household types. In doing so, I draw specific examples from the research.

The interviews, diaries and home tours indicated that men are engaged in interior design practices to create a comfortable environment for relaxation and rejuvenation that simultaneously enables self-expression. I contend that this concern originates in, but also reworks, a particular normative masculine engagement with the home: the idea that a man's home is his castle, a private place to retreat after a 'heavy' workday (Gorman-Murray 2011b). As a bulwark against the trials of public life, home enables the articulation of a man's 'private' or 'inner' sense of self; as Noble (2005: 113–114) argues, comfort 'is fundamental to the fashioning of identity' and 'is best seen in terms of an attachment to a place or context that makes acting in that setting possible'. This thesis is supported in my findings. When I asked respondents what home meant to them, all said it was (or should be) a private space secured against the public sphere and outside engagements, where they could 'be themselves' and express their personalities (Gorman-Murray 2013). Even if some worked at home sometimes, this was typically presented as an intrusion into private space and time. Sequestering a restful space was thus seen as important for personal and emotional wellbeing. Interior design was deployed as a key way of facilitating this environment, with comfort, self-expression and wellbeing achieved through control over colour, texture, furniture and arrangement.

This was apparent in bachelor apartments, where men lived alone, generating their own homemaking ideals (Pink 2004). These men's interior design practices arguably find their heritage in classic treatises on bachelor domesticity stretching back to the nineteenth century. In 1881, for instance, Oliver Bunce asserted in *Bachelor Bluff*: 'refined and perfect domestic comfort is understood by men only. … Women are … neat because they constitutionally hate dust, not because neatness is important to their own selfish comfort' (Bunce 1881: 19–20, cited in Snyder 1999: 41). Despite problematically essentialising gender subjectivities, such notions are nevertheless instructive about bachelor domesticity. Drawing on such evidence, Snyder (1999: 35) argues that bachelors are sometimes seen as 'exemplars of domestic life', especially skilled in creating a comfortable home environment as a framework for selfhood and personal wellbeing (see also Fraterrigo 2008). Some of the middle-class bachelors in this study embody this legacy, discussing how they made their homes comfortable and expressive through material refinements in design and furnishings, creating a private oasis from work and the public sphere, and buttressing their psychological and physical health.

For instance, Brett (30s, professional, renter) described his apartment as his 'sanctuary', a space where he could retreat from a range of outside pressures, including work and interpersonal relationships, and 'be himself'. Creating this sanctuary was heavily contingent upon interior design and material culture. He emphasised the need to craft an environment that was expressive, comfortable and beautiful, with these elements entwined through the choice and arrangement of furniture, texture and colour. Figure 13.1 shows his open-plan living area. Colour is important for generating a restful personal space, particularly 'earthy' greens and browns, which affirm his sense of connection to nature and bring this into the domestic. To this end, Brett has a balcony garden, and places a mirrored screen at the opposite end of the living area which reflects the greenery and draws it deep into the living space. The leather lounge is the centre of this scenic domain: even though it was over-budget, Brett said he had to purchase *this* lounge, providing two reasons which interleave self-expression and wellbeing. On the one hand, its colour, brown, complements and enhances Brett's ethos of using natural light and colour to create a restful space, bookended by real and reflective gardens. On the other hand, its textural softness induces rest: since he spends most of his time at home on the lounge, it was important that he could 'sink into' it and allow it to envelope his body. The combination of colour, texture and placement thus establishes an expressive and restful home environment designed to facilitate emotional and physical comfort (see also Gorman-Murray 2013).

Figure 13.1 Brett's living area: colour, texture and arrangement
Source: Andrew Gorman-Murray

Brett's example invokes design features that were important across other single men's apartments. When I asked Gavin (30s, professional, renter) and Tom (30s, professional, renter) what was the most important space in their homes, both focused on the lounge itself. The lounge was the specific site where most relaxation and recuperation from public and employment commitments took place, and was central to building a restful homelife. This was an explicitly material concern, utilising interior design to facilitate wellbeing. Size and texture were important for relaxing body and self, but so too was placement adjacent windows in order to access views and natural light seen as rejuvenating (Figure 13.2). Arrangement of other furnishing and use of colour were also important for bachelors' comfort and self-expression. To create an individual but harmonious environment, Ryan (30s, professional, owner) chose furniture which suited the colour of existing features (e.g. a red lounge to complement the maroon splashback), the unusual circular shape of the rooms (his apartment was in a 'silo' redevelopment) and emphasised space and flow (Figure 13.3). Limiting clutter was important here, and reflected his 'meticulous masculinity' (Pink 2004). But for others ornamentation equally engendered a personalised and emotionally healthful interior. For widower David (60s, professional, owner), this meant surrounding himself with furniture, ornaments, paintings and photos (of family) from his earlier home (Figure 13.4).

Expressive interior design was also enacted by men in heterosexual couple family households. This provides an interesting case of changing gendered meanings and practices of home. In this case, the underlying discourse of home-as-a-man's-castle is predicated on a traditional archetype of separate gendered spheres and divisions of domestic labour – a model which, as noted earlier, posits women (as wives-and-mothers) as (usually) unpaid homemakers whose duty is to create a secure and restful 'fortress' for their husbands, and serve their needs when they come home from work. This model has been rightly challenged and altered by the entry of women, wives and mothers into the paid workforce (McDowell 1999). In couple family households where both partners work full-time, there are both reduced expectations and opportunities for female partners to take charge of

Figure 13.2 Tom's living area: placement and light
Source: Andrew Gorman-Murray

creating a home environment as a haven from work. In this study, both partners worked (mostly) full-time in 25 out of 27 non-retired couple families; the female partner was a full-time homemaker in only two. In this contemporary context of dual careers, both husbands and wives work together to sculpt their domestic

Figure 13.3 Ryan's dining room: colour, shape and flow
Source: Andrew Gorman-Murray

Figure 13.4 David's living area: pictures and ornaments
Source: Andrew Gorman-Murray

retreat. Male and female participants reflected on how this diverged from their own parents' experience, where mothers had typically handled interior design. Consequently, I argue that men have taken – have *had* to take – considerably greater interest in interior design in order to fashion, together with their partners, a domestic refuge for the constitution, affirmation and wellbeing of both partners.

In many cases this was done in flexible and interesting ways, and such material homemaking practices were also significant for relationship-building. Planning and fashioning domestic interiors together, for the wellbeing of both partners, requires careful and often lengthy negotiations over colour, furnishings and arrangement. Sam (30s, professional, owner) and Lisa, for instance, planned and executed the renovation of their house over a three year period, enabling their individual and mutual likes and personalities to be materially reflected in their home (Figure 13.5). Similarly, Michael (40s, professional, owner, house) and Gina admitted to spending considerable time – months and even years – negotiating new colour schemes and furnishings. Aaron (20s, professional, renter, house) and Wendy demonstrated another style of partnered interior design. Wendy worked in a major furniture and homewares store, and used this situation to select the furnishings, paintings and ornaments for their home. However, it was Aaron who took responsibility for deciding where these acquisitions should go and arranging the appearance of their living space (Figure 13.6). This was a fascinating way of allocating aesthetic decision-making, and both emphasised that this process had effectively created a shared sanctuary from outside pressures and engagements – a home which reflected not just their separate personalities, but their relationship and joint aspirations.

Indeed, in all such cases in the study, the aim was to confer to partners, through an ongoing process of disagreement, compromise and alignment, a sense of investment in the appearance of domestic spaces (Reimer and Leslie 2004). These homemaking practices materialised both partnerships and individual personalities in couples' interiors, enabling a space of identification, comfort and wellbeing for both men and their partners, alone and in relationships. But in order to ensure this was so – and that the male partners' aspirations and identities were reflected in the home – the men themselves had to take an active involvement in interior design decisions and practices. This engagement reveals a change in men's relationships with domesticity, and moreover, loosening of the traditional gendering of the twentieth century domestic sphere. There is a shift away from both a parallel between femininity and domesticity, on the one hand, and the rhetoric of a man's home as his castle on the other. Instead, there is an emerging ethos of 'equal' gendered investment in the modern home, including its interior design and decoration. Equal does not mean a 50/50 split, but continual negotiation between male and female partners, whose individual interests in design and appearance could shift over time. In this study, partners' concerns were largely presented as more-or-less mutual, but not always: in two households the wife took greater interest, while in two others the husband devoted more time and thought to interior design, showing the variability of contemporary gendered investment in the home.

Figure 13.5 Sam and Lisa's dining room: negotiation and expression
Source: Andrew Gorman-Murray

Figure 13.6 Aaron and Wendy's living area: aesthetic decision-making
Source: Andrew Gorman-Murray

A final point about men's changing concern with interior spaces cuts across both single-occupancy and couple family households: the contribution of media messages to design practices. Earlier I argued that the media – especially homemaker magazines, lifestyle television and advice guides – constitutes a key space for articulating new relationships between masculinity and the home, prompting men's involvement in domestic aesthetics. The input of media commentaries into men's interior design activities was affirmed in this study. For both bachelors and partnered men, media discourses played an important role in encouraging design practices and providing information about possibilities. Most homes contained an assembly of homemaker magazines. These were prominent in bachelors' homes, often exhibited as aesthetic library displays. Both Brett and Harry (50s, professional, owner, apartment), for instance, housed collections of home design journals on living room shelves, including *The World of Interiors*, *Vogue Living* and *InDesign Magazine*. Partnered men also read such publications: Brendan (50s, professional, owner, house) had journals and books on domestic design (which were his, not his wife's). While these men applied ideas from magazines and books, others utilised advice from lifestyle television. *HomeMade* – a renovation show featuring teams of interior designers, and the new lifestyle programme for 2009 – was a favourite. Michael and Sean (40s, professional, owner, house), for instance, watched the show with their wives to glean creative ideas for their homes. These men, like most in the study, felt they should be equally involved in interior design, and found information and inspiration through lifestyle programmes. Such findings confirm contentions about the role of media discourses in re-gendering interior design and reconfiguring domestic masculinities (Attwood 2005).

Material relationality: reconfiguring masculinities and domesticities

This chapter has utilised a critical geographical perspective on homemaking to advance insight into interior design practices in contemporary Australia, and in turn understand the shifting relationship between masculinity and the home. Specifically, I have drawn together concepts about the materiality and gendering of homemaking to analyse reconfigured relationships between masculinity and interior design, focusing on the case of men's shifting patterns of homelife in inner-city Sydney. The spatial and temporal context of twenty-first century Sydney offers opportunities to explore meanings and practices of homemaking in a situation of changing gender, work, lifestyle and household configurations. Through a combination of interviews, diaries and home tours I have found that the majority of men in this study take a strong interest in the design and decoration of their domestic interiors. This is true for both bachelors and men in heterosexual relationships. Concern with material homemaking practices – with the style, appearance and arrangement of domestic space – is bound up with personal needs for comfort, wellbeing, self-expression and relationship-building. In the process, interior design and decoration is appropriated as a masculine activity. At the same time, the gendered meaning of the domestic sphere is reconfigured, and home becomes a site for materialising both masculine and feminine identity work.

These changes are bound up with trends unfolding across the West, including the continued entry of middle-class women into the paid workforce, the rise of personal 'lifestyle projects', and the centrality of domestic styling to those lifestyle goals (Bell and Hollows 2005). In other words, while the ideology of separate gendered spheres erodes, home is increasingly valued as a material site of comfort, wellbeing and self-expression. Advancing these desires has demanded a realignment of gender and space. Just as women are now firmly embedded in the public sphere, men are ever more present in the domestic sphere, taking up homemaking practices like cooking, designing and decorating. These emerging masculinised domesticities are apparent in lifestyle television across the West (Hollows 2003, Attwood 2005). Along with advice guides and wider media commentaries (Minor 2004, Kalyn 2008), these programs urge men to greater engagement with homemaking as part of an ethos of wellbeing and self-expression. Moving beyond the simple misogynistic logic of 'a man's home is his castle', masculinity and domesticity are entwined in increasingly complex relations, with consequent fluorescence of new (domestic) masculine subjectivities. Future work on these gendered performativities would find a fertile vein in intersections of class and sexuality with masculinity, comparing working-class and middle-class masculinities and gay and hetero-masculine domesticities. Nonetheless, the present discussion contributes to scholarship on masculinities and place, highlighting and analysing some of the social and material practices that co-constitute masculinity and domesticity in twenty-first century Sydney.

Acknowledgement

This chapter is an output of the project *Men on the home front: spatialities of domesticity and masculinity*, funded by an Australian Research Council Discovery Grant (DP0986666).

References

Aitken, S.C. 2009. *The Awkward Spaces of Fathering*. Aldershot: Ashgate.

Allon, F. 2008. *Renovation Nation: Our Obsession with Home*. Sydney: University of New South Wales Press.

Attwood, F. 2005. Inside out: men on the 'home front'. *Journal of Consumer Culture*, 5(1), 87–107.

Barker, C. 2007. *The Hearts of Men: Tales of Happiness and Despair*. Sydney: University of New South Wales Press.

Bell, D. and Hollows, J. (eds) 2005. *Ordinary Lifestyles: Popular Media, Consumption and Taste*. Maidenhead: Open University Press.

Blunt, A. and Dowling, R. 2006. *Home*. London: Routledge.

Brickell, K. 2012. 'Mapping' and 'doing' critical geographies of home. *Progress in Human Geography*, 36(2), 225–244.

Cameron, J. 1998. The practice of politics: transforming subjectivities in the domestic doman and the public sphere. *Australian Geographer*, 29(3), 293–307.

Carter, N. 2011. Man with a plan: masculinity and DIY house-building in post-war Australia. *Australasian Journal of Popular Culture*, 1(2), 165–180.

Chapman, T. 2004. *Gender and Domestic Life: Changing Practices in Families and Households*. Basingstoke: Palgrave Macmillan.

Cohan, S. 1996. So functional for its purposes: the bachelor apartment in *Pillow Talk*, in *Stud: Architectures of Masculinity*, edited by J. Sanders. New York: Princeton Architectural Press, 28–41.

Connell, R.W. 2005. *Masculinities*. 2nd edition. Crow's Nest: Allen and Unwin.

Cox, R. 2012. The complications of 'hiring a hubby': gender relations and the commoditization of home maintenance in New Zealand. *Social and Cultural Geography*, 14(5), 575–590.

Dolgopolov, G. 2003. Doing your block: TV's guide to lifestyle renovation. *Metro Magazine*, 138, 140–144.

Domosh, M. and Seager, J. 2001. *Putting Women in Place: Feminist Geographers Make Sense of the World*. New York: Guildford Press.

Dowling, R. 2008. Accommodating open-plan: children, clutter and containment in suburban houses in Sydney, Australia. *Environment and Planning A*, 40(3), 536–549.

Dowling, R. and Power, E. 2011. Beyond McMansions and green homes: thinking household sustainability through materialities of homeyness, in *Material Geographies of Household Sustainability*, edited by R. Lane and A. Gorman-Murray. Farnham: Ashgate, 75–88.

Fellows, W. 2004. *A Passion to Preserve: Gay Men as Keepers of Culture*. Madison: University of Wisconsin Press.

Fraterrigo, E. 2008. The answer to suburbia: Playboy's urban lifestyle. *Journal of Urban History*, 34(5), 747–774.

Friedman, A. 1998. *Women and the Making of the Modern House: A Social and Architectural History*. New York: Harry N. Abrams.

Gelber, S. 2000. Do-it-yourself: constructing, repairing, and maintaining domestic masculinity, in *The Gender and Consumer Culture Reader*, edited by J. Scanlon. New York: New York University Press, 70–93.

Gorman-Murray, A. 2006. Queering home or domesticating deviance? Interrogating gay domesticity through lifestyle television. *International Journal of Cultural Studies*, 9(2), 227–247.

Gorman-Murray, A. 2007. Contesting domestic ideals: queering the Australian home. *Australian Geographer*, 38(2), 195–213.

Gorman-Murray, A. 2008a. Reconciling self: gay men and lesbians using domestic materiality for identity management. *Social and Cultural Geography*, 9(3), 283–301.

Gorman-Murray, A. 2008b. Masculinity and the home: a critical review and conceptual framework. *Australian Geographer*, 39(3), 367–379.

Gorman-Murray, A. 2011a. 'This is disco-wonderland!' gender, sexuality and the limits of gay domesticity on *The Block*. *Social and Cultural Geography*, 12(5), 435–53.

Gorman-Murray, A. 2011b. Economic crises and emotional fallout: work, home and men's senses of belonging in post-GFC Sydney. *Emotion, Space and Society*, 4(4), 211–220.

Gorman-Murray, A. 2013. Urban homebodies: embodiment, masculinity, and domesticity in inner Sydney. *Geographical Research*, 51(2), 137–144.

Gosling, S., Craik, K., Martin, N. and Pryor, M. 2005. Material attributes of personal living spaces. *Home Cultures*, 2(1), 51–88.

Hart, K.P. 2004. We're here, we're queer – and we're better than you: the representational superiority of gay men to heterosexuals on *Queer Eye for the Straight Guy*. *Journal of Men's Studies*, 12(2), 241–253.

Hollows, J. 2003. Oliver's twist: leisure, labour and domestic masculinity in *The Naked Chef*. *International Journal of Cultural Studies*, 6(2), 229–248.

Jellie, D. 2005. Secret lives of us. *Sydney Morning Herald*, 30 August, 6.

Johansson, T. and Klinth, R. 2008. Caring fathers: the ideology of gender equality and masculine positions. *Men and Masculinities*, 11(1), 42–62.

Johnson, L. 2000. *Placebound: Australian Feminist Geographies*. South Melbourne: Oxford University Press.

Johnson, L. and Lloyd, J. 2004. *Sentenced to Everyday Life: Feminism and the Housewife*. Oxford: Berg.

Kalyn, W. 2008. *Guy Spaces: A Guide to Defining a Man's Personal Space*. New Jersey: Creative Homeowner.

Lambert, A. 2006. Stats please: gay men as mimics, robots, and commodities in contemporary cultural spaces, in *Gendered Outcasts and Sexual Outlaws: Sexual Oppression and Gender Hierarchies in Queer Men's Lives*, edited by C. Kendall and W. Martino. New York: Harrington Park Press, 61–77.

Lees-Maffei, G. 2008. Introduction: professionalization as a focus in interior design history. *Journal of Design History*, 21(1), 1–18.

Lewis, T. 2008. *Smart Living: Lifestyle Media and Popular Expertise*. New York: Peter Lang.

Martin, A. 2008. *How to Get Things Really Flat: A Man's Guide to Ironing, Dusting and Other Household Arts*. London: Short Books.

McDowell, L. 1999. *Gender, Identity and Place: Understanding Feminist Geographies*. Cambridge: Polity Press.

McDowell, L. 2000. The trouble with men? Young people, gender transformations and the crisis of masculinity. *International Journal of Urban and Regional Research*, 24(1), 201–209.

McDowell, L. 2002. Unsettling naturalisms. *Signs: Journal of Women in Culture and Society*, 27(3), 815–822.

McDowell, L. 2005. The men and the boys: bankers, burger makers and barmen, in *Spaces of Masculinities*, edited by B. van Hoven and K. Hörschelmann. London:

Routledge, 19–30.

Meah, A. and Jackson, P. (2013) Crowded kitchens: the 'democratisation' of domesticity? *Gender, Place and Culture: A Journal of Feminist Geography*, 20(5), 578–596.

Meth, P. 2003. Entries and omission: using solicited diaries in geographical research. *Area*, 35(2), 195–205.

Miller, D. 2008. *The Comfort of Things*. Cambridge: Polity Press.

Minor, C. 2004. A room of his own. *Sydney Morning Herald: Forty-Eight Hours*, 13–14 March, 4.

Noble, G. 2005. The discomfort of strangers: racism, incivility and ontological security in a relaxed and comfortable nation. *Journal of Intercultural Studies*, 26(1), 107–120.

Osgerby, B. 2005. The bachelor pad as cultural icon: masculinity, consumption and interior design in American men's magazines, 1930–65. *Journal of Design History*, 18(1), 99–113.

Pink, S. 2004. *Home Truths: Gender, Domestic Objects and Everyday Life*. Oxford: Berg.

Pitt, R and Borland, E. 2008. Bachelorhood and men's attitudes about gender roles. *Journal of Men's Studies*, 16(2), 140–158.

Ramsey, M. and Santiago, G. 2004. The conflation of male homosexuality and femininity in *Queer Eye for the Straight Guy*. *Feminist Media Studies*, 4(4), 353–355.

Reimer, S. and Leslie, D. 2004. Identity, consumption, and the home. *Home Cultures*, 1(2), 187–208.

Robinson, V. and Hockey, J. 2011. *Masculinities in Transition*. Basingstoke: Palgrave Macmillan.

Rosenberg, B.C. 2008. Masculine makeovers: lifestyle television, metrosexuals and real blokes, in *Exposing Lifestyle Television: The Big Reveal*, edited by G. Palmer. Aldershot: Ashgate, 145–157.

Singleton, A. 2007. Boys in crisis? Australian adolescent males beyond the rhetoric. *Journal of Men's Studies*, 15(4), 361–373.

Singleton, A. and Maher, J. 2004. The 'new man' is in the house: young men, social change, and housework. *Journal of Men's Studies*, 12(3), 227–240.

Snyder, K. 1999. *Bachelors, Manhood, and the Novel*. Cambridge: Cambridge University Press.

Sparke, P. 1995. *As Long as it's Pink: The Sexual Politics of Taste*. London: Harper Collins.

Tolia-Kelly, D. 2004. Locating processes of identification: studying the precipitates of re-memory through artefacts in the British Asian home. *Transactions of the Institute of British Geographers*, 29(3), 314–329.

Walsh, K. 2011. Migrant masculinities and domestic space: British home-making practices in Dubai. *Transactions of the Institute of British Geographers*, 36(4), 516–529

Young, I.M. 2005. *On Female Body Experience: 'Throwing Like a Girl' and Other Essays*. New York: Oxford University Press.

Chapter 14
Working on Masculinity at Home

Rosie Cox

Introduction

The home is so tenaciously tied to femininity and to women's traditional roles as wives, mothers, carers and nurturers that the importance of home to men and to the construction of masculinity is easily obscured. In discussions of masculinity and place, home is often seen as the 'private' sphere, to which the public, male, world exists in opposition. It is the space off stage, less than central to the action, when men go to relax and recuperate and create work for women. This chapter seeks to complicate this view. It uses the example of DIY (do-it-yourself) home improvement activities to explore home as a place where men labour too (see also Meah 2014: this volume, Gorman-Murray 2014: this volume) and where the tasks they carry out, like those women perform in the home, are expected of them because of their gender.

The chapter draws on research carried out with homeowners in New Zealand to examine the place that home improvement has in the negotiation of masculinities. Interviewees, both male and female, portrayed the ability to carry out home maintenance tasks as an important part of the right way to be a 'good Kiwi bloke'. For homeowners, notions of appropriate masculinity were at play in decision-making about home repairs and in the carrying out of DIY projects. Yet there was not a simple relationship between men, masculinity and enthusiastic engagement in DIY. Many women did DIY too and most heterosexual couples shared tasks between them. This chapter explores this negotiation of masculinity by looking at how men learn to take on this duty and how they pass it on to their children. I argue that there is a dissonance between the expressed ideal of men being capable, practical and responsible for home repairs and people's lived experiences of DIY activities, yet this dissonance does not challenge the strength of the ideal.

The chapter begins with a brief contextualisation outlining the importance of DIY to masculinity at specific times and then looks in more detail at the development of particular ideals of masculinity in New Zealand. It then outlines the methods used to gather the data that is drawn upon before turning to findings of the research. First I look at how masculinity is negotiated within households through DIY activity and then discuss home improvement as a form of male duty and a performance of fatherhood.

Domestic space, gender and work

Women's responsibility for reproductive labour is not only a material practice; it is part of a division of labour which is at the heart of theoretical analyses of women's oppression and gender inequalities (Friedan [1963] 2010, Oakley 1976). The work that women do in the home is not just any work; it is work that has profound effects on their standing outside the home. Because of their responsibility for reproductive labour, women practically have less time to devote to paid work or political careers, to leisure or other activities that would cement their standing in 'public' fora (Bryson 2007). Symbolically, women are associated with care work and cleaning and considered to be 'naturally' attuned to such activities in contrast to men's 'natural' acuity in the world of paid work. The close association between women and reproductive labour means that despite extensive gains in struggles for equality in most high-income countries, women still carry out the majority of domestic work regardless of how many hours they work outside the home (Bryson 2007). Who does what at home matters.

Women's responsibility for domestic labour is a key aspect of the construction of traditional femininities and men's avoidance of this work can be defining of them too. However, the home is an important site for the creation and maintenance of masculinities as well as femininities. Men's work on the home can be an element of this; 'work creates place' as Stuart Aitken (2009: 190) has commented. There is labour that takes place in the home which has traditionally been done by men and has, at some times and in some places, been embraced by them as contributing to certain culturally-valued versions of masculinity.

Traditionally masculine domestic activities such as home repairs, renovations, car maintenance, gardening and woodworking have been particularly important to the performance of masculinity at certain times and in certain places. Steven Gelber (1997: 67) has argued that in the early decades of the twentieth century in the United States of America (USA), the rise of DIY was a key component in men's renegotiation of their place in their homes and 'part of the definition of suburban husbanding'. Household repairs and maintenance were free from any hint of gender-role compromise and allowed men to reassert their masculinity at a time when the workplace was no longer a male preserve. DIY was not undertaken to save money but as a way to be a proper man and a good father. Similarly, Gorman-Murray (2011) has shown that an increased focus on home repairs and practical projects was a way for some men to negotiate anxiety produced in the world of work following the global financial crisis in Australia. This chapter reflects on how what happens in the world of work can also bear upon what men do at home and how they feel about home-based activities. Carolyn Goldstein (1998: 37), commenting on the expansion of the American suburbs in the 1950s, described home-improvement activities as transcending cost-benefit analysis, but rather providing a route to the house and lifestyle to which families aspired as 'a way of participating in the American dream'. Within this, DIY was represented as man's domestic duty and easy to use products were specifically developed so that men who had not learnt home-improvement skills could take on projects and so rise to familial expectations. It is not only women who have work to do at home.

Masculinity and home in New Zealand

When discussing relationships between home and masculinity it is worthwhile attending to geographical and historical specificities as well as shared experiences. New Zealand presents an interesting case where imaginings of both masculinity and home have been shaped by imperialism and where the home and the physically-capable man both developed as highly-valued ideals.

Extensive links have been documented between European imperialism and the (re)imagining of home in both colony and metropole (McClintock 1998, Tosh 2007). Aitken (2009: 215) notes 'colonialism took shape around the Anglo-American invention of domesticity and the idea of the home. […] Imperialism cannot be understood without theories of racialised and sexualised power in and through domestic spaces.' The 'civilised' European home was important as both symbol and means of imperialism. In New Zealand, settlement by whites was encouraged through the availability of housing. Annabel Cooper (2008) has written on home ownership as being part of the fabric of the New Zealand dream for emigrants from Europe in the nineteenth century. Advertising materials promised emigrants the possibility of home ownership on a sole breadwinner's wages – i.e., that only men would work for pay. Thus New Zealand offered the chance for both home ownership and a way of living in that house that was only available to the better off in Europe, but was also widely understood to be ideal (Cooper 2008). An ideal of home, made the European settlement of the islands possible.

Closely associated to such ideals of the single family home and male breadwinner were ideals of masculinity which were also developed in the light of colonial ambitions. Lawrence Berg (1999: 73) quotes Tosh (1994: 180), saying that manliness 'was treated as the essence of civic virtue and the root of heroic achievement, while at the same time being scaled down to everyday proportions for the little man'. Berg continues, 'manliness was one of the key concepts in the moral universe of Victorian Britain and its colonial outposts; New Zealand was no exception'.

European settlement of New Zealand was dominated by men for more than 150 years and the rural nature and frontier character of the settler experience provided fertile growth for the development of male institutions and of particular attitudes towards work, physical strength and comfort. Most occupations open to European settlers demanded hard, physical work and but not the application of high levels of particular skills, as would have been more common in Europe. Rather, the ability to learn on the job, turn one's hand to what needed doing, to rough it and 'make do and mend' were all practically useful as well as culturally celebrated. Thus the renowned Kiwi masculinity which developed is not just about brute strength or sporting prowess, but about a particular set of attitudes and ingenuity allied to physical ability (Bell 1996).

New Zealand has been described as 'a Man's country' (Phillips 1987); a country where male stereotypes and national identity have been intimately intertwined (Phillips 1987, Bell 1996) and where the male stereotype, to quote Phillips (1987: vii), 'has been unusually influential upon the lives of both women and men'. Claudia Bell (1996: 76–77) argues that the writing of New Zealand's history has often excluded women from the narrative, 'in fact New Zealand history as a sequence of eras is often recited in terms of male occupations: first the whalers and sealers, then the labourers who came to farm; then the gold-panners and gum-diggers, then the coal miners and so on'.

However, this story of masculinity as woven into New Zealand's history (Philips 1987) is not unproblematic for New Zealanders, nor is it uncontested (see for example Law, Campbell and Dolan 1999; see also special issues on sexuality and gender 'down under' in *Australian Geographer* and *New Zealand Geographer*, Gorman-Murray, Waitt and Johnston 2008 and Gorman-Murray and Morrison 2012). Michael King (1998: vii), writing in 1988 said: 'There is widespread agreement that traditionally held views of masculinity in New Zealand have contributed to a cycle of the emotional deprivation, use of alcohol and drugs, violence and violent crime, which is gathering momentum and threatens a whirlwind of social destruction if not checked.' While rumours of the death of masculinity appear to be exaggerated (Macinnes 1998) it is worth bearing in mind these comments and also that a specific type of masculinity, which has come to be taken for granted – rugby-loving, physically-able, emotionally-disengaged – is not an inevitable result of historical or material conditions (although it is rooted in them) but one which Phillips (1987) and Connell (2005) argue is also a product of government intervention in the light of global imperial rivalries. The image of the Kiwi bloke as practical, strong and sports-obsessed was nurtured in order to increase enlistments for the wars of the late nineteenth and twentieth centuries. It is a model of masculinity that sent men to their deaths as well as being one which has disguised racial and class inequalities (Phillips 1987).

This historical context is important for considering the place of DIY activities in New Zealand today. Authors have commented that home improvements are for some New Zealanders a close link to, or the last remnants of a self-sufficient, frontier past (Lovelock 1999, Mackay, Perkins and Gidlow 2007). Whether or not this is the case, a form of masculinity based on physical ability, ingenuity and practicality has deep roots in New Zealand's colonial history and is still culturally celebrated today.

Methods

This chapter draws on work for a larger project which has looked at both DIY and the commoditisation of home repairs in New Zealand (see for example Cox 2013).

Interviews were carried out with 30 homeowners and ten 'Hubbies' (franchise owners with the company Hire-A-Hubby) in New Zealand between 2007 and 2010 and a small amount of archival research was carried out to look at the changing discourses on home improvements during the twentieth century.

This chapter draws on the interviews with homeowners. They were asked what home repairs/building they paid for, what work they and other household members did for themselves, how they made decisions about who should do tasks and who else might help them with such tasks. Homeowners were interviewed in Auckland, Dunedin, Hamilton and Wellington. Interviewees were sought systematically through personal contacts in these cities, to give maximum variety in terms of household income, age, lifecycle stage and household size. All the homeowner interviewees were Pākehā, that is, white, of European Descent and many of them had lived outside New Zealand at least briefly. The majority of households contained two adults with or without resident children; three of these were lesbian couples. Four households were single people (two men and two women). The interviews were carried out with whichever members of the household agreed to be interviewed and these were relatively evenly split between men and women. In six cases, both adult partners agreed to be interviewed together. Interviews took place in a variety of locations including the participants' homes, workplaces and coffee shops. Interviews with homeowners lasted between 20 minutes and nearly two hours, with interviews in homes generally being longer and including some element of interviewees showing me the projects that they were telling me about.

The interviews were analysed using both pre-determined and emergent themes. The pre-determined themes were based on the original research aims and interview questions but I had not predicted many of the topics that would arise in discussions of home improvement and so also identified many emergent themes during the process of analysis. The topics of masculinity, fatherhood, duty to family and being a 'Kiwi bloke', which are discussed in this chapter, were all themes which emerged during interviews.

Working at DIY and masculinity

The intertwining of DIY skills and activities with ideals of masculinity came through during interviews in many ways. While the association between being able to tackle household repairs and renovations and being a proper 'Kiwi bloke' was strong, lived experiences did not simply reflect or reinforce this. Rather, both men and women worked on their homes and found ways for this to make sense to their gendered identities.

All the men that I talked to described their (female) partners as doing just as much, or almost as much, DIY as themselves and almost all the women interviewed were active DIYers too. Those where the balance was not totally equal were generally families with young children and childcare was falling to the woman while the man worked on the house. Most couples did work on their homes together and seemed to enjoy being able to spend time this way. However, there was a gendered division of tasks within households with women generally doing more painting and more inside work and men doing more heavy 'building' tasks, particularly those using power tools and more outdoor work (see also Morrison 2012). There was also a highly gendered *expectation* about knowing how to do things and this came through in many ways during interviews. For example, when asked if there were friends and/or family members who they could turn to, people searched their minds for *men* who they might consider and instantly dismissed women, as one put it when asked if his children helped, 'I've only got daughters'. The men I spoke to did not feel that they were expected to work on their homes alone, or maybe even at all, but they did feel that they were expected to have knowledge about what to do and how it should be done.

Masculinity is learnt, experimented with and negotiated in the home by women as well as men and in interactions between men and women as they consider DIY tasks. A conversation with two sisters-in-law, Homeowners 20 and 21 exposed the very different ways in which expectations of men could be played out when doing DIY. Even though they were members of the same extended family and social group these two homeowners had very different attitudes towards and experiences of doing home improvements. Yet, despite their differences, they and their husbands both thought about DIY in light of the understanding that this was a man's duty and their attitudes are instructive of how pervasive, yet contradictory such understandings were.

First I asked Homeowner 20 who did which tasks in her house, she was the only interviewee who claimed to do no home maintenance or DIY at all:

> **Interviewer**: So then have you done any of the …
>
> **HO20**: Nothing.
>
> **Interviewer**: Nothing?
>
> **HO20**: Nothing at all.
>
> Interviewer: Would you have if you weren't doing childcare, if you didn't have the kids to look after?
>
> **HO20**: No, it's not my thing […]
>
> **Interviewer**: I'm trying to think if there's anything else … you might have done that you're denying. Do you do any of the gardening?
>
> **HO20**: I planted a veggie garden that's now died [laughs] […] And it's a man – and I was brought up – it's a man's duty to do [laughs]. I just guess … I've just always had a … man to do the man stuff … really.

Homeowner 20 is clearly articulating the idea that DIY is both 'man stuff', something men are interested in and men's duty. Her family contains a large number of tradesmen and many of their friends are tradesmen too who not only do this kind of work for pay but also spend much of their spare time working reciprocally on each others' houses. She expects men to be capable of these tasks and not to have to think about them herself.

In contrast, her sister-in-law, Homeowner 21 told a very different story about who does what and why around the house. She is married to a South African man, who she met when they were both working in London and she described how her husband has had to learn to do DIY since their return to New Zealand:

HO21: He was just quite … keen to um … because it's not something he'd not really done before [right]. So he was quite keen to learn … how to do it. Yeah. And, um … and he was enjoying, so I thought 'well … ' Up until a point he was enjoying it anyway [laughs].

Interviewer: Right [yeah]. So you were the person who knew how to do it and he was learning how to do it, so you let him get on with it?

HO21: Yeah, yeah. For the most part [laughs]. I did have to fix some stuff up over on the stair and he knows that [laughs]. So … but my dad was also enjoying it too [right]. He'd come and join us and so then quite a nice time, yeah.

Interviewer: And is that because … because … [your husband] – is [your husband] from South Africa? So he hadn't been doing those things?

HO21: No, I don't think they did there [yeah]. He'd never painted a room before [right]. Um … and so … he did kind of help with that in the UK, he learned it there when I was redoing the house in my summer holidays. I think he … it was a big … challenge and it was, like, from scratch.

Interviewer: So did your dad and brothers think it was a bit odd that he didn't know how to do any of these things?

HO21: Yeah, it's a standing joke [laughs]. They loved it. He just had hassles all the time [laughs]. Especially in the bathroom, he was trying to nail down a floor and it was, like, 6 little taps to one of their whacks. It was just [laughs]. And we have video footage, actually [laughs].

Interviewer: So the things that you know how to do: how did you learn how to do them?

HO21: Umm … from … doing it growing up, I suppose. My mum liked to change the house. So we often were repainting rooms and stuff. Or she decided

> that she didn't like the hallway anymore, so it needed to be open plan, so all … walls got knocked out.

Homeowner 21's description of the gendered division of DIY activities is very different from that of Homeowner 20's but it reveals the importance of these tasks to masculinity and 'manliness' nonetheless. Homeowner 21's South African husband has used DIY to learn how to be a proper 'Kiwi bloke'. His father and brothers-in-law have teased him and shown him the 'right' way to do things. The message being circulated is that 'real' men can do this work (and do it efficiently with only a few whacks, not with little taps) yet this is despite the fact that Homeowner 21 is herself proficient at these tasks and learnt how to do them from her mother not her father.

The conversation with Homeowners 20 and 21 shows both that doing DIY is bound up with the performance of an idealised form of masculinity and that many people's lived experience conflicts with this ideal without in any way impairing it. Homeowner 20 says it is men's duty to do home repairs and Homeowner 21's husband is learning this new duty, even though he is learning how to do such things from his wife.

Masculinity, fatherhood and duty to family

As the discussion above suggests, being able to carry out home maintenance was understood by some interviewees as a male duty to their families. In other interviews this theme developed and it became clear that carrying out work on the home was also seen as an important element of fatherhood and an expression of adult manhood.

For a number of homeowner interviewees doing home repairs could be a way to express love and care for family and to physically look after them (see Cox 2013). For example, Homeowner 11 explained that when his wife was pregnant with their first child he felt the work he did on their home was something [he] could contribute to the making of their new family: 'I was not carrying the baby or giving birth, but this [painting the outside of the house] was something I could do.' Homeowner 11 went on to explain that he continues to work on the house himself despite being able to afford to pay for tasks to be done because of his ideals of fathering. He wants to be a role model to his children, he said: '[I do DIY] so that they know you can do things. They have helped a little bit with painting, they're not very good, but mostly I want to provide a model so that they will have a go.' Homeowner 11 understood this specifically as a gendered role, as something he would do as a *father*. This was a motivation that was also expressed by other interviewees. For example, Homeowner 9 said when asked if his children had learnt DIY skills: 'No, I think it's exactly the same situation as me and my father they've seen someone do it, they know it can be done and they'll learn it as they need it.' Interviewees felt that they should show their children both how to do DIY and show them that working on your home is something that you can do yourself (see also Jackson 2006 who comments on the importance of DIY to the development of 'healthy' father-son relationships).

When he did decide to pay for a professional, Homeowner 11 also expressed this in terms of his role as a husband and father. He said that over the years he has become happier to pay for people to do things: 'I think that I'm intelligent enough to work out what is good for my family and not take on something that is going to take six months to finish just because that is what a bloke is meant to do.' For Homeowner 11, caring for his house was about his role as a husband and father. The external appearance of his house, such as a neatly painted house and well-kept lawns, communicated his successful accomplishment of this role to the world. He did not expect to do all the work on his house but he did feel responsible for the upkeep of the house and thought that it reflected on him as a man and a father.

Geographers are increasingly paying attention to fathering as work and emotional engagement, something which is 'done' and which creates spaces, including homes, just as mothering does (see also Aitken 2009). As Aitken (2000: 582) writes: 'If we accept that the gender performances of caregivers are amongst the most influential in the evolving political identities of young children, then it is important to study those performances.' Fathering practices can challenge gender norms but, even when unconventional, Aitken (2000) found that fathering was done in the context of patriarchy which shaped fathers' expectations and attitudes towards their role. Homeowner 11 does not feel that he has to work on his house just because that is what 'a bloke is meant to do' but his attitudes towards DIY and his practices clearly developed within what he saw as wider social expectations on men and fathers.

As a socially-produced practice the norms and ideals of fatherhood and how they are played out in the home, around activities such as housework and DIY, can vary from place to place and across time. My research in New Zealand found that many interviewees were motivated to do DIY so that their children could learn from them, both because they had learnt this way from their parents, or because they had not and regretted it. This contrasts to Perrons, Plomien and Kilkey's (2010) findings from their research in the UK, where ideals of 'hands-on' fatherhood were more likely to be a motivation for paying a professional handyman in order to free up time to spend with kids.

Homeowner 11 was able to express his desire to pass on a particular 'can do' attitude to his children and this sort of inter-generational transfer of knowledge and skills was important to many interviewees. While both men and women learned how to do DIY from parents and taught these skills to children, men were also learning what was expected of them as men and fathers were negotiating their own masculinity as they taught their children.

Kirsten Lovelock (1999) has written about how men in the Southland of New Zealand learned masculinity through securing knowledge of machines both in the workplace ant at home. 'In this region [Southland], securing some knowledge of machines has been the chief way men have obtained employment for over a century. Skill with machines has become integral to what it means to be a man' (Lovelock 1999: 129). She goes on:

> It is possible that some of the young men in Mataura [a town in Southland] may never experience the employment opportunities that their fathers and grandfathers did, but they continue to be socialised by these men and so take on a certain understanding of the place that machines have in a social world. In their greatly expanding leisure time (due to unemployment and underemployment) they still tinker with cars and spend time learning and understanding machines – even if the scope of such knowledge has become restricted to their knowledge of cars and lawnmowers. (Lovelock 1999:132)

Lovelock was examining a form of masculinity related to paid work in local factories but her work shows how skills which are valued economically can also become part of life outside work and integrated into identities beyond the workplace. She reveals how some skills are important to masculine identities as they link to historical legacies and culturally valued abilities even when no longer directly used at work. DIY is about skills and practices which make home but it can also be about more than that because the skills involved are so unequivocally masculine (see also Jackson 2006).

Only one man mentioned in interviews had been discouraged from learning DIY skills by his parents. Homeowner 12 described her (male) partner as 'not a typical Kiwi bloke' when asked what DIY he did. She went on to explain that:

> His father didn't want them to know any kind of trade or work with their hands at all because his father saw it as very working class [right] and that's where he had come from and he didn't want his kids involved in that […] He saw that was beneath them and that that they should learn more intellectual things than physical things.

DIY activity can be about passing on skills, the practice of being a 'good Kiwi bloke' and passing on a 'can do' ethos. While in New Zealand this is a form of masculinity which is culturally celebrated and which has roots in a national and colonial history, it is also a form of masculinity which is classed and is not equally embraced by all. As this quote shows it is not masculinity per se that is practiced or negotiated during DIY but particular forms of masculinity which are valued by some people but threatening to the class position of others.

Conclusion

This chapter has examined the relationship between the production of masculinity and home maintenance activities in New Zealand. It has argued that there is a strong ideological association between home maintenance and men's duty to their family but in practice the gendering of DIY is not clear-cut. However, the participation of women in DIY (and the non-participation of some men) did not seem to decrease the association between ideals of manliness and being proficient at home improvements.

The gendering of responsibility for home repairs is, of course, not unique to New Zealand but it is important to consider current practices and attitudes in light of New Zealand's specific history; a history which strongly valued practicality, ingenuity and physically ability, particularly in men. A number of interviewees referred to what 'Kiwi blokes' were 'meant' to be like and this image of the capable, practical man is still at play when people think about their own home repairs. With this is mind, this case study highlights the connections between masculinity, everyday practices and place in a multi-scalar way. The practices of DIY link together the national cultural space of Pākehā New Zealand, the local and the domestic space of the home.

Carrying out DIY could also be about performing fatherhood at home. Forms of masculinity and practices of fatherhood are communicated within families and between generations in mundane ways. The work which men do in the home, like that of women, is constitutive of gendered identities. The home is a place where masculinities as well as femininities are produced and reproduced and routine acts, such as carrying out DIY, are ways in which this is done. Both men and women take part in these routine negotiations producing and communicating expectations for themselves and others and passing on practical knowledge and skills.

References

Aitken, S.C. 2000. Fathering and faltering: 'sorry, but you don't have the necessary accoutrements'. *Environment and Planning A*, 32(4), 581–598.

Aitken, S.C. 2009. *The Awkward Spaces of Fathering*. Aldershot: Ashgate.

Bell, C. 1996. *Inventing New Zealand*. Melbourne: Penguin Books.

Berg, L. 1999. A (white) man of his times? Sir George Grey and the narration of hegemonic masculinity in Victorian New Zealand, in *Masculinities in Aotearoa/New Zealand*, edited by R. Law, H. Campbell and J. Dolan. Palmerston North: Dunmore Press, 67–83.

Bryson, V. 2007. *Gender and the Politics of Time: Feminist Theory and Contemporary Debates*. Bristol: Policy Press.

Connell, R.W. 2005. *Masculinities*. 2nd edition. Cambridge: Polity Press.

Cooper, A. 2008. Poor men in the land of promises. *Australian Historical Studies*, 39(2), 245–261.

Cox, R. 2013. The complications of 'hiring a hubby': gender relations and the commoditisation of home maintenance in New Zealand. *Social and Cultural Geography*, 14(5), 575–590.

Friedan, B. [1963] 2010. *The Feminine Mystique*. London: Penguin Classics.

Gelber, S.M. 1997. Do-it-yourself: constructing, repairing and maintaining domestic masculinity. *American Quarterly*, 49(1), 66–112.

Goldstein, C. 1998. *Do It Yourself: Home Improvement in 20th-Century America*. New York: Princeton Architectural Press.

Gorman-Murray, A. 2011. Economic crises and emotional fallout: work, home and men's senses of belonging in post-GFC Sydney. *Emotion, Space and Society*, 4(4), 211–220.

Gorman-Murray, A., Waitt, G. and Johnston, L. 2008. Guest editorial – Geographies of sexuality and gender 'down under'. *Australian Geographer*, 39(3), 235–246.

Gorman-Murray, A. and Morrison, C.A. 2012. Revisiting geographies of sexuality and gender down under. *New Zealand Geographer*, 68(2), 77–80.

Jackson, A. 2006. Labour as Leisure: the Mirror Dinghy and DIY Sailors. *The Journal of Design History*, 19(1), 57–67.

King, M. 1988. *One of the Boys: Changing Views of Masculinity in New Zealand*. Auckland: Heinemann.

Law, R., Campbell, H. and Schick, R. 1999. Introduction, in *Masculinities in Aotearoa/New Zealand*, edited by R. Law, H. Campbell and J. Dolan. Palmerston North: Dunmore Press, 13–35.

Lovelock, K. 1999. Men and machines: manufacturing work sites in Mataura, Southland, in *Masculinities in Aotearoa/New* Zealand, edited by R. Law, H. Campbell and J. Dolan. Palmerston North: Dunmore Press, 121–134.

Mackay, M., Perkins, H. and Gidlow, B. 2007. *Constructing and maintaining a central element of housing culture in New Zealand: DIY (do-it-yourself) home building, renovation and maintenance*. Paper presented at Transformations in Housing, Urban Life and Public Policy Conference: Transformations in Housing, Urban Life and Public Policy Conference (Seoul, Korea: 30 August – 1 September).

Macinnes, J. 1998. *The End of Masculinity: The Confusion of Sexual Genesis and Sexual Difference in Modern Society*. Buckingham: Open University Press.

McClintock, A. 1995. *Imperial Leather: Race, Gender and Sexuality in the Colonial Contest*. New York: Routledge.

Morrison, C.A. 2012. Home and heterosexuality in Aotearoa New Zealand: the spaces and practices of DIY and home renovation. *New Zealand Geographer*, 68(2), 121–129.

Oakley, A. 1990. *Housewife*. New Edition. Melbourne: Penguin Books.

Perrons, D., Plomien, A. and Kilkey, M. 2010. Migration and uneven development within an enlarged European Union: fathering, gender divisions and male migrant domestic services. *European Urban and Regional Studies*, 17(2), 197–215.

Philips, J. 1987. *A Man's Country*. Auckland: Penguin Books.

Tosh, J. 2007. *A Man's Place: Masculinity and the Middle-Class Home in Victorian England*. Bury: St Edmundsbury Press.

PART 5
Masculinities and the Family

Chapter 15
Domestic Ageing Masculinities and Grandfathering

Anna Tarrant

Introduction

There is evidence of a burgeoning theoretical literature in the social sciences concerning the ways in which men are experiencing ageing in specifically gendered ways *as men* (Calasanti 2004, Featherstone, Rivett and Scourfield 2007, Hearn 2007, Arber and Timonen 2012). This literature remains in its infancy (van den Hoonard 2007), and more generally within theorising of masculinities, both the spatiality of masculinities (Hopkins and Noble 2009) and old age (Mowl, Pain and Talbot 2000) remain marginalised. This chapter argues that grandfatherhood, a familial life stage understood as paradoxically intersected by masculinities and old age (Davidson, Daly and Arber 2003, Mann 2007), offers potential to examine men's performances and constructions of ageing masculinities and consequently how this might inform experiences of different spaces, including home, in distinctive ways (Tarrant 2010a). The emplaced nature of these gendered experiences for men later in life also deserve greater attention, particularly by social geographers, who have indicated that the intersections and contradictions of ageing and masculinities are also produced and experienced spatially (e.g. McDowell 2003, Pain, Mowl and Talbot 2000, Tarrant 2010b).

The aim of this chapter is to examine the spatiality of the theoretically paradoxical performances of ageing domestic masculinities. I do this through an analysis of thirty-one qualitative, semi-structured interview narratives obtained from men who are grandfathers in the UK. I argue that these men's grandfathering practices, and consequently their performances of ageing masculinities, are simultaneously intersectional, relational and situated and are significant to the material and social relations that shape the home. Results demonstrate that men negotiate the intersections of their masculinities and ageing in multiple and variable ways that are spatially constituted.

Grandfatherhood, masculinities and old age

It was Sarah Cunningham-Burley (1984) who first identified gendered differences in women and men's orientations to grandparenting. Since then research on grandfathers has been piecemeal and it was not until some 20 years later that specific attention to the roles and relationships of grandfathers were critically appraised (Mann 2007). Mann's (2007) review of these patchy and limited existing literatures concerning grandfather identities was significant for reinvigorating interest in grandfathering and revealing the importance of the intersections of masculinities and old age as they construct grandfatherhood. In alignment with the convergence of sociological and gerontological literatures to study older men *as men* (see Calasanti 2004, Arber and Timonen 2012), this paved the way for developing knowledge about the identities and practices of grandfathers as old men.[1] This shift in focus represented a distinct departure from existing research about grandparents, which has since been criticised for making assumptions that men perform in opposite ways to grandmothers (Scraton and Holland 2006) or are not involved in their family lives at all. While the emergence of new norms of 'good grandfatherhood' (Mann and Leeson 2010) are being reported in contemporary research about grandfathers, further work needs to be done to assess whether or not the everyday activities and practices of grandfathers are actually changing (Mann 2007). Mann (2007) argues that these 'changes' in grandfathering, if they are indeed changing, are contingent on a range of contextual factors including age, gender, geographical proximity and so on, all of which shape individual experiences of grandfatherhood.

Of these factors, orientations to hegemonic masculinity[2] and ageing are significant and indicate that men's identities are subject to norms of both ageing and masculinity (Eman 2009, Spector-Mersel 2006). Current theoretical debates about ageing masculinities are complex and question the extent to which men are able to maintain semblance to models of hegemonic masculinity, as they get older. The intersection of old age, for example, erects barriers to old men's constructions of hegemonic masculinity, in relation to economics, sexuality and athleticism, and is thought to make men more dependent (Hearn 2011). However, men may also benefit from the resources they have accrued over the lifecourse on account of being men, especially financially (Hearn 2011). In referencing Whitehead (2002), Eman (2009) argues that the theoretical association of hegemonic masculinity with youthfulness automatically constructs growing old as a descent into decline and loss of power. Rather than a complete disconnection from hegemonic masculinity, however, Davidson, Daly and Arber (2003) consider grandfatherhood to be a paradox. Men become more nurturing and caring in their relationships with

1 I use the term old men as opposed to older men in this chapter, in alignment with Calasanti's (2004) arguments. She argues that the word 'old' is currently stigmatised. Using 'old' imbues it with meaning and attempts to reclaim it and construct it more positively.

2 A highly critiqued yet prolific concept in studies of masculinities, describing culturally exulted forms of masculinity and male identity (Connell 1995, Connell and Messerschmidt 2005). Hegemonic masculinity conceptualises the most powerful and ideal ways of being a man in a hierarchy of multiple masculinities but is never actually achievable by many men (Calasanti 2004).

grandchildren, but may also act the sage and have the resources to continue to enact hegemonic forms of masculinity. It is therefore difficult to come to any specific conclusions about the degree to which men become marginalised by their ageing.

The complexity of this issue is rooted in theoretical understandings of both masculinities and ageing as multiple, performative and social, shaped through social forces but also in social interaction (Connell and Messerschmidt 2005, Laz 1998). While individuals may be regulated by specifically gendered and aged norms, they also have agency to respond to these norms, in different places and at different times and in and through multiple interactions with others. This perspective portends to the diversity of ageing masculinity performances as well as their spatiality, to the extent that at any one time and in any one place various axes of difference that construct identities have different implications for men's inclusivity and belonging.

Both masculinities and age are also understood as axes of power, difference and similarity and are therefore relational. Connell (1995), for example, argues that masculinities are part of a broader system of gender relations that define power differentials between men and women, and between groups of men. This is significant especially to a study of grandfathers, because while grandfather identities are undoubtedly regulated by norms of masculinities and ageing that are also spatially experienced, they are also relational and familial identities, defined by their generational relationships. To be a grandfather is to have a grandchild.

Geographies of age have recently shifted to encompass these ideas, through conceptualising age as relational (Hopkins and Pain 2007). From this perspective, individuals and their identities are understood through their relationships with others of different age groups and generations. Intergenerationality, for example, suggests that individuals make sense of themselves partly on the basis of generational sameness or difference. In adopting this approach, generation is considered an important aspect of an individual's social identity as well as age. For familial generational identities such as grandfather, this is important to recognise given that difference from children and grandchildren, and shared identities with other grandfathers, all influence how older men experience different spaces at different time. Significant to Hopkins and Pain's (2008) conceptualisations of age as relational are that these aspects of people's lives are also consequential in shaping geographies at different scales.

Ageing, masculinities and the homespace

As previously discussed, geographical proximity and context are regarded as contingent factors in the performances of grandparenting (Mann 2007), and geographers have already made important contributions to revealing the spatiality of this identity paradox. From the perspective of existing gendered domestic imaginaries, family, care work and femininity, which also construct the gendered differences between grandmothers and grandfathers, have been more dominantly associated with, and even bound to the idea and literal form of, home (Gorman-Murray 2008, Domosh and Seager 2001). Chapman (2004) argues that while wives are positioned as 'homemaker', men are positioned directly opposite, in a gendered binary, as 'breadwinner'. This constructs a gendered division of labour that reproduces gendered inequalities and constraints, especially for women. This and the imaginary that men's identity is bound to a work identity (McDowell 1999) also construct a problematic separation between men, domesticity and home.

While there has been more attention to how meanings of home change as people get older (Blunt and Dowling 2006), geographers have also outlined the association of ageing bodies with different places, and in particular 'homespaces' (Varley 2008, Bhatti 2006, Harper and Laws 1995). Pain (2001) argues that the home and other sites all acquire meanings associated with age. According to Vanderbeck (2007: 206), the discursive emplacement of age identities reproduces 'patterns of age differentiation and segregation' that have important implications for the spatiality of intergenerational relationships. Older men, whose identities, as previously outlined, are regulated by age and gender norms, therefore occupy a paradoxical and contradictory relationship to home; one where their gendered identities are imagined as separate from the domestic sphere but where their age(ing) identities are associated with home.

Several geographers have explored this contradictory relationship and predominantly found that older men are more likely to have negative or ambivalent relationships to home later in life. Mowl, Pain and Talbot (2000) uncovered distinct gendered differences between older women and men and their perceptions of home. The women in their study were more likely to reinforce a positive female identity at home, while the men considered it to accelerate their ageing. Basing her arguments on the work of Varley and Blasco (2000), Brickell (2012) also argues that men's complicated relationship with home later in life is manifest in the loss of privacy from family members alongside the loss of connection to a work identity (McDowell 1993). In their study of ageing men in Urban Mexico, Varley and Blasco (2000) found that men felt particularly dislocated at home because their identities remained rooted in a breadwinning role. In particular they complained of being unable to be by themselves at home a lot of the time, and some even drove around in a car if they owned one to get some privacy.

Critique of dominant imaginaries of home as connected to femininity and family has resulted in a shift in focus more recently, to domestic masculinities and the ways in which male identities are co-constituted of, and interrelated with, home (Gorman-Murray 2008). Gorman-Murray (2008) argues for mutuality between domesticity and masculinity in which male identities reconfigure imaginaries of home, and home and homemaking practices shape male identities. This approach, he argues, provides insight into the diverse and fluid gendered meanings of home. The relationship between ageing masculinities as they construct older male identities, and how these intersections of difference complicate men's relationship to homespace, have yet to be considered.

Methodology and methods

A relational and interpretative approach to men's ageing masculinities is employed in this chapter to reveal that grandfather identities, and their diverse enactments, are products of the socially-constructed intersections of their identities and their intergenerational relationships, and are also co-constituted of the spaces in which they are enacted. The interpretative approach is necessary for understanding how *grandfather* is socially constructed and experienced by the participants in diverse ways, but also situated (Mann 2007) and understood at particular points in time. As such, the subjective meanings of grandfather for each individual are considered significant, as are the social structures that shape meanings of contemporary grandfatherhood.

The data presented in this chapter are from a larger project undertaken between July 2009 and July 2010 that sought to examine the meanings men construct about their identities as grandfathers, as well as the spatialities of contemporary grandfathering. Thirty-one in-depth, qualitative, semi-structured interviews were conducted with men who defined themselves as grandfathers in the Lancaster District region of the UK. In-depth, semi-structured interviews were deemed most appropriate for drawing interpretative conclusions about commonly held ideas about contemporary grandfatherhood by the men, as well as more exploratory work about the individual, subjective meanings men assigned to their identities, practices and intergenerational relationships. Similarities across the sample in terms of how grandfatherhood is currently constructed did emerge, but more interesting were the diversities in orientations to these ideas in the men's narratives and the reasons for this.

The research participants were recruited from a range of employers and social clubs in the local area, and snowballing was also employed. The aim of this was to target a diverse group of people from different age groups. The age range of the participants was 51–88 years, and so represented the broad age range of individuals grandfathering in contemporary Britain. Only one of the participants had grandchildren living with him in his home. The rest lived either locally or at large distances from their grandchildren. Diversity between the participants in terms of ethnicity, religion, social class and sexuality was more limited in the sample and future research could aim to recruit to accommodate these differences. The research was conducted ethically. All participants signed consent forms to confirm their participation and understanding of the project aims. This has become an accepted practice for ethical social research (Wiles et al. 2009) and I deemed it especially necessary because individuals were discussing personal information, not only about themselves but also others. All participants have been assigned a pseudonym to protect their identities. Similarly, place names, names of family members and any identifiable associations have been anonymised.

Analysis was an iterative process. I transcribed each interview and then coded the data using software program Atlas.Ti. A constructed grounded theory approach was adopted in alignment with Charmaz (2006), and a two-tiered coding system including axial and open codes was employed. While grounded theory has attracted critique, as with Sorensen and Cooper's (2010) contention, it was deemed important that the men discussed what they felt was important to them about their identities as grandfathers. As a result, the semi-structured interview format was most appropriate and no theoretical approach was applied in advance. Themes were generated through the coding system, and what emerged was the importance of a variety of spaces, including the home, to men's practices of grandfathering and their identities as older men. In this chapter I particularly discuss the themes of home, intergenerational interaction, and caring practices, that emerged from the data coding.

Performing ageing masculinities at home

In talking about their grandfathering, the men in this study described a range of practices and activities that they engage in with grandchildren, but also explicitly identified specific spaces of intergenerational encounter. In alignment with research on grandfathers and older men in leisure studies (Wiersma and Chesser 2011, Scraton and Holland 2006) men and women's practices of leisure as grandparents were not gender-neutral. The men particularly emphasised going outdoors and being active as central to their care work as grandfathers, and often constructed gendered spatial binaries between themselves and their wives. This represented a continued gendered division of labour/leisure later in life between grandfathers and their wives, who they described as responsible for domestic tasks (Tarrant 2013). Connection to public and outdoor leisure spaces also indicated that older men continue to construct and negotiate their identities as older men through spatial connections to norms of hegemonic masculinity – i.e., the public sphere as masculine space. Leisure and the use of outdoor spaces represent a continued disconnection of men from the home (McDowell 1999). However, as Smith and Winchester (1998) have argued the boundaries between work and home, and in this case leisure and home, are blurred, to the extent that men negotiate alternative masculine identities in these spaces and consequently re-define work/home, male/female binaries. For the majority of the men interviewed for this study, home was also deemed important, as a place for spending time with grandchildren and in informing their explanations of what it is that a grandfather (and grandmother) does for their grandchildren. Sam and Reg particularly describe providing a second home:

> I spend a lot of time with [grandchildren] in our house, so our house is like their second home. (Sam, age 51)

> [Being a grandfather] it's very special, because we hope that we'll have … a good relationship with our grandchildren, that they will see that we offer, almost

> a second home, that there's somebody else there to care, and to love them … it's quite special being a grandfather. (Reg, age 66)

Reg and Sam are surprisingly candid about their perceptions of home in the context of their relationships with grandchildren. Mowl, Pain and Talbot (2000) describe the home as an accelerant of ageing and approaching death for older men, but the home in grandfatherhood represents something alternative; it involved providing and being a 'good grandfather'. Reg, in particular, departs from hegemonic masculinity associated with breadwinning and not being involved in family life by describing his love for his grandchildren and his desire to maintain good relationships. Interestingly, however, the paradox of being nurturing but also masculine emerges in the need to provide a second home for grandchildren. Being a protector and provider typifies a middle-class fatherhood role (Morrell 2006) – a role that these grandfathers continue to consider important as older men.

While the provision of a home is deemed important, it is also a contradictory site where ageing is most acutely resisted by grandfathers through grandfathering practices. For the men in this study the home and becoming a grandfather was deemed a marker of old age (see Tarrant 2010a). However, grandchildren were also considered a source of opportunity for being active and fit and getting out of the house:

> [On becoming a grandfather] It was quite scary, what did Churchill say?, 'it's the beginning of the end' (laughs) yes I think, I think while it's a lovely and unique thing to happen, it's also a big dose of reality, because I mean you're not going to have any more of your own children and that's finished, I think it's a stage of your life that … I don't tend to dwell on, put it that way you know. (Philip, age 62)

> I think it's good for you as a grandparent to be held down and made to run after a football and stop being lazy and sat in front of a television so there's a positive sort of health dynamic there, and I think not just with the grandchildren but with children as well. A lot of our closer relationships are with the next generation down and I think in old age I think it keeps you younger and, wiser and your feet closer to the ground. I think there is a danger with the older generation of sort of nodding off into Coronation Street for the next 30 years. (Peter, age 65)

Kaufman and Elder (2003) found that individuals subjectively associate grandparenting with an old age identity, and men like Peter interpret this spatially; as being stuck in a sofa or wasting away at home. While only 62 years old, Philip relates becoming a grandfather to a specific lifestage; the beginning of the end, but not something he chooses to dwell on. Peter identifies intergenerational relations with grandchildren as central to keeping young and also to maintaining a link to the outdoor world. As such, both lifecourse and contemporary intergenerational relations shape orientations to the more negative associations of old age that are tied to the home, but also provide opportunities to maintain links to hegemonic masculinity such as keeping active and fit and engaging in leisure/sporting activities.

Intergenerational contact at home

The previous discussion reveals that while there is evidence of continued associations with outdoor and leisure spaces, the home is also a key space in defining contemporary grandfathering for the men and a key space for intergenerational practices of grandfathering. In terms of the intersections of masculinity and ageing, providing a home for children and grandchildren is deemed important, and yet spending too much time there is deemed to represent being old and unhealthy. The paradox of ageing as a man is clearly inherently spatial as well. But what about the relationships and intergenerational encounters men have with grandchildren at home? As outlined in a previous paper (Tarrant 2010a) and by others (Davidson, Daly and Arber 2003), men's interaction with grandchildren shows signs of becoming much more intimate and nurturing than previous research suggests. Davidson, Daly and Arber (2003) do not indicate the types of practices men conduct in becoming more nurturing, but my own study suggested that a small yet significant minority of the men were engaging in more intimate practices such as nappy changing, or what Twigg (2004) calls the 'dirty' care work usually reserved for women. There was also discussion of intimate practices, including hugging and kissing, that were described as highly gendered practices, especially contingent on the genders of grandchildren (see Tarrant 2010a). These kinds of practices are spatially paradoxical in relation to more traditional gendered expectations of men and home premised on fatherly discipline as opposed to nurturance and care.

While some evidence of this 'new grandfatherhood' (Leeson and Mann 2007) was discussed by a minority of the men as part of their practices, predominantly emphasis was on creating and providing spaces in the home suitable for grandchildren and interacting with them through, often, established gendered practices:

> I build him, we've given [grandson] a construction thing, where you build it, if you imagine Meccano?, yeah well got young, lots of pre-formed shapes and things like that. We're very happy to get down on the floor and crawl about and play with things. (Reg, age 66)

> With a small child you've got to be involved and directing and, helping and guiding, you know how these bits of Lego go and, 'shall we build a bus together?' and whatever.(Peter, age 65)

> We are starting to go through the stage of having to change things at home, like move things out of reach, fasten my grandfather clock to the wall so she doesn't pull it over and this sort of thing and move wires out of the way and, things which … you don't think about until the grandchild arrives you know. People say 'oh you'll have to move this you know' and then of course she moves in and you have to do it; catches on kitchen cupboards this sort of thing, change the glass in the door so it's all safety glass or something, yes. (James, age 62)

The narratives presented here indicate that, as grandfathers, men emphasise practices of care that are both activity-based and involve educating or being 'wise'. Rather than talk about caring work, the majority of the men were keen to discuss their home-based practices in terms of fixing, providing spaces and attending to practical tasks. Interactions with grandchildren allow them to extend their interests in making and doing. For James, part of this practice is to child-safe his home and to protect his granddaughter from the dangers therein. Ageing domestic masculinities consequently emerge through intergenerational encounters and construct the men's homes as sites of intergenerational care, albeit through more conventional, and less intimate domestic tasks, such as fixing (maintaining space) and protecting (controlling space).

Charles, who lives with his grandchildren, tells a different story. He places emphasis on finding space away from his grandchildren while at home. Brickell (2012) argues that a loss of privacy from family members when returning to the home post-retirement can be a source of disempowerment for older men; while this was certainly the case for Charles who lives with his grandchildren, he also employed strategies for creating his own space and some time for himself:

> we all need our own space at times, they're out at school most of the time, they're out of school from 8 o'clock in the morning and they have school activities and so it's often, all but one night a week, it's always after 5 o'clock, sometimes even as late as seven, when they come home. That's not purposely, they want to do these things … we're quite happy for the children to be there, but we all need space. Now they have their own bedrooms and we've fitted them all out, they've got their own gear, their own toys and gear and what have you and, me wife and I have our own room where I have my computer and everything as well, so, we have our own space if we want it, or we can be together. (Charles, age 65)

While not specifically gendered, Charles discusses the marking of particular spaces in his home as belonging only to him and his wife in order to get some privacy from their grandchildren. For Charles it is important to have his own space at home where intergenerational contact is limited and he can connect to what he deems important, such as his computer. Sibley (1995) argues that this patterning and ownership of space in the home actively separates out generational roles by marking particular spaces as adult. As such these practices of creating and negotiating particular spaces in the home can also contribute to defining men generationally and in constructing appropriate domestic spaces that balance intergenerational contact with grandchildren.

This negotiation of generational difference between grandfathers and their male grandchildren at home is also a powerful tool in the constitution of domestic ageing masculinities. In Ted's case, a generationally-organised hierarchy of masculinities emerges that shapes his power and disrupts his ability to perform hegemonic masculinities at home:

> Well, there's not a lot of difference between role of grandfather as father, only is you don't have the // the same power with your grandchildren you know, if I shout, when we have a meal and they do ought wrong and I shout at them they turn round and say 'I'll tell me dad!' (laughs). (Ted, age 66)

In alignment with Haywood and Mac an Ghaill (2003) and Gorman-Murray (2008), the occupation of the homespace does not mean that men let go of their masculinities altogether. However, family relationships with sons and grandsons in the homespace, and intergenerational encounters with them therein, are distinctly relational and have the capacity to construct older men as less powerful and therefore less capable of achieving the authority and mastery associated with ideals of hegemonic masculinity. In this case, Ted's ability to discipline is significantly reduced and he is marginalised in interactions with the younger men in his family. This results in a challenge to patriarchy and, from a feminist perspective, a desirable breakdown of hegemonic masculinity in the home, particularly in Ted's case. However the relational display of masculinities across generations is also stark, reinforcing the hierarchies between men of different generations that are, according to Connell (2005) at least, always organised in relation to hegemonic masculinity.

Discussion and conclusion

This chapter explored the performances of ageing domestic masculinities by men who are grandfathers, focusing on the men's descriptions of spaces of intergenerational encounter and practices. Taken together, existing research suggests that grandfather identities, and consequently the performances of ageing domestic masculinities, are relational, emplaced and constructed in and through relationships with grandchildren. An interpretative methodology and qualitative interviews were conducted with men who are grandfathers to examine this in further detail and to explore the realities of contemporary grandfathering beyond theoretical conjecture.

Evidently, older men's identities, as examined through their interactions with grandchildren at home are multiply negotiated so that men who are grandfathers perform their identities in diverse ways. Their performances of masculinities are much more varied than suggested in previous research that has focused on retirement transitions to home suggests (Brickell 2012, Varley and Blasco 2000). The men in this study, while associating grandfatherhood with being old, certainly did not explicitly consider home as a space that increased their negative relationships to stereotypes of age, even if they were aware of this connection. Instead, they interacted with children and grandchildren in active ways and created spaces at home through practices that reflected the more powerful facets of their identities – their masculinities. In this way, like older male athletes (Eman 2009), being an involved and active grandfather allows men to perform what they consider to be successful old age masculinities. Successful performances of grandfathering, including taking an active and involved role with grandchildren, were contingent on both lifecourse experiences and intergenerational interactions (see also Richardson 2014: this volume, Aitken 2014: this volume), which the men considered important in justifying and explaining their current attitudes to care work and spending time at home.

The relationship between home, masculinities and age are mutual to the extent that imaginaries of home can also be re-shaped by men's performances of identity (Gorman-Murray 2008). In this study, this was certainly not only gendered but also reflected the ways in which older men construct imaginaries of home through their experiences of ageing. The paradoxes of ageing masculinities shaping men's identities contributed to the ways in which they actively created and resisted their age identities through their use of home, and in their ongoing practices of identity work that seem to represent an enduring attachment to hegemonic masculinity. While associations with hegemonic masculinity and gendered divisions of labour were largely durable, there was also evidence for the redefinition of masculinities, and the home was significant to this later in life. The men considered their homes to be important spaces of intergenerational encounter, and a small, yet noteworthy, minority of these men also adopted more nurturing practices that challenged traditional expectations of male and female practices and roles at home. However, while these findings suggest some positivity in the redefinition of male identities, my analysis of constructions of ageing masculinities suggested gendered spatial divisions of labour remained dominant – both public/private distinctions and within the domestic sphere itself – and indicate that masculinities are thus still powerful and continue to reproduce gendered inequalities in the home. To some extent, negative associations with ageing encourage men to reinforce these masculinities even more so, stressing active, healthy and capable embodied masculinities (arguably hegemonic ideals) in their interactions with grandchildren.

This chapter perhaps brings us no closer to resolving the ageing masculinities paradox and debate, nor the extent to which men lose their relationship to hegemonic masculinity, as introduced in the literature review. However, the empirical findings of this research contribute evidence that men experience ageing and the spaces of later life in ways that allow them to negotiate the contradictory intersections of their identities. Some are likely to be more successful than others. The men in this sample, for example, were all able-bodied and arguably just leaving middle-age. They associated their identities as grandfathers with old age, and were even considered old by their grandchildren (as Ted's narrative reveals), but some of the more physical challenges of ageing were not yet pertinent to these men. They still had both embodied and discursive resources available to them to construct, align themselves with and reproduce hegemonic masculinity. Future research into much older grandfathering would be especially useful for examining how embodied ageing and associated decline impacts men's relationships to home and grandchildren, and how these are constructed, both socially and biologically.

Given the diversity of contextual factors that shape men's lives, including their biographies, movements through space and their relationships, debates concerning a complete loss of connection to hegemonic masculinity may never be fully resolved, although ageing men offer some hope in pursuing challenges to patriarchy and the durability of men's gendered practices. Men variably negotiate the social structures that constitute their identities and constructions of grandfatherhood, and to this end, they variably resist the 'decline' normatively associated with ageing. What I have shown is that there is a need for greater awareness of the relationality, spatiality and intersectionality of ageing domestic masculinities because this necessarily complicates geographers' understandings of multiple masculinities and performances of ageing, including their relationship to different spaces and their constitution in different contexts.

References

Arber, S. and Timonen, V. 2012. *Contemporary Grandparenting: Changing family Relationships in Global Contexts.* Bristol: Polity Press.

Bhatti, M. 2006. 'When I'm in the garden I can create my own paradise': homes and gardens in later life. *The Sociological Review*, 54(2), 318–341.

Blunt, A. and Dowling, R. 2006. *Home*. London: Routledge.

Brickell, K. 2012. 'Mapping' and 'doing' critical geographies of home. *Progress in Human Geography*, 36(2), 225–244.

Calasanti, T. 2004. Feminist gerontology and old men. *Journal of Gerontology: Social Sciences*, 59b(6), 5305–5314.

Chapman, T. 2004. *Gender and Domestic Life: Changing Practices in Families and Households*. Basingstoke: Palgrave Macmillan.

Charmaz, K. 2006. *Constructing Grounded Theory: A Practical Guide through Qualitative Analysis.* London: Sage Publications.

Connell, R.W. 1995. *Masculinities.* Berkeley: University of California Press.

Connell, R.W. 2005. *Masculinities*. 2nd edition. Cambridge: Polity Press.

Connell, R.W. and Messerschmidt, J.W. 2005. Hegemonic masculinity: rethinking the concept. *Gender and Society*, 19(6), 829–859.

Cunningham-Burley, S. 1984. 'We don't talk about it ... ': issues of gender and method in the portrayal of grandfatherhood. *Sociology*, 18(3), 325–338.

Davidson, K., Daly, T., and Arber, S. 2003. Exploring the social worlds of older men, in *Gender and Ageing: Changing Roles and Relationships*, edited by S. Arber et al. Maidenhead: Open University Press, 168–185.

Domosh, M. and Seagar, J. 2001. *Putting Women in Place: Feminist Geographers Make Sense of the World*. New York: Guildford Press.

Eman, J. 2009. Constructing successful old-age masculinities amongst athletes. *NORMA: Nordic Journal for Masculinity Studies*, 6(1), 46–58.

Featherstone, B., Rivett, M. and Scourfield, J. 2007. *Working with Men in Health and Social Care*. London: Sage Publications.

Gorman-Murray, A. 2008. Masculinity and the home: a critical review and conceptual framework. *Australian Geographer*, 39(3), 367–379.

Harper, S. and Laws, G. 1995. Rethinking the geography of ageing. *Progress in Human Geography*, 19(2), 199–221.

Haywood, C. and Mac an Ghaill, M. 2003. *Men and Masculinities: Theory, Research and Social Practice*. Buckingham: Open University Press.

Hearn, J. 2007. From older men to boys: masculinity theory and the life course(s). *NORMA: Nordic Journal for Masculinity Studies*, 2(1), 79–84.

Hearn, J. 2011. Neglected intersectionalities in studying men: age/ing, virtuality, transnationality, in *Framing Intersectionality: Debates on a Multi-Faceted Concept in Gender Studies*, edited by H. Lut, M.T.H. Vivar and L. Supik. Farnham: Ashgate, 89–104.

Hopkins, P. and Noble, G. 2009. Masculinities in place: situated identities, relations and intersectionality. *Social and Cultural Geography*, 10(8), 811–819.

Hopkins, P. and Pain, R. 2007. Geographies of age: thinking relationally. *Area*, 39(2), 287–294.

Van den Hoonard, D. 2007. Aging and masculinity: a topic whose time has come. *Journal of Aging Studies*, 21(4), 277–368.

Kaufman, G. and Elder, G.H. 2003. Grandparenting and age identity. *Journal of Aging Studies*, 17(3), 269–282.

Laz, C. 1998. Act your age. *Sociological Forum*, 13(1), 85–113.

Mann, R. 2007. Out of the shadows: Grandfatherhood, ageing and masculinity. *Journal of Aging Studies*, 21(4), 281–291.

Mann, R. and Leeson, G. 2010. Grandfathers in contemporary families: evidence from qualitative research. *Journal of Intergenerational Relationships*, 8(3), 158–172.

McDowell, L. 1993. Space, place and gender relations: Part II. Identity, difference, feminist geometries and geographies. *Progress in Human Geography*, 17(3), 305–318.

McDowell, L. 1999. *Gender, Identity, and Place: Understanding Feminist Geographies*. Minneapolis: University of Minnesota Press.

McDowell, L. 2003. *Redundant Masculinities? Employment Change and White Working Class Youth*. Oxford: Blackwell.

Morrell, R. 2006. Fathers, fatherhood and masculinity in South Africa, in *BABA: Men and Fatherhood in South Africa*, edited by L. Richter and R. Morrell. Cape Town: HSRC Press, 13–25.

Mowl, G., Pain, R., and Talbot, C. 2000. The ageing body and the homespace. *Area*, 32(2), 189–197.

Pain, R. 2001. Age, generation and life course, in *Introducing Social Geographies*, edited by R. Pain et al. London: Arnold, 141–163.

Pain, R., Mowl, G. and Talbot, C. 2000. Difference and negotiation of 'old age'. *Environment and Planning D: Society and Space*, 18(3), 377–393.

Scraton, S. and Holland, S. 2006. Grandfatherhood and leisure. *Leisure Studies*, 25(2), 233–250.

Sibley, D. 1995. Families and domestic routines: constructing the boundaries of childhood, in *Mapping the Subject: Geographies of Cultural Transformation*, edited by S. Pile and N. Thrift. London: Routledge, 123–319.

Smith, G. and Winchester, H. 1998. Negotiating space: alternative masculinities at the work/home boundary. *Australian Geographer*, 29(3), 327–339.

Sorensen, P. and Cooper, N. 2010. Reshaping the family man: a grounded theory study of the meaning of grandfatherhood. *The Journal of Men's Studies*, 18(2), 117–136.

Spector-Mersel, G. 2006. Never-aging stories: Western hegemonic masculinity scripts. *Journal of Gender Studies*, 15(1), 67–82.

Tarrant, A. 2010a. Constructing a social geography of grandparenthood: a new focus for intergenerationality. *Area*, 42(2), 190–197.

Tarrant, A. 2010b 'Maturing' a sub-discipline: the intersectional geographies of masculinities and old age. *Geography Compass*, 4(10), 1580–1591.

Tarrant, A. 2013. Grandfathering as spatio-temporal practice: conceptualizing performances of ageing masculinities in contemporary familial carescapes. *Social and Cultural Geography*, 14(2), 192–210.

Twigg, J. 2004. The body, gender and age: feminist insights in social gerontology. *Journal of Aging Studies*, 18(1), 59–73.

Vanderbeck, R. 2007. Intergenerational geographies: age relations, segregation and re-engagements. *Geography Compass*, 1(2), 200–221.

Varley, A. and Blasco, M. 2001. Exiled to the home: masculinity and ageing in urban Mexico, in *Men at Work: Labour, Masculinities, Development*, edited by C. Jackson. Oregan: Frank Cass, 115–138.

Varley, A. 2008. A place like this? Stories of dementia, home and self. *Environment and Planning D: Society and Space*, 26(1), 47–67.

Wiersma, E. and Chesser, S. 2011. Masculinity, ageing bodies, and leisure. *Annals of Leisure Research*, 14(2–3), 242–259.

Wiles, R., Crow, G., Heath, S. and Charles V. 2008. The management of confidentiality and anonymity in social research. *International Journal of Social Research Methodology*, 11(5), 417–428.

Chapter 16

Intergenerational Relations and Irish Masculinities: Reflections from the Tyneside Irish, in the North-East of England

Michael Richardson

Introduction – Irish masculinities

In her study probing the 'in-between spaces' of the Irish diaspora, Ni Laoire (2002: 183) contends that:

> Conventional understandings of the Irish diaspora assume a homogenous white, Catholic, 'straight' community with unproblematic ties to a romanticised homeland. The myth of the homogenous Irish diaspora has important implications for all migrants from the island of Ireland, as those migrants who do not conform to the myth may still find themselves interacting with it in various ways.

The present chapter advances research on the Irish diaspora by examining working-class masculinities in the context of intergenerational family relations. The discussion is based on a study with 38 men of Irish descent living on Tyneside, the regional term for the city of Newcastle upon Tyne and its surrounding areas to the North and South of the River Tyne, in the United Kingdom. The study was made up of 28 men within nine families and a further ten individuals from different families. All participants are white and heterosexual (though how 'white' they are has been debated in critical whiteness studies – see Nayak 2009, Hickman and Walter 1997); however, not all are Catholic (with Protestant, Atheist and Agnostic beliefs represented), nor are their connections to a 'romanticised homeland' necessarily 'unproblematic'. Building on earlier work on the geographies of family life, which studied the gender performances of fathers as well as mothers and children in the everyday, I note Aitken's remarks (1998: 195) that: 'it is important that we try to understand how these performances come together in a critical form of world making that is not constrained by myths'. In responding to both Ni Laoire and Aitken, then, the empirical work that follows goes beyond the imagined homogeneity of the Irish diaspora, generational lineage, family life and masculinities.

In discussing the cultural fusion of the Irish diaspora and indigenous Tyneside, I use the narratives of one family to chart how the legacies of working-class masculinities have changed over time. I focus upon three members of one participant family, who reflect the most linear family model present in my study and whose spoken evidence helps to reveal certain consequences of intergenerational relations on continuities and transitions in working-class masculinities in the diaspora. Out of the nine families, this is one of three examples where I met with the grandfather, father and son (though intergenerational relations were present in all other interactions involving uncles, nephews, cousins and so on).

This chapter details the intergenerational relations between Peter (a 5th generation Irishman born on Tyneside in the 1960s), his father (a 4th generation Irishman born on Tyneside in the 1940s) and his son (a 6th generation Irishman born on Tyneside in the 1990s). Peter is a working mechanic, his father a retired engineer and his son a chemist. I have chosen to talk about these men from Peter's standpoint so as not to prioritise age or youth in either a top-down or bottom-up approach to the study; in so doing, it supports the 'back and forth' nature of research across ages (Lundgren 2012, Tarrant 2010, 2014). How 'Irish' these three men feel varies, as later discussions of the intergenerational relations show. Across the 38 participants there is no set pattern of certain generations feeling more Irish than others, the most salient factor being family circumstance.

Masculinity is relational – to other masculinities (including my own as a young male researcher – see Horton 2001, Vanderbeck 2005) as well as to femininities (Connell 1995). In looking at masculinity 'intergenerationally' – that is, at the relationships between generations (Hopkins et al. 2011) – the chapter is structured around discussions of behavioural changes and continuities through the micro-level geographies of the pub, the home, the school, the body and the workplace (see also Tarrant 2014, this volume). The intergenerational approach to researching men's lives contributes to an emerging field within the geographies of masculinities literature that investigates the relationship between age and masculinities, as well as the intersections of masculinity with roles within the family, such as son, father and grandfather, etc. (Hopkins 2006, Tarrant 2010, 2014).

Intergenerational relations

By looking for generational differences in the perceptions and performances of Peter's family's masculinities, recorded evidence revealed that, over time, Peter's family have become 'less Irish'. Interacting with their daily lives across different geographic locations, my starting point was the pub, or more specifically an Irish club in South Tyneside. Such sites are key for the establishment of a diasporic community, and in this case the green painted walls, images of idyllic rural Ireland, posters advertising folk musicians and ceili dancing reinforced traditional notions of the 'homeland'. Furthermore, drinking and pub culture itself – an oft-cited component of working-class culture – is seen as a key signifier for establishing hegemonic masculine ideals (Nayak and Kehily 2008, Nayak 2003), with alcohol seen as 'asserting male togetherness' (Donkersloot 2012: 584).

My interactions supported this as Peter, who, in responding to my call for participants on the Tyneside Irish website, invited me to meet him and his family at the club. This is not a completely public place, as the club is based on membership (I had to be signed in as a guest), but I was nevertheless comfortable to meet the men in a 'public enough' place for our introductions. I was greeted by Peter and his father, and we were joined later in the evening by his son. I was told that Peter and his father often came here for a drink, whereas Peter's son had never been before – which seemed symptomatic of the club's membership, with a distinctly older clientele in the bar during my time there.

Over the course of the evening, pints of beer were consumed (mostly Guinness and Murphy's [Irish stouts], but also [the English bitter] John Smith's). We joked that these were 'old men's' drinks (compared to lager, vodka mixers, or 'shots' which are stereotypically consumed by younger generations). This practice of being 'selective with what I drink' is a factor in my own social life, as friends often accuse me of liking 'girly drinks'. All too aware of this, when meeting people for the first time, I choose not to order my usual Amaretto and Coke! In her work with the North American Irish diaspora, Marston (2002: 385) talks of the 'hyper-masculinised and the hyper-feminised, which carry with them an implicit assumption of heterosexuality', and I make this link to 'gender appropriate drinking practices'. In addition to carefully selecting what I drank, by driving myself to the venue I also controlled how much I drank. This deliberate decision allowed me to be able to join in with the pub culture, while avoiding a situation of drinking excessively.

The following week, I returned to the Irish club to interview Peter alone. Ideally, this would have taken place at his home, but he felt that there would not be enough quiet space for us to talk uninterrupted. While the discussions went well with Peter, it soon became apparent that interviewing in the pub was not particularly conducive to a quiet talk either; other customers' voices, noises from the till and the clinking of glasses featuring regularly on the digital recording. It was agreed that subsequent meetings would take place with Peter's father in his home a few weeks later and with Peter's son in his bedroom within Peter's house a few weeks thereafter. I note that the 'home' can be a contentious place: it is argued by some as a positive environment, as a sanctuary or escape (Blunt and Dowling 2006, Holloway and Hubbard 2001), but also as a negative space, a place of oppression (Skelton and Valentine 2005). Of particular note are ideas of the material and imaginative processes of making 'home' within a diaspora context (Walsh 2011, Tolia-Kelly 2010). 'Homes straddle the public and private' (Gorman-Murray 2012: 111): in Peter's father's home we sat in the living room, a place of comfort and familiarity to the participant but with a sense of public display, whereas in Peter's son's bedroom I gained insight to a more private space. The interaction in this instance was enhanced through discussions of items in the room including musical instruments, a games console and dumbbells (discussed later in the chapter).

'What the hell's a Shillelagh?'

> From point 1 way back in the 1800s in Ireland, which is about as far back as we could go in that field, there's something like five or six generations have elapsed and yet there is a feeling of feeling Irish, and Irish ancestry. (Peter's father, in his home in South Tyneside)

> Occasionally, things from Ireland would rear their head. When we were visiting Ireland (me Dad's siblings are all older than him as he said) and their houses were furnished differently to his, which was only natural. But on one occasion, in me uncle's house, there was this thing that hung upon the wall – it looked like a crude tobacco pipe, mounted on a bit of wood, 'Oh, it's a shillelagh' … 'What the hell's a shillelagh?' I still don't know, do you? (Peter, in an Irish club in South Tyneside)

> I've kind of watched my Granddad develop the family tree that he did and I was quite interested in that cos he started off with not a lot and he ended up going all the way back to like the 1820s and that was interesting and that's probably as far as it goes really. I don't feel particularly Irish. I've never been or anything, but yeah, it's definitely an Irish sounding name I suppose and that's about as far as it goes. In my daily kind of, day to day activities, it doesn't really affect me to be honest. (Peter's son, in his home in South Tyneside)

We see three contrasting levels of engagement with an Irish identity from these excerpts from the family narratives. While perhaps not surprising, it illustrates the complexities of intergenerational relations: while Peter's father believes that the feelings of 'Irishness' still exist across the family, Peter's son does not confirm this to be the case. Significantly, we see that while Peter's own father took him on visits to family in Ireland, enabling him to encounter such symbols of Ireland as the 'Shillelagh'[1], he has not done the same with his son, thereby facilitating more physical detachment from the 'homeland'. Peter asked me whether I knew what a shillelagh was and I did, because I had become familiar with many symbols of Ireland when visiting the homes of some of my participants. Unlike this family, many others within the study did have photographs, paintings and other artefacts. These 'visual and material cultures of the home' can be seen as 'cultural artefacts of diasporic heritage' (Tolia-Kelly 2010: 7). It is these constructions that help establish the 'romanticised homeland' (Ni Laoire 2002) of the Irish diaspora.

There is also an assumption that with age comes greater knowledge (Lundgren 2012), with both Peter and his son suggesting that they will not be as much 'use' as Peter's father in the research: 'that's the only thing I'm a little concerned about,

---

1 The Shillelagh is a wooden walking stick and is synonymous within the Irish diaspora as a symbol of Ireland. It is often incorporated into the logos of sports teams and also military emblems, for more on this see Sheen (1998).

as you might ask me something here and I might have to say, "I don't know"' (Peter, in a group discussion in an Irish club in South Tyneside); 'but … [pause] … to be honest, the whole Irish thing has not really been a massive part of my life' (Peter's son, in a group discussion in an Irish club in South Tyneside). It is this issue of self-doubt that reinforces the importance of interviewing individually. During the family group discussions, answers were deflected from the younger men to Peter's father. When I spoke with them individually they could not do this and often thought more carefully about their responses.

Intergenerational relations, though, do not just exist within and across the men of my study families; they also exist between my participants and me. I have written elsewhere about my positionality as a man researching men and masculinities (Richardson in press), and like Vanderbeck (2005: 398) believe that 'different men fit differently into different situations and places'. Drawing upon my interviews with Peter and his family, I wish to reflect in this chapter about the intergenerational nature of their interactions, which themselves are 'produced within particular times, spaces and cultures' (Hopkins et al. 2011: 314). We have seen above how, over time, generational changes have affected the levels of engagement with and understanding of family heritage, with age prioritised and valued in this context. Further evidence of 'experience as knowledge' follows in the next section.

'You'll find all this out one day'

> Well as a parent you are [a role model]. It's the role of hypocrite. I've never been such a breathtaking hypocrite in me life. You'll find all this out one day. It's just unbelievable. You could be a politician once you've been a parent, it's just so hypocritical, 'Don't do that, don't do that … don't speed!' 'But Dad?' It just goes on. It's not really worth going into. You'll just … you've got all this to come is what I can say really. (Peter, in an Irish club in South Tyneside)

It became apparent during the interactions with Peter that he saw me as a similar man to himself, with the major difference between us being our ages. Peter's remarks – 'you'll find this out one day' and 'you've got this all to come' – clearly position me in relation to himself as a fellow heterosexual man, who, though not yet having children, is expected to become a father at a later (older) stage. Peter is correct in his assumptions: I am a heterosexual man and plan to have children of my own one day. But was this interaction constructed around a performance of my heterosexuality? Possibly; though a more likely cause is Peter's heteronormative assumptions, leading him to adopt a fathering role, looking upon me as a younger man from a similar family background (I am close in age to his son, whom I also happen to resemble). A useful caveat is argued by Nash (1997: 109, citing Finn 1995), on studying the North American Irish diaspora: 'somehow being heterosexual is so wrapped up with being Irish that they simply can't imagine something being Irish and not being heterosexual.' Sexuality, though, was discussed with Peter after he mentioned there were two brothers he went to school with 'and one of them was gay'. He went on to say 'we didn't *know* that [he was gay], well we knew he was different, put it that way' (Peter, in an Irish club in South Tyneside); though the 'difference' Peter talks of is not in relation to any Irishness, inferring more generally to being a young boy in school on Tyneside in the 1960s. Contrary to some literature, which points out that in ageist societies 'ageing and old age are considered negatively' (Tarrant 2010: 192, cf. Yi et al. 2006), the next section illustrates how, for these men, ageing is seen more favourably.

Ageing masculinities

The effect of ageing on the participants' masculinities was a prominent theme throughout the interactions. For example, Peter said that once the young gay boy grew up and left school he successfully established a hairdressing business – an inverse example that highlights Messerschmidt's (1994: 87) argument that, within the school environment, many boys or young men assert their masculinity through 'participation in sports and academic success'. The implication is that those who do not demonstrate a toughness, resilience or endurance through competitive discourse (and choose not to construct their masculinity in such a way that parallels the traditional model of the 'hard and heavy' legacy of industrial work or of the family patriarch) are made to feel marginalised. The men in Peter's family had all left school, and their conforming to these traditions is shaped at least in part by their (Catholic) school experiences. While Peter's father still maintains strong connections to the Catholic Church, Peter's and his son's religiosity lessened upon leaving school. Peter talks of how, at the age of 16, he upset his father by turning his back on religion 'probably just to see what it was like' (though he has since returned by getting married in Church and Christening his son). Peter's son now actually identifies as an atheist and opines it was precisely because of his education in school that he now discredits an adherence to religious belief:

> I think it's just cos I've always been good at science at school and that's what I have always focussed on and been interested in. And obviously doing the degree in Chemistry. So it was just kinda everything I've ever wondered about has been answered by science. So I felt there was no real need for me. It just seemed like a whole farfetched idea with organised religion. So that's where I am. I haven't had it forced down my neck at home either. So I guess they've kind of just let us make my own mind up. That's my conclusion. I do quite like it though. It does a lot of good things like the Church and that. Charity work and stuff. The world's a better place for it; it's just not for me.

While conforming to traditions of family and industrial work, we see significant changes in the lives of these men in relation to their ageing masculinities. In looking across their own lives they were recognising that 'rather than following fixed and predictable life stages, we live dynamic and varied lifecourses which have, themselves, different situated meanings' (Hopkins and Pain 2007: 290). While Peter 'upset' his father by turning against religion (even if only for a short period of time) we see Peter's own more liberal (modern) attitudes to his own son's decision in letting his son 'make [his] own mind up'. They also recognise the attitudes of family members and it is this 'relationality' that Hopkins and Pain (2007: 288) state 'does not just pose interesting questions about age, but makes a fundamental change in ways which we approach and think about it'.

In addition to decreasing levels of religious sentiment we see changes in attitudes to health and work relative to their ageing masculine bodies:

> You're aware that at the age of 59 I had a heart attack and I overcome that and I'm on medication now and I workout and that. But then this job came up for the Far East and I went. The family were appalled you know. I had the words of me daughter ringing in my ear 'Just come back in one piece Dad' and I did. Bit of a challenge maybe. But I did it and I got away with it. No regrets. (Peter's father, in his home in South Tyneside)

Peter's father's decision was not taken lightly and ultimately the reason he took the job thousands of miles away was due to family pressures; these were financial, revolving around being the primary breadwinner. However, he also talked of how he:

> … felt that I was one of the lucky ones. I came out of it a lot better than a lot of people would, people the same age. So I was being given a chance. 'Use it. Exploit it. Don't just sit in your armchair' … and it worked out right. (Peter's father, in his home in South Tyneside)

I thanked Peter's father for sharing his story but he brushed this off by saying what he went through was nothing compared to what his ancestors went through; he says, 'like me father, Battle of the Somme, came through that without a scratch'. There is camaraderie in this military narrative (Atherton 2009) but there is also a son's respect for his father, and an acute awareness of the need to stay healthy. We see this theme expressed by Peter, who emphatically states, when talking about an opportunity to go for a promotion post in his workplace (which he turned down):

> I've seen the pressure and I've seen what it's done to people. Get a little bit extra, and they think 'I'm great' and then the pressure starts and it just has an effect – strokes, heart attacks, people going off with stress. It's not for me. You've just got to look at me father, you know. That is not for me. (Peter, in an Irish club in South Tyneside)

While Peter's father felt a need (no doubt spurred on by his father's efforts in the Battle of the Somme) to challenge himself both physically and mentally, Peter is influenced by *his own father* in a *different* way. Peter adopts a more careful and considered approach, which is different again to the more defiant response from *his own son*. Upon seeing some dumbbells in the corner of his room, I asked Peter's son about how important was keeping fit:

> I went through a period a while ago of going through like a proper health binge, 'Right, got to get in shape'. Doing loads of cycling. Lost loads of weight. Eating total rabbit food for weeks on end, and it got to a point where I thought, and it occurred to us, 'Right hang on. I'm doing all of this when I could just be hit by a bus tomorrow. Like 21 years of sheer boredom'. So yeah I'm just gonna like go out, not worry too much and eat what I want and just you know, exercise some of it off later. You know I'd rather live for 50 years having the time of my life and die of a heart attack 'cos I didn't do enough running, rather than live a little bit longer and just have like a boring life. But that might change as I hurl towards 50. We'll see. (Peter's son, in his home in South Tyneside)

What is evident in these narratives is how Peter's father's heart attack – to the sufferer, an obvious life-changing event – impacted significantly upon the lives of the two younger men. For them, also, it was not just an emotional experience, but one that has altered their life courses. Peter himself has admitted that, amongst other factors, the health scare discouraged him from taking more responsibility at work (with the consequent loss of extra income), whereas we see a more free-spirited, spontaneous attitude from Peter's son after he rejects his 'health binge'. Peter has himself had a relatively recent illness that impacted upon his capacity to work; while the intergenerational impact is without doubt a factor in his masculinity, it may only be contributing to a more complex set of relations. On speaking about his own illness he comments:

> So you tread a, it's like a tightrope, and you can fall off either way I can tell you. But that was an eye opener for me as a man. For to have to concede that, you know, these things aren't a given. It could quite easily happen where you're not in a position to bring the money in, you know. It's come at a time where my Son's now self-sufficient; wor [our] mortgage is paid, so it's not the major trauma that it would have been if he was still at college or something like that you know. But certainly it was a wake-up call; you know as a bloke, you know as a working bloke, I had quite a fright. (Peter, in an Irish club in South Tyneside)

We see the significance here of an embodied identity: the 'working bloke' is precisely that, working. And so what happens when this man cannot work? His identity is suddenly in crisis, his masculinity comes into question. This is an area of work within masculinity studies that has been well-documented (McDowell 2000, 2003), but not so much from the perspective of intra-familial relations *between* men. The above discussion illustrates how intergenerational relationships shape the way men both conform to, contest and rework the connections between masculine identities, workforce participation and career success. These intergenerational influences, legacies and transformations are explored further in the next section.

An inheritance of culture?

This form of working-class masculinity has been passed down through the generations and it best encapsulated by Peter's son who states:

> I think it's only just occurred to us now. Like in the family, like my Granddad has always worked in industrial, hands on, 'get your hands dirty' type of jobs, my Dad has as well. And I'm involved in industry as well. Like there's no one in our family has ever been like a graphic designer or a journalist or whatever, or a TV star. It always has been like the proper nitty, gritty 'grrr' manly sort of work, which I dunno, maybe is sort of a family link that I've not noticed before. But I couldn't see myself doing another type of job. I've always wanted to do a sort of job in the Chemical industry. (Peter's son, in his home in South Tyneside)

So Peter's son has been influenced by both his elder male relatives in his career trajectory. This narrative is rich with a visceral reaction to the men's employment status; the 'grrr' noise was made during the description of the 'manly sort of work' which Peter's family undertakes. He later mentions that his mother works in a bank but states he himself 'wouldn't ever be in an office-based job'. Peter's son is studying for a degree at university (unlike both his father and grandfather) though he is sponsored by an industrial company throughout the course which has a strong vocational component to it. While maintaining the working-class culture of a traditional family of Irish descent, his career is what Peter's father calls 'progress':

> You've also got to recognise the progress from way back when [my ancestors] were really struggling to survive. And that we've always said, 'Well I'm better off than my parents and their parents beforehand' … Let's just take the paint industry which my grandfather worked as a cooper – with lead paint which was hazardous – which burnt the paint off the bows [of ships]. Then there's [my Grandson] working in a lab for a paint company. So you can see how things progress?

In charting the work of men in the family, Peter's father tells us how, from dangerous manual labour in a shipyard to technical expertise in a laboratory, the family has 'progressed'. Working-class masculinities are still surviving but they have had to adapt to the changing workplace where 'brain has replaced brawn' in 'places that were once the engine room of the industrial revolution' (Miles 2005: 914). Work on the banks of the Tyne brought Peter's family to the region all those years ago – at one time Tyneside produced 40 per cent of the global output of shipbuilding which fell to around 7 per cent in 1960 (the time when Peter was growing up [see Tomaney, Pike and Cornford 1999]). Peter's son grew up in the post-industrial era (1990s), and much to the delight of his family, he managed to find work in one of the region's surviving legacies.

I return to one of the first conversations I had with Peter's father about the coming together of the Irish and Tyneside cultures in North East England – which was aptly coined by Cooter (2005) as *When Paddy Met Geordie* (in reference to the colloquial names for men from both Ireland [Paddy] and Tyneside [Geordie]). I found myself citing the historians Colls and Lancaster (1992: xii) who state that Geordie identity believes 'belonging is an act of affiliation and not of birth'. This seemed to be well-received by Peter's father, who also added the importance of Irish 'values' to this culture. He talked of 'fair play' and 'giving a man a chance' and explained this is why he felt there were so many men of Irish descent within the global diaspora who work within the police force and the legal profession. He states:

> There's been a lot achieved on Tyneside. Education. Education in the formal sense but also education out of the workplace, not forgetting again, education starts in the home. So it's the parents responsibility, it's the responsibility of siblings to educate and that's where it starts. Back to values and the values that's been developed. (Peter's father, in his home in South Tyneside)

By making specific reference to 'Tyneside' we see that Peter's father believes the area to be as important an influence on the family as the aforementioned 'Irish values'. The scope of this chapter cannot further discuss the relationship between the diaspora and the host environment; but certainly the narrative extracts suggest that the label of 'Tyneside Irish' is appropriate for this participant family.

Conclusion

In bringing together Peter's family narratives I have articulated how the places of Tyneside and the Irish diaspora have helped to shape their working-class masculinities. Through the micro-level geographies of the pub, the home, the school, the body and the workplace, I have outlined why Peter's family has become 'less Irish' over time, and that a significant factor in this evolution has been the ease in which they have become integrated with the host community. It has been the high levels of assimilation that have led so many of my participants to identify as 'Tynesiders' first and anything else second – whether, that is, Irish, English, British or European.

Through these interactions, I have reflected on the heteronormative assumptions that are rife within family studies and positioned myself as a researcher in relation to the men's familial, working and embodied masculinities. Their empirical evidence is rich and detailed, yet highly subjective, offering insights to life as men of Irish descent living in the North East of England. Their stories are not representative of this community but nor do they claim to be; rather they shed light on aspects of a community that is currently under-researched in scholarship.

Jackson (1991, 1994) wrote of masculine pluralities and the shifting spatial structures of gendered geographies, and two decades on, this collection, like the collection of van Hoven and Hörschelmann (2005), reveals different ways in which men perform and construct gender roles. Gender is socially and spatially (re)created and (re)organised in different ways by different generations (see also Aitken 2014, this volume). Through the intergenerational approach to researching men's lives adopted here, this study contributes to critical geographies of gender with a focus on the myriad everyday practices and shifting performances of masculinities enacted over generations of men from families of Irish descent.

References

Aitken, S.C. 1998. *Family Fantasies and Community Space.* New Jersey: Rutgers University Press.

Atherton, S. 2009. Domesticating military masculinities: home, performance and the negotiation of identity. *Social and Cultural Geography*, 10(8), 821–836.

Blunt, A. and Dowling, R. 2006. *Home.* London: Routledge.

Colls, R. and Lancaster, B. 1992. *Geordies: Roots of Regionalism.* Edinburgh: Edinburgh University Press.

Connell, R.W. 1995. *Masculinities.* Polity Press: Cambridge.

Cooter, R. 2005. *When Paddy Met Geordie: The Irish in Newcastle in County Durham and Newcastle, 1840–1880.* Sunderland: University of Sunderland Press.

Donkersloot, R. 2012. Gendered and generational experiences of place and power in the rural Irish landscape. *Gender, Place and Culture: A Journal of Feminist Geography*, 19(5), 578–599.

Gorman-Murray, A. 2012. Queer politics at home: gay men's management of the public/private boundary. *New Zealand Geographer*, 68(2), 111–120.

Hickman, M.J. and Walter, B. 1997. *Discrimination and the Irish Community in Britain.* London: Commission for Racial Equality.

Holloway, L. and Hubbard, P. 2001. *People and Place: The Extraordinary Geographies of Everyday Life*. Harlow: Pearson Education.

Hopkins, P. 2006. Youthful Muslim masculinities: gender and generational relations. *Transactions of the Institute of British Geographers*, 31(3), 337–352.

Hopkins, P. and Pain, R. 2007. Geographies of age: thinking relationally. *Area*, 39(3), 287–294.

Hopkins, P., Olson, E., Pain, R. and Vincent, G. 2011. Mapping intergenerationalities: the formation of youthful religiosities. *Transactions of the Institute of British Geographers*, 36(2), 314–327.

Horton, J. 2001. 'Do you get some funny looks when you tell people what you do?': muddling through some angsts and ethics of (being a male) researching with children. *Ethics, Place and Environment: A Journal of Philosophy and Geography*, 4(2), 159–166.

van Hoven, B. and Hörschelmann, K. (eds) 2005. *Spaces of Masculinities*. London: Routledge.

Jackson, P. 1991. The cultural politics of masculinity: towards a social geography. *Transactions of the Institute of British Geographers*, 16(2), 199–213.

Jackson, P. 1994. Black male: advertising and the cultural politics of masculinity. *Gender, Place and Culture: A Journal of Feminist Geography*, 1(1), 49–59.

Lundgren, A.S. 2012. Doing age: methodological reflections on interviewing. *Qualitative Research*, 1–17.

Marston, S.A. 2002. Making difference: conflict over Irish identity in the New York City St. Patrick's Day parade. *Political Geography*, 21(3), 373–392.

McDowell, L. 2000. Learning to serve? Employment aspirations and attitudes of young working class men in an era of labour market restructuring. *Gender, Place and Culture: A Journal of Feminist Geography*, 7(4), 389–416.

McDowell, L. 2003. *Redundant Masculinities?: Employment Change and White Working Class Youth*. Oxford: Wiley-Blackwell.

Messerschmidt, J.W. 1994. Schooling, masculinity, and youth crime by white boys, in *Just Boys doing Business? Men, Masculinity and Crime*, edited by T. Newburn and E.A. Stanko. London: Routledge, 81–99.

Miles, S. 2005. 'Our Tyne': iconic regeneration and the revitalisation of identity in Newcastle Gateshead. *Urban Studies*, 42(5/6), 913–926.

Nayak, A. 2003. 'Boyz to Men': masculinities, schooling and labour transitions in de-industrial times. *Educational Review*, 55(2), 147–159.

Nayak, A. 2009. Beyond the pale: chavs, youth and social class, in *Who Cares about the White Working Class?* edited by K.P. Sveinsson. London: Runnymede Trust, 28–35.

Nayak, A. and Kehily, M. 2008. *Gender, Youth and Culture: Young Masculinities and Femininities*. Basingstoke: Palgrave Macmillan.

Nash, C. 1997. Embodied Irishness: gender, sexuality and Irish identities, in *In Search of Ireland: A Cultural Geography*, edited by B. Graham. London: Routledge, 108–127.

Ni Laoire, C. 2002. Discourses of nation among migrants from Northern Ireland: Irishness, Britishness and the spaces in-between. *Scottish Geographical Journal*, 118(3), 183–199.

Richardson, M.J. (in press) Embodied intergenerationality: positioning yourself as a man researching men and masculinities. *Gender, Place and Culture: A Journal of Feminist Geography*.

Sheen, J. 1998. *Tyneside Irish: A History of the Tyneside Irish Brigade Raised in the North East in World War One*. Barnsley: Pen & Sword Books Ltd.

Skelton, T. and Valentine, G. 2005. *Cool Places: Geographies of Youth Cultures*. London: Routledge.

Tarrant, A. 2010. Constructing a social geography of grandparenthood: a new focus for intergenerationality. *Area*, 42(2), 190–197.

Tarrant, A. (2014) Negotiating multiple positionalities in the interview setting; researching across gender and generational boundaries. *The Professional Geographer*, 66(3), 493–500.

Tolia-Kelly, D.P. 2010. *Landscape, Race and Memory: Material Ecologies of Citizenship*. Aldershot: Ashgate.

Tomaney, J., Pike, A. and Cornford, J. 1999. The political economy of a shipyard closure: the case of Swan Hunter on Tyneside. *Regional Studies*, 33(5), 401–411.

Vanderbeck, R. 2005. Masculinities and fieldwork: widening the discussion. *Gender, Place and Culture: A Journal of Feminist Geography*, 12(4), 387–402.

Walsh, K. 2011. Migrant masculinities and domestic space: British home-making practices in Dubai. *Transactions of the Institute of British Geographers*, 36(4), 516–529.

Yi, C.C., Pan, E., Chang, Y. and Chan, C. 2006. Grandparents, adolescents, and parents: intergenerational relations of Taiwanese youth. *Journal of Family Issues*, 27(8), 1042–1067.

Chapter 17

Emotional Mappings and the Ethnopoetics of Fathering

Stuart C. Aitken

A lot of it had to do with making my dad proud
I worked my butt off
I didn't want anyone on the boat to say
Oh, it's that guy's son, he can't pull his weight
I would sometimes do extra
slice cable learning knots stacking tagging fixing nets
and a lot of times I helped my dad if there was nothing to do
down there
engines break down a lot

Felipe's stepfather came into his life when he was eight years old. Fishing consumes the work of the men in Felipe's family, extended out to cousins and uncles. As part of the Calderon family, Felipe's stepfather worked as chief engineer and medic with cousins and uncles on small shrimp boats and on larger boats that went in search of tuna far to the south of San Diego; sometimes they spent up to a year at sea. At 19, Felipe joined his stepfather on an extended voyage down through the Panama Canal to fish in the Pacific, the Gulf of Mexico, and the Atlantic. It is during this time that aspects of his manhood foment, and it is within the space of the boat that he builds an emotional bond with his stepfather and learns lessons that come into play when he has children of his own. The physical spaces of the boat combine with the length of the voyage to establish a crucial context for Felipe's transformation to manhood and to his connection to fathering.

I bunked with eight other guys
two to each bunk
my dad had his own room
so if I wanted some peace and quiet
I would go to my dad
I liked to spend time with my dad, which was a great experience
you know I was the only person who had that quality time with him
not even my mom would have that
because he would be gone nine months out of the year

With this chapter I bring together ideas of space, mobility and change, as elaborated by Henri Bergson with Elizabeth Grosz's ideas on geo-power, to help make sense of the deep emotional resonances of the fathering story that connects Felipe back to his father and forward to his children. I want to raise the importance of considering the work of fathering through emotions and stories, and ethnopoetry helps with this task. The first section of the chapter deals with the methodology of ethnopoetics, which I first used in *The Awkward Spaces of Fathering* (2009) as a way to describe and contextualise men's emotions and spatial stories, and I continue the practice here with Felipe's work first as a son and then as a father. I am committed to understanding men's lives spatially, and over a considerable period of time, to get a sense of how they accommodate and foment change. The methodological section is followed by a very specific theoretical defense of understanding men's lives through a focus on the spaces of emotion, mobility and change that pulls from the early work of Henri Bergson and the later work of Elizabeth Grosz and Giulliana Bruno. Throughout the chapter, I try to speak to the issue of how we can use emotion and affect to create deep mappings that challenge imperious notions of fatherhood. I end the chapter with an emotional mapping of Felipe's story as it unwinds and circles back on itself.

The ethnopoetics of space[1]

Spaces, and how we move through them, are lyrical events when they emplace and transform our connections to other people and the world around us in ways that are perhaps more centred, perhaps more spiritual, perhaps more politically-charged than our run-of-the-mill daily grind. If we think of spaces as events that have history and encourage change, then spaces and people can become something different through complex, emotionally-charged relations. In the discussion of Felipe's first voyage, I describe these relations lyrically and poetically so as not to diminish the importance of the emotions. In larger debates in the sciences and humanities it is clear that emotions matter to the extent that they transform the way we sense the past, present and future. If poetry is an emotive construction of language, then my arrogance as a creator of texts is to re-visualise, contort and arrange people's words and gestures to create something that speaks to their emotions. I call this ethnopoetry because it is derived from discussions, stories, narratives, biographies, interview transcripts, participant observation and experimentation through mapping and other visual methodologies (see Aitken 2009, 2014, in press).

I want to suggest a way of negotiating spatial politics through experiencing material relations as ongoing, affective and embodied. Spatial stories and their poetics pose in particular form the question of how biographies and power are

---

1 This discussion begins in Aitken 2009, is elaborated in Aitken in press, and is developed fully in a forthcoming book (Aitken 2014).

negotiated. Understanding the embeddedness of power relations in spatial stories helps us to see how change plays out in particular locales, but considering power alone is insufficient to understand the dynamic relations between people and places because, as a habituated aspect of our lives, everyday spaces are rarely envisaged as those parts of our lives that raise acuity. This tame and passive notion of space belies its affective and transformative properties, which are sometimes realised when we visit foreign cultures and places for the first time. At these times, acuity is at the forefront of our sensibilities as we are actively presented and emplaced. An active notion of space such as this positions it as permeable and fluid: space as an event. If we consider spaces as events in the Deleuzian sense that they are an assemblage of previously unrelated forces rather than things, then it changes the way we think about not only space and its transformative potential, but also its politics (Deleuze and Guattari 1983, 1988).

As part of my ethnopoetics, then, and to push what may be called a lyrical experiment, throughout the chapter I use different genres – mixing poetry with dialogue, maps and academic discussion – to transform fathering stories into what Pearson and Shanks (2001) call a deep mapping. Through the silences that join and link the narrative, dialogue and poetry, it is my hope that emotions foment and reveal themselves. These are the collective experiences of change, the content of which is always partial, incomplete, generative and creative. Further, there are quirky politics embedded and emanating from these ethnopoetics of space. What follows next is a consideration of the way spaces as events can be seen not only as personally transformative but as an important part of spatial politics.

Mappings, movements and the politics of emotions

Historian David Bodenhamer (2010: 26) points out that if we are interested in mapping people and their humanity in a deep and meaningful way then we need to articulate a combination of spatial stories, memory, images, knowledge and identity. He quotes Pearson and Shanks (2001: 64–65), who argue that deep and emotional mapping 'attempts to record and represent the grain and patina of place through juxtapositions and interpretations of the historical and the contemporary, the political and the poetic, the discursive and the sensual'. Emotional mapping anticipates a methodology that, I argue, borrows from a Bergsonian understanding of affect and emotion. Henri Bergson's *Introduction to Metaphysics* (1999) is a beginning plea for a coherent focus in movement, affect and emotion, which he calls intuition (as opposed to analysis) in the world of thought. Arguing against the Newtonian and Cartesian extraction of metaphysics from science, Bergson offers intuition as a way of placing more metaphysics in science and more science in metaphysics. Through his notion of intuition, he was one of the to look carefully at what Grosz (2011: 1) calls 'imperceptible movements, modes of becoming, forms of change, and evolutionary transformations that make up natural, cultural and political life'. Bergson was primarily interested in science and his point was that static positions for viewing the world are absolute and do not represent well the relationality of the material world. Bergson's point was that rather than looking at something from the outside and trying to represent it in absolute but fragmented terms, we can look at it from the inside and get in motion with it and, to this extent, he elaborates a philosophy of mobility and relationality.

Grosz (2011: 1) is particularly interested in Begsonian movement because, she argues, 'movement pre-exists the thing and is the process of differentiation that distinguished one object from another'. In other words, movement is about difference. Movement does not attach to a stable object, putting it in motion; and so it is the movement that defines the ways objects are differentiated. She goes on to point out that the process of movement makes and unmakes objects, including people, animals and institutions. As a consequence of this differentiation, movement is inherently political. It is also potentially emancipatory. Grosz is interested in the ways that material and living things overcome themselves and become something different. It is this context of difference that is about the relations between things. But, as Grosz and others have pointed out, the connections between emotions, places, power and difference are by no means straightforward and progressive.

Grosz argues that identity is created through processes that are virtual and, from Deleuze, she points out that it always comprises what we do in the virtual ever-present. The virtual ever-present is a variety of forces and valences, the most fundamental of which relate to what she calls geo-power (Grosz 2011). Put simply, the earth is framed through geo-power, which creates a condition for the plane of composition and thus for particular works. Framings cut through territories, break up systems of enclosure and performance, traverse territories and then reconnect with chaos, enabling something of the chaos outside to reassert and restore itself in and through bodies and their works. Emotional mappings are a form of framing that, to paraphrase Grosz, create and metabolise sensations that are released into the world and made to live a life of their own.

Understanding the deep emotional context of fathering begins with a frame that pushes against the creation of imperious patriarchal fatherhood as an institution that is intent upon disempowerment. The link between geography, imperialism and patriarchy is well established. I argue in *The Awkward Spaces* of *Fathering* (2009: 36–40) that patriarchal dominance comes out of institutionalised notions of fatherhood that derive from problematic interpretations of enlightenment thinkers such as Locke and Hume in their discussions of family values, which were focused more on reason than passion. My re-reading of Locke and Hume suggests that emotion, uncertainty and unknowability are equally as important as reason for understanding the contexts of lived experience, and the creation of society and the state. To the extent that our understanding of social life is influenced by representation, so part of social relations are mediated by science and academic debates that misplace the importance of emotions. Pushing through patriarchal desires for control, it seems to me that cartography – another problematic scientific representation – offers the possibility of redemption through what Guilliana Bruno

(2002) calls *carte du pays de tendre*, or tender mappings. There is a fundamental geo-power to these mappings that give voice to a language for feelings and memory.

It is clear that Western society has been characterised by an abstract spatial framing – a two-dimensional mapping – that is fragmented into sub-spaces devoted to the performance of specialised, homogeneous activities and to empire, but it is less clear how these may be transformed. The creation of ethnopoetic maps may be one way of understanding the production of language and meaning along with the production of space as part of a transformative anti-imperialist project. Ethnopoetic mappings are a halting and partial – and yet also a sincere and promising – attempt to represent the non-representable of a conversation, an interview, a narrative, a life.

In what follows, I embark on a voyage of discovery with Felipe that constitutes a partial, but nonetheless deep emotional mapping of his connection to his father. In so doing, he and I produce a map, whose material mapping is about emotionally-charged stories. The stories circumgyrate around an actual sea voyage that begins the weaving of a complex and irreducible map whose strands were already in place years before, and which encapsulates Felipe's later struggle with substance abuse and his own fathering issues.

A voyage of discovery

Felipe was raised within an extended family deeply contextualised by commercial fishing and, as a consequence, men were often leaving home for extended periods of time. San Diego has a long tradition of fishing, which was dominated by the tuna industry from 1920 until the 1980s. During that time a number of Portuguese and Italian fishermen immigrated to the area, and because of recent Iberian ethnic boosterism the importance of Mexican influences on the tuna industry is sometimes lost. The Calderon family comes from this latter tradition. By the time Felipe first sailed with his stepfather, the industry was struggling due to over-fishing and competition from an expanding Japanese fleet. When Mexico set its territorial waters to 200 nautical miles after the 1982 United Nations Convention on the Law of the Sea, San Diego fishermen had to sail further and for longer periods of time, and they had to find innovative ways to make extra money. One of these ways was to refurbish and sell fishing boats to South American companies. The voyage around which this story evolves is focused on a boat that was repaired in San Diego, fitted out in Panama, and then left to a new Venezuelan owner after several months of fishing.

Soon after he joined the Calderon family, Felipe and his brothers connect with their stepfather in good ways and within a short period they are calling him dad. Felipe recalls family traditions when dad took his leave for a year-long fishing trip.

> I am at the dock waving to my dad
> And after the boat would leave the dock

we would rush to go park
at Shelter Island
And wait for the boat to come by
When it did we would honk flash our lights and wave
And he would wave back
And that would be the last time I would see him
for a while

Felipe was always around fishermen and their boats. When he was eight years old, his stepfather would take him down to whatever boat he was working on and give him a little pole so that he could fish off the side. Later, when his older brother got to go on an extended trip Felipe was jealous. He was particularly covetous of his brother's 'Popeye arms' on his return. Felipe has five sisters and one brother, and he is the youngest; he describes the fraternal rivalry as fierce but good-natured.

I ask him, 'So … there is one brother and he's out fishing and you want to be like him?'

'Right, I wanted those little Popeye arms', replies Felipe. 'Yeah he came back a little stocky … he's a year and a half older than me. So I made a commitment to him that when I got back we were going to arm wrestle. So the whole time I was on the boat I was lifting when I could, harder and higher, thinking of him'.

'Is he a big guy like you?'

'Nope. Nope. Needless to say I won and he said he didn't get a good start but there was no competition. He tried to weasel his way out of it'.

This early rivalry between Felipe and his brother circled around physical prowess and dad's approval. The physical prowess was about a strong, hard, embodied masculinity and approval from dad circulated vaguely around the kind of life-choices the brothers' pursued and the way they showed up to make these choices. Integrity and family values were important but neither brother was entirely sure what happened on during those long months at sea. And for Felipe there was something more that related directly to the sea, the stories he heard and to how much he admired his father for who he was and what he did. Men live storied lives, and their children have proclivities to respond to those stories. Acclaimed Canadian writer Margaret Atwood (2011) argues that we have storied minds, hard-wired in 'template form, thus causing stories to generate semi-spontaneously if the epigenetic switch for them is turned on'. We are not hard-wired in this way to mathematics or science she goes on to argue. Atwood questions whether we are slaves to stories, whether we are compelled to re-enact them. Are they part of the matrix of a shared humanity? Are they are a large part of what make us men and fathers?

I always wanted to go to sea 'cause
I looked up to my dad
I heard all the stories
My brother had some good stories

Seeing what it did to him physically
I always just wanted to go out to the ocean
and check it out, you know?
It was a big part of our lives and the whole family, you know?
I love the water

Felipe's first trips with his dad were moving shrimp boats down to San Diego from San Pedro.

I would do the back and forward
Just little trips
I would get sea sick
So I knew what was in store for me

At 19, Felipe was afforded the opportunity to test what was in store on a long-distance voyage on a boat that was being fixed up in San Diego for sale in Venezuela. To make money, the crew were to fish for tuna in the Pacific, the Atlantic and the Gulf of Mexico for several months before leaving the boat in Caracas. His stepfather was chief engineer and Felipe got a position as rookie deckhand. As the boat was being refurbished, the rest of the crew was flown in from Chile, Brazil and Portugal. In February 1982 they left San Diego harbor for the nine month voyage. Felipe talks about the thrill of leaving port and having members of his family drive to Shelter Island to wave goodbye to him: 'so it was cool to be on the other side, to be on the boat this time and heading out of the harbor and to see the flashing lights and stuff … it was cool.'

When not fishing, time on board the boat was filled with repair work, watching the weather and, for Felipe, learning new skills. The space of the boat, and the cramped quarters of the regular crew provided ample opportunities for Felipe and his dad to engage in quality time:

'So you headed off to Panama?' I ask Felipe.

'Yup'.

'And that was just straight sailing?'

'Nope, we got into trouble on the way'.

On their way to Panama the boat was stopped off the coast of Costa Rica by 'a military boat'.

'They got on the radio and told us to stop', Felipe tells me.

'You were in international waters?' I ask.

'Apparently not', he laughs, ' … they get paper work from each place, get permission to go through the waters, you know? And the paper work got messed up and we weren't allowed to go through Costa Rica and we were going there and …

That's when they pulled us over
Told us we needed to stop

kinda scary
I didn't know what to do, you know?
They just come up and take over the boat … total military style
take over
I was like, wow, what's going on here?
And they take the captain upstairs
The next thing I hear is gun-fire

I think they're killing the captain

I get under the table
started to hide
One of the crew comes and says:
What are you doing?
And I said
I am hiding
And he said
Get up, it's just the guy on their boat
with the 50 caliber
Shooting at a shark.

… and they determined we didn't have permission under the new international law of the sea and that they were going to have to take us in. By next morning the office was open. They did the paper work. Took all day and it was solved. Then we threw a big party with the military [and] with everyone that was involved. I think the captain gave them some booze and cigarettes and I traded something with some guy who asked if I had some Pepsi or Coke cause it's rare down there to have that and I was like, yea, I have a six-pack and he was all excited and he gave me one of his bullets from the 50 caliber that was a misfire.'

The boat was 200 feet long and had a crew of ten that did not include the captain, mate and engineer. Felipe bunked with eight other guys, right over the engine forward of the main cabin and below the captain's berth. The space was cramped and always noisy. On the voyage south Felipe was busy with two hour watches day and night. He'd check gauges, check for leaks, and if he saw anything out of the ordinary he'd go get his dad.

One time
I saw water spitting out
and I grabbed him
and he said
good thing
I grabbed him because the water was going right into the air filter going into the engines
hitting one of the generators … and if I would have just left it would have burn the motor
We switched it and fixed the pipe

The next time it was pretty rough I was looking all over the place and as I am
walking through the hall and there was a doorway right here and the hatch was
open and it popped off and I had to jump up in the air so it wouldn't hit my
legs and I landed on it and went for a ride all the way across the boat ... slid
through the whole boat and rolled off it
So I went to get dad up because there were things flying everywhere and he
said go wake up the captain and he said to ring the bell and wake up everyone
to tie everything down and we had the dye and it was spilling all over the deck
and it was about to get to the tank and that would damage the fish.
My dad said
I did good

As the boat was fitted with a net in Panama City, Felipe had about a week to enjoy the city and its 'pretty cool nightlife'. After Panama City they headed to Venezuela through the Canal. Felipe's dad had just finished working on the speed boat and asked him if he'd be interested in testing it out in the lake on the east side of the canal: 'I was, like, yeah. Pretty cool.' The boat was provisioned in Caracas, which is where the new owner resided.

Out of Venezuela they did a two month trip around the Caribbean. Felipe remembers the first time they set the net and being told to sit on his hands – don't do anything! – just watch. It is dangerous on deck when nets are being set and pulled in if you do not know where to go or what to do: from fish free-falling on you out of the stack of the net to sharks getting in amongst the catch. Felipe told me a story of trouble on a previous voyage. It was a time of new legislation to protect porpoises that got caught in the nets with the tuna. There was an observer on board and the crew had to be seen to be doing all they could to help save entangled porpoises. Short of cutting away their nets, a member of the crew was sent out in the water to help with disentanglements. This was two years prior to Felipe's voyage. The captain's son was in the water trying to free a porpoise when a shark attacked him, taking out two biceps and a calf. (Felipe tells me that during his voyage he was out in the water many times on the same task: 'That is when the adrenaline kicked in.') Over the next four hours the captain's son bled out and died. For much of that time he was on ship-to-shore radio with his mother. After four hours the captain said to his wife over ship-to-shore, 'he's gone'. They put the body in the freezer and headed home. Many fishing families in San Diego, including the Calderons, monitored the event on their radios. Tragedies of this kind dog the lives of fishermen and hugely affect family members on shore.

During the voyage, Felipe was part of four fishing trips in nine months. Once the boat had about 30 tons fish – the ship can hold up to 110 tons of fish – they'd take the catch to port, re-provision and head back out. If fishing dropped off in the Atlantic or the Caribbean they'd sail through the canal and fish in the Pacific. They unloaded twice in Panama, once in Venezuela and once to a Japanese factory ship. Sometimes they would sail for two weeks without catching any fish. Felipe's favourite part was when it got really rough – 'like in that movie *The Perfect Storm* when the water would completely submerge the pilot house' – and they headed to a safe anchorage, usually in the lee of an island.

Deserted islands were the best
We were there until the storm was gone
And my dad would give me the speed-boat
And I would go all over the island
collect shells   lay on the sand
I would be like wow if only my friends could see me
That was the best

Most of the time, they were really busy. When fishing was good Felipe might get less than two hours sleep and be working hard all the time. Stacking the net was one of the hardest tasks, taking eight crew members. Even if they did not catch anything, it took an hour to bring in the net. With a full load it would take up to four hours. Felipe particularly liked going below to help his dad. The fish went down chutes and sometimes they got jammed so Felipe's job was to clear the passages.

As the voyage progressed Felipe's dad began to have issues with the captain: 'it got political'. On the ship-to-shore radio with his mom, Felipe would chat about coming home but his mother urged him to stay on for another trip: 'I finished unloading one day and she said you know I think you should take another trip and she said that because she knew that it would make me a better person because I would grow from it and I would be with my dad.'

Felipe tells me that crew members were also a huge part of his growing up. One time some plain-clothed police came into a bar where he was partying with three other crew members. Felipe and his colleagues had some drugs. Everyone was put up against the wall and the police pulled their guns. Felipe is waiting to feel the pain of a gunshot. They asked for his papers and said 'okay let's go'. The police put them in the back of a truck and one of them jumped in the back with his gun and said 'don't try anything stupid'. Felipe was wondering if they were going to be taken to a quarry and killed. After 20 minutes the truck stopped and they are at the boat and Felipe thought 'ooh, this is good'. They asked them which boat was theirs and said that they would come back tomorrow to check out the story. One of the policemen then asked if he could get a fish and Felipe said 'oh yea' and gave him the biggest fish he could find, one that would feed his family for a couple weeks.

On another occasion they were at 'a place where the guys go, you know, with women and stuff'. Felipe confesses that he has been there a couple of times. On this occasion, his dad walks in and Felipe exclaims 'oh Jeez, what's he doing there?' Felipe and the other crew members run out the back, jump in a cab and are gone. Later, back at the boat Felipe is making a sandwich before going to bed and his dad returns. Felipe thinks, I wonder what he's got to say for himself; up to that point Felipe had assumed his dad's faithfulness to his wife. Felipe's dad is fuming but not because he has seen his son in the brothel. He tells his son he is really pissed off at the captain because they were out to dinner and then, 'he took me to this hooker place'. Felipe raises an eyebrow, 'oh really?' And that is when the 'political' issues started between Felipe's dad and the captain.

Towards the end of the voyage Felipe was getting tired – 'but it took nine months for me to say I'd had enough' – and he and his dad were having financial difficulties.

We went to Cumana, Venezuela
The money was devalued so we flew in a little plane to Caracas
And the money devaluated again
We only had enough to get to New York
We were just like …
get us home

Once we hit Kennedy my mom wired Western Union
and got us money
Because the money we made we sent home
But the last trip hadn't paid us yet
That's why we didn't have enough money

Felipe talks about how the fishing trip, being with his dad and the crew, shaped him as a man and a father but not all his life experiences during the voyage served him well. He talks about 'running amuck' with drugs and alcohol, and when he got back that continued. He 'bounced from job to job, from the east coast to the west coast'. During this time, Felipe had a son and two daughters with different women. His son is now 21 and his youngest daughter is 16. Felipe's relationships with the mothers fell apart because of his issues with substance abuse. He tells me that towards the end he was trying to get caught by doing stupid things. Felipe was done; rather than living up to the image of his stepfather's faithfulness to his mum, he had succumbed to the drug and alcohol excesses of his crew-mates. Felipe got into a recovery program and, as he had learnt at sea, he took suggestions and worked hard. He got back together with an old girlfriend but struggled at the beginning of this relationship with his substance abuse, going in and out of recovery programs. With the threat of losing his long-time sweetheart he went to a four-month treatment program and has been sober since that time.

Felipe reflects back to his stepfather's storied life as a fisherman who stayed faithful to his mother, and of the stories generated by his own voyage into manhood and wonders at the ways they constructed him as father. His life today is good and he credits his current successes to sobriety and the example of his step–father, whose work ethic and family values eventually came through to Felipe.

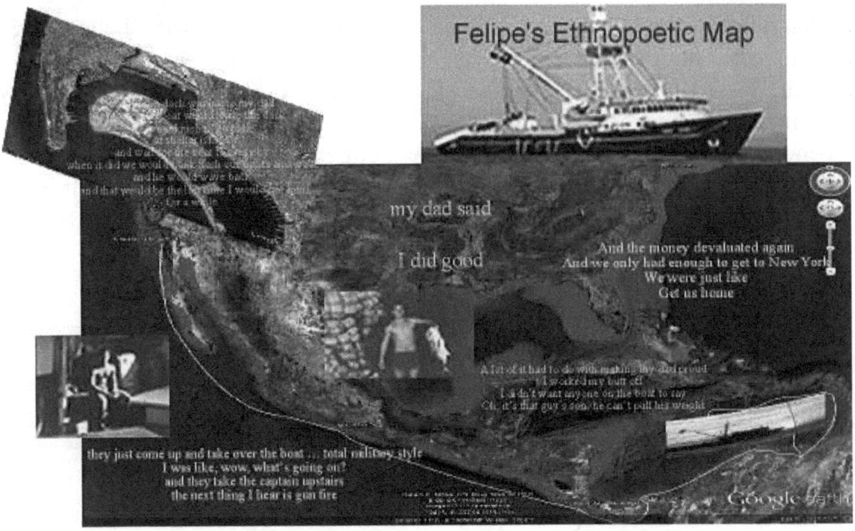

Figure 17.1 Felipe's ethnopoetic map

Deep mappings of storied lives

My understanding of Felipe's voyage of discovery begins with a push against the creation of imperious patriarchal fathering with its intent upon disempowerment. My story of Felipe's voyage of discovery is augmented with a tender mapping, replete with poetic language that suggests feelings and memories that makes some small sense of complexity, affects and emotions in a way that is meaningful for the work of fathering. With ethnopoetry and emotional mapping, I do not claim the annihilation of the altogether overwhelming imperial abyss of patriarchy (nor would I want to because it is out of this chaos, Grosz (2011) argues, that creativity and art arises), but the possibility of redemption – at least for a moment – from imperious notions of fathering. For Felipe, this reworking moves him away from an abusive and neglectful form of fathering where he loses his children to something softer from where he can reach his son and daughters through stories.

Felipe and I tried to create a map of tenderness that re-focuses concern onto movement and the production of space, and the degree to which ideology is inscribed in space and then acted out upon it and with it, while not missing the material and relational nuances of change, flexibility, freedom and surprise that is the opening of political possibilities. It is clear that possibilities erupt from stories: their generation, mapping, accommodation and transference. Langellier and Peterson (2004: 112) argue forcefully that families produce life by creating and consuming stories about themselves. There is a politics to this, because family storytelling is about a movement that has the capacity to order group and personal identities. Moreover, although it may be argued that contemporary families are asked to create their own myths, rituals and representations which children can reject or upon which they might build (Teather 1999), the stories that families create are always complicatedly enmeshed in larger societal values and mores. In performing narrative and creating maps of lived experience, we struggle over personal and family identities that are simultaneously destabilising, deferred and looking towards the future. Our stories are always in motion and that movement pre-exists the content of the stories and is the process of differentiation that distinguishes one family from another. In other words, to return to Grosz's argument, stories in motion – moving stories – are about difference. For Felipe, thankfully, this movement cannot easily attach to a stable notion of patriarchy, putting it in motion; and so it is the movement that defines the ways fathering as a practice is differentiated. It is the process of movement – deep mappings and moving stories – that offers hope because it makes and unmakes objects, including fathers, in ways that are potentially liberating.

The last time I met with Felipe was a Sunday morning. We had a coffee and he told me he was looking forward to meeting up with his son that afternoon to go to a shooting range. Now five years clean and sober Felipe is working on his relationship with his son, which has been fraught with tension as each struggled with alcoholism. The two of them go to AA meetings together where they share stories of their substance abuse and recovery. Today, Felipe is happy to share an afternoon hanging out with his son, shooting rounds at the firing range and perhaps sharing a few stories.

References

Aitken, S.C. 2009. *The Awkward Spaces of Fathering*. Aldershot: Ashgate.

Aitken, S.C. (in press) Quelling imperious urges: deep emotional mappings and the ethnopoetics of space, in *Deep Maps and Spatial Narratives*, edited by D.J. Bodenhamer, J. Corrigan and T.M. Harris. Bloomington: Indiana University Press.

Aitken, S.C. 2014. *The Ethnopoetics of Space and Transformation: Young People's Engagement, Activism and Aesthetics*. Farnham: Ashgate.

Atwood, M. 2011. The stories we tell. *The National Post* [Online, 17 October]. Available at: http://arts.nationalpost.com/2011/10/17/margaret-atwood-the-stories-we-tell/ [accessed 17 October 2011].

Bergson, H. 1999. *An Introduction to Metaphysics*. Translated by T.E. Hulme. Indianapolis and Cambridge: Hacket Publishing Company.

Bodenhamer, D.J. 2010. The potential of spatial humanities, in *The Spatial Humanities: GIS and the Future of Humanities Scholarship*, edited by D.J. Bodenhamer, J. Corrigan and T.M. Harris. Bloomington: Indiana University Press, 14–30.

Bruno, G. 2002. *The Atlas of Emotion: Journeys in Art, Architecture, and Film*. London and New York: Verso.

Deleuze, G. and F. Guattari. 1983. *Anti-Oedipus: Capitalism and Schizophrenia.* Minneapolis: University of Minnesota Press.

Deleuze, G. and F. Guattari. 1988. *A Thousand Plateaus: Capitalism and Schizophrenia.* London: The Athlone Press.

Grosz, E. 2008. *Chaos, Territory, Art: Deleuze and the Framing of the Earth.* New York: Columbia University Press.

Grosz, E. 2011. *Becoming Undone: Darwinian Reflections on Life, Politics and Art.* North Carolina: Duke University Press.

Langellier, K. and Peterson, E. 2004. *Performing Narrative: Storytelling in Daily Life.* Philadelphia: Temple University Press.

Pearson, M. and Shanks, M. 2001, *Theatre/Archeaology: Disciplinary Dialogues.* London and New York: Routledge.

Teather, E. 1999. *Embodied Geographies: Spaces, Bodies and Rites of Passage.* London and New York: Routledge.

PART 6
Masculinities, Place and Care

Chapter 18
Masculinities, Embodiment and Care

Kim England and Isabel Dyck[1]

The feminisation of care is well established in the literature. However, there is a relative neglect of the increasing involvement of men in both paid care work and family caregiving. Given the naturalisation of care as feminine and the devaluing of care work in general, this lacuna provides an opportunity to explore the plurality of masculinities and everyday lived experiences of men 'doing gender' outside the boundaries of conventional gender conduct (see also Brown et al. 2014: this volume, Trell and van Hoven 2014: this volume). Feminist geographers have argued for some time now that subjectivities and spaces are recursively (re)created, and underscore the myriad ways that power and knowledge are reproduced through subjectivities, representations, bodies and space. In introducing their collection *Masculinities and Space*, Bettina van Hoven and Kathrin Hörschelmann (2005: 1) remarked 'geography has long been a discipline dominated by men and one about men'. Feminist geographers' interventions have prompted other geographers to rethink gender and most fundamentally to accept that gender is constructed in specific spatial contexts and at particular historical moments rather than as something that is fixed and stable.

Although feminist geographers have focused primarily on women and femininities, there is increasing scholarship on men and masculinities (such as this edited collection) that explores men as men, rather than as an idealised, disembodied masculinity against which women are othered (Berg and Longhurst 2003, Van Hoven and Hörschelmann 2005, Hopkins and Noble 2009). Raewyn Connell's work on hegemonic masculinities has been especially influential. In her now classic book, *Masculinities* (1995: 29) she argued, 'definitions of masculinity are deeply enmeshed in the history of institutions and economic structures. Masculinity is not just an idea in the head or a personal identity. It is also extended in the world, merged in organised social relations.' Thus masculinity is conceptualised as both a social practice and a social process, and there are a variety of ways that masculinities are shaped and reshaped within broader changing economic, political and gender relations. For Connell, the history (and we would add geography) of masculinity is not linear, but instead 'dominant, subordinated and marginalised masculinities are in constant interaction, changing

1 In this chapter we draw on previously published work that we have written together (especially Dyck and England 2012, and England and Dyck 2011, 2012) and separately (especially Dyck 2011 and England 2010).

the conditions for each other's' existence and transforming themselves as they do' (1995: 198). While Connell's initial framework has been critiqued and revised, the key point remains: there are a plurality of masculinities that are overlapping, contested and contingent.

Dismantling masculinity as a taken-for-granted monolithic category has become an important project. And for us the contributions of feminist theorists have been critical to that project. As with femininities, there are multiple ways of 'doing' masculinities. We understand 'doing gender' partly via Judith Butler's idea of performativity: gender is not based on an ontological essentialism, but is grounded in stylisations of the body requiring constant repetition (Butler 1993). We are also influenced by Candace West and Sarah Fenstermakers' (1995) insistence that 'doing difference' involves a *relational* aspect in that gender (and other systems of difference) comes about in ongoing interpersonal interactions that reaffirm and reproduce broader social structures.

The conceptually and empirically rich work on masculintities is careful about engaging with the historical contingencies and specificities of masculinity, but less so about the spatial contingencies and specificities. Given masculinity is socially, culturally *and* spatially constructed, the discourses, meanings and experience of masculinity change from one place to another, as well as across time (Berg and Longhurst 2003, Hopkins and Noble 2009). Thus geographers' unique contribution is to explore how masculinities play out differently in different places and how those places are shaped based on the experience of masculinities.

Care and embodiment

In this chapter, we advocate for strengthening conceptual, theoretical and empirical links between masculinities and 'the body'. In particular we do this by considering the embodied care relations associated with the long-term care of people in their homes. We follow Diemut Bubeck's (1995: 160) 'restrictive definition of care as an activity' as specifically 'meeting the needs of one person by another person where face-to-face interaction between carer and cared for is a crucial element of the overall activity and where the need is of such a nature that it cannot possibly be met by the person in need herself' (Bubeck 1995: 129). She intends her definition to capture 'the more active and face-to-face aspects of care' including body work activities such as feeding, bathing, and toileting. In turn this means we are primarily focussing on care work that is face-to-face, hands-on and usually involves the intimate space of the body.

Care, especially daily care work, is, of course, heavily gendered, both in terms of the discourses underpinning it and the people actually providing it. Women have long held primary responsibility for providing care, in their homes, in their communities and in their paid jobs. This gendering of work has its discursive and material roots in the social and spatial separation of waged work from social reproduction, obscuring activities defined as 'women's work'. Thus a longstanding theme of feminist scholarship has been to make visible the pivotal role of women's *unpaid* care work and its necessary value to society. Initially considered as something unremunerated and occurring in the family home, care work, as a concept and an analytical tool, is now used in provocative analyses of the porous boundaries between paid and unpaid work, as well as public and private spheres. For instance, Pei-Chia Lan (2003: 189) uses the concept of 'continuity of domestic labour' to describe, 'the affinity between unpaid household labour and waged domestic labour – both are feminised work attached with moral merits and yet undervalued in cash'.

Geographers have made key interventions into understandings of the spatiality of the processes and practices of care and the difference that space, scale and sites make in the processes and practices of care (e.g., Milligan and Wiles 2010, Conradson 2011). Some address the provision of care such as access to health care provision, child care, or how working parents (especially mothers) negotiate their home and paid work responsibilities (Perrons et al. 2006). More recent attention has turned to formal and informal care for older people and the changing locations where that care occurs. While a fair amount of attention has addressed the experience of family caregivers, increasing research, including our own, focuses on both the care recipients and paid care workers, along with the implications of the home becoming a major site in the landscape of care provision (Wiles 2003, Milligan 2009, Milligan and Wiles 2010, Conradson 2011). But there has been limited attention paid to masculinities, care and space (but see Thein and Del Casino 2012).

In our collaborative work we have addressed the interrelationships between gender, care and space through an emphasis on the relationality of care and its embeddedness in complex social relations and materialities of home care. In so doing we are guided by the work of Elizabeth Grosz (1994) who argues:

> (T)he body, or rather, bodies cannot be adequately understood as ahistorical, precultural, or natural objects in any simple way; they are not only inscribed, marked, engraved, by social pressures external to them but are the products, the direct effects, of the very social constitution of nature itself. It is not simply that the body is represented in a variety of ways according to historical, social, and cultural exigencies while it remains basically the same; these factors actively produce the body as a body of a determinate type. (Grosz 1994: x)

Feminist and post-structural scholars emphasise the intertwining of the corporeality of the body with powerful discursive 'readings' of the body that etch materiality with social meanings of gender, race, sexuality and other dimensions of differentiation. Much of the scholarship on bodies zooms in on women's bodies, and early studies of masculinities often tended to essentialise particular characteristics of men, male-female differences and naturalised men's bodies. However recent approaches in masculinities studies often take a more relational approach to gender and call for a more robust engagement with theorising embodiment. For instance, Connell and Messerschmidt (2005: 851) argue that:

> Bodies are involved more actively, more intimately, and more intricately in social processes than theory has usually allowed. Bodies participate in social action by delineating courses of social conduct – the body is a participant in generating social practice. It is important not only that masculinities be understood as embodied but also that the interweaving of embodiment and social context be addressed.

For our conceptual framework, we are drawn to the concept of embodiment (rather than the body as a docile surface of inscription) because we want to avoid the tendency to consider bodies as somehow separate from their constitutive material and discursive processes. Thus we use embodiment to refer to both the discursive constructions of bodies *and* the fleshy materiality of actually existing bodies. As geographers, we are particularly keen to highlight the spatialities of bodies, including seeing the body itself as a space and scale. For us, bodies are defined and created in and through discursive and material spaces, and embodiment is an active process, constituted in and through social relations *and* space (Moss and Dyck 2002). Thus the spatiality of embodiment means the interaction of bodies in the production of lived experience is central to the cultural and social processes whereby powerful discourses are embodied in 'the lived body' of everyday encounters in particular spaces.

Men and care relations

There is an extensive literature exploring the complex interactions that form care relations (e.g. Bondi 2008, Milligan 2009). The bodily practices of care, connected as they are with the emotional relations of care along with the intimacies of care work, are pivotal to the construction of the care and bodies of care recipients, family caregivers and paid care workers and in the spaces where everyday practices occur. We frame our discussion in the remainder of the chapter around the three groups of people who together form 'care triads' – an analytical concept increasingly deployed in the health sciences to describe the experiences and interrelations between the care recipient, the family caregiver and the health or social care professional. This captures the relational character of care relations and the interactive, dynamic processes that constitute them. In each instance we draw on an illustrative example from our collaborative research about home care in Ontario, Canada, to make broader points about the different ways that masculinities are embodied by focussing on men 'doing gender' in the context of practices of home care.

Our study of home care was conducted as part of a larger interdisciplinary team[2] that investigated the experience of care giving and care receiving in Ontario's publicly funded long-term care services. Seventeen cases were recruited from across Ontario in which the home-care recipients were interviewed along with their paid home-care providers and their family caregiver (if they had one). In what follows we use the everyday lived experiences of three men to illustrate discursive and material understanding of bodies, care and masculinities in the putatively private, domestic settings of the care recipients' homes.[3]

Men as care recipients

> We have supper about six o'clock. Then I'll go and watch the television 'til (the care workers) come to put me to bed. On Wednesday and Thursday it's six-thirty because I don't lie down in the afternoon. But the rest of the time it's late, eight-thirty.

Robert is 69 years old and has Multiple Sclerosis (MS); he has difficulties walking and receives care from his wife, Doris, a Personal Support Worker (PSW) and an attendant. He requires help getting in and out of bed, and with bathing and toileting. This quote illustrates that Robert is keen to have consistency and routine in his daily (and weekly) schedule. At various points in his interview Robert described his schedule of bodily practices in intricate detail – what time he gets up, when he has a shower, which paid care worker came on which days and at what time to do what sorts of care tasks. His wife, Doris also remarked:

> He's one that likes things on schedule and it's upsetting to him if (the routine is broken). It's better for him if you can just keep things right on time … like going to bed at the same time. And he likes – and even little details, he likes to do things his way. Like he wants his coffee before he shaves.

One explanation of Robert's need for routine might be that as a man used to his role as the sole family breadwinner, he has lost much control of his own body and

---

2 The research team was led by Principal Investigator, Patricia McKeever, Faculty of Nursing, University of Toronto; co-investigators were J. Angus, M. Chipman, A. Dolan, I. Dyck, J. Eakin, K. England, D. Gastaldo, and B. Poland. The research co-ordinator was K. Osterland and the research assistants were P. Kontas and T. Irvine. Funding was provided by the Social Sciences and Humanities Research Council of Canada. The names of the participants are pseudonyms.

3 Elsewhere we have discussed the home as a discursive and material site in the process and practices of care (see also Dyck and England 2012).

also over the daily temporal and spatial rhythm of his everyday life laid down over his course of his paid work life. A timetabled regime of activities associated with his bodily care (getting up, meals, sleeping – even those that require assistance) provides familiar guideposts for the organisation of his day and provides continuity in the midst of his increasingly unreliable body. And, of course, he may well be reworking his version of hegemonic masculinity to maintain some degree of control over his time, his wife and the paid care workers (of whom the regulars are all women).

Reading masculinities through care also suggests additional interpretations. Julia Twigg (2000) in her important book, *Bathing*, describes the temporal and spatial ordering of care, pointing to the 'conflicting times' that:

> arise when the world of service delivery attempts to map its logic onto domestic life ... Scientific medicine measures out hours exactly but domestic time moves to a different rhythm. The conflict between *the rationalized world of formal services* and the day-to-day lives of individuals is particularly visible in relation to body time; and the needs of the body present recurring *problems for service delivery*. (2000: 100)

Thus Robert (and Doris) have had to adapt to 'conflicting times' associated with scheduling publicly funded home care. Obviously, the shift of homespace to also act as a workplace for the paid care workers has an impact on care recipients' and family caregivers' use of their own homes. Throughout their married life, Robert and Doris had a more traditional gendered familial division of labour – Doris had been a full-time mother, and both had retained elements of their routines from when he was in paid employment. Doris, for instance, was keen to cook their meals and refused help preparing them (although she was eligible for some assistance) and described being annoyed when she found one paid care worker cleaning the bathroom. But they have had to adapt to accepting that his bodily needs mean that at least for the time the care workers are in their home, it is transformed into a paid workplace. Both family caregivers and paid caregivers have similar goals in terms of the care of the care-recipient, but their respective experiences of the same material space is tempered by the tensions emerging as the meaning of 'home' is re-worked when it is also enacted as a paid workplace.

The bodies of 'ill men' often get constructed as culturally undesirable and beyond the hegemonic bodily norm, both by the men themselves and by those around them. O'Brien, Hunt and Hart (2007: 194) suggest that 'the losses men experience through illness can reveal what men think masculinity is and expose the practices of masculinity that participants engaged in prior to their illness'. When masculinities are unsettled by illness, men often reflect on taken-for-granted embodied processes, particularly when their body is impacted long-term. The experience of prolonged illness or disability realigns their relationships to time and space in profoundly embodied ways.

Robert's bodily care work included intimate bodily care – the care workers bathe him and give him bowel treatments (he still does some of his own body care: shaving himself and cutting his nails, for instance). And this has necessitated a major adjustment on his part. When the care-recipient requires such extensive personal care that, as Bubeck puts it, 'cannot possibly be met by the person in need herself', the care recipient is often reduced to merely an ill, frail or damaged body in need of care and dependent on others. This is suggestive of a docile body that remains permanently static, bounded and fixed in ways that are curiously incongruent with theoretical discussions of embodied subjectivities as always in the process of becoming. Many of the care recipients in the larger home care project we draw on here insisted that they were more than merely a person 'in need' of care: 'I still want to be a person unto myself', said one. All too often care is presented as one-directional, something performed on a passive recipient. Of course there has been changed bodily capabilities, nevertheless bodies are not singular, bounded and closed and are open to being affected and affecting others.

Moreover, if we take seriously the implications of the now popular feminist care ethics literature, then the care recipient is seen differently: they are located within socially embedded relational networks of care. Care ethics challenge the existence of the independent, rational subject and instead focus on human *inter*dependence of people. Needing and giving care is deeply implicated in human life (Tronto 1993, Kittay 1999). Seen through this framing it becomes possible to see care recipients as not only receivers of care but also as giving care to others and also as *active* co-constitutors of their own care. Robert, for instance, even with his advanced MS, still provides care for his grandchildren as he has since they were born. In fact, his relative 'spatial entrapment' at home means Robert has become a relatively static and dependable part of his children and grandchildren's daily schedules. Similarly Robert, and many other care recipients we interviewed, provide emotional support for their partners and, at various points, for their care workers too – calming the nerves of a newly trained attendant and offering 'tips' to a personal support worker on how best to move them (which the care workers then fold into their own routines with other clients).

Men as caregivers

> I think one of the things that bothers me is that I have to be at a certain place at a certain time. Mum needs her injections twice a day, Donna doesn't like to do it, (Mum) needs her medications, she needs her meals pretty much on time, and proper balanced diet. […] So it's just ah, from morning to night it's rush, rush, rush. Get this done, get that done. I'm just bone weary.

Ben, aged 59, who is a school teacher, cares for his mother-in-law, Glenda, aged 82, who lives with him and his wife, Donna (Glenda's daughter). Glenda is housebound and suffers from diabetes and arthritis, and has terminal lung cancer.

Donna also has cancer and is frequently bed-bound. Oftentimes Ben provides most of the care, not only for his mother-in-law, but also for his wife when she is less well. Ben finds caring for 'the ladies', as he calls them, as well as working full time, very demanding, leaving him 'bone weary'.

Home care policy is built on cultural assumptions about home, and that there is (or should be) a 'family caregiver' or 'informal carer' available to provide care. As Janine Wiles (2003: 191) remarks, '(f)amilies, particularly daughters, may be strongly encouraged or pressured to be "available" whether they are willing or feel able, or not'. This suggests a strong normative expectation that families will step in and provide care at home. Numerically, more men are doing unpaid family caregiving: as partners, fathers and sons, and sometimes, as in Ben's case, a combination of these. In 2007, 28 per cent of employed men in Canada aged 45 and older were providing care for a family member or friend. The proportion of women was still higher (37 per cent) and women do more hours of care, but the gender gap in each case is smaller than in the past (Fast et al. 2011).

There has been a proliferation of scholarship on family caregivers in numerous disciplines. Most of it focuses on women and their 'struggle to juggle' paid work, child care and elder care (Folbre 2012). Conventional gender scripts infuse the academic (and policy) literature on caregivers. A slew of time-use studies show that statistically men's care falls at the practical or instrumental end of the spectrum, such as trips to the doctor, organising finances and medicine management, whereas women are repeatedly found to be more likely to provide bodily care activities, such as feeding and dressing, and giving emotional support. Based on these gendered division of caregiving activities, much of the literature on family caregiving tends to reinscribe responsibilities for care tasks as firmly divided along normativised and stereotypic gendered lines (Russell 2007). While Ben is only one case, it is clear from his description of a typical day that he is doing caring activities from across the spectrum (for instance, giving insulin shots and cooking dinner). In an effort to care for his mother-in-law and support his wife's grief at her mother's impending death, Ben is also attempting to manage the emotional as well as the corporeal dimensions of care relations. In what amounts to essentialist associations of caregiving with women, men's caregiving is implicitly if not overtly compared unfavourably to women's, and some accounts even suggest men caregivers are ineffective and insignificant. More sensitive readings of masculinities and caregiving are needed (see Aitken (2009) for an example of this in relation to fatherhood).

In the quote above, Ben describes not only some of his numerous care giving tasks, but also the stress and strain on his body – he feels rushed and is frequently so exhausted he is 'bone weary'. His experience of caregiving is deeply embodied. As Michael Fine (2007: 171) argues, 'recognition of the body and the precarious vulnerability of physical life provide a powerful conceptual tool with which to explore the central place that issues of care occupy in human societies'. Certainly narratives of 'vulnerable bodies' abound, but usually only in reference to care recipients: for instance, the older care-recipients are frequently described as 'frail elderly'. Ben's explicitly embodied description of his lived experience of caregiving captures elements of what is often described as the 'caregivers' burden' – the negative physiological, psychological, and behavioural effects on their daily lives and health (Folbre 2012). Like other caregivers, Ben's lived experience is complex and complicated by multiple competing priorities (caring for his mother-in-law and his wife, maintaining the household and working full-time). A relational understanding of care, underpinned by the human interdependency highlighted by care ethics, point to multiple embodied vulnerabilities: not only are care recipients' bodies vulnerable but also those of the family caregivers (and the paid care workers for that matter). The family caregivers' bodies are vulnerable to injuries from, for example, lifting or moving the care recipient. This impacts their ability to care for their loved one, which in turn increases the vulnerability of the care recipient.

Men as care workers

> I got a little old lady and I go, 'Hi, you know, your nurse is here'. And they open the door, she thought I would be a woman, you know. So that can, yeah, it takes time for (the clients) to adjust. I remember one lady, first thing she said was, 'Whoa, you're a big fella'.

Dan is 43 years old and retrained as a Registered Nurse in his thirties after finding other work less satisfying. Nursing had 'always been at the back of my mind when I think about it', then he paused and cleared his throat, 'maybe it was just that whole thing of guys don't nurse'. Paid care work remains heavily gendered, both in terms of who does the work and the feminised attributes associated with it. Although more men are going into nursing, they remain a small minority. In 2006, men represented 53 per cent of the Canadian labour force, but only six per cent of registered nurses and eight per cent of Registered Practical Nurses (Statistics Canada 2006). As Dan put it: 'Well I'm not a nurse, right; I'm a *male* nurse. Yes, I'm not a nurse; I'm a *male* nurse' (the emphasis was his).

Feminist scholarship spotlights the gendered boundaries constructed around the concept of work and how different sorts of work get socially constructed and differentially valued as 'men's work' or 'women's work'. Geographers have underscored how spaces and occupations gender workers, and have conceptualised worker identities and subjectivities through the ways in which women and men are transgressing the gendered boundaries of work. Several studies explore how women and men, as corporeal subjects, 'do gender' in the paid workplace. More commonly attention is on the everyday, embodied practices through which women are marked as 'other' and 'out of place' in masculinised workplaces such as the steel industry (Tonkins 2000) and the information and communication technology sector (Raghuram 2008). Other work has considered how masculinities are constructed in the workplace, such as Linda McDowell's work on merchant banking and low-income service work (McDowell 2009).

In the social sciences, there is a growing body of research about men 'doing gender' in feminised jobs such as temporary clerical work and nursing. Such men disrupt the gender order because their gender performances do not match with gendered expectations generated by hegemonic masculine normativity. Men in feminised jobs face challenges to their masculinity, including suggestions they are not 'real men', assumptions that they are gay, or in some way are positioned as lacking (Williams 2013). Thus men in paid care work can find themselves being held accountable for both challenging established normative masculinity and as changing the feminine identification of care work. For instance, in their work on immigrant men working in low paid jobs in London, Datta et al. (2009) found a range of masculinities unfolding in different sorts of jobs. Generally men in feminised jobs, like care work or cleaning, tended to 'develop a range of compensatory strategies and rationales for coping with the challenges such work presented to their masculinity' (Datta et al. 2009: 865). Similarly, Batnitzky et al. (2009) argue that migrant men enact 'flexible and strategic masculinities' as a strategy for making sense of their employment in low-paid 'women's work'. These scholars underscore practices and strategies of negotiation and resistance associated in the complex processes whereby migrant men perform and (re) evaluate their masculinity in the context of gender relations in their home country compared with their destination country.

Although Dan did not migrate across national boundaries, it is not insignificant that Dan became a nurse in his thirties, presumably once he felt more secure in his masculinity. He went through a period of self-examination and was drawn to palliative care. He talked of enjoying helping people manage their health and felt community nursing offered him more autonomy in his work than hospital-based nursing would. Dan described his job as primarily 'fly in and out visits' – adjusting medications and checking medical technology – as he visited up to as many as 40 care recipients in a week. This meant that in a regular workweek he was visiting people in a range of neighborhoods, sometimes after dark and sometimes in locations that did not feel safe. In these instances he engaged in a complex and multi-layered 'flexible and strategic' masculinity in which he both used his body to emphasize his size (at several points in his interview he described himself as a 'big' man) *and* the gendered, embodied discourses surrounding 'male nurses'. He recounted a story where he was visiting a care recipient in a rooming house in the late evening. After knocking several times on the door, the building owner:

> opened the door and he had this baseball bat and he was gonna let me have it. Because he'd been having all kinds of problems with crack dealers and customers and that. I just went: 'Whoaaa! I'm a nurse, I'm a nurse to see so-and-so'. He knew this guy needed – had a nurse. He went, 'Oh, oh, come right in! Oh, it's nice to meet you!' If they know you're a nurse they … they know

> you're not threatening. You're not there to threaten them, you know, they know you're there to help.

Dan's story reminds us that embodiment is an active process, constituted in and through social relations *and* space. And that masculinities involve actually existing people engaged in *situated*, grounded practices that produce and are produced in particular places.

Conclusion

Over a decade ago, Robyn Longhurst (2000: 439) urged geographers to 'engage not just with femininity but also with masculinity and the relation between these binary constructs'. In the intervening years several have responded to her call and research on the geographies of masculinities has flourished. In this chapter we too have responded by thinking about masculinities through the lens of care and embodiment. We highlight the complex processes that unfold as men 'do gender' when engaging in practices more commonly associated with women. In telling the stories of Robert, Ben and Dan we have kept in plain sight the corporeal aspects of masculinity as we explored how they perform and actively rework their particular hue of masculinity in non-gender typical processes, practices and even places (i.e. the home). We suggest that linking together masculinities, embodiment and care opens up and expands future possibilities for others to take up more research on the lived experience of men (and women). Moreover by revisiting the relationship between gender and domestic space through the lens of masculinities it becomes apparent that specific spatialities of masculine performance are not only embedded in broader cultural change but also contextualised in policy formulated in particular political-economy moments that vary over time and space. Further research on men who care and men's involvement in care work would further open the fractures and sticking points in power within gender relationships and what women and men do – and where – which would further reveal the dynamic, ongoing formulation of places.

References

Aitken, S.C. 2009. *The Awkward Spaces of Fathering*. Aldershot: Ashgate.

Batnitzky, A., McDowell, L. and Dyer, S. 2009. Flexible and strategic masculinities: the working lives and gendered identities of male migrants in London. *Journal of Ethnic and Migration Studies*, 35(8), 1275–1293.

Berg, L.D. and Longhurst, R. 2003. Placing *masculinities* and *geography*. *Gender, Place and Culture: A Journal of Feminist Geography*, 10(4), 351–360.

Bondi, L. 2008. On the relational dynamics of caring: a psychotherapeutic approach to emotional and power dimensions of women's care work. *Gender, Place and Culture: A Journal of Feminist Geography*, 15(3), 249–265.

Bubeck, D. 1995. *Care, Gender and Justice*. Oxford: Clarendon Press.

Butler, J. 1993. *Bodies That Matter: On the Discursive Limits of 'Sex'*. London and New York: Routledge.

Connell, R.W. 1995. *Masculinities*. Berkeley: University of California Press.

Connell, R.W. and Messerschmidt, J.W. 2005. Hegemonic masculinity: rethinking the concept. *Gender and Society*, 19(6), 829–859.

Conradson, D. 2011. Care and caring, in *A Companion to Social Geography*, edited by V. Del Casino, et al. Oxford: Wiley-Blackwell, 454–471.

Datta, K., McIlwaine, C., Herbert, J., Evans, Y., May, J. and Wills, J. 2009. Men on the move: narratives of migration and work among low-paid migrant men in London. *Social and Cultural Geography*, 10(8), 853–873.

Dyck, I. 2011. Embodied life, in *A Companion to Social Geography*, edited by V. Del Casino, et al. Oxford: Wiley-Blackwell, 454–471.

Dyck, I. and England, K. 2012. Home for care: reconfiguring care relations and practices, in *Home, Care, Practices: Critical Perspectives on Care at Home for Older People*, edited by C. Ceci, K. Bjornsdottir and M.E. Purkis. New York: Routledge.

England, K. 2010. Home, paid care work and geographies of responsibilities themed issue on 'care-full geographies. *Ethics, Place and Environment*, 13(2), 131–150.

England, K. and Dyck, I. 2011. 'Managing the body work of home care' themed issue 'body work'. *Sociology of Health and Illness*, 33(2), 206–219.

England, K. and Dyck, I. 2012. Migrant workers in home care: responsibilities, routes and respect. *Annals of the Association of American Geographers*, 101(5), 1076–1083.

Fast, J., Lero, D., Duncan, K., Dunlop, C., Eales, J., Keating, N. and Yoshino, S. 2011. *Employment Consequences of Family/Friend Caregiving in Canada: Research on Aging, Policies and Practice* [Online: University of Alberta]. Available at: http://www.rapp.ualberta.ca/Publications/~/media/E1E0F4EFD4F849B79D278FAB1AE5F7C8.pdf [accessed 30 March 2013].

Fine, M. 2007. *A Caring Society?: Care and the Dilemmas of Human Service in the Twenty-First Century*. New York: Palgrave Macmillan.

Folbre, N. 2012. *For Love and Money: Care Provision in the United States*. New York: Russell Sage Foundation.

Grosz, E. 1994. *Volatile Bodies: Toward a Corporeal Feminism*. London: Allen and Unwin.

Hopkins, P. and Noble, G. 2009. Masculinities in place: situated identities, relations and intersectionality. *Social and Cultural Geography*, 10(8), 811–819.

van Hoven, B. and Hörschelmann, K. 2005. *Spaces of Masculinities*. London and New York: Routledge.

Kittay, E.F. 1999. *Love's Labor: Essays on Women, Equality and Dependency.* New York: Routledge.

Lan, P.C. 2003. 'They have more money but I speak better English': transnational encounters between Filipina domestics and Taiwanese employers. *Identities: Global Studies in Culture and Power*, 10(2), 132–161.

Longhurst, R. 2000. *Geography* and *gender: masculinities,* male identity and men. *Progress in Human Geography,* 24(3), 439–444.

McDowell, L. 2009. *Working Bodies: Interactive Service Employment and Workplace Identities*. Malden: Wiley-Blackwell.

Milligan, C. 2009. *There's No Place like Home: People, Place and Care in an Ageing Society*. Farnham: Ashgate.

Milligan, C. and Wiles, J. 2010. Landscapes of care. *Progress in Human Geography*, 34(6), 736–754.

Moss, P. and Dyck, I. 2003. *Women, Body, Illness: Space and Identity in the Everyday Lives of Women with Chronic Illness*. Lanham: Rowman and Littlefield.

O'Brien, R., Hunt, K. and Hart, G. 2007. Standing out from the herd: men renegotiating masculinity in relation to their experience of illness. *International Journal of Men's Health*, 6(3), 178–200.

Perrons, D., Fagan, C., McDowell, L., Ray, K. and Ward, K. (eds) 2006. *Gender Divisions and Working Time in the New Economy.* London: Edward Elgar.

Raghuram, P. 2008. Migrant women in male-dominated sectors of the labour market: a research agenda. *Population, Space and Place*, 14(1), 43–57.

Russell, R. 2007. The work of elderly men caregivers: from public careers to an unseen world. *Men and Masculinities*, 9(3), 298–314.

Thien, D. and Del Casino, V.J. 2012. (Un)healthy men, masculinities, and the geographies of health. *Annals of the Association of American Geographers*, 102(5), 1146–1156.

Tonkins, L. 2000. Women of steel: constructing and contesting new gendered geographies of work in the Australian steel industry. *Antipode*, 32(2), 115–134.

Tronto, J. 1993. *Moral Boundaries: A Political Argument for an Ethic of Care.* New York: Routledge.

Twigg, J. 2000. *Bathing, the Body and Community Care*. London: Routledge.

West, C. and Fenstermaker, S. 1995. Doing difference. *Gender and Society*, 9(1), 8–37.

Wiles, J.L. 2003. Daily geographies of caregivers: mobility, routine, scale. *Social Science and Medicine*, 57(7), 1307–1325.

Williams, C. 2013. The glass escalator, revisited: gender inequality in neoliberal times. *Gender and Society*, 6(3), 178–201.

Chapter 19
The Gay Bar as a Place of Men's Caring

Michael Brown, Stefano Bettani, Larry Knopp and Andrew Childs

Introduction

Within queer studies gay bars have long had a bad rap. As longstanding territories of dissident sexualities, they have been frequent targets in queer scholarship's aggressive and relentless critique. For instance, gay bars are characterised as spaces of exploitation. As commercial enterprises run for profit, unequal class relations structure relations between gay bars' owners and workers. They also enable the commodification and assimilation of alternative culture (Rushbrook 2002, Bell and Binnie 2004, Brown 2009). Similarly, they can be part of the displacement process of gentrification (Knopp 1987, 1990). Gay bars are also characterised as racist. They privilege whiteness and white bodies in them (Caluya 2008, Teunis 2007, Salcedo 2009). They are seen as misogynistic as well, or at least sites for the production/reproduction of normative masculinities (Valentine 1994, Johnson and Samdahal 2005). Men use bars to exclude women. And gay bars are seen as ableist (fit, able bodies are privileged and welcomed while non-normative bodies are not – see Butler 1999, Field 1993) and ageist (they exclude elders – see Weinberg 1970, Binnie 1995, Casey 2007).

Collectively, these characterisations portray gay bars as homonormative. They welcome and privilege an unforgiving normality: wealthy, white, young, beautiful able-bodied gay men. Furthermore, gay bars are seen as quite unhealthy places (Steiner, Lemke and Roffman 1994, Greenfield, Midanik and Rogers 2000, Valentine and Skelton, 2003). They are renowned for excessive drug and alcohol use, sexual exploitation and STD transmission (Rosario, Schrimshaw and Hunter 2004, Slavin 2004, Parsons, Kelly and Weiser 2007). Collectively, these negative characterisations have led scholars to theorise gay bars as uncaring and careless.

In the spirit of queer theory's quest to critique every doxa, the purpose of this chapter is to open this consensus itself – however insightful – to critique. Drawing on theories of masculinity and care (which are ascendant in critical human geography) and our historical-geographic research project on gay spaces in Seattle, USA, we argue that gay bars can be a place of men's caring – including caring across difference (see also England and Dyck 2014: this volume). Our aim is not to wholly deny the critiques summarised above, nor to blunt the critical will of queer theory and scholarship. Rather, our aim is to modulate that theoretical consensus with a more nuanced historical-geographic perspective. Furthermore, we argue that appreciating the care relations manifest in gay bars historically pushes recent work on the geographies of care in new gendered ways.

We conceptualise gay bars here not as abstract locations, but as places. By this we mean culturally and densely signified sites and situations that have both spatial and temporal dimensions. Evidence for our argument comes primarily from two sources.[1] The first is a large research project on the governmentalities of gay men's health in mid-twentieth century (pre-AIDS) Seattle, Washington (cf. 1943–1983). We draw here on interviews (n=72) focused on biopolitical relations between gay men, the Washington State Liquor Control Board and the Seattle-King County Department of Public Health. While questions of care and caring were not central to the larger research project for which those interviews were collected, they nonetheless emerged as crucial dimensions in respondent's chronicles of gay life and experiences in Seattle during that era. When we asked interviewees to describe their relations with the two government agencies, the geographies of their accounts frequently involved bars and taverns. Second, we draw data from the oral history collection of the Northwest Lesbian and Gay History Museum Project (NWLGHMP). This local all-volunteer, non-profit group undertook in-depth interviews with local LGBTQ individuals from around the region roughly 10–15 years ago (n=96). Their interviews tend to focus on the post-war era, when Seattle's gay community was forming (see also Atkins 2003). A frequent line of discussion in these oral histories was the social and cultural dimensions of bars. What these data offer then, is an historical-geographical reflection on the saliencies of these places to our respondents. Gay bars emerge as places of care in quite multidimensional ways. Our findings suggest that care took both immaterial and material forms (often simultaneously). Bars were places of identity – formation and community – building and emotional caring was key to these processes. More materially, gay bars were sites of employment, health promotion, education and activism.

Men's caring

Tronto (1994: 103), of course, provides the starting point with her conceptualisation of care as:

> … a species of activity that includes everything that we do to maintain, continue and repair our world so that we can live in it as well as possible. That world includes our bodies, our selves and our environment, all of which we seek to interweave in a complex life-sustaining web.

1 A third but much more minor source is a collection of user comments on the website discomusic.com (see below).

Care is both an affective orientation towards the world (caring for, caring to) and also action and work (taking care of, care-work). The immaterial (cultural, emotional and affective) and material dimensions of care are imbricated in order to maintain life and well-being. In the past decade there has been an explosion of excellent work by geographers on care and caring. These scholars stress that the geographies of care and caring are deeply gendered and place-based (England 2000, 2010, Milligan 2001, 2003, Wiles 2003a, 2003b). Simply put, caring is associated with women, the feminine and femininity and is spatially structured through particular forms of work in particular places, such as the private sphere. Women care in the home (but not necessarily their own), or as care workers in institutional facilities for low wages or care for the body itself.

A small, parallel literature outside of geography reminds us that men can and do care (Arber and Gilbert 1989, McFarland and Sanders 1999, Kramer and Thompson 2002, Vuori 2007). This literature stresses the particular challenges and constraints for male carers in a patriarchal society (Evans 2002). This care work and affect occurs in both private (Bywaters and Harris 1998, Mays and Lund 1999) and public spaces (MacDougall 1997) and associates particular masculinities of caring with particular identities. For example there is a vast literature on older men as carers for ill spouses (Riberio, Paul and Nogueira 2007, Russel 2007a, 2007b, Baker, Robertson and Connelly 2010). There is also a strong literature on the care work that gay men have performed around HIV/AIDS (Wrubel and Folkman 1997, Sidwell Sipes 2002, Munro and Edward 2008, Kia 2012).

That gay men do care work is less taken up in geography, with some exceptions. In his work on AIDS activism in Vancouver, Brown (1997) argued that caring work and ethics mapped a new space of urban politics. Later in his work on home hospice care, he noted how men still did care work, though in lesser amounts and at greater distance to the dying body (for example, taking care of insurance while women did more 'hands on' care) (Brown 2003). He also found gay men were used by hospice workers to argue for the possibility that men could care (though they certainly could do a whole lot more!).

From this literature we take the following points. First, men *do* care: both in terms of emotion and labour (see also Simpson 2004). Second, hegemonic masculinity (Connell 2005) can be reinforced, redefined, or resisted through men's care. Third, *gay* men are particularly theorised as carers (see Vanderbeck 2005). These insights conceptually open up the possibility for considering the possibility of men/masculine/masculinity gendering care in all its dimensions, but especially by gay men. So if gay bars are presently theorised as exploitative and exclusionary, but literature on men's care and caring suggests important but often hidden forms of relations that resist such oppressions, how do we reconcile these? This literature conceptually opens up the possibility for considering the possible geographies of men's caring that have yet to be conceptualised or investigated.

Men's care and caring in gay bars

Identity formation and community building[2]

It is important to recall that not so long ago bars and taverns that catered to (or even merely tolerated) 'homosexuals' were almost the only public places where they could come together with even a modicum of safety. Without homosexual bars, community could not form because the recognition of a shared identity was almost impossible without place to bring people together. As such, bars and taverns centrally provided a means by which people could link themselves with others through the formation of community. Community provided care by showing people they were not alone or isolated in the closet and bars allowed people a place to focus on careful community building. They became nodes around which community moved and newcomers were mentored. While seemingly an obvious point, Sedgwick (1993) reminds us that the uniqueness of homosexual oppression is the intensity of isolation and loneliness of the closet. As one trans* person put it about bars generally, 'Yeah because it was a place for the community to be. Where we could go and be amongst our own'. Or as a gay man in his 50s explained: 'I remember going into the Dancing Machine and Shelly's Leg and just being awestruck that there were thousands of people like me. Because I thought I was – my – total minority – like there was five of us and I was one of the five.'

This sense of identity and community extended to and educated non-gay participants too, as a straight female contributor to the website discomusic.com demonstrates:

> A fellow student gave me the address and direction (name too) for the Monastery but didn't tell me anything else about it. So there I was … seventeen years old and rather 'innocent' … That night was the beginning of an ongoing expansion of consciousness for me. The first people in Seattle who mentored me and made me feel welcome, beautiful and a part of a larger loving community were the dwellers of the Monastery … Now I have two gorgeous daughters who benefited from the love I experiences as a member of The Monastery. (http://www.discomusic.com/clubs-more/3845_0_6_0_C/)

The first disco in Seattle, Shelly's Leg (1973–1976) exemplified this caring affect for mid-1970s Seattle gays and lesbians. It was noteworthy because, as Seattle's first disco, heterosexuals for the first time were drawn to a gay bar because of the celebration of identity and community – so much so, in fact, that its

2 'Identity' and 'community' are of course complex, contested and problematic concepts. We use the terms advisedly here, both to signify the sense of connection and belonging that was engendered amongst diverse populations of gay people patronizing bars at the time and because of the resonance of the terms in these people's lives.

management placed this large placard on the wall (Figure 19.1). In the words of one baby boomer gay man:

> With Shelley's Leg, something was really changing. That was to the Seattle Gay Community probably as a whole, that truly was a point of demarcation. It was something is changing in the bar life of gay and lesbian people. Bright lights inside, dancing, everyone having a great time. No sense of, you know, secrecy. It was – And from there on, many, many bars developed and I think there are probably a couple that still sort of resembled the old days that went under, but mostly, they were moving forward to sociable environments.

Different, simultaneous constructions of 'gay' helped identity-formation, too, by specifying one's position in and relationship to amorphous notions of 'the gay community'. These striations commonly took the form of different types of gay bars, which corresponded to different performatives of masculinity and femininity. We see this in the following quote that describes the complex geographies of gay masculinity in 1970s Seattle:

Figure 19.1 Sign inside of Shelly's Leg disco 1973–1976. (Photo courtesy of the Northwest Lesbian and Gay History Project – used with permission)

> The Park Bench crowd was more going off to a disco afterwards. Whereas, some of the Daddy patrons would – that would be their destination and they would go and stay and then go home from there. It was just more masculine, manly. Many of the bar tenders I think would wear like blue jeans and then a leather vest or something sort of and like work boots. So more of that kind of butch. Seattle has never really had a true leather bar. I've known several people in the leather community and they refer to it as kind of naugahyde and 'pleather'. Pleather, plastic leather, rather than a real leather bar. The J&L Saloon that became the Eagle and it kind of flip flopped back and forth between Ego and J&L and I know a couple of leather people that referred to it as the Judy and Laverne Lounge and that's what J&L meant. Brass Connection was one of the main discos when I first moved into town. Young twenties, very much more the preppy, the polo shirt with the collar turned up. At that time there were also Tugs down in Belltown and that was more kind of new wave and punk. It wasn't real punky. We didn't have safety pins in our cheek and wearing garbage bags and things like that but they would play music like Nina Hagen and things like that where Brass Connection was playing the kind of top 40s pop dance music.

Attaching oneself to community in order to bolster one's identity is of course part and parcel of caring for the self. Gay bars provided men opportunity to improve how they felt about themselves, which in turn could augment their emotional and even physical health. Gay bars and taverns could often be places – the only ones sometimes – where people felt welcomed, in place (as opposed to feeling out of place) and accepted. Recalling his terror at entering a gay bar in the 1960s for the very first time, an elderly man said: 'It was very interesting to go into that bar that first night and know that I was home. I knew I wasn't alone anymore'. In a context where there were very few gay or lesbian places per se, 'coming out of the closet' literally meant entering a gay bar. As one man put it, 'Now in those days "coming out" meant: I went to gay bars, mixed with gay people and identified as gay'.

So in an otherwise heteronormative and homophobic city, gay bars could be environments where people augmented their self-worth. It wasn't only a matter of finding a meeting place: gay bars allowed people to look at themselves and see something different from the diseased, sinful bodies with which mainstream media and families often hegemonically forced them to identify. Seattle's gay bars were places of resignifications and self-acceptance where human beings took care of themselves and each other in the most fundamental way: learning to feel that they had the right to exist. In the words of one baby boomer, 'There's been something there [in bars] of a musical, tribal kind of togetherness amongst strangers that heterosexual people do not have and have not found amongst themselves'.

Emotional caring

Most gay bars in Seattle were not actually owned by gays or lesbians, especially the further back in time you go. Bars often 'turned' gay because such clientele were tolerated or because actual caring friendships developed between owners and patrons. Velma recalls that the owners of The Casino in the mid-twentieth century were a heterosexual couple, but cared for gays in what was one of the first gay bars in the city:

> [The owners of The Casino] John and Margaret wouldn't let anyone mess with the queens. A queen was anyone who was gay and didn't try to hide it. They protected us and we loved them for that. … The Casino was the only place on the West Coast that was so open and free for gay people. (Paulson and Simpson 1996: 23)

Intergenerational caring relations were also manifest in bars and taverns. Often alienated and far away from families of origin, gay men took care of one another in familial terms. One man recalled being under-age in Seattle gay bars in the 1960s and how he was cared for by an older man: 'I think in the old days it was a lot easier to be around the old people. I loved being around the old "aunties". That was the term: "aunties" that referred to an older usually nelly male'.

> **Interviewer**: How old?
>
> **Interviewee**: From my perspective back then, someone forty [laughs]. But the old people were like the old aunties. And one of them that I can remember was Francine. She was an old drunk and a bartender of the Pioneer Square era. She'd worked in a number of bars – Double Header, Stage Door, when we were going there. That's when I first met her. And she was an old drunk and disheveled – hair always messed up – very platinum blonde type-of-thing. She'd done shows in the old bars and stuff … She gave advice. Sage advice.
>
> **Interviewer**: What kinds of stuff did she say?
>
> **Interviewee**: One of the things that I found most amusing was when a friend of mine asked her, 'Well what's the secret of developing the right kind of perfect relationship? And how do you make a lasting relationship?' And she goes, 'Oh honey! That's simple. You just sleep with him til you get used to him.' Which I think is one of the sagest things that I've ever heard.

Relations between lesbians and gay men could also embody this form of care. Seattle's homosexual bars were typically gender-integrated throughout most of the twentieth century. While there have been women's bars in the city since the mid-1950s and especially during the lesbian separatism of the 1970s, women and men cared for one another in these spaces quite often. This might take the form of deep friendships, but it also could take the form of 'beards': fake boyfriend-and-girlfriend relationships that concealed homosexuality from outsiders, or allowed men – but especially women – to come-and-go from bars without harassment outside the door.

Caring also meant having the chance to experience joy and desire without feeling pain or shame. Dancing together, hugging and kissing, sharing a drink or just a few words: gay bars, in different ways according to different venues, allowed people to have a social and sexual life under the sun and out of the closet. They were places where friends met to chat and have fun and where partners could share moments of public intimacy. People felt the joy of standing in a crowd without feeling afraid and had the opportunity to express and live desires labelled as clandestine and diseased by the world outside the gay bars. One man described it thusly: 'That feeling of, being with other people you liked and enjoyed in daylight, you know dancing or whatever and – and, you know, just watching the crowd, but that it was no – it was not a clandestine activity.'

The layout of gay bars also worked towards facilitating cruising and intimacy amongst otherwise lonely and isolated individuals. The 611, for example, a small tavern that opened in the early 1960s deliberately hung large mirrors behind the bar so that men could make eye contact with one another surreptitiously. This discretion was vital because direct verbal or physical contact could risk an arrest from undercover police officers from the vice squad.

Finally, bars were often places where caring and loving relationships began. Several men recalled meeting long-term partners at such places in a context of otherwise lonesome and alienated lives. We quote one oral history at length to convey the importance of the gay bar as the catalyst for such long-term care:

> I met him in 1975. I met him at Shelly's Leg … I looked down to the dance floor from the balcony and I saw Jon[3] and I said, jokingly-but-somewhat-seriously, 'I want that one!' Like I was shopping for a toy or something. And my friend said, 'That one?' And I said, 'Yes'. And he rushes down the steps without – I didn't encourage this! He grabs Jon on the dance floor by the arm. He apparently met him once before but I didn't know that. He drags him upstairs and says, 'What's your name?' And the guy says, 'Jon'. And my friend goes, 'Jon, I'd like you to meet [the interviewee]'. And I said, 'Oh great'. Well, I'm so embarrassed now, but I can't lose by taking the final step. So I said, 'Would you like to go home with me and have sex?' And he said, 'Sure!' We've been together ever since.

This oral history was taken in 2000. It's important to note that not only did the bar facilitate lust and love between two gay men, but also the friendship behind the very abrupt introduction!

3 A pseudonym.

Material caring

Employment

Imagine you are a nellie queen or butch lesbian at a time when not only paid employment was tightly gendered, but also the division of labour. Imagine as well that there is no fair employment legislation in place to protect you from being fired (which was the case in Seattle until 1973). Thus for some gays and lesbians – especially the unskilled and semi-skilled – bars and taverns were some of very few places that would hire them. According to one lesbian, during the 1950s and 1960s:

> Butch women were so outrageous in their looks that they were pretty much unemployable. And so they were being supported by their [femme partners]. … Well, most of those that I knew, including some really so called stone-butch worked in jobs where they could wear pants. Bartenders, some of them were bartenders in gay bars.

Working in a gay bar meant living close to the community, feeling its social and political heart beating, knowing what was happening and how people felt. It was a chance to earn a wage, certainly, but it was also an opportunity to develop a strong sense of stability. Working in places they could call their own, no matter what side of the counter they were standing on, people felt useful: they were giving something to the community while receiving something from it. It was an exchange of resources that kept the community alive and made many people feel alive. Some people spent their entire working career in bars, such as a recently retired manager of a gay bar:

> I worked at Daddy's, I worked at the Marshall's office, I worked at the original Bus Stop, which is now Changes. I worked at the Eagle which was then just switching over from the J&L Saloon. Worked at Mike's on Madison, Mom's, then CC's

The owner of Tugs, a small popular gay tavern in the early 80s tied these themes all together in the following conversation:

> **Interviewer**: As someone who has owned a bar for a while, what gave you the most satisfaction from that experience? The money?
>
> **Interviewee**: It definitely wasn't the money!
>
> **Interviewer**: What then?
>
> **Interviewee**: It was just beer and wine only – and the money would have been in liquor only. But Tugs supported itself. It paid the employees. It paid the rent.

> I think it was just a sense of accomplishment, a dream that I've always had. And I did it with the help of my friends. I couldn't do it by myself. I'm not an artistic person. They created the atmosphere that made it so special'.

Fundraising

From the 1960s through the 1980s, Seattle's gay community produced a wide and typical array of organizations, community centres, political initiatives and campaigns. Homophile movements like the Dorian Society (from the mid-1960s), gay and lesbian community centres, campaigns for fair housing and employment and repeal of the state sodomy laws. In some respects the centrality of bars to the community was being displaced by a new, broader geography of services and activism. But in other respects bars played an important role in this new geography. They provided early spaces for meetings. Most importantly, however, they provided the space for fundraising, which was a material form of caring at a time when both the public sphere of the welfare state and the private sphere of the family could be quite uncaring. As one activist reminisced:

> We had a terrific grassroots kind of creative campaign and we did fundraisers for the campaign. And I was very involved in the campaign. I lived and breathed it for many months. And so one time we were doing a fundraiser, as we did in those days and we got a liquor license for one of our events that was held, I believe, at the Monastery, which was a gay club, but it might have been for people under the age of 21 or something.

As early as 1971, The Imperial Court system of Seattle existed. It involved a competitive pageant for drag queens and gay men (and later women) after which they would be crowned Emperor and Empress of Seattle. These royalties would then host fundraisers throughout the year to benefit various local causes and charities, including scholarships. This financial form of caring, at least in one case, extended to helping a regular patron make bail. Continuing Velma's recollection of the owners of the Double Header, she recalled: 'But you didn't mess with them or take advantage of their kindness. They'd do anything for you if they liked you, even bail you out of jail, but if you crossed John he'd throw you out in a minute, gay or straight'.

Health promotion

Go to any gay bar today and you will invariably find some materials promoting safer sex: information kiosks, condoms, even free HIV testing. But this form of caring did not just emerge from the AIDS crisis. Long before, gay bars were places where caring for people's physical health was undertaken. Before AIDS, STDs typically meant syphilis and gonorrhoea. Especially for syphilis, testing was done at least occasionally by the Seattle-King County Health Department in bars (and also bathhouses). Information brochures and pamphlets on STDs – with a rather caring tone – were available in gay bars (Figure 19.2). More frequently the department's Disease Intervention Specialists, or Disease Investigators (contact tracers), used bars and taverns to locate suspected infected individuals and talk to them discretely about the need to come in for testing. For example, one Disease Investigator from the 1970s recalled: 'We, very often, would offer to do testing in bars, gay bars. They would agree to it for the most part. You would first go to the bar tender but sometimes he'd refer you to the owner or whatever, whoever. Sometimes they were the same person. Yeah, very often'.

Figure 19.2 Veneral Disease Education Pamphlet distributed by the Seatte-King County Public Health Department, in conjunction with the Seattle Gay Community Center circa 1978

Source: King County Archives

The role of gay bars in the promotion of health must not be underestimated. In the pre-cellular phone, pre-internet, pre-social media era, the fact that gay bars functioned as a social node within the community was absolutely vital for the job of volunteers and doctors. STD testing was often offered in gay bars or just outside of them. They were places where posters and leaflets from the health department circulated and where contact tracers worked. One doctor from the Health Department confirmed these pre-AIDS safer sex efforts in the bars:

> There was an attempt to educate them through a myriad of things. It was literature. It was trying to put up notices in the gay bars. We put posters up in the gay bars – not me personally, but you know, some of the people from the Health Department – and in the bathrooms – And wanting them – we tried to urge condoms and whatnot – so there was a proactive stance among that group.

In the era of the sexual revolution, gay bars stood on the front lines of its contradictions and extremes, simultaneously embodying hedonism and health, lust and education.

Education/politics

Along with fundraising and health promotion, political movements and activism also worked through bars. Again, as one of the places gays congregated, it was an obvious efficiency to educate patrons there. As one activist described it:

> Whatever we happened to be doing at the time: We would leaflet wherever we knew gay people were and that was at all bars and then you would give them leaflets. At all the bath houses and then you would give them leaflets and in the parks. Then you go in the parks and you would pass out leaflets and then you pass out leaflets on Capitol Hill for whatever it was you were doing.

Education was not just for gays in bars. Among the caring efforts of Seattle Counseling Center for Sexual Minorities was their field-trips for heterosexuals to gay bars and taverns. While there was surely a risk of a patronising Othering in such excursions, when asked why they were taken on such a tour, one of the founders replied, 'We were teaching them to be sensitive'.

Conclusion: caring masculinities in place

The themes above inductively emerged from our data when we considered the most salient forms and expressions of gay men's caring in twentieth-century Seattle. In what follows we analyse the multidimensionality of care across these empirical patterns. Beyond her definition of care, Tronto identifies four dimensions of caring relations: caring about, taking care of, caregiving and care receiving. Each of these dimensions appeared throughout the different empirical forms of care in Seattle's gay bars.

'Caring about' refers to the initial recognition of need in a situation. One cannot realise any of the other four phases if this phase is not met. Its corresponding value is attentiveness. In other words, 'caring about' means suspending your own concerns to recognise the needs of others. For example, realising that Seattle needed gay bars was a response to a yearning for the sense of community. Gay folks longed to create and establish meeting places that allowed people to feel welcomed, accepted, 'places for the community to be', in the words of one interviewee.

'Taking care of' is moving from recognising the need to undertaking action to address it. Its corresponding virtue is responsibility and it involves the assumption of obligation on the part of the carer. Taking care of is about assuming the needs of the first phase and how best to react and meet them. Institutions, in our case bars, play important roles in this phase because they are the primary means of realising care. Activities such as fundraising, flyering for political and health issues, or offering jobs, all of which took place in Seattle's gay bars, are examples of assuming responsibility.

Caregiving often involves material forms of care. Competence is the corresponding virtue. Often caregiving involves professionals or people with some degree of training in a particular area like the doctors and STD screeners that used bars as spaces to provide care. At the same time, a less formal means to deliver care is also simple physical contact. In our study then, dancing together or touching each other are instances of exchanging care, both at a material and immaterial level. Although casual encounters in bars do not require the same professional competence that say, phlebotomy does, the people involved in these encounters still give immediate or intimate actions of care.

Finally 'care receiving' signifies the situation where the care recipient's situation improves because of the completion of the caring circle. Responsiveness is the corresponding virtue. In more than one occasion our respondents expressed their feelings of relief, fulfilment and belonging after they experienced the kinds of material and immaterial care, that gay bars can offer. Sayings like, 'I didn't feel alone anymore. I met my partner there. I finally felt like I wasn't a diseased person anymore'. Such comments were common among patrons of gay bars.

We do not intend to over-draw these points, however. This chapter is a modest intervention rather than an alternative metanarrative to queer thought. We also do not mean to be naive or romantic. None of the evidence presented here disqualifies the critiques of these kinds of spaces in the literature. Furthermore, we think there are consequential theoretical insights from acknowledging these findings. For queer geography it means appreciating the forms of caring that gay men use to perform their masculinities. For feminist geography, it means considering the possibility of rethinking masculinity in ways that acknowledge care and carework by taking seriously places that sustain them (see also England and Dyck 2014: this volume, Trell and van Hoven 2014: this volume). And for scholars of men's care and especially gay men's care, we note that these themes have a longer history than merely gay carers of AIDS patients. The gay bar has historically been a place where gay men cared for each other, their worlds and were cared for by others across differences. Indeed, our insistence that gay bars be conceptualised as places asks that the multiple – and contradictory – meanings be appreciated in all their dissonance and complexity.

Acknowledgements

Support for this research was provided by the National Science Foundation (Award # 1059732). Thanks to the Northwest Lesbian and Gay History Project, the Puget Sound Branch of the Washington State Archives and the Special Collections Division of the University of Washington for their help. Thanks especially to Jeff Henness for his insight and recollections and to Trace Adams for his comments.

References

Arber, S. and Gilbert, N. 1989. Men: the forgotten caregivers. *Sociology*, 23(1), 111–118.

Atkins, G. 2003. *Gay Seattle: Stories of Exile and Belonging*. Seattle: University of Washington Press.

Baker, K.L., Robertson, N. and Connelly, D. 2010. Men caring for wives or partners with dementia: masculinity, strain and gain. *Aging and Mental Health*, 14(3), 319–327.

Bell, D. and Binnie, J. 2004. Authenticating queer space: citizenship, urbanism and governance. *Urban Studies*, 41(9), 1807–1820.

Binnie, J. 1995. Trading places: consumption, sexuality and the production of queer space, in *Mapping Desire*, edited by D. Bell and G. Valentine. London: Routledge, 182–199.

Brown, G. 2009. Thinking beyond homonormativity: performative explorations of diverse gay economies. *Environment and Planning A*, 41(6), 1496–1510.

Brown, M. 1997. *RePlacing Citizenship: AIDS Activism and Radical Democracy*. New York: Guilford Press.

Brown, M. 2003. Hospice and the spatial paradoxes of terminal care. *Environment and Planning A*, 35(5), 833–851.

Butler, R. 1999. Double the trouble or twice the fun? Disabled bodies in the gay community, in *Mind and Body Spaces: Geography of Illness, Impairment and Disability*, edited by R. Butler and H. Parr. London: Routledge, 446–461.

Bywaters, P. and Harris, A. 1998. Supporting carers: is practice still sexist? *Health and Social Care in the Community*, 6(6), 458–463.

Caluya, G. 2008. 'The rice steamer': race, desire and affect in Sydney's gay scene. *Australian Geographer*, 39(3), 283–292.

Casey, M. 2007. The queer unwanted and their undesirable 'otherness', in *Geographies of Sexualities: Theory, Practice and Politics*, edited by K. Browne, J. Lim and G. Brown. Farnham and Burlington: Ashgate, 137–149.

England, K. 2000. 'It's really hitting home': the home as a site for long-term health care. *Women and Environments International Magazine*, 48/49, 25.

England, K. 2010. Home, work and the shifting geographies of care. *Ethics, Place and Environment*, 13(2), 131–150.

Evans, J.A. 2002. Cautious caregivers: gender stereotypes and the sexualization of men nurses' touch. *Journal of Advanced Nursing*, 40(4), 441–448.

Field, J. 1993. Coming out of two closets (lesbians with disabilities). *Canadian Women's Studies*, 13(4), 18–19.

Greenfield, T., Midanik, L. and Rogers, J.D. 2000. A 10-year national trend study of alcohol consumption, 1984–1995: is the period of declining over? *American Journal of Public Health*, 90(1), 47–52.

Johnson, C.W. and Samdahal, D.M. 2005. 'The night they took over': misogyny in a country-western gay bar. *Leisure Sciences*, 27(4), 331–348.

Kia, H. 2012. 'I'm part of this family': how five care-giving partners of gay men story their experience. *Journal of Gay and Lesbian Social Services*, 24(2), 140–157.

Knopp, L. 1987. Social theory, social movements and public policy: recent accomplishments of the gay and lesbian movements in Minneapolis, Minnesota. *International Journal of Urban and Rural Research*, 11(2), 243–261.

Knopp, L. 1990. Some theoretical implications of gay involvement in an urban land market. *Political Geography Quarterly*, 9(4), 337–352.

Kramer, B.J. and Thompson Jr, E.H. 2002. *Men as Caregivers: Theory, Research and Service Implication*. New York: Springer Publishing Company.

MacDougall, G. 1997. Caring – a masculine perspective. *Journal of Advanced Nursing*, 25(4) 809–813.

Mays, G.D. and Lund, C.H. 1999. Male caregivers of mentally ill relatives. *Perspectives in Psychiatric Care*, 35(2), 19–28.

McFarland, P.L. and Sanders, S. 1999. Male caregivers: preparing men for nurturing roles. *American Journal of Alzheimer's Disease*, 14(5), 278–282.

Milligan, C. 2001. *Geographies of Care: Space, Place and the Voluntary Sector.* Aldershot: Ashgate.

Milligan, C. 2003. Location or dis-location? Towards a conceptualization of people and place in the care-giving experience. *Social and Cultural Geography*, 4(4), 455–470.

Munro, I. and Edward, K. 2008. The lived experience of gay men caring for others with HIV/AIDS: resilient coping skills. *International Journal of Nursing Practice*, 14(2), 122–128.

Parsons, J.T., Kelly, B.C. and Weiser, J.D. 2007. Initiation into methamphetamine use for young gay and bisexual men. *Drug and Alcohol Dependence*, 90(2), 135–144.

Paulson, D. and Simpson, R. 1996. *An Evening at the Garden of Allah*. New York: Columbia University Press.

Riberio, O., Paul, C. and Nogueira, C. 2007. Real men, real husbands: caregiving and masculinities in later life. *Journal of Aging Studies*, 21(4), 302–313.

Rosario, M., Schrimshaw, E.W. and Hunter, J. 2004. Predictors of substance use over time among gay, lesbian and bisexual youths: an examination of three hypotheses. *Addictive Behaviors*, 29(8), 1623–1631.

Rushbrook, D. 2002. Cities, queer space and the cosmopolitan tourist. *GLQ: A Journal of Lesbian and Gay Studies*, 8(1–2), 183–206.

Russell, R. 2007a. Men doing 'women's work': elderly men caregivers and the gendered construction of care work. *The Journal of Men's Studies*, 15(1), 1–18.

Russell, R. 2007b. The work of elderly men caregivers: from public careers to an unseen world. *Men and Masculinities*, 9(3), 298–314.

Salcedo, J. 2009. Deconstructing the outreach experience: renegotiating queer and Latino masculinities in the distribution of safe sex materials. *Journal of Gay and Lesbian Social Services*, 21(2/3), 151–170.

Sedgwick, E. 1993. *Epistemology of the Closet*. Berkeley: University of California Press.

Sidwell Sipes, C. 2002. The experiences and relationships of gay male caregivers who provide care for their partners with AIDS, in *Men as Caregivers: Theory, Research and Service Implication*, edited by B.J. Kramer and E.H. Thompson Jr. New York: Springer Publishing Company, 151–189.

Simpson, R. 2004. Masculinity at work: the experience of men in female-dominated occupations. *Work, Employment, Society*, 18(2), 349–368.

Slavin, S. 2004. Drugs, space and sociality in a gay nightclub in Sydney. *Journal of Contemporary Ethnography*, 33(3), 265–295.

Steiner, S., Lemke, A.L. and Roffman, R.A. 1994. Risk behavior for HIV transmission among gay men surveyed in Seattle bars. *Public Health Reports*, 109(4), 563–566.

Teunis, N. 2007. Sexual objectification and the construction of whiteness in the gay male community. *Culture, Health and Sexuality*, 9(3), 263–275.

Tronto, J. 1994. *Moral Boundaries: A Political Argument for an Ethic of Care*. New York: Routledge.

Valentine, G. 1994. Toward a geography of the lesbian community. *Women and Environments*, 14(1), 8–10.

Valentine, G. and Skelton, T. 2003. Finding oneself, losing oneself: the lesbian and gay `scene' as a paradoxical space. *International Journal of Urban and Regional Research*, 27(4), 849–866.

Vanderbeck, R. 2005 Masculinities and fieldwork: widening the discussion. *Gender, Place and Culture*, 12(4), 387–402.

Vuori, J. 2007. Men's choices and masculine duties: fathers in expert discussions. *Men and Masculinities*, 12(1), 45–71.

Weinberg, M.S. 1970. The male homosexual: age-related variations in social and psychological characteristics. *Social Problems*, 17(4), 527–537.

Wiles, J. 2003a. Informal caregivers' experiences of formal support in a changing context. *Health and Social Care in the Community*, 11(3), 189–207.
Wiles, J. 2003b. Daily geographies of caregivers: mobility, routine, scale. *Social Science and Medicine*, 57(7), 1307–1325.
Wrubel, J. and Folkman, S. 1997. What informal caregivers actually do: the caregiving skills of partners of men with AIDS. *AIDS Care*, 9(6), 691–706.

Chapter 20

'It's a place where all friends meet'[1]: Shared Places, Youth Friendships and the Negotiation of Masculine Identities in Rural Estonia

Elen-Maarja Trell and Bettina van Hoven

Introduction

Interest in young people's lives in East and Central Europe (ECE) has often centred around exploring the broader social, political and economic processes and their impact on youth well-being and living conditions (Taimalu et al. 2007, Stenning and Hörschelmann 2008, Krevs 2008, Blazek 2011). Considering the extent of the post-socialist transformations it is not surprising that in this context research has been 'more frequently preoccupied with […] solving problems of economic, social, political and environmental survival' (Krevs 2008: 146). Therefore, to date, an absence of academic engagement with *everyday lives* of young people in East and Central Europe can be observed (Blazek 2011, Stenning and Hörschelmann 2008). Research into youth kinship networks in provincial Russia by Walker (2010: 647) reveals that local social networks, family and friends are central in shaping the life-chances and helping young people to 'get by' (see also Habeck 2007). The special role of friendship in young people's daily lives and relationships has been often emphasised, especially in the field of developmental and social psychology (e.g. Erwin 1998, Schneider 2000, Dunn 2004). While the psychological approach to studying young people and their peer relations has been concerned primarily with the impact of friendship on youths' immediate well-being and on their transitions to adulthood, importantly for this chapter, social scientists have also highlighted the central role of friendships in young people's ongoing negotiation of their social identities (Nayak and Kahily 1996, Dyson 2010, Blazek 2011). For example, in his research in an urban neighbourhood in Slovakia, Blazek (2011) found that it is children's practices of friendship which are the enacting and transforming medium of their identities (see also Goodwin 2008). Other authors such as Nayak and Kehily (1996, 1996), Morris-Roberts (2001, 2004), Renold (2006) and Dyson

1 Olav (16).

(2010), furthermore show the significance of embodied practices that accompany friendship in the formation of young people's gendered subjectivities.

In this chapter, we focus on friendships as one of the key aspects in the everyday lives of young men in rural Estonia. More specifically, our aim is to emphasise the role of *place* in negotiating and performing young men's friendships (see also Gorman-Murray 2013).

According to social psychologists Bowlby (1969) and Erikson (1968), in youth the influence of friends surpasses the influence of parents. For young people, friends become the main points of reference, persons of identification, affirmation, as well as sources of support and understanding. Peer and friendship groups are the main social context within which youths learn to 'mark themselves out as same or different from others and to manage tensions between conformity and individuality' (Valentine 2000: 258). Pugh and Hart (2007) show that with the support of friends, young people are more likely to engage in new and alternative activities through which they can express and explore their various identities (see also Blazek 2011). By opening up alternative ways of being, enabling favourable social comparisons to be made and strengthening positive self-esteem, friendships can give individuals the confidence to resist dominant norms and values and bring about change (Dyson 2010, Bunnell et al. 2012). For young people, friends and peers also play a central role in their ongoing negotiation of gendered identities (Evans and Holt 2011).

However, there are studies that indicate that instead of empowering young people, friendship can reproduce exclusionary cultural patterns and function as a form of social control, through which dominant, 'acceptable' ways of being and doing can be enforced and reproduced (Dyson 2010, Bunnell et al. 2012). As Bunnell et al. (2012) argue, 'given that friendship connotes a relation to others, it always involves racial, class, sexual and gender dynamics which (re)create what is acceptable and what is not'. In his research focusing on gendered friendships and homophobia, Hooghe (2011) found that the norms of masculinity that are practiced in friendship networks of male adolescents can contribute to the development of prejudice against homosexuality. Within teenage, male peer networks, norms of masculinity are fostered that are 'antithetical to the development of tolerant attitudes toward homosexuality' (Hooghe 2011: 548, see also Hesp and Brooks 2009).

Underlying these norms is what Connell (1990: 83) defines as the leading pattern of masculinity, which is the 'standard-bearer of what it means to be a 'real' man or boy' (Kenway and Fitzclarence 1997: 119–120). This 'hegemonic masculinity' generally defines the norm, and many boys find that they have to fit into, and conform to, its demands. In many ways, the localised, hegemonic mode of masculinity serves as an idealised form of behaviour that boys are able to measure themselves against to discover the extent of their manliness (Mills 2001, Swain 2006). Since different locations provide different resources for (young) men to draw on, each location creates different options and opportunities to perform different aspects of masculinity and, in the context of this chapter, interactions with friends.

Studies such as the above imply that friendships can have a controversial influence on individual lives and identities (Dyson 2010, Bunnell et al. 2012). Bunnell et al. (2012: 494), for example, observed that, while friendships can enable 'boundary crossing' socio-spatial relations, they may also reinforce geographies of exclusion. At some moments, friendships can support and empower individuals to 'generate critique and novel practice and at other moments mirror and reinforce dominant structures' (Dyson 2010: 484).

In this chapter, we will first outline the theoretical framework guiding the analysis of our data, specifically addressing the role of young people's living environments, as a mix of physical and social affordances, in the construction and performance of gendered identities and friendship relations (Gibson 1979). We then briefly introduce our research location, participants and methods of data collection. In the discussion, we focus on youths' performance of masculinities in their key shared places of friendship and interaction, outside school and the familial home. Through reference to different ways in which masculine identities are performed and negotiated in these key places together with friends, we explore the influence of friendship on young people as well as the role of place in young men's identity negotiations.

The construction of gender-identity: masculinity, performance and place

Butler (1990) argues that gender is not a given static structure, but rather a performance that is enacted continually at specific social sites. Butler (1990) sees gender as multiple, perfomatively constituted and in a constant flux. Within their everyday lives and local places, people constantly (re)define themselves and negotiate their identities in interaction with others (Hopkins and Pain 2007). Lysaght (2002: 59) illustrates that different audiences, locations and circumstances can 'ensure a highly divergent and even contradictory performance'. Lysaght (2002) observes that the men in her research continually shifted between what she calls 'dominant' and 'subordinate' masculinities depending on their location in either their relatively safe residential communities in Belfast or outside these boundaries. When gender is conceptualised as something that individuals 'do', in contrast to something that they are (born into), gender is viewed as relational, contingent and subject to transformation depending upon locational and positional change (Lysaght 2002, van Hoven and Hörschelmann 2005, Hopkins and Pain 2007).

The closed cultural circle of the friendship and peer-group has become increasingly recognised as a key area of influence in performing masculinities (Connell 2000, Connolly 1998, Gilbert and Gilbert 1998, Mac an Ghaill 1994, Pollard 1985, Woods 1990). Friends are the point of reference, where boys get their information about how they are supposed to be and how they are supposed to act as a boy (and future man), and there are 'constant pressures on individuals to perform and behave to expected group norms' (Swain 2006). Masculinities, thus, 'have an existence beyond the individual and are, primarily, a collective enterprise' (Swain 2006: 334, see also Connell 2000, Pattman, Frosh and Phoenix 1998, Lesko 2000).

In addition to social context, the physical setting influences the performance of masculinity and can favour certain types of performances over others (see research on prison masculinities by van Hoven 2011). Nature and the outdoors, for example, provide a context where men can demonstrate their ability to cope with extreme weather conditions and hostile landscapes or to 'control' the environment (Saugeres 2002, Little 2002, Little and Panelli 2007). In this chapter, we draw on Gibson's (1979) theory of affordances as a starting point for exploring relations between identity performance and space. Gibson (1979) argues that elements in the environment have functional significance for individuals and can afford various opportunities for action and interaction. Gibson (1979) terms this significance and the resulting opportunities 'affordances'. Affordances can be physical, such as a stream affording water and cooling, but can also be social, for example the presence of other people affording opportunities for social interaction, playing or nurturing (Clark and Uzzell 2002). For example, in their study of adolescent places, Clark and Uzzell (2002) compared the affordances of a town centre, neighbourhood, school and home. They found that in contrast to the town centre and the neighbourhood, the home, as a closed indoor environment shared with family, does not afford young people opportunities for social interaction (Clark and Uzzell 2002). The home environment has the most affordances for different types of retreat, retreat together with close friends and retreat involving security-seeking (Clark and Uzzell 2002, Trell and van Hoven 2012). The town centre, as a public, adult-dominated place, is subject to formal symbolic and physical mechanisms of exclusion, such as signs or the 'mosquito' device meant to 'protect' adult places from (deviant) young people 'hanging out' (Trell and van Hoven 2012). Public and commercial places do not offer all social groups the same kinds of resources or amount of freedom of action and interaction.

Valentine (2007: 19) argues that 'the ability to enact some identities or realities rather than others is highly contingent on the power-laden spaces in and through which our experiences are lived'. All groups have specific geographies within the community, their own spaces in which they exert, perform and establish their identities. Compared to young people, the legal and societal status of adulthood affords adults more influence, a greater voice and more freedom of action in the use of places (and the definition of barriers to places) (Hay 1998).

Research location and approach

The data informing this chapter were collected during a participatory research project in the town of Järva-Jaani (see Figure 20.1). Järva-Jaani is located in one of the most agricultural and least densely populated areas of Estonia (14.7 ppl/km2 compared to Estonian average 30.9 ppl/km2) (Regional Portrait of Estonia: Järvamaa 2010). Employment in agriculture is the main source of income for

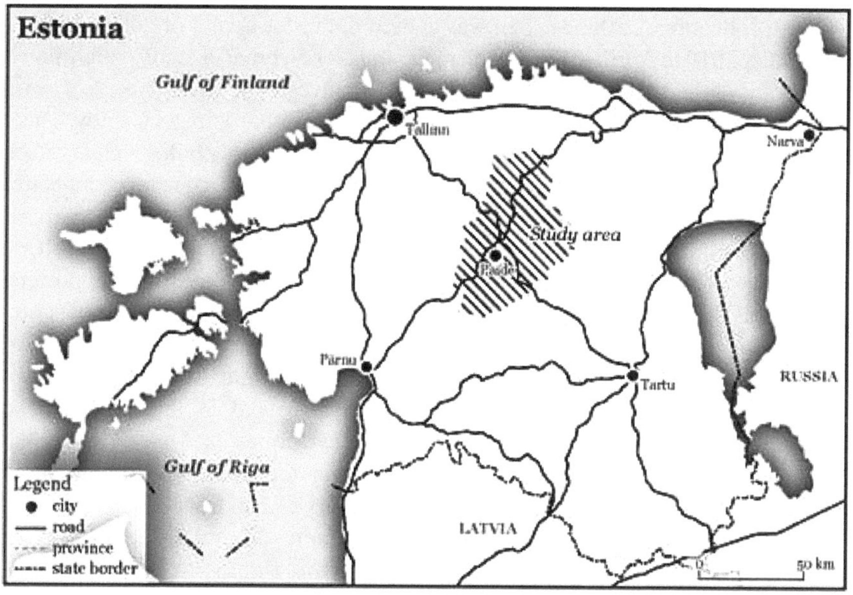

Figure 20.1 The study area

local people, followed by employment in the food processing and forestry sectors. In 2008, approximately 1000 people lived in Järva-Jaani town (Järva-Jaani municipality development plan 2008).

Similar to other peripheral rural areas in Estonia, during the past decades the population of Järva-Jaani municipality has been steadily decreasing (Statistics Estonia 2012). In the past two decades (1989–2009), the decrease was greater than 30 per cent (Järva-Jaani municipality development plan 2008). The rural periphery in Estonia in general is characterised by decline – decline in employment opportunities, services, infrastructure as well as population (Estonian Human Asset Report 2010). The national migration trend in Estonia is out-migration from the rural periphery and small towns to regional urban centres, particularly into two big cities – Tallinn and Tartu, and their hinterlands (Statistics Estonia 2009, Estonian Human Asset Report 2010). Young (and ambitious) people are among the most active movers from rural areas to bigger towns and cities (Statistics Estonia 2009). In 2007, for instance, nearly 40 per cent of youth in Estonia changed residence and it was the rural periphery of counties that lost the largest number of young people (Statistics Estonia 2009, Jõeveer 2003). Among the young people, women are more active movers from rural to urban areas than men (Estonian Human Asset Report 2010, Statistics Estonia 2012). As a result, a male–female imbalance among youth in rural areas exists and young rural men face a so-called 'bride problem' (Estonian Human Asset Report 2010).

Data collection for this chapter was carried out in the spring of 2009 and from September 2010 to April 2011. This chapter is a part of a broader study which aimed to map the key places and practices of youth and investigate young people's sense of belonging and well-being in rural Estonia. It was a participatory study where a mix of visual and (inter)active research methods (video, photography, walks, mental mapping, peer-led and researcher-led interviews, peer-led questionnaire) were used (Trell and van Hoven 2010). We focused on young people in their last three years of high school. Potential participants were contacted via teachers, the activity councillor of Järva-Jaani high school, as well as information posters. During the first meeting with the potential participants, the aims, activities and research methods of the project were introduced by the researcher. Informed consent was sought and information about confidentiality and use of the data given.

Eight boys between 15–18 years old were involved in this project. The researcher and the participants met on average two times each week, mostly at Järva-Jaani high school, but occasionally at other locations, such as the town square, culture-house or the hamburger kiosk in Järva-Jaani town. Data collection occurred in the Estonian language (therefore all quotes from the research used in this chapter are translated).

Places of friendship for youths in Järva-Jaani

In order to explore the ways in which friendship-groups influence masculinity, and the ways in which masculinities are performed in different spaces, we focus on two key shared places of the young men in our study (outside school and familial homes). Those key shared places are the boat trips organised by the boys with their friendship-group, and the dance classes and performances at the House of Culture (a centre for social and cultural activities, inherited from Soviet times; for a more detailed description see Habeck 2007). The experiences and activities in these places together with friends were considered highlights in the boys' current lives. We focus on these key shared spaces because it was in the context of these places that the different roles that friendship can play in influencing performances of masculinity appeared most readily. In addition, examining the characteristics of these places enables us to better outline the affordances that different places provide for young people for interaction, as well as the role of place in identity performance.

'The trip is a serious business actually'[2]*: men's friendship in the outdoors*

The bi-annual boat trips on different rivers of Estonia emerged as one of the highlight-activities for the boys in our research. A selected group of people, usually eight to ten boys, is invited to participate by senior boys (on a few occasions

2 Urmo (18).

the girlfriends of the older boys were involved as well). Six of the eight boys in our research group have participated or organised the boat trips on one or more occasions. The trip, which takes place in spring and/or autumn during high water, lasts for two to three days and consists of travelling along a river on a rubber boat, camping outside, making food on a fire and building shelter (see Figure 20.2).

Figure 20.2 Boys on a boat trip

The trips are strictly limited to the group that is involved and invited to join. It does not provide many opportunities for interaction with other people, except for some unexpected meetings with, for example, the military organising their exercise in the forest, and a few local farmers or nature observers. In order to join the trip, one has to be known to be physically fit and handy. As Tõnis (16) explains:

> I think you have to choose the people who will join you on such a trip really carefully. That they would know that they are doing and would not be some clumsy losers. If you take a clumsy airhead … they may be your friends and all but you'll still get in trouble.

Being on the river means, for the boys, space that they have created for themselves to spend time with their friends. It implies the absence of adult surveillance and the freedom to make own decisions and act accordingly. However, the absence of adults as authority figures does not mean that everybody can do as they wish. Instead, a hierarchy based on seniority and experience is established within the group. Appropriate behaviour and solidarity in, for example, building up a camp and contributing to making food and fire was important. Friends controlled and enforced these rules. It seemed to be important for everybody to know their place, role, rights and duties. One of the organisers of the trip explains:

> If I, for example, take my cousin Tiit with me and I have been on the trip for four times and it's his first and if I then say, 'go to the forest to get some firewood',

> he goes to the forest and does not start arguing with me. You have to know your place. (Urmo, 18)

The appropriate behaviour for the boys on the boat trips was closely connected to the resources, opportunities and restrictions imposed by the physical environment. The unknown natural environment appeared to be an important 'actor' in the boat trip experience. It provided the possibility for unexpected, even dangerous moments to occur. Such moments, which the boys labelled 'adrenaline moments' or moments of 'humour', gave them the possibility to demonstrate their abilities of being in charge, to show their toughness and courage, and by doing so, to distinguish themselves as men (Woodward 2000). In the research by Woodward (2000) on military masculinities, the physical characteristics of the rural landscape, i.e. ruggedness and harshness, are central elements for the military for 'making' the so called warrior-hero solider. The rough rural landscape is 'the setting for the provision of circumstances in which emotions – excitement, fear, and a sense of challenge – can be stimulated and then overcome by acquiring the necessary mental attributes' (Woodward 2000: 650). Urmo (18) describes one of the adrenaline moments on the river:

> There was this incident once with a bridge. The current was so strong it pulled the first boat under but the bridge appeared to be too low, so the boat could fit under but the people on the boat could not. On the first boat there was a boy and a girl and they tried to hold on to the bridge and the boat, to prevent the boat from drifting under. But the current was too strong. And then, there they were, hanging on to the bridge, in the icy water. And then I came around the curve with my boat, I was the closest, and oh I was proud. My partner in the boat had not even seized the situation when I was already in the water, ready to pull my own boat ashore. The girl in the water was yelling, I jumped in and dragged the girl out of the water. The boy was able to climb out by himself. The girl wanted to go home at once, it was obvious she was in shock so we called their parents to find us and pick them up.

Urmo (18) prided himself on being in control of the situation and reacting to the challenge in a fast and courageous manner, showing his ability to defy an extreme condition (the icy water). Importantly, Urmo's friends had witnessed him taking action, and that provided him a central and honourable role and affirmed some aspects of his masculine identity, such as strength and fearlessness. His reaction and being in control also put him in the central position in the stories that were told about the incident to other friends (and to the researcher) for many months after. Some authors have associated ideas of control over the environment with hegemonic masculinity in general and rural masculinity in particular (Little 2002, Saugeres 2002). As the quote above indicates, in a similar vein, in the context of the boat trips, being in control, alert, and not afraid to endure uncomfortable and tough situations was considered appropriate behaviour for a man. The natural landscape enabled the boys of our research to demonstrate such qualities. In addition, despite their absence from most of the boat trips, the quote above indicates that girls play a key role in the construction of men as brave adventurers. Whitehead (2002: 119) indeed argues that the women are crucial for enabling men to exercise their 'heroic male project'.

In the context of the boat trips in general, the boys made a distinction between feminine and masculine based on the ability to put up with the 'rough' conditions (Woodward 2000). Explaining the reasons for the girls not being involved in the boat trips, Urmo (18) says:

> Well, boys are able to take things better, how do I put it, they don't give a damn, they don't care if the fire is low and the food sucks and … the ground is also hard you see but it is less important for us. For girls, you have to make everything comfortable.

In sum, the boat trips show that friendships can enable young people to expand their mobilities and experience different spatialities. The feature that made the boat trips attractive for young people was the ability to be together with a group of friends without adult control and surveillance, in a context where exciting and unexpected things could happen. As the above indicates, being on the river does not mean the absence of any rules, rather, control is important and it is the friendship-group that is in charge of the rules. Inter-group relations and hierarchy are established, and appropriate practices for men determined within the peer-group. In the context of the boat trips, masculinity is constructed in relation to the natural environment and the opportunities it affords for the boys for action and interaction. The natural environment enables the boys to show certain practical skills as well as the ability and willingness to endure rough conditions. Those characteristics set them apart as real men, strong, tough, skilful and in control, in contrast to the girls and the city-boys. Valentine (1996) argues that visibility to friends and peers is an important aspect for young people for establishing themselves and affirming their identity (see van Hoven and Sibley (2008) for a discussion on the significance of seeing and being seen in interpersonal relations and the relations between vision and power). In the case of the boat trips, indeed, an important aspect for the young men for performing different aspects of masculinity was the possibility to demonstrate it to their friends. By providing exciting and somewhat dangerous situations as described above, together with the possibility to be visible to their friends, the boat trips enabled the boys to demonstrate very specific, 'tough' aspects of their masculinity.

'I have always been dancing, as long as I can remember[3]': exploring different opportunities together with friends.

The House of Culture was considered by the respondents as one of the central places in young people's lives because friendships developed there during dance practice. In Järva-Jaani, dancing is a key social activity which crosses age and gender groups. Local people consider dancing a 'trademark' of Järva-Jaani (interview Silva Kärner, see also Trell, van Hoven and Huigen 2012), and the town is renowned for its dancing since the dance groups have attained success at competitions at the national level. Six of the eight boys in our research group were either actively participating in dancing or had previously been members of dancing groups, and named dancing at the local House of Culture as a key activity in their lives (see Figure 20.3) (Trell, van Hoven and Huigen 2012, Habeck 2007). The House of Culture provides a different context for social activities compared to the boat trips. It is a place where most activities are provided for young people by adults who also supervise the activities. For young people then, the House of Culture represents a somewhat controlled environment in which dancers spend many hours practising together. Interestingly, in this context, boys experience masculinities as quite flexible performances.

Figure 20.3 Boys at their dancing performance
Source: Egon Tintse

3 Kalle (16).

The members of the dance group experience a strong sense of belonging in the context of their dancing-group-friends and use the terms 'home' and 'family' in their descriptions. Eneli (female, 18) adds: 'We have a great group, we've become a family.' 'We dance for the sake of it but also because we want to belong somewhere', another member of a dancing group explains (Mõttus 2009). For the young men in our study, this sense of belonging attained as a result of their participation in dancing, was the main reason to continue dancing throughout in their teenage years. Madis (19) explains: 'I have stayed in the dancing group because it's impossible to leave such a good company'.

Dancing and its role in the boys' life illustrate the importance of friends and peers in influencing what is cool and acceptable. Showdance is not something that could in general be considered a typical or popular activity for either rural or urban men in Europe (Risner 2007). As Risner (2007: 140) argues, 'European cultural paradigm situates dance as primarily a 'female' art form' (see also Hasbrook 1993). For adolescent boys, in particular, dancing is often associated with homosexuality (Pascoe 2005). Considering the dominant notions of masculinity and 'pervasive homophobia', for teenage boys, being engaged in dancing can result in bullying, neglect and harassment (Risner 2007: 143, see also Kimmel 2001). Therefore, in general, boys are not likely to engage in dancing or consider it an appropriate activity for real men (Risner 2007).

Indeed, in our research, too, boys picked up on such stereotyping. The following exchange between the boys from an in-class discussion illustrates that making fun of each other for characteristics that they associated with homosexuality (e.g. wearing a purple sweater or watching certain movies) was not unusual for the boys in this research:

> **Neeme** (16): I watched you perform last week, haha, you totally messed up your move.
>
> **Olav** (16): A question here is, why did you watch ME dance? Are you into guys?? *(The whole group laughs)*

However, during the research project, none of the boys or other young people at the local school expressed in any way that it could be unusual for heterosexual boys to perform showdance. Instead, in the context of Järva-Jaani, boys' dancing was seen as compliant with local performances of masculinity, and also as an activity that carried with it a certain prestige, which was not the case for the more stereotypically masculine sport of football in town. The tradition of dancing in Järva-Jaani places the boy-dancers within a local tradition of masculinity. Because 'everybody is doing it' (Oliver, 18), the boys are neither singled out nor harassed for being dancers. Instead, the accomplishments of the dancers are used to promote the local high school in the primary schools all over the municipality, and some young men have transferred to the local school because of the dancing-opportunity. Boys' engagement in and preference for dancing groups illustrates that there is flexibility in the construction of masculinity and that the friendship group, as point of reference, plays an important role in achieving this. Male friends perform dance together, compete together and experience the positive response from the community together. Dancing has become a part of their narratives of what it is to be 'good rural men'.

In sum, in the context of dancing, what is masculine seems to be constructed in relation to adult role-models encountered at the House of Culture, friends and local traditions. At the House of Culture, the presence of adults was considered important and desirable by the young people, as adults facilitated the young people's activities and the accomplishment of success. The boys spoke of their (adult) dance teacher with much respect. At the House of Culture and within the local community, dancing is in-place and appropriate for men. Through dancing, some flexibility in terms of expanding the selection of activities appropriate for men was created, although traditional masculine characteristics such as competitiveness and success were important for making that flexibility possible.

Conclusion

In this chapter, we discussed two key shared places of friendship for young men in rural Estonia: boat trips and dancing in the House of Culture. Young rural men in our study actively performed different dimensions of masculinities in relation to available physical resources and social groups in both locations. The ability to perform some identities rather than others was influenced by the 'power-geometries' and societal regulations of different places (Valentine 2007). Our data illustrate that, depending on the physical setting, but also opportunities stemming from, for example, the presence or absence of adults or girls, different practices and opportunities for different expressions of masculinities arise and are actively constructed by young men. The key shared spaces discussed above illustrate some specific opportunities and restrictions afforded by the rural physical environment, as well as the social context, for the boys' negotiation of masculinities. They also illustrate the demands of boys for excitement, achievement and acknowledgement. Our respondents were actively using the local resources at their disposal to feel capable, accomplished, popular, and in control. In that sense, the exemplary places and activities reflect some traditional dominant characteristics of masculinity: masculinity as representing power, competitiveness, adventure and strength.

The presence of friends and activities engaged in with friends appeared influential in setting the boundaries of what is considered masculine in different contexts. Activities with friends provided a frame of reference for positioning oneself as a young, rural man and for assessing the boundaries of what can be considered masculine. In interaction with friends, ideas about masculinity were constantly (re)produced, formed and negotiated (Connell 1990).

Earlier studies suggested that, in the case of small rural communities in particular, it might be difficult for young people to explore alternative identities

(Glendinning et al. 2003, Nairn, Panelli and McCormack 2003). Young people are very visible in their small rural communities, and as Valentine (2000: 265) points out, the fear of being socially excluded or marginalised 'limits the choices individuals are prepared to make'. This would suggest that young men are most likely to reproduce stereotypical rural masculinities (e.g. Bye 2009, Stenbacka 2011). Indeed, our research shows that boys value some of the features associated with hegemonic masculinity. In their boat trips, the boys' interaction with friends appeared to involve a set of rules and a hierarchy, and in order to belong one had to adhere to certain 'entry criteria', for example, be physically tough or skillful in order to join the trip.

However, our research also demonstrates that, in the rural town studied, there are locations that offer boys a space to nurture friendships which allow for the exploration of 'alternative' versions of masculinity (see also England and Dyck 2014: this volume, Brown et al. 2014: this volume). Such versions involve activities such as dancing and might open up possibilities for young people to explore alternative ways of being (a man) (Pugh and Hart 2007).

We wish to note that, our findings illustrate that it is fruitful to focus on the everyday level, because a more varied picture of what it is like to be(come) a rural man can be revealed. In the context of rural decline, and the scarcity of places of socialising, we found that friendship groups encouraged young people to demonstrate organisational and planning skills in order to create positive spaces for themselves. In contrast to the larger-scale studies where rural places are often considered homogenous spaces with relatively passive populations (Kay, Shubin and Thelen 2012), our focus on the everyday level shows that rural realities are diverse, and rural young people are active agents in the construction of their identities.

References

Blazek, M. 2011. Place, children's friendships, and the formation of gender identities in a Slovak urban neighbourhood. *Children's Geographies*, 9(3–4), 285–302.

Bowlby, J. 1969. *Attachment and Loss*, Vol. 1: Attachment. New York: Basic Books.

Bunnell, T., Yea, S., Peake, L., Skelton, T. and Smith, M. 2012. Geographies of friendships. *Progress in Human Geography*, 36(4), 490–507.

Butler, J. 1990. *Gender Trouble: Feminism and the Subversion of Identity*. London: Routledge.

Bye, L.M. 2009. 'How to be a rural man': young men's performances and negotiations of rural masculinities. *Journal of Rural Studies*, 25(3), 278–288.

Clark, C., Uzzell, D.L. 2002. The socio-environmental affordances of adolescents' environments, in *Children and Their Environments Learning, Using and Designing Spaces*, edited by C. Spencer and M. Blades. Cambridge: Cambridge University Press, 176–197.

Connell, R.W. 1990. An iron man: the body and some contradictions of hegemonic masculinity, in *Sport, Men and the Gender Order: Critical Feminist Perspectives*, edited by M.A. Messner and D.F. Sabo. Champaign: Human Kinetics.

Connell, R.W. 2000. *The Men and the Boys*. Cambridge: Polity Press.

Connolly, P. 1998. *Racism, Gender Identities and Young Children: Social Relations in a Multi-Ethnic, Inner-City Primary School*. London: Routledge.

Dunn, J. 2004. *Children's Friendships: The Beginnings of Intimacy*. Oxford: Wiley-Blackwell.

Dyson, J. 2010. Friendship in practice: girls' work in the Indian Himalayas. *American Ethnologist*, 37(3), 482–498.

Erikson, E.H. 1968. *Identity: Youth and Crisis*. New York: Norton.

Erwin, P. 1998. *Friendship in Childhood and Adolescence*. London: Routledge.

Estonian Human Asset Report, 2010. Tallinn, Estonian Cooperation Assembly and Committee for Sustainable Development.

Evans, R. and Holt, L. 2011. Diverse spaces of childhood and youth: gender and other socio-cultural differences. *Children's Geographies*, 9(3–4), 277–284.

Gibson, J.J. 1979. *The Ecological Approach to Visual Perception*. Michigan: Houghton Mifflin.

Gilbert, R. and Gilbert, P. 1998. *Masculinity Goes to School*. London: Routledge.

Glendinning, A., Nuttall, M., Hendry, L., Kloep, M. and Wood, S. 2003. Rural communities and well-being: a good place to grow up? *The Sociological Review*, 51(1), 129–156.

Goodwin, M. 2008. The embodiment of friendship, power and marginalization in a multi-ethnic, multi-class preadolescent U.S. girls' peer group. *Girlhood Studies*, 1(2), 72–94.

Gorman-Murray, A. (2013) Straight-gay friendships: relational masculinities and equalities landscapes in Sydney, Australia. *Geoforum*, 49, 214–223.

Habeck, J.O. 2007. Enacting 'culture' and 'culturedness': why people may or may not want to spend their free time in the house of culture. *Kultura: Russian Cultural Review*, 1, 14–18.

Hasbrook, C. 1993. Sociocultural aspects of physical activity. *Research Quarterly for Exercise and Sport*, 64, 106–115.

Hay, R. 1998. Sense of place in developmental context. *Journal of Environmental Psychology*, 18(1), 5–29.

Hesp, G. and Brooks, J. 2009. Heterosexism and homophobia on fraternity row: a case study of a college fraternity community. *Journal of LGBT Youth*, 6(4), 395–415.

Hooghe, M. 2011. The impact of gendered friendship patterns on the prevalence of homophobia among Belgian Late adolescents. *Archives of Sexual Behavior*, 40(3), 543–550.

Hopkins, P. and Pain, R. 2007. Geographies of age: thinking relationally. *Area*, 39(3), 287–294.

van Hoven, B. 2011. 'We were just testing what kind of man you are'– negotiating masculinities in a New Mexico prison [Online: *Spatial Justice*. Special Issue: Gender, sexual identities and Spatial Justice] Available at: http://www.jssj.org/media/dossier_focus_vo5.pdf [accessed: 16 January 2013].

van Hoven, B. and Hörschelmann, K. (eds) 2005. *Spaces of Masculinities*. London and New York: Routledge.

van Hoven, B. and Sibley, D. 2008. 'Just duck': the role of vision in the production of prison spaces. *Environment and Planning D: Society and Space*, 26(6), 1001–1017.

Jõeveer, J. 2003. Siserände vanuserisused [Internal migration by age], in *Ränne üleminekuaja Eestis [Migration in Estonia during the Transition Period]*, edited by T. Tammaru and H. Kulu. Tallinn: Statistics Estonia.

Järva-Jaani Municipality. 2008. *Development Plan for 2009–2015* [Online] Available at: http://www.riigiteataja.ee/ert/act.jsp?id¼13090293 [Accessed: 16 November 2010].

Kay, R., Shubin, S. and Thelen, T. 2012. Rural realities in the post-socialist space. *Journal of Rural Studies*, 28(2), 55–62.

Kehily, M.J. and Nayak, A. 1996. The Christmas kiss: sexuality, story-telling and schooling. *Curriculum Studies*, 4(2), 211–227.

Kenway, J. and L. Fitzclarence. 1997. Masculinity, violence and schooling: challenging poisonous pedagogies. *Gender and Education*, 9(1), 117–133.

Kimmel, M. 2001. Masculinity as homophobia: fear, shame, and silence in the construction of gender identity, in *The Masculinities Reader*, edited by S. Whitehead and F. Barrett. Cambridge: Polity Press, 266–287.

Krevs, M. 2008. Sense of place and quality of life in post-socialist societies, in *Sense of Place, Health and Quality of Life*, edited by J. Eyles and A. Williams. Aldershot: Ashgate, 135–152.

Lesko, N. 2000. *Masculinities at School*. London: Sage Publications.

Little, J. 2002. Rural geography: rural gender identity and the performance of masculinity and femininity in the countryside. *Progress in Human Geography*, 26(5), 665–670.

Little, J. and Panelli, R. 2007. 'Outback' romance? A reading of nature and heterosexuality in rural Australia. *Sociologia Ruralis*, 47(), 173–188.

Lysaght, K. 2002. Dangerous friends and deadly foes – performances of masculinity in the divided city. *Irish Geography*, 35(1), 51–62.

Mac an Ghaill, M. 1994. *The Making of Men: Masculinities, Sexualities and Schooling*. Buckingham: Open University Press.

Mills, M. 2001. *Challenging Violence in Schools: An Issue of Masculinities*. Buckingham: Open University Press.

Morris-Roberts, K. 2004. Girls' friendships, 'distinctive individuality' and socio-spatial practices of (dis)identification. *Children's Geographies*, 2(2), 237–255.

Mõttus, A. 2009. Ülle Vaas ja tema tantsukogukond. Journal for Teachers [Online: Journal for Teachers] Available at: http://www.opleht.ee/?archive_mode=article&articleid=1801&print=1 [accessed: 1 November 2010].

Nairn, K., Panelli, R. and McCormack, J. 2003. Destabilizing dualisms. young people's experiences of rural and urban environment. *Childhood*, 10(1), 9–42.
Nayak, A. and Kehily, M.J. 1996. Playing it straight: masculinities, homophobias and schooling. *Journal of Gender Studies*, 5(2), 211–230.
Pascoe, C.J. 2005. 'Dude, you're a fag': adolescent masculinity and the fag discourse. *Sexualities*, 8(3), 329–346.
Pattman, R., Frosh, S. and Phoenix, A. 2005. Constructing and experiencing boyhoods in research in London. *Gender and Education*, 17(5), 555–561.
Pollard, A. 1985. *The Social World of the Primary School*. London: Cassell.
Pugh, M.J.V. and Hart, D. 2007. Identity development and peer group participation. *New Directions for Child and Adolescent Development*, (84), 55–70.
Regional Portrait of Estonia: Järvamaa. 2010. *Regional Portrait of Estonia: Järvamaa* [Online: Statistics Estonia] Available at: http://www.stat.ee/ppe-jarva-maakond [accessed: 1 November 2010].
Renold, E. 2006. 'They won't let us play unless you're going out with one of them': girls, boys and Butler's 'hetero-sexual matrix' in the primary years. *British Journal of Sociology of Education*, 27(4), 489–509.
Risner, D. 2007. Rehearsing masculinity: challenging the 'boy code' in dance education. *Research in Dance Education*, 8(2), 139–153.
Saugeres, L. 2002. Of tractors and men: masculinity, technology and power in a French farming community. *Sociologia Ruralis*, 42(2), 143–159.
Schneider, B.H. 2000. *Friends and Enemies: Peer Relations in Childhood*. London: Arnold.
Statistics Estonia. 2009. *Migration [Ränne]*. Tallinn: Statistics Estonia.
Statistics Estonia. 2012. *Statistics Estonia* [Online] Available at: www.stat.ee [Accessed: 11 June, 2012].
Stenbacka, S. 2011. Othering the rural: about the construction of rural masculinities and the unspoken urban hegemonic ideal in Swedish media. *Journal of Rural Studies*, 27(3), 235–244.
Stenning, A. and Hörschelmann, K. 2008. History, geography and difference in the post-socialist world: or, do we still need post-socialism? *Antipode*, 40(2), 312–335.
Swain, J. 2006. Reflections on patterns of masculinity in school settings. *Men and Masculinities*, 8(3), 331–349.
Taimalu, M., Lahikainen, A.R., Korhonen, P. and Kraav, I. 2007. Self-reported fears as indocators of young children's well-being in societal change: a cross-cultural perspective. *Social Indicators Research*, 80(1), 51–78.
Tallinn, 2010. *Estonian Human Asset Report*. Tallinn, Estonian Cooperation Assembly & Committee for Sustainable Development.
Trell, E. and van Hoven, B. 2010. Making sense of place: exploring creative and (inter)active research methods with young people. *Fennia*, 188(1), 91–104.
Trell, E. and van Hoven, B. 2012. Place attachment in rural areas: a participatory research project with youth in Cedar, British Columbia, in *Re-Exploring*

Canadian Space/Redécouvrir l'espace Canadien, Issue 14 of Cahiers: Canada, edited by J. den Toonder and B. van Hoven. Eelde: Barkhuis Publishing, 27–44.

Trell, E., van Hoven, B. and Huigen, P. 2012. 'It's good to live in Järva-Jaani but we can't stay here': youth and belonging in rural Estonia. *Journal of Rural Studies*, 28(2), 139–148.

Valentine, G. 1996. Children should be seen and not heard? The role of children in public space. *Urban Geography*, 17(3), 205–220.

Valentine, G. 2000. Exploring children's and young people's narratives of identity. *Geoforum*, 31(2), 257–267.

Valentine, G. 2007. Theorizing and researching intersectionality: a challenge for feminist geography. *The Professional Geographer*, 59(1), 10–21.

Walker, C. 2010. Space, kinship networks and youth transition in provincial Russia: negotiating urban–rural and inter-regional migration. *Europe-Asia Studies*, 62(4), 647–669.

Whitehead, S.M. 1998. *Men and Masculinities: Key Themes and New Directions*. Cambridge: Sage Publications.

Woods, P. 1990. *The Happiest Days?* London: Falmer.

Woodward, R. 2000. Warrior heroes and little green men: soldiers, military training, and the construction of rural masculinities. *Rural Sociology*, 65(4), 640–657.

PART 7
Masculinities, Health and Wellbeing

Chapter 21
'Being a Man' in Treatment: Health, Masculinity and the Drama of Independence

Robert Wilton and Joshua Evans

Introduction

Over the past two decades, a vibrant social science scholarship has developed on men's health and masculinity. This work draws inspiration from a number of sources, including the diverse strands of feminist scholarship and the broader field of critical men's studies (see Sabo and Gordon 1995, Courtenay and Keeling 2000, Connell 2000, Sabo 2005, Courtenay 2009, O'Brien, Hunt and Hart. 2009, Evans et al. 2011). Despite the growth of this scholarship in other social science disciplines, health geographers have been largely silent on the question of masculinity and its significance for men's health and well-being (see also Lewis 2014: this volume). As Thien and Del Casino (2012: 2) have argued recently, the sub-discipline has: 'yet to interrogate men's overall (un)healthiness, their health behaviours, experiences, and outcomes, including how socio-spatial practices of hegemonic masculinities affect men's health, men's spatial and affective relationships with and in support systems for health, and the contexts within which men's health takes place'. In this chapter, we explore the utility of a geographic imagination for the topic of men's health (see also Keppel 2014: this volume), using a case study of men's drug and alcohol treatment. Our specific focus is on how treatment settings are staged and what implications such places hold for the enactment of masculinity.

The chapter is organised into three main sections. First, we review recent developments in the field of men's health, with particular attention to men's consumption of drugs and alcohol. Work here has pointed to the contradictory impacts of alcohol and drug use, both allowing for an enactment of a locally valued gender identity while at the same time potentially undermining the health of individual men. A key question concerns how, and to what extent, men might be encouraged to adopt healthier drug/alcohol practices, and the implications of any change for masculinity. We argue that a sensitivity to place, and its role in shaping, constraining and mediating gender identities/relations is critical to an understanding of the challenges of, and possibilities for, health-related change. We then illustrate this point using a case study of men's experiences in a drug treatment program. Qualitative data drawn from observation and interviews with staff and clients are used to examine the connections between masculinity and alcohol/drug use, and the challenges involved in reworking men's daily practices in the interests of better health.

Men's health

Since the early 1990s, there has been a rapid growth in the literature on men's health. This work has been characterised in part by quantitative studies concerned with differences in mortality and morbidity between women and men, and among men, but it has also drawn upon theories of gender to explore the social construction of masculinity in relation to health (see Courtenay and Keeling 2000, Connell 2000, Sabo 2005, Courtenay 2009, Evans et al. 2011). A review of the breadth and depth of the men's health literature is beyond the scope of this chapter, but several insights are directly relevant.

First, many studies have drawn on Connell's (1995, 2000) concept of 'hegemonic masculinity' to explore the ways in which *practices* associated with culturally valued gender identities impact men's health. As Connell (2000: 178) argues, this approach allows for an understanding of health effects not as 'mechanical consequences of either the physiological or the social condition of being a man [but as] the product of human practice, of things done, in relation to the gender order'. Moreover, as Courtenay (2009) has recently argued, health beliefs and behaviours need to be understood as one part of the broader range of social and cultural practices used to construct gender. In this sense, we can think about both gender and health as being actively made in the context of men and women's daily lives. Connell (2000) uses the example of why young men drink and drive. For him, young men who drink and drive are not driven by uncontrollable hormones or an uncontrollable male role; rather the act of dangerous driving can be understood as a resource for constructing masculinity. In this sense, 'the active construction of masculinity is key to the risk-taking behaviour, and to strategies of prevention' (Connell 2000: 192).

Second, a key finding of recent work on men's health is that many practices linked to, and constitutive of, valued forms of masculinity can be harmful to men's health. For example, the association of hegemonic (and other forms of) masculinity with risk-taking manifests in many activities including sports, driving, smoking, alcohol and drug consumption, diet, and violence, all of which result in higher rates of morbidity and mortality for men (Courtenay 2000, Sabo 2005, Schrock and Schwalbe 2009). At the same time, rates of mortality and morbidity differ signficantly *among* men, reflecting varying opportunities and resources, and the locally valued masculinites to which different men aspire (de Visser and Smith 2007).

Recognising the health effects of 'doing' masculinity is important for several reasons, not least that it sheds light on the way in which masculinity as gender identity is an embodied accomplishment. The body serves as an 'arena for the making of gender patterns' (Connell 2000: 12) within particular historically and geographically contingent settings. Bodies can be used as resources in the pursuit of a valued masculinity (Schrock and Schwalbe 2009), although some male bodies may be limited in their capacity to act in ways deemed normatively masculine (e.g. Longhurst 2005). At the same time, practices associated with hegemonic masculinity can produce negative health effects, thereby undermining the capacity of the body to 'pull off' or sustain a particular performance.

The consumption of alcohol and drugs represents one area of practice in which these complex relations between masculinity, the body and health play out (Harnett et al. 2000, Capraro 2007 de Visser and Smith 2007). As Willott and Lyons (2012: 331) argue, the 'excessive and public consumption of alcohol with other men' has long been a practice associated with masculinity in Western cultures (also De Visser, Smith and McDonnell 2009). Drinking is gendered with respect to the places in which it occurs (public houses and other sites), the types of beverage, and the volume of alcohol consumed. The way in which alcohol is consumed is also critical to masculinity. Campbell (2000: 571) points to how the successful performance of drinking as a form of 'pub(lic) masculinity' requires the disciplining of the body to display control over alcohol; what he labels 'drinking fitness'.

Yet drinking and drug use also embody what Capraro (2007) identifies as a central paradox of masculinity in that while men as a group dominate women in a patriarchal society, individual men may not feel powerful. In this sense, heavy drinking and drug use may be part of an attempt to conform to valued norms of masculinity but also motivated by a perceived individual inadequacy. As Capraro (2007: 194) suggests: 'On the one hand, heavy drinking may result from men attempting to conform to traditional norms of masculinity … on the other, men drink because of a perceived inadequacy as individual men … The distinction between these two motives may not exist in practice.' Capraro's argument connects to Connell's (2000) broader point about the contradictory nature of masculinities. It also connects to the multiple differences that exist among men, and the varied resources available to these men in the pursuit of a valued gender identity (de Visser, Smith and McDonnell 2009). Work by Willott and Lyons (2012) on drinking found that middle-class men in professional careers were able to exercise more choice – drinking less and expressing preferences for wine rather than beer – when compared with other men; the social class and financial status of these men provide other immediate evidence of their masculinity. By contrast, for younger, working-class men in post-industrial settings the ability to 'master' the heavy consumption of drugs and alcohol may represent one of a limited number of pathways to 'local' respect (Connell 1995, Nayak 2006). Similarly, de Visser and Smith (2007) argue that although men are often 'acutely aware' of the equation of alcohol consumption and hegemonic masculinity, there are other masculinities linked to abstinence or more moderate alcohol consumption. Some of these may be complicit with hegemonic masculinity (e.g., using competence in other domains such as sport to excuse little or no alcohol consumption). Others may be more resistant to the hegemonic norm (directly rejecting alcohol).

There is good evidence, then, that the consumption of drugs and alcohol can be understood as a way of doing gender/masculinity, and that this consumption can be associated with a variety of negative health effects (e.g., de Visser and Smith 2007, O'Brien, Hunt and Hart 2009). Despite the interest in masculinity and drug/alcohol consumption, there has been significantly less work completed on the ways in which men might be encouraged to re-think unhealthy drug/alcohol practices (O'Brien, Hunt and Hart 2009), and what this might mean for performances of masculinity. As these authors note, further research can usefully provide:

> … a more detailed examination of the social circumstances and characteristics of those men who appear able to embrace the idea that a concern with men's health is 'manly' [and] the inequalities between men that currently mean that only some are free to embrace 'new' ways of articulating their masculinity which bring health benefits. (O'Brien, Hunt and Hart 2009: 377)

It is important, therefore, to think about how gender identity, gender relations, and gender performances are implicated in health-related change.

Placing men's health

In this chapter, we ask how the complex relationship between masculinity and health is mediated by place. Following Thien and Del Casino (2012), we suggest that sensitivity to the role of place in shaping, constraining and mediating gender identities is critical to an understanding of the challenges of, and possibilities for, health-related change. While there has been some recognition of the importance of geography in the broader literature on masculinity (e.g., Connell and Messerschmidt 2005), the specific role of 'place' in shaping and constraining the performance of masculinity remains under-developed (Atherton 2009). We conceptualise the role of place using Hopkins and Noble's (2009: 814) notion of masculinities as *strategic performances* that 'emerge within local networks and respond to and shape social circumstances, mediating and negotiating relations with others'. The emphasis on strategy and performance permits us to think about how the varying capacities of different men (in terms of bodily capacities, material resources, etc.) intersect with the distinctive characteristics of particular places to define the range of possible masculine performances at a given point in time. At the same time, we employ a dramaturgical metaphor to suggest that these gendered performances can be thought of, in this particular instance, as 'staged'. In the analysis that follows we approach drug and alcohol treatment settings as very specific social settings that operate as a 'stage' for the enactment of different masculinities. This is not to suggest that these settings are a passive backdrop; rather, they are infused with a very specific set of rules, expectations, and obligations that invite men to think and act differently.

The case study

Methods: data collection

The data in this chapter are drawn from a larger research project on the geographies of drug/alcohol treatment. In this chapter, we focus on a single program as a case study. This focus allows for an in-depth exploration of the ways in which men in treatment are encouraged to rework masculinity in the interests of leading healthier (drug/alcohol-free) lives. The program in question is a six-week, community-based treatment program for men. Being a community-based program, men did not live at the program site but rather came to the program site every day to participate in therapy. Data collection for the case involved one-week spent in program with a cohort of ten men. All of the men were aware of the researcher's identity and the nature of the study. Much of the observation was spent in intensive group counselling sessions, as well as time spent more informally with men during breaks. Extensive field notes were taken and transcribed. Counselling materials were also collected (e.g., workbooks, session handouts). In addition, interviews were conducted with the program director, the counsellor, and six male clients.

Program clients

The men ranged in age from late twenties to early sixties. With respect to income/class, only one of the ten men had a professional/managerial job. Two others had unionised blue-collar work and had been referred to treatment by employee assistance programs. Two others worked periodically in the construction trade and one was a truck driver. The remaining four were not working and were living at a nearby 'dry' shelter operated by the same service organisation. One of these four was receiving disability benefits, while the other three men were reliant on general social assistance. With respect to race/ethnicity, nine of the ten men were white and one was South Asian. Cocaine and alcohol were the most commonly reported current 'drugs of choice' within the group. Two men said their primary problems were with prescription medications. Two men said they also used crystal meth and heroin in addition to cocaine and/or alcohol.

In the analysis that follows we look first at men's use of alcohol and drugs, and the ways in which past use comes to be experienced in the present as 'excessive' or 'problematic'. We then look at how the treatment program is staged in such a way to position alternative performances of masculinity as both permissible and essential for recovery. Finally, we consider the 'strategic performances' of men in the program as they encounter, engage with, and struggle over these programmatic norms, a struggle we call the 'drama of independence'.

Analysis

Masculinities in crisis

Statements from the men begin to shed some light on the role of drugs and alcohol in their lives. Significantly, they point both to the consumption of alcohol and drugs as part of an enactment of a locally valued masculinity, and the role that these substances play in helping men to cope with problems and disappointments in everyday life. For example, Jeff, who was in his late thirties, talked about being socialised into drug use at school:

> It was a social thing for me first, social acceptance 'cause I'd go out in the smoking pit at high school, right. People smoking cigarettes, okay but there's also people in the corner, and I want to see what the corner group is all about. Stupid thing, oh, I'll have a couple of tokes before I go into class or something, and then I started using, I tried acid, LSD, that's quite a good trip. Don't get me going on that! Somebody cracks open some cocaine at a party, well you're a pot smoker but lets do that. That's the way you think.

While schoolyard drug use is not exclusively the domain of young men, the role that such drug use plays in demonstrating 'maturity, defiance, and authority to their peers' can help to construct a form of 'dominant masculinity' that is valued within a particular social/group context (Kulis, Marsiglia and Hecht 2002: 469). Moreover, as Connell (2000) and others have noted, these practices are not adopted uniformly, but are more likely to be used by poor and marginalised young men as a form of protest. For instance, Bob, in his late fifties, talked about drinking as a way to challenge authority. In this instance, the authority figure was Bob's father, who was himself a heavy drinker and a domineering presence at home:

> Nobody poured the drink in me. I did it. I made a decision to pick up the bottle. I made a decision to show my dad, 'I'm going to fix you!' So I'd go out and drink, started as a kid, which is a dumb thing looking back but that's the way I did it.

Bob's statement highlights the social role of drinking as a means of enacting a particular form of masculinity – 'I'm going to fix you!' – but also reflects Capraro's (2007) contention with respect to the paradoxical relationship between drug use and masculinity. During the interview, Bob talked repeatedly about the difficulties of home life with this father, and the fact that he was profoundly hurt by the experiences of his childhood; in this sense, drinking offered an escape from the problems of his home life. Other men made similar statements about the role of drugs and alcohol as way of coping with problems, failures and feelings of inadequacy. For example: 'I've had some disappointments with personal problems, relationships, attempts at business that didn't work. Every time there was a failure in my life I turned back to using just to drown the sorrow and the feelings' (Mick).

While drugs and alcohol provide a means to establish a locally valued masculinity *and* a way to deal with the disappointments and failures confronting individual men, excessive consumption of these substances over time can also erode the bases of men's embodied identities. In this study, all of the men had come to see their consumption of drugs and/ or alcohol as 'excessive' or 'problematic' principally because of the negative impact this consumption was having on the physical, social and emotional bases of their lives and the lives of those around them. Moreover, in the context of the treatment program, most of the men had come to understand their lives as having reached a 'crisis point' in relation to drug and alcohol use. The impact of drug and alcohol use on men's physical health and appearance was a common topic of discussion in interviews. Doug, for example, talked about his recent use of opiates:

> Two years ago I started using needles. I was using cocaine and stuff before that ... and then I started using opiates with the needles and before I knew it I was injecting cocaine and opiates, together. It was getting quite serious. Like I said, I've been close to death several times. I was just sick of it. It just disgusts me, the way I have become.

Doug's statement also points to the strong emotional impacts of drug use. His expression of disgust with his circumstances is illustrative of a broader crisis narrative and the sense that a workable identity had been compromised. Tom also spoke of a crisis point when his drinking led to the end of his marriage and, subsequently, serious impacts on his health: 'After my separation, maybe three months I went, after [my wife] left, we sold the house, and I drank really hard for three months. Started having seizures when I tried to stop, and I had three seizures, had two while I was driving. So I was hospitalised.' For Tom, the ending of his marriage, coupled with the earlier loss of employment, eroded an existing gender identity. After a stay in hospital, Tom admitted himself to a detox facility and then sought treatment for his drinking. At the time of the interview, he was living at the homeless shelter and was struggling to cope with the disjuncture between his previous sense of self and his current circumstances: 'I was taking clothes down [to the shelter] six months before, to drop them off down there as donations and now I'm staying down there. Oh god, it's hard. It's just, I feel low for being there.'

Approached critically, the language of 'addiction as crisis' can be understood as a mechanism for problematising drinking and drug using (Fairbanks 2009). This is not to deny or downplay the difficult circumstances in which the men find themselves, or the fact that the sense of crisis may be deeply felt by individual men. Indeed, as Gorman-Murray (2011: 214) notes, the internalisation of such a crisis discourse 'provides an opportunity for some men to actively question their lives, roles and identities, and explore alternative formations of "being a man"'. In this study, men's sense that their drinking and/or drug use had become 'unmanageable' was often a primary motivation to seek treatment. The internalisation of crisis discourse was further consolidated through the treatment process, a topic to which we turn next.

Staging old and new masculinities

In this section, we look at how treatment staff try to engage men in a process of critical self-analysis that focuses not just on the use of drugs and alcohol, but is concerned more broadly with the nature of men's identity and daily practice. Place plays a critical role here in that the treatment program is staged in such a way that men are encouraged (and, to some extent, required) to think and act differently. This process of place-making happens simultaneously through the enactment of rules of conduct, the design of physical surroundings, and the orchestration of social relations.

Rules of conduct can provide an important source of external restraint for people struggling with drugs and alcohol. This program, like most we studied, requires abstinence during treatment, and uses random drug-testing and staff surveillance to ensure men's compliance with the requirement. The significance of this rule had become apparent in recent months when staff had proposed eliminating drug testing but clients had opposed the move. The director commented: 'It does make you realise that there is that feeling of "I'm not safe with myself". They want proof, something tangible. Here's a piece of paper that says I have not used.' With respect to the programme's physical surroundings, staff members had considerable input into the design of the treatment centre. The director spoke at length about the type of environment they had tried to create: 'We wanted it to look very professional, to have a professional but comfortable air about it [Interviewer: Is the professional theme important?] It's very important ... They've lost their self-respect and we're trying to provide respect to them, and we feel that a professional environment conveys respect.'

From a gender perspective, the link between professionalism and respect resonates with a particular kind of middle-class masculinity. Several of the clients commented favourably about the program's 'professional' atmosphere:

> The night before I came, I had it in my mind I was coming to a hospital, you know what I mean? So when I came in and it was more of an office, you don't, I guess it's hard to explain but you didn't feel so down. Like, there was a sense of professionalism about this. Like I have a job to do, and you're here to do a job really, you really are. (Sean)

Sean's sense that drug treatment constitutes a form of 'professional' work is significant in that it offers an effective way of constructing this self-care activity as appropriately masculine. There are parallels here with Sloan, Gough and Conner (2010), who found that men engaged in health-promoting practices tend to use other discursive repertoires to construct these practices, avoiding the connotation of vulnerability linked to an explicit discussion of health concerns. For Sloan,

Gough and Conner (2010) sport was a key repertoire. Here, a language of work offers a similar alternative.

There are also parallels with Heath's (2005: 432) work on the Christian men's movement, the Promise Keepers. She argues that the use of sports arenas as venues for PK rallies offered a 'bounded masculine space' in which men could display emotion – crying, hugging, holding hands – without undermining their masculinity. The professional, all-male treatment program might be understood as a similar setting in which expressions of emotion and other alternative practices are permissible.[1] Jeff talked about the importance of the programme being all-male.

> Women have their groups and I think they're great for women, but men also need it. It allows them to express themselves without having any hesitation about (.) I've seen guys cry, not cry, weep about what they're trying to say. Do you think these guys would do that stuff in front of women? Maybe, maybe not, but it allows the man to be able to express his feelings the way he feels without having any qualms about it.

Here the treatment setting, staged as it is, affords men the opportunity to break with hegemonic masculine norms (i.e. real men do not cry) and perform masculinity in a socially valued yet different way (i.e. weeping).

These performances are not limited to outward expressions of emotion. Within this bounded masculine space, men engage in a 'client-centred' program of treatment that draws heavily on a cognitive-behavioural model of lifestyle change aimed at cultivating practices for healthy (clean and sober) living. Over the course of six weeks, men work as a group on topics that include relationships, stress, anger management, relapse prevention, guilt and shame, and exercise and nutrition. A series of techniques are used to collectively engage men in a process of self-reflection, through which they learn to critically examine their thoughts, feelings and actions.

Examples of these techniques include *Seemingly Irrelevant Decisions* (SIDs) and *Relapse Prevention*. SIDs is a technique of self-analysis that requires men to question the mundane choices they make, to consider why they make those choices and how such choices place them at risk for drinking or using. In groups, men recount 'small' choices from their own past, which are then scrutinised by the group members. *Relapse Prevention* focuses on subtle changes in mood, emotional state and practice that might signal an increased risk of drinking or using. Men are asked to consider how a suite of 48 different 'warning signs' might be applied to their own situations. Like SIDs, this technique necessitates critical self-analysis; details of past experiences must be divulged and critiqued by peers, and interventions devised and rehearsed.

---

1 There is, of course, an assumed heterosexuality here, which was common throughout the treatment system.

The drama of independence

In the remainder of the analysis we look at how men's independence is problematised as they engage these and other techniques. Independence can be understood as a key facet of hegemonic masculinity, and one that is constructed relationally in opposition to women as dependents. The privilege accorded independence suggests that 'real' men are self-reliant and autonomous (Gerschick and Miller 1995, Smith et al. 2007). The emphasis on independence can also be linked specifically to concerns about men's health, where an assumed self-reliance can lead men to avoid seeking help for health concerns or to eschew the acquisition of health-related knowledge (Connell 2000, Courtenay 2004, Smith et al. 2007). For many men in treatment, the ability to enact independence had been compromised by past failures to control drinking and using by themselves. Yet they were reluctant to acknowledge this failure explicitly. For program staff, unpacking the ideal of independence is thus a key treatment task. As the director explained: 'They need relationships and most of them don't realise that. Especially the ones who have chronic addictions, they will try to just tough it out, "I don't need anyone, I can do it myself" and that never works, not for very long.'

During observation, discussions of independence and the importance of healthy, supportive relationships were commonplace. The following field note describes part of a session on relapse prevention:

> The assignment in class today was to talk about three critical warning signs [for relapse]. After each guy had identified his signs, Alan [counsellor] picked one and asked them to describe the signs or evidence … Then guys had to list the interventions they'd use. For example, Dave's three critical warning signs of relapse were: 1) compulsive behaviour; 2) worrying about other people rather than yourself; and 3) irregular attendance at meetings … Alan asked Dave about the third warning sign. Dave's solutions were largely focused on needing to catch himself and get himself to a meeting. Alan's response was that he needed to have someone actively intervene; to come over and take him to the meeting. [He said] 'You need someone to kick your ass back into gear'. (Field notes)

Here, the counsellor uses the group discussion of relapse prevention to critique the assumption of self-reliance that underpins Dave's proposed solution. In subsequent discussions, men began to articulate the ways in which relationships with other people were critical to their recovery. They also talked about ways in which the practice of daily life could be transformed by relationships with other people. For example, the following field note offers an example of a practice that challenges norms of independence and autonomy in relation to personal finances:

> Later, we talked more about Seemingly Irrelevant Decisions that may lead to 'high risk' behaviours. Guys talked about things like taking the long way or the wrong way home so as to pass by a dealer or a bar. Then Brian talked about

> taking too much money out from the bank. He thought about this and talked about the problem he has with money. He says that his sister gets his money right now and gives him some every so often (field notes).

As a truck driver in his early forties, Brian's relationship with his sister and his willingness to cede control over his money can be seen as a significant change in his enactment of masculinity, one that he believes is critical to the process of recovery.

Notwithstanding these efforts to unpack independence, our data also point to 'mismatches, tensions and resistances' between the model of healthy masculinity articulated by the program, and individual men's own plans for recovery (Connell and Messerschmidt 2005: 841). Sometimes this 'drama' reflected the difficulties of surrendering independence as a deeply embedded part of men's sense of self. In interviews, several men recognised their need for other people but tended to fall back on the language of an autonomous self: 'One thing I know (.) the only way I know I am going to stay away from drugs is I have to not want to do it. I have to not want to do drugs' (Doug).

In group sessions, there was frequent recognition of the importance of other people as sources of support; this was particularly true of relationships with women (wives, mothers, sisters). Yet there were also repeated efforts by men to discursively position themselves as 'burdened by' their relationships with women. For example:

> Alan asks people to make a list of the emotions they were feeling. This is what they came up with: envy, sadness, jealousy, guilt, shame, anxious. Alan notes these are all negative ones and so adds joy, excitement. Then Ray suggests 'ecstatic'. Guys laugh and he says: 'Trust me, I've never felt it; at least not since I was at the altar!'

This statement sits in clear contradiction to men's admission of their need to ask for help from the women in their lives. Such statements can be seen as 'compensatory manhood acts' – acts designed to signify a valued masculine self despite, and because of, an inability to approximate a hegemonic ideal (Schrock and Schwalbe 2009). As Schrock and Schwalbe note, compensatory acts can have contradictory effects. In the context of the group, they permit the discursive reproduction of a sense of masculine independence. Yet, they carry health-related risks to the extent that they discourage men's admission of their need for support.

Conclusion

This chapter has explored how drug and alcohol treatment programs encourage men in treatment to adopt different relationships towards themselves and others in the name of health, and the implications of these changes for masculinity. Our examination focused attention both on the strategic performances of individual men and the active role of the treatment setting as place in 'staging' the enactment of old and new masculinities. We also highlighted one revealing drama that unfolded – the drama of independence – as men enacted these masculinities over the course of their treatment.

The analysis sheds light on drug and alcohol treatment programs as one paradoxical context where men's 'health takes place' (Thien and Del Casino 2012). First, 'masculinities in crisis' speak to how drug and alcohol use, for some men, is a paradoxical, and ultimately unsustainable, practice. Drug and alcohol use provided men with a means to cope with disappointment (in some cases with central male figures in their lives) and personal failure while simultaneously granting entry to locally valued masculinities; however, these 'compensatory manhood acts' (Schrock and Schwalbe 2009) eventually proved unsustainable insofar as they contributed, over time, to the deterioration of men's self-identity and physical health. Second, the way in which treatment practices were 'staged' in terms of program rules and techniques engendered both 'manly' (professional work) and 'unmanly' performances (the outward expression of emotion). While these performances may appear in tension in relation to hegemonic masculine norms, they were nonetheless constructed as appropriately masculine in the program setting. Third, reconciling these performances proved problematic when it came to one key anchor point of hegemonic masculinity: independence. From the point of view of hegemonic masculinity and the value placed on self-reliance and autonomy, the treatment process requires men to acknowledge a double failure: the recognition of the 'self in crisis' *and* the subsequent acceptance of one's dependence on others. Surrendering an ideal of independence is thus central to treatment but is difficult to acknowledge and even harder to enact. Men's struggles to confront deeply held assumptions about the value of masculine independence constituted a drama that played out in the context of treatment, but one whose outcome was often uncertain.

We conclude by noting that in the realm of drug/alcohol treatment and recovery men's failure to approximate norms of hegemonic masculinity is conceived as a 'productive' failure. If one accepts that 'compensatory manhood acts' exemplify a type of 'hollowed out' masculinity (insofar as the enactment of locally valued masculinities hinge upon a sense of individual inadequacy) then recovery can be read as a process of filling in these hollowed out spaces. Recovery is fundamentally a project about the individual in which clients seek to build a new, more responsible and healthy self. Drug and alcohol treatment programs afford men a 'stage' for practicing and different 'props' for managing their emotional and social lives without alcohol or drugs. As detailed here, the way in which the treatment process is staged requires men to act and think differently about themselves and others, particularly in relation to independence. Thus, drug and alcohol treatment cannot be understood apart from the prevailing gender order and how it comes to be 'placed' through the staged performances of gender identities that are themselves so instrumental for health-related change.

References

Atherton, S. 2009. Domesticating military masculinities: home, performance and the negotiation of identity. *Social and Cultural Geography*, 10(8), 821–836.

Campbell, H. 2000. The glass phallus: pub(lic) masculinity and drinking in rural New Zealand. *Rural Sociology*, 65(4), 562–581.

Capraro, R.L. 2007. Why college men drink: alcohol, adventure and the paradox of masculinity, in *Men's Lives* (7th Edition), edited by M. Messner and M. Kimmel. Don Mills: Pearson Education.

Connell, R.W. 1995. *Masculinities.* Crow's Nest: Allen and Unwyn.

Connell, R.W. 2000. *The Men and The Boys.* Berkeley: University of California Press.

Connell, R.W. and Messerschmidt, J.W. 2005. Hegemonic masculinity: rethinking the concept. *Gender and Society*, 19(6), 829–59.

Courtenay, W. 2000. Constructions of masculinity and their influence on men's well-being: a theory of gender and health. *Social Science and Medicine*, 50(10), 1385–1401.

Courtenay, W. 2004 Making health manly: social marketing and men's health. *Journal of Men's Health and Ggender*, 1(2), 275–276.

Courtenay, W. 2009. Theorizing masculinity and men's health, in *Men's Health*, edited by A. Broom and P. Tovey. West Sussex: Wiley-Blackwell, 9–32.

Courtenay, W. and Keeling, R. 2000. Men, gender, and health: toward an interdisciplinary approach. *Journal of American College Health*, 48(6), 243–246.

de Visser, D. and Smith, J. 2007. Alcohol consumption and masculine identity among young men. *Psychology and Health*, 22(5), 595–614.

de Visser, R., Smith, J. and McDonnell, E. 2009. 'That's not masculine': masculine capital and health-related behaviour. *Journal of Health Psychology*, 14(7), 1047–1058.

Evans, J., Blye, F., Oliffe, J. and Gregory, D. 2011. Health, illness, men and masculinities: a theoretical framework for understanding men and their health. *Journal of Men's Health*, 8(1), 7–15.

Fairbanks, R. 2009 *How it Works: Recovering Citizens in Post-Welfare Philadelphia.* Chicago: University of Chicago Press.

Gerschick, T. and Miller, A. 1995. Coming to terms: masculinity and physical disability, in *Men's Health and Illness: Gender, Power and the Body*, edited by D. Sabo and D. Gordon. Thousand Oaks: Sage Publications, 183–204.

Gorman-Murray, A. 2011. Economic crises and emotional fallout: work, home and men's senses of belonging in post-GFC Sydney. *Emotion, Space and Society*, 4(2), 211–220.

Harnett, R., Thom, B., Herring, R., and Kelly, M. 2000. Alcohol in transition: towards a model of young men's drinking styles. *Journal of Youth Studies*, 3(1), 61–77.

Heath, M. 2005. Soft-boiled masculinity: renegotiating gender and racial ideologies in the Promise Keepers Movement. *Gender and Society*, 17(3), 423–444.

Hopkins, P. and Noble, G. 2009. Masculinities in place: situated identities, relations and intersectionality. *Social and Cultural Geography*, 10(8), 811–819.

Kulis, S., Marsiglia, F. and Hecht, M. 2002. Gender labels and gender identity as predictors of drug use among ethnically diverse middle school students. *Youth and Society*, 33(3), 442–475.

Longhurst, R. 2005. 'Man breasts': spaces of sexual difference, fluidity and abjection, in *Spaces of Masculinities*, edited by B. van Hoven and K. Hörschelmann. Abingdon and New York: Routledge, 165–178.

Nayak, A. 2006. Displaced masculinities: chavs, youth and class in the post-industrial city. *Sociology*, 40(5), 813–831.

O'Brien, R., Hunt, K. and Hart, G. 2009. Prospects for change in Scottish men's constructions of masculinity and their health-related beliefs and behaviours. *Critical Public Health*, 19(3–4), 363–381.

Sabo, D. 2005. The study of masculinities and men's health, in *Handbook of Studies on Men and Masculinities*, edited by M. Kimmel, J. Hearn and R.W. Connell. Thousand Oaks: Sage Publications, 326–352.

Sabo, D. and Gordon, D. 1995. *Men's Health and Illness: Gender, Power, and the Body.* Thousand Oaks: Sage Publications.

Schrock, D. and Schwalbe, M. 2009. Men, masculinity and manhood acts. *Annual Review of Sociology*, 35(1), 227–295.

Sloan, S., Gough, B. and Conner, M. 2010. Healthy masculinities? How ostensibly healthy men talk about lifestyle, health and gender. *Psychology and Health*, 25(8), 783–803.

Smith, J., Braunack-Mayer, A., Wittert, G., and Warin, M. 2007. Independence, masculinity and aging in a help seeking context. *Journal of Aging Studies*, 21(4), 325–335.

Thien, D. and Del Casino, V. 2012. (Un)Healthy men, masculinities and the geographies of health. *Annals of the Association of American Geographers*, 102(5), 1146–1156.

Willott, S. and Lyons, A. 2012. Consuming male identities: masculinities, gender relations and alcohol consumption in Aotearoa New Zealand. *Journal of Community and Applied Social Psychology*, 22(4), 330–345.

Chapter 22
Masculinities, Life Courses and Sexual Health: Unpacking HIV Risk and Prevention among Gay Men in Halifax, Nova Scotia, Canada

Nathaniel M. Lewis

Introduction

Increasingly, gender is considered a fundamental determinant of health outcomes and behaviours (Denton, Prus and Walters 2004, Hankivsky 2012). The emergent field of 'men's health', has thus sought to understand how maleness and masculinity inform health risks and health-seeking behaviours among men. Here, masculinity has often been framed as a singular, implicitly heterosexual attribute with negative health consequences; for example, excessive risk-taking, a 'superman' sense of confidence in one's health and a reluctance to be checked or tested for various illnesses (Schofield et al. 2000, Courtenay 2003, Connell and Messerschmidt 2005). More recently, however, health research has reconceived masculinity as a set of multiple masculinities that develop over the life course and intersect with other characteristics (e.g., ethnicity, sexuality) to influence health (Evans et al. 2011, Hankivsky 2012). This more nuanced approach has been adopted widely in areas of men's health such as nutrition, substance use, and chronic disease management (see also Wilson and Evans 2014: this volume, Keppel 2014: this volume).

In the field of HIV/AIDS risk and prevention, the focus of this chapter, masculinities tend to fade away in favour of ostensibly concrete determinants such as sexual orientation, sexual behaviour, and treatment adherence. This medicalised research approach, coupled with the labelling of HIV/AIDS as a 'gay disease' in the 1980s and 1990s, historically has cast gay men's bodies as disease vectors rather than complex, social beings (Brown 1995, 2006). Moreover, because homosexuality is sometimes implicitly associated with the lack or absence of masculinity (Connell and Messerschmidt 2005), little research considers how the constructions of masculinities that gay men experience throughout their lives might influence their sexual health. Integrating masculinities into sexual health research, however, requires more than simply linking men's self-ascribed identities with sexual behaviour. It should also consider how masculinities are shaped and performed at different points in the life course, and how they diffuse through place-specific institutions such as homes, schools, and health authorities (Foucault 1979, Brown 2006, Lewis 2012).

The following chapter presents masculinities as one component of a regional 'ecology' of HIV/AIDS (Brown 2006, King 2010), in which the risk and prevention of HIV/AIDS is considered in relation to both a particular place and multiple analytical scales, such as the individual, the gay community, local institutions, and the provincial health system. In Canada, this ecological approach – in which masculinities are one component – is central to understanding the transmission and prevention of HIV/AIDS outside of known high-prevalence epicentres such as Montreal, Toronto, and Vancouver. In these cities, research has focused on gay communities characterised by a backdrop of extensive health infrastructure and 'cosmopolitan' acceptability for gay identities, leaving the emphasis on specific *sites* (e.g., bath houses) or *behaviours* (e.g., drug use) rather than the broader social and contextual aspects of the places that men live in or traverse across the life course (e.g., Weber et al. 2001).

The following case study of Nova Scotia thus seeks to (1) shed light on gay men's sexual health in a region of Canada where it is rarely studied, and (2) understand gay men's masculinities as products and components of individual life courses and place-specific ecologies of sexual health. After a brief discussion of methods and the social and historical context of the Halifax region, the chapter turns to: (1) ruptures of masculinities and encounters with risk; (2) the fragmentation of the gay men's health system; and (3) the aggregate impact of masculinities messaging on the gay community itself.

Methods

This is an ethnographic study involving research at the Nova Scotia Public Archives and semi-structured interviews with equally sized groups of HIV/AIDS-related service providers and individual gay-identified men. All of the interviewees were located in Halifax County, a mixed urban–rural county including the cities of Halifax and Dartmouth, and Colchester County, a largely rural county. Between September 2012 and February 2013, eight service providers and seven individual men were recruited via targeted e-mailing or electronic posting of a recruitment poster on service organisation websites. Interviews lasted 35–75 minutes and were held at service agencies or by telephone. The service provider interviews focused on client experiences and the challenges of doing HIV/AIDS-related work in Nova Scotia. The interviews with individual men, who ranged in age from their twenties to their sixties, focused more broadly on individual life histories (see Cohler and Hostetler 2003) and the ways in which they encountered HIV risk and alternately, learned about and practiced HIV prevention. The archival sources included back copies of *Wayves*, Atlantic Canada's gay and lesbian monthly magazine, and the archives of the Nova Scotia Gay and Lesbian Association (NS GALA). The interviews were fully transcribed and then coded by the author for themes such as 'risk contexts' or 'health care experiences'. While the frequency of each theme was recorded, the analytic process placed greater emphasis on how the themes related to one another in an iterative manner (Charmaz 2006). Masculinity was not a discrete theme; rather, it comprised the various messages, and modes of masculinities inflected in each theme.

Setting the context: the region of Halifax, Nova Scotia

Halifax is the largest city in Atlantic Canada (Newfoundland and Labrador, New Brunswick, Nova Scotia, and Prince Edward Island), comprising a population of just over 100,000 in the city centre and 400,000 in Halifax County, also known as the Halifax Regional Municipality (HRM). HRM also comprises several towns of less than 5,000 people, and is situated at the centre of a province that is about 55 per cent rural and is often characterised as 'have not': its economy was historically based in fishing, mining, and agriculture, and it typically receives equalisation payments from 'have' provinces (Tomblin 1995). The broader region, to some extent, still reflects an Atlantic Canadian milieu of rurality, physical labour in resource-based industries, and often, heteronormativity and traditional gender roles (Bulman 2005).

As Connell and Messerschmidt (2005) observe, however, even places suffused with a traditional hegemonic masculinity still experience ruptures of dominant gender norms. Halifax was the site of the first conferrals of same-sex surviving partner pension benefits in the late 1990s and Nova Scotia became the first province to establish a domestic partnership law in 2001 (see Wile 1998, Lewis 2014). At the same time, it is important to note that these laws were pushed forward largely by well-connected lawyers, lobbyists and professionals in Halifax (rather than wider grassroots campaigns), as well as governing bodies that have been historically conscious of *not* perpetuating notions of Nova Scotia as socially and culturally peripheral (Marontate 2000). These changes have also tended to benefit a specific demographic of coupled, openly gay men, while the day-to-day visibility of gay masculinities in the region has been more contested. During Halifax's first gay pride parade in 1988, for example, many marchers concealed their identity by wearing bags over their heads (CBC 2012).

HIV/AIDS activism, too, has followed a less steady path in Halifax compared to cities such as Vancouver, where thousands of AIDS-related deaths in the gay community had sparked both dense networks of local HIV/AIDS activism and the emergence of 'gay men's health' as distinct sector worthy of resources, personnel, and public messaging (Brown 1997). Halifax, in contrast, has been hesitant to place HIV/AIDS – and consequently, gay masculinities – in the public's purview. In 1995, the first HIV/AIDS service organisation (ASO) in Halifax, Metro Area AIDS coalition (MacAIDS) splintered into a second group (the Nova Scotia Coalition of People with AIDS) after the MacAIDS executive director refused to fund targeted initiatives aimed at gay men and African Nova Scotians (Boutilier

1996). Today, the tensions around gay men's visibilities remain. The Nova Scotia Advisory Commission on AIDS, which provides support for people living with HIV/AIDS (PLHWA), receives provincial funding. In contrast, the organisations engaged in community-based prevention – which demands the acknowledgement of both a gay/MSM population and male-male sex more generally – are funded by donations and grants. With these tensions in mind, the following chapter seeks to understand both the diffusion and perpetuation of certain masculinities through local and regional institutions and the impact of these constructions on the sexual health of gay-identified men across the life course.

Coming out and getting out there (or not)

The relationships between rurality and the notion of a traditional, hegemonic 'masculinity' have been discussed elsewhere (Williams, Bowen and Horvath 2005, Bulman 2005) but still bear mention here because of their impact on the trajectory of men's individual development trajectories and sexual health behaviours. Early-in-life messages about masculinity comprised a dominant theme in the interviews, and were mentioned by almost every participant. Some participants focused on family life, usually pointing to masculinities messaging from individual family members (e.g., 'my father tried to teach me to hunt and tried to make me work in the wood pile') or the pressure to perform traditional masculinities expected by multi-generational family networks that were also their primary sources of social support. Others focused on schools, which were sites of both individual experiences of bullying and name-calling, but also the profoundly structural marginalisation of gay identities in terms of employee terminations, bans on gay-straight alliances (GSAs), and the exclusion of 'controversial' (i.e. sex-positive and gay-positive) sex education materials from the curriculum (Stoddard 1991, Beagan 2004, McKinnon 2006, van Berkel 2006, Mombourquette 2011, Hinchliffe 2012).

The effects of early-in-life heteronormative and homophobic messaging on the mental health of gay-identified men are well established (Flowers and Buston 2001, Lewis 2009). Although many studies have suggested an association between isolation, self-esteem, mental health, and sexual risk-taking or drug use, less is known about the distinct ways in which place-based experiences of gender normativity or homophobia lead to risk for HIV and other sexually transmitted infections (STIs). Many of the participants discussed subsequent sexual behaviour changes stemming from attempts to form or negotiate a gay identity, or alternately, from seeking out sex while attempting to remain closeted. As research on the gay life course has suggested, delays in coming out or activities such as dating – especially in homophobic environments – may make men feel pressured to 'catch up' or, alternately, to negotiate same-sex activity while maintaining a straight identity (Kertzner 2001, Cohler and Hostetler 2003, Lewis 2014). One participant described reacting to identity suppression earlier in life:

> … and then I just got to 30 and realised I had no sexual confidence, I had no sexual, like I don't even really know what I like or what's kind of weird, or what I want and so it was just a beautiful revolving door for like three years, hundreds I feel like, I just went totally crazy … it was fun and I'm just so thankful I came out of that and then now I'm in a place of comfort and pick and choose, and date, and do what I want. (Mark, 30s, Halifax County)[1]

The re-negotiation of masculinities not only potentially 'ramps up' sexual activity, as Mark describes, but also introduces specific coping strategies (online hook ups or traveling) that may also be associated with higher HIV risk. For men seeking out same-sex sexual contact, the online world can provide a buffer or boundary to set the terms of the sexual experience in relation to one's identity (i.e. maintaining a straight identity by only *receiving* oral sex) or to access modes of intimacy that they wouldn't otherwise. Mark, for example, also 'learned there was definitely a huge desire out there for sort of straight-identified men to seek a gay man or a cross dresser or drag queen'. In a preliminary programme of online outreach via online cruising sites, one of the HIV/AIDS service organisations in Halifax found that most men seeking same-sex contact online identified in ways that defied gay-straight binaries.

> … whether they were asking me questions or not … almost 60 per cent [of the profiles] identified as bisexual, with almost 12 per cent identifying as straight and just under 30 per cent presenting as gay … Is it just people who are not gay-identified who are using cruising sites, or disproportionately skewed that way … Are they newly out and it's still unsure, the cachet of being bi in some instances, for that matter the cachet being straight in some instances? Then I thought maybe it shouldn't be that surprising, maybe, for openly out gay men cruising sites aren't the go-to place … to the same degree that they are for people who might identify as bi and maybe bi means, well I have a girlfriend, but I play on the side and this is how I hook up with guys. (Outreach worker, Halifax County)

Previous studies have suggested, however, that online encounters also more commonly involve unprotected anal intercourse or other risky activities like substance use in conjunction with sex (Bolding et al. 2005, Liau, Millett and Marks 2006). Many service providers agreed:

> Meeting online is certainly something that has increased over the years … there's less people probably who are going to hook up on [Citadel Hill][2] or hook up wherever because they're meeting online … but it's, the same fears are still there because now they're hooking up online and then they're meeting

1 Respondents are anonymised to protect their identities.

2 Citadel Hill, the site of a British colonial fortress, is also well-known historical and current cruising site for gay men in downtown Halifax.

somewhere and there's even less of a relationship than perhaps prior to. (Youth outreach worker, Halifax County)

Depending on where you are, I mean some people feel like they can't come out, so they're doing things that may be riskier because perhaps they don't even want to really talk about it … if they're not talking, they're not comfortable talking to [sex] partners or going and getting condoms … I suppose you're doing things a little bit more spur of the moment that you hadn't planned on. (HIV nurse A, Halifax County)

For other men, the renegotiation of masculinities across the life course involved traveling or relocating. While migration and travel have long been framed as liberating and even necessary components of gay identity formation (Weston 1995); a growing body of research also suggests that the social displacement, stress, and isolation that occurs with relocation creates scenarios (e.g. more frequent, more rushed, and sometimes anonymous sexual encounters in less familiar settings) during which sexually transmitted infections are spread (Bianchi et al. 2007, Bruce and Harper 2011). While Nova Scotia itself is not a place with a high HIV prevalence rate, the accounts of the participants suggest that they encounter higher HIV risk – in terms of both places with higher prevalence *and* their own behavioural shifts – when traveling or relocating.

For men coming from rural surrounding areas to seek out sexual encounters the city of Halifax, temporarily relocating might involve a shift from a more restrained sexual disposition to a more active, flexible one (see also Williams, Bowen and Horvath 2005).

What we're seeing is that we're seeing people from rural areas and outside of Halifax flocking to this urban area because there is no place close to them. So they flock here and either they're – they may not be out or they may have you know pent up energy or whatever – and they come here and all hell breaks loose sometimes. So it may not be the first thing on people's minds and then they're going home … they're going back and they're living their lives whether that's gay relationships or whether that's married to the opposite gender and potentially the spread. (Youth outreach worker, Halifax County)

There certainly is a pattern of people going to larger centers whether it's somebody in Cape Breton coming to Halifax for the weekend, whether it's somebody in Halifax going to Montreal for a weekend, or people taking vacations as a way to have sex and push boundaries that they wouldn't push in their own back yard. (ASO outreach worker, Halifax County)

For others, the shifts may occur when traveling between the Halifax region and other places in Canada or North America. Although the trips may or not be explicitly for the purpose of sexual exploration, the act of leaving a place where one mode of masculinity is maintained can temporarily free up the mental space to perform or enact another. Rodney, who earlier in life had married a woman, began using travel as a way to maintain a straight life at home while exploring the possibility of emotionally healthier sexual relationships with men:

> So whenever I would go away to a conference, I could feel myself transforming into this other person within me … if I was landing in Toronto, or Montreal, or Vancouver, wherever, and I just … went crazy … I could just feel myself changing and then I could also feel myself changing when I came home. I just sort of reverted back to that other person that I was. So I was actually living two lives, two identities … I'm assuming that I actually contracted HIV someplace else, not in Nova Scotia. … before I would even get to the hotel, I would actually head to the steam bath. So I was in a marriage, so I could get all the penetrative sex that I wanted … but I could not get anal sex, I couldn't be on the receiving end … I think it was more of a physical need, but it was also, more also … I met some really wonderful men who actually really loved me in the way I wanted to be loved for those 15, 20 minutes. (Rodney, 50s, Colchester County)

Although Rodney was describing events from more than a decade earlier, the service providers suggested that the shifting masculinities (and thus, sexual behaviour) that gay men experienced between 'home' in Nova Scotia and other big cities were still fairly commonplace.

> I've had many conversations with, you know, gay men, that might be around the 30, 32 age who have spent a number of years, you know, in the Toronto, Vancouver area, who talk about the minute they got there they were like, in fantasy land right, and they took every advantage they could of course and nothing wrong with that, but we're not prepared for the emotions, the responsibilities of any of that associated with it. (ASO director, Halifax County)

> [I worked with] certainly young guys who went to big cities and encountered a whole other realm and level of party scene, of gay party scene. Well it was like candy you know, it was like wow fun but no tools. Ah, and also going, moving forward with the belief that you know HIV, that really HIV is okay, it's not really a big deal anymore, and that they don't have to be super conscious or careful and then they ended up with HIV. (LGBT health coordinator, Halifax County)

Although men leaving the Halifax region for say, Toronto, may, on one hand, be escaping an environment that they perceive to be heteronormative, they also encounter new risk scenarios as they attempt to negotiate new forms of masculinities in a new place. These scenarios might involve contextual changes, such as greater availability of sex or substances and higher prevalence of HIV and other STIs, as well as stressors (e.g. coming out, lack of familiarity with how to negotiate safer sex) that might affect how they deal with those contextual shifts.

Experiences with HIV/AIDS and sexual health services

In the Halifax region, the lack of historical experience with the HIV/AIDS epidemic, economic constraints, and ongoing conceptions of non-normative sexualities as abnormal or peripheral have all created a sexual health system that remains heteronormative *de facto*. Services for gay men are lacking, their experiences in the 'mainstream' system are frequently negative, and the lack of access they experience may exacerbate some of the disparities (e.g. lower service uptake) associated with men's health more generally. Currently, there are few mental health services for gay men in the Halifax region, excepting those in the youth or PLWHA populations. In addition, there are only two permanent, anonymous HIV testing (AHT) sites in Nova Scotia (1 per 450,000 people) compared with seven in New Brunswick (1 per 100,000 people) or over 50 in British Columbia (1 per 88,000 people). Rapid point-of-care (POC) HIV testing, which shortens the testing time and is available in most provinces, is not available in Nova Scotia (PHAC 2010a; Lewis, Gahagan and Stein 2013).

Since gay/MSM-specific services are sparse, men often engage with a health system where the heteronormative and homophobic messaging they may have experienced earlier in life is sometimes reiterated. Two providers recounted the experiences of some of their clients:

> Many men who would go to the [hospital-based] clinic and basically would come away feeling like they could never have any kind of sex again … or the only sex they could ever have was with a condom even if it's just a hand job … a lot of the stuff that we did was trying to really … unpack that information so that men – who are not stupid – can actually have all the information to actually make informed decisions. (LGBT health coordinator, Halifax County)

> This young fella drove all the way from Truro to a walk-in clinic … saw a doctor who … just chastised him and never did help him. And he ended up feeling worse when he left … thank god he came here. I forget, I don't know if he came from there to here, dropped in, or walked in, whatever, I saw him and he told me about that experience. I mean I wanted it written up, I wanted some action on it … and he didn't want to do anything because you know he was afraid, fear, he's young. He drove from Truro to Halifax to get judged by a health professional. (HIV nurse A, Halifax County)

Men's willingness or unwillingness to engage with available HIV services is also influenced by concerns about their anonymity, particularly in the context of communities (e.g., small communities, the gay community) where – to borrow a phrase used in several interviews – the 'six degrees of separation is more like two'. Tom, for example, discussed a friend who had avoided being tested for HIV:

> You know like he'd probably been with I'm guessing over 100 guys and almost always unprotected sex … he didn't feel comfortable when he was at home in Pictou [County] with his family doctor to go and [get tested], and he wasn't really aware of how to go about doing it here in Halifax. (Tom, 30s, Colchester County)

Importantly, he sees the lack of testing as not just an individual fear about anonymity, but also a general problem of testing not being normalised or visible, even in the city of Halifax. Mark (30s, Halifax County) agreed that testing among gay men remains limited because of the lack of specific services (e.g. rapid POC testing) and a general silence about gay men's HIV risk from public health authorities:

> [In bigger cities] you can just go right in, no stress, no fuss, no muss. It takes me weeks to get into my doctor, and then I get in and he's got to give me a rec and then I've got to go here and go there and all … over the place … [In Toronto] I mean they have those men's health centers and you see the billboards up everywhere a little bit more … [there are] some prevalent branding and marketing and things going on, on bus shelters and the sides of buses, and you know I see some things like that going on that keep it sort of in the forefront.

Finally, some providers saw the lack of specific attention to gay men's health as exacerbating the lower rates of health-seeking behaviour among men more generally.

> I guess that's one thing that makes Halifax sadly different from other places, one provider said, 'there's not a lot of places to go for support really … once you get past [youth] age, there's not a lot for gay men in particular … in general, women get together, right, and they talk and they do stuff. It's harder for the men … I think it's a lot of the old fashioned attitude, it's not my problem … you know I'm fine. (HIV nurse B, Halifax County)

> Men are not necessarily socialised to talk about problems, so I think that in itself just seems a base issue. I think if you look at cultural overtones, especially men in rural communities that are heterosexist, you know, men don't have problems, they don't want to talk to you about problems, sets men whether they be gay or not, up for failure. (ASO director, Halifax County)

The lack of a widespread gay men's health movement in Nova Scotia both perpetuates and stems from the presumption of hetero-masculinity in the health system, which creates both ongoing incidents of outright homophobia as well as the more subtle relegation of HIV/AIDS to a peripheral position on the spectrum of regional public health concerns. Consequently, there may be less of what one provider called 'cultural awareness' about sexual health in the gay community, despite the realistic risk of HIV and other STIs.

Normative masculinities, HIV/AIDS, and the gay community

To this point, the analysis has focused on the ways in which the various institutions that gay men encounter in Nova Scotia (families, schools, communities, health systems) have privileged or marginalised particular masculinities in ways that influence gay men's development trajectories and sexual health. Many participants observed, however, that normative masculinities had also become entrenched within the gay community *itself*, resulting in the delineation of HIV/AIDS as an abnormal and therefore unspeakable topic.

According to some participants, the desire to portray normalised gay masculinities in social and community contexts was an outgrowth of early-in-life messaging. Mark suggested that the sense of loyalty to family and the way they were raised produced a 'very straight gay masculinity' (Connell 1992), even among men who were 'out'. He described it as:

> This sort of unwillingness to be comfortable with their own sexuality. And just hating the gays that are … it's more prevalent here I feel like … 'cause maybe there's this undercurrent or this tone in our community where we're still striving to be either for their families or their dads, or you know, somewhat masculine and not want to change.

According to Tom, this desire for a widely acceptable, inoffensive gay masculinity creates a lack of speakability around HIV/AIDS and other 'controversial' topics. To discuss or acknowledge HIV, Tom explained, would force men to self-reflect in a way that would disrupt their performance of 'normal' gay masculinity, or potentially implicate them as someone irresponsible and unacceptable to the community:

> There's still a lot of judgement about sexuality even within the gay community and it's sort of like, you know there's sort of this badge of honor for normal gays like you know, I'm a normal gay, I want a monogamous relationship and I want to get married. [My HIV–positive friend] was an example of what they *could* be and by sort of casting him aside you know it allowed them to sort of look back to their sort of cocoon of … we're all in open relationships, we all fuck around with everybody, we do engage in unprotected sex … there's sort of this, like if we dismiss it and push it away and you know don't think about it, then we can keep on going and living our lives.

Tom's narrative not only reflects men's anxieties over a portraying an overtly sexual (or polyamorous) masculine identity, but also the way in which gay men – as a community – might replicate the silencing of HIV/AIDS occurring in the institutions around them.

When acknowledging and discussing HIV/AIDS conflicts with men's desired representations of gay masculinities, as it seems to in the Halifax region, the type of informal information-sharing that has emerged as a protective factor in other communities is less frequent. 'We don't have an environment of openness in talking about HIV within the gay community', one provider said. 'There's a lot of stigma and discrimination within the gay community and I know that people would rail against that, but it's true, I heard it over and over again. And if you talk to men who have HIV they will most likely tell you the same thing' (LGBT health coordinator, Halifax County). Interestingly, even providers worried that more visible public messaging would reinforce extant stigma toward gay men:

> But we also need to consider who [billboards and posters] are directed at? I mean, yeah, the overall community may not like a bus ad, but it's not directed specifically to the overall community, it's directed towards, potentially, in this example, gay men. But then a deeper level of that is it's not helping if we're causing a stigma, a further stigma on this. (Youth outreach worker, Halifax County)

Masculinities and intersecting anxieties

This chapter is one of the first to address gay men's sexual health in Canada outside of Montreal, Toronto, and Vancouver, where HIV and STI transmission for this population typically has been framed by specific high-risk behaviours (e.g., substance use) and spaces (e.g., bath houses, circuit parties) rather than broader social and political ecologies of disease. While ecological approaches to HIV/AIDS that look at the intersections of life courses, institutions, and local politics are potentially useful in many contexts, they are particularly relevant for places like Nova Scotia, where HIV risk among gay men/MSM cannot be explained solely through the behaviour-outcome models applied to other 'gay community' studies. The findings here show that masculinities and health are connected not just through the vehicle of 'maleness' or 'masculine' health behaviours, but from the active construction, perpetuation, and negotiation of masculinities as ideas and identities in multiple social and institutional contexts.

Although the accounts of the participants are generally critical, they do not necessarily reflect the *purposeful* maintenance of traditionalist, hegemonic, or repressive masculinities. Rather, they seem to suggest the presence of historically and socially grounded anxieties around masculinity, sexuality, and HIV/AIDS, which occur at multiple scales and reinforce one another. For large, extended families living in small communities, acknowledging the possibility of gay identities within the family – even if not outright rejected by all family members – could be seen as threatening. In communities, many of which may have not recorded an HIV/AIDS case, introducing outreach programming on same-sex identities or HIV/AIDS itself might introduce a sense of panic that they are not 'immune' to epidemics, that gay masculinities are not solely urban, or that urban health personnel are challenging established (e.g., family-centred) modes of health education. For individual men, the anxiety may arise over 'getting out' to escape perceived hegemonic masculinities, how to shape new gay masculinities through sexual encounters, or how to negotiate both milieux at once. Later in life, even when part of an 'out' gay community, they might struggle to acknowledge or discuss HIV/AIDS, which could potentially brand them as abnormal or undesirable. For policymakers, the need for HIV/AIDS gay men's prevention services and programming might be tempered by anxieties over the potential disapproval of constituents in some communities, or that drawing attention to HIV/AIDS as a public health concern would further paint Nova Scotia – a 'have not' province on the Canadian periphery – as backward and dysfunctional.

The future of gay men's health in Nova Scotia is, in many ways, an uncertain one. On the one hand, the prevalence of HIV is low (just over 700 HIV-positive tests ever recorded in the province), which has tended to implicitly justify the relative silence on HIV/AIDS (PHAC 2010b). On the other, the emergence of other STI epidemics (e.g., syphilis) among gay men in the region suggests that the risk of HIV is far from absent (CBC 2013). Consequently, ecological approaches to HIV prevention pay interest to communities of gay men/MSM that fall outside the standard (i.e., urban and metropolitan) geographic milieu of gay men's health, yet remain susceptible to the same health crises being experienced elsewhere. Careful consideration of these contextual factors in HIV prevention efforts within the region will ultimately bolster gay men's communities and improve the conflicted, sometimes anxious institutions and systems that support and serve them.

References

Beagan, D. 2004. Sex ed book furor in Nova Scotia. *The Interim* [Online, December 10]. Available at: http://www.theinterim.com/issues/sex-education/sex-ed-book-furor-in-nova-scotia [accessed: 21 August 2013].

Bianchi, F., Reisen, C., Zea, M., Poppen, P., Shedlin, M. and Penha, M. 2007. The sexual experiences of Latino men who have sex with men who migrated to a gay epicentre in the USA. *Culture, Health and Sexuality*, 9(5), 505–518.

Bolding, G., Davis, M., Hart, G., Sherr, L. and Elford, J. 2005. Gay men who look for sex on the internet: is there more HIV/STI risk with online partners? *AIDS*, 19(9), 961–968.

Boutilier, R. 1998. Nova Scotia leads the way. *Wayves*, June, 1.

Boutilier, R. 1996. Perspectives: AIDS, homophobia, and other stories. *Wayves*, December/January, 4.

Brown, M. 1995. Ironies of distance: an ongoing critique of the geographies of AIDS. *Environment and Planning D: Society and Space*, 13(2), 159–183.

Brown, M. 1997. *RePlacing Citizenship: AIDS Activism and Radical Democracy*. New York: Guilford Press.

Brown, M. 2006. Sexual citizenship, political obligation and disease ecology in gay Seattle. *Political Geography*, 25(8), 874–898.

Bruce, D. and Harper, G.W. 2011. Operating without a safety net: gay male adolescents and emerging adults' experiences of marginalization and migration, and implications for theory of syndemic production of health disparities. *Health Education and Behavior*, 38(4), 367–378.

Bulman, D. 2005. A constructivist approach to HIV/AIDS education for women within the Maritime Provinces of Canada. *International Journal of Lifelong Education*, 24(6), 475–487.

Charmaz, K. 2006. *Constructing Grounded Theory: A Practical Guide Through Qualitative Analysis*. London: Sage Publications.

Cohler, B.J. and Hostetler, A.J. 2003. Linking life course and life story: social change and the narrative study of lives, in *Handbook of the Life Course*, edited by J. Mortimer and R. Shanahan. New York: Kluwer Academic/Plenum, 555–578.

Connell, R.W. 1992. A very straight gay: masculinity, homosexual experience and the dynamics of gender. *American Sociological Review*, 57(6), 735–751.

Connell, R.W. and Messerschmidt, J.W. 2005. Hegemonic masculinity: rethinking the concept. *Gender and Society*, 19(6), 829–859.

Courtenay, W.H. 2003. Key determinants of the health and well-being of men and boys. *International Journal of Men's Health*, 2(1), 1–30.

Denton, M., Prus, S. and Walters, V. 2004. Gender differences in health: a Canadian study of the psychosocial, structural and behavioural determinants of health. *Social Science and Medicine*, 58(12), 2585–2600.

Evans, J., Frank, B., Oliffe, J. and Gregory, D. 2011. Health, illness, men and masculinities (HIMM), a theoretical framework for understanding men's health. *Journal of Men's Health*, 8(1), 7–15.

Flowers, P. and Buston, K. 2001. 'I was terrified of being different': exploring gay men's accounts of growing-up in a heterosexist society. *Journal of Adolescence*, 24(1), 51–65.

Foucault, M. 1979. On governmentality. *Ideology and Consciousness*, 6, 5–21.

Hankivsky, O. 2012. Gender and health: relational, intersectional, and biosocial approaches. *Social Science and Medicine*, 74(11), 1712–1720.

Hinchliffe, A. 2012. Gay/straight alliance group to promote awareness. *The Advance*, [Online, March 13]. Available at: http://www.theadvance.ca/Living/Education/2012–03–13/article-2925386/Gay-straight-alliance-group-to-promote-awareness [accessed: 1 October 2012].

Kertzner, R. 2001. The adult life course and homosexual identity. *Annual Review of Sex Research*, 12(1), 75–92.

King, B. 2010. Political ecologies of health. *Progress in Human Geography*, 34(1), 38–55.

Lewis, N.M. 2009. Mental health in sexual minorities: recent indicators, trends, and their relationships to place in North America and Europe. *Health and Place*, 15(4), 1029–1045.

Lewis, N.M. 2012. Gay in a 'government town': the settlement and regulation of gay-identified men in Ottawa, Canada. *Gender, Place and Culture: A Journal of Feminist Geography*, 19(3), 291–312.

Lewis, N.M. 2014. Moving 'out', moving on: gay men's migrations through the life course. *Annals of the Association of American Geographers*, 104(2), 225–233.

Lewis, N.M., Gahagan, J.C. and Stein, C. 2013. Preferences for rapid point-of-care HIV testing in Nova Scotia, Canada. *Sexual Health*, 10(2), 124–132.

Liau, A., Millett, G. and Marks, G. 2006. Meta-analytic examination of online sex-seeking and sexual risk behvior among men who have sex with men. *Sexually Transmitted Diseases*, 33(9), 576–584.

Marontate, J. 2002. Les rapports d'appartenance aux lieux de creation et l'art contemporain en région périphérique: le cas de la Nouvelle-Ecosse (1992–2002). *Sociologie et Sociétés*, 34(2), 139–161.

McKinnon, B. 2006. HRM School Board Wants to Know. *Wayves*, March, 4.

Mombourquette, A. 2011. For gay teachers, coming out is a lot harder than it sounds. *The Chronicle Herald* [Online, November 14]. Available at: http://thechronicleherald.ca/hcw/32713–gay-teachers-coming-out-lot-harder-than-it-sounds [accessed: 7 September 2012].

Public Health Agency of Canada. 2010a. *HIV Testing and Surveillance Systems in Canada* [Online: Public Health Agency of Canada]. Available at: http://www.phac-aspc.gc.ca/aids-sida/publication/epi/2010/pdf/EN_Chapter3_Web.pdf [accessed: 21 August 2013].

Public Health Agency of Canada. 2010b. *HIV/AIDS Surveillance Report to 31 December 2009* [Online: Public Health Agency of Canada]. Available at: http://www.phac-aspc.gc.ca/aids-sida/publication/survreport/2009/dec/3–eng.php [accessed: 21 August 2013].

Schofield, T., Connell, R.W., Walker, L., Wood, J. and Butland, D. 2000. Understanding men's health and illness: a gender-relations approach to policy, research, and practice. *Journal of American College Health*, 48(6), 247–256.

Stoddard, M. 1991. *Press Statement from Shelburne County School Board, 8 May. Gay Alliance for Equality/Gay and Lesbian Association of Nova Scotia Fonds*. Nova Scotia: Nova Scotia Public Archives.

Tomblin, S. 1995. *Ottawa and the Outer Provinces: The Challenge of Regional Integration in Canada*. Toronto: James Lorimer and Company.

van Berkel, L. 2006. The destruction, rebuilding, vindication, and progression of Lindsay Willow. *The Coast* [Online, July 20]. Available at: http://www.thecoast.ca/halifax/the-destruction-rebuilding-vindication-and-progression-of-Lindsay-Willow [accessed: 11 September 2012].

Weber, A., Chan, K., George, C., Hogg, R., Remis, R., Martindale, S., Otis, J., Miller, M., Vincelette, J., Craib, K., Masse, B., Schecter, M., LeClerc, R., Lavoie, R., Turmel, B., Parent, R. and Alary, M. 2001. Risk factors associated with HIV infection among young gay and bisexual men in Canada. *JAIDS Journal of Acquired Immune Deficiency Syndromes*, 28(1) 81–88.

Weston, K. 1995. Get thee to a big city: sexual imaginary and the great gay migration. *GLQ: A Journal of Lesbian and Gay Studies*, 2(3), 253–277.

Williams, M.L., Bowen, A.M. and Horvath, K.J. 2005. The social/sexual environment of gay men residing in a rural frontier state: implication for the development of HIV prevention programs. *Journal of Rural Health*, 21(1), 48–55.

Chapter 23
Masculinities and Mental Health: Geographies of Hope 'Down Under'

Jessica Jean Keppel

Introduction

The 'kiwi bloke' is often represented as a stubbie-wearing[1], beer-drinking, sheep-shearing, 'do-it-yourself' heteronormative masculinity (Phillips 1987, Longhurst and Wilson 1999):

> I think there's an aspect of New Zealand culture and upbringing that's sort of macho, and because of that, males in particular struggle to come to grips with their own true emotions. What they think they should be feeling has a lot of weight, and they can find it really hard to deal with full-on emotion. (Kirwan and Thomson 2010: 52).

This quote describes the nature of hegemonic masculinity in Aotearoa New Zealand and characteristics associated with the 'typical kiwi bloke'. This hyper-masculinisation is well-recognised in New Zealand culture. The 'kiwi bloke' is celebrated by the nation which leaves little room for the emergence and acceptance of alternative gender identities (Campbell, Law and Honeyfield 1999). Hardy (2007) maintains that this exclusive identity is achieved through participating in 'hard man activities' such as playing rugby union and beer-drinking. Indeed, '[t]he social construction of masculinity, in both developed and many developing countries, highlights the idea that men must present themselves as physically and emotionally strong' (Payne 2004: 206).

Expressing emotion or desire is not a facet of the 'kiwi bloke' mythology. He is a 'diamond in the rough', hard-working and 'manly'. The 'kiwi bloke' is the dominant cultural stereotype and hegemonic masculinity in New Zealand. Alternative male subjectivities are often feminised as 'soft' and made to feel as though they don't belong in certain spaces. The New Zealand Ministry of Health recognises that such masculine ideologies may avert men from engaging with their

1 Stubbies are shorts which sit above the knee at the mid-thigh. Stubbies are usually firm around the waist and buttocks and share a history of being worn by Australian and New Zealand men. Notorious for being an unattractive choice of public attire, stubbies are more commonly worn when playing sports or relaxing in private dwellings.

mental health and emotional wellbeing. Actually, '[t]he traditional view that men should be tough and self-reliant is also held by some women. Men may fear that admitting to their depression [for example] will result in being rejected by their partner' (Ministry of Health 2008).

This chapter provides a critical reading of men's mental health geographies in Aotearoa New Zealand. The research, which was conducted over nine months in 2012, comprised interviews and diary work with a small group of men who experience depression and/or anxiety, as well as an analysis of government-sponsored mental health campaigns. The participants live in New Zealand or strongly identify as New Zealanders. The findings are organised around two spatial scales. First, through an analysis of recent gendered mental health campaigns, I examine the discursive space of men's mental health promotion in New Zealand. I assert that there is a new national imaginary unfolding – a discursive geography of hope – which encourages 'kiwi bloke' personalities to be aware of their mental health and emotional wellbeing. Second, I discuss how the research participants negotiate pressurised spaces and seek meaning in, and attachment to, alternative places. Healthy places and homely spaces permit men to nurture their emotions and mental health without the fear of being objectified by others, especially those embedded in hegemonic masculine ideals. By examining these spatial scales, in contrast with one another, I tease out how discursive representations of mental health and New Zealand machoism affect men's everyday spatial interactions. The empirical material cultivates a deeper understanding of the relationships between New Zealand masculinities, emotions and mental health-in-place and bridges critical geographical scholarship with health and gender studies. Before engaging in this case study, I begin with the contextual and conceptual framing for the analysis.

Masculinities and health geographies: emotions, embodiment and place

Connell and Messerschmidt (2005) describe hegemonic masculinity as the pattern or practice of patriarchy. Through the representation of dominant discourses these patterns and practices help normative (male) identities sustain their control over women and alternative gender subjectivities. Gendered power relations operate to define and marginalise difference through discursive, material and symbolic spaces. In other words, the discursive body of representation affects the material body of experience and the ways in which people are politically involved in space and place (Jackson 1991). Masculinities that do not discursively live-up to the 'un-written' characteristics of socially acceptable 'manhood' are usually labelled as the Other, socially displaced and spatially excluded (Sibley 1995, Wolch and Philo 2000). Even so, hegemonic masculinity is problematic to maintain. Masculinities are plural, open to deconstruction and subject to change through social spaces, institutions and mass media (Connell and Messerschmidt 2005); '[a]lthough individuals are constituted by discourse, they are still capable of critically reflecting on how certain discourses have developed' (Pringle 2002: 63). 'Masculine' patterns and practices can be manipulated, mimicked and temporarily occupied by multiple genders to elicit power, domination and control. Wherever there is power there is resistance, and thus, individuals can exercise social influence on varying socio-spatial platforms (Pringle 2002). Foucault (1972) wrote that power is negotiated at the micro-level though everyday socio-spatial interactions. Masculinities are perpetually (re)constructed and (re)presented as men experience difference through space and place.

Since 2001 the Mental Health Foundation of New Zealand and the Ministry of Health have been consistent in promoting men's mental health. The New Zealand government defines depression as more than just a low mood or a bad day. Depression is a complicated state of mind that can cause a person to experience cognitive, emotional, social and physical difficulties (Ministry of Health 2008). Symptoms of depression[2] vary and adversely affect how a person interacts with other people and places. Depression and anxiety are often experienced simultaneously, which further complicates a person's daily existence. In general, anxiety is a natural response from the mind and body to escape danger. At the onset of an anxiety attack, adrenaline is released into the blood stream to enable 'fight or flight'. Physical and emotional symptoms of anxiety[3] can make people feel out of control, as though they are going 'crazy', or as if they are going to die. A person who has an anxiety disorder will experience symptoms more regularly or at a more intense rate than someone who is responding to mild stress or worry (Mental Health Foundation 2008).

Mental ill-health experiences render unpleasant emotions, feelings of fear and a sense of isolation within different social contexts. As a result, mental ill-health often creates terrifying and upsetting realities. Davidson (2003) maintains that social spaces threaten to dissolve an anxious person's sense of self (control), their reality and their being-in-the-world through a fear of being objectified. Therapeutic places, or environments that contribute to a person's wellbeing, alleviate the pressures felt in 'peopled' or pressurised places (Gesler 2009). Therapeutic spaces allow people to reconstruct their psychocorporeal boundaries in safe, comfortable environments (Davidson 2003).

Men's socio-spatial relations are complex and this case study does not aim to simplify these involvements. In response to fear and stigma, associated with

2 Symptoms of depression can include: irritability; lack of mental, emotional and physical energy; sadness, guilt and/or anger; cognitive difficulties; disruptions to sleeping and eating patterns; loss of interest in previously-enjoyed activities; feelings of dejection or emotional numbness; and thoughts about death and suicide/attempts (www.depression.org.nz).

3 Symptoms of anxiety can include: bodily trembling; sweating; respiratory complications; aches and pains; dizziness; feeling out of control or as though one is 'crazy'; feeling scared, worried and panicked; repetitive thoughts; derealisation and depersonalisation (http://www.mentalhealth.org.nz).

mental ill-health, the goal of this research is to give voice to men's mental ill-health experiences. The men in this research shape 'geographies of hope' as they elicit power, resistance and autonomy through their lived understandings of space and place. Lawson (2007b) alerts us to the ways in which growing global concerns of political instability, natural hazards, climate change and health endemics are shaping geographies of fearfulness. In response, scholars are beginning to theorise the powerful emotions of hope as they permeate geographical phenomena. Recent investigations have examined hope in relation to ethnicity and place (Duruz 2010, Johnston and Longhurst 2012, Wise 2005). While there is a wealth of value in these 'multicultural geographies of hope' there is also room for expansion. If scholars are to build geographies of hope, critical to our survival, then they need to look closely at a nexus of relationships that contribute to experience in place (Lawson 2007a, 2007b).

To unearth a greater understanding of men's alternative health realities the research is underpinned by feminist-poststructuralist ideologies and scholarship contributing to holistic health geography. Health geography as a sub-discipline, incorporates a wide range of perspectives that seek to investigate and explain the relationships between mental health and place (Curtis 2010, Kearns and Moon 2002). Curtis (2010) theorises individual mental health as fluctuating on a complex spectrum and intimately affected through a myriad of personalities and places. Furthermore, psychological, embodied and emotional responses to place are significant for sense of identity and wellbeing. 'Emotional wellbeing is the ability to cope with everyday demands – life's "ups and downs" – and poor emotional wellbeing correlates with stress, anxiety, and depression' (Gorman-Murray 2013:138). Fleuret and Atkinson (2007) call for geographers to more thoroughly conceptualise geographies of wellbeing. The participants and I appreciate that definitions of wellbeing are relative to an individual's being-in-the-world. Not only is wellness place-specific, it cannot always be separated from ill-health (Moss and Dyck 2003).

The research stresses that state-of-mind has physical and emotional effects on a person. In other words, the mind and body operate simultaneously, not in isolation. Cartesian health interpretations impose binary divisions and thereby assert fault to the individual. Dichotomising mind/body as separate entities means disregarding the ways in which lived experience of space and place affects an individual's mental health (Moss and Dyck 2003). A more inclusive and holistic perspective scrutinises that mental ill-health is affected by a person's social position as well as their psychological 'make-up' and biological characteristics (Curtis 2010, Moss and Dyck 2003, Robbins 2004, 2006). Mental ill-health experiences can also be theorised through the 'three bodies of experience'. The body is not only a material entity: it is a discursive formation and a site of political contestation. Meaning is created through the body as it is tied up in spatial webs of power, domination and control (Moss and Dyck 2003). Men experience mental ill-health differently from women, and indeed there is difference within masculinities, since subjectivities are unique (Robbins 2004, 2006). Men's mental health realities are complicated and spatially diverse which justifies the call for further research in this area. New Zealand scholars have already contributed insightful investigations which examine men's health geographies. O'Connor (2002), for example, analyses the sociological aspects of Pākehā[4] men's healthcare practices, and more recently Myers (2010) conducted research on gay men's experiences of HIV in Auckland, New Zealand. Predominantly, research has concentrated on post-asylum geographies, and the re-development and de-institutionalisation of mental healthcare facilities (Gleeson, Hay and Law 1998, Kearns and Joseph 2000, Joseph, Kearns and Moon 2013). Men's mental health geographies in the Antipodes are underdeveloped sites of analysis.

Methodology

The intersectional research lens – between masculinities, emotions, embodiment and place – necessitated flexible methodology. Critical social analyses can empower and enhance understandings of the complex relations constructing mental health experiences and socio-spatial interactions (Wolch and Philo 2000, Kearns and Moon 2002). An adaptable qualitative framework was thus employed to gather empirical material: seven semi-structured interviews and five solicited diaries were provided by nine respondents. Of the interviews, five were face-to-face and two over the telephone, for convenience, anonymity and accessibility. Three interviewees wrote diaries, and two other men (not interviewed) also undertook diary work. Following Meth (2003), the participants and I negotiated the content of the solicited diaries, which allowed for individual reflexivity within a collaborative framework. Solicited diaries are helpful in gauging emotional actualities or events that would otherwise be inaccessible to researchers through other methods (Morrison 2012). Diaries can also be a therapeutic outlet for participants (Meth 2003). Additionally, I designed a follow-up questionnaire, which established connections between the behaviours, attitudes and beliefs of participants. Questions were open-ended to allow participants flexibility in sharing their perspectives.

Mixed and multiple qualitative methods were chosen for the purpose of giving voice to participants, building reflexivity and enhancing researcher/participant relations. These aims coincide with feminist research agendas (Renzetti 1997, Meth 2003). It is important to note that each participant identified as mentally healthy during the stages of data collection, and pseudonyms were chosen for anonymity. I gave participants a list of accessible mental healthcare services in case they wanted to discuss their experiences with a professional.

Furthermore, a critical reading of recent gendered mental health texts enabled me to map the men's relationships with, and responses to, mental health

4 Pākehā is the Maori term for a New Zealander of European decent (www.maoridictionary.co.nz).

discourses circulating in the New Zealand media. Discourse analysis permits a deeper understanding of the social structures which legitimise masculinities and mental health information. 'It is men's and boy's practical relationships to collective images or models of masculinity, rather than simple reflections of them, that is central to understanding gendered consequences in violence, health and education' (Connell and Messerschmidt 2005: 841). I was particularly concerned with Sir John Kirwan's 'discourses of hope' and material produced by the Ministry of Health and Mental Health Foundation of New Zealand. I developed a qualitative coding structure to thematically analyse the texts. I studied the audio and visual imagery of six *Depression: There is a way through it* advertisements. The advertisements feature John Kirwan and have been showcased on Television New Zealand since 2007. I viewed the advertisements on the online video community YouTube Broadcast Yourself. I then undertook a close reading of the Mental Health Foundation's *Get in the Game: Training for Happiness* poster. This facilitated an understanding of how masculinity and mental health is positioned to the 'typical kiwi audience'. John Kirwan's autobiography *All Blacks Don't Cry: A Story of Hope* provided the final resources for content analysis. I adapted Gordon Waitt's (2010: 227, 229, 230) questions for conducting critical discourse analysis and worked to answer a number of questions about the authorship, the audience, and the content of the data. I found that the mixed methodology afforded me a range of well-positioned qualitative information.

As I engaged with the empirical material I reflected on my positionality throughout the research. By acknowledging positionality, researchers substantiate that knowledge is relative and the research becomes more rigorous (Longhurst 2009). I conclude that I upheld a 'closeted' positionality throughout the research. I did not 'come out' to participants about my own experiences of anxiety and depression. Akin to other health geographers (Parr 2001) my intention was not to pose or be deceitful. Rather, I felt that our time was better placed on the participant's narratives. I observed that the men had strong political motives of social justice that drew them to participate in the research. These motivations draw a strong correlation with the socially-mediated discourses that are examined in the next section.

Re-imaging the 'kiwi bloke': a discursive geography of hope

The slogan for Mental Health Awareness Week 2011 was *Get in the Game, Training for Happiness*. This discourse was produced by the Mental Health Foundation to coincide with the 2011 Rugby World Cup which was hosted in New Zealand at the time. Relying on the 'national compliance' that New Zealanders strongly relate to rugby union, the representation uses rugby and 'hard man' themes to inform the audience of everyday actions applicable to enhancing their mental health.

Applying 'hard man' themes to the context of mental health positions the poster as a parody. The promotion relates mental health to 'kiwi bloke' identities but men who do not respond to rugby and sport are excluded. Visual imagery presides over the text in this representation. A black and white rugby jersey is the dominant image. Splattered with dirt, the jersey is symbolic of the All Blacks (the national rugby union team). White stars frame the capitalised words 'GET IN THE GAME: TRAINING FOR HAPPINESS' which are shaped to form a crest. The crest, which is a standard feature on sports jerseys and school uniforms, signifies conformity. The crest is strategically placed on the chest, to emblemise notions of national pride and hegemonic masculinity. The mud-splattered jersey verifies a tough, working-class masculinity which is both privileged and eroticised in Aotearoa. The poster's text is positioned to strengthen the visual discourse. To assert a disciplined way of managing mental ill-health, the discourse invokes notions of team work, strategy and control, and thereby collapses Cartesian dualisms which alienate rationality from emotion, masculine from feminine, and illness from health. The poster utilises and reflects facets of New Zealand machoism to unshackle discourses which position men with anxiety and depression as somehow effeminate.

Kirwan's mental health advocacy also upsets Cartesian thinking by urging men to embrace their emotions and address their mental ill-health. It is no coincidence that Sir John Kirwan, former All Black and currently the coach of the Auckland Blues rugby team, is situated at the forefront of men's mental health promotion in New Zealand. All Black rugby players and sportsmen are rendered prime examples of 'healthy' masculinities (O'Connor 2002). Having proven himself as a strong, able-bodied rugby player, Kirwan is a well-respected sporting figure in New Zealand, Italy and Japan. His rugby union background renders him as a privileged body and therefore his identity predominantly goes unchallenged. Since 2007 Kirwan has appeared in several television commercials for the Ministry of Health, which support the National Depression Initiative.[5] The campaign introduces a new dialogue around masculinities and mental health. In these advertisements Kirwan is seen wearing a cleanly-pressed, white, Italian dress-shirt and jeans. Kirwan appears less like an All Black in these advertisements. His face is smooth-shaven and he appears well-groomed. In one of the advertisements Kirwan is shown on a beach (with his jeans rolled-up to avoid getting these wet and dirty) and with a large stick he carefully draws the word HOPE into the wet sand. Kirwan occupies a position between being in-place and out-of-place. Through his openness to mental and emotional wellbeing and the presentation of his clothed embodiment, Kirwan depicts aspects of the 'new man' identity. Jackson (1991) professes that the 'new man' is gentle, caring and self-confident in his masculinity as he embraces new emerging gender performances. Kirwan creates a space for men to emotionally express themselves and to actively nurture, request and accept support for their mental ill-health.

---

5 The National Depression Initiative is part of the New Zealand Government's commitment to addressing mental ill-health and suicide prevention. For more information about the goals, objectives and key strategies of the National Depression Initiative visit www.health.govt.nz.

Six main themes emerge in Kirwan's advertisements: hang on to hope; reach out; have a plan; know your triggers; stay active; and enjoy the little things. These themes reinforce how non-medicalised methods of achieving wellbeing are becoming more desirable in New Zealand (Collins and Kearns 2010). Significantly, the advertisements, together with their themed messages, were especially meaningful to the research participants. Joe said:

> I think the John Kirwan ones mean the most to me. Given not only that he is a bloke but the fact that he is an ex-All Black and he epitomises, I guess, what New Zealand is not willing to stand up and look at. He's a guy, he's a sportsman, he's a 'hard man' but he's had a mental 'illness'. I think that, for me, meant a lot.

Joe also said that at times he'd personally felt restrained and as though he'd be judged for experiencing depression and being in touch with his emotions. Joe recognises how hegemonic masculinity has affected his own political and material actuality and his above quote reinforces how discursive constructions affect people's lived experiences. Similarly, Andrew's lived experience draws a parallel to the discourse 'know your triggers'. Recognising his warning signs, positively impacts Andrew's mental health. Andrew says: 'It's much faster now and I think that is why I have had such a good run health-wise recently because I have learnt to understand my processes a lot more, stopped blaming myself and also started recognising where my weak spots are'.

Michael's narrative coincides with the 'staying active' theme: 'I used exercise, whether it was with a team every week or going to the gym every other day. This helped me stay not only physically active but helped me stay mentally fresh.' The advertisements portray healthy spaces as active, outdoor and social places – primarily the site of the beach. Coastal sites and nature spaces are heavily associated with the promotion of physical, psychological and social wellbeing in New Zealand (Collins and Kearns 2010). Frank agrees that (promoting) an active lifestyle is a positive method for improving men's mental health. Both Frank and Joe embody active spaces to enhance their wellbeing. Frank discussed the release he feels when tramping in the hills and Joe explained that his running space helps him ease his anxious worries. Kahu finds that gardens and native walking spaces are beneficial for alleviating his depressive episodes. Nature spaces offer Kahu a therapeutic environment away from his isolated, chaotic and physically-inactive workplace. By using outdoor spaces to nurture their mental health, the men challenge the idea that rough, rural spaces in New Zealand are strictly associated with 'hard man' performances. Occupying therapeutic spaces facilitates men's inner desires of a healthy, more positive self.

'Reach out' was another important message for participants. Harry says: 'I really try very much to have positive-thinking people around me. That can definitely have an impact.' Kirwan emphasises the importance of reaching out for support by saying: 'You need to tell someone – loved ones, doctors, psychologists, psychiatrists – just reach out. And if you tell someone and they don't get it, go and tell someone else, until you get someone who gets it' (Ministry of Health, 2007).

In 2010 Kirwan published his autobiography *All Blacks Don't Cry: A Story of Hope*. The book details his personal journey through anxiety and depression and plays on the masculine idea of 'conquering the beast'. Kirwan discusses his paradoxical journey to emotional control and fearlessness through a willingness to understand and embrace his emotions. Kirwan (2010) uses a medical lens to destabilise illness as weakness and through the use of rugby metaphors he juxtaposes physical injury with mental ill-health (whereby the former is privileged over the later). Joe also seizes a medical lens to make sense of how his mental health has changed. Joe says: 'I'd say to people "Look, I've got severe depression" and they wouldn't understand that there is actually some sort of chemical imbalance in my brain and that I need medication to bring that back to normal. My way of explaining it to people would be really simple.' Using a medical lens to simplify mental ill-health is less threatening to men's sense of self and their social relationships. This method is one of the coping mechanisms men use to maintain mental stability and resist oppressive discourses of weakness. 'Men can adopt hegemonic masculinity when it is [spatially] desirable but the same men can, at other moments, choose to distance themselves from hegemonic masculinity at other moments' (Connell and Messerschmidt 2005: 841). Kirwan's narrative exemplifies how masculine ideologies are persistently re-worked. Dualisms, which position emotion and nurturing as the behavioural characteristics of women, operate to feminise New Zealand men who accept their emotions and practise mental healthcare. This philosophy is being counteracted through Kirwan's emotional discourse. Kirwan resists and upholds the feminisation of emotions by stating: 'When life throws its challenges and disappointments at you, it's okay to have an emotional response. It's really important to understand that you can be angry, you can be sad, you can want to cry, and all it means is that you're angry, or sad, or need to cry' (Kirwan and Thomson 2010: 161).

In these discourses, emotions are accordingly re-imaged as simplistic 'kiwi bloke' attributes. The stigmatisation of mental ill-health produces a fear of the 'mad'. 'Discourses of fear emerge in different cities and societies at particular historical moments and are linked to profound structural changes of a socio-spatial as well as economic kind' (Sandercock 2002: 208). Kirwan's hybrid positionality counteracts this fear and redefines masculinity as bearing the courage to address mental ill-health. This is 'true toughness, true courage' (Kirwan and Thomson 2010: 56). I term these discourses the 'new national imaginary' of men's mental health in New Zealand. This new national imaginary influences a discursive geography of hope by encouraging men to identify their ill-health and their need for support. Next, I discuss how the men use space and place to personify these geographies of hope.

Healthy places and homely spaces

The participants in this research recognise that their mental health and emotional responses differ from hegemonic masculine ideals. I asked Andrew how he felt when anxious and depressed. He responded:

> Feeling like I am out of control with my feelings and I can't do anything about it and often I'll just have to wait, ride it out, and be patient. When I was first going through those depressive states, I'd beat myself up quite a bit and not understand why it was that I couldn't be well. I think it's just a feeling of being really dark and foggy. You can't see clearly and your thoughts aren't straight. It's kind of hard to describe the emotional state because when you're there, there is no real logic to that space. It just feels like you're numb and empty.

Andrew's mentality and cognitive expression is complex. His state of mind is quite distinct from the assumed simplicity of the 'kiwi bloke'. Andrew's quote disrupts Cartesian thinking which seeks to divide reason from emotion and mind from body. Bondi (2009) theorises that reason and emotion are intertwined and powerfully articulated, rising in us, through embodiment. Robbins (2006) adds that mental and emotional symptoms of depression and anxiety are physically expressed through mental construction.

At times when the men feel depressed or panicked, they are conscious of their social, embodied behaviours in the gaze and presence of others. To avoid social objectification some men, like Andrew, perform the 'absence of emotion' in public spaces:

> I conceal them from my friends and from the people that I associate with and sometimes, if I'm going out, if there is a social function or if there is something on, if I don't want to talk about it often I can over-compensate by being louder. The anxiety I can't cover up at all but I won't talk about it with people because, again, it's that stigma.

Andrew expresses how the symbolism of social space is tied up, conceptually and experientially, in emotion. Emotional places are infused with mediation and articulations of the self (Bondi, Davidson and Smith 2005). Andrew fears becoming 'Other', so he constrains himself to normalised performances of New Zealand masculinity. By performing a hegemonic masculinity and mentality, Andrew hopes to resist social and spatial exclusion. Fear is often based on social perceptions of threat, which shape people's mental maps and everyday geographies (England and Simon 2010). Andrew's mental map of fear is suffused with the threat of hegemonic others, which affects how he spatially expresses himself and consumes peopled-places. His passage through space is carefully enacted to ensure that his masculinity and mental health go unchallenged. If necessary, he enters public space through a 'subjective space of protection'. He creates this space by encasing his body in clothing and accessories:

> When I'm feeling anxious, depressed, or both, and I have to be in public for some reason, one strategy I found helpful is to wear sunglasses, a hat, and earphones. Doing so makes it feel like I'm in a bubble and insulated from everything around me. The effects of the presence of people on my anxiety are less if I'm listening to music, behind glasses and under a hat. Somehow it feels like armour in a way, and the negative thoughts that sometimes arise from being around people don't get out of control.

Andrew's corporeality constitutes his experience of social space. His 'costume' asserts him as simultaneously present in and absent from place. Although he is physically embodying the public sphere, his 'armour' makes him feel as though he is invisible and impenetrable. Over time and influenced by previous exposure, Andrew has learnt how to negotiate place through his clothed embodiment. Manzo (2005) maintains that spatial relationships are based on a history, regardless of whether place affiliations are positive or negative. Andrew's narrative underlines how past engagements have affected his contemporary spatial relationships as well as his emotional knowing – that is, what he knows about himself and what he knows about himself-in-place.

Social spaces are highly pressurised places that 'intrude on the boundaries of fragile selves' (Davidson 2003: 141). Demonstrating this as a lived experience, Harry knows that he needs to spend time away from highly pressurised places when he feels unwell:

> I love being around positive people and happy places and places where there is a lot of people but when I've been depressed that's the last thing I want to be doing like you don't want to be in a library or a pub or anything … everything feels like 'not you' like you don't want to be there, you don't belong … plus you have other people penetrating into your space.

Harry describes the de-personalisation he feels through his ill-health at times when people are piercing his personal space. Meaningful spaces, that empower men with a sense of hope, are therefore extremely important for the upkeep of their mental and emotional health. Men embody healthy places and homely spaces to mend their psychocorporeal boundaries which become fractured through an exposure to angst and panic in public places. Coming to terms with mental ill-health is both an unsettling and an awakening journey. The evolution to a state of self-knowing, realisation and regained mental health is fraught with an assembly of different emotions which are felt, resisted, avoided, and sometimes nurtured paradoxically in the home.

The home is not merely a material construct. The home is built by experience, social relationships, memories and everyday practices that affect a range of responses (Peil 2009). Michael creates a sense of home beyond his residential dwelling. In his diary narrative, Michael wrote about how finding a meaningful homely space, with a person who could offer him support, contributed to his recovery from a deep state of depression: 'I made a new friend who helped me through what I was dealing with. It was at her home that I felt most at home, comfortable, warm and at peace'. Michael exemplifies how 'a house is not necessarily nor automatically a home, and personal relations that constitute home extend beyond those of the household' (Blunt and Dowling 2006: 3).

The home is a space where men can be emotionally vulnerable, idle and prepare themselves for interactions outside of the home (Gorman-Murray 2013). Yet spaces within the home are also fraught with complex emotional entanglements such as mutual feelings of liberty and imprisonment. During Andrew's interview, for example, I asked him to discuss the places that he feels most comfortable in when he is anxious or depressed:

> A bed – definitely bed with depression. It's kind of like a good and bad space. It's good because you feel safe but then you feel guilty and you feel trapped because you can't get out of bed. You just feel exhausted and low energy as if you have run a marathon but it certainly beats being up or outside your home. In flatting situations definitely because I guess the way I associate a flatting experience is that anything that's not your bedroom is public space and you can't necessarily control who's going to be in that space, you don't want to talk and you look like crap. Being in bed, under the duvet, is definitely the place and that really helps with anxiety as well … it's kind of like hiding.

This extract certifies that home spaces are instilled with a plurality of positive and negative emotions and mixed feelings of health and ill-health. Andrew embodies his bedroom to nourish a positive state of mind. He hopes that his bedroom space will relieve him of negative emotions but at the same time Andrew is faced with feelings of guilt and confinement because he feels like leaving his bedroom is not an option. Jim's experience of home is also marked by competing emotions. Although the house that Jim and his wife live in has all the typical characteristics which make up a home (possessions, furnishings, relationships, memories and spaces), in his experience of anxiety and depression the house feels un-homely and stressful. The family-man ideology that Jim is expected to uphold in the home sways him to escape and nurture his mental health in the country.

> I think the identity [of the kiwi bloke] had to be re-mediated around my wife because she is not from New Zealand. Her experience of New Zealand males is very much the family man, stereotypical 'kiwi bloke' as well as the Asian expectations of what is expected from a husband or a man. For me now, it's mostly places in the countryside, by a lake or by a river. I find after a while, that buildings start closing in on me and even though I love cities … I can't stay

> there for too long … I have to drive to the countryside and get out and sit there for an hour.

There is no house physically situated in the country but Jim experiences comfort, safety, privacy and wellbeing there.

Frank's home narrative is also instructive of the complex entwining of emotional, imaginative and material dimensions in therapeutic place-making. When Frank feels depressed he imagines a new home space which he hopes will become his most positive and healthy space. In this way, Frank's home is in a process of becoming. Blunt and Dowling (2006) maintain that home can also be an idea or an imaginary which is infused with feelings, inspiration and emotion. Frank desires his home imaginary to have native flora and fauna. He explains how such elements would create a 'retreat' as well as a sense of belonging, health, positivity, and rootedness. Frank's home imaginary is emotionally imbued with feelings of desire, belonging and hope. It is in these instances that the home appears as an array of spaces, emotions, imaginaries and relationships which shift over time.

Conclusion

Masculinities are in a constant state of flux, from the site of body to the ways in which they are discursively represented on a greater national scale. This research has highlighted an emerging national imaginary which discursively produces new masculinities and mental health in New Zealand. I have argued that this imaginary produces a discursive geography of hope which men embody through place. I have elicited how the participants respond and relate to these new discourses of hope and the ways in which men resist mental illness stigma through their place-based relations. The men who participated in this research challenge the discourses which have historically constructed hard and fast meanings around what constitutes New Zealand masculinity.

Social spaces affect men to perform a hegemonic masculine identity. In turn, men constantly negotiate their relationships with people and place, through methods of sartorial embodiment and by visiting meaningful places that reflect hope, health and homeliness. Their socio-spatial performances affect temporalities of autonomy, resistance and control, and reflect their desire to be well. Some men find wellbeing through embodying their home spaces, while others seek attachment to place outside of their residential dwellings. This study is by no means comprehensive. However, it is my hope that knowledge will continue to be cultivated in a response to geographies of fear and the marginalisation of difference. As Jim asserted: 'We should find ways to make people functional in society. Assist people to find a place where their unique brain wiring is a benefit and not a negative. It's possible.'

Acknowledgements

I am grateful to the participants for having the courage to share their unique stories with me. I would like to thank Andrew Gorman-Murray and Peter Hopkins for their encouragement and acknowledge the ongoing support of Lynda Johnston who supervised this study. Thanks to the Mental Health Foundation of New Zealand, Progress to Health Hamilton, Wise Group Hamilton and Healthy Christchurch for endorsing this project.

References

Blunt, A. and Dowling, R. 2006. *Home*. New York: Routledge.

Bondi, L. 2009. Emotional knowing, in *International Encyclopedia of Human Geography*, edited by R. Kitchin and N. Thrift. Oxford: Elsevier, 446–452.

Bondi, L., Davidson, J. and Smith, M. 2005. Introduction: geography's 'emotional turn', in *Emotional Geographies*, edited by L. Bondi, J. Davidson and M. Smith. Aldershot: Ashgate, 1–17.

Campbell, H., Law, R. and Honeyfield, J.E. 1999. 'What it means to be a man': hegemonic masculinity and the reinvention of beer, in *Masculinities in Aotearoa/New Zealand*, edited by R. Law, H. Campbell and J. Dolan. Palmerston North: Dunmore Press, 166–186.

Collins, D. and Kearns, R. 2010. 'Pulling up the tent pegs?' the significance and changing status of coastal campgrounds in New Zealand. *Tourism Geographies*, 12(1), 53–76.

Connell, R.W. and Messerschmidt, J.W. 2005. Hegemonic masculinity: rethinking the concept. *Gender and Society*, 19(6), 829–859.

Curtis, S. 2010. *Space, Place and Mental Health*. Farnham: Ashgate.

Davidson, J. 2003. *Phobic Geographies: The Phenomenology and Spatiality of Identity*. Aldershot: Ashgate.

Duruz, J. 2010. Floating food: eating Asia in kitchens of the diaspora. *Space and Society*, 3(1), 45–49.

England, M.R. and Simon, S. 2010. Scary cities: urban geographies of fear, difference and belonging. *Social and Cultural Geography*, 11(3), 201–207.

Fleuret, S. and Atkinson, S. 2007. Wellbeing, health and geography: a critical review and research agenda. *New Zealand Geographer*, 63(2), 106–118.

Foucault, M. 1972. *The Archaeology of Knowledge*. London: Tavistock Publications.

Gesler, W.M. 2009. Therapeutic landscapes, in *International Encyclopedia of Human Geography*, edited by R. Kitchin and N. Thrift. Oxford: Elsevier, 229–230.

Gleeson, B., Hay, C. and Law, R. 1998. The geography of mental health in Dunedin, New Zealand. *Health and Place*, 4(1), 1–14.

Gorman-Murray, A. 2013. Urban homebodies: embodiment, masculinity, and domesticity in inner Sydney. *Geographical Research*, 51(2), 137–144.

Hardy, N.A. 2007. A *real (wo)man's beer: gendered spaces of beer drinking in New Zealand*. Masters. University of Waikato.
Jackson, R. 1991. The cultural politics of masculinity: towards a social geography. *Transactions of the Institute of British Geographers*, 16(2), 119–213.
Johnston, L. and Longhurst, R. 2012. Embodied geographies of food, belonging and hope in multicultural Hamilton, Aotearoa New Zealand. *Geoforum*, 43(2), 325–331.
Joseph, A., Kearns, R. and Moon, G. 2013. Re-imagining psychiatric asylum spaces through residential redevelopment: strategic forgetting and selective remembrance. *Housing Studies*, 28(1), 135–153.
Kearns, R. and Joseph, A.E. 2000. Contracting opportunities: interpreting post-asylum geographies of mental health care in Auckland, New Zealand. *Health and Place*, 6(3), 159–169.
Kearns, R. and Moon, G. 2002. From medical to health geography: novelty, place and theory after a decade of change. *Progress in Human Geography*, 26(5), 605–625.
Kirwan, J. and Thomson, M. 2010. *All Blacks Don't Cry: A Story of Hope*. Auckland: Penguin Books.
Lawson, V. 2007a. Geographies of care and responsibility. *Annals of the Association of American Geographers*, 97(1), 1–11.
Lawson, V. 2007b. Introduction: geographies of fear and hope. *Annals of the Association of American Geographers*, 97(2), 335–337.
Longhurst, R. and Wilson, C. 1999. *Heartland* Wainuiomata: rurality to suburbs, black singlets to naughty lingerie', in *Masculinities in Aotearoa/New Zealand,* edited by R. Law, H. Campbell and J. Dolan. Palmerston North: Dunmore Press, 215–228.
Longhurst, R. 2009. Interviews: in-depth and semi-structured, in *International Encyclopedia of Human Geography*, edited by R. Kitchin and N. Thrift. Oxford: Elsevier, 580–584.
Manzo, L. 2005. For better or worse: exploring multiple dimensions of place meaning. *Journal of Environmental Psychology*, 25(1), 67–86.
Mental Health Foundation of New Zealand. 2008. *Anxiety and how to handle it* [Online: Mental Health Foundation of New Zealand]. Available at: http://www.mentalhealth.org.nz/file/downloads/pdf/file_90.pdf [accessed: 7 March 2012].
Mental Health Foundation of New Zealand. 2008. *Men and depression* [Online: Mental Health Foundation of New Zealand]. Available at: http://www.mentalhealth.org.nz/file/downloads/pdf/file_87.pdf [accessed: 7 March 2012].
Meth, P. 2003. Entries and omissions: using solicited diaries in geographical research. *Area*, 35(2), 195–205.
Ministry of Health. 2007. *Depression: there is a way through it* [Online: Ministry of Health]. Available at: http://www.youtube.com/watch?v=vXMLXfFmaM0 [accessed: 13 June 2012].

Ministry of Health. 2008. *Men and depression* [Online: Ministry of Health]. Available at: http://www.mentalhealth.org.nz/file/downloads/pdf/file_87.pdf [accessed: 13 June 2012].

Morrison, C.A. 2012. Solicited diaries and the everyday geographies of heterosexual love and home: reflections on methodological process and practice. *Area*, 44(1), 68–75.

Moss, P. and Dyck, I. 2003. *Women, Body, Illness: Space and Identity in the Everyday Lives of Women with Chronic Illness*. Lanham: Rowman and Littlefield.

Myers, J. 2010. Health, sexuality and place: the different geographies of HIV–positive gay men in Auckland, New Zealand. *New Zealand Geographer*, 66(3), 218–227.

O'Connor, A.M. 2002. Young Pakeha men's conceptions of health, illness and healthcare, in *The Life of Brian: Masculinities, Sexualities and Health in New Zealand*, edited by H. Worth, A. Paris and L. Allen. Dunedin: University of Otago Press, 139–157.

Parr, H. 2001. Feeling, reading, and making bodies in space. *Geographical Review*, 91(1–2), 158–167.

Payne, S. 2004. Gender influences on men's health. *The Journal of the Royal Society for the Promotion of Health*, 124(5), 206–207.

Peil, T. 2009. Home, in *International Encyclopedia of Human Geography*, edited by R. Kitchin and N. Thrift. Oxford: Elsevier, 180–184.

Phillips, J. 1987. *A Man's Country? The Image of Pakeha Male, A History*. Auckland: Penguin Books.

Pringle, R. 2002. Living the contradictions: a Foucauldian examination of my youthful rugby experiences, in *The Life of Brian: Masculinities, Sexualities and Health in New Zealand*, edited by H. Worth, A. Paris and L. Allen. Dunedin: University of Otago Press, 57–72.

Renzetti, C. 1997. Confessions of reformed positivist: feminist participatory research as good social science, in *Researching Sexual Violence Against Women: Methodological and Personal Perspectives*, edited by M. Schwartz. Thousand Oaks: Sage Publications, 131–143.

Robbins, A. 2004. Introductions to men's mental health. *The Journal of Men's Health and Gender*, 1(4), 359–364.

Robbins, A. 2006. Biopsychosocial aspects in understanding and treating depression in men: a clinical perspective. *The Journal of Men's Health and Gender*, 3(1), 10–18.

Sandercock, L. 2002. Difference, fear and habitus: a political economy of urban fears, in *Habitus: A Sense of Place*, edited by J. Hillier and E. Roooksby. Aldershot: Ashgate, 203–218.

Sibley, D. 1995. *Geographies of Exclusion: Society and Difference in the West*. London: Routledge.

Waitt, G. 2010. Doing Foucauldian discourse analysis – revealing social realities, in *Qualitative Research Methodologies in Human Geography*, edited by I. Hay. Toronto: Oxford University Press, 217–240.

Wise, A. 2005. Hope and belonging in a multicultural suburb. *Journal of Intercultural Studies*, 26(1–2), 171–186.

Wolch, J. and Philo, C. 2000. From distributions of deviance to definitions of difference: past and future mental health geographies. *Health and Place*, 6(3), 137–157.

PART 8
Masculinities and Work

Chapter 24

Representations, Respect and Resentment: Labour Market Change and Discourses of Masculine Disadvantage

Linda McDowell, Esther Rootham and Abby Hardgrove

Introduction

In this chapter, which focuses on Britain, we explore the marginality of working-class young men in a service-dominated economy where youth unemployment rates are high. We trace the historical continuities in the construction of these young men as dangerous and out of control in the public arena: attributes that did not necessarily disqualify them from employment in manufacturing jobs, where the jobs themselves were often dangerous or dependent on embodied attributes associated with masculinity such as strength and determination. However, as interactive service occupations based on customer contacts have become increasingly numerous, their disadvantage correspondingly became greater as the acceptable deferential performance associated with many servicing jobs at the bottom end of the labour market often ruled out working-class young men as potential employees. Nevertheless young men do work in the service sector in poorly-paid and often low status jobs in, for example, retail or in call centres, but for too many working-class young men unemployment is more common.

Since the financial crisis in 2008, and the consequent years of recession and austerity, youth unemployment has risen significantly and the social construction of working-class young men as unacceptable or as failures as employees and as citizens, has become even more significant than in previous decades. This is reflected in an unpleasant discourse about youth out of control and unemployable and in rhetoric about 'sad' and depressed young men. However, as ethnographic research in deprived areas in British towns and cities has documented, many young men resent these constructions. Their lives are complex and variable. For some, their aim is to work and to become respectable and respected members of society, despite the difficulties of finding work during a recession. For others, their assessment of employment prospects leads to resignation or to anger and to decisions to get by and find a way of making sense of themselves as men in ways other than seeking waged employment in the formal economy. Yet others find ways of constructing an acceptable version of masculinity through participation in other areas of daily life. We draw on two interviews with white young men in Swindon, a town in southern England, to explore these representations and responses.

Discursive continuities: dangerous youth

There has been a long history in Britain, and elsewhere in the world (Kaplan 1996), in which working-class young men are discursively constructed in the press and in policy documents, and to an extent in academic texts, as disorderly, out of control, if not dangerous to know. The effects of their presence on the streets as part of an urban crowd, as potential and actual rioters and as threatening just by loitering on corners have been documented over time by Pearson (1983) as well as explored in contemporary accounts by social scientists (Nayak 2003, McDowell 2003, 2012, Noble 2007). Here the figure of the street-wise, rampantly masculine, often out of control 'lad' has been a pervasive figure: an identity Connell (1995) termed protest masculinity. As Delamont (2000) noted at the start of the new millennium, it is the 'bad boys', the working-class rebels, from the Mods and Rockers of the 1960s, to the 'mugger' in the 1980s (Crichter 2006) and more recently minority gang members (Alexander 2000), who occupy centre stage. Versions of youthful, middle class, hetero-normative masculinity are taken for granted as the unmarked norm and so remain relatively unexplored. And, as Delamont continued, there is a distinct miasma of envy in the sociological accounts constructed by 'good boys', academics who succeeded at school, but enjoy danger by association as they survey the worlds of young male rebels.

In the last two decades or so, however, a second version of troublesome masculinity has become common. A new or alternative moral panic (Cohen 1973) about working-class youth has entered popular representations of young men – the boys who fail (McDowell 2003). In this version the focus is on the comparative failure of school-boys as their success in school leaving exams falls compared to the results achieved by girls at the age of 16. There is also concern about rising rates of depression, anxiety, anorexia and suicide among young men. As youth unemployment rates remain high these two versions of masculinity are connected by the decreasing possibility of participation in the first version of masculinity. Participation in a culture often fuelled by fashion, drink, and drugs is difficult as ways of earning a living, at least legitimately, decline. In both discourses, working-class young men are presented both as a problem to be controlled or solved, through for example, regulation such as anti-social behaviour orders or special treatment at school or in programmes to 'encourage' labour market participation, and as a group that is outside commonly accepted definitions of active citizenship. Class condescension also grew in Britain from the 1990s as the middle class mocked and parodied the working class, subjecting them to regulation through the law and through cultural practices (Mount 2004). Young men were the particular object of this condescension, illustrated in the figure of the 'chav' (Jones 2011).

In an exploration of the continuing significance of these two versions of masculinity, we monitored British press coverage for 2010 and 2011, when the implications of rising youth unemployment had become an issue of key concern. In Britain, one in five young people between 16 and 24 were out of work at the end of 2010, compared to a total unemployment rate of 7.9 per cent (ONS 2011). Youth unemployment continued to rise in 2011 and in the first part of 2012 rose to just over one million, but fell slightly (to 945,000) by October 2012. Despite the significance of unemployment and its clear impact on young people's opportunity to find waged work, in many of the media discussions worklessness among young people was represented as if it were their own fault or a consequence of an over-generous benefit system. Common descriptions of youth were as failures, unfit, inactive, without respect and too idle to search for employment. White British youth fared especially poorly in comparisons with East European migrants who had entered the country from 2004 onwards, as the extract below illustrates:

> Britain has produced a lost generation of young people who lack essential literacy, numeracy and communication skills and cannot be trusted to turn up to work on time, an influential report has warned. It says failing schools have left employers no option but to hire foreign workers, who are punctual, work harder and have a more positive attitude. (Gallagher 2011 n.p.)

The notion that unemployed young people constitute a 'lost generation' became common following an influential, and largely sympathetic, speech in 2005 by Frank Field, a former Labour minister with a particular interest in poverty and inequality. He suggested, in an analogy with the loss of young men in two World Wars, that young people not in employment, education or training (NEET) in the new millennium represented the 'the first non-violent loss of a generation' as social mobility stalled. As unemployment rose after 2008, the concern shifted from lack of mobility to exclusion from the labour market altogether. In February 2011, Ed Miliband, leader of the Labour Party, repeated Frank Field's claim in a speech about workless young people and Demos, a policy think tank, issued a report on youth unemployment called *The Forgotten Half* (Birdwell 2011).

While commentators from the left of the political spectrum were largely supportive, elsewhere a vicious rhetoric of dislike and blaming the victim was more common. In a survey of articles about young men published in the British redtop and blacktop press in 2010 and 2011 the following terms were used to describe working-class young men: youths (73), yobs (101) and lads (34). These terms typically were used in the context of reports about violence, drunkenness and other forms of anti-social behaviour and were almost always qualified by pejorative adjectives. Thus the term yob was most frequently associated with mindless, hooded, racist, armed, gang of, drunk, brick throwing, and gun carrying. The term youth was associated with terms such as feral, rampaged, masked, hooded, disenfranchised, trapped, disaffected, and lost: with only the last four of these terms being used sympathetically. Lads too were more likely to be represented in these last four ways, but overall sympathy for the plight of young men was unusual.

Press coverage in the later part of this period undoubtedly reflected the urban unrest in Britain's major cities in August 2011 and the level of disbelief and shock this created among the general public. There was relatively little positive coverage of the plight of unemployed and disenfranchised urban youth in the main stream media, as this report in 2012 in *The Guardian*, a left of centre serious broad sheet paper, reveals. The comment is about a European survey of popular opinions among older people:

> For many, the riots confirmed what a decade of antisocial behaviour legislation has been suggesting already: that young people show 'no respect'. … A definitive European social survey conducted over the last decade found that young people are much more likely to be viewed as 'incompetent' and 'unfriendly' in Britain than in any other European country. They are also considered to be 'less moral' by their elders. Being young in Britain affords a pariah status all of its own. (Howker 2012 n.p.)

This pariah status was reflected in legislative proposals. In January 2011, Teresa May, Home Secretary in the Coalition Government, announced a consultation paper on anti-social behaviour and at the end of the same month she introduced new measures, including forbidding walking aggressive dogs and wearing certain cloths or colours in to attempt to reduce gang membership. These negative and aggressive versions of masculinity – of young men as bad, as failures, as feral or as forgotten – that dominate the popular media and are reflected in legislation by a right wing Government also influence potential employers. Too often, they are reluctant to consider either swaggering or dejected youth as prospective workers in the now service-dominated economy of the UK. For many prospective employers, the young men that they interview when filling vacancies are less appealing prospects than either young women from the same class position or the growing number of older women returning to work as their children go to school, often to make up for the declining incomes of their husband and partners who are also affected by declining opportunities for employment regarded as appropriate for men (Alcock et al. 2003). In the next section we explore the ways in which the types of jobs expanding in a service-dominated economy disadvantage unskilled young men.

Masculine disadvantage in a service economy

From the influential work of Willis (1977) onwards, there has been a long history of research on the connections between class, gender and employment opportunities and status. Willis documented the ways in which working-class boys were educated to move straight into unskilled and semi-skilled but reasonably well-paid and relatively secure manufacturing jobs, whereas more recent work has explored the disadvantages for men of deindustrialisation. Studies of UK and US labour markets (Bourgois 1995, Fine and Weiss 1998, Nayak 2003), especially those where the effects of industrial decline has been most severe, have shown how disadvantage is connected to the categorical inequalities of age, class, race and gender (Tilly 1998). In the US, Roediger's (1999) historical analyses have illustrated how the 'wages of whiteness' advantaged white men, but have also shown how whiteness itself is a malleable and socially-constructed category, as Southern European in-migrants as well as Irish men (Ignatiev 1996) had to earn their inclusion in the privileged category of whiteness. In the second half of the twentieth century, as service employment became more significant, it became increasingly clear that the ways in which the social construction of class, raced and gendered bodies intersect with ideas about suitable workers disadvantaged working-class men, both white men and men of colour. In service employment, especially in what is often termed interactive work (Leidner 1993), or by some body work (Cohen 2010, Wolkowitz 2002, 2006), the social attributes of masculinity that had constructed men as the preferred employees in industrial occupations began to become a disadvantage, especially at the bottom end of the labour market. Furthermore, in service sector work the provider and consumer of the service often are both present as an exchange takes place. As a consequence, personal attributes of the body – its height, weight, posture, its presentation – affect the social interaction between the seller and buyer and so the embodied performativity of identity becomes crucial.

Feminist theorists of employment change (Adkins 2002, McRobbie 2011, Skeggs 2004) and scholars interested in youth employment and unemployment (Bourgois 1995, MacDonald 2008, MacDonald, Shildrick and Blackman 2010) have shown how the intersection of class, gender, ethnicity and the construction of an idealised serving body produces a hierarchy of eligibility for different types of employment, disadvantaging working-class young men of colour in particular. The financial crisis in 2008 made brutally evident how hollow were about claims of continuous economic growth on the basis of 'new knowledge' industries including financial services. Key adherents of the new knowledge economy had argued that class and gender had become less significant. Ulrich Beck (2000: 151), for example, identified an era of a 'new modernity', in which 'older' divisions based on class and gender were likely to wither away, as individuals were increasingly dis-embedded from stable class-based communities and traditions. In an aside, he noted as 'gender is part of an older modernity ... women find it difficult to remove themselves from these social traditions and become individualised subjects'. He failed to recognise that many men too would find it hard to 'remove themselves' as class and gender differences failed to wither away.

These claims have never had a great deal of purchase in the sort of working-class communities that Rob MacDonald (2008, MacDonald, Shildrick and Blackman 2010) has analysed over more than a decade of empirical work in the north east of the UK. Here, and as one of us (McDowell 2003) found on an outer estate in

Sheffield, 'traditional' divisions remain significant as young working-class men and women enter gender-segregated forms of employment if they are fortunate, or the dole queue if not. Crompton (2010: 22), in an analysis of the continuing salience of class divisions, concluded that 'although both the contours of this [class] structure have changed, differentiated and unequal rewards to relative positions within it have remained comparatively stable'. Similarly, McRobbie (2009: 1) identified '"new-old" dependences and anxieties' that continue to structure women's lives in post-millennium Britain. Her claim, we suggest, is equally relevant to the position of young men in the labour market.

At the bottom end of the labour market, class, gender, age and ethnicity have a continuing salience in the explanation of who gets which jobs (McDowell 2009). As many scholars (see Brush 1999, Castells 2000, Goos and Manning 2003) have argued, the growing dominance of service employment in the UK has been associated with an increasingly bifurcated labour market. Despite the rhetoric about the knowledge-based information economy, in the UK at least as many low status and poorly paid jobs have been created over the last two decades. Although the extent of polarisation has been disputed, there is no doubt of the significance of low-waged work. Among the fastest growing jobs in the last two decades are retail assistants, catering workers, and hotel workers. Astonishingly, more than a quarter of all 18–21 year olds in employment in 2010 worked in the retail sector, albeit many on a part-time basis. Other jobs include, for example, work in bars, in fast food outlets, and in all sort of care, whether for children or for the growing numbers of elderly people.

Jobs in care work, in particular, are ones where the attributes of white working-class masculinity are seen as diametrically opposed to the skills needed to provide the types of close personal care for bodies that constitutes such a large part of the work involved. Women, however, are assumed to be ideal workers as they are assumed to be more at ease with the messy, leaky boundaries of the human body and the demands it makes for comfort and solace. Other jobs at the low paid end of the service sector demand a particular type of deferential performance. They too are 'feminised' forms of employment, drawing on stereotypical attributes of femininity included docility, empathy with the needs of others, and an ability to produce a courteous 'smiling' performance in exchanges with customers and clients, often under stressful conditions. These are attributes that many working-class young men find offensive to the sense of themselves as men (Connell 2000, Mac an Ghaill 1994). Thus they are excluded by their class, gender and embodied performance of masculinity from the only jobs available to them. In the penultimate section of the chapter, we turn to a recent empirical exploration of patterns of exclusion and the consequences for young men on the margins of the labour market, showing how their construction either or both as yobs and as failures, in official discourse and in their own narratives, exacerbates their labour market marginality.

In and out of work in Swindon

In 2012, ACEVO produced an analysis of youth unemployment 'hot spots' in the UK, places where the rates of young people claiming Job Seekers' Allowance were twice the national average. As well as the 'usual suspects' (deindustrialised towns in Britain's peripheries, certain London Boroughs and inner areas of major cities), Swindon, in Wiltshire, was on the list. Despite its location in the south of the UK and its reasonably buoyant local economy, the fastest expanding jobs in Swindon, as in many British towns and cities, were those at the bottom end of the labour market. Especially for young men with few educational credentials, little social capital and/or workplace-related skills, jobs in the consumer services sector including fast food, work in hotels and catering and in the retail sector, were the only options. Unqualified either for skilled jobs in the car industry (Honda in Swindon employed 3500 in April 2012) or for clerical employment in local government services or for other forms of state employment (the UK Research Council in Swindon is a major employer), working-class young men found their prospects limited. As the recession deepened in 2012, the labour market in Swindon became increasingly inhospitable: Honda introduced a four day week at the end of the year, the public sector began a programme of cuts and declining disposable incomes hit the consumer services sector. For these reasons, we decided to investigate the consequences of the financial crisis and austerity for working-class young men, both British-born and in-migrants, whose labour market disadvantage was increasing. In the context of a general crisis of youth unemployment, it seemed important not to neglect the sort of 'ordinary towns' like Swindon.[1] Our aim was not only to explore the ways in which young men's labour market attachments have become increasingly precarious but also to address the extent of or exclusion from forms of civic engagement. In this chapter we look in particular at the ways in which young men expressed their own sense of their construction as masculine as a disadvantage or a social problem. Although we did not discuss the different representations of youth in the media with the young men to whom we talked, their own interpretation of how they are perceived both fell into and challenged the binary stereotypes we outlined above. Through the words of two young men, we explore the rhetoric of blame, the use of terminology such as yobs, and the resentment, resignation and coping strategies common among both 'bad boys' and 'sad boys' on the margins of Swindon's labour market.

---

1 This study is the first part of a comparative analysis of youth unemployment and marginality in Swindon and Luton, funded by the Leverhulme Trust as part of the Oxford Diasporas Programme. The first stage in Swindon in 2012 involved interviews with 38 young men, as well as a small number of interviews with employment agencies, college and other youth service providers and employers. A similar survey will be carried out in Luton in 2013. The interviewees include white British, white EU, and men from BME communities, born in and outside the UK.

Masculinity as a threat

Tom is a 25-year-old British-born white man, who was unemployed and living in a hostel in September 2012. He was adopted at the age of ten when his birth mother began a jail sentence. Tom had been living independently since the age of 18 when he left the home of his adoptive parents after a major disagreement. He had been working in casual jobs but became homeless when an arrangement with friends fell through. After living on the streets for a short while, Tom found hostel accommodation, but as the rent exceeded his weekly earnings, he stopped looking for work and so qualified for job seekers allowance and housing benefit. At the time of the interview he was volunteering at a charity, organised through the local Job Centre. Despite emphasising that he was a reformed character as he was the father of a three year old son, Tom told us he had been involved in various sorts of illegal activities, including theft and arson. He also had what he termed 'a little crack habit'. He acknowledged that he might be seen as 'bad' but justified the reputation of young men like him as follows:

> There's nothing [jobs] out here and I reckon that's why the crime's gone up … I go round town and I drop a cv in there, there, there and it's always in the back of my mind at the end of the day, are they going to get in contact with me again? And it just feel like it's I give them the cv and they are just screwing it up and chucking it in their pocket. So at the end of the day, that's why crime's gone up. Young people like myself … are committing crime to support, getting money for a habit or doing anything else possible.

He later expanded on this comment:

> It depends what young people, like younger than myself, are willing to do at the end of the day just to get their point across. And that's just like smashing something up or breaking the law somehow, just to think, 'Look at me. I'm doing this just to break the peace'. So it is quiet [now] but sometimes it does get out of control.

There is an interesting echo here of some of the comments made by the young people involved in the urban unrest in English cities in August 2011 and their claim that policy makers ignored them until they made trouble (Newburn 2011).

Despite Tom's insistence that he was a responsible father, he recognised that his life was, in his words, 'a bit rough'. One of his friends died recently 'one of my mates died outside of town, got stabbed'. Although his aim is to 'just try to step back' when trouble arises, he knows he has a reputation as trouble maker and is likely to be picked up by the police:

> They all know me, that's the thing … It's not good but it's the situations I've been in at the end of the day when I've broken the law. And the thing is, I can't

> blame nobody else … If I didn't get myself a name, if I kept out of trouble by the police then I'd be walking down the road like a normal person and they wouldn't even acknowledge me … [but] I got myself a label when I was younger as a thug, as a yob. Now I have stepped back … the best label I've got now is to be a Dad. Before it was a thug, druggie, alcy, whatever.

Despite Tom's change of heart he feels that he is judged as a trouble-maker by others, not only the police but potential employers and the general public:

> People probably look at me like 'ah, he's just a yob, he's a yob' … you go around town, you hang around in a big group and nobody knows your inside story, like what I went through, what I have done in my life. They just thinks 'oh, he's a yob; he's a thug; he causes trouble; he gets in trouble with the police; he does this every single day. He gets drunk, he gets drugged up and all that lot' and people just judge you before they see you.

And he concluded, despite his resolution to step aside, 'If something really bad happens on the street and it involves me, then obviously I have to deal with it.' As many of the other young men told us, 'We go out drinking and then we cause a little trouble.'

Masculine failure

Tom's narrative of his own life is a classic example of a particular form of working-class protest masculinity, although it is not without contradictions. The tenderness which infused his comments about his young son, for example, belied his tougher, macho version of himself. Nevertheless he fell into, and to an extent concurred with, the public view of young men as yobs. In the next sketch, we explore the other side of the popular discourse: boys as 'sad lads' or failures as individualised neo-liberal subjects.

Darren, also white and born in Britain, who was 21 in 2012, falls into the category of young men as failures, as the sort of 'sad lad' identified in the media as at risk of depression or worse. He was permanently excluded from school from the age of 13 but was later offered a place in a special unit for difficult pupils where, with the help of individual tuition, he passed several GCSEs and began, but did not complete, an A level course.[2] As he explained:

---

2 GCSEs are the qualification taken at the end of the period of compulsory schooling in England that is aged 16 and A levels are a higher level qualification usually taken after two years of further study.

> I went to a place for kids who've got kicked out of school and I went for five hours a week. At school I never did well in my lessons but I went there and I did amazing. I got Bs and Cs and stuff, just because I had nothing to distract me.

However, once he left, his life fell apart again, as he developed a serious drug habit which resulted in ineligibility for Job Seeker's Allowance. Instead he was classified as sick and so receives a sickness allowance which prohibits him from waged work, although volunteering is permitted. His life between 16 and 21 was marked by homelessness, a short period in prison, and unemployment: 'My Mum kicked me out when I was 15 and I started living in hostels when I was 16.' Between the ages of 16 and 21, he lived in the main in a hostel for homeless men – 'they have been housing me since I was 16 for three months at a time and they've seen me homeless. I have lived here [a particular hostel] ten times since I was 16.' However, as he told us he had recently been offered the chance to live in 'move-on' accommodation, where 'they only put the people who are doing well at the moment'.

As Darren went on to explain, in the hostel where he had been living, which accepts anyone (if there is a vacancy) 'you get alcoholics, drug addicts, it's for literally homeless, living on the streets homeless' and so it is hard to construct anything approaching a regular life. He was currently on probation as 'I am what is called a PPO, persistent and prolific offender, so I've got to see a probation officer'. Despite his failure at school, in the labour market, and to stay clean, Darren accepted that it was his responsibility to try and turn his life round:

> If I don't do anything with my life then I'll lose that place [the move-on accommodation]. All the stuff I am doing now (volunteering and writing for a local magazine started by his drug worker) I've organised myself … you have to be doing something, you can't just do nothing.

In a society that values individual success and financial self-sufficiency, especially for men, as a marker of worth, Darren might appear as a failure. Nevertheless, his own optimism and his local knowledge of ways to survive through access not only to the welfare system but also forms of voluntary aid (for example, soup kitchens, places to sleep when homeless) meant that he is hanging in on the margins of society in a cruel climate for young men with no material advantages. In many ways, Tom and Darren's lives were similar and the distinctions between them small. Tom's own categorisation of himself as a 'bad boy' lay in his greater susceptibility to involvement in petty crime and involvement in threatening behaviour in public spaces. Both of them were significantly disadvantaged, and yet both retained an optimism that things would look up eventually.

Conclusions: responses to youth unemployment

In both of the popular discursive constructions of young men there is a strong moral and judgemental strand. In a neo-liberal world in which individuals are assumed to be the narrators of their own lives, young men are expected to be active agents in the production of themselves as satisfactory employable subjects. Neither Tom nor Darren is able to measure up. In this concluding section we briefly address two sides of the same issue: the response of official providers to youth unemployment and the decisions made by young men in the face of their disadvantaged position in the labour market. Through training, participation in 'work-ready' programmes and constant job search, the presumed aim of young men's lives is to find waged work. As Connell (2000) argued, the very definition of masculinity assumes employment and the willingness to provide through work. This notion infuses official schemes and the rhetoric of many providers of youth training services, although their success in an era of high unemployment is not guaranteed. Indeed, critics of current schemes have suggested that the aim of many of them is simply to warehouse young men, removing them, at least temporarily from the figures for those who are NEET. Among the 38 young men we talked to in Swindon, more than half had been recruited to at least one training programme. Tom's experience is interesting, although atypical. He found when he turned up at the local college that he had been enrolled, he assumed by mistake, on a childcare course where he was the only man in a class of young women. He did stick the course out and found a number of temporary short term jobs in related areas but found being a man in a feminised field was often an issue for potential employers and so he could not obtain secure employment. In an ironic echo of the arguments that employment in the new economy is increasingly based on the construction 'portfolio' pathways (Carnoy 2000) in which individuals sell themselves on the basis of diverse experience in different jobs, Darren explained that he was required by the housing agency to produce 'a resettlement folio'. 'I have to build up a folder of evidence of the things that I have done … the work and whether I was good or not go in that'.

Among many of the young men themselves, we found a resigned acceptance of their marginality and a perhaps not irrational decision to make a life for themselves outside the boundaries of the labour market. Although MacDonald (2008) makes strong claims about the willingness of young people on the margins of the labour market to search for and persist with employment, even in boring ill-paid jobs, we found an alternative rhetoric to the stalwart clinging to a view that being a man means labour market participation. A number of the young men we spoke to wove strands of protest and 'worthy' manliness into their narratives in complex and contradictory ways in the face of not holding conventional paid work, and not necessarily seeking it. These men on the margins of the labour market constructed an alternative version of masculine respectability through fatherhood and friendship, valuing and enjoying life and living in the moment, or simply through their capacity to survive in difficult circumstances. In this way, young men often positioned themselves in ambivalent ways in relation to the neoliberal norm of acceptable masculine subjectivity and citizenship as equated with self-sufficiency and self-responsibility. While many, like Darren, held themselves accountable for their marginality, at the same time, some resisted their marginality and dependency as necessarily implying masculine inadequacy by highlighting other ways of performing masculinity. There is a tendency in popular discourse to represent young men as if they are either good or bad, angels or devils: a temptation which Back (2007: 157) noted is particularly prevalent in writing about marginal and excluded groups. As we have shown here, binary distinctions deny the complexity of the lives of young men struggling in the margins of an austere new world.

References

Adkins, L. 2002. *Revisions: Gender and Sexuality in Late Modernity*. Buckingham: Open University Press.

Alcock, P., Beatty, C., Fothergill, S., Macmillan, R. and Yeandle, S. 2003. *Work to Welfare: How Men Become Detached from the Labour Market.* Cambridge: Cambridge University Press.

Alexander, C. 2000. *The Asian Gang: Ethnicity, Identity, Masculinity*. Oxford: Berg.

ACEVO Commission on Youth Unemployment. 2012. *Youth Unemployment: The Crisis We Cannot Afford.* London: ACEVO Commission on Youth Unemployment.

Back, L. 2007. *The Art of Listening*. Oxford: Berg.

Beck, U. 2000. *The Brave New World of Work.* Cambridge: Polity Press.

Birdwell, J. 2011. *The Forgotten Half.* London: Demos.

Bourgois, P. 1995. *In Search of Respect: Selling Crack in El Barrio*. Cambridge: Cambridge University Press.

Brush, L. 1999. Gender, work, who cares?, in *Revisioning Gender*, edited by M.M. Ferree, J. Lorber and B. Hess. London: Sage Publications, 18–42.

Carnoy, M. 2000. *Sustaining the New Economy: Work, Family and Community in the Information Age.* New York and Cambridge Mass: Russell Sage Foundation and Harvard University Press.

Castells, M. 2000. Materials for an exploratory theory for the network society. *British Journal of Sociology*, 51(1), 5–22.

Critcher, C. (ed.) 2006. *Critical Readings: Moral Panics and the Media.* Buckingham: Open University Press.

Cohen, R. 2010. Rethinking 'mobile' work: boundaries of space, time and social relation in the working lives of mobile hairstylists. *Work, Employment and Society*, 24(1), 65–84.

Cohen, S. 1973. *Folk Devils and Moral Panics* London: Routledge.

Connell, R.W. 1995. *Masculinities.* Berkeley: University of California Press.

Connell, R.W. 2000. *The Men and the Boys*. Cambridge: Polity Press.

Crompton, R.W. 2010. Class and employment. *Work, Employment and Society*, 24(1), 9–26.

Delamont, S. 2000. The anomalous beasts: hooligans and the sociology of education. *Sociology*, 34(2), 95–111.

Fine, M. and Weiss, L. 1998. *The Unknown City: The Lives of Poor and Working Class Young Adults*. Boston: Beacon Press.

Gallagher, I. 2011. Generation betrayed by bogus promises: Our failing schools are 'forcing UK films to choose foreign workers. *Daily Mail* [online: 20 November] Available at: www.dailymail.co.uk/news/article-2063739 [accessed 17 December 2012].

Goos, M. and Manning, A. 2003. McJobs and MacJobs: the growing polarisation of jobs in the UK, in *The Labour Market Under New Labour*, edited by R. Dickens, P. Gregg and J. Wadsworth. Basingstoke: Palgrave Macmillan, 70–85.

Howker, E. 2012. It'll take more than back-combing tutorials to bridge the generation gap. *The Guardian* [online 16 August] Available at: http://www.theguardian.com/commentisfree/2012/aug/15/bridge-generation-gap?INTCMP=SRCH [accessed 17 December 2012].

Ignatiev, N. 1996. *How the Irish Became White*. London: Routledge.

Jones, O. 2011. *Chavs: The Demonization of the Working Class*. London: Verso.

Kaplan, R. 1996. *The Ends of the Earth: A Journey at the Dawn of the 21st Century*. New York: Random House.

Leidner, R. 1993. *Fast Food, Fast Talk: Service Work and the Routinization of Everyday Life*. Berkeley: University of California Press.

Mac an Ghaill, M. 1994. *The Making of Men: Masculinities, Sexualities and Schooling*. Buckingham: Open University Press.

MacDonald, R. 2008. Disconnected youth? Social exclusions, the 'underclass' and economic marginality. *Social Work and Society*, 6(2), 236–248.

MacDonald, R., Shildrick, T. and Blackman, S. (eds) 2010. *Young People, Class and Place*. London: Routledge.

McDowell, L. 2003. *Redundant Masculinities?* Oxford: Wiley-Blackwell.

McDowell, L. 2009. *Working Bodies: Interactive Service Employment and Workplace Identities*. Oxford: Wiley-Blackwell.

McDowell, L. 2012. Post-crisis, post-Ford and post-gender? Youth identities in an era of austerity. *Journal of Youth Studies*, 15(5), 573–590.

McRobbie, A. 2009. *The Aftermath of Feminism: Gender, Culture and Social Change*. London: Sage Publications.

McRobbie, A. 2011. Reflections on feminism, immaterial labour and the post-Fordist regime. *New Formations*, 70(1), 60–76.

Mount, F. 2004. *Mind the Gap: The New Class Divide in Britain*. London: Short Books.

Nayak, A. 2003. Last of the 'real Geordies'? White masculinities and the subcultural response to deindustrialisation. *Environment and Planning D: Society and Space*, 21(11), 7–25.

Newburn, T. 2011. *Reading the Riots: Investigating England's Summer of Disorder.* London: London School of Economics and Political Science (LSE) and The Guardian.

Noble, G. 2007. Respect and respectability amongst second generation Arab and Muslim Australian men. *Journal of Intercultural Studies*, 28(3), 331–344.

Office of National Statistics (ONS). 2011. *Statistical Bulletin*, 19 January, London.

Pearson, G. 1983. *Hooligan: A History of Respectable Fears*. London: Palgrave Macmillan.

Roediger, D. 1999. *The Wages of Whiteness: Race and the Making of the American Working Class.* London: Verso.

Skeggs, B. 2004. *Class, Self, Culture*. London: Routledge.

Tilly, C. 1998. *Durable Inequality*. Berkeley: University of California Press.

Willis, P. 1977. *Learning to Labour: How Working Class Kids get Working Class Jobs*. London: Hutchinson.

Wolkowitz, C. 2002. The social relations of body work. *Work, Employment and Society*, 16(4), 497–510.

Wolkowitz, C. 2006. *Bodies at Work*. London: Sage Publications.

Chapter 25
Masculinity in the Marketplace: Geographies of Post-Colonial Gender Work in Modern Fiji

Geir-Henning Presterudstuen

Introduction

Although many Fijians construct ideal notions of social life and organisation outside the market economy and often explicitly argue that Fijian tradition was incompatible with the capitalist economy, modernity has brought an increasing amount of Fijians into direct and more frequent contact with the marketplace.

However, throughout this development the native Fijians remained in a cultural sphere largely independent and separate from these modern dynamics until quite recently, 'insulated by colonial policy from the workings of the capitalist market' (Kelly 1992: 98). In fact, even in contemporary Fiji, the relationship between Fijians and the dynamics of the modern economy has remained ambiguous and conflictual, based on an ideology which draws a distinct dividing line between Fijian traditional practices and 'the way of money'. By focusing my discussion on these two spheres as 'domains of difference' (Bhabha 1994: 2), I argue that the modern marketplace is a site for complex, ongoing negotiations between conflicting discourses about masculinity which frame indigenous Fijian men's gender identification in post-colonial Fiji.

Based on observations and field studies I discuss findings pointing to the continuous, complex relationship between notions of Fijian tradition and the dynamics of the market economy and how Fijian men attempted to negotiate these two concepts to perform valorised masculine performances in a changing, social context.

In fact, men's complicated relationship to waged work and money appears to be at the core of many men's struggle to position themselves as dominant men within the changing Fijian social sphere, highlighting the interplay between notions of tradition, modernity and masculinity.

A key argument of this chapter is that colonial and post-colonial policies have discursively created the modern marketplace and village Fiji as two diametrically opposite domains of difference. Urban, commercial space and exogenous, Western culture are conflated concepts in this discourse, where modernity is constructed in direct contrast to traditional Fiji. The Fijian post-colonial condition, then, is at once temporal and spatial, in the sense that modernity is explained based on these two interrelated metaphors. Drawing upon postcolonial theories, I propose the argument that it is in these in-between spaces, the third spaces 'where the negotiation of incommensurable differences create a tension peculiar to borderline existences' (Bhabha 1994: 312), that notions of masculine and ethno-cultural identities are articulated and performed.

Postcolonial theorists have, despite their pre-supposition with identities, cultural transformations and nationalism, often focussed their attention on texts rather than social practice. There is, however, much in postcolonial theory that can aid us in thinking 'beyond narratives of originary and initial subjectivities', such as gender, race or ethnicity, and challenge officialised histories by focusing on 'moments and processes that are produced in the articulation of cultural differences' (Bhabha 1994: 2). These frameworks, I suggest, are particularly useful in understanding the formations of gendered and ethno-cultural self-identities in particular contexts.

Maintaining that masculinity is a social performance, attained through a complex process of socialisation which comprises historical, geographical, social, economic, political and ethno-cultural factors, I consequently set up my discussion with a brief analysis of the emergence of the capitalist economy in Fiji and its impact on discourses about gender and masculinity. This chapter thus draws upon the principles of historical anthropology, which seeks to combine a trans-historical analysis with thick, ethnographic description. The ethnographic data utilised here was collected by means of participant observation and informal interviews in urban settlements and villages in the western parts of Fiji's main island, Viti Levu, in 2009 and 2010.

Capital and colonialism in Fiji

Although processes of globalization and international capitalism have recently intensified the impact of the market economy on Fijians' everyday lives, the relationship between different economic spheres has been somewhat continuous since European capitalism started to significantly influence Fijian islands at the turn of the eighteenth century. The influx of foreign capital from sandalwood and beche-de-mer trade in eastern Fiji created a duality which came to be a central force in the shaping of modern Fiji; Anglo-Australasian industrial and settler capital and local, predominantly eastern, chiefs' control over land and labour resources (Britton 1980: 254). The cession of Fiji's sovereignty to Great Britain in 1874, and the following arrival of the first cargo ship with Indian recruits on Fijian shores in March 1879 marked the advent of modernity and formalised the union between the eastern Fijian chiefs and international capital forces.

The colonial history of Fiji stands out in many ways, most strikingly in this sense the extensive complicity local elites showed in implementing new power regimes. In return, colonial administrators set up a system of indirect rule, where the eastern Fijian chiefs were given paramountcy and recognition for their immediate interest. Indeed, British colonial domination in Fiji was not characterised by formal coercion as much as by 'the ability of the imperial system to have its main social tenets accepted as appropriate forms of behaviour and ordering' by, if not the bulk of the colonised population at least the local elite (Stoddart 1988: 650).

In practical terms this meant developing an economic system equally concerned about preserving the viability of the village-based subsistence economy and ensuring prosperity for European settlers and investors. This seemingly incongruous economic situation was a direct reason for the decision to import Indian labourers, and has been a defining aspect of Fijian economics and development since.

From the outset of colonialism, the modern Fijian state was structured around the notion of Fiji as a three-legged stool, resting upon European money, Indian labour and Fijian land as equally important sources of national prosperity. This was a central aspect of the national ethos throughout the twentieth century, and became entrenched as the way to understand economic dynamics (Kelly 1992, Trnka 2005). Under these provisions Fijians' traditional economy and subsistence-based village lifestyles were to be protected from capital forces and modernity, while the imported Indian labour class would bear the brunt of manual labour and production work. The vast majority of Fijian land consequently became inalienable by law and came to be viewed by native Fijians as their guarantee to economic prosperity as well as political supremacy (France 1969, Lawson 1996).

Land has famously been crucial in the discourses surrounding the political conflicts that have affected modern Fiji, and remains at the core of discussions of economic distribution and social organisation. In Indigenous Fiji, 'money must often be tied discursively to social locations such as "clans", villages, and church congregations' (Tomlinson 2004b: 190). Through these complex interactions between Fijian tradition and modernity land consequently became inscribed with a multitude of meanings. In fact, land came to be discursively constructed as the entity which simultaneously connected indigenous Fijians with modernity and distinguished indigenous Fijians from others.

The concept of land which became officialised in Fijian tradition and legislation during this process is encompassed in the notion of *vanua*. Although frequently translated directly as land or place (Capell 1991: 255), *vanua* has far wider connotations, socially, culturally as well as politically (Ravuvu 1987: 14–15). As a discursive concept it signifies larger groups of people who recognise social or political allegiances and their relationship to the land. It thus 'embodies the values and beliefs which people of a particular locality have in common' (Ravuvu 1987: 14–15). More so, the relationship between Fijians and the *vanua* is all-encompassing and sacred; often summarised by the notion of *I cauviti*, meaning 'Man and land are one' (Tuwere 1992: 34).

Tradition in the Fijian sense is understood through the concept of *cakacaka vakavanua*, often translated as 'acting in accordance with the land' in this extended sense (Toren 1988: 712). Contrary to Western perceptions of tradition then, it refers to culturally appropriate behaviour rather than a notion of 'objectified structures' in the past (Toren 1988: 696). Hence, just as 'events and the presence of past events in the present are determined by the way a group or an individual is related to the past in an ongoing process of symbolic mediation' (Dickhardt 2005: 344), tradition is understood and constructed in contemporary Fiji as praxis which is beneficial and in accordance with the *vanua*. Fijian villages thus became the crucial site for the maintenance of Fijian tradition and the construction of ethno-cultural identities in opposition to alien cultural forces.

Conversely, whatever is spatially located outside the village settings may also be ideologically and culturally removed from indigenous Fiji. Underpinned by the idea that modern life and engagement in the market economy was intrinsically detrimental to Fijian culture and their well-being, these principles was crucial in the development of the particular space-economy which remains a central aspect of everyday life in contemporary Fiji; indigenous Fijians desire to 'live off the land' while European and Indo-Fijians profess the *bula vaka ilavo*, 'the life of money'.

Domains of difference

Symbolically these two spheres are constructed as diametrically opposed, a dichotomy which takes on both spatial and ideological meanings. While the *bula vaka ilavo* is performed in an urban market place and centred on material gains, selfishness and individuality (Williksen-Bakker 1995: 220), 'the Fijian way' is played out in the village and the *vanua*, and represents ideas and values such as respect, care, love and selflessness (Ravuvu 1987).

I focus on this dichotomy and how it influences gendered and cultural self-identification for contemporary Fijian men through their everyday practices. What is particularly interesting is that while contemporary Fijian urban spaces provide room for more frequent, intensive and consequential confrontations with the marketplace, discourses about the intrinsic opposition between Fijianness and the market economy remains. While most indigenous Fijians today consider the market economy an inevitable force of contemporary society and business a social reality which everyone needs to engage with, notions that business and money is ultimately antithetical to traditional Fijian values and structures circulate widely in everyday discourses.

Although arguably an inversion of colonial discourses using spatial metaphors to designate 'the global south' both temporally and geographically distant from modernity and progress, these discourses reinforce similar dichotomies. As with most other social dynamics in Fiji, a society marked by its 'obsession with race' (Lal 2003: 347), these demarcations are strictly racialised. In indigenous Fijian discourses, moral evaluations ascribed to the different economic spheres are generally transposed onto the individuals 'at home' there and given meaning in racial terms; Indo-Fijians and Europeans are money-driven, individualistic and shifty, while Fijians are communal, selfless and non-materialistic.

It is tempting to see this as an inverted consequence of the colonial discourse of protectionism based on racial categorisation. Rather than being a benign strategy to protect Fijian interests, Emberson-Bain argues that colonial economic policies were based on 'imperial notions of cultural superiority and paternalism' that promoted a modern Fijian nation state in which 'racialist values legitimised divergent forms of social and economic discrimination' (Emberson-Bain 1994: 82). Indeed, Fijian men were considered unsuitable for effective economic production because they were, in the words of an inspector of mines, 'careless, unreliable, inclined to take unnecessary risks and mentally lethargic' (quoted in Emberson-Bain 1994: 82).

Many Fijians have both internalised and embraced these racialised colonial assumptions about their ability and willingness to complete work and conduct labour in a timely manner. The distinction between 'Fiji time' and 'European time' is commonly articulated, and explained as being a fundamental aspect of a set of culturally specific reasons why Fijians perceive themselves at odds with modern labour processes. Joe explained how visiting teachers from the United States who were placed in their village school outside Lautoka for six months as part of a development programme had to rely upon 'European workers' to complete their living quarters, because he and his village comrades were unable to complete it in 'European time' rather than 'spend five, six months … doing bits and pieces here and leaving it for a while … while we do other bits and pieces' according to Fijian time.

The Fijian labour pattern was often displayed in the villages I visited, where a group of men could frequently spend the whole working day completing a very limited amount of work. Masi[1] explained this by the notion that village life was often organised around a principle of 'doing what's necessary today, and everything else tomorrow'. Having caught enough fish or gathered sufficient vegetables for one day's consumption, the men involved in the task would then spend the rest of the day drinking *yaqona*[2] or relaxing.

Similarly, the racialised notions of lazy native Fijians are selectively used to affirm manhood and male power in Fijian village settings. 'In Fiji, the man is the boss', Samuel proclaimed, 'so while we discuss matters and have *yaqona*, the women have to do the farm work and cooking.' In a separate village, some of my male respondents pointed out how they were napping during the day while their women completed their housework or other domestic duties such as weaving or cleaning, and teased me with the point that 'European women make you guys run around' completing chores. The colonial perception of laziness, or at least reluctance to do hard manual work, enabled them to construct a notion of the unreliable native Fijian. This, in turn, is embraced and selectively utilised by

1 All respondents are referred to via pseudonyms.

2 Yaqona is the Fijian name for the root of the piper methysticum plant which is dried, pounded and mixed with water to create a slightly narcotic drink of significant ceremonial and social importance throughout Oceania.

Fijian men as an emblematic symbol of male power in the contemporary Fijian villages I visited.

These dynamics are thus also gendered. In the indigenous pre-capitalist subsistence economy which characterises village, the cultivation and gathering of substantial foods, namely root crops and other hearty vegetables are generally considered masculine pursuits, making men at once the main breadwinners and the ones more closely connected to the *vanua* than women. This is of course underpinned by the patriarchal nature of officialised Fijian tradition where both symbolic and actual power are closely linked to culturally specific notions of masculinity to the extent that masculinity is seen as emblematic of Fijianness.

Indeed, the trinity of *turagaism*, the notion of inherent chiefly rights to leadership, *lotu* – which is the Fijian Christian ideology – and militarism, which is at the core of Fijian power structures, is integral to what I call Fijian notions of hegemonic masculinity. Hegemonic masculinity is best defined as an 'ideal type of masculinity that imposes upon all other masculinities (and femininities) coherence and meaning about what their own identities and positions within the gender order should be' (Howson 2006: 3, Connell 1987: 98–99). In Fiji, then, this ideal is discursively linked to Fijian history and tradition and both geographically and ideologically located within the village setting.

In practical terms this means that men go to great lengths to emphasise their understanding of Fijian tradition. Respect for the chiefly office and devotion to Christianity are performed through both rituals and everyday social practices, through both words and actions. Posture, gestures and more elaborate bodily movements, such as working the land, keeping in shape and playing sport, a modern link to traditional martial prowess (see Presterudstuen 2010), are all constructed as constitutive practices for masculinity and ways to act out Fijian ethno-cultural identity. Masculinity is also spatially linked to the village, and villages clearly reflect the gendered hierarchy. Men are generally more visible in the village common areas and are responsible for the cultivation and protection of communal land. Positions of dwellings within the village parameters follow relatively strict conventions in relation to power hierarchies and divisions of labour which are largely based on masculine status positions, such as *turaga* (chief), *matanivanua* (herald), *bati* (warrior) or *gonedau* (fisherman). Similarly, the positioning of bodies within buildings follow both gender and status demarcations emphasising male authority.

Many of my respondents extended this logic to include the notion that it is more problematic for men to engage in market ventures than women. 'A man's place is in the *koro* (village)', one local chief explained, 'as he needs to attend to his traditional obligations full time.' He contrasted directly with women, who, while undeniably important to life in the village, 'have much weaker ties to the village … and less important positions in the traditional system' and thus can more easily do tasks and take on responsibilities outside the village.

Men's engagement in the modern economic sphere is understood as more problematic, as their absence from the traditional village exacerbates the risks and vulnerabilities associated with 'the way of money'. Just as it is clear that this demarcation is, at least partly, a colonial product it is obvious that it is a defining aspect of post-colonial Fiji, and was a common theme in my discussion with Fijian men and their ambiguity towards the market economy.

The infirmity of the model of the three-legged stool to sustain a national policy on economy post-colonisation became apparent with the withdrawal of colonial money, and most villagers today experience increasing difficulties in living off their own produce. The frailty of land as a guarantee for economic prosperity has been effectively demonstrated through the lack of monetary rewards that followed re-indigenisation of previously leased agricultural land and the increasing level of poverty in contemporary Fijian villages. It consequently becomes increasingly difficult to sustain a space-economy based on a distinction between traditional Fiji and the modern 'life of money'.

Additionally, young Fijian men in urban locations are under growing pressure from broader social dynamics to engage more directly with international market forces in terms of gaining education, employment or take part in cultural and material consumption. While the importance of tradition and custom remains important in most Fijian men's understanding and construction of their masculine identity, the impact of modernity is becoming increasingly evident in contemporary Fiji. Brij V. Lal (2009: 428) recently pointed this out in relation to the role of the chiefs: 'The power of chiefs to decide the destinies of their people, to be their sole spokesmen and intermediaries with the outside, has long gone as travel, technology, education, the effects of competitive market economy and exposure to broader forces of change have altered the fabric of Fijian society.'

While the traditional power structures provide status and authority for the higher strata of chiefs, clergy and elders, I encountered many young Fijian men during my fieldwork whose experience of the traditional village system was that it could not provide opportunities for developing the competency and capital necessary to succeed in modernising, urban Fiji. They struggled to negotiate the traditional expectations associated with manhood in modern settings, often experiencing traditional responsibilities as constraining them from fully participating in contemporary settings.

Hence, while village Fiji and the modern marketplace are constructed as two markedly different social spheres both geographically and ideologically, the relationship between these domains of difference is continuous rather than strictly separated. Bhabha (1994: 2) asserts that the 'social articulation of difference, from the minority perspective, is a complex, on-going negotiation that seeks to authorize cultural hybridities that emerge in moments of historical transformation' rather than a one-way process of cultural domination. When Fijians maintain the idea that the Fijian village is nucleus of traditional life and a spatial site removed from the cash economy and urban centres are not only the geographical space of market transactions but also ideologically linked to the pursuit of wealth and profit, while also engaging with the market economy is an example of such cultural negotiation. Ultimately these practices have the potential to 'intervene and dislocate processes of domination through re-interpreting and redeploying dominant discourses', highlighting how the 'spaces where differences meet becomes important' (McEwan 2009: 65, Bhabha 1994).

In practical terms these hybrid constructions take on peculiar forms. In discussions with my respondents money often came to symbolise everything that was un-Fijian and thus everything which was morally questionable in the Fijian context. While village life is considered free, in touch with nature, harmonious and conflict free, based on community, respect and reciprocal exchange, the 'way of money' that allegedly characterises the lives of Indo-Fijians and Europeans is seen to be driven by greed and selfishness, to be exploitative and associated with a lifestyle full of stress and moral contamination. However, most of these respondents would actively seek out opportunities for obtaining cash, including taking part in regular employment.

While the process of attaining money in a capitalist system, through such means as being employed full-time and receiving a pay check from wage work, was seen as undesirable and morally detrimental by many of my respondents, having money 'in their hand' on occasions, was often enviable. In fact, such respondents as Jimmy and Ione could spend considerable time criticising my way of 'chasing money' and label the perceived Western focus on money and wealth as 'shallow and wrong' in stark contrast to their own village-based righteous and selfless communalism. They would then end the conversation by asking me for a 20 dollar note to buy take-away food, beer or *yaqona*, and, if successful, another two dollars for transportation home.

This was a rather common occurrence during my fieldwork, particularly when I spent time with respondents outside the village setting. At times I enquired about the moral viability of such a practice based on their frequently articulated ethical reservations about making money, and it was explained that 'Fijians know money is gonna do no good' and that was why they did not want to 'fill the pockets' on regular basis. Joe, after obtaining ten dollars from a generous, and generously intoxicated, Australian tourist, told me he 'better rid [him]self' of them fast before they were lost, and maintained that he was glad he did not have access to cash very often because when he did he 'got into bad habits … drinking beer, playing pool and roaming around town'.

By associating money with an un-Fijian, Western aspect of modern life and viewing spending money as intrinsically detrimental to their own Fijian values, these men paradoxically afforded themselves a license to freely spend cash they obtained in town on goods and practices they themselves labelled problematic. This practice was only acceptable because of the fluidity of the money and because they did not 'normally chase money', and as a result of their articulated aversion against 'filling [their] pockets with cash'. A major point also appeared to be that money that did not enter the village circulation had only limited ability to do moral damage; indeed, money appeared to be considered a negative force only when they 'begin to consort promiscuously, erasing in the shuffle the many boundaries between kinds of persons and kinds of relationship that people have worked hard to create through their exchange' (Robbins and Akin 1999: 7).

Matt Tomlinson has elaborated on this, based on what he called a 'metacultural complaint' he frequently heard during his fieldwork on the island of Kadavu; that commoners who are successful in business and make lots of money 'thought they were chiefs, and began acting like chiefs' (2004b: 193). Money in this sense became understood not only as a source of illegitimate power and inauthenticity, but also as a possible disturbance to the social system as the locus of the 'Fijian way'.

Although many Fijians are thoroughly Protestant, there is little resonance with the Weberian protestant ethic to use success in business as a personal, moral barometer in native Fijian discourse (Tomlinson 2004b: 194). Instead, material success and notions of being good in business are determined by how a person's 'handling of money benefits his or her kin group, church or other emblematic social institution' (Tomlinson 2004b: 194).

Chiefs, capital and moral decay

On the other hand, many contemporary Fijians have reversed these types of criticisms and directed them against chiefs who failed to act according to their position. This was often exemplified by their perception of the chiefs' mismanagement of communal funds and self-enriching enterprises at the expense of the wider *vanua*. Cash dividends yielded from land leased for tourism or industrial purposes were sometimes not used to benefit the *vanua*, but 'goes right in the pocket of the chief' as one respondent claimed, symbolising the deterioration of chiefly integrity in modern Fiji.

For many Fijian commoners in the village this moral decay of their chiefs is associated with their engagement with modernity or Western culture, both at a spatial and cultural level. As chiefs have, to an increasing extent, migrated towards the urban centres, many commoners such as Sefa, experienced 'a lost connection … [and] have no longer any idea what's happening in the village'. Moses, a farmer in a village in the highlands at the outskirts of Nadi, said his chief could no longer serve them well because 'he [was] never [t]here to listen' but was preoccupied with 'money issues and politics' in Suva. A third farmer from an urban village in western Viti Levu claimed the chief would 'shoot off as soon as lease money comes in [from leaseholders in the agricultural or tourism industry]' and was only in the village for 'ceremonies and presentations'.

The chiefly role in Fiji has traditionally been centred on the concept of *vakaturaga*, best translated as 'acting in chiefly manner', which is 'the most important concept depicting ideal behaviour among Indigenous Fijians' (Ravuvu 1987: 18). The *turaga*, the chief, is responsible for, and holds authority over, every matter related to the *vanua*, and the efficacy of his governance was at least partly based on his ability to know his place in the community and act out this authority appropriately (Halapua 2003: 111–112, Nayacakalou 1975). At the core of these notions was the idea that the chief would act selflessly according to the interests of his people, and the concept of *vakaturaga* ideally embodies 'respect and deference, compliance and humility, loyalty and honesty' (Ravuvu 1987: 18). A strong sense of these ideologies remained among the respondents I met in 2009, but I was surprised by the strength and intensity of dissatisfaction with the current state of the chiefly office in many villages.

The common theme in these narratives was one of decline and disruption, where the chiefly office and the concept of *vakaturaga* have both been spatially removed from the traditional setting by modernity and urbanism, and ideologically contaminated by capitalism. Williksen-Bakker has written insightfully on the importance of the spatial metaphor of business as a path followed by non-Fijians, located outside the village, in Fijian discourses (1995: 220). I argue that, rather than mere metaphor, this can be understood in more physical and real terms as the absence of chiefs, because they are pursuing business in Suva or sometimes overseas and this is seen as crucial to moral deterioration and social problems in the village.

While, as Tomlinson has argued, modernity in the spatial sense can be evaded and negotiated, by shunning Indo-Fijians and European traders and capitalism or simply not bringing money into the village (2004b: 191), this chiefly urban migration is a reality in many villages. Moreover, in a practical sense this lack of chiefly authority forces other villagers into the capital spheres to provide basic supplies for the village, such as fuel, kerosene and sugar.

More importantly though, a chief's efficacy is derived from the attention he receives from his subjects. This is played out in most practical settings, as the chief is sitting at the top of the room or in front of the *tanoa* (the wooden bowl in which *yaqona* is mixed and served) so everyone can face him and thus attend to him in any ceremonial or social setting (Tomlinson 2004a, Toren 1988, 1994). An absent chief cannot be attended upon, something which helps explain the frustration many commoners feel about these issues. Iko, a villager from a small agricultural village outside Nadi, lamented his chief's absence in this matter, claiming it made it 'impossible to keep up traditional life and obligations' and difficult to 'solve problems and make decisions the right way'.

Ideologically, it is also clear that chiefly authority loses some of its power when removed from the traditional setting and integrated into the competing cultural sphere of the market economy and the 'way of money'. By indulging in practices which are seen as benefiting themselves at the expense of the greater *vanua*, many contemporary chiefs were deemed both immoral and un-Fijian.

Ultimately the same critique is extended to most men who for one reason or another engage in the modern marketplace at the expense of their traditional village life. As bearers of Fijian tradition their absence is at once seen to undermine the welfare of the village and the power of their traditional leaders as well as weaken their own ethno-cultural identity.

However, the modernisation of Fijian society and the growth of primary and secondary industries have made it increasingly difficult for Fijian men to remain content with a traditional Fijian way of life that strictly limits their market participation. The rhetoric of pride in the 'Fijian way' as opposed to European and Indo-Fijians who presumably 'worship money' rings hollow when many Fijian men find that material paucity and financial hardships jeopardise their ability to partake in modern leisure activities, fulfil traditional village roles or look after their family. Urbanisation has accentuated these processes. In town, 'low wages become even more depressed owing to the costs of food and accommodation' and cities were often referred to as places that *kania nai lavu*, eat up money (Chapman 1991: 273).

Conclusions

Hence, while most Fijian men still subscribe to the ideology known since the outset of colonisation, claiming that engagement in the modern economy is both a practically and ethically incongruous enterprise for Indigenous Fijians, it is becoming increasingly difficult to construct an everyday life outside the modern marketplace. Modernity, and particularly the accumulation of wealth for personal use, is thus at once considered un-Fijian and in conflict with the 'Fijian way' and an inevitable fact that needs to be dealt with on a daily basis.

Paradoxically some engagement in trade or wage-work became a necessity in order to fulfil their traditional obligations as men towards kinship groups, family and church organisations for many of my respondents. This ambiguity comes to highlight their ambiguity towards modernity and tradition. Indeed, Fijian men's engagements with modernity and the market economy as well as their social constructions of such practices are manifestations of what Connell and Messerschmidt have poignantly referred to as the layering or 'potential internal contradiction' which is intrinsic to all practices used to construct masculinities (2005: 852).

Fijian men's apprehension against engaging in waged work or capitalist trade is also in marked contrast to how dominant notions of masculinity in the global north often are intrinsically linked to financial success and participation in the marketplace. For Fijian men, constructing and understanding their masculinities at the edge of the global, the relationship between gender, power and money is mediated by competing, local discourses about manhood and tradition that locate masculine power outside the market. Hence, it is clear that while local constructions of masculinity, to an increasing extent, are shaped and transformed by the workings of global capitalism, a sustained focus on local discourses and patterns of engagement with transnational market forces remains crucial for an understanding of culturally-specific masculinities that goes beyond classical dualisms like tradition and modernity, local and global (see also McDowell, Rootham and Hardgrove 2014: this volume, Warren 2014: this volume).

References

Bhabha, H. 1994. *The Location of Culture.* London: Routledge.

Britton, S. 1980. The evolution of a colonial space-economy: the case of Fiji. *Journal of Historical Geography*, 6(3), 251–74.

Capell, A. (ed.). 1991 [1941]. *The Fijian Dictionary.* Suva: Government Printer.

Chapman, M. 1991. Pacific Island movement and socioeconomic change: metaphors of misunderstanding. *Population and Development Review*, 17(2), 263–292.

Connell, R.W. 1987. *Gender and Power: Society, the Person, and Sexual Politics.* Cambridge: Polity Press.

Connell, R.W. and Messerschmidt, J.W. 2005. Hegemonic masculinity: rethinking the concept. *Gender and Society*, 19(6), 829–859.

Dickhardt, M. 2005. *Viti*, the soil from Eden: on historical praxis as a mode of connecting Kadavu. *Oceania*, 75(4), 342–353.

Emberson-Bain, A. 1994. *Labour and Gold in Fiji.* Cambridge: Cambridge University Press.

France, P. 1969. *The Charter of the Land: Custom and Colonization in Fiji.* Melbourne: Oxford University Press.

Halapua, W. 2003. *Tradition, Lotu and Militarism in Fiji.* Lautoka: Fiji Institute of Applied Studies.

Howson, R. 2006. *Challenging Hegemonic Masculinity.* London and New York: Routledge.

Kelly, J.D. 1992. Fiji Indians and 'commoditization of labor'. *American Ethnologist*, 19(1), 97–120.

Lal, B.V. 2003. Heartbreak islands: reflections in Fiji in transition. *Asia Pacific Viewpoint*, 44(3), 335–350.

Lal, B.V. 2009. One hand clapping: reflections on the first anniversary of Fiji's 2006 coup, in *The 2006 Military Takeover in Fiji: A Coup to End All Coups?*, edited by J. Fraenkel, S. Firth and B.V. Lal. Canberra: Australian National University E-press, 425–447.

Lawson, S. 1996. *Tradition Versus Democracy in the South Pacific: Fiji, Tonga and Western Samoa.* Cambridge: Cambridge University Press.

McEwan, C. 2009. *Postcolonialism and Development.* London and New York: Routledge.

Nayacakalou, R.R. 1975. *Leadership in Fiji.* Melbourne: Oxford University Press.

Presterudstuen, G.H. 2010. The mimicry of men: rugby and masculinities in post-colonial Fiji. *The Global Studies Journal*, 3(2), 237–248.

Ravuvu, A.D. 1987. *The Fijian Ethos.* Suva: Institute of Pacific Studies.

Robbins, J. and Akin, D. 1999. An introduction to Melanesian currencies: agency, identity, and social reproduction, in *Money and Modernity: State and Local Currencies in Melanesia*, edited by D. Akin and J. Robbins. Pittsburgh: University of Pittsburgh Press, 1–40.

Stoddart, B. 1988. Sport, cultural imperialism, and colonial response in the British Empire. *Comparative Studies in Society and History*, 30(4), 649–673.
Tomlinson, M. 2004a. Perpetual lament: kava-drinking, Christianity and sensations of historical decline in Fiji. *The Journal of the Royal Anthropological Institute*, 10(3), 653–673.
Tomlinson, M. 2004b. Memes and metaculture: the politics of discourse circulation in Fiji. *The Australian Journal of Anthropology*, 15(2), 185–197.
Toren, C. 1988. Making the present, revealing the past: the mutability and continuity of tradition as process. *Man*, 23(4), 696–717.
Toren, C. 1994. The drinker as chief or rebel: kava and alcohol in Fiji, in *Gender, Drink and Drugs*, edited by M. McDonald. Oxford: Berg, 153–174.
Trnka, S. 2005. Land, life and labour: Indo-Fijian claims to citizenship in a changing Fiji. *Oceania,* 75(4), 354–367.
Tuwere, I.S. 1992. *Making Sense of Vanua in the Fijian Context: A Theological Exploration.* PhD. Melbourne University of Divinity.
Williksen-Bakker, S. 1995. Ceremony and embodied memory in urbanized Fijian culture. *Bijdragen tot de Taal-, Land- en Volkenkunde*, 151(2), 218–234.

Chapter 26
Crafting Masculinities: A Cultural Economy of Surfboard-Making

Andrew Warren

Introduction

This chapter explores the versions of masculinity embodied and performed by men working in commercial surfboard factories. Since the 1960s surfboards have been manufactured in industrial-style workshops. Boards are hand-made for local surfers and prevailing marine geographies. Recent global expansion of surfboard manufacturing has occurred with a transition to automated production technologies. However, in popular surfing places customisation via craft-based production is an enduring ritual of the surfboard industry. Lurking next to craft production is the equally stubborn legacy of commercial surfboard-making: a profoundly gendered division of labour.

Corresponding to other capitalist industries, jobs in the surfboard industry 'are not gender neutral; they are created as suitable for particular sexed bodies' (McDowell 1997: 25). In advanced economies the social attributes of 'working bodies' are increasingly important features of labour market relations (McDowell 2009, Nixon 2009, Banks and Milestone 2011). With the rise of interactive service industries, features aligned to social constructions of femininity – aesthetic performance, team work, holistic thinking, empathy and persuasiveness – have become more important for accessing jobs and completing economic transactions (Simpson 2004). Meanwhile declining employment in manufacturing informs discussion about a 'crisis' of masculinity (McDowell 2003). Notions of idealised hegemonic masculinities, bound-up with labour market participation, are being challenged (Connell 2005). From the juncture of masculinities and work this chapter focuses on a self-defined manufacturing industry. Nevertheless performances of work and commercial transactions in surfboard manufacturing are flushed with close, personal interaction; not only between workers but also through engagements with customers who purchase end products. Drawing from cultural economy theory this chapter reveals how waged work comprises alternative and often conflicting masculinities, shaped in working relations and performance.

In the following section I outline the chapter's conceptual framework. Cultural economy is used to explore the masculinities of surfboard-makers, prioritising analysis of the way values, practices and skills shape economic relations. In the surfboard industry, mapping of work to particular sexed bodies is influenced by wider surfing subculture. After framing the analytical approach I describe research methods. Ethnographic engagements with workers and workshops focuses on the three global 'hubs' of surfboard innovation and production: southern California, O'ahu, Hawai'i and east coast Australia. Empirical insights follow and are organised in two overarching sections.

The first empirical section focuses on performances of 'blokey' masculinities articulated by male workers in relations with one another (Wheaton 2004, Hopkins and Noble 2009). Co-worker interactions on factory floors valorise the exploits of heterosexual men. The reproduction of surfing's subcultural discourses resonates strongly in commercial workshops and offers an explanation for persistent divisions of labour along gender lines. The second empirical section explores alternative versions of masculinity observed in crafting work and in relations between workers and customers. Surfboard shaping and glassing – the two main labour specialisations – depend on embodied and emotive acuities. Workers also know customers personally, making boards to suit body shapes, surfing abilities and favourite waves. Finally, I draw conclusions, arguing for the usefulness of cultural economy approaches in making sense of the relational, intersecting and often competing nature of workplace masculinities.

Cultural economy: working relations in surfboard-making

Surfing subculture is a US$10 billion a year global industry (Global Industry Analysts 2011). Aside from boards, selling of the surf incorporates an assortment of branded fashion products: clothing, swim, eye and footwear, jewellery, film and tourism. Surfboards are the essential element of the wider surf industry, authenticating the efforts of corporate firms Quiksilver and Billabong. Since the 1970s surf brands have internationalised the distribution of a range of consumer products, as global consumption of surf fashion has enabled the corporatisation of surfing. At the same time surfboard manufacturing remains dominated by small and medium-sized firms operating in close proximity to popular surfing places. Multi-national surf companies use labelled boards – via contracting of independent manufacturers and retail networks – to help buttress their status as 'genuine' surf labels (Warren and Gibson 2013). Credibility is a crucial ingredient for successful surf business.

Analysing surfboard-making as an industry through classical economic and orthodox economic geographical theories (of profit and loss, vertical integration, agglomeration dependencies, rational choice theory etc.) can't enunciate how the industry works, what factors shape production or what the key issues are facing workers and workshops. Maintaining sensitivity to the 'cultural' logics and values at play within industries situates surfboard manufacturing within a cultural economy framework (Warren and Gibson 2013). Cultural economy is used here to examine the human dimensions shaping commercial production; the relationships between and among workers and the 'things' they produce and sell.

Over the last two decades the phrase cultural economy has emerged in several guises. Because 'the' cultural economy is most evident in certain sectors it has come to stand for the cultural industries (Scott 2000) – widely re-branded as 'creative industries' and incorporating an expanding list of activities defined by innovation and entrepreneurialism (O'Connor 2013). These are industries in every sense, consisting of small and large firms, with inputs and outputs, workers, workplaces and sometimes unions. However, they differ from other forms of capitalist production. Cultural (and creative) industries rely on immaterial and embodied processes such as innovation and resourcefulness to create 'symbolic content' – the work by musicians, artists, directors, actors, and designers (Reimer 2009).

Surfboard-making itself is a cultural industry. Production involves high levels of creative skill; a substantial symbolic component (ascribed meanings of the surfboard within the surfing subculture); knowledge of fashions and subcultural preferences; constant updates and adaptations of design. Custom manufacturers offer high value-added boards personalised to individual surfers and local marine conditions. Custom boards are infused with artistic and rarity value. Independent surfboard firms survive despite growing competition from corporate players whose sub-contracted production is concentrated offshore in cheaper labour locations (see Warren and Gibson 2013). Local workshops contribute to, and utilise, regional reputations within global surfing culture. As cultural goods surfboards entangle regional identities, physical geography, popular local pastimes, creative design and material production (Molotch 2002). But the cultural economy *as* cultural/creative industries approach relies on a different mode of thinking to the original framework. Culture is treated as an economised component of advanced post-industrial societies, rather than a constituent input actively shaping capitalist relations.

In this chapter I use cultural economy theory as an epistemological approach to trouble dichotomies of 'culture' and 'economy' as discrete 'natural' categories (Gibson-Graham 2008, Mitchell 2008, Gibson 2012). Cultural economy theory stresses the entwined nature of economic, cultural, social and political relations (Barnes 2001). The goal is to change the epistemology of economic knowledges away from the premise of underlying, abstract market-driven forces towards theorising the relations between cultures and economies (Peet 2000). Channelling the arguments of Karl Polanyi (2001 [1944]), it becomes impossible to think of economies as autonomous in relation to broader social structures and cultural processes. Cultural economy thus attempts to unravel how economies are made and remade through resources, actions, symbols, signs, discourses, technologies and theories (Amin and Thrift 2007). By questioning what it is that constitutes the fabric of 'economies' cultural economy allocates no ontological privilege. Instead the aim is to promote the inclusion of actors, activities, knowledge and resources situated outside traditional notions of economy.

The polysemy and conceptual looseness of cultural economy as a framework is helpful for examining the versions of masculinity constructed and performed within the workplace. The surfboard industry has its origins as do-it-yourself (DIY) craftwork performed in coastal suburban tool sheds and organised around waged day jobs (see Warren and Gibson 2013). This 'backyard' work was informed by desires to go surfing, demonstrating how human actions are much more than the sum of different tactics implemented to gain economic advantage. Cultural values, personal passions and relationships, competitiveness, and local geography shape surfboard-making as an industry as much as wages, prices and rents. Nonetheless core 'economic' matters of market share and proximity, exploitation, agglomeration and labour markets still have primacy. Cultural economy frameworks can't simply reverse a binary, making culture primary and economy secondary. The argument is economies are open, porous entities influenced as much by culture, as culture is by the economic. Using cultural economy to examine the construction and performance of masculinities in paid workplaces thus brings into dialogue perspectives, interests and arguments pioneered by post-structural feminism (Gibson-Graham 2008). Culture and embodiment are constituent features of economies, particularly for the (re)production of unevenness and inequality.

Methodological approach: ethnography and locating workshops

Empirical research in this chapter was undertaken with surfboard-makers inside their work spaces. Research centred on the three most renowned surfing regions globally: southern California, O'ahu, Hawai'i and east coast Australia (Warren and Gibson 2013). Between 2008 and 2012, some 120 workers from 33 workshops took part in the study. A total of 12 workshops were located along Australia's expansive east coast; 11 in southern California (between Los Angeles and San Diego) and ten on O'ahu, Hawai'i. Surfboard workshops in each region employed between two and 25 workers, operating in close proximity to popular breaks. Participating workshops reflected the diverse scales of surfboard production globally. Overall, 12 labels exported surfboards internationally with a further 15 selling to combined regional and national markets. The six smallest workshops serviced surfing communities within their immediate locations.

In each factory ethnography took the form of extended 'workplace tours' (see Burawoy 1998, Warren and Gibson 2013). Spending several days in each workshop the approach included completing basic duties alongside workers – helping to unload trucks, carrying tools and equipment, sanding surfboards. More technical work designing, crafting and sealing surfboards was closely observed so that shapers and glassers could discuss their jobs in situ. Semi-structured interviews were also conducted with the 33 workshop owners/managers.

Ethnography benefited from the residual positioning of surfboard-making within the wider surfing subculture. As an active member of that subculture I was able to establish a measure of 'insider' status. My positionality became crucial for eliciting and interpreting responses from participants that 'outside' researchers might have ignored or misinterpreted. My gender and sexuality was also significant. As a white, heterosexual male body I was granted a level of acceptance and access by male workers unlikely for a non-surfing 'outsider' or female researcher. Simultaneously, it was crucial to recognise the potential for influencing relations and actions in workshops (Burawoy 1998). Conversations and interviews in the workplace were captured with a hand-held audio recorder. Detailed fieldwork diaries were also maintained to document important observations. A final point: to maintain privacy pseudonyms are used for workshops, owners and workers throughout the chapter.

Making boards and 'blokey' masculinities

In this first empirical section I aim to show how male working bodies in surfboard workshops perform 'blokey' masculinities in relations with one another.

The gendered origins of commercial surfboard workshops

The surfboard industry's labour process was divided into a small number of specialisations. Workers known as shapers – the most prestigious jobs in the industry – created designs and sculpted boards from casts of 'blank' foam[1] (Figure 26.1). Glassers were responsible for sealing finished foam shapes using woven fibreglass cloth, layered over the board and evenly coated with a liquefied resin (Figure 26.2). The hardening agent mixed into the resin created a sealed finish and once cured the porous foam was waterproof. In larger factories two further tasks were devolved from shaping and glassing. Sanders were employed to finish the final stages of shaping. Polishers ensured boards were 'clean and shiny' before collection by a customer or transport to surf retail stores (Pete, mid-20s, California). Sanders and polishers were usually 'biding their time' performing more remedial jobs in anticipation for opportunities to shape or glass (Tony, sander, late 20s, O'ahu). Across the three surfing regions a professionally recognised trade certificate or accredited diploma didn't exist for surfboard manufacturing. Informality was yet another persistent legacy of commercial production.

Since the late 1950s, when a viable industry congealed, commercial surfboard-making has been organised around a manual labour process. Jobs in this manufacturing industry accordingly mapped neatly onto male working bodies (Collinson 1992, McDowell 2011). An experienced board-maker in Australia outlined the gendered landscapes of surfboard-making:

---

1 Foam replaced wood in surfboard manufacturing during the late 1950s. Surfing entrepreneurs Hobie Alter and Gordon Clark widely introduced foam in southern California and helped to significantly reduce the labour intensiveness of surfboard manufacturing. Foam was important to the expansion from DIY board-making practices to organized, larger-scale commercial production (see Warren and Gibson 2013).

Figure 26.1 Shaping a custom surfboard from a foam blank using an electric planer, southern California

Source: Andrew Warren

Figure 26.2 Glassing a custom surfboard with liquefied resin using a squeegee, east coast Australia

Source: Sean Maguire

> The industry is very old school in a lot of ways. Some of the things that go on in here, well you wouldn't get away with them in other workplaces. Not just health and safety but the conversations and pranks; that sort of thing. We like to call it manufacturing and it's very blokey … Making surfboards is messy. It gets hot and sweaty in the workshop, especially in summer. It's [surfboard-making] suited to blokes that aren't afraid to get their hands dirty and who are surfers of course. (Joe, shaper, early 50s)

In recent decades the growth of knowledge intensive industries has transformed employment landscapes for men and women alike. Masculine identity work bound-up with labour market participation is being transformed (Gorman-Murray 2011). Nonetheless in the surfboard industry gender segregation in the workplace was ubiquitous. Where women were employed in workshops (ten across 33 workshops), it was in defined roles aligned to supposedly natural feminine attributes: 'looking after the books' (Trent, workshop owner, mid-50s, O'ahu), making sure 'the place [workshop] is neat and tidy' (Brett, shaper, 40s, southern California), or in the case of an Australian workshop, 'handling our retail orders and dealing with any complaints' that came from customers (Jimmy, workshop manager, mid-30s).

From engagements with workers it became apparent that subcultural membership, values and beliefs explained gender relations in commercial surfboard-making (Evers 2009) – as much as the nature of the labour. Commercial production was, ostensibly, an extension of Western surfing subculture. Pre-colonial forms of Hawaiian surfing were, if anything, aligned to what Westerners would categorise as a feminine reading of the body – the ocean was valued as a nurturing, spiritual space (Walker 2011). Surfing among Pacific Island cultures prioritised elegance and gracefulness by riding surfboards in rhythm with the wave's natural movements. Men and women participated on even terms. Meanwhile, early surfing in California and Australia was experimental and new: in the 1910s and 1920s women participated unselfconsciously as much as men did, in a comparatively liberated era (Warren and Gibson 2013). After World War II, surfing was increasingly influenced by more conservative cultural value and societal norms.

In the 1950s and 1960s the surf zone became increasingly stereotyped as a wild and dangerous space where brave and courageous bodies tested themselves in large and powerful waves (Booth 1995). A growing surf media (magazines and surf-based film production), along with judging at professional events, prioritised the performance of fast and aggressive surfing in barreling waves, or riding the biggest surf possible. Surfing came to privilege masculine attributes of aggression, courage and fearlessness (Evers 2009). Women and their surfing styles, always an underestimated presence on Californian and Australian beaches, were considered weak by male counterparts (Evers 2009). Surfing's wider gender values washed into commercial surfboard workshops at the same time a viable industry was coalescing in coastal California, Hawai'i and Australia.

Co-worker relations and doing 'blokey' masculinity

Social relations between workers concentrated in shaping bays, sanding and glassing rooms, where production was carried out during the day. However, worker interaction in each of the three case study regions flowed into other local spaces: popular surfing spots, beachside car parks, social bars and pubs. Fellow workers from a business, local customers and workers from competing labels were, in each case study region, part of wider social groups. In terms of in-house production, friendship was a key feature of the job. While creative secrets were at times fiercely protected by older expert craftsman, because many workers had been shaping and glassing alongside the same individuals for many years they nevertheless came to form strong social bonds with colleagues. These relations extended after a day's work was finished and flowed well beyond the factory.

Workplaces and social hangouts combined paid labour and a subculture united by enthusiasm for surfing. Here, 'blokey' mateship had become an ever-present feature in the production of surfboards:

> The blokes who work in here – we're all pretty close mates, you know. We work hard during the week and every Friday we crack open some beers and we have a joke and share some stories. That's a big part of the job. It's a small crew here, just six of us, so we become pretty close. We're always talking about our next surf trip or the latest chick one of the boys is rooting. [laughs] You know how it is. (Cameron, shaper, late 30s, Australia)

Masculinities observed in co-worker relations frequently involved the exclusion and sexualisation of women. Here blokey performances by surfboard-makers were similar to Belinda Wheaton's (2004) 'laddish' masculinity identified among young male windsurfers in the UK. One example of the sexualisation of women within surfboard-making cultures occurred in a southern California workshop. A young female surfer walked into the workshop seeking help from a shaper to fix her damaged board. Word quickly travelled around the factory that a 'hot chick' was 'out front' (Brian, shaper, mid-30s). Three other men moved to the retail section of the workshop so they could 'check her out' (Brian). When the young woman left, the men joked about 'what she would be like in bed' (Todd, glasser, 40s). Rather than a legitimate surfing body, the male workers reduced the young woman to a sexual object.

Other conversations observed in male-dominated workshops included the regular discussion of sex with women. Rarely talked about in terms of surfing abilities – unlike male counterparts – women were discussed in terms of sexual desire. The sexual objectification of women was a shared feature of surfboard workshops. Sexist discourses flooded into factories as surfing culture shaped economic landscapes: worker relations, values and accepted practices.

The relational nature of blokey surfboard-making masculinity was also demonstrated at a workshop on O'ahu (Hopkins and Noble 2009). One quiet afternoon a conversation had begun between five male workers over the small number of female surfboard shapers now making their own surfboards as hobbyist activity. A respected shaper interjected into the conversation:

> Yeah man, my two favourite things right there: women and surfboards. I picture this hot little female shaper right ... She jumps out of bed in the morning and races down to her shaping room. There she is bending over the blank, slowly caressing her fingers along the stringer [centre line of the board]. Big (emphasises)! Big and wide she screams. And when she leans over the blank her panties creep up her tight butt and her tits pop [motions with his hands] out just a little. (Billy, shaper, late 40s, O'ahu)

The exchange kicked off a series of new conversations between the male workers. Surrounded by laughter, other workers explained how there was: 'nothing quite like the thought of a hottie shaping a blank is there?' (Eddy, shaper, late 40s); 'In a little bikini would do it for me' (Pete, sander, early 30).

Subcultural credibility was not only achieved by demonstrating quality work and a surfing identity. Open discussion of sex reinforced membership in the social make-up of workshops, while also excluding women from surfboard-making (Wheaton 2004). To be 'one of the boys' – as several Australian workers described it – involved the sharing of stories and adventures. In addition to surfing ability, sex with women, particularly for younger men, became a way to gain peer acceptance. Yet, older men also openly shared experiences from their own youth – partying, drinking, surfing trips and sex. In this way a sense of camaraderie was generated in workshops across generations.

Underpinning talk of women, sex and blokey surfing cultures was the intensely heteronormative construction of space (Waitt and Warren 2008). Homophobic undercurrents were readily detectable in surfboard workshops. It was acceptable for men within a workshop to 'have a perv' on the 'hot chick', yet on another occasion male workers used terms like 'poofters', 'homos' and 'fags' in describing two male customers being served in a workshop that were interpreted as being gay (Research diary entry, April 2010). The thought of a fellow surfboard-maker being queer, for most workers, disrupted normalised understandings of their job and workplace as heterosexual and blokey (Embrick, Walther and Wickens 2007). For the men, 'strong' heterosexual bodies were wrapped up with understandings of surfing subculture and surfboard-making as a paid career.

Worker masculinities were performed and negotiated through the spaces of surfboard workshops. Overall surfboard-making was seen to be characterised by what Chino called 'strong bodies' (shaper, early 50s, California). Strong bodies were, however, both physical and embodied attribute, negotiated by male workers in relations with one another. While the sexualisation of women permeated work spaces, and co-worker interaction in workshops valorised male heterosexuality, alternative and often competing masculinities were readily detectable.

'A soulful pursuit': crafting alternative masculinities

In talking with customers, sketching out new surfboard designs, using tools to shape or glass a board, participant's revealed complex lived experiences of masculinity. Alternative masculinities were uncovered in the production of custom surfboards and in the close, personal exchanges between makers and wider surfing subcultures.

Performing work and use of the body

Embodied senses (feel, touch and sight) were critical for making customised surfboards. Hard work and what Mark Paterson (2009) referred to as haptic knowledge, not mere reproduction, were the over-riding symbols of quality workmanship. Bobby, a native Hawaiian (*Kanaka Maoli*), explained the process for performing his work:

> After I meet with my customer I start to visualise their board. Then I get my hands on the blank. I have to imagine that board coming to life and I need to feel it with my body. I use the measurements I've designed to check each shape but you picture it in your mind, the different elements of the board; its tail shape, width, thickness, rocker, rails all of this. You put all the different elements together and make something that brings all this joy. That is so cool [laughs]. (Early 70s)

The skills needed to hand-make custom surfboards were deeply embodied. Shapers emphasised abilities to 'feel', 'visualise' and bring 'joy' to customers through their work. Surfboard-making drew from unique crafting abilities:

> I work like this [shifts his hands up and down the board] to feel the rail, you know I can feel the difference between this rail [left hand side of the board] and this rail [right hand side]. Looking at it, I can also see the difference between this part of the board [near the tail] and this part of the board [near the nose]. All that comes down to feel, sight and time in the shaping bay. If I was to measure it and only go off those measurements then it doesn't necessarily feel right. The job is hands on, and what feels good. (Stu, shaper, early 50s, Australia)

It was also essential to be accomplished with different manual tools, and equally, tactile control of, and feel with, the hands. The importance of felt senses in performing and evaluating work was also articulated by Taylor:

> If you want to be a good designer and shaper you must learn how to feel the board, see how it is going to turn out before you've even started making it. You have to imagine the design in your mind and picture how you'll shape it together for your customer … I have found that I rely most on my senses and how a board

> feels. I visualise and really get into the right frame of mind where I feel good about how the board is coming together. (Mid-60s, Australia)

Bodily skills were used by surfboard-makers to produce unique and original products. Surfboard-makers materialised their designs into physical, finished products. The combination of craft skills ingrained rarity and artistic value in each custom surfboard.

Individual board-makers were renowned for their haptic talents to design and make a variety of different board styles. Dave, Wayne and Toby in Australia were experts in designing and crafting light, fast and maneuverable boards – a reflection of local waves and surfing style. Meanwhile, in Hawai‘i, Jeff, Ken and Richie were experts at making boards refined for large and powerful waves that frequented the Hawaiian Islands. Underlying physical geography was important for surfboard design and manufacture. In southern California, Greg, Gary and Shane were skilled at shaping 'hybrid' boards: fusing design concepts from longboarding (increased paddling and buoyancy) with those of shortboard maneuverability.

Many other board-makers, including Charlie (O‘ahu) and Timmy (California), expressed deep felt connections between their work and their bodies. Rather than control and discipline of bodies – attributes traditionally ascribed to masculine identities – male surfboard-makers demonstrated the shifting emotional terrain upon which surfboards were manufactured. Shapers relied on embodied knowledge, imparted on a blank through the skilled use of specialised tools. The creative labour of surfboard-makers ran parallel to other forms of craft production such as furniture or musical instrument-making; all of which require specific embodied, haptic abilities (Sennett 2008). For example, several workers used a certain brand of electric planer to sculpt their blanks because it provided a 'fine sense of touch' compared to other models (Greg, shaper, mid 50s, California).

Planers themselves were motioned in long, flowing strokes to delicately and uniformly sculpt sections of the foam blank. Any adverse movement in the hands or body caused the shaper to gouge into the foam and risked destroying the design or entire blank. Similarly, glassers moved along each board with a rubber squeegee, careful to spread liquid resin evenly over fiberglass cloth to achieve a smooth and uniformed finish. Applying just the right amount of pressure ensured no air bubbles were left in the glass, while resin didn't remain too thin in any part of the board. Basic tools such as electric planers and squeegees were consequently cherished, essential instruments – an extension of working bodies.

Through repetitive and sustained use of their tools, shapers and glassers developed heightened senses of feel and touch. Such haptic talents, refined over years of work, became ritual features of working identities (Paterson 2009). A shaper in southern California outlined the significance of embodiment for working in the surfboard industry:

> The main thing for shapers that do it by hand is trying to get this rail and that rail the same … I'm constantly working by feel and touch. I've been in restaurants

> where I'm sitting at a table and I grab the table and I start feeling it to see if it's the same shape on each side. I talk to other shapers who do the same thing. (Graham, shaper, mid-50s)

Hand-makers used attuned haptic knowledge to establish whether designs were symmetrical. Many shapers told how they could accurately locate the smallest imperfections in foam shape or thickness in a fiberglass coat, by feel. Such imperfections were invisible to untrained senses and measuring tools such as calipers.

Being a surfboard-maker also legitimised, to the wider world, passions for surfing – a means to turn a subcultural pastime into a 'proper job' (Dean, early 40s, shaper, O'ahu). Because no formal training pathways existed into surfboard manufacturing, the ability to find meaningful paid work in the industry was driven by personal ambitions and desires. In discussing the nature of their employment during interviews and in performing work, participants explicitly described the 'artistic', 'magical', 'inspiring' and 'soulful' process of 'making surfboards for a living' (Paul, early 30s, shaper, O'ahu). These felt, emotional expressions aligned to a feminine reading of the body and contrasted the 'blokey' masculinities defined in relations between male co-workers.

Jim, an experienced hand-shaper from southern California in his 50s explained the 'soulful' nature of shaping work:

> Shaping – it's, you know … a collective experience. That is what surfboard design is … [it] basically started off as a two by four [piece of timber] and morphed into something much more progressive. And it might sound silly, but really that evolution of surfboards and surfing has been a soulful process. It's come from the artistic way surfers have made boards to ride waves. It's where they've put everything, their bodies and creativity into designing and shaping that magical board for someone.

Embodied skills, knowledge of surfboard design and crafting were developed progressively over time through personal experiences within surfing subcultures. The requisite talents for shapers and glassers didn't blend together quickly or easily. Different customers required different designs, and as new materials became popular old ones were rendered outdated.

Worker/customer relations

Designing and materialising custom surfboards drew from close interactions between customers and shapers. This was a relationship that started out in a workshop. But spaces. The close relations established between many workers and their customers were a unique feature of the industry. Surfboard-makers often knew customers intimately – especially their surfing abilities – as they returned year after year for new surfboards.[2] Close worker/customer relationships were a cultural legacy of customised production as the boundaries between identities as worker and surfer blurred. One exchange in Hawai'i demonstrated the close relations that existed between makers and local customers:

> **Author**: Ok, you've been getting boards here for 30 years, so can I ask why you keep coming back?
>
> **Customer**: Nearly 40 years actually. [laughs] Bobby made my first board in 1973. We have been friends surfing together for all that time and we're from the same neighbourhood … the thing is I watch him sometimes working and we talk about how my board is riding and what we can do for my next one. [laughs] His boards are perfect … classic thing is Bobby is still so stoked on surfing, it's infectious to be around.

Pleasures of the job were not gained from financial rewards. Despite unique skill sets, surfboard-makers were modestly paid workers. Full wages were only earned during the busiest few months of the year when, in each region, local orders peaked. Instead social and cultural factors were at play in motivating and informing paid careers:

> It has got to be a passion [surfboard-making], otherwise you should just go make some money. [laughs] You don't make money in this game. It's a terrific business though, I love it. I get all my rewards through the relationships I've built with my customers. Simple as that. (Bruce, shaper, mid-60s, Australia)

Similarly, Beau, a Hawaiian shaper in his early 30s, spoke about the emotional rewards that motivated his surfboard-making:

> Oh man, I shape each board like I want the thing to be perfect. Shaping is not just a job – okay, it is – but [pauses] it has something much more behind it. [exhales] Oh man, it's kind of like a feeling you know that you get when you're making a board for someone and you see it come together, even watch it being used to ride a wave. That is such a cool, special thing.

In each of the three regions, surfboard-making was a form of social and cultural membership as much as paid profession. While a competitive commercial

2 Regular surfers can go through two or three surfboards each year as waves and surfing bodies take a substantial physical toll on foam and fiberglass. The continual turnover of boards is an important feature of the industry and ensures a regular demand among groups of avid local surfers in each case study region.

environment, surfboard manufacturing was also a collective of sorts, of craftsmen, who felt great pride in, and passion for, their work.

Despite masculinised work cultures and pretensions, surfboard-making was clearly an emotionally loaded form of work. Male surfboard-makers discussed their work in openly emotional ways. This was a 'passion' and 'soulful' occupation. Older workers in their 50s and 60s were more willing to articulate an understanding of their work in emotional ways, compared with younger men. Macho posturing remained mostly a young man's conceit. Careers in the surfboard industry were not, in the end, especially glamorous either. Instead, what a career making surfboards provided was a sense of mateship and cultural membership, and pride in making functional, high quality and artful things workers got to see being used. Here was an occupational group dominated by men who experienced lively working conditions in emotionally extroverted workplaces. Masculine identity work was much more than blokey posturing and egocentrism; performance was deeply marked by embodied skills and emotional experiences.

Conclusions

This chapter has attempted to draw out the versions of masculinity performed by male workers in the surfboard industry. Spaces of work (paid and unpaid) are saturated with gendered meanings and discourses. In polarised and segmented economies, different types of work become congruent with particular gendered identities (McDowell 2011). Jobs in any capitalist industry are not 'empty slots to be filled', but nor do workers 'enter the labour market … with fixed and immoveable gender attributes' (McDowell 1997: 25). With the social attributes of workers increasingly important features of labour market relations, surfboard-makers illustrate the relational and contested nature of masculine identity work (Hopkins and Noble 2009). Performances of blokey masculinity are omnipresent in commercial surfboard workshops. Yet, when men perform work they constantly utilise embodied skills and emotional perceptions. Male working bodies are not devoid of emotions. The study of masculinities and work can't, therefore, rely upon neat material divisions between 'new' economy service sector jobs and 'old' economy manual work. To do so neglects the multifarious lived experiences of performing human labour. Embodied and deeply emotive senses are crucial, even for industries and jobs organised around a manual labour process.

A final point to underscore echoes the arguments of Linda McDowell (2011): embodiment matters for doing (and researching) workplace masculinities. In pushing this point I add that cultural economy offers much to the study of masculinities and work because focus is directed to the human dimensions and relations furnishing capitalist labour markets. For men and their work, alternative masculinities are embodied as talents, knowledge, beliefs and values. Personal subjectivities are constantly deployed to carry out work no matter how the activity is categorised economically. Cultural economy approaches are valuable for exploring the relational, intersecting and often competing nature of masculine identity work.

References

Amin, A. and Thrift, N. 2007. Cultural economy and cities. *Progress in Human Geography*, 31(2), 143–161.

Banks, M. and Milestone, K. 2011. Individualisation, gender and cultural work. *Gender, Work and Organisation*, 18(1), 73–89.

Barnes, T.J. 2001. Retheorizing economic geography: from the quantitative revolution to the 'cultural' turn. *Annals of the Association of American Geographers*, 91(3) 546–565.

Booth, D. 1995. Ambiguities in pleasure and discipline: the development of competitive surfing. *Journal of Sport History*, 22(3), 189–206.

Burawoy, M. 1998. The extended case method. *Sociological Theory*, 16(1), 4–33.

Collinson, D.L. 1992. *Managing the Shopfloor: Subjectivity, Masculinity and Workplace Culture*. Berlin: De Gruyter.

Connell, R.W. 2005. *Masculinities*. Second edition. Crow's Nest: Allen and Unwin.

Embrick, D.G., Walther, C.S. and Wickens, C.M. 2007. Working class masculinity: keeping gay men and lesbians out of the workplace. *Sex Roles*, 56(11–12), 757–766.

Evers, C. 2009. 'The Point': surfing, geography and a sensual life of men and masculinity on the Gold Coast, Australia. *Social and Cultural Geography*, 10(8), 893–908.

Gibson, C. 2012. Cultural economy: achievements, divergences, future prospects. *Geographical Research*, 50(3), 282–290.

Gibson-Graham, J.K. 2008. Diverse economies: performative practices for 'other worlds'. *Progress in Human Geography*, 32(5), 613–632.

Global Industry Analysts 2011. *Surfing: A Global Strategic Business Report* [Online: Global Industry Analysts]. Available from: http://www.strategyr.com/Surfing_Market_Report.asp [accessed 25 August 2012].

Gorman-Murray, A. 2011. Economic crises and emotional fallout: work, home and men's senses of belonging in post-GFC Sydney. *Emotion, Space and Society*, 4(4), 211–220.

Hopkins, P. and Noble, G. 2009. Masculinities in place: situated identities, relations and intersectionality. *Social and Cultural Geography*, 10(8), 811–819.

McDowell, L. 1997. *Capital Culture: Gender at Work in the City*. Oxford: Wiley-Blackwell.

McDowell, L. 2003. *Redundant Masculinities? Employment Change and White Working Class Youth*. Melbourne: Wiley-Blackwell.

McDowell, L. 2009. *Working Bodies: Interactive Service Employment and Workplace Identities*. Oxford: Wiley-Blackwell.

McDowell, L. 2011. Doing work, performing work, in *The Sage Handbook of Economic Geography*, edited by A. Leyshon et al. London: Sage Publications, 338–349.

Mitchell, T. 2008. Rethinking economy. *Geoforum*, 39(3), 1116–1121.

Molotch, H. 2002. Place in product. *International Journal of Urban and Regional Research*, 26(4), 665–688.

Nixon, D. 2009. 'I can't put a smiley face on': working-class masculinity, emotional labour and service work in the 'new economy'. *Gender, Work and Organisation*, 16(3), 300–322.

O'Connor, J. 2013. Intermediaries and imaginaries in the cultural and creative industries. *Regional Studies* [Online DOI:10.1080/00343404.2012.748982].

Paterson, M. 2009. Haptic geographies: ethnography, haptic knowledge and sensuous dispositions. *Progress in Human Geography*, 33(6), 766–788.

Peet, R. 2000. Culture, imaginary, and rationality in regional economic development. *Environment and Planning A*, 32(7), 1215–1234.

Polanyi, K. 2001[1944]. *The Great Transformation: The Political and Economic Origins of Our Time*. Boston: Beacon Press.

Reimer, S. 2009. Geographies of production III: knowledge, cultural economies and work (revisited). *Progress in Human Geography*, 33(5), 677–684.

Scott, A.J. 2000. *The Cultural Economy of Cities*. London: Sage Publications.

Sennett, R. 2008. *The Craftsman*. New Haven: Yale University Press.

Simpson, R. 2004. Masculinity at work: the experiences of men in female dominated occupations. *Work, Employment and Society*, 18(2), 349–368.

Waitt, G. and Warren, A. 2008. 'Talking shit over a brew after a good session with your mates' surfing, space and masculinity. *Australian Geographer*, 39(3), 353–365.

Walker, I. 2011. *Waves of Resistance: Surfing and History in Twentieth-Century Hawai'i*. Honolulu: University of Hawai'i Press.

Warren, A. and Gibson, C. 2013. *Surfing Places, Surfboard-makers: Craft, Creativity and Cultural Heritage in Hawai'i, California and Australia*. Honolulu: University of Hawai'i Press.

Wheaton, B. 2004. New lads: competing masculinities in the windsurfing culture, in *Understanding Lifestyle Sports: Consumption, Identity and Difference*, edited by B. Wheaton. Oxon: Routledge, 131–153.

Chapter 27
Performing Rural Masculinities: A Case Study of Diggers and Dealers

Barbara Pini and Robyn Mayes

Introduction

This chapter examines what Parpart and Zalewski (2008) label 'the man question' in terms of the rural. That is, 'how masculinity comes to be "made" as a continuing process within the social context' of rural places and spaces (Kerfoot and Knights 1993: 662). Our understanding of masculinities as discursively produced, relational, multiple and changing is given empirical force through a case study of the annual resource conference, Diggers and Dealers. The conference, held in the remote mining town of Kalgoorlie in Western Australia since 1992, is today the largest international meeting for the resource sector, attracting over 2000 attendees. Through an analysis of 120 texts related to the conference from 2006 to the present, including media reports, blogs and conference programs and speeches, we demonstrate how, what is essentially a corporate event, is *imported* into the rural and constructed through the intersecting discourses of rurality, masculinity and heterosexuality. That is, though the first such meeting may have taken place spontaneously in Kalgoorlie, the delegates, and the 'skimpy' barmaids who serve patrons in their underwear or sometimes topless and are seen as central to the event, are flown into town for the conference. Kalgoorlie, as a working mining community on the edge of the desert, provides both spectacle and conditions for the enactment of frontier masculinity not possible in the metropole.

Constructing Kalgoorlie and frontier masculinities

As Hogan and Pursell (2008) observe in an analysis of representations of Alaska, places are imagined in particular ways and these imaginaries are imbricated in the formation of specific gendered identities. Alaska, for example, through its landscape and history, is connected to wilderness and physicality and thus deeply coded as masculine. In a similar respect, the masculinities that are performed at and associated with Diggers and Dealers are embedded in broader constructions of Kalgoorlie. With a population of 30,000 and located 595 kilometres (370 miles) east-northeast from the state capital of Perth is clearly a remote place. It also has a distinct landscape and is therefore seen as exotic, with its open plains, wide blue skies and rich red dirt. Kalgoorlie is located in Western Australia, which is itself understood as illustrative of the last frontier, given its vast size (covering a third of the continent), its physical distance from the capital cities of the eastern states (requiring five to six hour flights), and its economic dependence on mineral extraction.

Kalgoorlie is also strongly associated with resource extraction – an endeavour that further conjures images of masculine strength and endeavour, and ultimately, masculine conquest over nature (Mayes and Pini 2011). The first European discovery of gold in Kalgoorlie was in the nineteenth century and deposits of gold are still incredibly rich. When a number of small underground mines close to the town were consolidated into a single open pit mine in 1989, Kalgoorlie became home to what is colloquially known as the 'Super Pit'. At 3.5 kilometres long, 1.5 kilometres wide and 360 metres deep, the Super Pit has become a significant tourist attraction for the town and helped cement broader images of the place as exceptional.

Along with geography and gold, a further element in the mythologising of Kalgoorlie as a masculine frontier town is its connection with sex-workers. Indeed, the three factors – rurality, mining and prostitution – are largely conflated without question or explanation in representations of the place. As a travel writer explains:

> The outback mining city of Kalgoorlie is famous for two things – goldmining and the red light district on Hay Street. In fact, the two go pretty much hand in hand. It was because of the miners who settled the town that a demand for the second profession arose, with men vastly outnumbering women in the early days of the town's history. Some of the old 'tin shed' brothels still stand, and even though they double as a tourist attraction these days, they are still utilised by the locals and visitors to escape the hardships of living a miner's life. (Anonymous 2012)

The assumptions inherent in the above quotation relating to masculinity, and a particular version of rural masculinity, require highlighting. Critically, masculinity is unquestionably conflated with heterosexuality. As such, prostitution is constructed as an inevitable and natural outcome of the absence of women. The presence of sex-workers confirms the heterosexuality of the rural man in an environment that is largely homosocial. Importantly, the rural masculine heterosexuality naturalised is not the benign and unthreatening rural masculine heterosexuality associated with farming men and the sustainability and reproduction of family agriculture (Little 2003, 2007). This is the voracious and unbridled rural masculine heterosexuality of the frontier man.

What is particularly interesting in the above quotation in terms of our analysis in this chapter is the way in which the dominant tropes associated with the masculinity of an historical construction – the frontier man – are conjured to be part of the present. In the following sections of the chapter, we see an extension of this process as urban corporate mining men take up the scripts of frontier masculinity as attendees of the Diggers and Dealers conference.

Performing frontier masculinities

As suggested by its title, Diggers and Dealers brings together mining and exploration companies and financers, brokers and/or bankers. The three day event involves representatives from the former enumerating a case for investment. The process by which attendees, almost all of them men, are 'trying to stand out from the crowd' and 'trying to put their story in front of everyone else' (Wynne 2010) has obvious homoerotic possibilities. The homosocial relations between the mining men extend to the large contingent of male journalists attending to report on the event annually.

Both 'the digger' and 'the dealer' are represented on the conference logo. It's a logo that suggests a much longer history than the establishment date of 1992. It is a circular shape with the words 'Mining Forum: Kalgoorlie Western Australia' on the outer rim. In the inside of the circle are the words 'Diggers & Dealers' in a traditionally styled font. On the left-hand side of an elongated ampersand is an illustration of a 'Digger' while on the right is the figure of the 'Dealer'. Both are men and are drawn as if stepping from the early nineteenth century. The 'Digger' leans forward panning for gold with shovel alongside him while the 'Dealer' sits on a bar stool attending to his books and dressed in spats. Such a representation of mining is not only far removed from contemporary times, but also from two decades ago when it would have been chosen as the official logo of the event. However, branding the conference in such a way explicitly links it to a long past as well affords the event a sense of heritage and tradition. Indeed, words such as 'institution' and 'legacy' pepper descriptions of the event by organizers, participants and commentators.

Given the considerable emphasis on the past and tradition, Diggers and Dealers advocates must work to navigate the reality of change as manifest in the event and in the minerals sector. The event may, for example, have started as a 'humble' and 'spontaneous' affair 'with a dozen blokes in a pub' (McHugh 2011), but today it is a very large, corporate affair. The 2012 program provides a representative sample of the content of the proceedings. Without exception, program presenters are resource company leaders with titles such as Chief Executive Officers, Managing Directors, Chief Operating Officers, Vice-President, President, Chairman or Executive Chairmen (sic). The conference's transformation has mirrored changes in the minerals industry which have distanced it from its frontier foundations. These changes include substantial technological advancement requiring an increasingly skilled, highly-educated and 'corporate' workforce, the use of a fly-in fly-out rather than residential workforce, a move to continuous production and compressed work shifts, and the ongoing global consolidation of the minerals industry through mergers (McDonald, Pini and Mayes 2012). Thus, the stereotypical mining figure as 'blue-collar' has been displaced along with notions of the emblematic national/local mining corporation (such as BHP Billiton, which was once referred to as 'The Big Australian').

The disparity between the Diggers and Dealers past (and the heritage of mining and identity of 'the miner') and the present is often noted in the texts, but is then muted or dismissed. A feature in the *Sydney Morning Herald*, for example, begins with the journalist Jamie Freed (2006) asking: 'Mining has gone global and respectable, but do pinstripes really change a miner?' The reporter goes on to quote a mining executive: 'This (conference) all started off going bush and getting dirty and getting minerals out of dark holes and now we put on suits and talk to you about it.' However, Freed (2006) reassures readers the same executive talks to him wearing jeans. In addition, he tells us that in choosing such attire this CEO is 'far from alone among Australian mining chiefs' who ultimately 'still enjoy living it up and drinking hard in Kalgoorlie'. Another journalist recounts with admiration: 'For three straight nights the moneymen from Sydney and Melbourne have been drinking in many cases until 5 am or later – alongside local miners in dusty work clothes' (O'Keefe 2007). In another story a writer comments:

> Late at night, in the front bar of the Palace (Hotel), there no longer is a segregation between mining company bosses, fund managers, well-heeled private investors, analysts and members of the media pack. Friendships are struck and relationships renewed, seeds are sown for deals of the future as well as story idea. (Klinger 2012)

Positioning excessive drinking as emblematic of Diggers and Dealers does considerable discursive work in terms of anchoring the event to masculinity. Through an analysis of texts ranging from advertisements to fiction, Kirkby (2003: 254) demonstrates that Australian nationalism, beer drinking in pubs and masculinity are considered a 'religious trinity' in popular discourse. As is evident in the above quotations, the pub is mythologised as an egalitarian and inclusive arena despite its exclusivity to men, and indeed, particular groups of men. Conflations between drinking and masculinity are magnified in a rural context where pubs have been described as 'no place for a girl' because they are a key site for masculine identity construction (Leyshon 2005: 166). Ultimately, the repeated references to alcohol in the texts work to assure us that despite the radical changes to the mining industry, the authentic masculine identity of the contemporary miner as frontier man remains intact.

Alongside drinking, skimpies are also presented as a means of shoring up Diggers and Dealers as a frontier event and, by association, confirming the masculine frontier credentials of attendees. After all, it is not just drinking which unites men across social divides in the pub, but the implicit and naturalised assumption of their shared heterosexuality. Drinking thus offers a public practice through which collective identification around masculine heterosexuality is sought along with the complicity of and dominance of (willing) women.

Even purportedly broadsheet publications and the public broadcaster, the Australian Broadcasting Commission, dismiss other substantial changes to the mining industry (and, by association the mining man) by reference to the skimpie and reaffirm the normativity of frontier masculine heterosexuality. In 2011, for example, an ABC reporter asserted that the conference had changed considerably in taking a political stance over a proposed mining tax when its organisers had always presented it as an apolitical event. He completed a serious analysis of the changing political focus of the meeting with the statement that:

> But not everything has changed, and certainly not the unique aspects of a mining conference in a mining town that make a ticket to Diggers one of the most sought after items in the international mining and finance companies. The massive open cut Super Pit gold mine on the edge of town and Kalgoorlie-Boulder itself on the edge of the Nullarbor Plain give the delegates a genuine look beyond the profit-forecast spread sheets, and into the heart of a living, breathing, working, mining community. And then there's the legendary friendliness of the hundreds of skimpy barmaids who have been flown in especially for the event. (McHugh 2011)

In the above quotation, urban corporate masculinity – as signified by profit-forecast spread sheets – is repudiated as superficial, lacking and inauthentic. It is one's emplacement in a working mining town and, of course, the presence of sex-workers, which affords a man access to legitimate discourses of rural masculinity. The need for urban men to break free of the feminising influences of the city in order to become more authentic masculine men is a theme taken up throughout the texts. Such a move may actually improve profits according to some texts, which suggest that citified business practices impede men's business. A journalist writes, for example, that in the authentically masculine environment of the rural pub 'many multi-million-dollar transactions have been clinched' only to be 'sealed with a handshake and little other fanfare' (Le May 2012).

In another commentary on the urban/rural dichotomy and the libratory potential of the rural for men, a conference organiser told ABC radio:

> Kalgoorlie really changes because if we do a comparison with what we have here on most weekdays – seven days a week for that matter is you'll see a lot of fluoro walking around the streets here whereas at the moment there's a heck of a lot of dark blue pin striped suits and black pin striped suits and people with ties on today. But as we spoke earlier this morning they'll probably be all off now and they won't wear any more ties until they go back to Sydney or Melbourne or Perth. (Gallagher 2012)

The reconfiguration of the otherwise urban/corporate mining man by the rural occurs at a symbolic level as he removes his suit and tie, as well as at a material level as he engages in large amounts of drinking and enjoys the presence of the skimpie girls in the company of other men. He is liberated from the control and restraint of the feminised, domesticated urban and able to inhabit a wild untamed masculinity. It is perhaps for these reasons that a former conference Chairman (sic) described the conference as akin to a 'religious retreat' (Hurley 2010).

The rural as a place of ritual and ceremony where men may come together to find and reclaim their 'real' masculine selves away from the overly feminised world has been given considerable force in the recent decade through the popularity of the mythopoetic men's movement (Kimmel and Kaufman 1994). In fact, as Bonnett (1996) explains, the type of envisaging of the rural associated with this movement – that is, as a place where an authentic essential masculinity may emerge in a community of men otherwise entrapped by femininity – has a longer history naturalised in movements dating back to the earliest part of the twentieth century, such as the Boy Scouts and the Masonic Clubs (Bonnett 1996). There is, consequently, considerable discursive scaffolding on which Diggers and Dealers can build a discourse of the rural as a place for the materialisation of 'true' manhood.

Becoming a frontier man

Becoming a frontier man is not simply a matter of attending Diggers and Dealers. Rather the types of paternalistic discourses woven into the text suggest that the event requires initiation and that this in turn provides entry to the mining industry. One senior male journalist, for example, reflects on his attendance at the conference over a number of years before defining the event as a 'rite of passage for those entering the resources industry' (Piper 2010: 23). Another is referred to as a 'veteran' of 'the infamous three day event' and highlights his insider status with claims such as 'Diggers – as it is known to regular attendees' (Leys 2012). Those new to the event are identified in a range of ways, such as, for example, not knowing to 'pace themselves': 'We all smile at them and think, "Well it'll be interesting to see how they look on Wednesday". … Some of the new ones try to play through on Wednesday night and the seven o'clock plane on Thursday is a pretty interesting place to be' (Wynne 2010).

The paternal relations which surround Diggers and Dealers are rendered explicit in terms of the conference and the Western Australian School of Mines (WASM), which is based in Kalgoorlie, and through its parent institution, the Curtin University of Technology. WASM offers tertiary education to mining engineers, and as is noted in the texts, schooled numerous attendees and speakers. Business reporter Rania Spooner (2012) demonstrates the way the event is positioned as a rite of (masculine) passage in the mining industry:

> Northern Star Resources managing director Bill Bearment who is a graduate from the School of Mines, recalls a time when he was a struggling Uni student who worked at Diggers and Dealers 'pouring a lot of drinks for a lot of thirsty men'. Today, during his maiden Diggers presentation he sounds like he has been

> a very thirsty man these past three days – his profile margin may be strong but he's almost lost his voice completely.

In his opening speech to the conference in 2011, the event Chairman (sic) Barry Eldridge (2012) spoke warmly of the relationship between Diggers and Dealers and WASM:

> For many years Diggers and Dealers has been a quiet but we hope relevant supporter of the School of Mines and we expect to continue this. We provide a dozen free student passes to the School which allows students to attend and mingle and meet industry leaders … WASM does and has done for many years excellent industry research in partnership with companies. Diggers and Dealers also provide other support to the School and students but we won't dwell on this.

Overall, Diggers and Dealers is inculcated with a sense of old-style paternalism with its hints of an exclusive male club and fatherly figures overseeing and guiding new generations while smiling knowingly at their foibles and indiscretions (Pini 2008). The fact that this paternalism is institutionalised in the relationship between WASM and the conference is problematic for women's equal participation in the minerals sector as the following section will demonstrate.

Frontier masculinities and the 'problem' of women in mining

Diggers and Dealers is an event for and about men, as a cursory perusal of the annual program demonstrates. In 2011 and 2012, for example, all speakers were male. Interestingly, the main website image on the Diggers and Dealers homepage suggests otherwise, with an unnamed female photographed at a podium positioned (collage fashion) to the right and front of an unnamed male speaker also standing at a podium. Despite this, anyone in the audience for the three day event would be left in absolutely no doubt that this is a 'man's sector'. Images of men dominate in the presentation texts. A number of slides, for example, show all male boards while others repeatedly present the mine employer as male – driving machinery, working in a processing plant or surveying an exploration site. Further, since its inception in 1997, the recipients of the conference award, the G.J. Stokes Memorial Award, have all been men.

Alongside the masculine dominance of the minerals sector, government and industry in Australia have undertaken numerous inquiries on the 'problem of women in mining', largely because of the economic imperative to increase the labour pool and address a skill shortage in the sector (Mayes and Pini in press). What is of interest is that Diggers and Dealers has remained off-limits in terms of critique. Despite declarations by the Minerals Council of Australia (2007: 135) that 'the industry now has access to a significant body of knowledge about female employment', such knowledge is clearly highly circumscribed in that it does not examine men and masculinities, particularly as they are manifest in such a venerated and high-profile annual resource sector event. This is curious given that Diggers and Dealers is referred to as 'one of the biggest dates on the global resources calendar' (Keenan 2006), involves a 'who's who of the mining industry' (Varischetti 2007) and essential to 'understand the Australian minerals industry' (Klinger 2012).

Women are mentioned by journalists in terms of their work as skimpies, but even then they fare badly, represented largely as objects of ridicule or even as a source for abuse as 'gold-digging' sex-workers (Clarke 2012a, 2012b). As attendees, their lack of presence is noted by a few reporters, but little queried. In fact, we found only one case where an ABC female reporter questioned women's absence and asked for a reply from a CEO of a minerals company. He invokes the 'pipeline' argument, treading the familiar ground of absolving men and corporations of responsibility for gender equality and of the need to address masculine power and privilege (Pini 2005). More extraordinary is his apparent puzzlement at the paucity of women attendees:

> We really do need to see more women turning up. I don't know what you do, mining is still very male dominated not because of any predication to have it all men only, but the women are working their way into it and it would be good to see a lot more women here. (McLaren 2008)

It certainly appears there is little tolerance for criticising the major global mining event for promoting and celebrating 'skimpies', as a female blogger found out in nominating Diggers and Dealers for her 'ass of the week award'. She explained:

> Why Kalgoorlie? Some would say its proximity to mine sites; but ask the mostly male 3000 participants and they'll tell you it's the after hours programme in the town's eleven topless bars that's the big drawcard. Gives you an idea why it's a mostly-male event when the jugs of beer come with the option of having the barmaid's own 'jugs' dipped or undipped in the beer's frothy head. (Anonymous 2011a)

In response, a self-confessed 'long term supporter and an ex-Western Australian female executive' writes:

> It is with disappointment that I read this piece. Your comments show a lack of knowledge and understanding around the origins and impetus of the event. The event is about bring [sic] the industry back to 'where it all began' which was indeed Kalgoorlie and networking/ensuring future successes of the industry. (Anonymous 2011b)

In the above response, the poster legitimises the masculine hegemony of Diggers and Dealers, and even renders it laudable through claims to 'the origins and impetus of the event'. However, terms such as 'history' and 'tradition' are not gender-neutral, but deeply entwined with articulations and practices of a frontier-based masculinity, which is defined by the subjugation of women and femininities.

Conclusion

This chapter has used a case study of the minerals conference Diggers and Dealers to explore rural masculinities. It is a rich illustration of the interconnectedness between rurality and masculinity for three inter-related reasons. Firstly, it reveals the performative nature of rurality and masculinity. It is not just gender, but also rurality which is a 'verb' (Butler 1990: 24). This is a deeply embodied performance requiring attention to practices of dress, drinking and male/male and male/female interactions. It is also a performance requiring distancing and differentiation. Again, it is not just the feminine, but the urban (as feminine) which is key to this process. The metropole and its associated values, practices and discourses are central to the lives of the types of elite transnational male managers who attend Diggers and Dealers, yet this primacy is undermined or discounted in conference texts. Instead, the urban is feminised and becomes a point for distinction as conference participants take up the scripts of frontier masculinity. As Bell (2000: 559) found in a reading of a range of feature films, the countryside is 'naturalized as the space to be (or become) a man'.

Secondly, the case study reveals how place-related aspects of masculinity and rurality are enrolled in the process of gender identity formation (see also Presterudstuen 2014: this volume, Warren 2014: this volume). It is the encoding of Kalgoorlie as a particular type of place steeped in romanticised, nostalgic notions of frontier masculinity, which provides the discursive platform for conferring to male conference participants that they are 'real' rural men. Unsurprisingly, when accessibility and venue concerns have been used to suggest a change in location for the conference, it has been vehemently rejected by organisers as well as previous attendees. They know that place matters.

A final dimension of the case study's worth is that it has juxtaposed the mobilisation of frontier masculinities at Diggers and Dealers against the mineral sector's repeated claims to be committed to gender equality. While research suggests that recent socio-economic and political changes have wrought shifts in rural masculinities with some more egalitarian and inclusive discourses coming to the fore (e.g., Bryant and Pini 2011, Sherman 2011), there is no evidence of this at Diggers and Dealers. Rather, in the conference tradition we can see what Connell (2003: 52) has referred to as the reassertion of dominance-based masculinity in the arena of global capitalism. This aggressive and retrograde performance of masculinity by senior corporate mineral industry figures has not been remarked upon, let alone critiqued in the multitude of gender equity studies, policies and strategies that have been produced by industry in recent years (Mayes and Pini in press).

References

Anonymous. 2011. *Ass of the Week Award: Diggers and Dealers and their After Conference Activities* [Online: August 9]. Available at: http://thesheeoblog.com/_blog/The_SheEO_Blog/post/Ass_of_the_Week_Award_The_Diggers_and_Dealers_and_their_after_conference_activities. [accessed: 20 December 2012].

Anonymous. 2011. *Comment* [Online: August 10]. Available at: http://thesheeoblog.com/_blog/The_SheEO_Blog/post/Ass_of_the_Week_Award_The_Diggers_and_Dealers_and_their_after_conference_activities. [accessed: 20 December 2012].

Anonymous. 2012. *A walk through Kalgoorlie's red light district* [Online: iTourist]. Available at: www.itourist.com/guides/destinations/article/110057 [Accessed: 20 December 2012].

Bell, D. 2000. Farm boys and wild men: rurality, masculinity, and homosexuality. *Rural Sociology*, 65(4), 547–561.

Bonnett, A. 1996. The new primitives: identity, landscape and cultural appropriation in the mythopoetic men's movement. *Antipode*, 28(3), 273–291.

Bryant, L. and Pini, B. 2011. *Gender and Rurality*. London: Routledge.

Butler, J. 1990. *Gender Trouble: Feminism and the Subversion of Identity*. London: Routledge.

Clarke, J. 2012a. Lose your top, add to your back pocket: the next generation skimpy. *Canberra Times* [Online, 10 August]. Available at: http://www.canberratimes.com.au/lifestyle/life/blogs/my-jennaration/lose-your-top-add-to-your-back-pocket-the-next-generation-skimpy-20120810–23xmm.html [accessed: 22 October 2012].

Clarke, J. 2012b. Welcome to the topless and gold digging jungle. *WA Today* [Online, 6 August]. Available at: www.watoday.com.au [accessed: 22 October 2012].

Connell, R.W. 2003. Globalisation and the future of gender, in *Future Imaginings: Sexualities and Genders in the New Millennium*, edited by D. Bird, W. Were and T.A. White. Perth: University of Western Australia Press, 1–10.

Eldridge, B. 2012. *Diggers and Dealers Conference: Opening Address* [Online: Diggers and Dealers]. Available at: www.diggersndealers.com.au/ [accessed: 6 November 2012].

Freed, J. 2006. Let's get loded – it's a whole new show. *The Sydney Morning Herald*, 12 August, 39.

Gallagher, H. 2012. The ties soon disappear at Diggers and Dealers. *WA Regional Drive ABC* [Online, 6 August]. Available at: www.abc.net.au/local/audio/2012/08/06/3561817.htm [accessed: 2 January 2013].

Hogan, M.P. and Pursell, T. 2008. The 'real Alaskan': nostalgia and rural masculinity in the 'last frontier'. *Men and Masculinities*, 11(1), 63–85.

Hurley, B. 2010. Diggers and Dealers conference kicks off in Kalgoorlie. *ABC News* [Online, 7 August]. Available at: www.abc.net.au/local/audio/2010/07/08 [accessed: 26 October 2012].

Keenan, R. 2006. Kalgoorlie ready for diggers forum. *Sydney Morning Herald* [Online, 6 August]. Available at: www.smh.com.au/news/BUSINESS/Kalgoorlie-ready-for-Diggers-forum/2006/08/06/1154802738112.html [accessed: 2 January 2013].

Kerfoot, D. and Knights, D. 1993. Management, masculinity and manipulation: from paternalism to corporate strategy in financial services in Britain. *Journal of Management Studies*, 30(4), 659–677.

Kimmel, M. and Kaufman, M. 1994. Weekend warriors: the new men's movement, in *Theorising Masculinities*, edited by H. Brod and M. Kaufman. Thousand Oaks: Sage Publications, 259–288.

Kirkby, D. 2003. Beer glorious beer: gender politics and Australian popular culture. *Journal of Popular Culture*, 32 (2), 244–256.

Klinger, P. 2012. Diggers critical to understanding mining. *The West Australian* [Online, August 5]. Available at: www://au.news.yahoo.com/thewest/business/a/–/wa/14437497/ [accessed: 29 October 2012].

LeMay, R. 2012. *Kalgoorlie Comes Alive for Mine Conference. Australian Stock, Share and Commodity Markets News* [Online: Trading Room]. Available at: www.tradingroom.com.au [accessed: 22 October 2012].

Leys, N. 2012. Diggers not Dealers. *The Australian* [Online, 13 August]. Available at: www.theaustralian.com.au/media/media-diary/diggers-not-dealers/story-fnab9kqj-1226448728602 [accessed: 22 October 2012].

Leyshon, M. 2005. No place for a girl: rural youth, pubs and the performance of masculinity, in *Critical Studies in Rural Gender Issues*, edited by J. Little and C. Morris. London: Asghate, 104 122.

Little, J. 2003. 'Riding the rural love train': heterosexuality and the rural community. *Sociologia Ruralis*, 43(4), 401–417.

Little, J. 2007. Constructing nature in the performance of rural heterosexualities. *Environment and Planning D: Society and Space*, 25(5), 851–866.

Mayes, R. and Pini, B. 2010. The 'feminine revolution in mining': a critique. *Australian Geographer*, 41(1), 233–245.

Mayes, R. and Pini, B. (in press) Unearthing new resources: a critique of the business case for gender equity in the Australian mining industry. *Journal of Industrial Relations*.

McDonald, P., Pini, B. and Mayes, R. 2012. Mining, work, family and community: a spatially oriented approach to the impact of the Ravensthorpe nickel mine closure in remote Australia. *Journal of Industrial Relations*, 54(1), 22–40.

McHugh, B. 2011. It's politics, stupid: Diggers and Dealers 2011. *ABC Rural* [Online, 1 August]. Available at: http://www.abc.net.au/site-archive/rural/content/2011/s3282781.htm [accessed: 2 January 2013].

McLaren, R. 2008. A man's world. *ABC Radio* [Online, 6 August]. Available at: http://www.abc.net.au/local/stories/2008/08/05/2325097.htm [accessed: 2 January 2013].

Minerals Council of Australia. 2007. *Unearthing New Resources: Attracting and Retaining Women in the Australian Minerals Industry* [Online]. Available at: http://minerals.org.au/__data/assets/pdf_file/0016/20275/MCA_Women_In_Mining_WebVersion.pdf [accessed: 2 January 2013].

O'Keefe, B. 2007. Australia's new gold rush, courtesy of China. *Fortune* [Online, November 19]. Available at: www://money.cnn.com/2007/11/19/news/international/australia_mining_boom.fortune [accessed: 2 January 2013].

Parpart, J. and Zalewski, M. 2008. Introduction: rethinking the man question, in *Rethinking the Man Question: Sex Gender and Violence in International Relations*, edited by J. Parpart and M. Zalewski. London and New York: Zed Books, 1–22.

Pini, B. 2005. Progress not pipelines: a case study of the need for the strategic management of equity in an Australian agricultural organisation. *Strategic Change*, 14(3), 133–140.

Pini, B. 2008. *Masculinities and Management in Agricultural Organisations Worldwide*. Aldershot: Ashgate.

Pini, B. and Mayes, R. 2011. Configurations of gender, class and rurality in resource affected rural Australia, in *Reshaping Gender and Class in Rural Spaces*, edited by B. Pini and B. Leach. Surrey: Ashgate Publishing Limited, 113–128.

Piper, D. 2010. Into the diggers mix once again. *Gold Mining Journal*, 1(104), 22–23.

Sherman, J. 2011. Men without sawmills: job loss and gender identity in rural America, in *Economic Restructuring and Family Well-Being in Rural America*, edited by K.E. Smith and A.R. Tickamyer. University Park: The Pennsylvania State University Press, 82–102.

Spooner, R. 2012. *The latest updates from day three of Diggers and Dealers* [Online: August 7]. Available at: www.watoday.com.au/business/the-latest-updates-from-day-three-of-diggers-and-dealers-20120808–23tgx.html [accessed: 2 January 2013].

Varischetti, B. 2007. Mining executives talk and play hard at Diggers and Dealers. *ABC Radio* [Online, 8 August]. Available at: www.abc.net.au/rural/telegraph/content/2006/s1999851.htm [accessed: 2 January 2013].

Wynne, E. 2010. Diggers for dummies – what actually happens in the big tent. *ABC Radio* [Online, 5 August]. Available at: www.abc.net.au/local/photos/2010/08/05 [accessed: 2 January 2013].

Index

Kolibri 360 GmbH
Ferdinand-Jühlke-Straße 7
99095 Erfurt, Deutschland
produktsicherheit@kolibri360.de